CAPTAIN AMERICA AND THE FALCON

THE SWINE

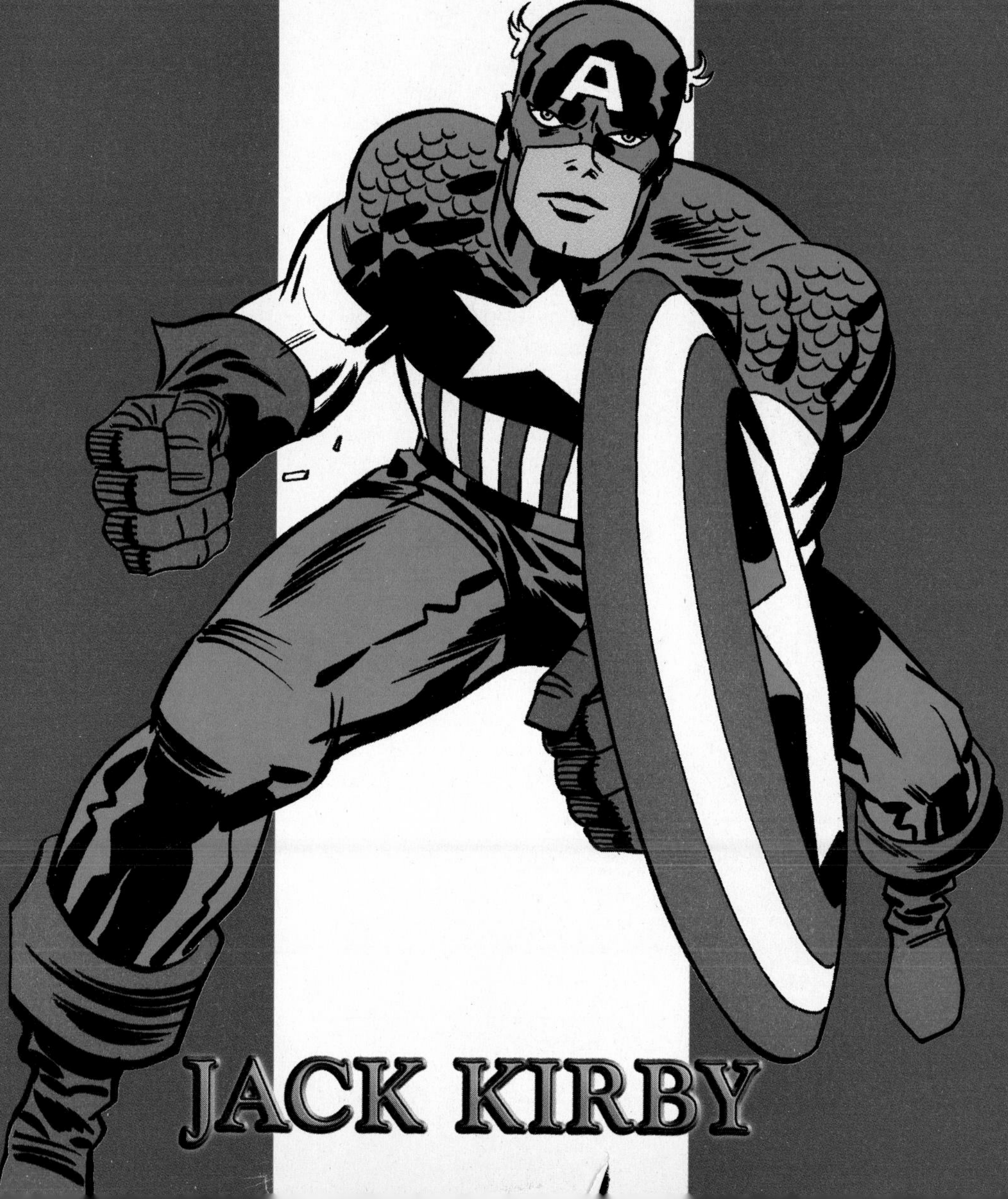

JACK KIRBY

CAPTAIN AMERICA ®
AND THE FALCON
THE SWINE

Writer/Artist/Editor
Jack Kirby
Inks
Frank Giacoia, Mike Royer, Dan Green,
John Verpoorten & John Tartaglione
Letters
Jim Novak, Mike Royer, Joe Rosen & Gaspar Saladino
Colors
Petra Goldberg, George Roussos, Glynis Wein,
Sam Kato & Janice Cohen

Consulting Editors
Archie Goodwin & Marv Wolfman
Color Reconstruction
Jerron Quality Color
Cover Colors
Avalon's Andy Troy

Senior Editor, Special Projects
Jeff Youngquist
Associate Editors
Jennifer Grünwald
& Mark D. Beazley
Assistant Editor
Michael Short
Vice President of Sales
David Gabriel
Production
Jerron Quality Color
Vice President of Creative
Tom Marvelli

Special thanks to Pond Scum
& Tom Brevoort

Editor in Chief
Joe Quesada
Publisher
Dan Buckley

Captain America created by
Joe Simon & Jack Kirby

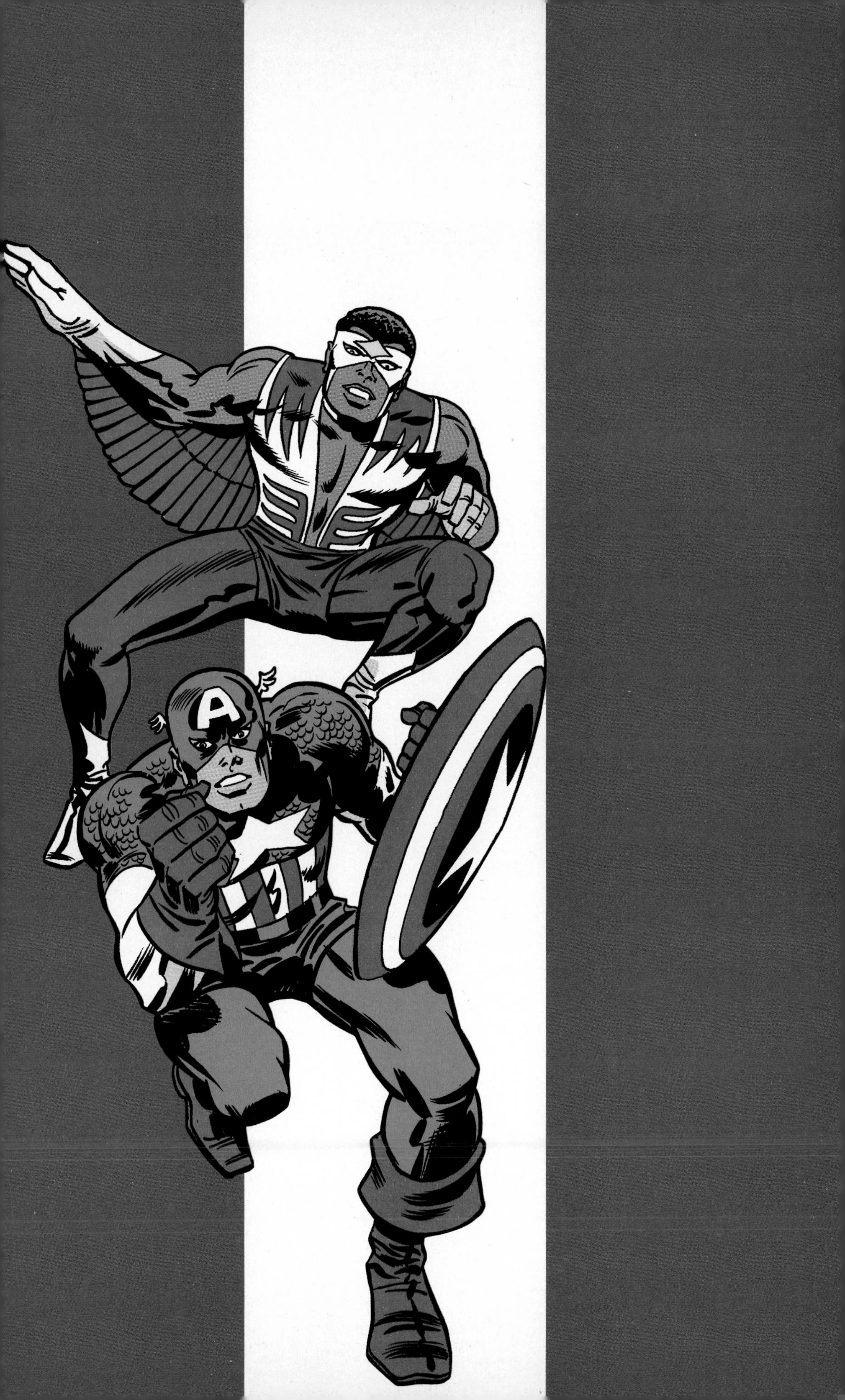

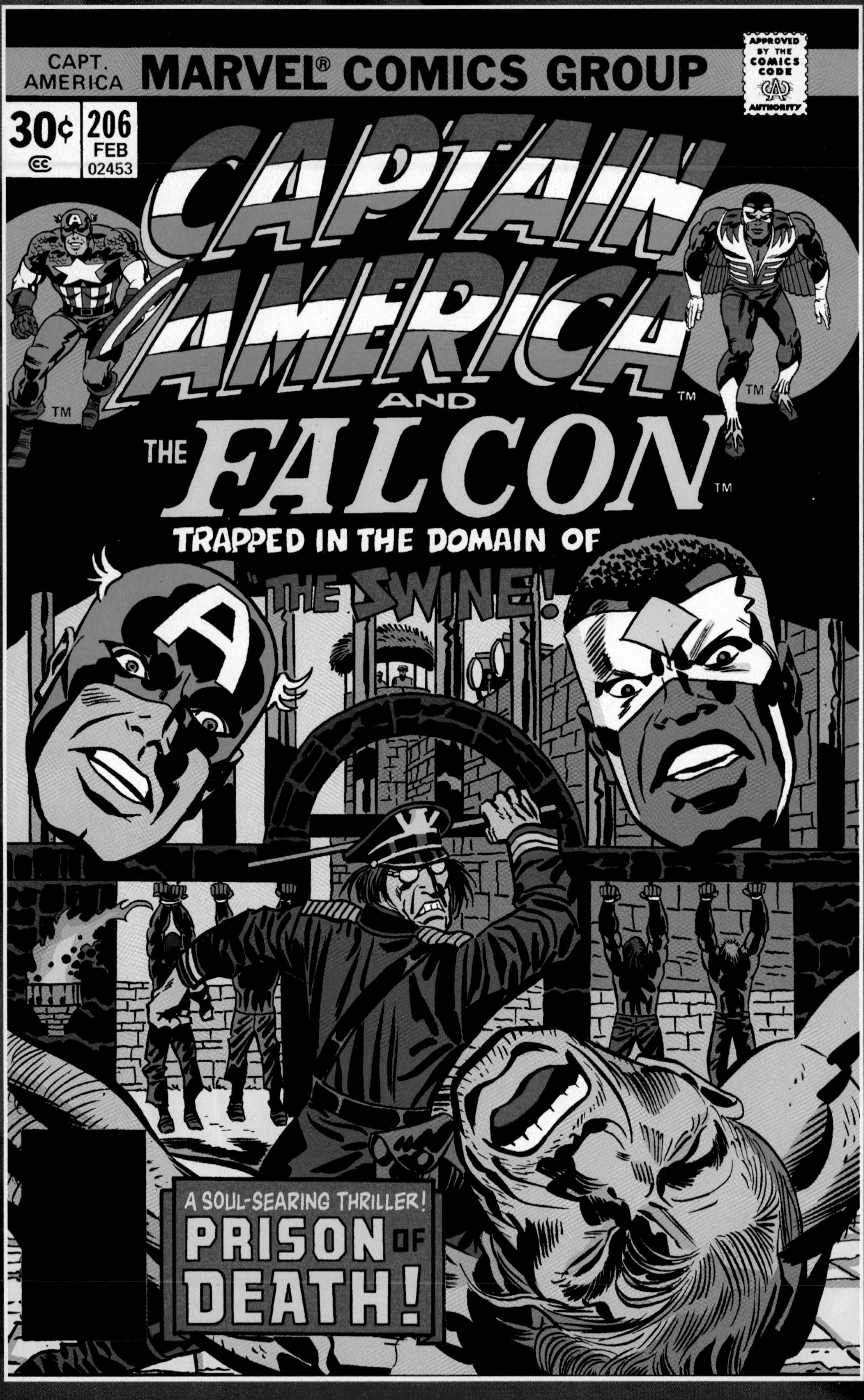
CAPT. AMERICA
MARVEL® COMICS GROUP
APPROVED BY THE COMICS CODE AUTHORITY
30¢
CC
206
FEB
02453
CAPTAIN AMERICA
AND
THE FALCON
TRAPPED IN THE DOMAIN OF
"THE SWINE!"
A SOUL-SEARING THRILLER!
PRISON OF DEATH!

1941! The world at *war!* And in a secret laboratory, frail *Steve Rogers* became the American *super-soldier!* For four thrilling years, he fought the Axis powers—until a freak stroke of fate threw him into *suspended animation.* He woke in the mid-1960s, a man *twenty years out of his time.* Since that fateful day, Steve Rogers has sought his *destiny* in this brave new world.

Stan Lee PRESENTS: CAPTAIN AMERICA AND THE FALCON™

EDITED, WRITTEN & DRAWN BY:	INKED BY:	LETTERED BY:	COLORED BY:	PEEKED AT BY:
JACK KIRBY	F. GIACOIA	J. NOVAK	P. GOLDBERG	A. GOODWIN

AFTER RECOVERING FROM THE PSYCHOLOGICAL *BACKLASH* OF A BIZARRE ADVENTURE, THE FALCON IS REUNITED WITH LEILA IN A *SHIELD* HOSPITAL WHERE MINDS ARE MENDED AND HUMAN SPIRITS ARE BROUGHT *BACK* FROM THE ABYSS OF DESPAIR. IN STARK CONTRAST TO THIS HOUSE OF HEALING, FAR AWAY THERE IS A PLACE WHERE SPIRITS ARE *CRUSHED* AND *BROKEN,* WHERE VICTIMS *PLEAD* FOR DEATH—A PLACE WHERE *CAPTAIN AMERICA* WILL FIND HIMSELF—

FACE TO FACE WITH THE SWINE!

LEILA! W-WE'RE *WELL!!* WE KNOW WHERE WE'RE AT!! *WE'RE YOU AND ME!*

A LITTLE BRAIN-WASHING DOESN'T LAST FOREVER!! YOU'VE BOTH GOT YOUR HEADS *STRAIGHT, NOW!!*

I-IT'S LIKE RUSHING INTO THE *SUNLIGHT* AFTER RIDING THROUGH A *DARK TUNNEL!!*

HI, FALCON! HI, *BIG SAM WILSON!*

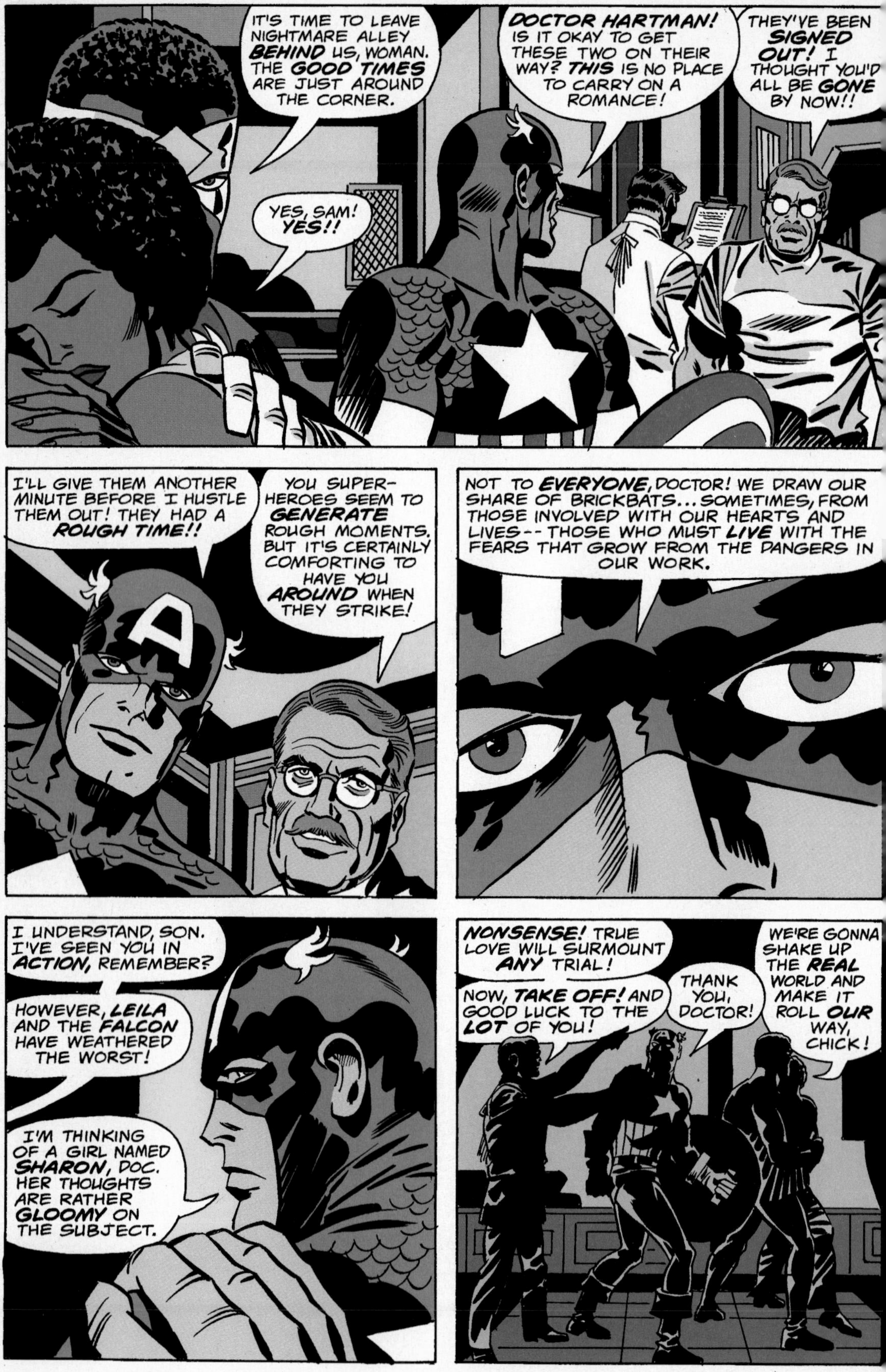
IT'S TIME TO LEAVE NIGHTMARE ALLEY BEHIND US, WOMAN. THE GOOD TIMES ARE JUST AROUND THE CORNER.
YES, SAM! YES!!
DOCTOR HARTMAN! IS IT OKAY TO GET THESE TWO ON THEIR WAY? THIS IS NO PLACE TO CARRY ON A ROMANCE!
THEY'VE BEEN SIGNED OUT! I THOUGHT YOU'D ALL BE GONE BY NOW!!
I'LL GIVE THEM ANOTHER MINUTE BEFORE I HUSTLE THEM OUT! THEY HAD A ROUGH TIME!!
YOU SUPER-HEROES SEEM TO GENERATE ROUGH MOMENTS. BUT IT'S CERTAINLY COMFORTING TO HAVE YOU AROUND WHEN THEY STRIKE!
NOT TO EVERYONE, DOCTOR! WE DRAW OUR SHARE OF BRICKBATS... SOMETIMES, FROM THOSE INVOLVED WITH OUR HEARTS AND LIVES-- THOSE WHO MUST LIVE WITH THE FEARS THAT GROW FROM THE DANGERS IN OUR WORK.
I UNDERSTAND, SON. I'VE SEEN YOU IN ACTION, REMEMBER?
HOWEVER, LEILA AND THE FALCON HAVE WEATHERED THE WORST!
I'M THINKING OF A GIRL NAMED SHARON, DOC. HER THOUGHTS ARE RATHER GLOOMY ON THE SUBJECT.
NONSENSE! TRUE LOVE WILL SURMOUNT ANY TRIAL!
NOW, TAKE OFF! AND GOOD LUCK TO THE LOT OF YOU!
THANK YOU, DOCTOR!
WE'RE GONNA SHAKE UP THE REAL WORLD AND MAKE IT ROLL OUR WAY, CHICK!

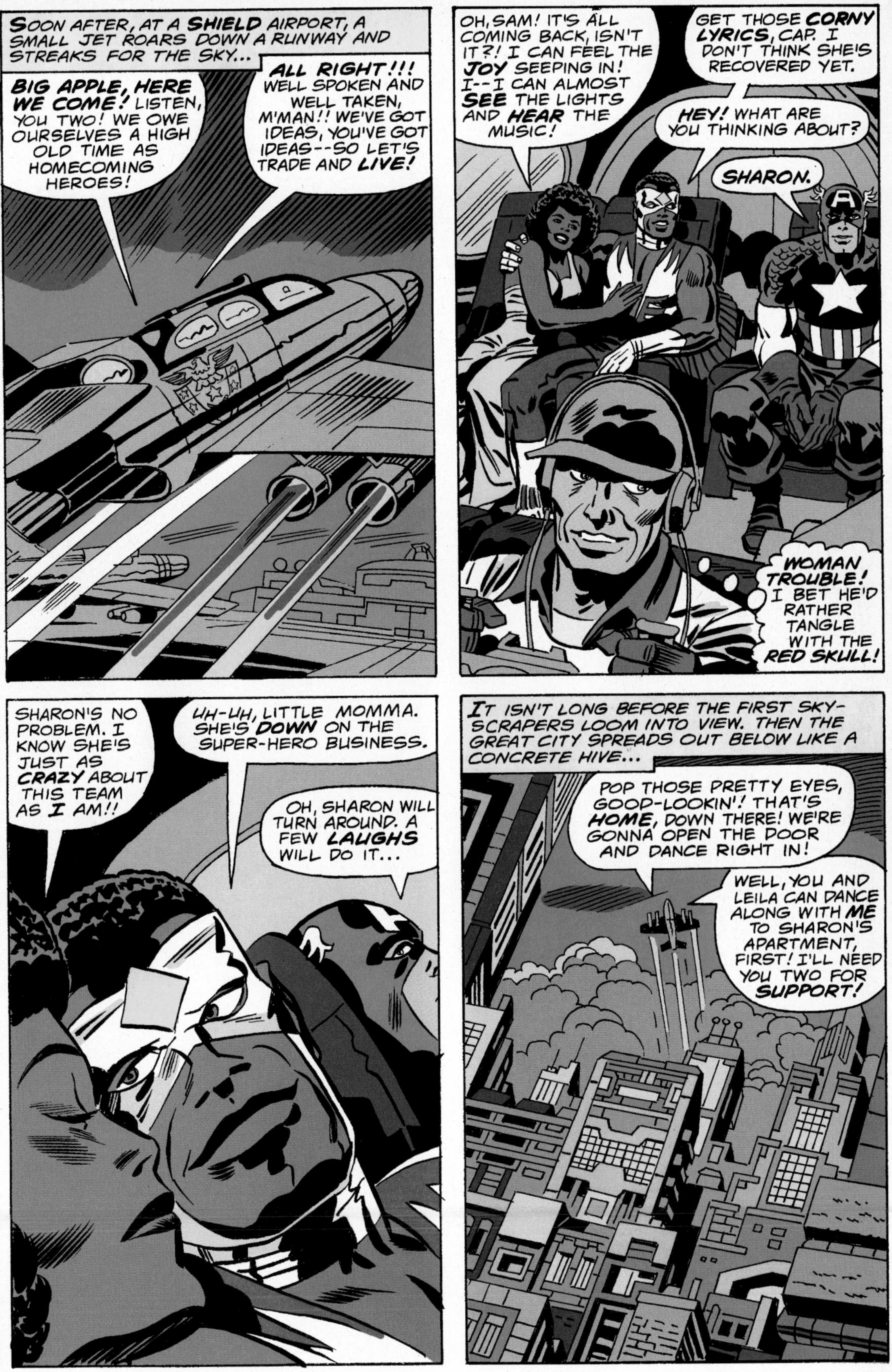
SOON AFTER, AT A SHIELD AIRPORT, A SMALL JET ROARS DOWN A RUNWAY AND STREAKS FOR THE SKY...
BIG APPLE, HERE WE COME! LISTEN, YOU TWO! WE OWE OURSELVES A HIGH OLD TIME AS HOMECOMING HEROES!
ALL RIGHT!!! WELL SPOKEN AND WELL TAKEN, M'MAN!! WE'VE GOT IDEAS, YOU'VE GOT IDEAS--SO LET'S TRADE AND LIVE!
OH, SAM! IT'S ALL COMING BACK, ISN'T IT?! I CAN FEEL THE JOY SEEPING IN! I--I CAN ALMOST SEE THE LIGHTS AND HEAR THE MUSIC!
GET THOSE CORNY LYRICS, CAP. I DON'T THINK SHE'S RECOVERED YET.
HEY! WHAT ARE YOU THINKING ABOUT?
SHARON.
WOMAN TROUBLE! I BET HE'D RATHER TANGLE WITH THE RED SKULL!
SHARON'S NO PROBLEM. I KNOW SHE'S JUST AS CRAZY ABOUT THIS TEAM AS I AM!!
UH-UH, LITTLE MOMMA. SHE'S DOWN ON THE SUPER-HERO BUSINESS.
OH, SHARON WILL TURN AROUND. A FEW LAUGHS WILL DO IT...
IT ISN'T LONG BEFORE THE FIRST SKY-SCRAPERS LOOM INTO VIEW. THEN THE GREAT CITY SPREADS OUT BELOW LIKE A CONCRETE HIVE...
POP THOSE PRETTY EYES, GOOD-LOOKIN'! THAT'S HOME, DOWN THERE! WE'RE GONNA OPEN THE DOOR AND DANCE RIGHT IN!
WELL, YOU AND LEILA CAN DANCE ALONG WITH ME TO SHARON'S APARTMENT, FIRST! I'LL NEED YOU TWO FOR SUPPORT!

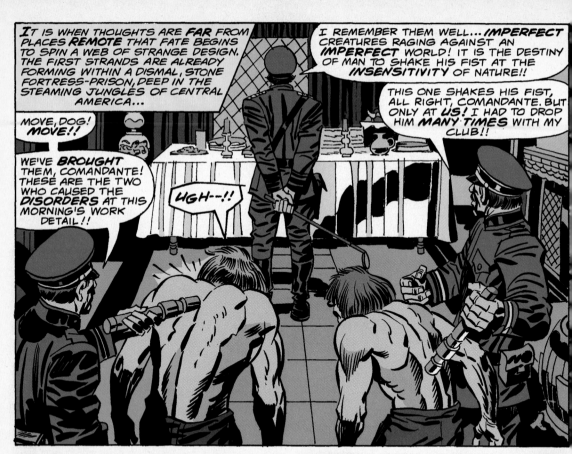

IT IS WHEN THOUGHTS ARE *FAR* FROM PLACES *REMOTE* THAT FATE BEGINS TO SPIN A WEB OF STRANGE DESIGN. THE FIRST STRANDS ARE ALREADY FORMING WITHIN A DISMAL, STONE FORTRESS-PRISON, DEEP IN THE STEAMING JUNGLES OF CENTRAL AMERICA...

MOVE, DOG! *MOVE!!*

WE'VE *BROUGHT* THEM, COMANDANTE! THESE ARE THE TWO WHO CAUSED THE *DISORDERS* AT THIS MORNING'S WORK DETAIL!!

UGH--!!

I REMEMBER THEM WELL... *IMPERFECT* CREATURES RAGING AGAINST AN *IMPERFECT* WORLD! IT IS THE DESTINY OF MAN TO SHAKE HIS FIST AT THE *INSENSITIVITY* OF NATURE!!

THIS ONE SHAKES HIS FIST, ALL RIGHT, COMANDANTE. BUT ONLY AT *US!* I HAD TO DROP HIM *MANY TIMES* WITH MY CLUB!!

THE COMANDANTE TURNS TO STUDY THE PRISONERS. HIS FACE *BELIES* HIS WORDS. IT IS *HARDLY* A BADGE OF COMPASSION...

HE SHOUTS AND CURSES, COMANDANTE! HE DOES NOT LIKE *THIS*, HE DOES NOT LIKE *THAT!* HE SOON HAS THE *OTHERS* SHOUTING WITH HIM!

WHY, THAT'S MOST *SURPRISING!* HE DOESN'T *LOOK* LIKE A TROUBLEMAKER!

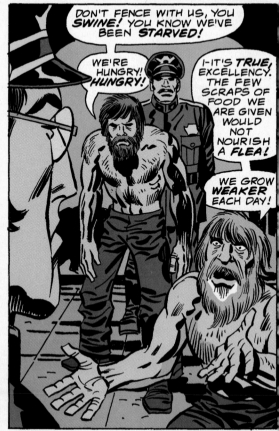

DON'T FENCE WITH US, YOU *SWINE!* YOU KNOW WE'VE BEEN *STARVED!*

WE'RE HUNGRY! *HUNGRY!*

I-IT'S *TRUE*, EXCELLENCY. THE FEW SCRAPS OF FOOD WE ARE GIVEN WOULD NOT NOURISH A *FLEA!*

WE GROW *WEAKER* EACH DAY!

8

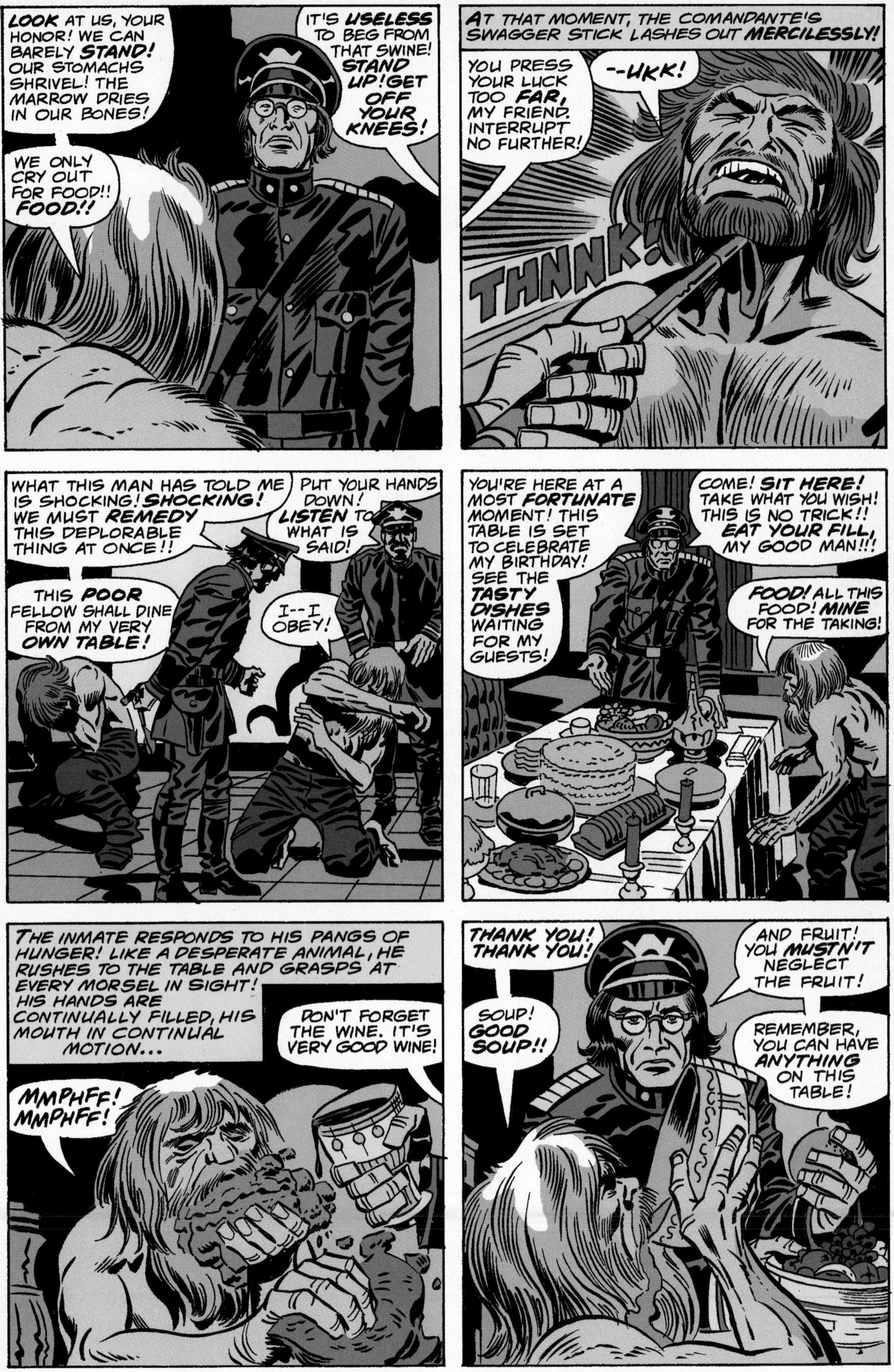
LOOK AT US, YOUR HONOR! WE CAN BARELY STAND! OUR STOMACHS SHRIVEL! THE MARROW DRIES IN OUR BONES!
IT'S USELESS TO BEG FROM THAT SWINE! STAND UP! GET OFF YOUR KNEES!
WE ONLY CRY OUT FOR FOOD!! FOOD!!
AT THAT MOMENT, THE COMANDANTE'S SWAGGER STICK LASHES OUT MERCILESSLY!
YOU PRESS YOUR LUCK TOO FAR, MY FRIEND. INTERRUPT NO FURTHER!
--UKK!
THNNK!
WHAT THIS MAN HAS TOLD ME IS SHOCKING! SHOCKING! WE MUST REMEDY THIS DEPLORABLE THING AT ONCE!!
PUT YOUR HANDS DOWN! LISTEN TO WHAT IS SAID!
THIS POOR FELLOW SHALL DINE FROM MY VERY OWN TABLE!
I--I OBEY!
YOU'RE HERE AT A MOST FORTUNATE MOMENT! THIS TABLE IS SET TO CELEBRATE MY BIRTHDAY! SEE THE TASTY DISHES WAITING FOR MY GUESTS!
COME! SIT HERE! TAKE WHAT YOU WISH! THIS IS NO TRICK!! EAT YOUR FILL, MY GOOD MAN!!!
FOOD! ALL THIS FOOD! MINE FOR THE TAKING!
THE INMATE RESPONDS TO HIS PANGS OF HUNGER! LIKE A DESPERATE ANIMAL, HE RUSHES TO THE TABLE AND GRASPS AT EVERY MORSEL IN SIGHT! HIS HANDS ARE CONTINUALLY FILLED, HIS MOUTH IN CONTINUAL MOTION...
DON'T FORGET THE WINE. IT'S VERY GOOD WINE!
MMPHFF! MMPHFF!
THANK YOU! THANK YOU!
AND FRUIT! YOU MUSTN'T NEGLECT THE FRUIT!
SOUP! GOOD SOUP!!
REMEMBER, YOU CAN HAVE ANYTHING ON THIS TABLE!

MEANWHILE, IN NEW YORK, OTHER STRANDS OF FATE'S WEB ARE WOVEN AND ANCHORED IN SMILE AND JEST AND THE SPARKLE OF THE NIGHT...

--FINALLY GOT YOUR ORDER, FOLKS! IT'S A *BUSY* NIGHT!

WE *UNDERSTAND*, FELIX. MMM, SMELLS *GOOD*!

I THOUGHT WE'D *NEVER* BE SERVED!

THE MANAGEMENT WOULD *BEND* THE RULES A BIT IF THEY KNEW THEY HAD *FAMOUS* GUESTS--

--BUT IT ISN'T *FAIR* TO CASH IN ON STEVE AND SAM THAT WAY!

OH, *HUSH UP*, MOMMA! STOP CHATTIN' AND *START CHOMPIN'*!

YOU CAN'T GET THIS KIND OF MENU IN THE FIELD!! I'D GIVE ANYTHING TO TACKLE A *POWER-MAD* CHEF, WHOSE CHIEF WEAPON IS A *TWENTY-COURSE GOURMET DINNER!*

I *WOULDN'T* JOKE ABOUT THE PEOPLE YOU MEET IN *YOUR* BUSINESS. THEY'RE INVARIABLY INCLINED TO *MASS MURDER!*

I--I'M SORRY. BUT STEVE *DID* BRING UP THE SUBJECT...

IT SURE IS *HARD* TO KEEP IT OUT OF THE CONVERSATION, *ISN'T* IT, SHARON HONEY!?

LEILA--!

OF COURSE, I'D BE DELIGHTED IF SAM, HERE, TAUGHT SCHOOL OR DELIVERED MILK. BUT, I'LL TAKE HIM AS HE IS-- EVEN IF HE DOES GO OFF TO SAVE THE WORLD TWICE A WEEK!!

KNOW WHAT I'M READY FOR? A BIG SLAB OF *APPLE PIE* WITH TWO SCOOPS OF *ICE CREAM* RIDING SHOTGUN!

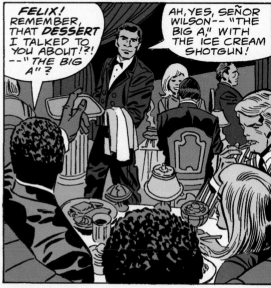

FELIX! REMEMBER, THAT *DESSERT* I TALKED TO YOU ABOUT!?! --"THE BIG A"?

AH, YES, SEÑOR WILSON-- "THE BIG A," WITH THE ICE CREAM SHOTGUN!

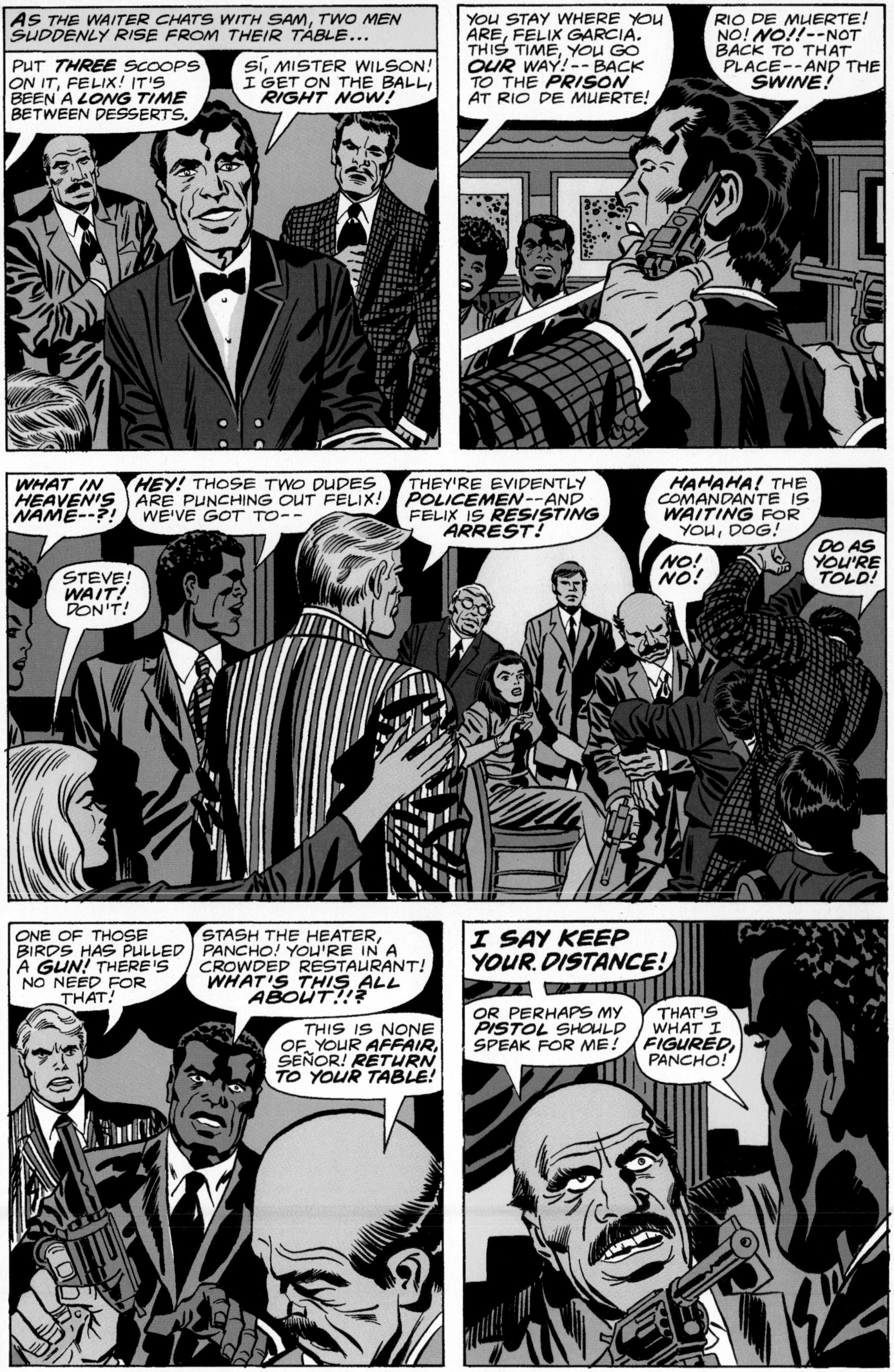
AS THE WAITER CHATS WITH SAM, TWO MEN SUDDENLY RISE FROM THEIR TABLE...
PUT THREE SCOOPS ON IT, FELIX! IT'S BEEN A LONG TIME BETWEEN DESSERTS.
SÍ, MISTER WILSON! I GET ON THE BALL, RIGHT NOW!
YOU STAY WHERE YOU ARE, FELIX GARCIA. THIS TIME, YOU GO OUR WAY!--BACK TO THE PRISON AT RIO DE MUERTE!
RIO DE MUERTE! NO! NO!!--NOT BACK TO THAT PLACE--AND THE SWINE!
WHAT IN HEAVEN'S NAME--?!
HEY! THOSE TWO DUDES ARE PUNCHING OUT FELIX! WE'VE GOT TO--
STEVE! WAIT! DON'T!
THEY'RE EVIDENTLY POLICEMEN--AND FELIX IS RESISTING ARREST!
HAHAHA! THE COMANDANTE IS WAITING FOR YOU, DOG!
NO! NO!
DO AS YOU'RE TOLD!
ONE OF THOSE BIRDS HAS PULLED A GUN! THERE'S NO NEED FOR THAT!
STASH THE HEATER, PANCHO! YOU'RE IN A CROWDED RESTAURANT! WHAT'S THIS ALL ABOUT!!?
THIS IS NONE OF YOUR AFFAIR, SEÑOR! RETURN TO YOUR TABLE!
I SAY KEEP YOUR DISTANCE!
OR PERHAPS MY PISTOL SHOULD SPEAK FOR ME!
THAT'S WHAT I FIGURED, PANCHO!

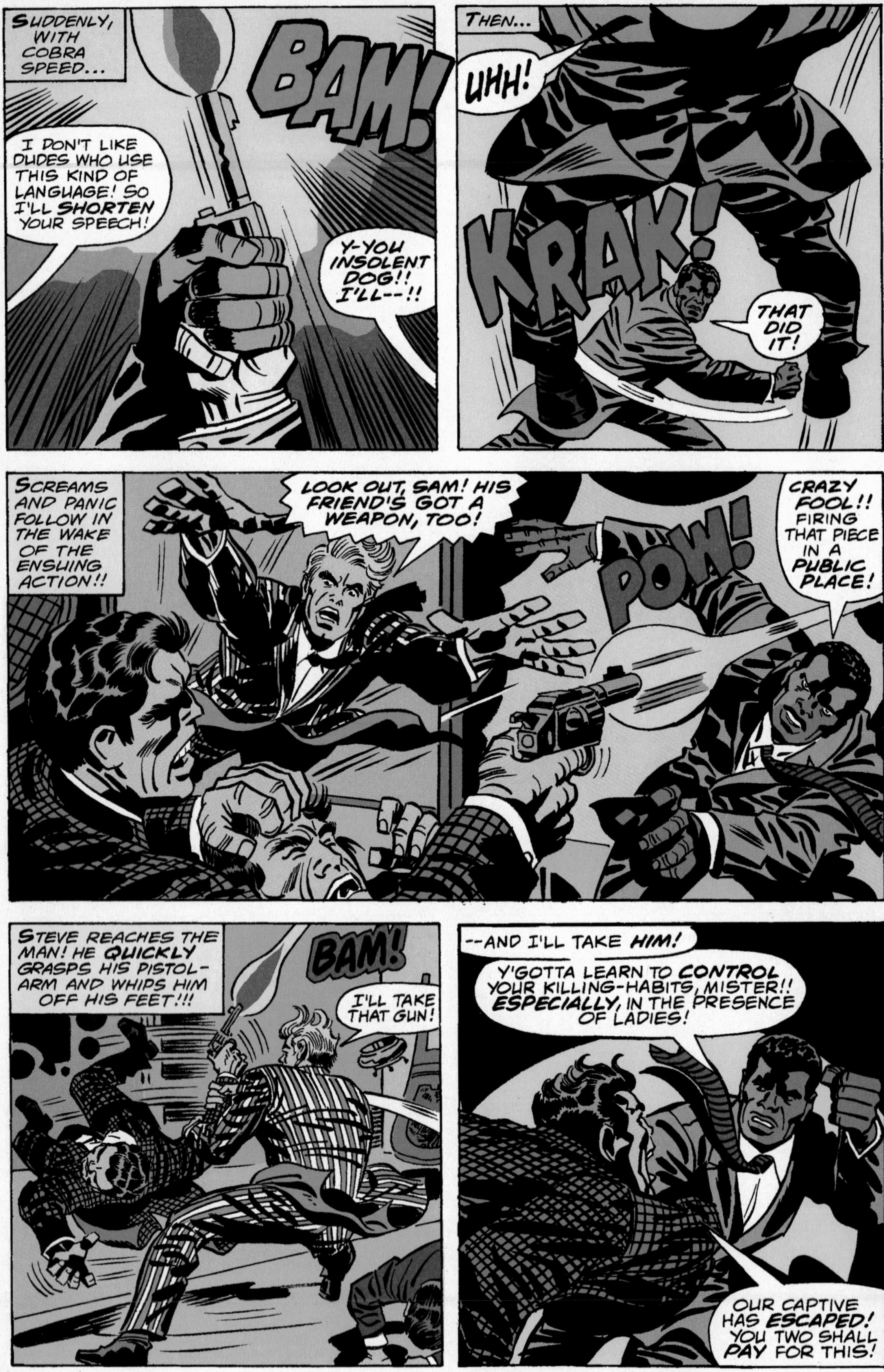
SUDDENLY, WITH COBRA SPEED...
BAM!
I DON'T LIKE DUDES WHO USE THIS KIND OF LANGUAGE! SO I'LL SHORTEN YOUR SPEECH!
Y-YOU INSOLENT DOG!! I'LL--!!
THEN...
UHH!
KRAK!
THAT DID IT!
SCREAMS AND PANIC FOLLOW IN THE WAKE OF THE ENSUING ACTION!!
LOOK OUT, SAM! HIS FRIEND'S GOT A WEAPON, TOO!
POW!
CRAZY FOOL!! FIRING THAT PIECE IN A PUBLIC PLACE!
STEVE REACHES THE MAN! HE QUICKLY GRASPS HIS PISTOL-ARM AND WHIPS HIM OFF HIS FEET!!!
BAM!
I'LL TAKE THAT GUN!
--AND I'LL TAKE HIM!
Y'GOTTA LEARN TO CONTROL YOUR KILLING-HABITS, MISTER!! ESPECIALLY, IN THE PRESENCE OF LADIES!
OUR CAPTIVE HAS ESCAPED! YOU TWO SHALL PAY FOR THIS!

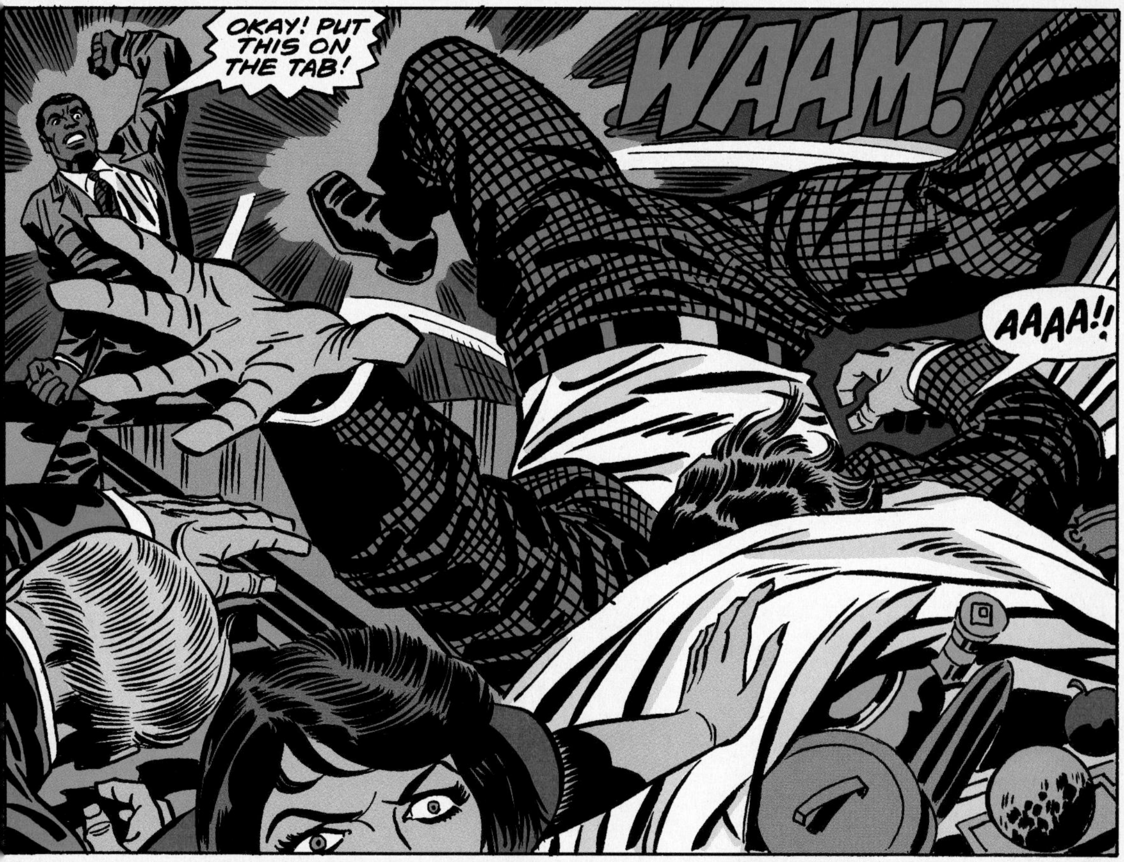
OKAY! PUT THIS ON THE TAB!
WAAM!
AAAA!!

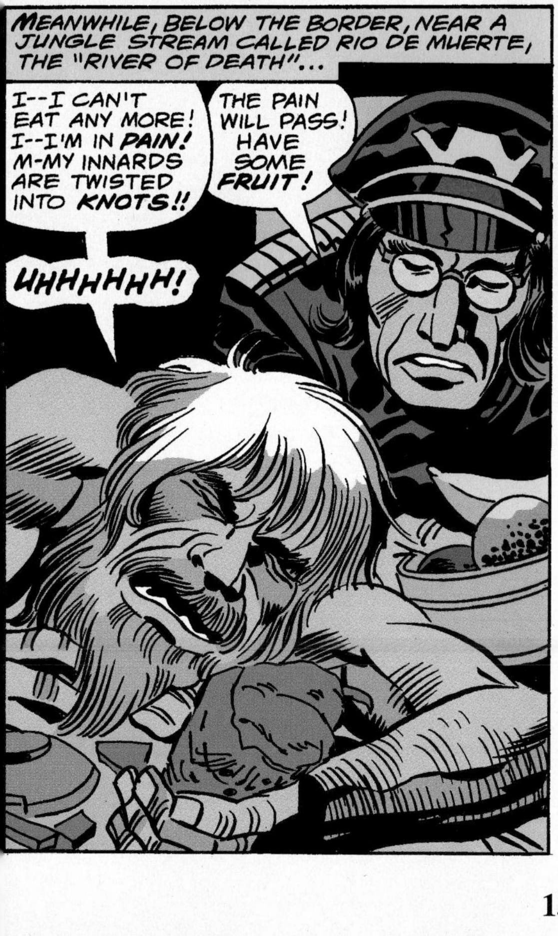
MEANWHILE, BELOW THE BORDER, NEAR A JUNGLE STREAM CALLED RIO DE MUERTE, THE "RIVER OF DEATH"...
I--I CAN'T EAT ANY MORE! I--I'M IN PAIN! M-MY INNARDS ARE TWISTED INTO KNOTS!!
THE PAIN WILL PASS! HAVE SOME FRUIT!
UHHHHHH!

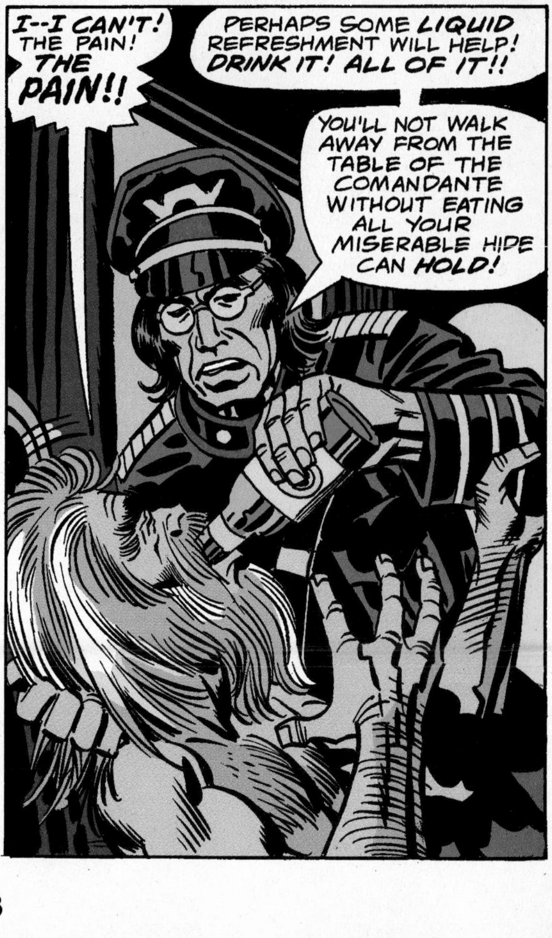
I--I CAN'T! THE PAIN! THE PAIN!!
PERHAPS SOME LIQUID REFRESHMENT WILL HELP! DRINK IT! ALL OF IT!!
YOU'LL NOT WALK AWAY FROM THE TABLE OF THE COMANDANTE WITHOUT EATING ALL YOUR MISERABLE HIDE CAN HOLD!

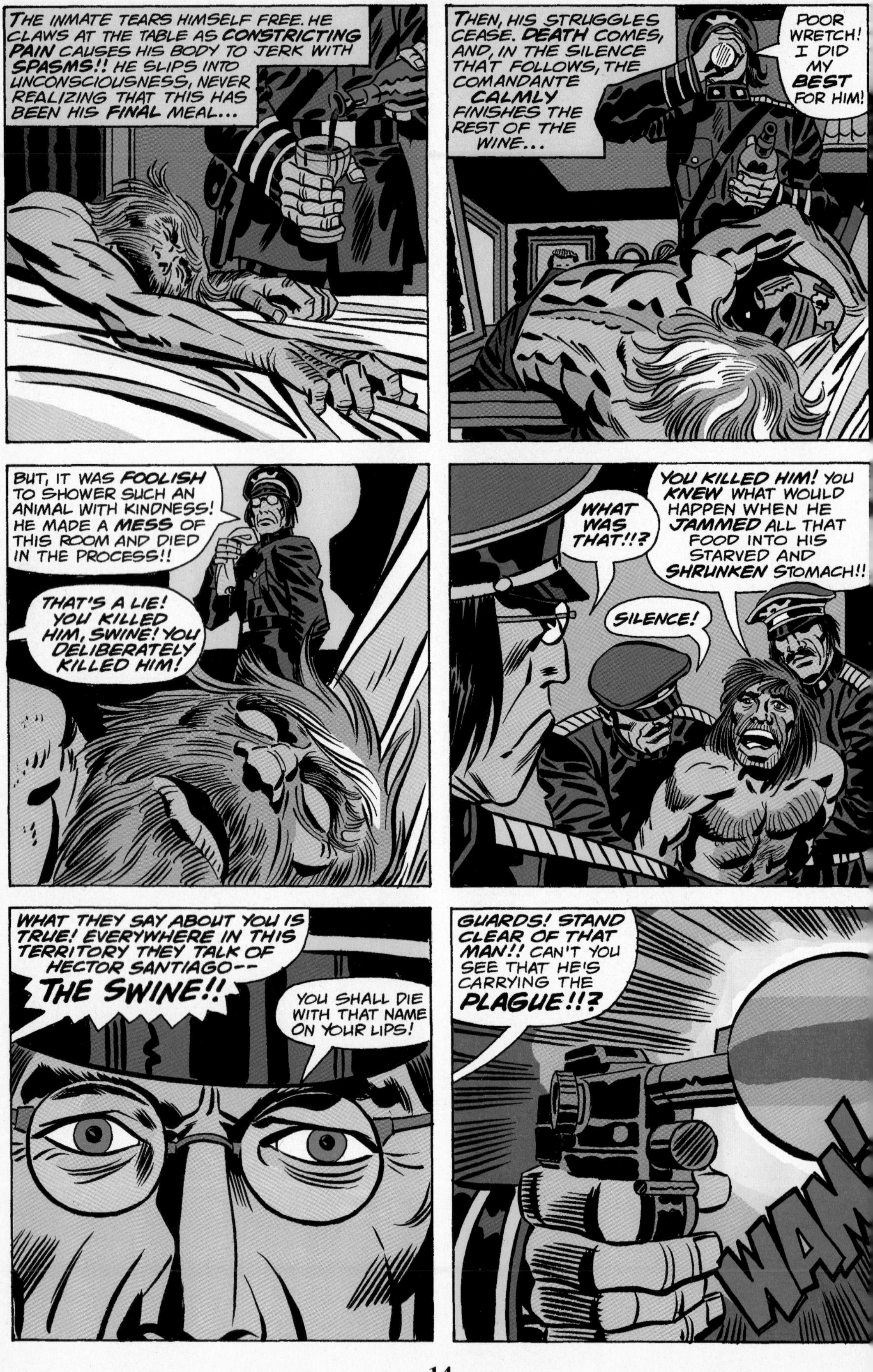
THE INMATE TEARS HIMSELF FREE. HE CLAWS AT THE TABLE AS CONSTRICTING PAIN CAUSES HIS BODY TO JERK WITH SPASMS!! HE SLIPS INTO UNCONSCIOUSNESS, NEVER REALIZING THAT THIS HAS BEEN HIS FINAL MEAL...
THEN, HIS STRUGGLES CEASE. DEATH COMES, AND, IN THE SILENCE THAT FOLLOWS, THE COMANDANTE CALMLY FINISHES THE REST OF THE WINE...
POOR WRETCH! I DID MY BEST FOR HIM!
BUT, IT WAS FOOLISH TO SHOWER SUCH AN ANIMAL WITH KINDNESS! HE MADE A MESS OF THIS ROOM AND DIED IN THE PROCESS!!
THAT'S A LIE! YOU KILLED HIM, SWINE! YOU DELIBERATELY KILLED HIM!
WHAT WAS THAT!!?
YOU KILLED HIM! YOU KNEW WHAT WOULD HAPPEN WHEN HE JAMMED ALL THAT FOOD INTO HIS STARVED AND SHRUNKEN STOMACH!!
SILENCE!
WHAT THEY SAY ABOUT YOU IS TRUE! EVERYWHERE IN THIS TERRITORY THEY TALK OF HECTOR SANTIAGO-- THE SWINE!!
YOU SHALL DIE WITH THAT NAME ON YOUR LIPS!
GUARDS! STAND CLEAR OF THAT MAN!! CAN'T YOU SEE THAT HE'S CARRYING THE PLAGUE!!?

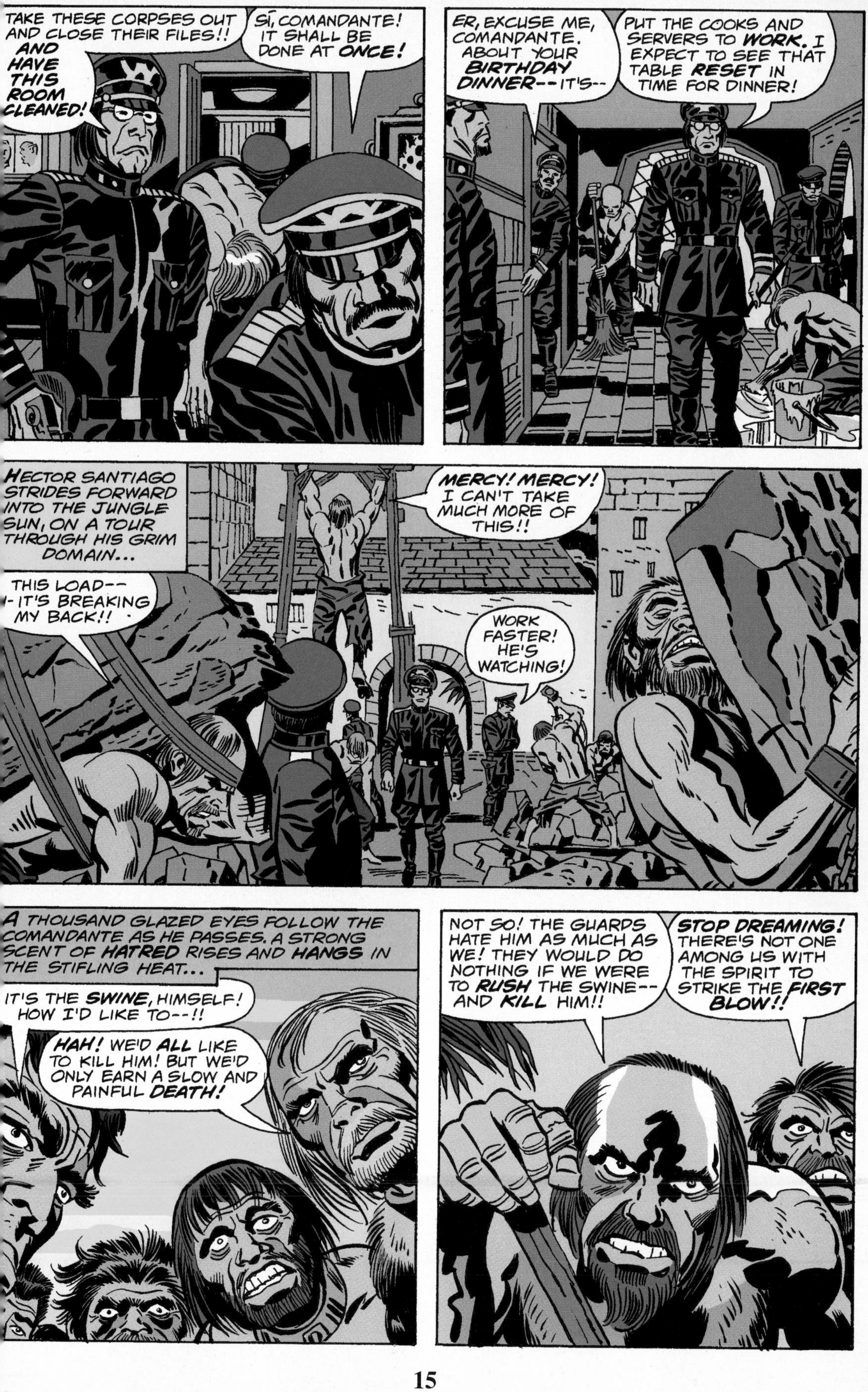

TAKE THESE CORPSES OUT AND CLOSE THEIR FILES!! AND HAVE THIS ROOM CLEANED!
SÍ, COMANDANTE! IT SHALL BE DONE AT ONCE!
ER, EXCUSE ME, COMANDANTE. ABOUT YOUR BIRTHDAY DINNER--IT'S--
PUT THE COOKS AND SERVERS TO WORK. I EXPECT TO SEE THAT TABLE RESET IN TIME FOR DINNER!
HECTOR SANTIAGO STRIDES FORWARD INTO THE JUNGLE SUN, ON A TOUR THROUGH HIS GRIM DOMAIN...
MERCY! MERCY! I CAN'T TAKE MUCH MORE OF THIS!!
THIS LOAD-- --IT'S BREAKING MY BACK!!
WORK FASTER! HE'S WATCHING!
A THOUSAND GLAZED EYES FOLLOW THE COMANDANTE AS HE PASSES. A STRONG SCENT OF HATRED RISES AND HANGS IN THE STIFLING HEAT...
IT'S THE SWINE, HIMSELF! HOW I'D LIKE TO--!!
HAH! WE'D ALL LIKE TO KILL HIM! BUT WE'D ONLY EARN A SLOW AND PAINFUL DEATH!
NOT SO! THE GUARDS HATE HIM AS MUCH AS WE! THEY WOULD DO NOTHING IF WE WERE TO RUSH THE SWINE-- AND KILL HIM!!
STOP DREAMING! THERE'S NOT ONE AMONG US WITH THE SPIRIT TO STRIKE THE FIRST BLOW!!

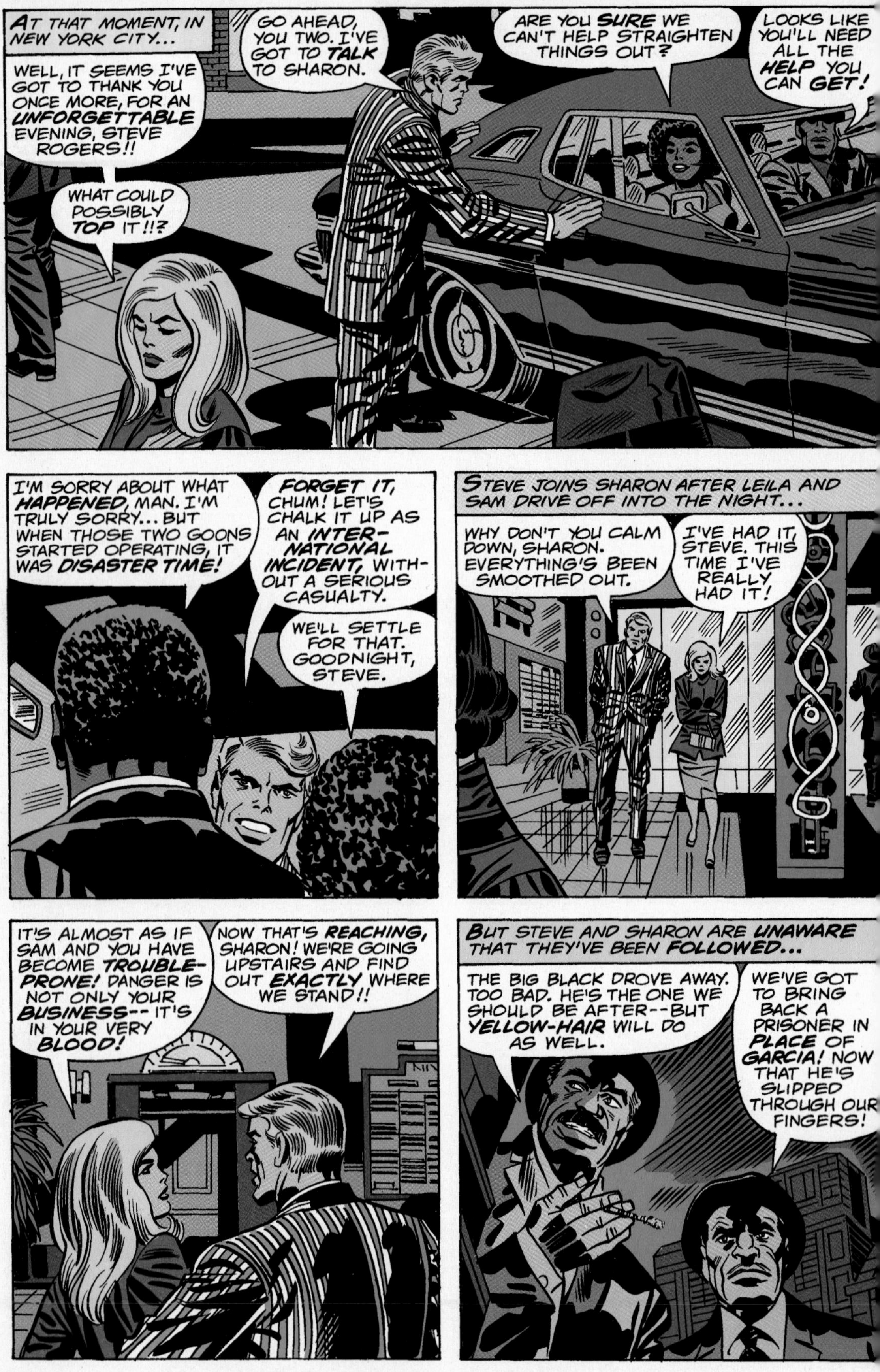
AT THAT MOMENT, IN NEW YORK CITY...
WELL, IT SEEMS I'VE GOT TO THANK YOU ONCE MORE, FOR AN UNFORGETTABLE EVENING, STEVE ROGERS!!
WHAT COULD POSSIBLY TOP IT!!?
GO AHEAD, YOU TWO. I'VE GOT TO TALK TO SHARON.
ARE YOU SURE WE CAN'T HELP STRAIGHTEN THINGS OUT?
LOOKS LIKE YOU'LL NEED ALL THE HELP YOU CAN GET!
I'M SORRY ABOUT WHAT HAPPENED, MAN. I'M TRULY SORRY... BUT WHEN THOSE TWO GOONS STARTED OPERATING, IT WAS DISASTER TIME!
FORGET IT, CHUM! LET'S CHALK IT UP AS AN INTER-NATIONAL INCIDENT, WITH-OUT A SERIOUS CASUALTY.
WE'LL SETTLE FOR THAT. GOODNIGHT, STEVE.
STEVE JOINS SHARON AFTER LEILA AND SAM DRIVE OFF INTO THE NIGHT...
WHY DON'T YOU CALM DOWN, SHARON. EVERYTHING'S BEEN SMOOTHED OUT.
I'VE HAD IT, STEVE. THIS TIME I'VE REALLY HAD IT!
IT'S ALMOST AS IF SAM AND YOU HAVE BECOME TROUBLE-PRONE! DANGER IS NOT ONLY YOUR BUSINESS-- IT'S IN YOUR VERY BLOOD!
NOW THAT'S REACHING, SHARON! WE'RE GOING UPSTAIRS AND FIND OUT EXACTLY WHERE WE STAND!!
BUT STEVE AND SHARON ARE UNAWARE THAT THEY'VE BEEN FOLLOWED...
THE BIG BLACK DROVE AWAY. TOO BAD. HE'S THE ONE WE SHOULD BE AFTER--BUT YELLOW-HAIR WILL DO AS WELL.
WE'VE GOT TO BRING BACK A PRISONER IN PLACE OF GARCIA! NOW THAT HE'S SLIPPED THROUGH OUR FINGERS!

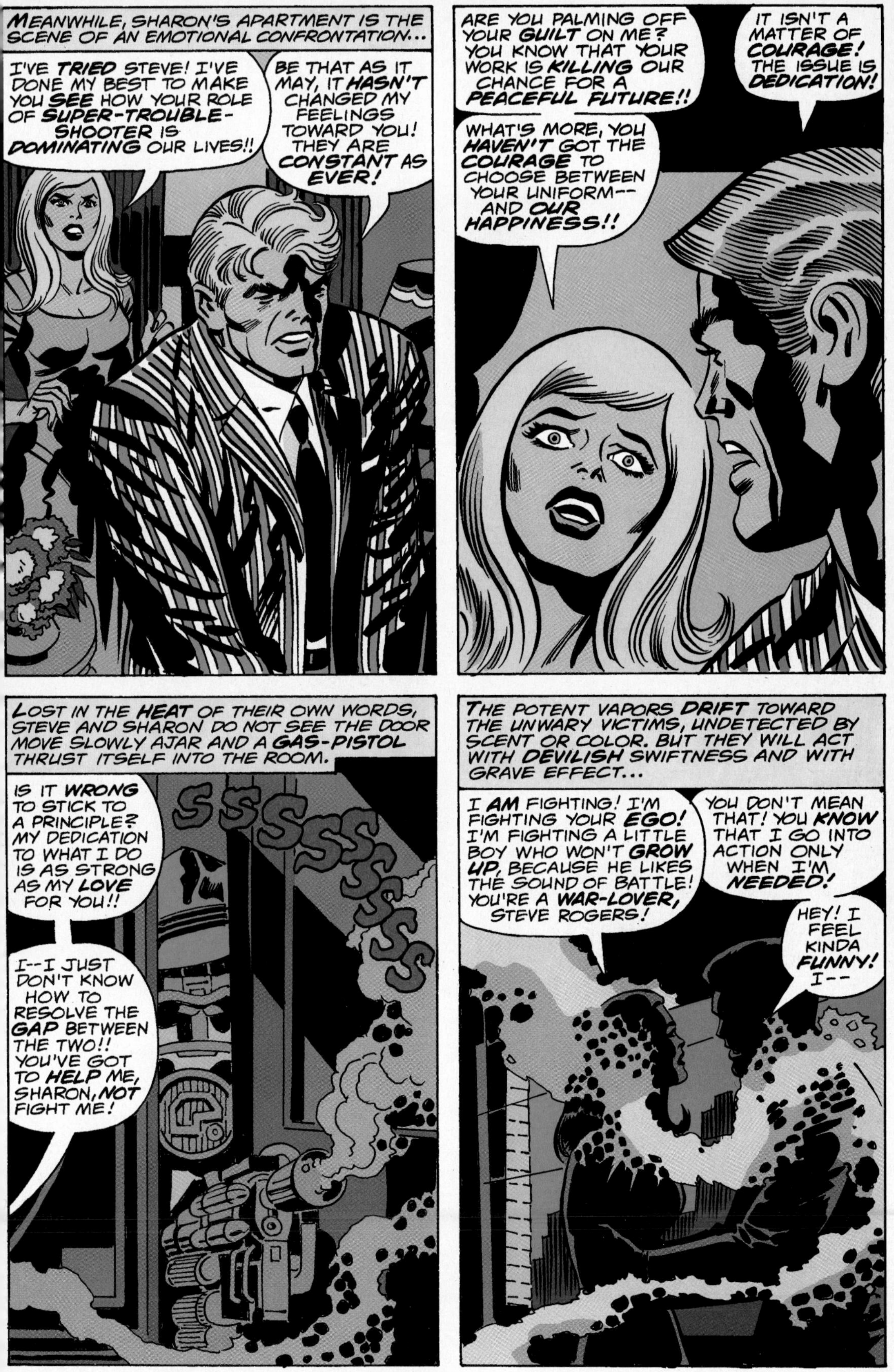
MEANWHILE, SHARON'S APARTMENT IS THE SCENE OF AN EMOTIONAL CONFRONTATION...
I'VE TRIED STEVE! I'VE DONE MY BEST TO MAKE YOU SEE HOW YOUR ROLE OF SUPER-TROUBLE-SHOOTER IS DOMINATING OUR LIVES!!
BE THAT AS IT MAY, IT HASN'T CHANGED MY FEELINGS TOWARD YOU! THEY ARE CONSTANT AS EVER!
ARE YOU PALMING OFF YOUR GUILT ON ME? YOU KNOW THAT YOUR WORK IS KILLING OUR CHANCE FOR A PEACEFUL FUTURE!!
WHAT'S MORE, YOU HAVEN'T GOT THE COURAGE TO CHOOSE BETWEEN YOUR UNIFORM-- AND OUR HAPPINESS!!
IT ISN'T A MATTER OF COURAGE! THE ISSUE IS DEDICATION!
LOST IN THE HEAT OF THEIR OWN WORDS, STEVE AND SHARON DO NOT SEE THE DOOR MOVE SLOWLY AJAR AND A GAS-PISTOL THRUST ITSELF INTO THE ROOM.
IS IT WRONG TO STICK TO A PRINCIPLE? MY DEDICATION TO WHAT I DO IS AS STRONG AS MY LOVE FOR YOU!!
I--I JUST DON'T KNOW HOW TO RESOLVE THE GAP BETWEEN THE TWO!! YOU'VE GOT TO HELP ME, SHARON, NOT FIGHT ME!
SSSSSSSSSSS
THE POTENT VAPORS DRIFT TOWARD THE UNWARY VICTIMS, UNDETECTED BY SCENT OR COLOR. BUT THEY WILL ACT WITH DEVILISH SWIFTNESS AND WITH GRAVE EFFECT...
I AM FIGHTING! I'M FIGHTING YOUR EGO! I'M FIGHTING A LITTLE BOY WHO WON'T GROW UP, BECAUSE HE LIKES THE SOUND OF BATTLE! YOU'RE A WAR-LOVER, STEVE ROGERS!
YOU DON'T MEAN THAT! YOU KNOW THAT I GO INTO ACTION ONLY WHEN I'M NEEDED!
HEY! I FEEL KINDA FUNNY! I--

THERE IS NO TIME FOR ALARM OR ACTION. THE VOICES OF STEVE AND SHARON ARE SUDDENLY *STILLED* AS THE INTRUDERS INVADE THE ROOM...

THUMP!

IT'S *DONE!* THEY'VE PASSED OUT!

LET'S GET TO WORK!

SEÑOR YELLOW-HAIR WILL FACE A MUCH *GREATER* PROBLEM WHEN HE *AWAKENS!*

IT'S *HIM* OR *US,* AMIGO!

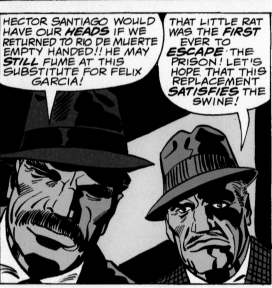

HECTOR SANTIAGO WOULD HAVE OUR *HEADS* IF WE RETURNED TO RIO DE MUERTE EMPTY HANDED!! HE MAY *STILL* FUME AT THIS SUBSTITUTE FOR FELIX GARCIA!

THAT LITTLE RAT WAS THE *FIRST* EVER TO *ESCAPE* THE PRISON! LET'S HOPE THAT THIS REPLACEMENT *SATISFIES* THE SWINE!

HE'LL *DO,* ALL RIGHT! THE SWINE WILL *ENJOY* BREAKING HIS SPIRIT!!

SOMETHING *WRONG?*

WH--!? WHAT'S *THIS!!?*

STRANGE! THERE'S A *HARDNESS* BENEATH HIS JACKET! CAN THIS *HOMBRE* BE WEARING AN *ARMORED VEST?*

ROLL UP THE JACKET! LET'S HAVE A *LOOK!*

THEN--!!!

WHAT DO YOU MAKE OF THIS!!? YELLOW-HAIR CONCEALS A YANKEE *SHIELD* AND *COSTUME!!*

HE IS A STRANGE ONE *INDEED,* AMIGO!

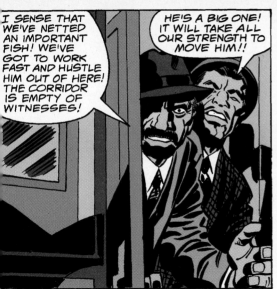

I SENSE THAT WE'VE NETTED AN IMPORTANT FISH! WE'VE GOT TO WORK FAST AND HUSTLE HIM OUT OF HERE! THE CORRIDOR IS EMPTY OF WITNESSES!

HE'S A BIG ONE! IT WILL TAKE ALL OUR STRENGTH TO MOVE HIM!!

QUICKLY! WE'LL TAKE HIM DOWN THE *FREIGHT* ELEVATOR. THERE'S LESS CHANCE OF DISCOVERY!

HAHAHA! THIS IS A STROKE OF *LUCK,* AMIGO.

HECTOR SANTIAGO WILL RAISE OUR *PAY* FOR BRINGING THIS ONE TO HIM. I THINK YELLOW-HAIR IS ONE OF THOSE SUPER-HEROES!

OF COURSE! A *SUPER-HERO!* THE SWINE WILL *LOVE* TO WORK ON A SUPER-HERO!

DANGER SEEMS TO SEND ITS OWN SIGNALS WHEN THERE IS RAPPORT BETWEEN INDIVIDUALS WHO LIVE WITH IT-- LIKE STEVE ROGERS AND SAM WILSON-- FOR AT THAT MOMENT IN LEILA'S APARTMENT...

NO, YOU DON'T SAM!! *DON'T TOUCH THAT PHONE!*

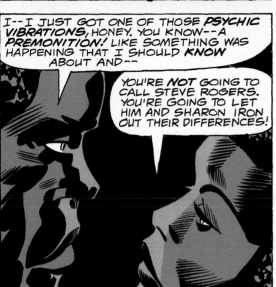

I-- I JUST GOT ONE OF THOSE *PSYCHIC VIBRATIONS,* HONEY. YOU KNOW-- A *PREMONITION!* LIKE SOMETHING WAS HAPPENING THAT I SHOULD *KNOW* ABOUT AND--

YOU'RE *NOT* GOING TO CALL STEVE ROGERS. YOU'RE GOING TO LET HIM AND SHARON IRON OUT THEIR DIFFERENCES!

WHILE *WE* MAKE THE *MOST* OF OUR COMPATABILITY!! WE *ARE* COMPATIBLE, AREN'T WE SAM?

WOMAN, IT WOULD TAKE AN *EARTH-QUAKE* TO SHAKE ME LOOSE FROM THIS *VELVET TRAP!!*

THUS, FATE'S WEB IS SPUN. THUS, THE SPIDER AWAITS THE COMING OF THE FLY...

COMANDANTE! I CAN DO *NOTHING* WITH THIS ONE!

HE FEIGNS, FATIGUE, NO DOUBT.

HE CLAIMS THAT HE WANTS A LIGHTER TASK. HE CANNOT CONTINUE WITH THIS ONE!

OF COURSE! IT'S QUITE *UNDER-STANDABLE!*

THE STONES GROW *HEAVIER,* EXCELLENCY. I CAN *NO LONGER* CARRY THEM.

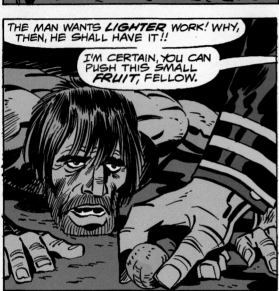

THE MAN WANTS *LIGHTER* WORK! WHY, THEN, HE SHALL HAVE IT!!

I'M CERTAIN, YOU CAN PUSH THIS SMALL *FRUIT,* FELLOW.

HE SHALL PUSH IT WITH HIS *NOSE! TEN MILES* EACH DAY, FOR A *MONTH!!* AND, IF HE PROTESTS, THEN RETURN HIM TO THE *BOULDERS!*

HAHAHAHA! HE'LL WEAR HIS NOSE DOWN IN A *WEEK!!* HAHAHA!

AND, OBSERVING NEARBY--

HECTOR, THE SWINE TRULY *EARNS* HIS NAME! ONLY SATAN *HIMSELF* COULD MATCH HIS SENSE OF HUMOR!

THERE IS A *DEVIL* INSIDE HIM, ALL RIGHT.

A DEVIL OF A *WOMAN!*

NO! IT IS *FEAR* AND *HATE* THAT DRIVES THE SWINE! BUT THE WOMAN HELPS! SHE FANS THE FIRES THAT WILL SOMEDAY *DESTROY* HIM!

AND TO THINK THAT HECTOR HAS SUCH A DESTROYER IN HIS VERY *OWN FAMILY...*

I WONDER HOW SHE WILL FINALLY DO HIM IN!!?

DONNA MARIA! I WARNED YOU ABOUT TAKING THESE SUN-BATHS WITHIN SIGHT OF THE GUARDS AND INMATES!!

MY WORK AT THE ADMINISTRATIVE OFFICE IS *DONE* FOR THE DAY, COUSIN. SO, I RELAX WHERE I *CHOOSE!*

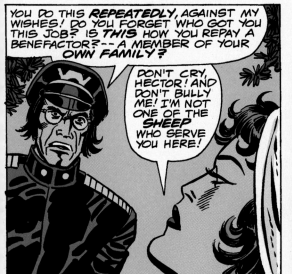

YOU DO THIS *REPEATEDLY*, AGAINST MY WISHES! DO YOU FORGET WHO GOT YOU THIS JOB? IS *THIS* HOW YOU REPAY A BENEFACTOR? -- A MEMBER OF YOUR *OWN FAMILY?*

DON'T CRY, HECTOR! AND DON'T BULLY ME! I'M NOT ONE OF THE *SHEEP* WHO SERVE YOU HERE!

AND I'M NOT A PATIENT MAN, COUSIN! *MY WORD IS LAW IN THIS PLACE!*

I KNOW IT WELL, HECTOR. I *KNOW* HOW YOU USE IT TO *AMUSE* YOURSELF WITH *BROKEN SPIRITS!*

IF YOU *DISAPPROVE* OF MY METHODS HERE, YOU ARE ALWAYS WELCOME TO *LEAVE* RIO DE MUERTE!

NO, HECTOR! I'LL *WAIT!* I KNOW THAT A *REAL* MAN WILL ONE DAY COME HERE AMONG US TO BREAK *YOU* -- AS YOU HAVE BROKEN *OTHERS!!!*

NEXT ISSUE: THE TIGER AND THE SWINE!

21

CAPT. AMERICA
MARVEL® COMICS GROUP
APPROVED BY THE COMICS CODE AUTHORITY
30¢
207 MAR 02453
CAPTAIN AMERICA AND THE FALCON
© 1976 MARVEL COMICS GROUP
THEY HUNT THE MOST DANGEROUS PREY OF ALL-- A SUPERHERO!
"THE TIGER AND THE SWINE!"

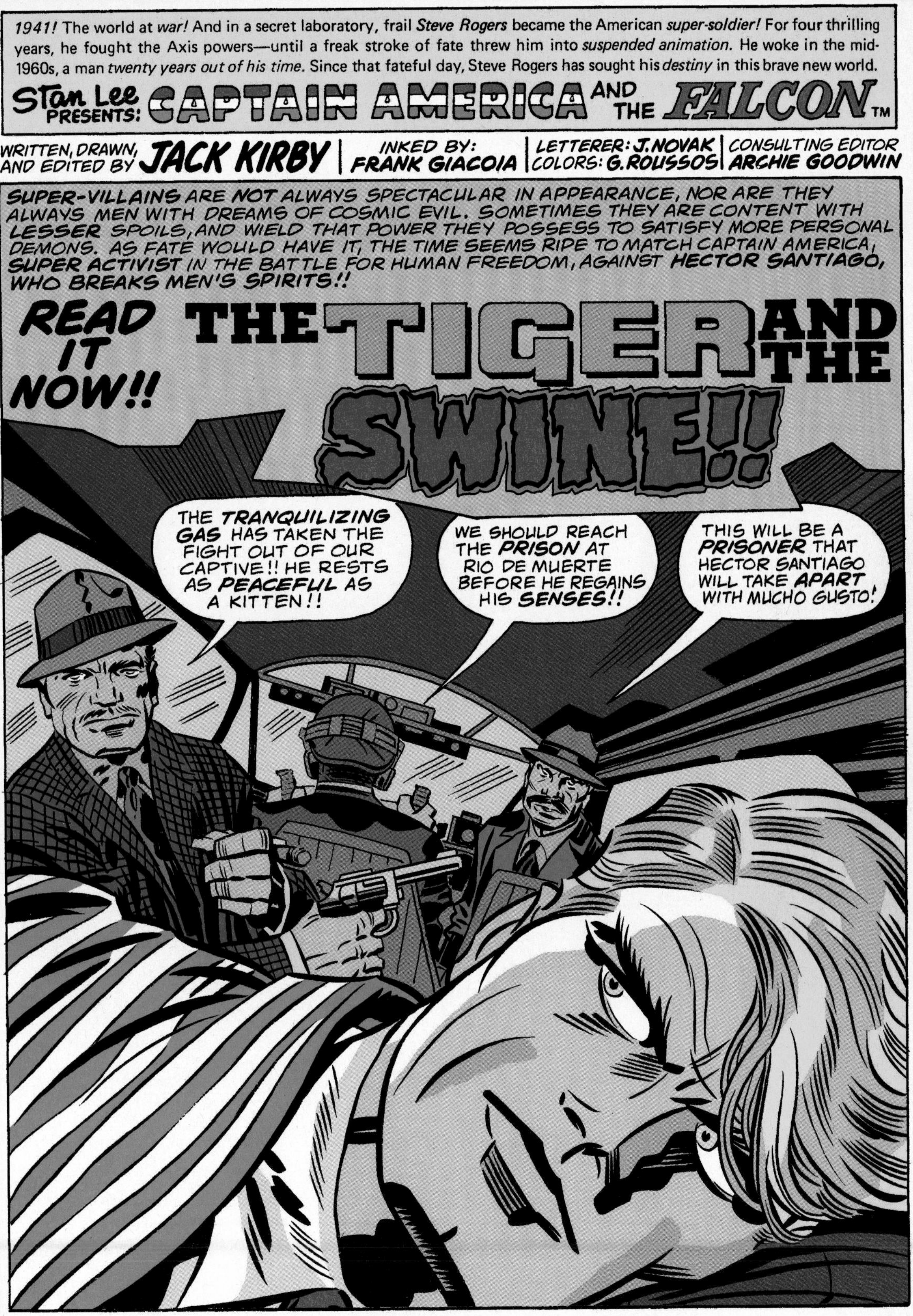

1941! The world at war! And in a secret laboratory, frail Steve Rogers became the American super-soldier! For four thrilling years, he fought the Axis powers—until a freak stroke of fate threw him into suspended animation. He woke in the mid-1960s, a man twenty years out of his time. Since that fateful day, Steve Rogers has sought his destiny in this brave new world.
Stan Lee PRESENTS: CAPTAIN AMERICA AND THE FALCON TM
WRITTEN, DRAWN, AND EDITED BY JACK KIRBY
INKED BY: FRANK GIACOIA
LETTERER: J. NOVAK COLORS: G. ROUSSOS
CONSULTING EDITOR ARCHIE GOODWIN
SUPER-VILLAINS ARE NOT ALWAYS SPECTACULAR IN APPEARANCE, NOR ARE THEY ALWAYS MEN WITH DREAMS OF COSMIC EVIL. SOMETIMES THEY ARE CONTENT WITH LESSER SPOILS, AND WIELD THAT POWER THEY POSSESS TO SATISFY MORE PERSONAL DEMONS. AS FATE WOULD HAVE IT, THE TIME SEEMS RIPE TO MATCH CAPTAIN AMERICA, SUPER ACTIVIST IN THE BATTLE FOR HUMAN FREEDOM, AGAINST HECTOR SANTIAGO, WHO BREAKS MEN'S SPIRITS!!
READ IT NOW!!
THE TIGER AND THE SWINE!!
THE TRANQUILIZING GAS HAS TAKEN THE FIGHT OUT OF OUR CAPTIVE!! HE RESTS AS PEACEFUL AS A KITTEN!!
WE SHOULD REACH THE PRISON AT RIO DE MUERTE BEFORE HE REGAINS HIS SENSES!!
THIS WILL BE A PRISONER THAT HECTOR SANTIAGO WILL TAKE APART WITH MUCHO GUSTO!

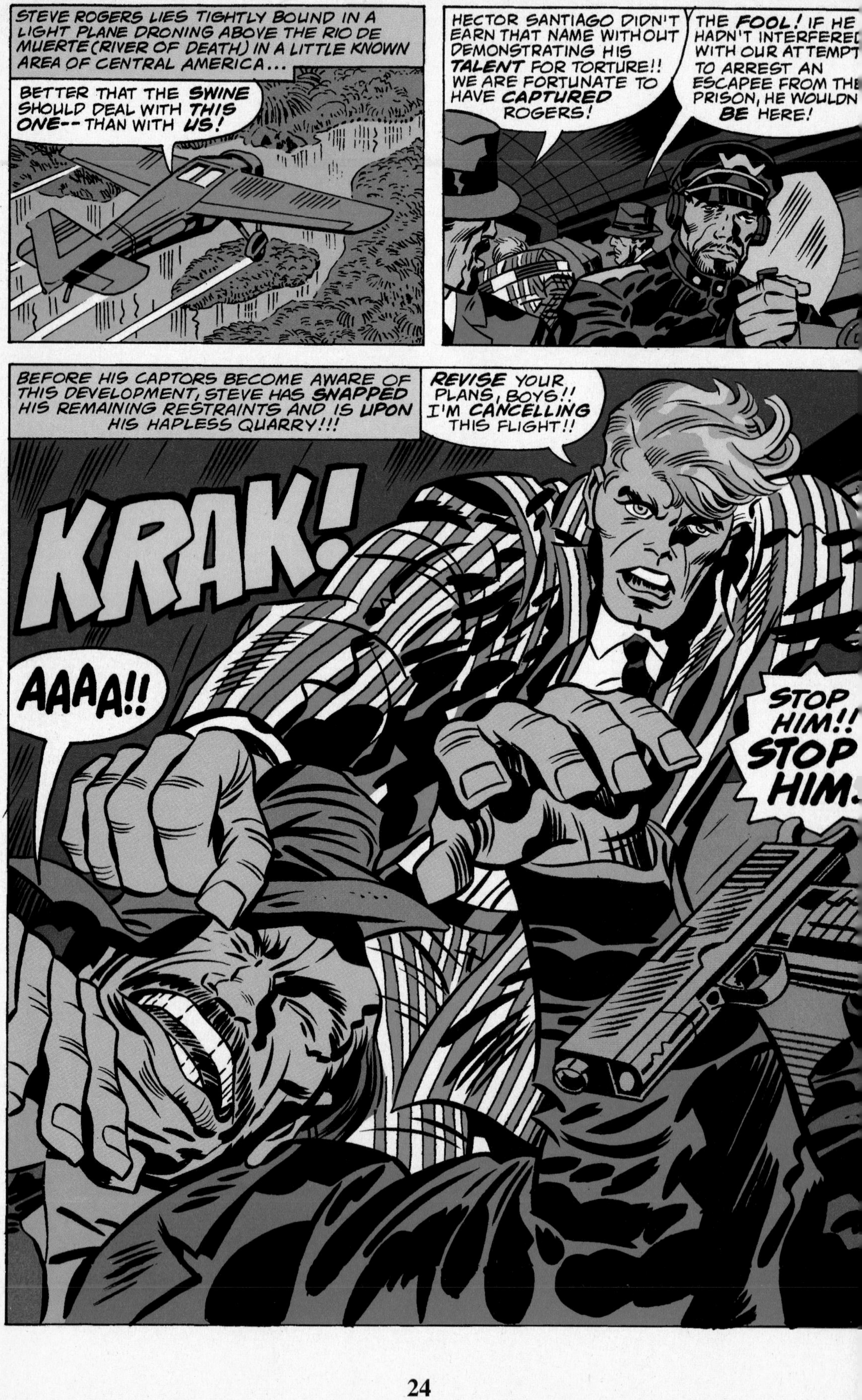
STEVE ROGERS LIES TIGHTLY BOUND IN A LIGHT PLANE DRONING ABOVE THE RIO DE MUERTE (RIVER OF DEATH) IN A LITTLE KNOWN AREA OF CENTRAL AMERICA...
BETTER THAT THE SWINE SHOULD DEAL WITH THIS ONE-- THAN WITH US!
HECTOR SANTIAGO DIDN'T EARN THAT NAME WITHOUT DEMONSTRATING HIS TALENT FOR TORTURE!! WE ARE FORTUNATE TO HAVE CAPTURED ROGERS!
THE FOOL! IF HE HADN'T INTERFERED WITH OUR ATTEMPT TO ARREST AN ESCAPEE FROM THE PRISON, HE WOULDN BE HERE!
BEFORE HIS CAPTORS BECOME AWARE OF THIS DEVELOPMENT, STEVE HAS SNAPPED HIS REMAINING RESTRAINTS AND IS UPON HIS HAPLESS QUARRY!!!
REVISE YOUR PLANS, BOYS!! I'M CANCELLING THIS FLIGHT!!
KRAK!
AAAA!!
STOP HIM!! STOP HIM.

ROGERS' MISFORTUNE IS OUR SALVATION! IT WOULD HAVE BEEN UNTHINKABLE TO RETURN TO THE SWINE WITHOUT A PRISONER.

WE'RE NOT THERE YET, YOU CREEPS!

STEVE'S FISTS CLENCH AND CAUSE A PRESSURE WHICH RELEASES A MINIATURE FLAME DEVICE ATTACHED TO HIS INNER SLEEVE. IT DROPS INTO HIS PALM AND ACTIVATES-- LITERALLY BURNING AWAY HIS BONDS...

MUST REMEMBER TO THANK NICK FURY FOR THIS GADGET.

WHA--!?!? WUMPHH!!

SMASH!

25

STEVE QUICKLY DISABLES HIS SURPRISED GUARDS AND SEIZES THE PILOT IN A STEEL GRIP...

NOW, USE WHAT FUEL YOU'VE GOT LEFT TO GET US *BACK* TO THE BORDER!!

YOU TURN THIS CRATE AROUND-- AND *I'LL* THINK ABOUT RELAXING THIS HOLD!

I--I CAN'T! I CA--!

YOU'LL DO AS I *TELL* YOU, MISTER!! OR I'LL *COOL* YOU OFF AND TAKE THE CONTROLS *MYSELF*!!

Y-YOU *DON'T* UNDERSTAND! I-IF WE DON'T DELIVER YOU TO THE *SWINE*--HE WILL TAKE OUR *HEADS*!!

AT THAT MOMENT, ONE OF THE GUARDS RECOVERS AND RETRIEVES HIS WEAPON...

IF WE CAN'T BRING YOU IN ALIVE--YOUR *CORPSE* WILL DO AS WELL!!

POW!

UGH--!

H-HE SHOT THE PILOT!

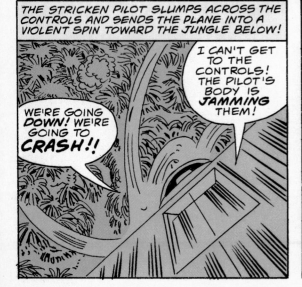

THE STRICKEN PILOT SLUMPS ACROSS THE CONTROLS AND SENDS THE PLANE INTO A VIOLENT SPIN TOWARD THE JUNGLE BELOW!

I CAN'T GET TO THE CONTROLS! THE PILOT'S BODY IS *JAMMING* THEM!

WE'RE GOING *DOWN*! WE'RE GOING TO *CRASH*!!

WHAT HAPPENS NEXT IS *INEVITABLE*! THE PLANE HURTLES INTO THE MASS OF GREENERY, AMID SHATTERING ECHOES THAT ARE SOON *SMOTHERED* BY THE JUNGLE...

WAAMM!!

THERE IS A PERIOD OF *SILENCE*... THE *SIBILANT* WISPS OF RISING VAPOR ARE THE ONLY SIGNS OF MOVEMENT FROM THE WRECKAGE... *THEN*--

SCORE *ANOTHER* NARROW MISS FOR MRS. ROGERS' BOY. I-I'M *ALIVE!*

E-EVERYTHING *SEEMS* IN PLACE. MY BONES ARE WHERE THEY SHOULD BE! BUT, IT WILL TAKE A MINUTE OR TWO BEFORE I GET MY *WIND* BACK...

I'LL CHECK ON THE OTHERS. *CAN'T* LEAVE THEM IN THE WRECK!

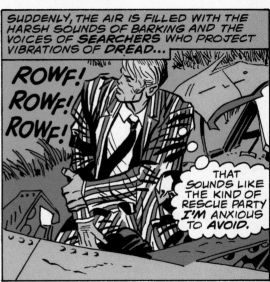

SUDDENLY, THE AIR IS FILLED WITH THE HARSH SOUNDS OF BARKING AND THE VOICES OF *SEARCHERS* WHO PROJECT VIBRATIONS OF *DREAD*...

ROWF! ROWF! ROWF!

THAT SOUNDS LIKE THE KIND OF RESCUE PARTY *I'M* ANXIOUS TO *AVOID.*

THE DOGS HAVE *GOT* THE SCENT!

WE SHOULD BE *SIGHTING* THE WRECK ANY MINUTE NOW!!

ROWF! ROWF! ROWF!

STEVE CATCHES A FLEETING GLIMPSE OF UNIFORMS IN THE DENSE VEGETATION BEFORE HE DASHES FOR THE COVER OF THE JUNGLE!!

THOSE WERE *PRISON GUARDS*, ALL RIGHT!! BUT THEY'RE *NOT* GOING TO FIND THE PACKAGE THEY'RE EXPECTING!!

STEVE ROGERS HAD BETTER MAKE A *QUICK EXIT* AND *YIELD* TO SOME- ONE WHO CAN HANDLE THIS CRISIS IN THE RIGHT MANNER.

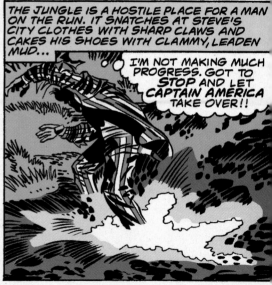

THE JUNGLE IS A HOSTILE PLACE FOR A MAN ON THE RUN. IT SNATCHES AT STEVE'S CITY CLOTHES WITH SHARP CLAWS AND CAKES HIS SHOES WITH CLAMMY, LEADEN MUD...

I'M NOT MAKING MUCH PROGRESS. GOT TO *STOP* AND LET *CAPTAIN AMERICA* TAKE OVER!!

AS THE GREEN SHADOWS ENVELOPE HIM, STEVE PAUSES TO MAKE THE *FABLED* CHANGE THAT TRANSFORMS HIM INTO A *SUPER-HERO OF REKNOWN.*

GOT TO GET *ORIENTED* AS SOON AS POSSIBLE. GOT TO FIND OUT WHERE THAT PRISON IS AND HEAD THE *OTHER* WAY!!

WHOEVER RUNS THAT *BANANA* JAIL SEEMS TO GET HIS KICKS OUT OF *KICKING* THE INMATES!

THIS MAN THEY CALL "THE SWINE" MUST BE *TYPICAL* OF THE KIND OF BULLY THAT FLOURISHES IN THESE *TWO- BIT* DICTATORSHIPS.

BUT, THIS IS *NOT MY* COUNTRY AND NOT MY PLACE TO FIGHT FOR CAUSES I KNOW *NOTHING* ABOUT.

MY IMMEDIATE PROBLEM IS TO *BEAT* THIS JUNGLE-- FIND MY WAY TO A FAIR- SIZED TOWN AND... *HOME!*

HOME IS WHERE *SHARON* IS-- WHERE FRIENDS LIKE SAM WILSON AND LEILA PITCH IN TO HELP WHEN TROUBLE STRIKES...

GAS! I--I SMELL-- GAS!

SHE'S COMING OUT OF IT, SAM. HERE, TAKE THIS, HONEY!

SHARON'S *RIGHT* ABOUT THE GAS. THERE ARE *STILL* TRACES OF IT IN THE APARTMENT.

WHAT IN BLAZES HAPPENED HERE?!

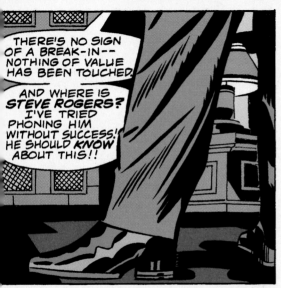

THERE'S NO SIGN OF A BREAK-IN-- NOTHING OF VALUE HAS BEEN TOUCHED.

AND WHERE IS *STEVE ROGERS?* I'VE TRIED PHONING HIM WITHOUT SUCCESS! HE SHOULD *KNOW* ABOUT THIS!!

IT'S THE GAS THAT BOTHERS ME. IT'S GOT A SORT OF *ETHER* SCENT!

I-IT COULD BE A *TRANQUILIZING* GAS!

I-IT MUST HAVE BEEN VERY *STRONG.* SHARON *CAN'T* SEEM TO SHAKE IT OFF!

TRANQUILIZING GAS!! THERE'S ONLY ONE GOOD REASON FOR USING TRAN-QUILIZING GAS!! ESPECIALLY IF YOUR TARGET IS A *ROUGH* AND *READY* DUDE LIKE--

SAM! DO YOU MEAN THAT *STEVE ROGERS* WAS HERE WHEN THIS HAPPENED?

IT DOESN'T MAKE SENSE ANY *OTHER WAY!!* WHOEVER SPREAD THIS GAS WANTED TO TAKE STEVE WITH THE *LEAST* POSSIBLE DIFFICULTY!!

THAT'S WHY STEVE DOESN'T ANSWER MY CALLS! HE'S MISSING! HE'S BEEN *KIDNAPPED!!*

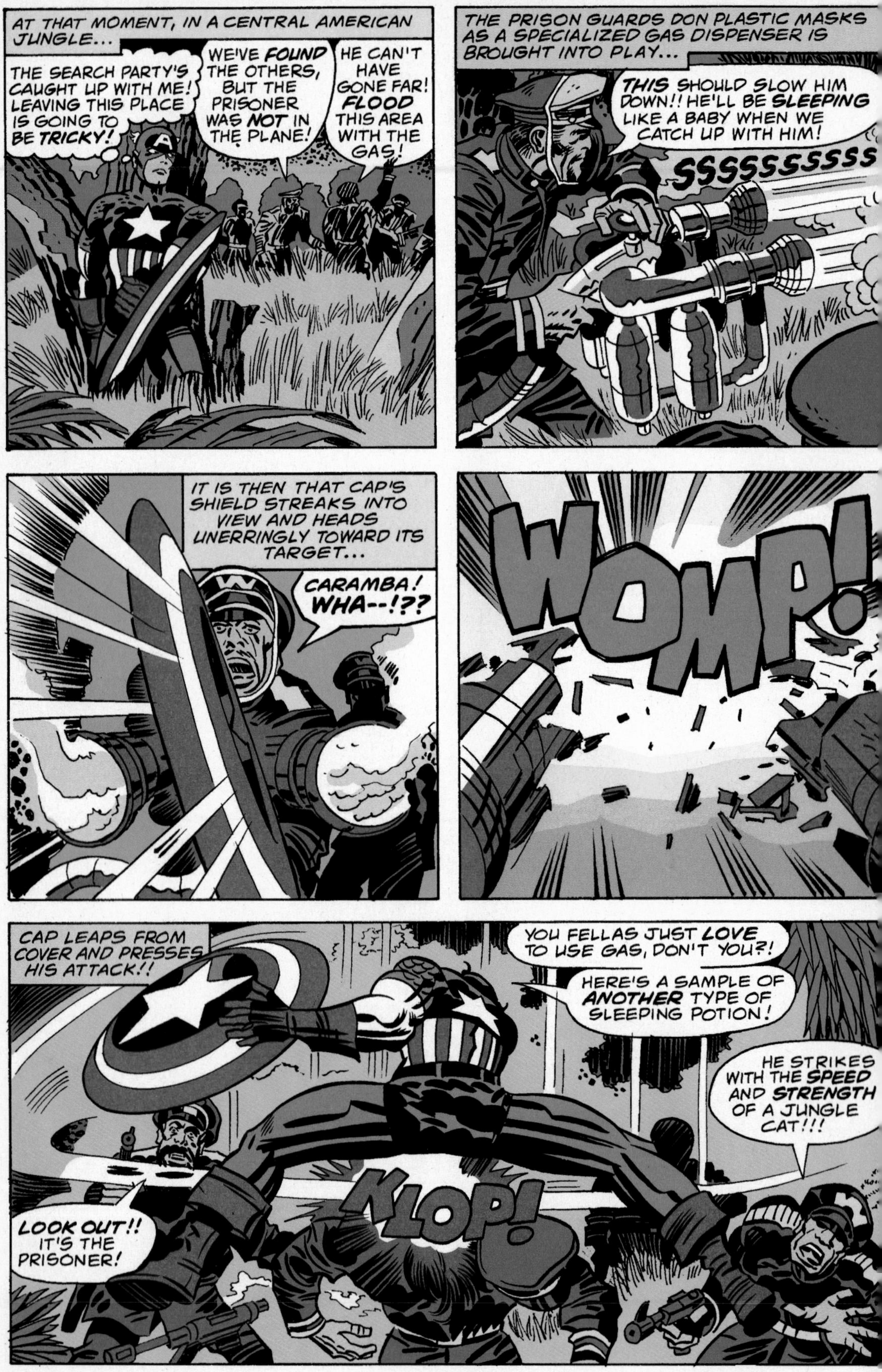
AT THAT MOMENT, IN A CENTRAL AMERICAN JUNGLE...
THE SEARCH PARTY'S CAUGHT UP WITH ME! LEAVING THIS PLACE IS GOING TO BE TRICKY!
WE'VE FOUND THE OTHERS, BUT THE PRISONER WAS NOT IN THE PLANE!
HE CAN'T HAVE GONE FAR! FLOOD THIS AREA WITH THE GAS!
THE PRISON GUARDS DON PLASTIC MASKS AS A SPECIALIZED GAS DISPENSER IS BROUGHT INTO PLAY...
THIS SHOULD SLOW HIM DOWN!! HE'LL BE SLEEPING LIKE A BABY WHEN WE CATCH UP WITH HIM!
SSSSSSSSSS
IT IS THEN THAT CAP'S SHIELD STREAKS INTO VIEW AND HEADS UNERRINGLY TOWARD ITS TARGET...
CARAMBA! WHA--!??
WOMP!
CAP LEAPS FROM COVER AND PRESSES HIS ATTACK!!
YOU FELLAS JUST LOVE TO USE GAS, DON'T YOU?!
HERE'S A SAMPLE OF ANOTHER TYPE OF SLEEPING POTION!
HE STRIKES WITH THE SPEED AND STRENGTH OF A JUNGLE CAT!!!
LOOK OUT!! IT'S THE PRISONER!
KLOP!

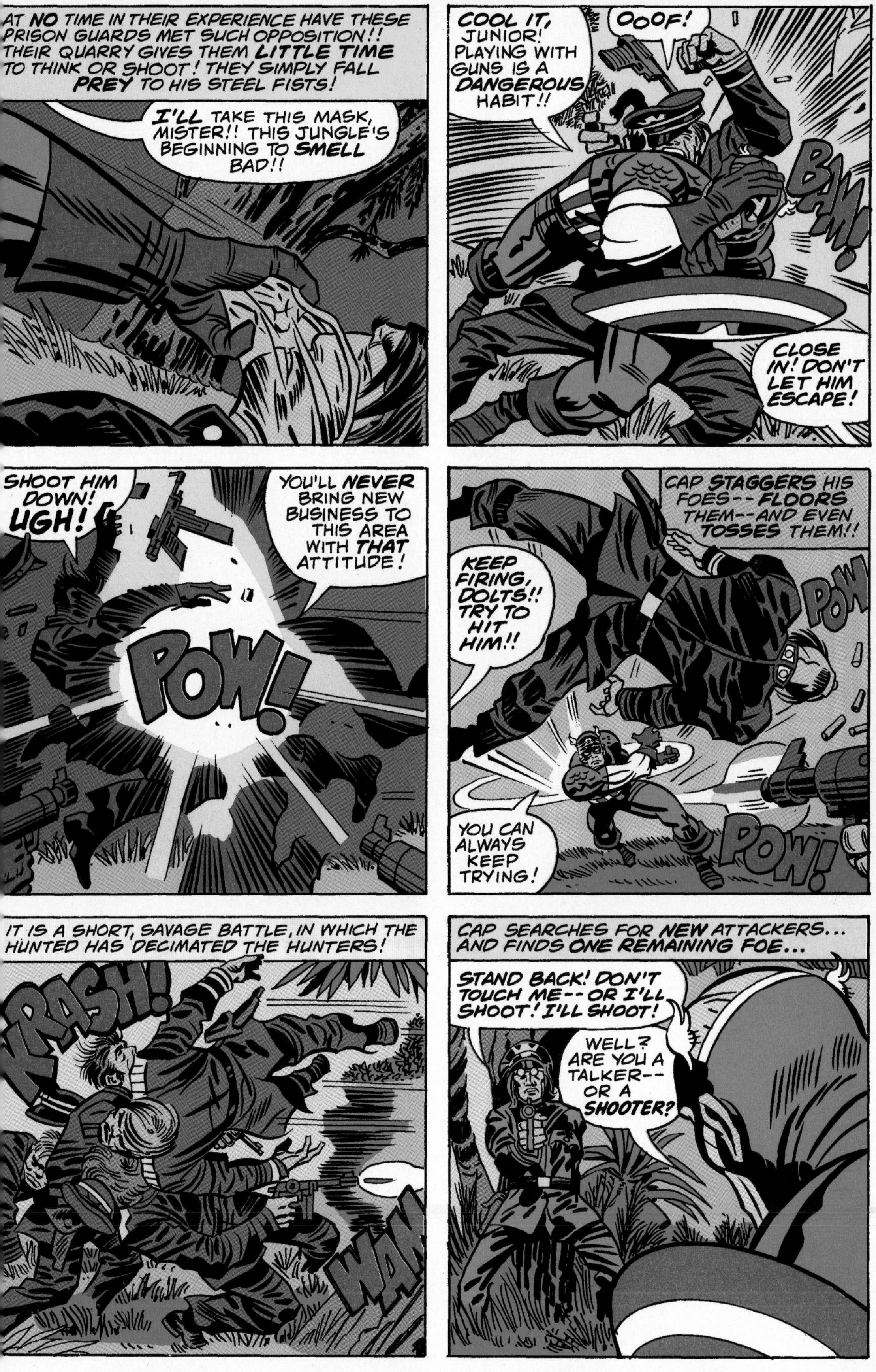
AT NO TIME IN THEIR EXPERIENCE HAVE THESE PRISON GUARDS MET SUCH OPPOSITION!! THEIR QUARRY GIVES THEM LITTLE TIME TO THINK OR SHOOT! THEY SIMPLY FALL PREY TO HIS STEEL FISTS!
I'LL TAKE THIS MASK, MISTER!! THIS JUNGLE'S BEGINNING TO SMELL BAD!!
COOL IT, JUNIOR! PLAYING WITH GUNS IS A DANGEROUS HABIT!!
OOOF!
BAM!
CLOSE IN! DON'T LET HIM ESCAPE!
SHOOT HIM DOWN! UGH!
YOU'LL NEVER BRING NEW BUSINESS TO THIS AREA WITH THAT ATTITUDE!
POW!
CAP STAGGERS HIS FOES--FLOORS THEM--AND EVEN TOSSES THEM!!
KEEP FIRING, DOLTS!! TRY TO HIT HIM!!
POW
YOU CAN ALWAYS KEEP TRYING!
POW!
IT IS A SHORT, SAVAGE BATTLE, IN WHICH THE HUNTED HAS DECIMATED THE HUNTERS!
KRASH!
CAP SEARCHES FOR NEW ATTACKERS... AND FINDS ONE REMAINING FOE...
STAND BACK! DON'T TOUCH ME--OR I'LL SHOOT! I'LL SHOOT!
WELL? ARE YOU A TALKER--OR A SHOOTER?

THERE IS SOMETHING IN THE *FEATURES* AND *MANNER* OF THE MAN THAT BRINGS BACK SNATCHES OF WHAT CAP OVERHEARD IN THE PLANE...

I *WARN* YOU! TAKE ONE MORE STEP AND *I'LL*--

YOU CAN ONLY BE *HECTOR SANTIAGO* --THE ONE THEY CALL *THE SWINE!*

I'VE *EXECUTED* MEN FOR CALLING ME THAT!! YOU SHALL *DIE* FOR IT AS WELL!

WAM WAM

SANTIAGO'S BULLETS MEET ONLY CAP'S *RESISTANT SHIELD!* A MOMENT AFTER CAP CHARGES, THE FIRING *ENDS*...

POW POW POW!!

THAT'S *ALL* THE SHOOTING YOU'RE GOING TO DO, MISTER!

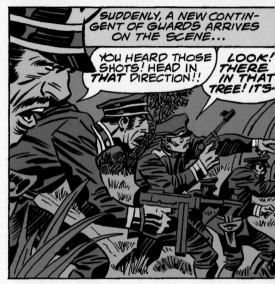

SUDDENLY, A NEW CONTINGENT OF GUARDS ARRIVES ON THE SCENE...

YOU HEARD THOSE *SHOTS!* HEAD IN THAT DIRECTION!!

LOOK! THERE IN THAT TREE! IT'S--

IT'S THE *COMANDANTE!* HOW COULD THIS HAVE HAPPENED!?

HURRY, MEN!

YES, *HURRY*, YOU FOOLS!! GET ME OFF THIS CURSED BRANCH!!

A-AT ONCE, SIR!!

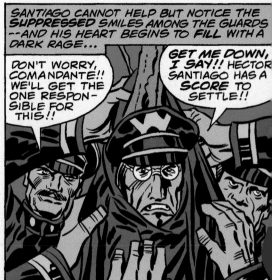

SANTIAGO CANNOT HELP BUT NOTICE THE *SUPPRESSED* SMILES AMONG THE GUARDS --AND HIS HEART BEGINS TO FILL WITH A *DARK RAGE*...

DON'T WORRY, COMANDANTE!! WE'LL GET THE ONE RESPONSIBLE FOR THIS!!

GET ME DOWN, I SAY!! HECTOR SANTIAGO HAS A *SCORE* TO SETTLE!!

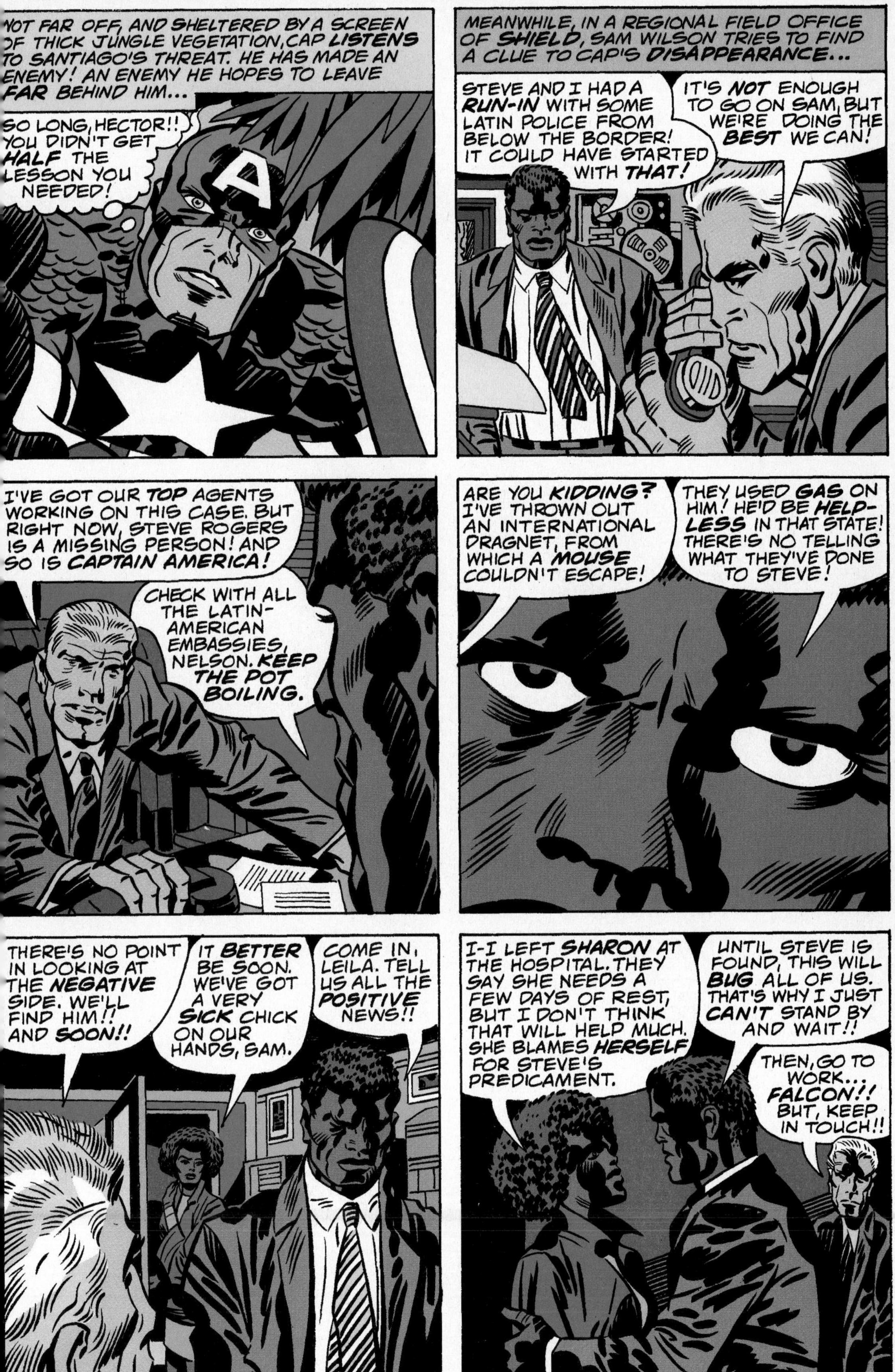
NOT FAR OFF, AND SHELTERED BY A SCREEN OF THICK JUNGLE VEGETATION, CAP LISTENS TO SANTIAGO'S THREAT. HE HAS MADE AN ENEMY! AN ENEMY HE HOPES TO LEAVE FAR BEHIND HIM...
SO LONG, HECTOR!! YOU DIDN'T GET HALF THE LESSON YOU NEEDED!
MEANWHILE, IN A REGIONAL FIELD OFFICE OF SHIELD, SAM WILSON TRIES TO FIND A CLUE TO CAP'S DISAPPEARANCE...
STEVE AND I HAD A RUN-IN WITH SOME LATIN POLICE FROM BELOW THE BORDER! IT COULD HAVE STARTED WITH THAT!
IT'S NOT ENOUGH TO GO ON SAM, BUT WE'RE DOING THE BEST WE CAN!
I'VE GOT OUR TOP AGENTS WORKING ON THIS CASE. BUT RIGHT NOW, STEVE ROGERS IS A MISSING PERSON! AND SO IS CAPTAIN AMERICA!
CHECK WITH ALL THE LATIN-AMERICAN EMBASSIES, NELSON. KEEP THE POT BOILING.
ARE YOU KIDDING? I'VE THROWN OUT AN INTERNATIONAL DRAGNET, FROM WHICH A MOUSE COULDN'T ESCAPE!
THEY USED GAS ON HIM! HE'D BE HELPLESS IN THAT STATE! THERE'S NO TELLING WHAT THEY'VE DONE TO STEVE!
THERE'S NO POINT IN LOOKING AT THE NEGATIVE SIDE. WE'LL FIND HIM!! AND SOON!!
IT BETTER BE SOON. WE'VE GOT A VERY SICK CHICK ON OUR HANDS, SAM.
COME IN, LEILA. TELL US ALL THE POSITIVE NEWS!!
I-I LEFT SHARON AT THE HOSPITAL. THEY SAY SHE NEEDS A FEW DAYS OF REST, BUT I DON'T THINK THAT WILL HELP MUCH. SHE BLAMES HERSELF FOR STEVE'S PREDICAMENT.
UNTIL STEVE IS FOUND, THIS WILL BUG ALL OF US. THAT'S WHY I JUST CAN'T STAND BY AND WAIT!!
THEN, GO TO WORK... FALCON!! BUT, KEEP IN TOUCH!!

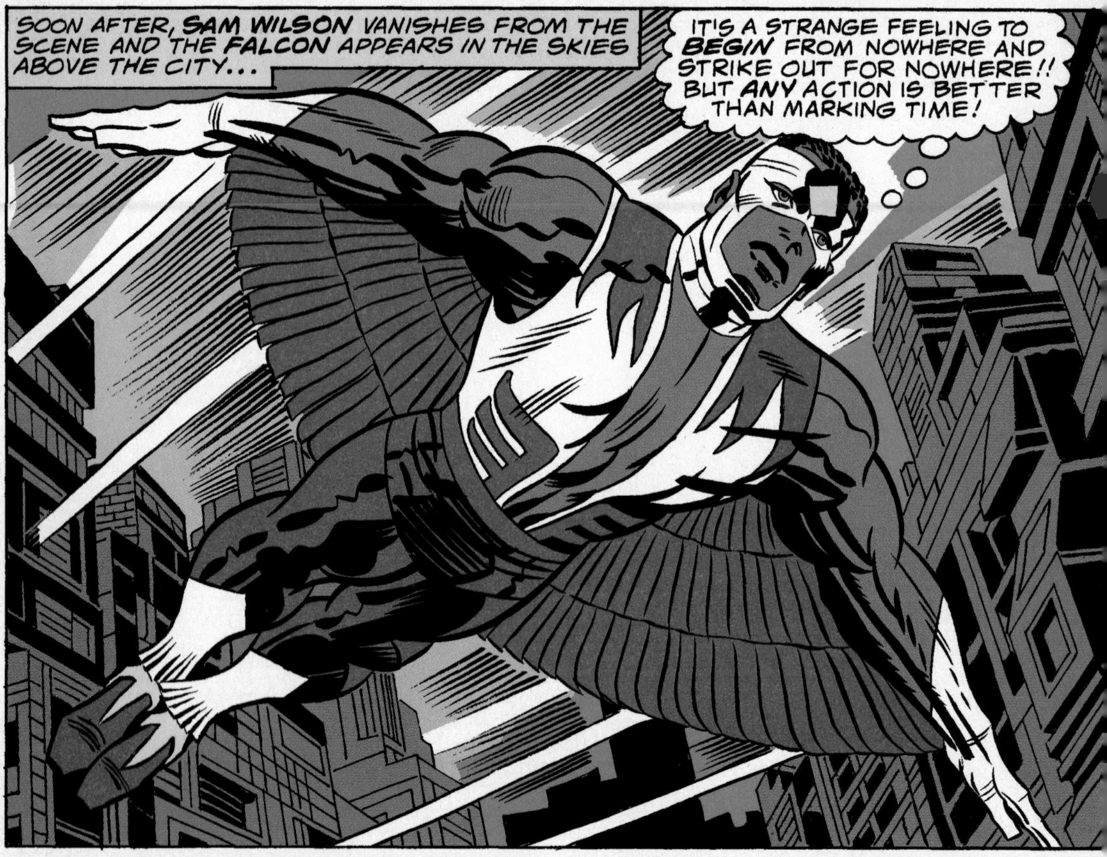
SOON AFTER, SAM WILSON VANISHES FROM THE SCENE AND THE FALCON APPEARS IN THE SKIES ABOVE THE CITY...
IT'S A STRANGE FEELING TO BEGIN FROM NOWHERE AND STRIKE OUT FOR NOWHERE!! BUT ANY ACTION IS BETTER THAN MARKING TIME!

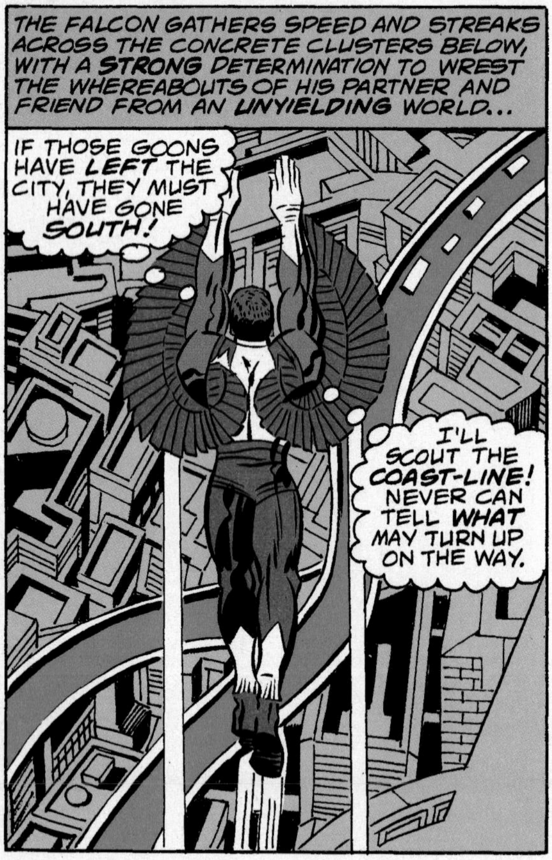
THE FALCON GATHERS SPEED AND STREAKS ACROSS THE CONCRETE CLUSTERS BELOW, WITH A STRONG DETERMINATION TO WREST THE WHEREABOUTS OF HIS PARTNER AND FRIEND FROM AN UNYIELDING WORLD...
IF THOSE GOONS HAVE LEFT THE CITY, THEY MUST HAVE GONE SOUTH!
I'LL SCOUT THE COAST-LINE! NEVER CAN TELL WHAT MAY TURN UP ON THE WAY.

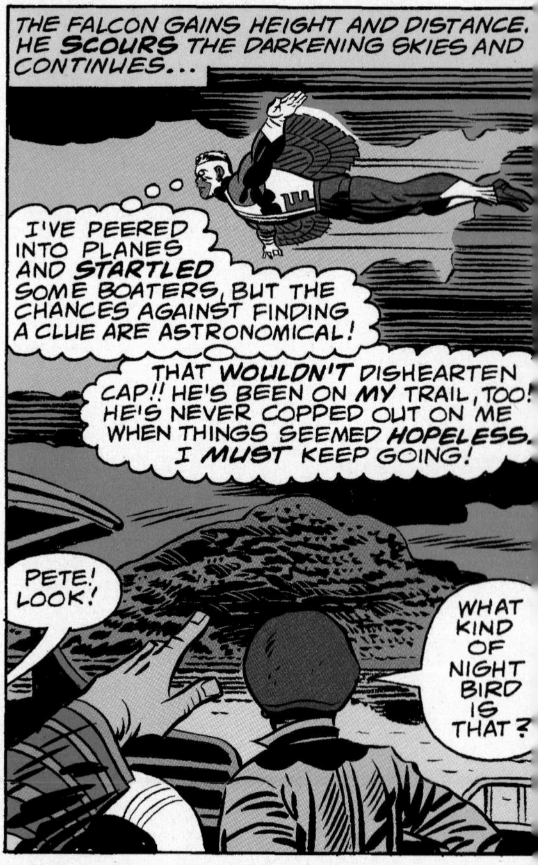
THE FALCON GAINS HEIGHT AND DISTANCE. HE SCOURS THE DARKENING SKIES AND CONTINUES...
I'VE PEERED INTO PLANES AND STARTLED SOME BOATERS, BUT THE CHANCES AGAINST FINDING A CLUE ARE ASTRONOMICAL!
THAT WOULDN'T DISHEARTEN CAP!! HE'S BEEN ON MY TRAIL, TOO! HE'S NEVER COPPED OUT ON ME WHEN THINGS SEEMED HOPELESS. I MUST KEEP GOING!
PETE! LOOK!
WHAT KIND OF NIGHT BIRD IS THAT?

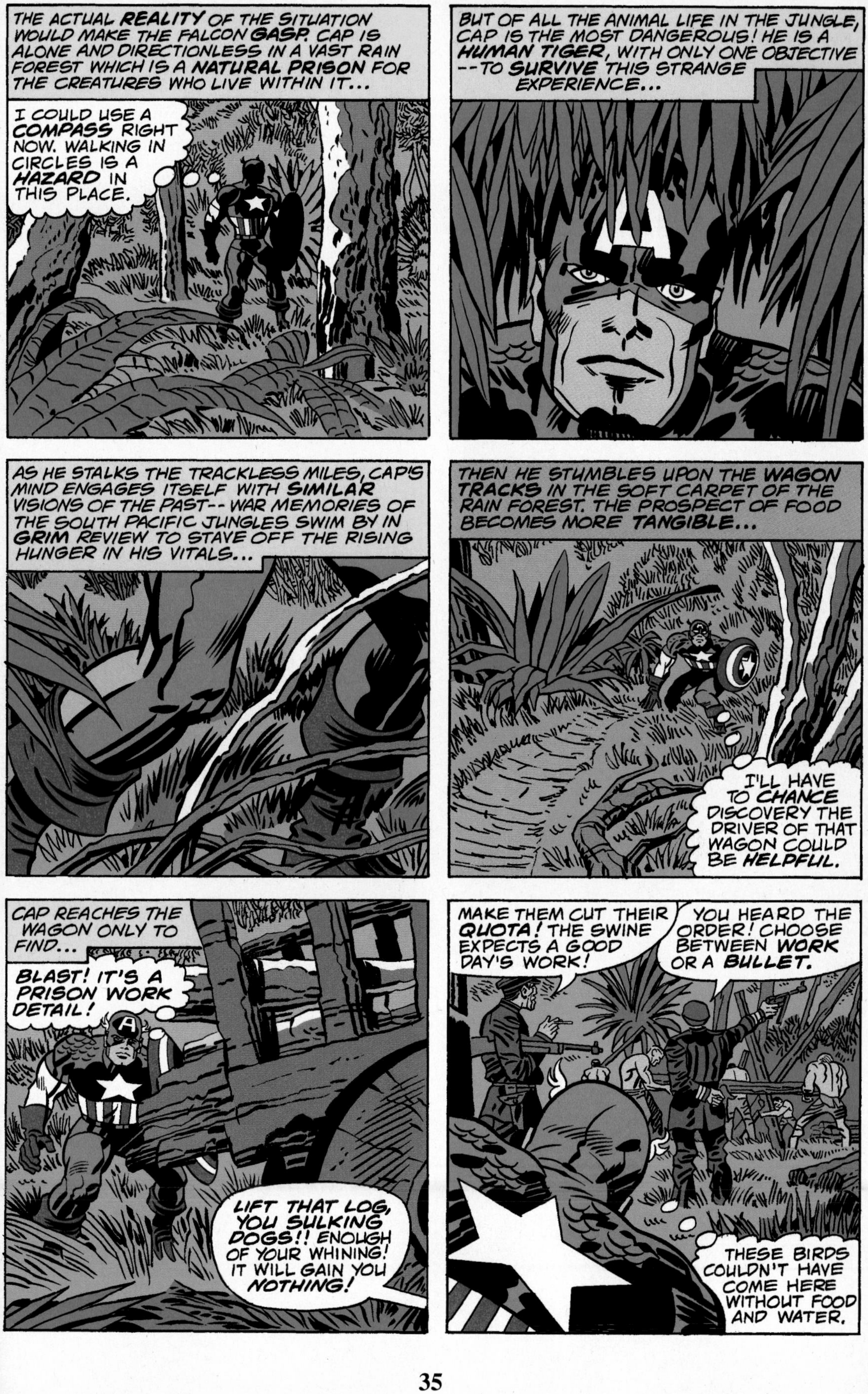
THE ACTUAL REALITY OF THE SITUATION WOULD MAKE THE FALCON GASP. CAP IS ALONE AND DIRECTIONLESS IN A VAST RAIN FOREST WHICH IS A NATURAL PRISON FOR THE CREATURES WHO LIVE WITHIN IT...
I COULD USE A COMPASS RIGHT NOW. WALKING IN CIRCLES IS A HAZARD IN THIS PLACE.
BUT OF ALL THE ANIMAL LIFE IN THE JUNGLE, CAP IS THE MOST DANGEROUS! HE IS A HUMAN TIGER, WITH ONLY ONE OBJECTIVE --TO SURVIVE THIS STRANGE EXPERIENCE...
AS HE STALKS THE TRACKLESS MILES, CAP'S MIND ENGAGES ITSELF WITH SIMILAR VISIONS OF THE PAST-- WAR MEMORIES OF THE SOUTH PACIFIC JUNGLES SWIM BY IN GRIM REVIEW TO STAVE OFF THE RISING HUNGER IN HIS VITALS...
THEN HE STUMBLES UPON THE WAGON TRACKS IN THE SOFT CARPET OF THE RAIN FOREST. THE PROSPECT OF FOOD BECOMES MORE TANGIBLE...
I'LL HAVE TO CHANCE DISCOVERY THE DRIVER OF THAT WAGON COULD BE HELPFUL.
CAP REACHES THE WAGON ONLY TO FIND...
BLAST! IT'S A PRISON WORK DETAIL!
LIFT THAT LOG, YOU SULKING DOGS!! ENOUGH OF YOUR WHINING! IT WILL GAIN YOU NOTHING!
MAKE THEM CUT THEIR QUOTA! THE SWINE EXPECTS A GOOD DAY'S WORK!
YOU HEARD THE ORDER! CHOOSE BETWEEN WORK OR A BULLET.
THESE BIRDS COULDN'T HAVE COME HERE WITHOUT FOOD AND WATER.

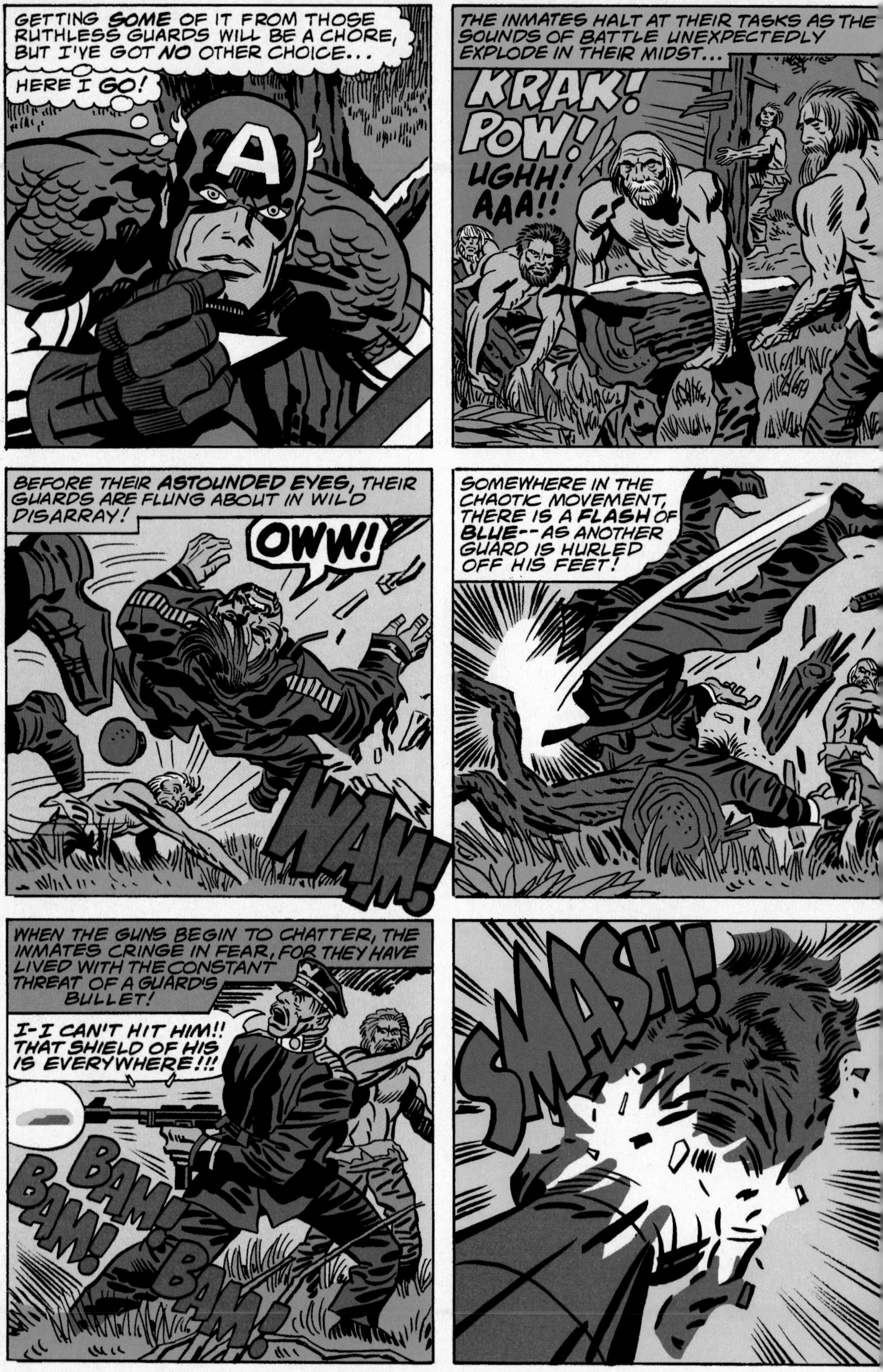
GETTING SOME OF IT FROM THOSE RUTHLESS GUARDS WILL BE A CHORE, BUT I'VE GOT NO OTHER CHOICE...
HERE I GO!
THE INMATES HALT AT THEIR TASKS AS THE SOUNDS OF BATTLE UNEXPECTEDLY EXPLODE IN THEIR MIDST...
KRAK! POW! UGHH! AAA!!
BEFORE THEIR ASTOUNDED EYES, THEIR GUARDS ARE FLUNG ABOUT IN WILD DISARRAY!
OWW!
WAM!
SOMEWHERE IN THE CHAOTIC MOVEMENT, THERE IS A FLASH OF BLUE--AS ANOTHER GUARD IS HURLED OFF HIS FEET!
WHEN THE GUNS BEGIN TO CHATTER, THE INMATES CRINGE IN FEAR, FOR THEY HAVE LIVED WITH THE CONSTANT THREAT OF A GUARD'S BULLET!
I-I CAN'T HIT HIM!! THAT SHIELD OF HIS IS EVERYWHERE!!!
BAM! BAM! BAM! BAM!
SMASH!

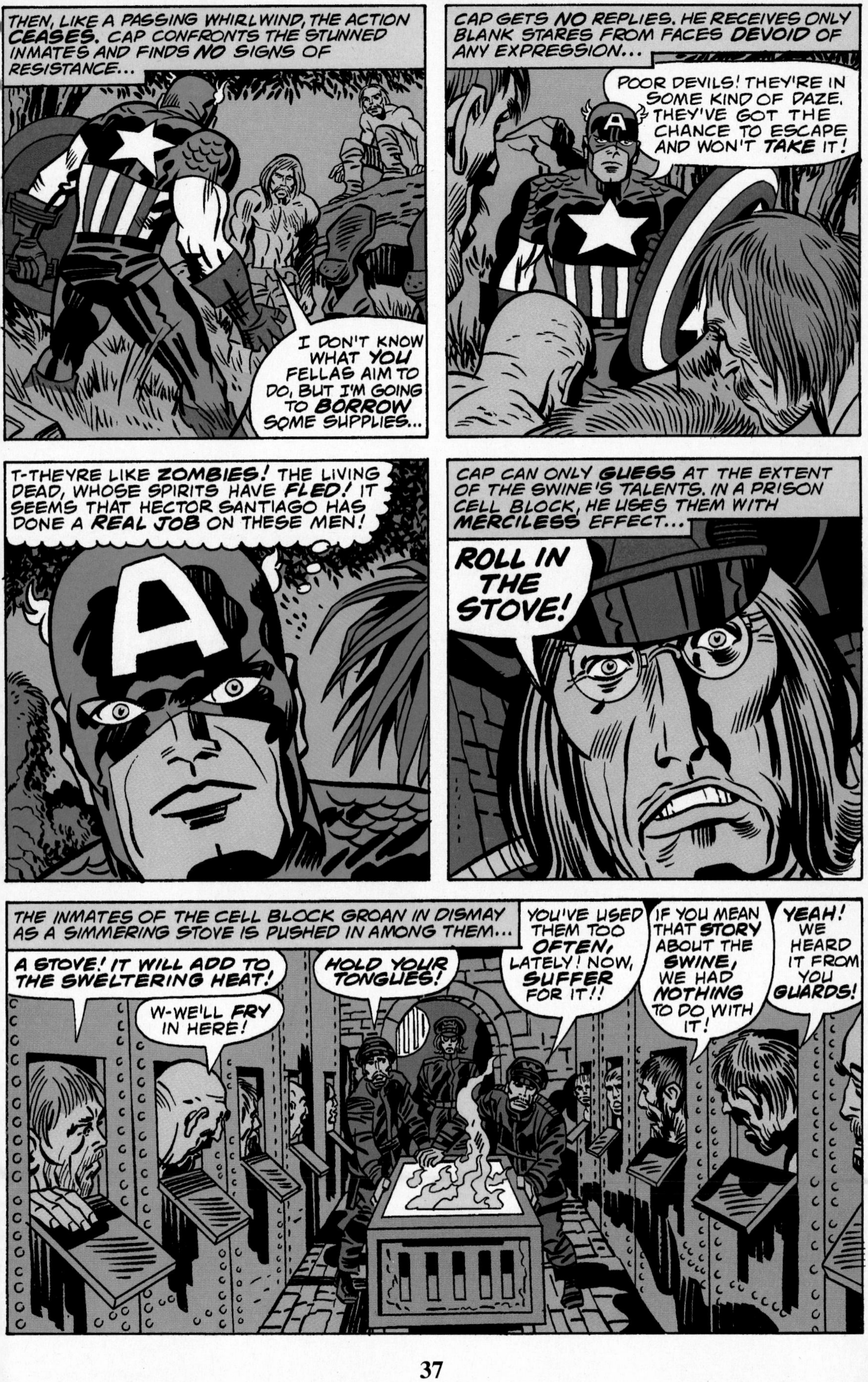
THEN, LIKE A PASSING WHIRLWIND, THE ACTION CEASES. CAP CONFRONTS THE STUNNED INMATES AND FINDS NO SIGNS OF RESISTANCE...
I DON'T KNOW WHAT YOU FELLAS AIM TO DO, BUT I'M GOING TO BORROW SOME SUPPLIES...
CAP GETS NO REPLIES. HE RECEIVES ONLY BLANK STARES FROM FACES DEVOID OF ANY EXPRESSION...
POOR DEVILS! THEY'RE IN SOME KIND OF DAZE. THEY'VE GOT THE CHANCE TO ESCAPE AND WON'T TAKE IT!
T-THEYRE LIKE ZOMBIES! THE LIVING DEAD, WHOSE SPIRITS HAVE FLED! IT SEEMS THAT HECTOR SANTIAGO HAS DONE A REAL JOB ON THESE MEN!
CAP CAN ONLY GUESS AT THE EXTENT OF THE SWINE'S TALENTS. IN A PRISON CELL BLOCK, HE USES THEM WITH MERCILESS EFFECT...
ROLL IN THE STOVE!
THE INMATES OF THE CELL BLOCK GROAN IN DISMAY AS A SIMMERING STOVE IS PUSHED IN AMONG THEM...
A STOVE! IT WILL ADD TO THE SWELTERING HEAT!
W-WE'LL FRY IN HERE!
HOLD YOUR TONGUES!
YOU'VE USED THEM TOO OFTEN, LATELY! NOW, SUFFER FOR IT!!
IF YOU MEAN THAT STORY ABOUT THE SWINE, WE HAD NOTHING TO DO WITH IT!
YEAH! WE HEARD IT FROM YOU GUARDS!

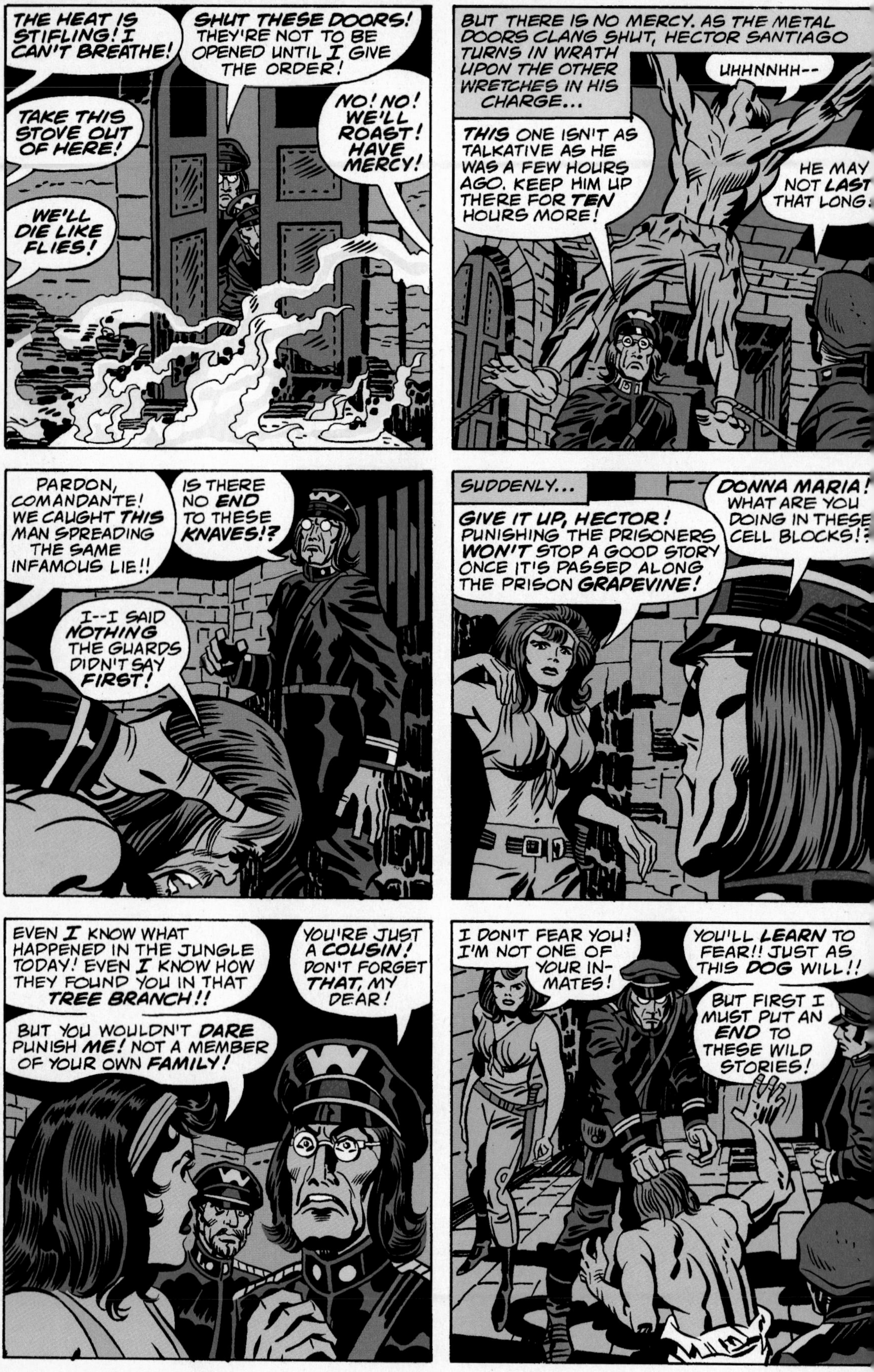
THE HEAT IS STIFLING! I CAN'T BREATHE!
SHUT THESE DOORS! THEY'RE NOT TO BE OPENED UNTIL I GIVE THE ORDER!
TAKE THIS STOVE OUT OF HERE!
NO! NO! WE'LL ROAST! HAVE MERCY!
WE'LL DIE LIKE FLIES!
BUT THERE IS NO MERCY. AS THE METAL DOORS CLANG SHUT, HECTOR SANTIAGO TURNS IN WRATH UPON THE OTHER WRETCHES IN HIS CHARGE...
UHHNNHH--
THIS ONE ISN'T AS TALKATIVE AS HE WAS A FEW HOURS AGO. KEEP HIM UP THERE FOR TEN HOURS MORE!
HE MAY NOT LAST THAT LONG!
PARDON, COMANDANTE! WE CAUGHT THIS MAN SPREADING THE SAME INFAMOUS LIE!!
IS THERE NO END TO THESE KNAVES!?
I--I SAID NOTHING THE GUARDS DIDN'T SAY FIRST!
SUDDENLY...
GIVE IT UP, HECTOR! PUNISHING THE PRISONERS WON'T STOP A GOOD STORY ONCE IT'S PASSED ALONG THE PRISON GRAPEVINE!
DONNA MARIA! WHAT ARE YOU DOING IN THESE CELL BLOCKS!?
EVEN I KNOW WHAT HAPPENED IN THE JUNGLE TODAY! EVEN I KNOW HOW THEY FOUND YOU IN THAT TREE BRANCH!!
BUT YOU WOULDN'T DARE PUNISH ME! NOT A MEMBER OF YOUR OWN FAMILY!
YOU'RE JUST A COUSIN! DON'T FORGET THAT, MY DEAR!
I DON'T FEAR YOU! I'M NOT ONE OF YOUR IN-MATES!
YOU'LL LEARN TO FEAR!! JUST AS THIS DOG WILL!!
BUT FIRST I MUST PUT AN END TO THESE WILD STORIES!

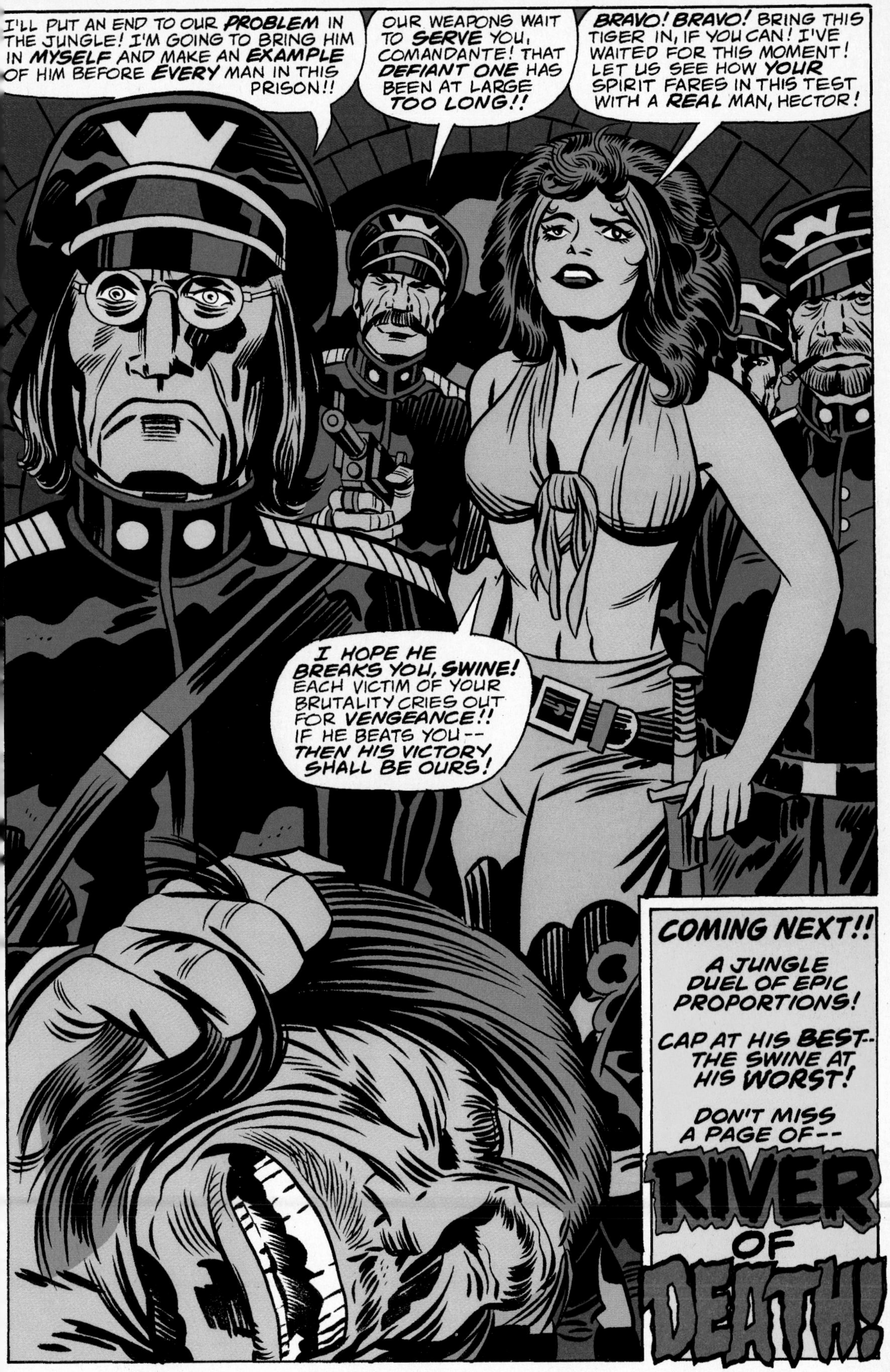
I'LL PUT AN END TO OUR PROBLEM IN THE JUNGLE! I'M GOING TO BRING HIM IN MYSELF AND MAKE AN EXAMPLE OF HIM BEFORE EVERY MAN IN THIS PRISON!!
OUR WEAPONS WAIT TO SERVE YOU, COMANDANTE! THAT DEFIANT ONE HAS BEEN AT LARGE TOO LONG!!
BRAVO! BRAVO! BRING THIS TIGER IN, IF YOU CAN! I'VE WAITED FOR THIS MOMENT! LET US SEE HOW YOUR SPIRIT FARES IN THIS TEST WITH A REAL MAN, HECTOR!
I HOPE HE BREAKS YOU, SWINE! EACH VICTIM OF YOUR BRUTALITY CRIES OUT FOR VENGEANCE!! IF HE BEATS YOU -- THEN HIS VICTORY SHALL BE OURS!
COMING NEXT!!
A JUNGLE DUEL OF EPIC PROPORTIONS!
CAP AT HIS BEST-- THE SWINE AT HIS WORST!
DON'T MISS A PAGE OF--
RIVER OF DEATH!

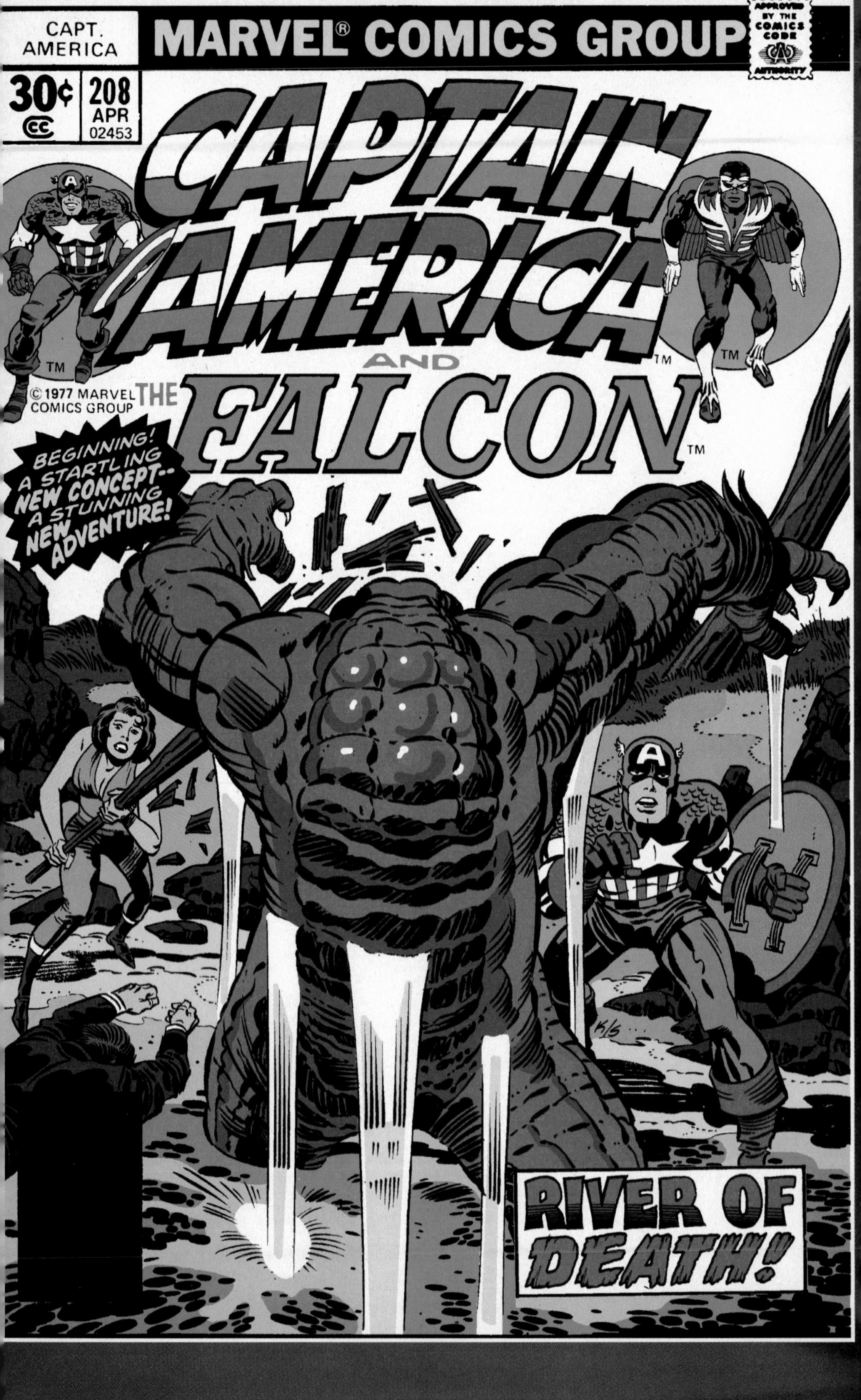

CAPT. AMERICA
MARVEL® COMICS GROUP
APPROVED BY THE COMICS CODE AUTHORITY
30¢ 208 APR 02453
CAPTAIN AMERICA AND THE FALCON
© 1977 MARVEL COMICS GROUP
BEGINNING! A STARTLING NEW CONCEPT-- A STUNNING NEW ADVENTURE!
RIVER OF DEATH!

1941! The world at *war!* And in a secret laboratory, frail *Steve Rogers* became the American *super-soldier!* For four thrilling years, he fought the Axis powers—until a freak stroke of fate threw him into *suspended animation.* He woke in the mid-1960s, a man *twenty years out of his time.* Since that fateful day, Steve Rogers has sought his *destiny* in this brave new world.

STAN LEE PRESENTS: CAPTAIN AMERICA AND THE FALCON™

EDITED, WRITTEN & DRAWN BY **JACK KIRBY**   INKED BY **FRANK GIACOIA**   LETTERED BY **JIM NOVAK**
COLORED BY **G. ROUSSOS**   ADMIRED BY **ARCHIE GOODWIN**

WHAT BEGAN AS A NIGHTMARISH *ABDUCTION* TO A PRISON FORTRESS IN THE UNCHARTED WILDS OF CENTRAL AMERICA, SUDDENLY CHANGES FROM A SINISTER INCIDENT INTO A FAR-OUT SAGA OF OVERWHELMING TERROR!!! IT BEGINS HERE--ON A SHORE OF THE RIO DE MUERTE--

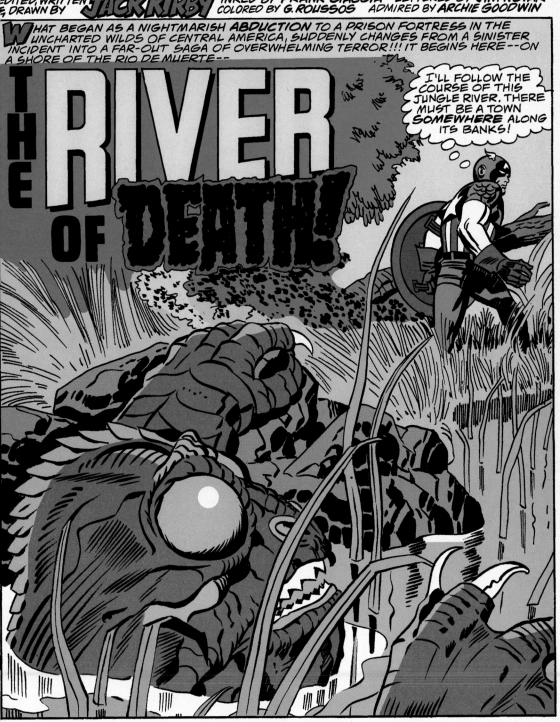

THE RIVER OF DEATH!

I'LL FOLLOW THE COURSE OF THIS JUNGLE RIVER. THERE MUST BE A TOWN *SOMEWHERE* ALONG ITS BANKS!

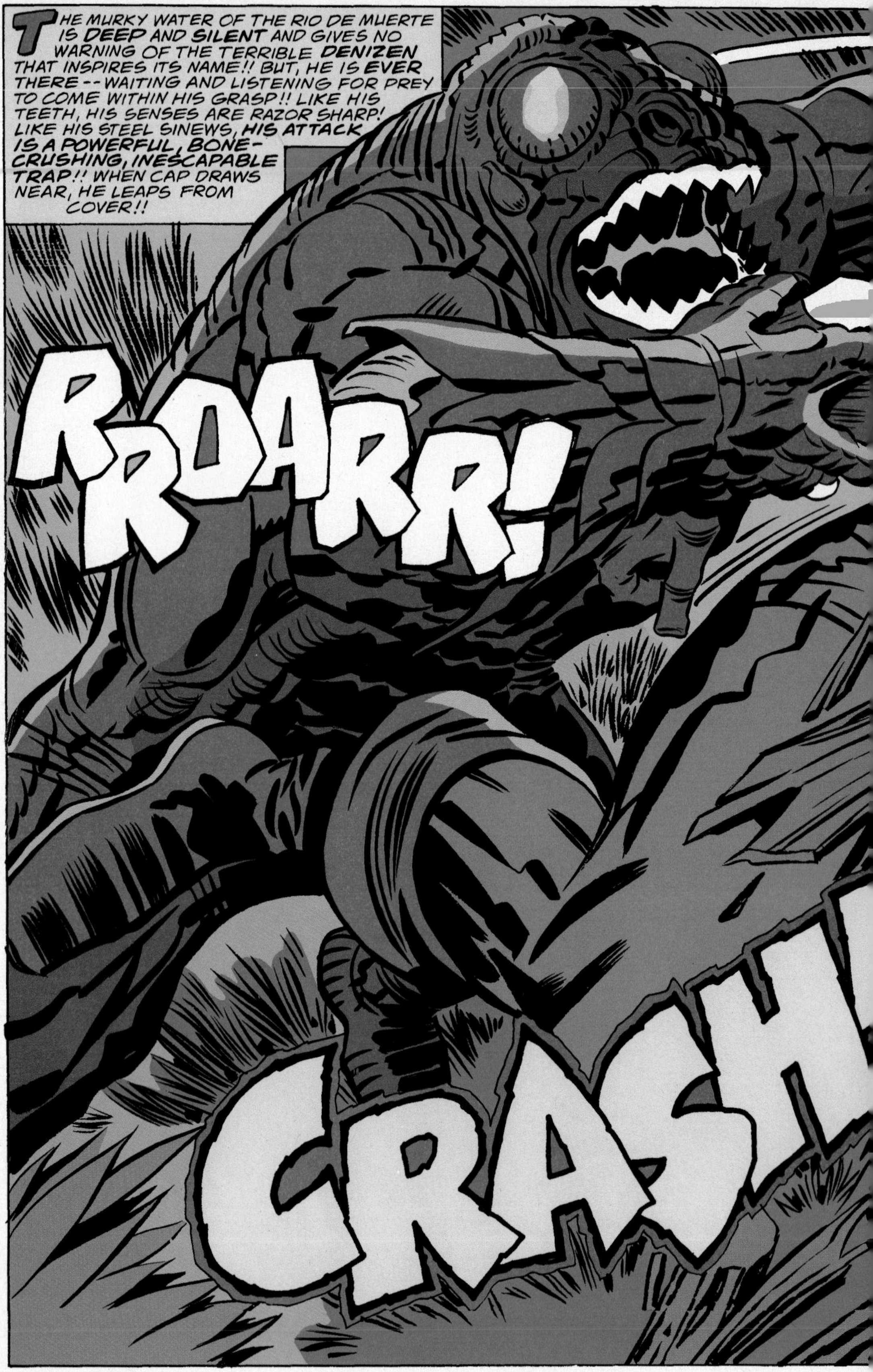

THE MURKY WATER OF THE RIO DE MUERTE IS DEEP AND SILENT AND GIVES NO WARNING OF THE TERRIBLE DENIZEN THAT INSPIRES ITS NAME!! BUT, HE IS EVER THERE -- WAITING AND LISTENING FOR PREY TO COME WITHIN HIS GRASP!! LIKE HIS TEETH, HIS SENSES ARE RAZOR SHARP! LIKE HIS STEEL SINEWS, HIS ATTACK IS A POWERFUL, BONE-CRUSHING, INESCAPABLE TRAP!! WHEN CAP DRAWS NEAR, HE LEAPS FROM COVER!!
RROARRR!
CRASH

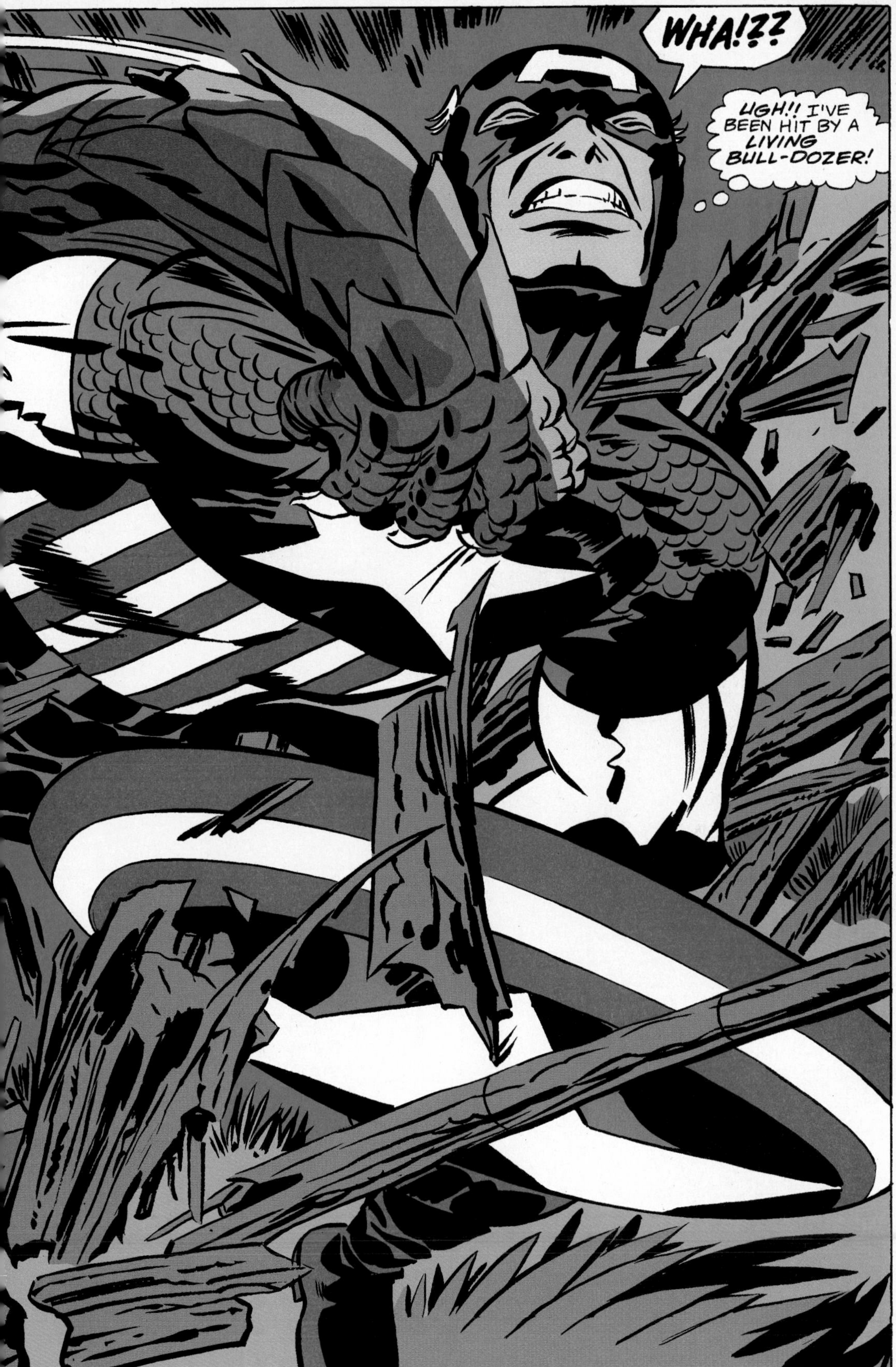
WHA!??
UGH!! I'VE BEEN HIT BY A LIVING BULL-DOZER!

THE THING FROM THE RIVER GIVES NO PAUSE FOR RECOVERY! ITS BODY COURSES WITH A PRIMITIVE FURY WHICH BLAZES UNTIL THE VICTIM EXPIRES!!!

RRROAR!

KRAK!

CAP STRUGGLES LIKE A *MADMAN* TO FREE HIMSELF! HE CATCHES HORRIFYING GLIMPSES OF HIS ATTACKER AND *FORCES* HIS STRENGTH TO ITS LIMITS!

GOOD GOD!! W-WHAT IS IT!? WHAT IS IT!?

A THOUSAND DEATH ENCOUNTERS HAVE *NOT* PREPARED CAP FOR THIS. HIS KNEES BUCKLE UNDER THE *CRUSHING WEIGHT* OF THE CREATURE!! HE IS THROWN TO THE JUNGLE FLOOR!!

NAARRR!

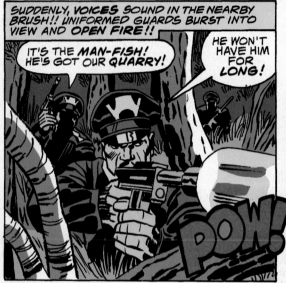

SUDDENLY, VOICES SOUND IN THE NEARBY BRUSH!! UNIFORMED GUARDS BURST INTO VIEW AND *OPEN FIRE!!*

IT'S THE *MAN-FISH!* HE'S GOT OUR *QUARRY!*

HE WON'T HAVE HIM FOR LONG!

POW!

A *DEADLY FUSILADE* IS HURLED AT THE STARTLED MONSTER! HE *HALTS* HIS SAVAGE WORK TO ROAR AT THE INTRUDERS!

BULLETS CAN'T PENETRATE THAT ARMORED SKIN, BUT THE SOUND OF GUNFIRE DISTURBS HIM!!

POW! POW! PO

SCREEEE!

44

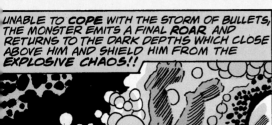

UNABLE TO **COPE** WITH THE STORM OF BULLETS, THE MONSTER EMITS A FINAL **ROAR** AND RETURNS TO THE DARK DEPTHS WHICH CLOSE ABOVE HIM AND SHIELD HIM FROM THE **EXPLOSIVE CHAOS!!**

THE BATTLE ON THE RIVER SHORE ENDS ABRUPTLY AS THE GUARDS ADVANCE ON THE **REAL** OBJECT OF THEIR SEARCH...

THE MAN-FISH IS **GONE!** WE CAN STAKE OUR **CLAIM** TO HIS VICTIM!

FORTUNE IS **WITH** US! THIS WILL BE AN **EASY** CAPTURE!

HA HA HA! SO THE TIGER HAS BEEN **WEAKENED** BY THE STRUGGLE!! **SEIZE HIM!**

HE OFFERS NO RESISTANCE...

ONE **RARELY** DOES AFTER MEETING THE **MAN-FISH!**

CAP IS LIFTED TO HIS FEET AND PROPPED AGAINST A TREE...

SPEAK, TIGER! HAVE YOU NO WORD OF **THANKS** FOR YOUR RESCUERS!?

YEAH! **BLOW IT OUT YOUR MOUSTACHE!**

THOSE ARE **HARDLY** WORDS OF GRATITUDE!

MANY PRISON ESCAPEES HAVE COME THIS WAY-- AND **PERISHED!!** YOU ARE THE **FIRST** TO KEEP YOUR SKIN INTACT!!!

NOW YOU KNOW **WHY** THIS INVITING BODY OF WATER IS CALLED THE "**RIVER OF DEATH**"! THE MAN-FISH GUARDS IT **WELL!**

ESCAPE IS **IMPOSSIBLE,** TIGER. WE'RE TAKING YOU TO OUR COMMANDANTE... **HE** WILL TREAT YOU AS DID THE MAN-FISH...BUT YOUR DEATH WILL BE-- **SLOWER!**

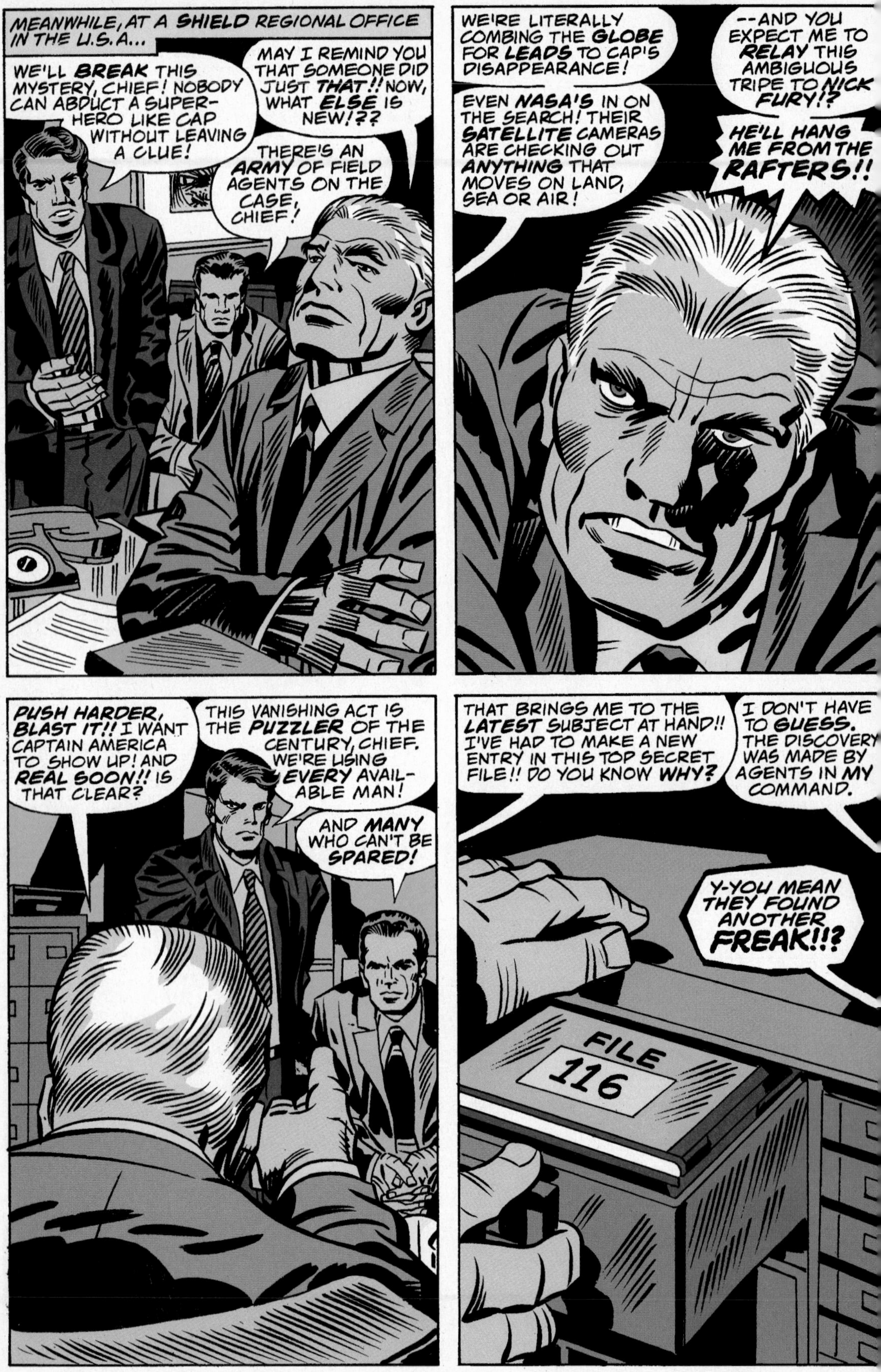
MEANWHILE, AT A SHIELD REGIONAL OFFICE IN THE U.S.A...
WE'LL BREAK THIS MYSTERY, CHIEF! NOBODY CAN ABDUCT A SUPER-HERO LIKE CAP WITHOUT LEAVING A CLUE!
MAY I REMIND YOU THAT SOMEONE DID JUST THAT!! NOW, WHAT ELSE IS NEW!??
THERE'S AN ARMY OF FIELD AGENTS ON THE CASE, CHIEF!
WE'RE LITERALLY COMBING THE GLOBE FOR LEADS TO CAP'S DISAPPEARANCE!
EVEN NASA'S IN ON THE SEARCH! THEIR SATELLITE CAMERAS ARE CHECKING OUT ANYTHING THAT MOVES ON LAND, SEA OR AIR!
--AND YOU EXPECT ME TO RELAY THIS AMBIGUOUS TRIPE TO NICK FURY!?
HE'LL HANG ME FROM THE RAFTERS!!
PUSH HARDER, BLAST IT!! I WANT CAPTAIN AMERICA TO SHOW UP! AND REAL SOON!! IS THAT CLEAR?
THIS VANISHING ACT IS THE PUZZLER OF THE CENTURY, CHIEF. WE'RE USING EVERY AVAIL-ABLE MAN!
AND MANY WHO CAN'T BE SPARED!
THAT BRINGS ME TO THE LATEST SUBJECT AT HAND!! I'VE HAD TO MAKE A NEW ENTRY IN THIS TOP SECRET FILE!! DO YOU KNOW WHY?
I DON'T HAVE TO GUESS. THE DISCOVERY WAS MADE BY AGENTS IN MY COMMAND.
Y-YOU MEAN THEY FOUND ANOTHER FREAK!!?
FILE
116

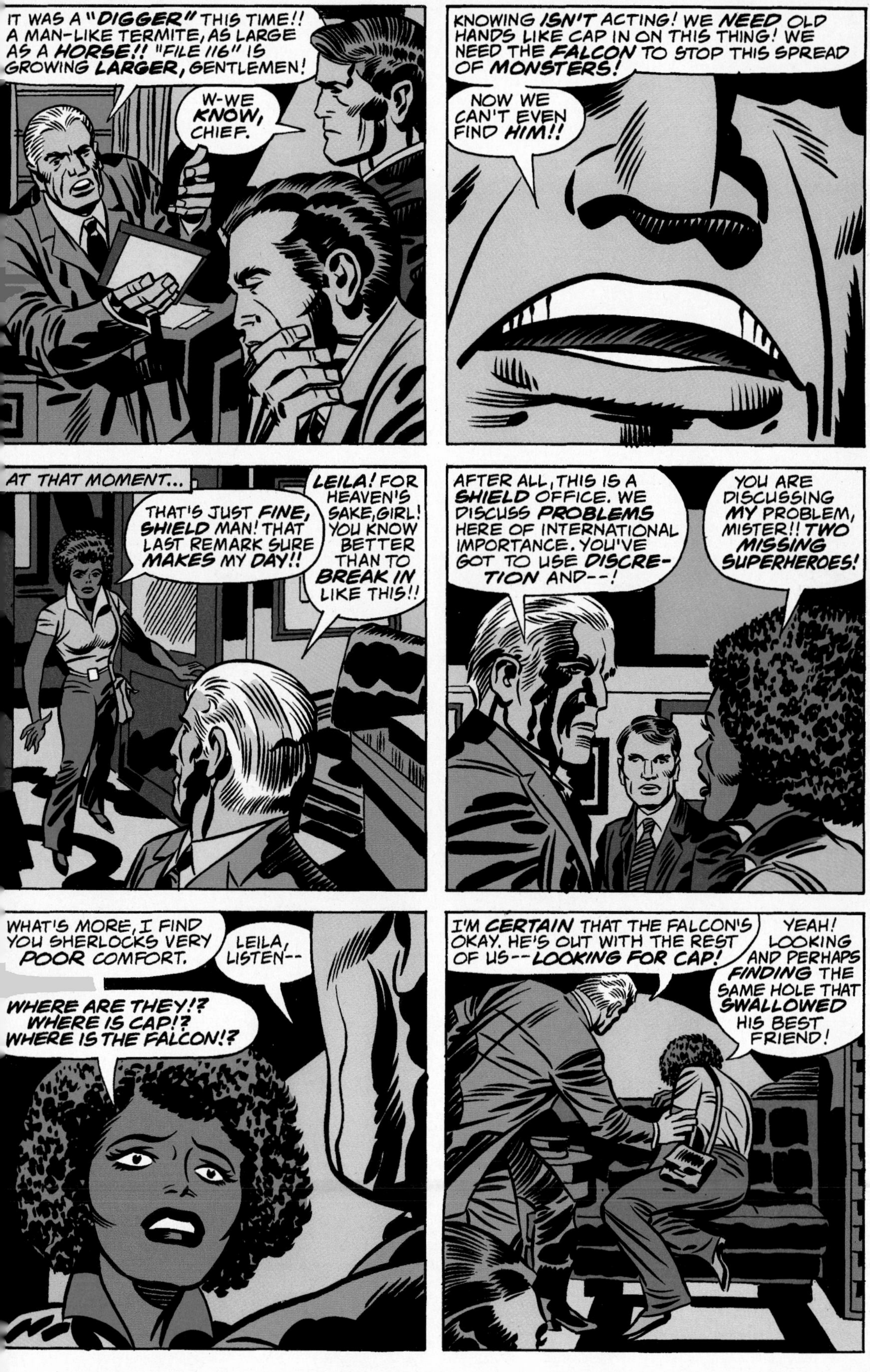

IT WAS A "DIGGER" THIS TIME!! A MAN-LIKE TERMITE, AS LARGE AS A HORSE!! "FILE 116" IS GROWING LARGER, GENTLEMEN!
W-WE KNOW, CHIEF.
KNOWING ISN'T ACTING! WE NEED OLD HANDS LIKE CAP IN ON THIS THING! WE NEED THE FALCON TO STOP THIS SPREAD OF MONSTERS!
NOW WE CAN'T EVEN FIND HIM!!
AT THAT MOMENT...
THAT'S JUST FINE, SHIELD MAN! THAT LAST REMARK SURE MAKES MY DAY!!
LEILA! FOR HEAVEN'S SAKE, GIRL! YOU KNOW BETTER THAN TO BREAK IN LIKE THIS!!
AFTER ALL, THIS IS A SHIELD OFFICE. WE DISCUSS PROBLEMS HERE OF INTERNATIONAL IMPORTANCE. YOU'VE GOT TO USE DISCRETION AND--!
YOU ARE DISCUSSING MY PROBLEM, MISTER!! TWO MISSING SUPERHEROES!
WHAT'S MORE, I FIND YOU SHERLOCKS VERY POOR COMFORT.
LEILA, LISTEN--
WHERE ARE THEY!? WHERE IS CAP!? WHERE IS THE FALCON!?
I'M CERTAIN THAT THE FALCON'S OKAY. HE'S OUT WITH THE REST OF US--LOOKING FOR CAP!
YEAH! LOOKING AND PERHAPS FINDING THE SAME HOLE THAT SWALLOWED HIS BEST FRIEND!

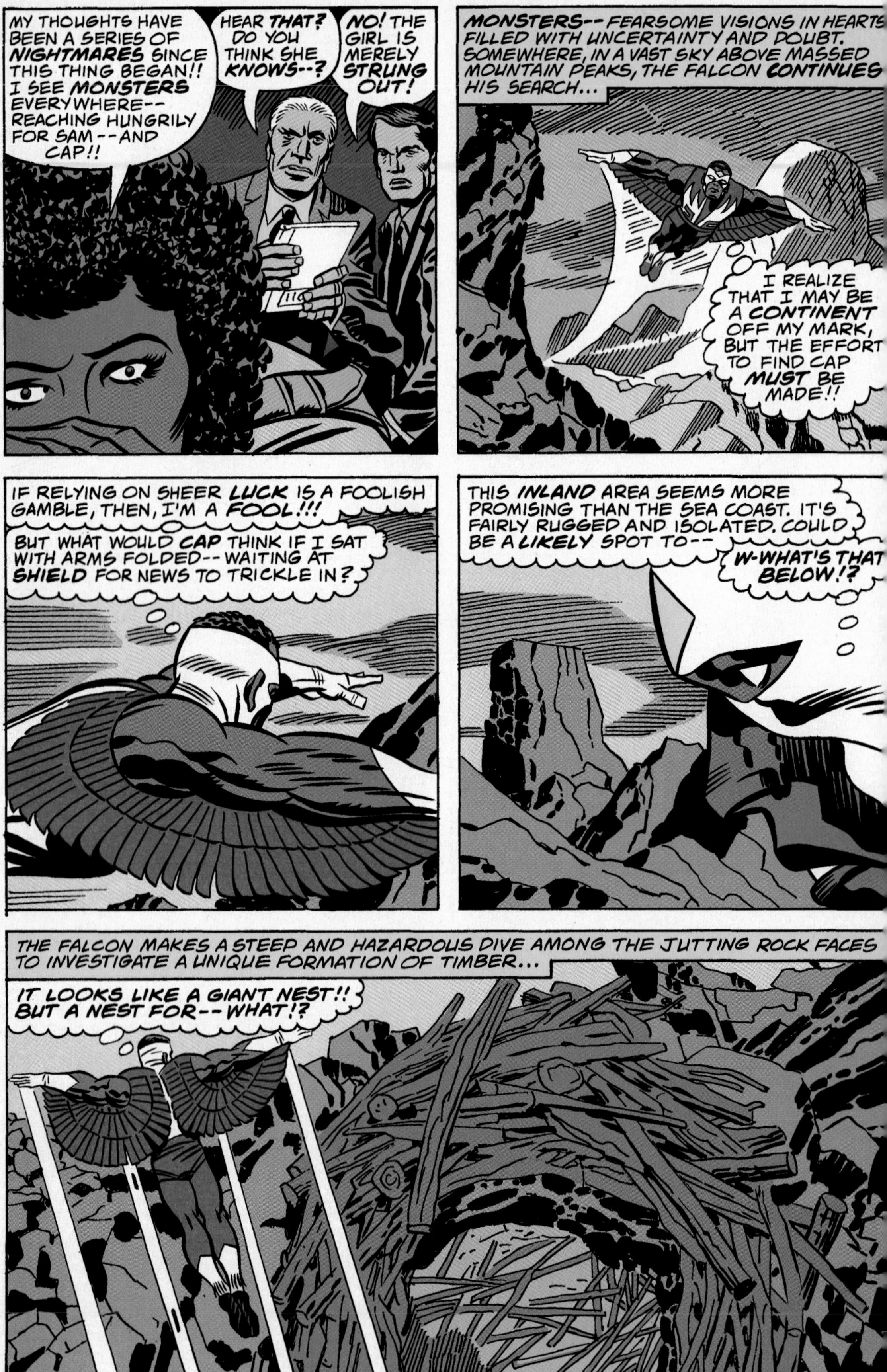
MY THOUGHTS HAVE BEEN A SERIES OF NIGHTMARES SINCE THIS THING BEGAN!! I SEE MONSTERS EVERYWHERE-- REACHING HUNGRILY FOR SAM --AND CAP!!
HEAR THAT? DO YOU THINK SHE KNOWS--?
NO! THE GIRL IS MERELY STRUNG OUT!
MONSTERS-- FEARSOME VISIONS IN HEARTS FILLED WITH UNCERTAINTY AND DOUBT. SOMEWHERE, IN A VAST SKY ABOVE MASSED MOUNTAIN PEAKS, THE FALCON CONTINUES HIS SEARCH...
I REALIZE THAT I MAY BE A CONTINENT OFF MY MARK, BUT THE EFFORT TO FIND CAP MUST BE MADE!!
IF RELYING ON SHEER LUCK IS A FOOLISH GAMBLE, THEN, I'M A FOOL!!!
BUT WHAT WOULD CAP THINK IF I SAT WITH ARMS FOLDED-- WAITING AT SHIELD FOR NEWS TO TRICKLE IN?
THIS INLAND AREA SEEMS MORE PROMISING THAN THE SEA COAST. IT'S FAIRLY RUGGED AND ISOLATED. COULD BE A LIKELY SPOT TO--
W-WHAT'S THAT BELOW!?
THE FALCON MAKES A STEEP AND HAZARDOUS DIVE AMONG THE JUTTING ROCK FACES TO INVESTIGATE A UNIQUE FORMATION OF TIMBER...
IT LOOKS LIKE A GIANT NEST!! BUT A NEST FOR-- WHAT!?

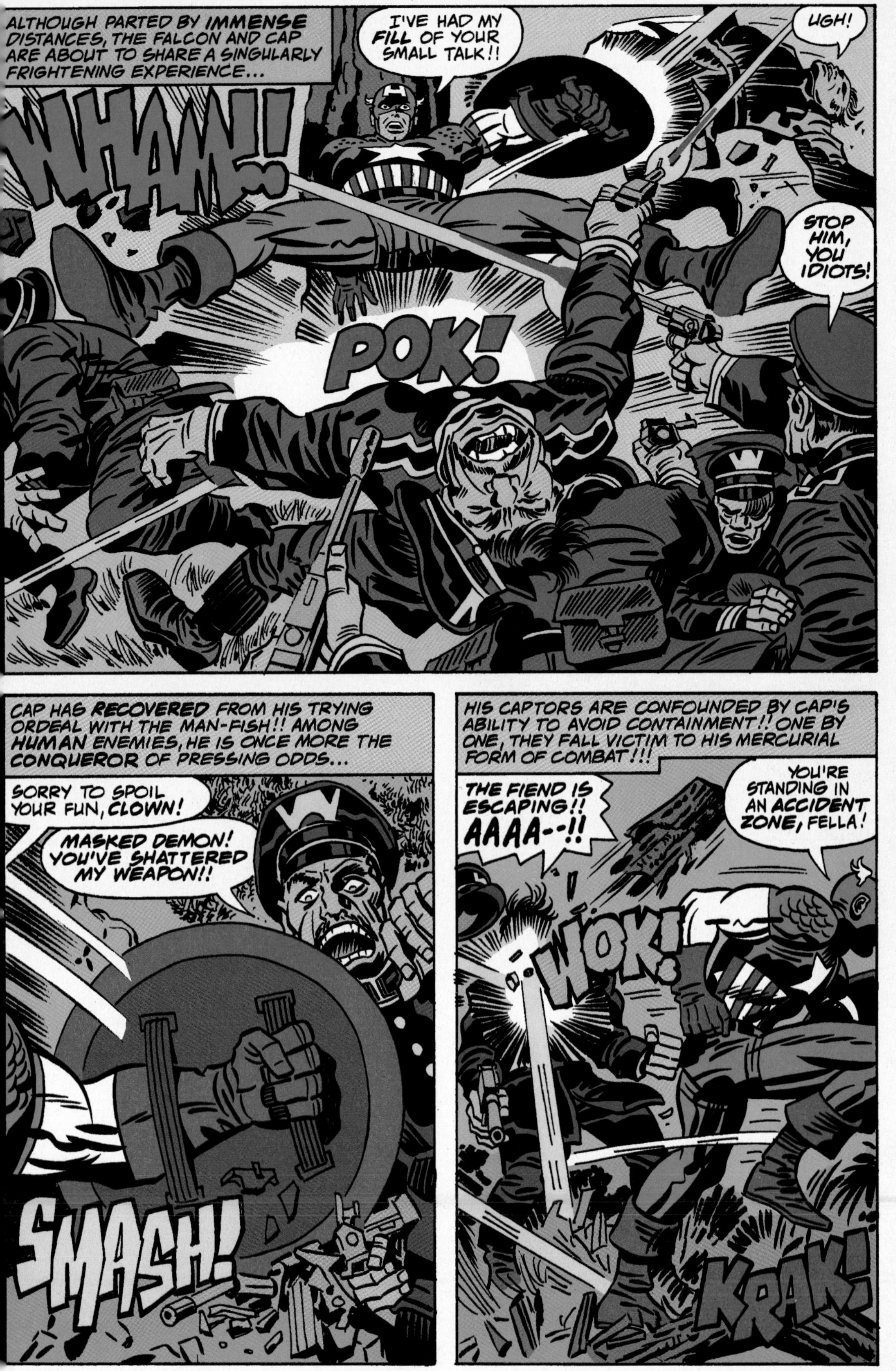
ALTHOUGH PARTED BY IMMENSE DISTANCES, THE FALCON AND CAP ARE ABOUT TO SHARE A SINGULARLY FRIGHTENING EXPERIENCE...
I'VE HAD MY FILL OF YOUR SMALL TALK!!
UGH!
WHAM!..
POK!
STOP HIM, YOU IDIOTS!
CAP HAS RECOVERED FROM HIS TRYING ORDEAL WITH THE MAN-FISH!! AMONG HUMAN ENEMIES, HE IS ONCE MORE THE CONQUEROR OF PRESSING ODDS...
SORRY TO SPOIL YOUR FUN, CLOWN!
MASKED DEMON! YOU'VE SHATTERED MY WEAPON!!
SMASH!
HIS CAPTORS ARE CONFOUNDED BY CAP'S ABILITY TO AVOID CONTAINMENT!! ONE BY ONE, THEY FALL VICTIM TO HIS MERCURIAL FORM OF COMBAT!!!
THE FIEND IS ESCAPING!! AAAA--!!
YOU'RE STANDING IN AN ACCIDENT ZONE, FELLA!
WOK!
KRAK!

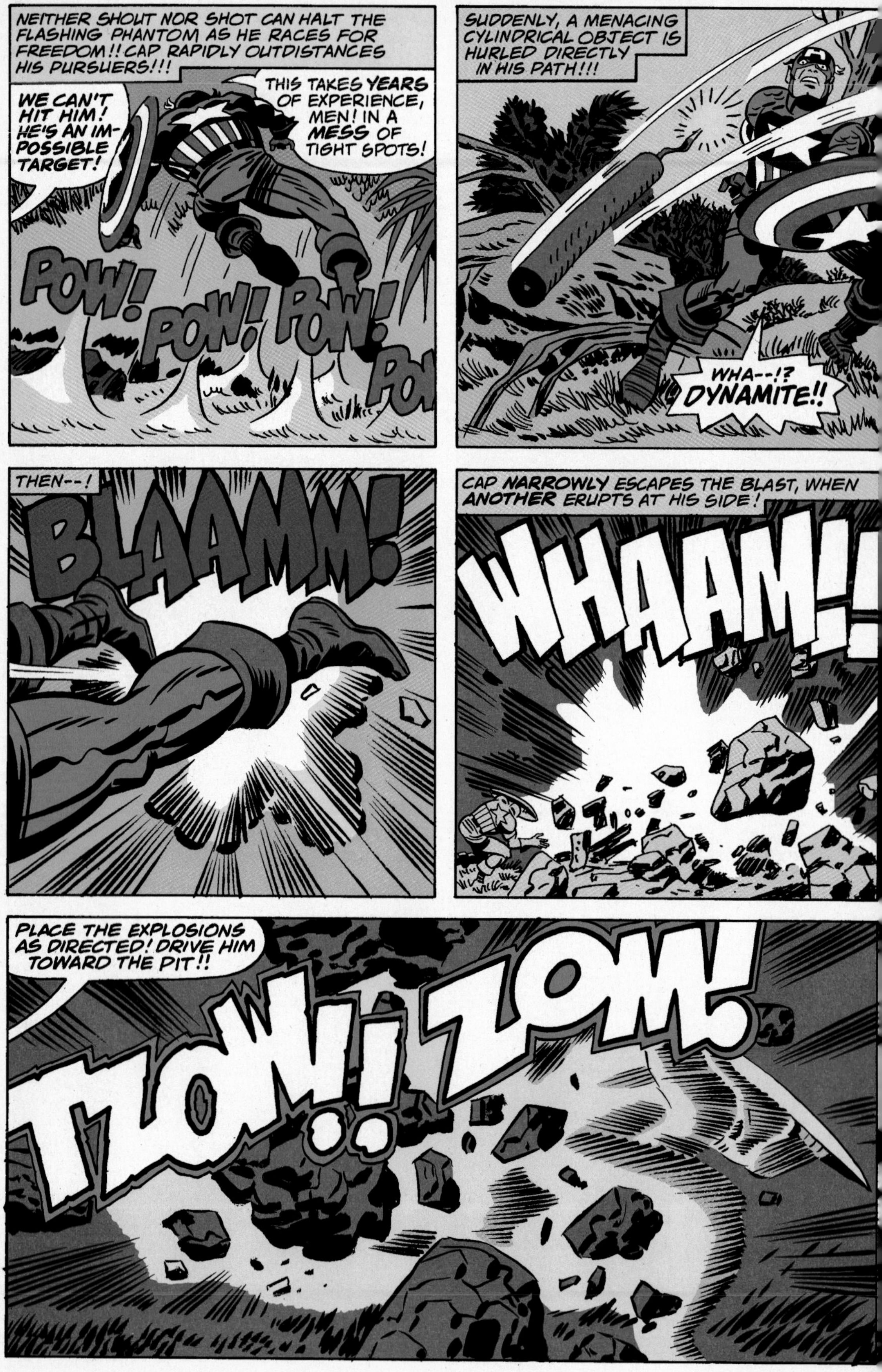
NEITHER SHOUT NOR SHOT CAN HALT THE FLASHING PHANTOM AS HE RACES FOR FREEDOM!! CAP RAPIDLY OUTDISTANCES HIS PURSUERS!!!
WE CAN'T HIT HIM! HE'S AN IM-POSSIBLE TARGET!
THIS TAKES YEARS OF EXPERIENCE, MEN! IN A MESS OF TIGHT SPOTS!
POW! POW! POW!
SUDDENLY, A MENACING CYLINDRICAL OBJECT IS HURLED DIRECTLY IN HIS PATH!!!
WHA--!? DYNAMITE!!
THEN--!
BLAAMM!
CAP NARROWLY ESCAPES THE BLAST, WHEN ANOTHER ERUPTS AT HIS SIDE!
WHAAM!!
PLACE THE EXPLOSIONS AS DIRECTED! DRIVE HIM TOWARD THE PIT!!
TZOM!! ZOM!

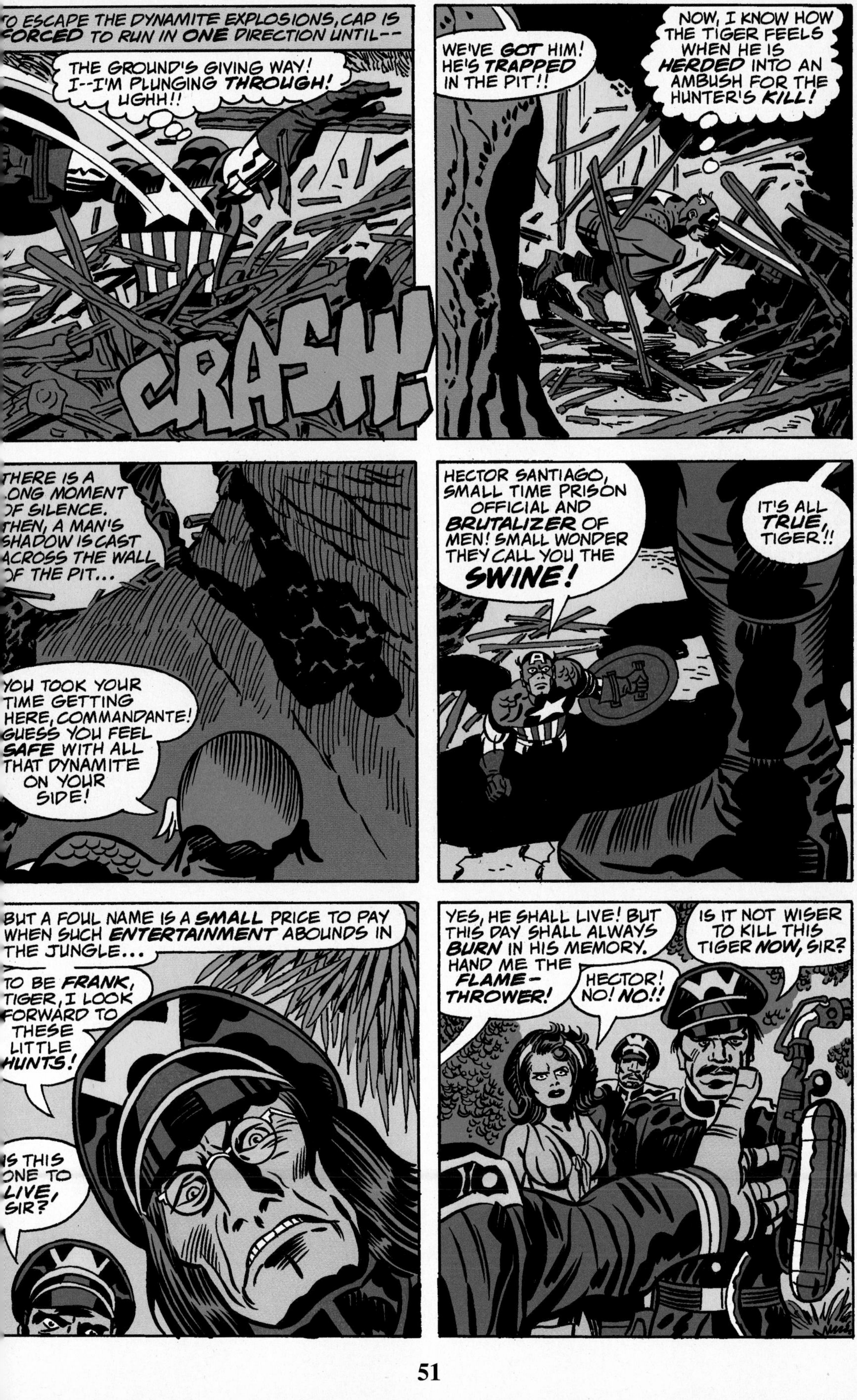
TO ESCAPE THE DYNAMITE EXPLOSIONS, CAP IS FORCED TO RUN IN ONE DIRECTION UNTIL--
THE GROUND'S GIVING WAY! I--I'M PLUNGING THROUGH! UGHH!!
CRASH!
WE'VE GOT HIM! HE'S TRAPPED IN THE PIT!!
NOW, I KNOW HOW THE TIGER FEELS WHEN HE IS HERDED INTO AN AMBUSH FOR THE HUNTER'S KILL!
THERE IS A LONG MOMENT OF SILENCE. THEN, A MAN'S SHADOW IS CAST ACROSS THE WALL OF THE PIT...
YOU TOOK YOUR TIME GETTING HERE, COMMANDANTE! GUESS YOU FEEL SAFE WITH ALL THAT DYNAMITE ON YOUR SIDE!
HECTOR SANTIAGO, SMALL TIME PRISON OFFICIAL AND BRUTALIZER OF MEN! SMALL WONDER THEY CALL YOU THE SWINE!
IT'S ALL TRUE, TIGER!!
BUT A FOUL NAME IS A SMALL PRICE TO PAY WHEN SUCH ENTERTAINMENT ABOUNDS IN THE JUNGLE...
TO BE FRANK, TIGER, I LOOK FORWARD TO THESE LITTLE HUNTS!
IS THIS ONE TO LIVE, SIR?
YES, HE SHALL LIVE! BUT THIS DAY SHALL ALWAYS BURN IN HIS MEMORY. HAND ME THE FLAME-THROWER!
IS IT NOT WISER TO KILL THIS TIGER NOW, SIR?
HECTOR! NO! NO!!

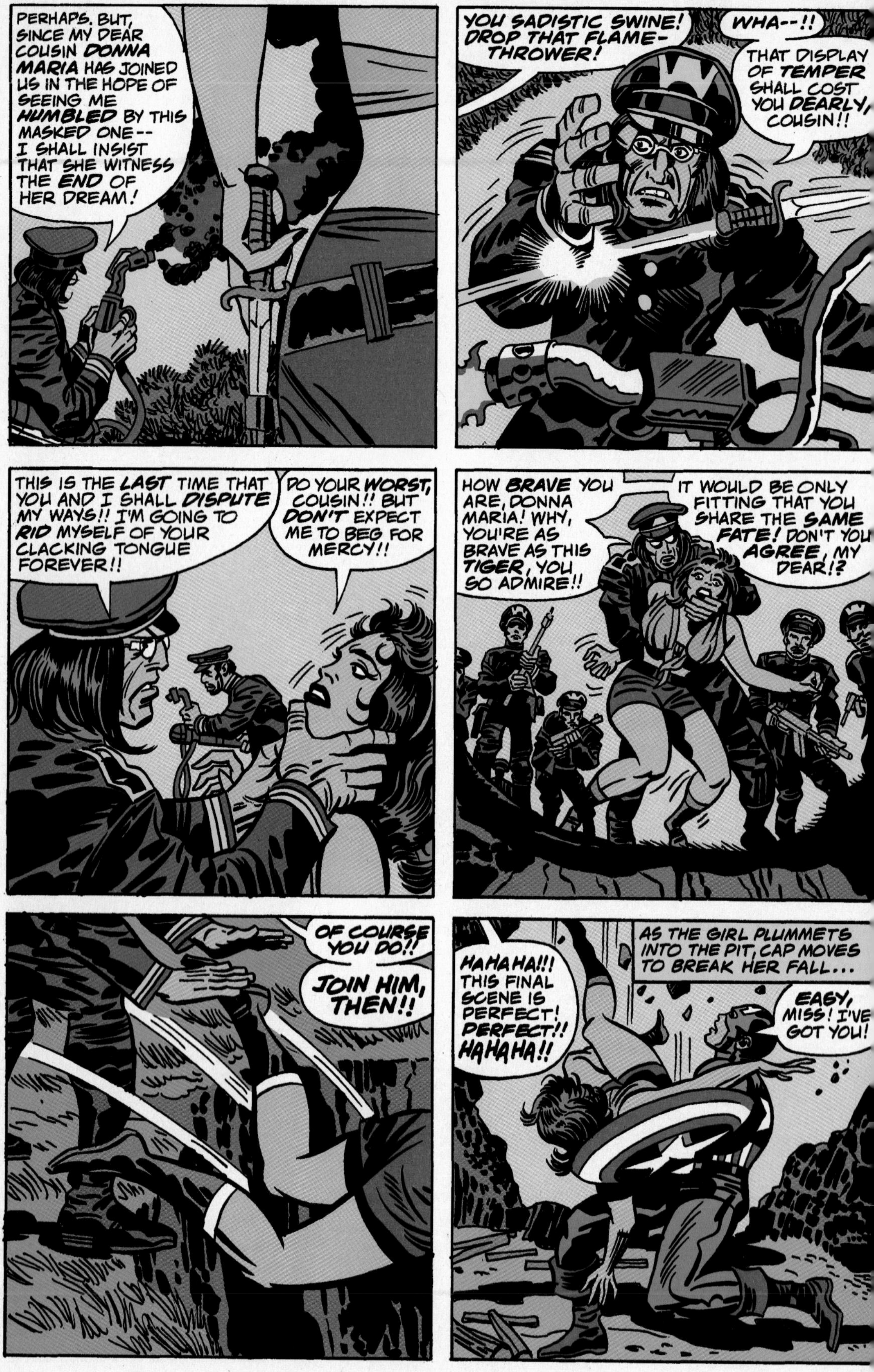
PERHAPS. BUT, SINCE MY DEAR COUSIN DONNA MARIA HAS JOINED US IN THE HOPE OF SEEING ME HUMBLED BY THIS MASKED ONE-- I SHALL INSIST THAT SHE WITNESS THE END OF HER DREAM!
YOU SADISTIC SWINE! DROP THAT FLAME-THROWER!
WHA--!!
THAT DISPLAY OF TEMPER SHALL COST YOU DEARLY, COUSIN!!
THIS IS THE LAST TIME THAT YOU AND I SHALL DISPUTE MY WAYS!! I'M GOING TO RID MYSELF OF YOUR CLACKING TONGUE FOREVER!!
DO YOUR WORST, COUSIN!! BUT DON'T EXPECT ME TO BEG FOR MERCY!!
HOW BRAVE YOU ARE, DONNA MARIA! WHY, YOU'RE AS BRAVE AS THIS TIGER, YOU SO ADMIRE!!
IT WOULD BE ONLY FITTING THAT YOU SHARE THE SAME FATE! DON'T YOU AGREE, MY DEAR!?
OF COURSE YOU DO!!
JOIN HIM, THEN!!
AS THE GIRL PLUMMETS INTO THE PIT, CAP MOVES TO BREAK HER FALL...
HAHAHA!!! THIS FINAL SCENE IS PERFECT! PERFECT!! HAHAHA!!
EASY, MISS! I'VE GOT YOU!

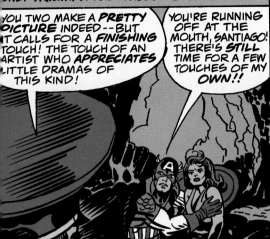

IN THE WARPED MIND OF THE SWINE THERE IS NO SENSE OF EVIL IN THIS DEED. HE KNOWS ONLY TRIUMPH AND A NEED FOR HASTE...

YOU TWO MAKE A PRETTY PICTURE INDEED--BUT IT CALLS FOR A FINISHING TOUCH! THE TOUCH OF AN ARTIST WHO APPRECIATES LITTLE DRAMAS OF THIS KIND!

YOU'RE RUNNING OFF AT THE MOUTH, SANTIAGO! THERE'S STILL TIME FOR A FEW TOUCHES OF MY OWN!!

WRONG, TIGER! YOUR TIME IS AT HAND!! THIS FLAME BURNS HOT AND BRIGHT--AND IS CONTROLLED BY THE HAND OF A SKILLED MASTER!!

IF I WERE YOU, TIGER, I SHOULD PRAY AT THIS MOMENT-- OR, PERHAPS, FUMBLE FOR THE PROPER WORDS TO APPEASE MY ANGER!

BUT, AS DONNA MARIA CAN TELL YOU, THERE IS NOTHING YOU CAN DO THAT WILL STOP WHAT IS ABOUT TO HAPPEN!!

SUDDENLY, THE JUNGLE ERUPTS WITH THE LOUD CRACK OF GUNFIRE AND THE SOUNDS OF STARTLED MEN!!!

LOOK! THE MAN-FISH! HE'S COMING OUT OF THE RIVER!

HE'S ATTACKING! SHOOT! SHOOT!

BAM! BAM!

POK! POK! POK!

HECTOR SANTIAGO REMAINS SPEECHLESS AT THIS SUDDEN TURN OF FATE!! HE WATCHES, ALMOST MESMERIZED, AS HIS MEN FALL-- AS SCALY DEATH WHEELS IN HIS DIRECTION...

NO! NO!

DEATH IS SWIFT AND SAVAGE! IT ROARS LIKE A BEAST AND SNATCHES SANTIAGO OFF HIS FEET!! HIS GLOWING, TWISTED VISION OF TRIUMPH VANISHES IN A SCREAM OF FRIGHT!

AAAAA!!

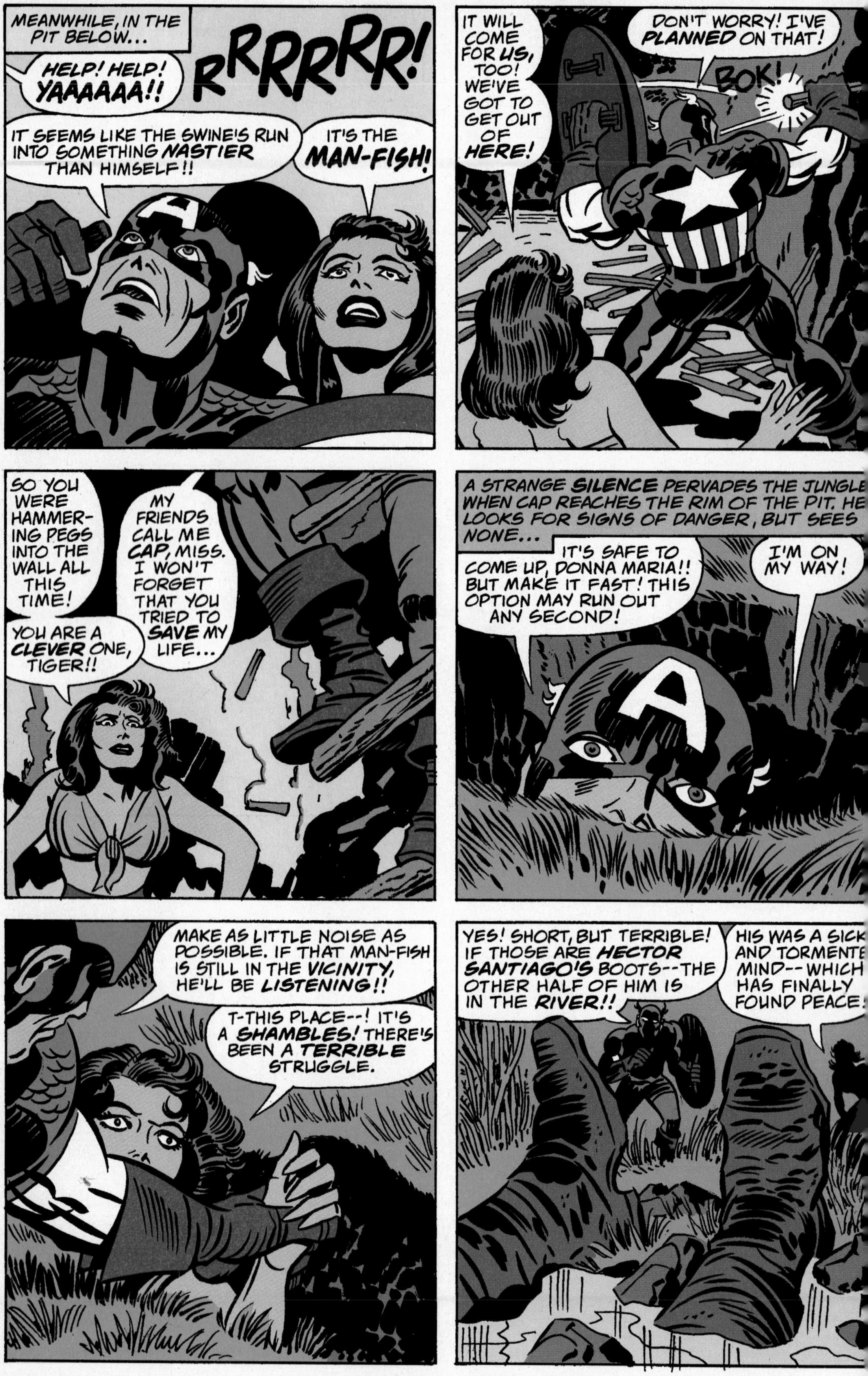
MEANWHILE, IN THE PIT BELOW...
HELP! HELP! YAAAAAA!!
RRRRRRR!
IT SEEMS LIKE THE SWINE'S RUN INTO SOMETHING NASTIER THAN HIMSELF!!
IT'S THE MAN-FISH!
IT WILL COME FOR US, TOO! WE'VE GOT TO GET OUT OF HERE!
DON'T WORRY! I'VE PLANNED ON THAT!
BOK!
SO YOU WERE HAMMERING PEGS INTO THE WALL ALL THIS TIME!
YOU ARE A CLEVER ONE, TIGER!!
MY FRIENDS CALL ME CAP, MISS. I WON'T FORGET THAT YOU TRIED TO SAVE MY LIFE...
A STRANGE SILENCE PERVADES THE JUNGLE WHEN CAP REACHES THE RIM OF THE PIT. HE LOOKS FOR SIGNS OF DANGER, BUT SEES NONE...
IT'S SAFE TO COME UP, DONNA MARIA!! BUT MAKE IT FAST! THIS OPTION MAY RUN OUT ANY SECOND!
I'M ON MY WAY!
MAKE AS LITTLE NOISE AS POSSIBLE. IF THAT MAN-FISH IS STILL IN THE VICINITY, HE'LL BE LISTENING!!
T-THIS PLACE--! IT'S A SHAMBLES! THERE'S BEEN A TERRIBLE STRUGGLE.
YES! SHORT, BUT TERRIBLE! IF THOSE ARE HECTOR SANTIAGO'S BOOTS--THE OTHER HALF OF HIM IS IN THE RIVER!!
HIS WAS A SICK AND TORMENTE MIND--WHICH HAS FINALLY FOUND PEACE!

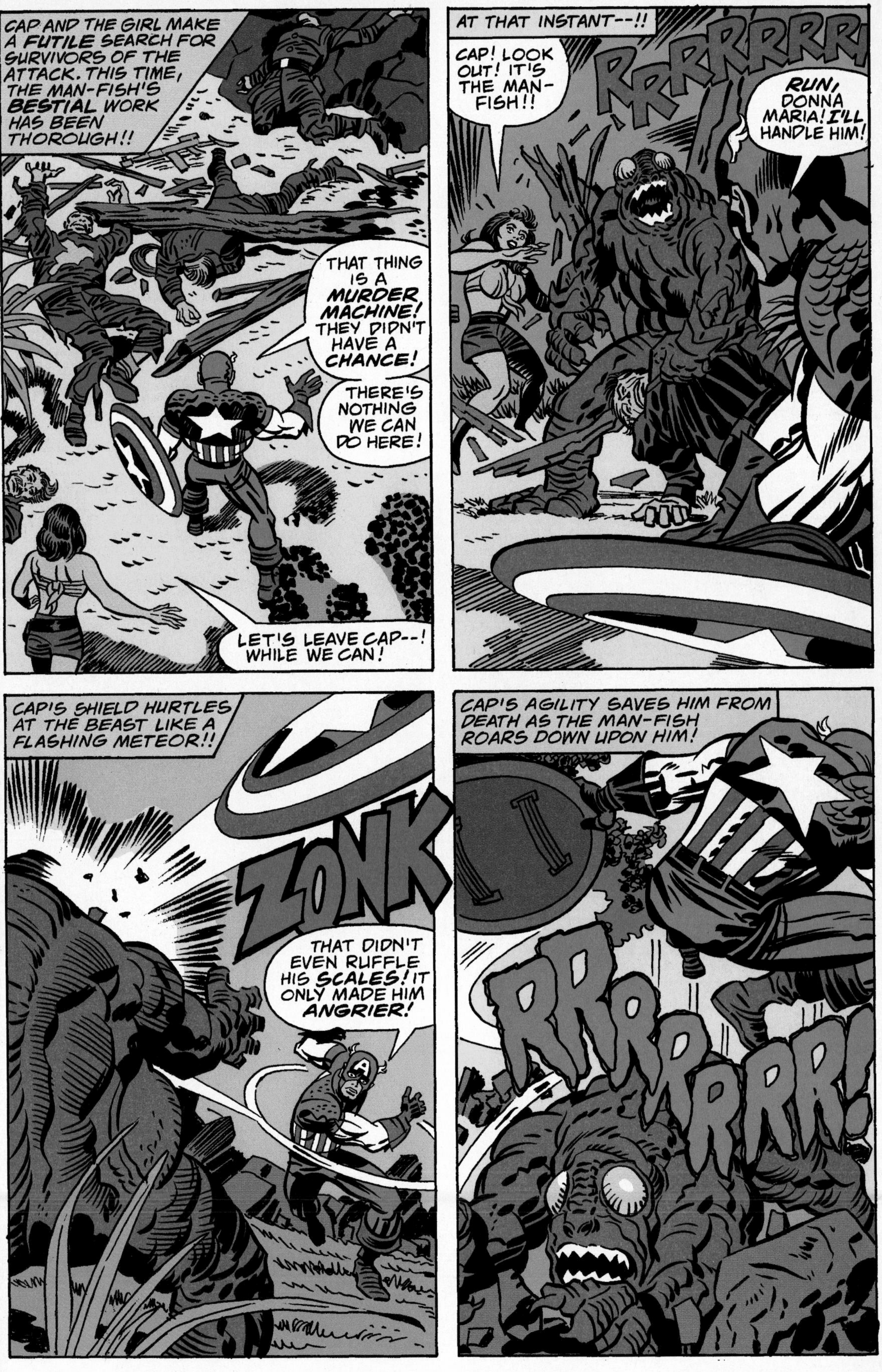
CAP AND THE GIRL MAKE A FUTILE SEARCH FOR SURVIVORS OF THE ATTACK. THIS TIME, THE MAN-FISH'S BESTIAL WORK HAS BEEN THOROUGH!!
THAT THING IS A MURDER MACHINE! THEY DIDN'T HAVE A CHANCE!
THERE'S NOTHING WE CAN DO HERE!
LET'S LEAVE CAP--! WHILE WE CAN!
AT THAT INSTANT--!!
CAP! LOOK OUT! IT'S THE MAN-FISH!!
RRRRRRRR
RUN, DONNA MARIA! I'LL HANDLE HIM!
CAP'S SHIELD HURTLES AT THE BEAST LIKE A FLASHING METEOR!!
ZONK
THAT DIDN'T EVEN RUFFLE HIS SCALES! IT ONLY MADE HIM ANGRIER!
CAP'S AGILITY SAVES HIM FROM DEATH AS THE MAN-FISH ROARS DOWN UPON HIM!
RRRRRRRR!

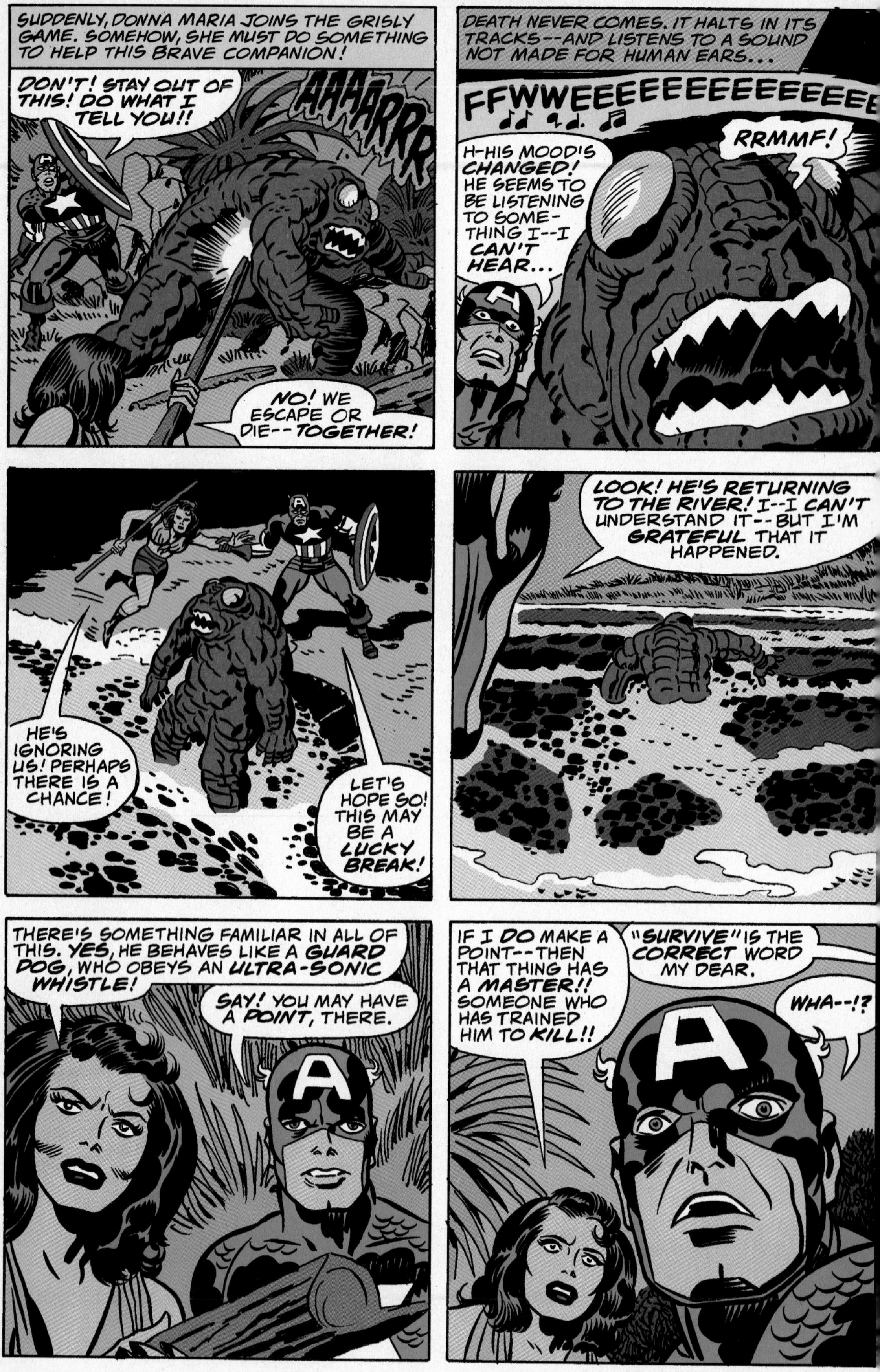
SUDDENLY, DONNA MARIA JOINS THE GRISLY GAME. SOMEHOW, SHE MUST DO SOMETHING TO HELP THIS BRAVE COMPANION!
DON'T! STAY OUT OF THIS! DO WHAT I TELL YOU!!
AAAARRR
NO! WE ESCAPE OR DIE--TOGETHER!
DEATH NEVER COMES. IT HALTS IN ITS TRACKS--AND LISTENS TO A SOUND NOT MADE FOR HUMAN EARS...
FFWWEEEEEEEEEEEEEEE
RRMMF!
H-HIS MOOD'S CHANGED! HE SEEMS TO BE LISTENING TO SOME-THING I--I CAN'T HEAR...
HE'S IGNORING US! PERHAPS THERE IS A CHANCE!
LET'S HOPE SO! THIS MAY BE A LUCKY BREAK!
LOOK! HE'S RETURNING TO THE RIVER! I--I CAN'T UNDERSTAND IT--BUT I'M GRATEFUL THAT IT HAPPENED.
THERE'S SOMETHING FAMILIAR IN ALL OF THIS. YES, HE BEHAVES LIKE A GUARD DOG, WHO OBEYS AN ULTRA-SONIC WHISTLE!
SAY! YOU MAY HAVE A POINT, THERE.
IF I DO MAKE A POINT--THEN THAT THING HAS A MASTER!! SOMEONE WHO HAS TRAINED HIM TO KILL!!
"SURVIVE" IS THE CORRECT WORD MY DEAR.
WHA--!?

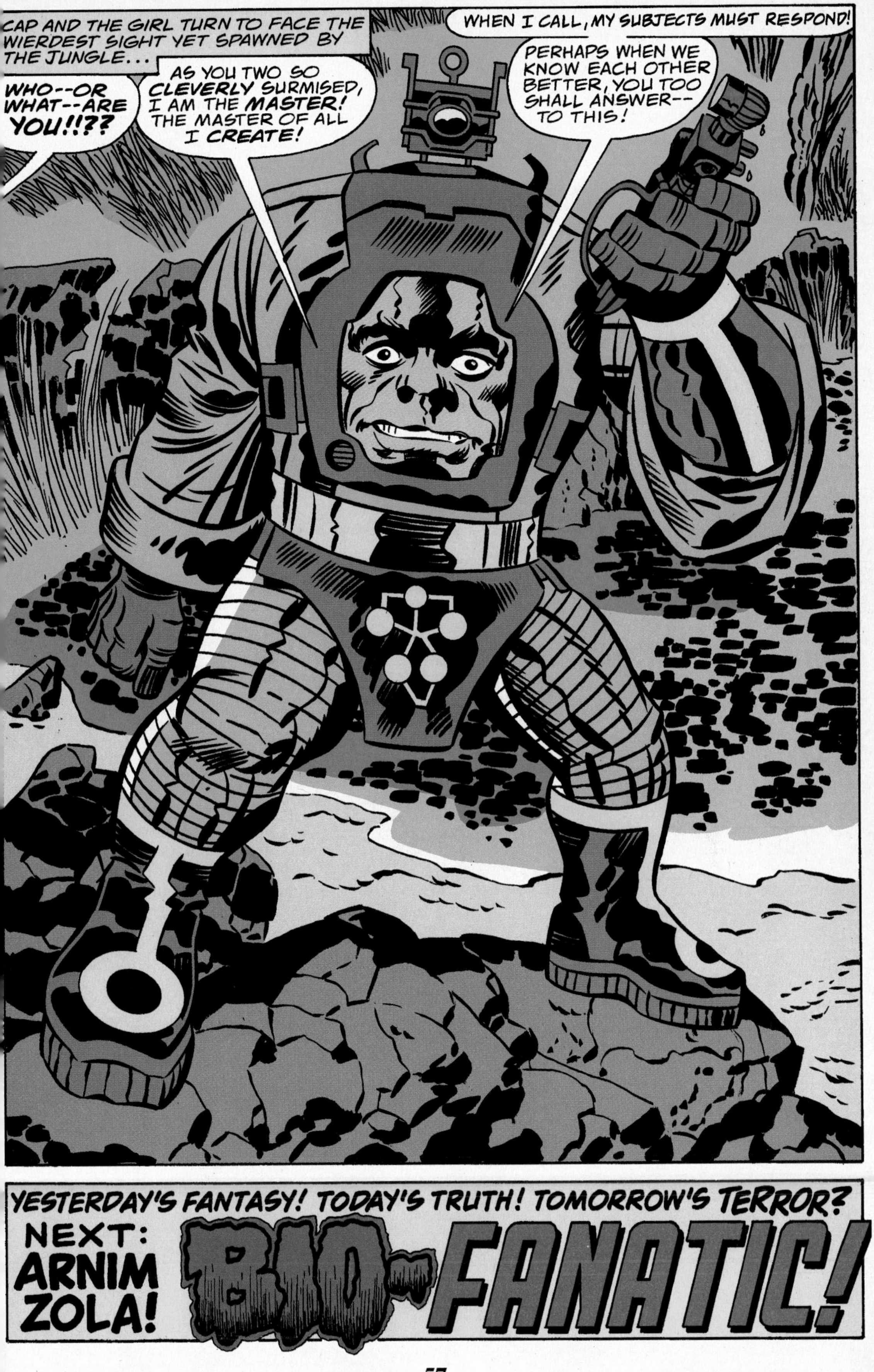
CAP AND THE GIRL TURN TO FACE THE WIERDEST SIGHT YET SPAWNED BY THE JUNGLE...
WHO--OR WHAT--ARE YOU!!??
AS YOU TWO SO CLEVERLY SURMISED, I AM THE MASTER! THE MASTER OF ALL I CREATE!
WHEN I CALL, MY SUBJECTS MUST RESPOND!
PERHAPS WHEN WE KNOW EACH OTHER BETTER, YOU TOO SHALL ANSWER-- TO THIS!
YESTERDAY'S FANTASY! TODAY'S TRUTH! TOMORROW'S TERROR?
NEXT: ARNIM ZOLA!
BIO-FANATIC!

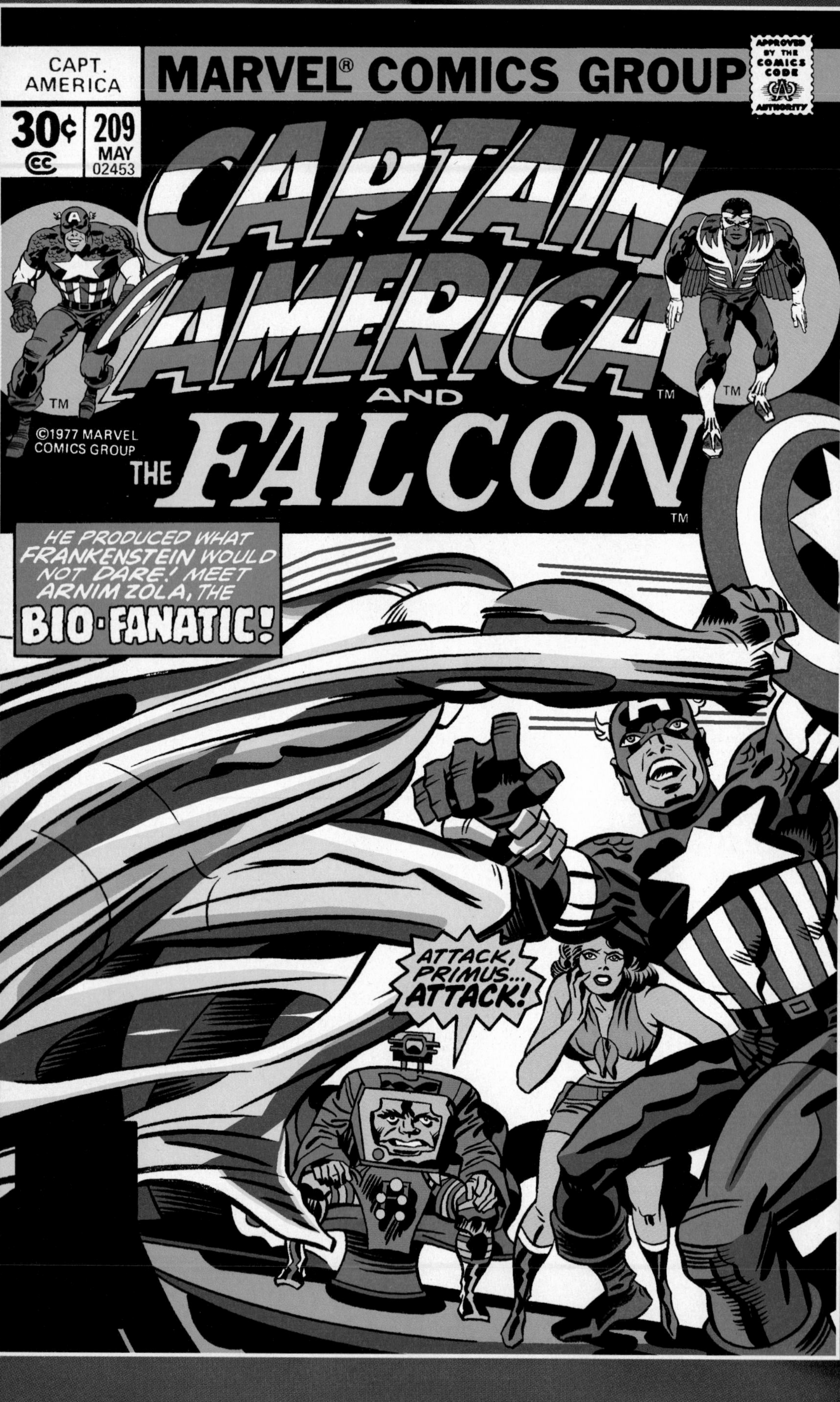
CAPT. AMERICA
MARVEL® COMICS GROUP
APPROVED BY THE COMICS CODE AUTHORITY
30¢ CC
209 MAY 02453
CAPTAIN AMERICA™ AND THE FALCON™
©1977 MARVEL COMICS GROUP
HE PRODUCED WHAT FRANKENSTEIN WOULD NOT DARE! MEET ARNIM ZOLA, THE BIO-FANATIC!
ATTACK, PRIMUS... ATTACK!

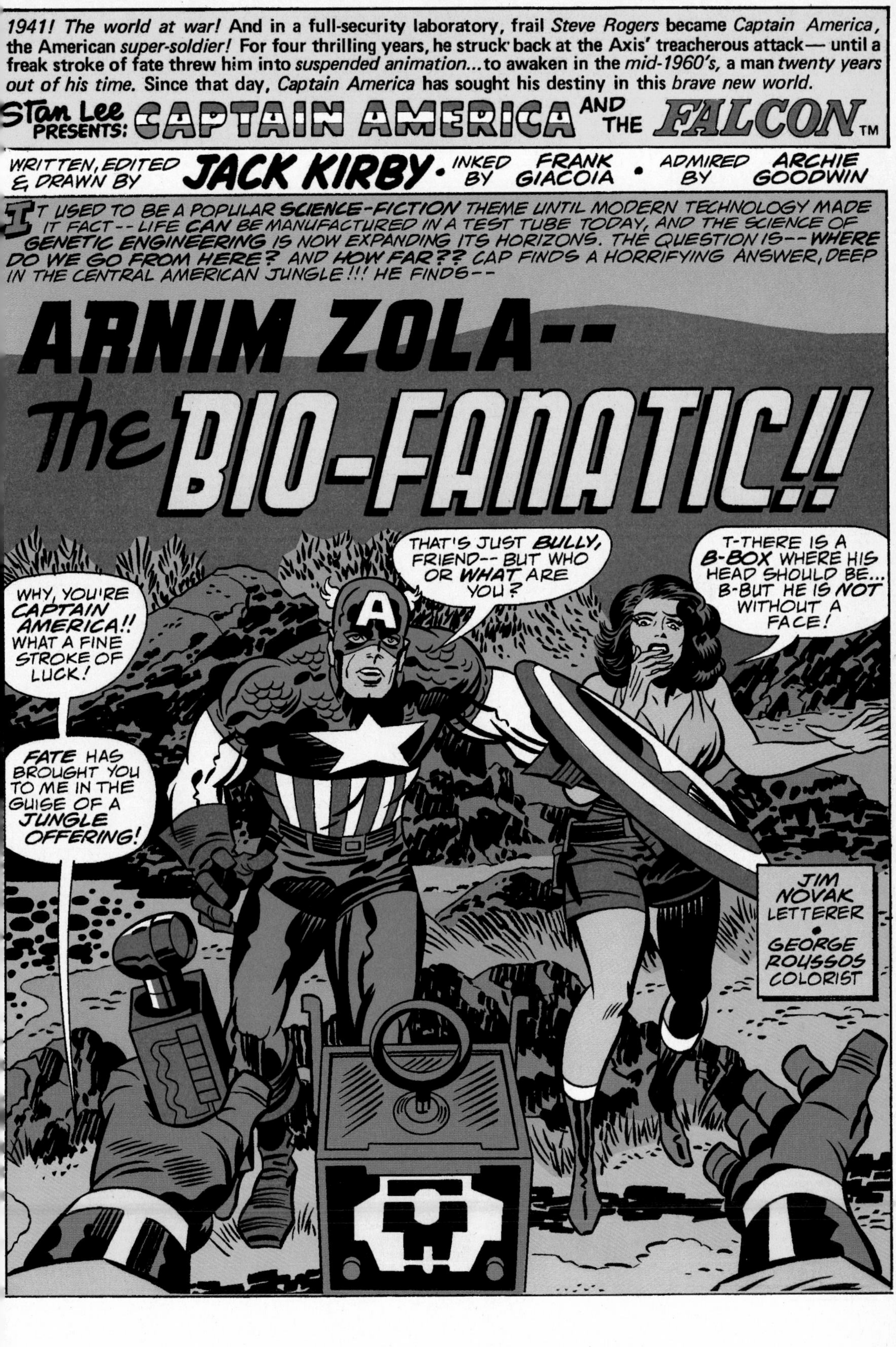

1941! The world at war! And in a full-security laboratory, frail Steve Rogers became Captain America, the American super-soldier! For four thrilling years, he struck back at the Axis' treacherous attack— until a freak stroke of fate threw him into suspended animation...to awaken in the mid-1960's, a man twenty years out of his time. Since that day, Captain America has sought his destiny in this brave new world.
Stan Lee PRESENTS: CAPTAIN AMERICA AND THE FALCON TM
WRITTEN, EDITED & DRAWN BY JACK KIRBY • INKED BY FRANK GIACOIA • ADMIRED BY ARCHIE GOODWIN
IT USED TO BE A POPULAR SCIENCE-FICTION THEME UNTIL MODERN TECHNOLOGY MADE IT FACT-- LIFE CAN BE MANUFACTURED IN A TEST TUBE TODAY, AND THE SCIENCE OF GENETIC ENGINEERING IS NOW EXPANDING ITS HORIZONS. THE QUESTION IS-- WHERE DO WE GO FROM HERE? AND HOW FAR?? CAP FINDS A HORRIFYING ANSWER, DEEP IN THE CENTRAL AMERICAN JUNGLE!!! HE FINDS--
ARNIM ZOLA-- The BIO-FANATIC!!
WHY, YOU'RE CAPTAIN AMERICA!! WHAT A FINE STROKE OF LUCK!
FATE HAS BROUGHT YOU TO ME IN THE GUISE OF A JUNGLE OFFERING!
THAT'S JUST BULLY, FRIEND-- BUT WHO OR WHAT ARE YOU?
T-THERE IS A B-BOX WHERE HIS HEAD SHOULD BE... B-BUT HE IS NOT WITHOUT A FACE!
JIM NOVAK LETTERER • GEORGE ROUSSOS COLORIST

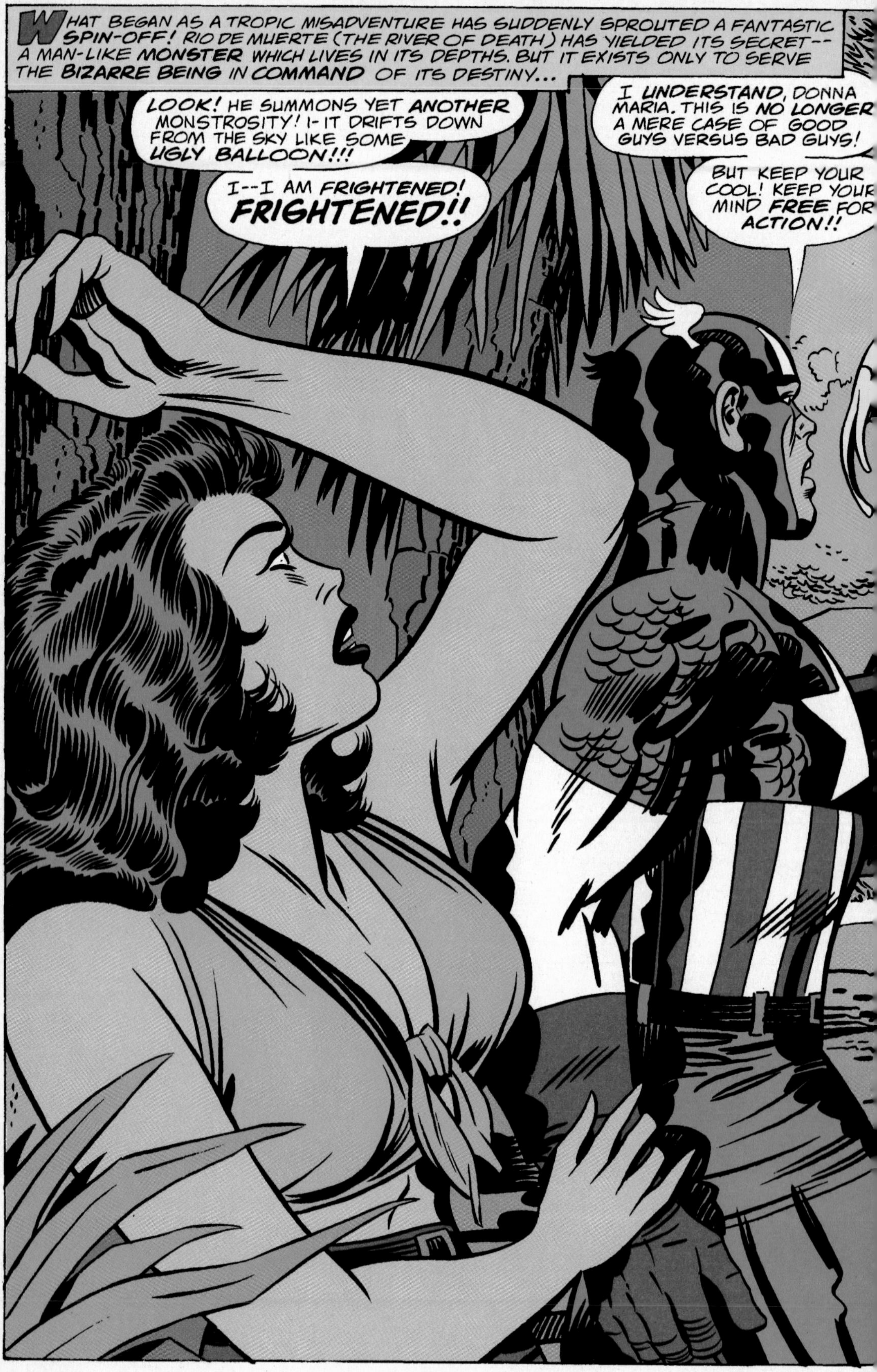
WHAT BEGAN AS A TROPIC MISADVENTURE HAS SUDDENLY SPROUTED A FANTASTIC SPIN-OFF! RIO DE MUERTE (THE RIVER OF DEATH) HAS YIELDED ITS SECRET-- A MAN-LIKE MONSTER WHICH LIVES IN ITS DEPTHS. BUT IT EXISTS ONLY TO SERVE THE BIZARRE BEING IN COMMAND OF ITS DESTINY...
LOOK! HE SUMMONS YET ANOTHER MONSTROSITY! I-IT DRIFTS DOWN FROM THE SKY LIKE SOME UGLY BALLOON!!!
I--I AM FRIGHTENED! FRIGHTENED!!
I UNDERSTAND, DONNA MARIA. THIS IS NO LONGER A MERE CASE OF GOOD GUYS VERSUS BAD GUYS!
BUT KEEP YOUR COOL! KEEP YOUR MIND FREE FOR ACTION!!

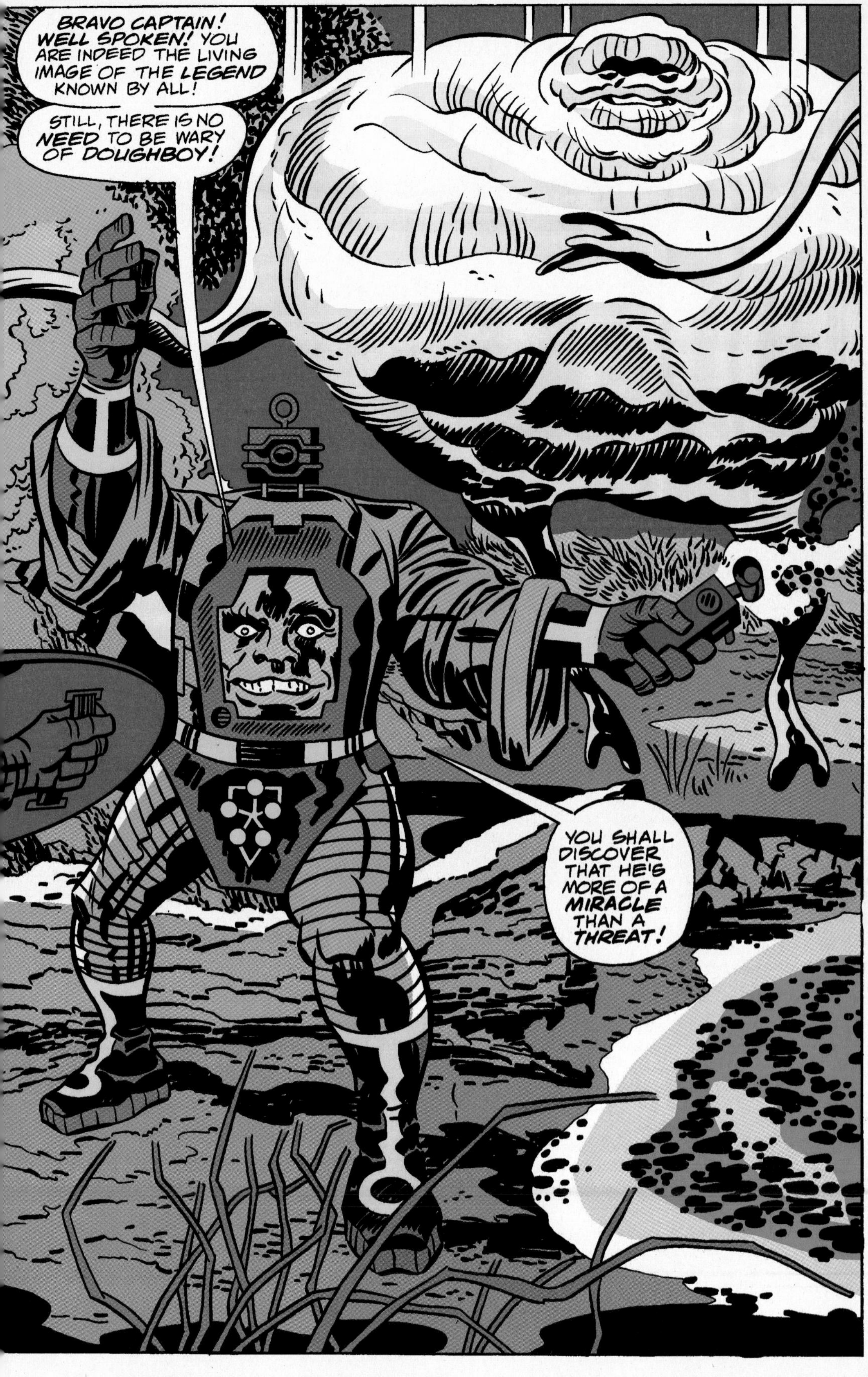
BRAVO CAPTAIN! WELL SPOKEN! YOU ARE INDEED THE LIVING IMAGE OF THE LEGEND KNOWN BY ALL!
STILL, THERE IS NO NEED TO BE WARY OF DOUGHBOY!
YOU SHALL DISCOVER THAT HE'S MORE OF A MIRACLE THAN A THREAT!

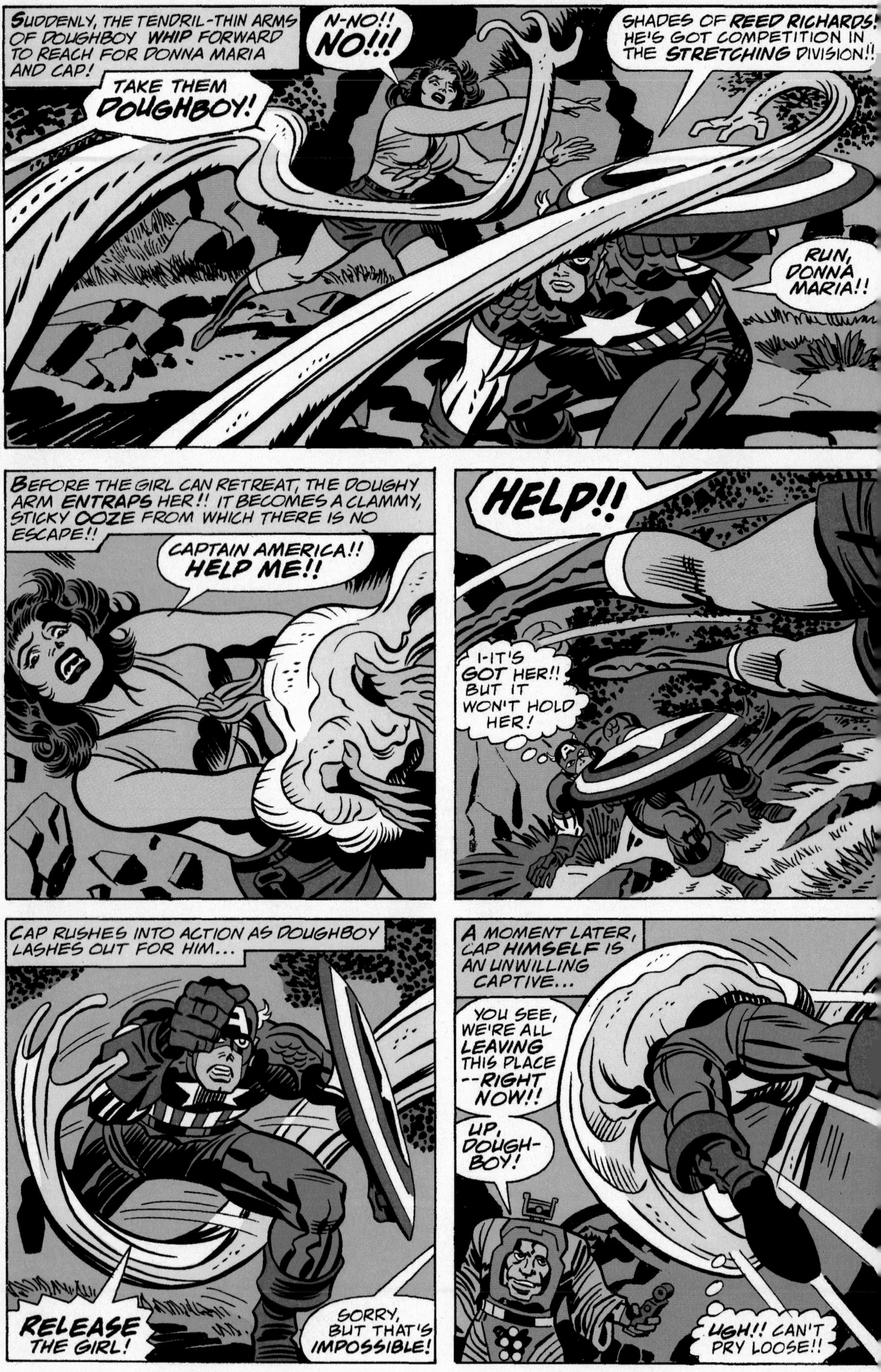

SUDDENLY, THE TENDRIL-THIN ARMS OF DOUGHBOY WHIP FORWARD TO REACH FOR DONNA MARIA AND CAP!
TAKE THEM DOUGHBOY!
N-NO!! NO!!!
SHADES OF REED RICHARDS! HE'S GOT COMPETITION IN THE STRETCHING DIVISION!!
RUN, DONNA MARIA!!
BEFORE THE GIRL CAN RETREAT, THE DOUGHY ARM ENTRAPS HER!! IT BECOMES A CLAMMY, STICKY OOZE FROM WHICH THERE IS NO ESCAPE!!
CAPTAIN AMERICA!! HELP ME!!
HELP!!
I-IT'S GOT HER!! BUT IT WON'T HOLD HER!
CAP RUSHES INTO ACTION AS DOUGHBOY LASHES OUT FOR HIM...
RELEASE THE GIRL!
SORRY, BUT THAT'S IMPOSSIBLE!
A MOMENT LATER, CAP HIMSELF IS AN UNWILLING CAPTIVE...
YOU SEE, WE'RE ALL LEAVING THIS PLACE --RIGHT NOW!!
UP, DOUGH-BOY!
UGH!! CAN'T PRY LOOSE!!

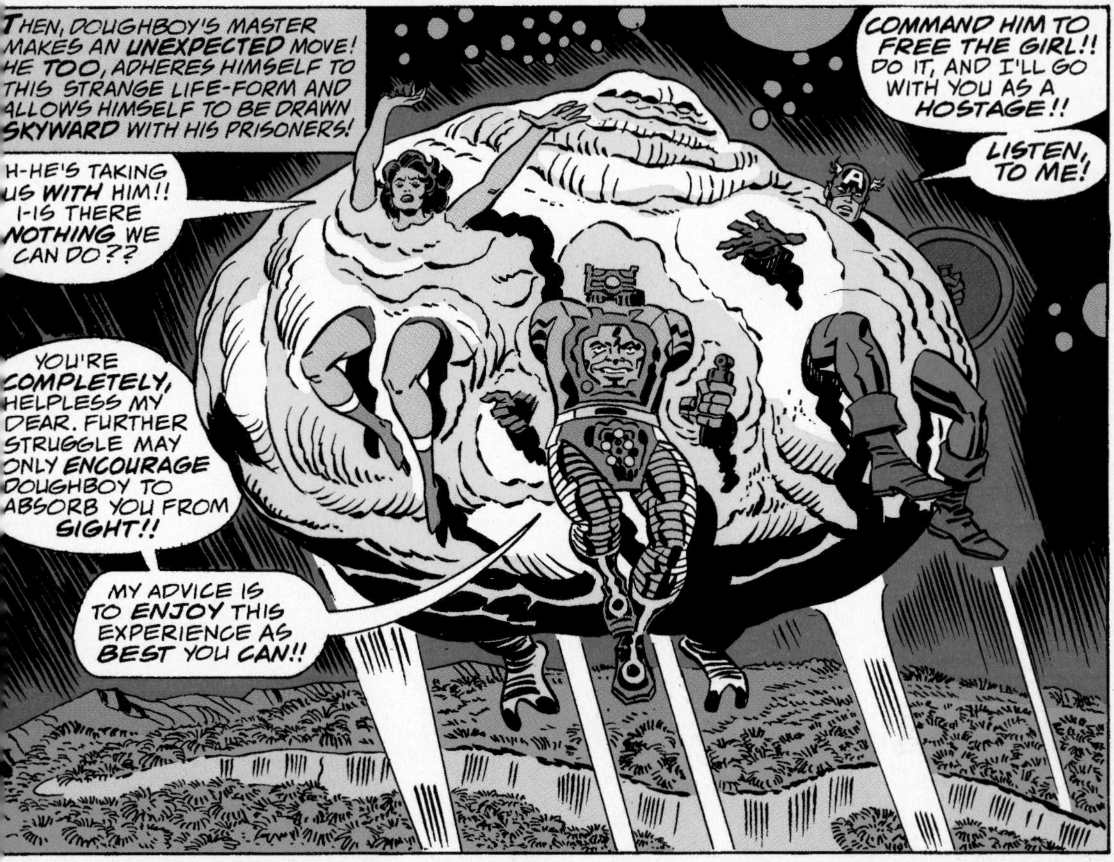
THEN, DOUGHBOY'S MASTER MAKES AN UNEXPECTED MOVE! HE TOO, ADHERES HIMSELF TO THIS STRANGE LIFE-FORM AND ALLOWS HIMSELF TO BE DRAWN SKYWARD WITH HIS PRISONERS!
H-HE'S TAKING US WITH HIM!! I-IS THERE NOTHING WE CAN DO??
YOU'RE COMPLETELY, HELPLESS MY DEAR. FURTHER STRUGGLE MAY ONLY ENCOURAGE DOUGHBOY TO ABSORB YOU FROM SIGHT!!
MY ADVICE IS TO ENJOY THIS EXPERIENCE AS BEST YOU CAN!!
LISTEN, TO ME!
COMMAND HIM TO FREE THE GIRL!! DO IT, AND I'LL GO WITH YOU AS A HOSTAGE!!

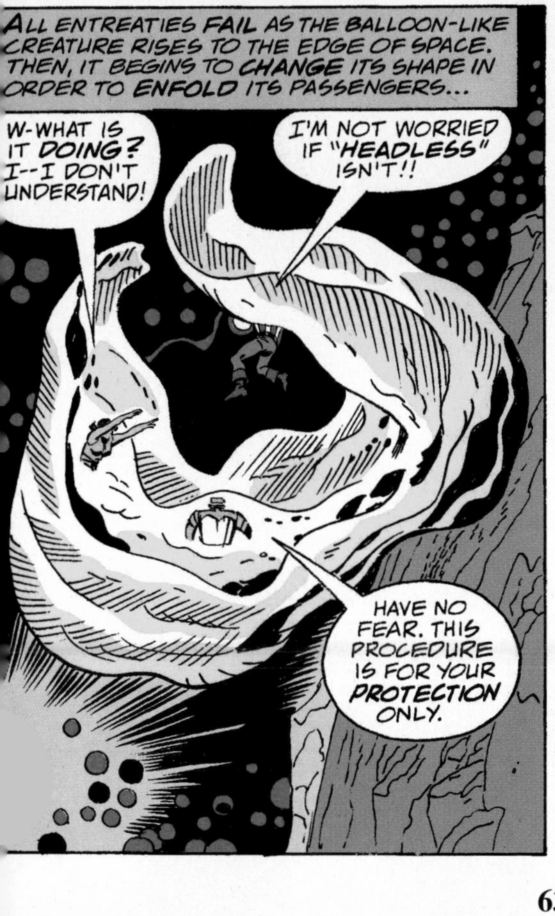
ALL ENTREATIES FAIL AS THE BALLOON-LIKE CREATURE RISES TO THE EDGE OF SPACE. THEN, IT BEGINS TO CHANGE ITS SHAPE IN ORDER TO ENFOLD ITS PASSENGERS...
W-WHAT IS IT DOING? I--I DON'T UNDERSTAND!
I'M NOT WORRIED IF "HEADLESS" ISN'T!!
HAVE NO FEAR. THIS PROCEDURE IS FOR YOUR PROTECTION ONLY.

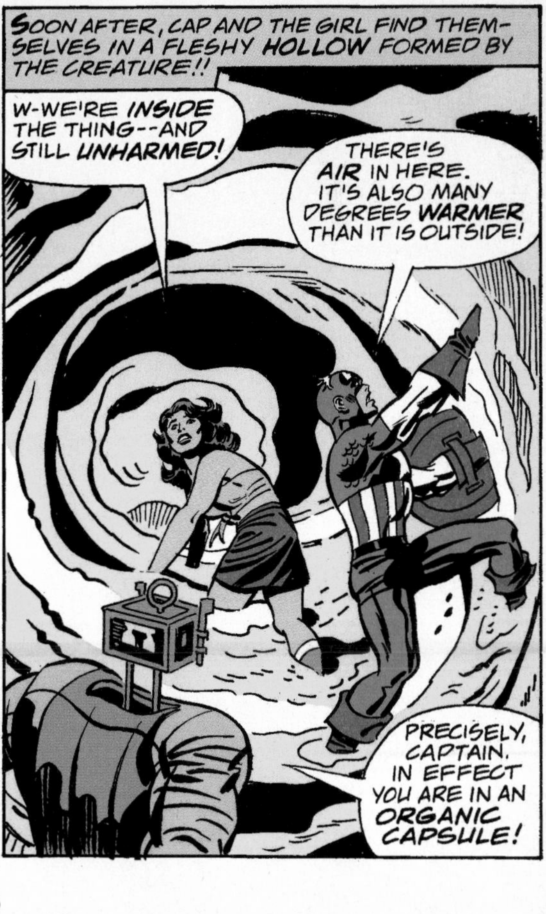
SOON AFTER, CAP AND THE GIRL FIND THEMSELVES IN A FLESHY HOLLOW FORMED BY THE CREATURE!!
W-WE'RE INSIDE THE THING--AND STILL UNHARMED!
THERE'S AIR IN HERE. IT'S ALSO MANY DEGREES WARMER THAN IT IS OUTSIDE!
PRECISELY, CAPTAIN. IN EFFECT YOU ARE IN AN ORGANIC CAPSULE!

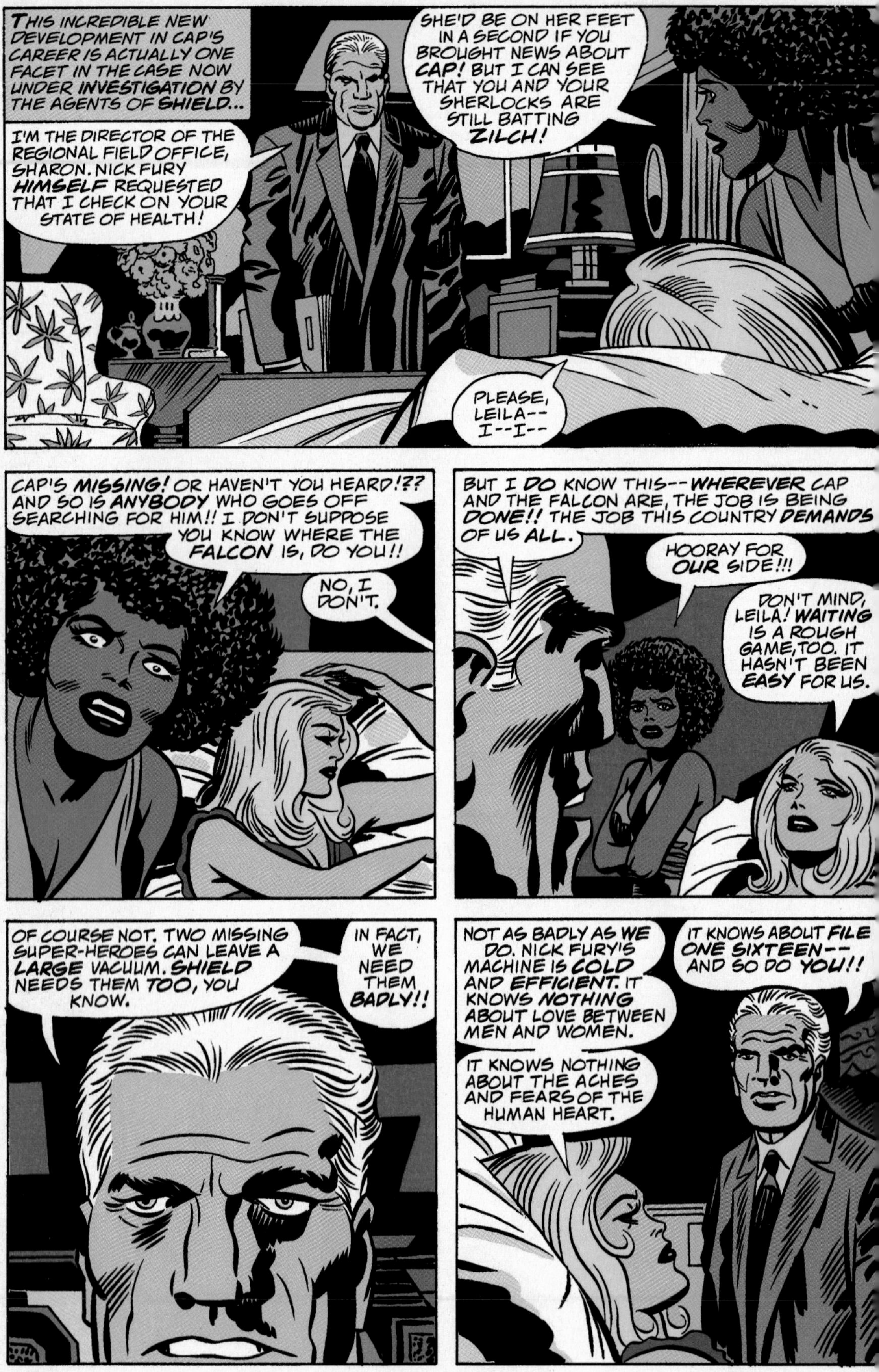
THIS INCREDIBLE NEW DEVELOPMENT IN CAP'S CAREER IS ACTUALLY ONE FACET IN THE CASE NOW UNDER INVESTIGATION BY THE AGENTS OF SHIELD...
I'M THE DIRECTOR OF THE REGIONAL FIELD OFFICE, SHARON. NICK FURY HIMSELF REQUESTED THAT I CHECK ON YOUR STATE OF HEALTH!
SHE'D BE ON HER FEET IN A SECOND IF YOU BROUGHT NEWS ABOUT CAP! BUT I CAN SEE THAT YOU AND YOUR SHERLOCKS ARE STILL BATTING ZILCH!
PLEASE, LEILA-- I--I--
CAP'S MISSING! OR HAVEN'T YOU HEARD!?? AND SO IS ANYBODY WHO GOES OFF SEARCHING FOR HIM!! I DON'T SUPPOSE YOU KNOW WHERE THE FALCON IS, DO YOU!!
NO, I DON'T.
BUT I DO KNOW THIS--WHEREVER CAP AND THE FALCON ARE, THE JOB IS BEING DONE!! THE JOB THIS COUNTRY DEMANDS OF US ALL.
HOORAY FOR OUR SIDE!!!
DON'T MIND, LEILA! WAITING IS A ROUGH GAME, TOO. IT HASN'T BEEN EASY FOR US.
OF COURSE NOT. TWO MISSING SUPER-HEROES CAN LEAVE A LARGE VACUUM. SHIELD NEEDS THEM TOO, YOU KNOW.
IN FACT, WE NEED THEM BADLY!!
NOT AS BADLY AS WE DO. NICK FURY'S MACHINE IS COLD AND EFFICIENT. IT KNOWS NOTHING ABOUT LOVE BETWEEN MEN AND WOMEN.
IT KNOWS NOTHING ABOUT THE ACHES AND FEARS OF THE HUMAN HEART.
IT KNOWS ABOUT FILE ONE SIXTEEN-- AND SO DO YOU!!

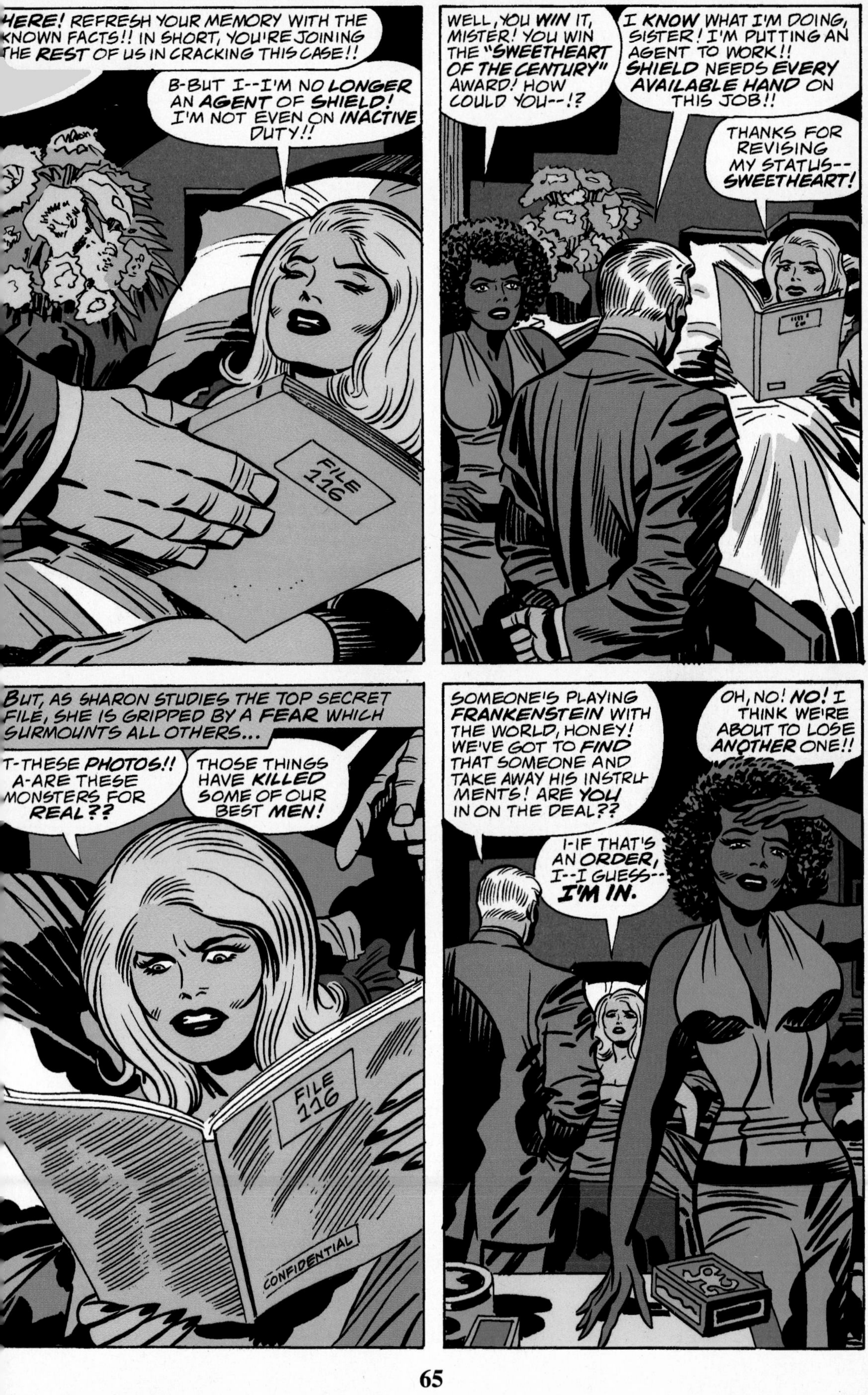
HERE! REFRESH YOUR MEMORY WITH THE KNOWN FACTS!! IN SHORT, YOU'RE JOINING THE REST OF US IN CRACKING THIS CASE!!
B-BUT I--I'M NO LONGER AN AGENT OF SHIELD! I'M NOT EVEN ON INACTIVE DUTY!!
FILE 116
WELL, YOU WIN IT, MISTER! YOU WIN THE "SWEETHEART OF THE CENTURY" AWARD! HOW COULD YOU--!?
I KNOW WHAT I'M DOING, SISTER! I'M PUTTING AN AGENT TO WORK!! SHIELD NEEDS EVERY AVAILABLE HAND ON THIS JOB!!
THANKS FOR REVISING MY STATUS-- SWEETHEART!
BUT, AS SHARON STUDIES THE TOP SECRET FILE, SHE IS GRIPPED BY A FEAR WHICH SURMOUNTS ALL OTHERS...
T-THESE PHOTOS!! A-ARE THESE MONSTERS FOR REAL??
THOSE THINGS HAVE KILLED SOME OF OUR BEST MEN!
FILE 116
CONFIDENTIAL
SOMEONE'S PLAYING FRANKENSTEIN WITH THE WORLD, HONEY! WE'VE GOT TO FIND THAT SOMEONE AND TAKE AWAY HIS INSTRU-MENTS! ARE YOU IN ON THE DEAL??
OH, NO! NO! I THINK WE'RE ABOUT TO LOSE ANOTHER ONE!!
I-IF THAT'S AN ORDER, I--I GUESS-- I'M IN.

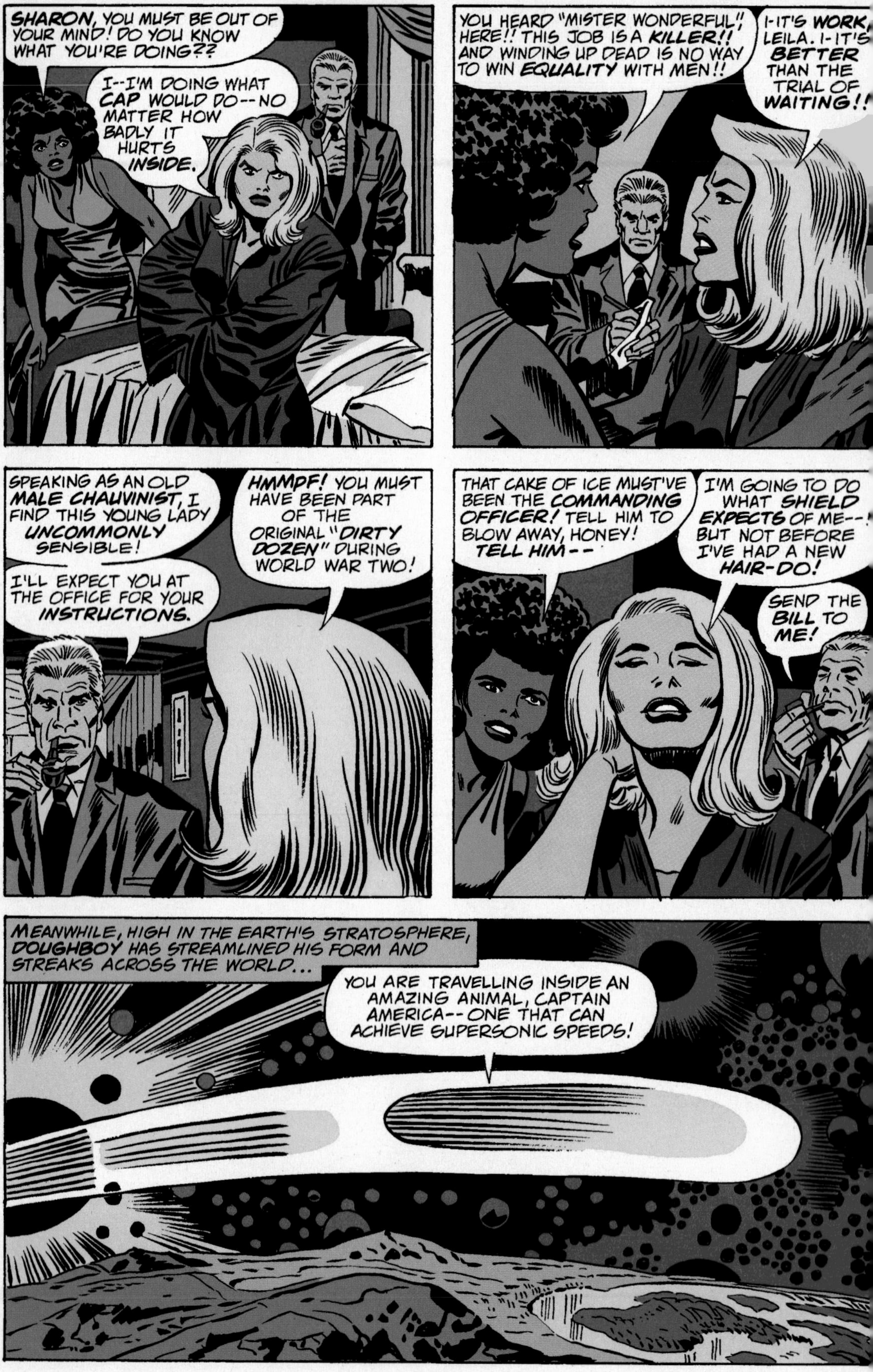
SHARON, YOU MUST BE OUT OF YOUR MIND! DO YOU KNOW WHAT YOU'RE DOING??
I--I'M DOING WHAT CAP WOULD DO--NO MATTER HOW BADLY IT HURTS INSIDE.
YOU HEARD "MISTER WONDERFUL," HERE!! THIS JOB IS A KILLER!! AND WINDING UP DEAD IS NO WAY TO WIN EQUALITY WITH MEN!!
I-IT'S WORK, LEILA. I-IT'S BETTER THAN THE TRIAL OF WAITING!!
SPEAKING AS AN OLD MALE CHAUVINIST, I FIND THIS YOUNG LADY UNCOMMONLY SENSIBLE!
I'LL EXPECT YOU AT THE OFFICE FOR YOUR INSTRUCTIONS.
HMMPF! YOU MUST HAVE BEEN PART OF THE ORIGINAL "DIRTY DOZEN" DURING WORLD WAR TWO!
THAT CAKE OF ICE MUST'VE BEEN THE COMMANDING OFFICER! TELL HIM TO BLOW AWAY, HONEY! TELL HIM--
I'M GOING TO DO WHAT SHIELD EXPECTS OF ME--BUT NOT BEFORE I'VE HAD A NEW HAIR-DO!
SEND THE BILL TO ME!
MEANWHILE, HIGH IN THE EARTH'S STRATOSPHERE, DOUGHBOY HAS STREAMLINED HIS FORM AND STREAKS ACROSS THE WORLD...
YOU ARE TRAVELLING INSIDE AN AMAZING ANIMAL, CAPTAIN AMERICA--ONE THAT CAN ACHIEVE SUPERSONIC SPEEDS!

...OUGHBOY MOVES ABOUT LIKE THE SQUID OR OCTOPUS, WITH NATURAL AIR JETS-- ONLY MY PET IS MUCH FASTER!

HE CAN APPARENTLY *HARDEN* HIS HIDE, TOO! THESE WALLS LOOK PRETTY SOLID!

VERY OBSERVANT, MY DEAR FELLOW! IF YOU WERE TO SEE DOUGHBOY FROM THE *OUTSIDE* RIGHT NOW, HE'D SEEM VERY SIMILAR TO A *FLYING SAUCER!*

I WOULDN'T *MIND* A LOOK OUTSIDE--IF ONLY TO PROTECT MY SANITY!!

I'M *CERTAIN* THAT DOUGHBOY WILL OBLIGE. ALL HE NEEDS IS A BIT OF *PRODDING* --WITH *THIS!!*

T-THE WALL--! I-IT'S GROWING *THINNER* WHERE THAT BEAM STRIKES!

SOON...

THIS SPOT IS NOW COMPLETELY TRANSPARENT!

I-IT'S LIKE A *WINDOW!* WE CAN SEE THE LAND RUSH BY BELOW US!!!

YES, YOU'RE FLYING OVER HILL AND DALE! HAPPILY *ADJUSTING* TO A MARVEL WHICH ONLY A *CHOSEN FEW* HAVE BEEN FORTUNATE TO SEE!!

YES...TELL US *MORE*--ABOUT THE *OTHERS!!*

T-THERE HAVE BEEN *OTHERS*--? LIKE *US?*

WHAT HAPPENED TO THEM!? WHAT DID YOU DO TO THEM!?

WELL, THAT'S PART OF A LONG BUT *VERY* INTERESTING TALE! I'D SUGGEST A *SEAT* FOR EACH OF YOU -- LIKE THIS ONE.

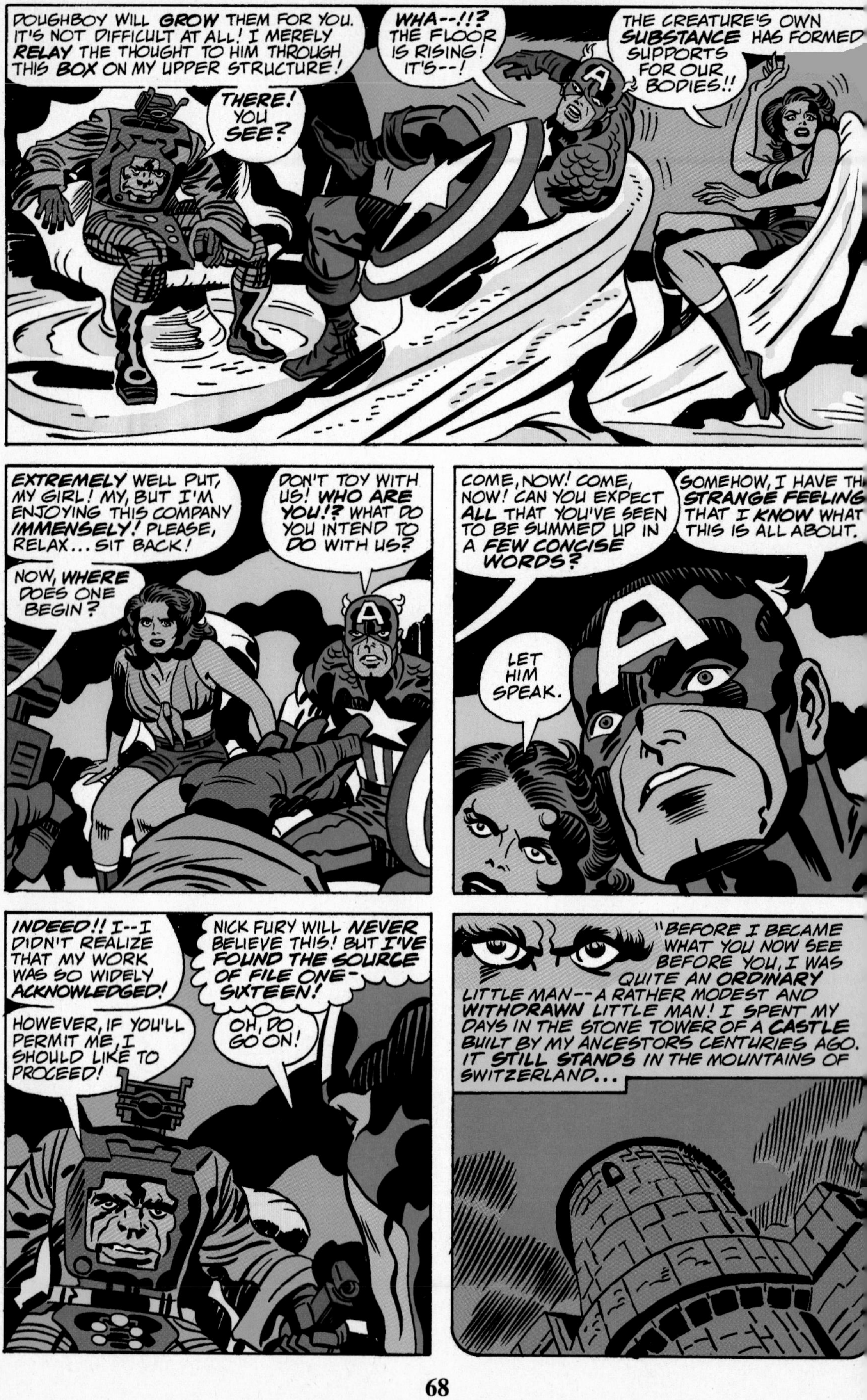
DOUGHBOY WILL GROW THEM FOR YOU. IT'S NOT DIFFICULT AT ALL! I MERELY RELAY THE THOUGHT TO HIM THROUGH THIS BOX ON MY UPPER STRUCTURE!
THERE! YOU SEE?
WHA--!!? THE FLOOR IS RISING! IT'S--!
THE CREATURE'S OWN SUBSTANCE HAS FORMED SUPPORTS FOR OUR BODIES!!
EXTREMELY WELL PUT, MY GIRL! MY, BUT I'M ENJOYING THIS COMPANY IMMENSELY! PLEASE, RELAX... SIT BACK!
NOW, WHERE DOES ONE BEGIN?
DON'T TOY WITH US! WHO ARE YOU!? WHAT DO YOU INTEND TO DO WITH US?
COME, NOW! COME, NOW! CAN YOU EXPECT ALL THAT YOU'VE SEEN TO BE SUMMED UP IN A FEW CONCISE WORDS?
SOMEHOW, I HAVE TH STRANGE FEELING THAT I KNOW WHAT THIS IS ALL ABOUT.
LET HIM SPEAK.
INDEED!! I--I DIDN'T REALIZE THAT MY WORK WAS SO WIDELY ACKNOWLEDGED!
NICK FURY WILL NEVER BELIEVE THIS! BUT I'VE FOUND THE SOURCE OF FILE ONE-SIXTEEN!
HOWEVER, IF YOU'LL PERMIT ME, I SHOULD LIKE TO PROCEED!
OH, DO GO ON!
"BEFORE I BECAME WHAT YOU NOW SEE BEFORE YOU, I WAS QUITE AN ORDINARY LITTLE MAN--A RATHER MODEST AND WITHDRAWN LITTLE MAN! I SPENT MY DAYS IN THE STONE TOWER OF A CASTLE BUILT BY MY ANCESTORS CENTURIES AGO. IT STILL STANDS IN THE MOUNTAINS OF SWITZERLAND...

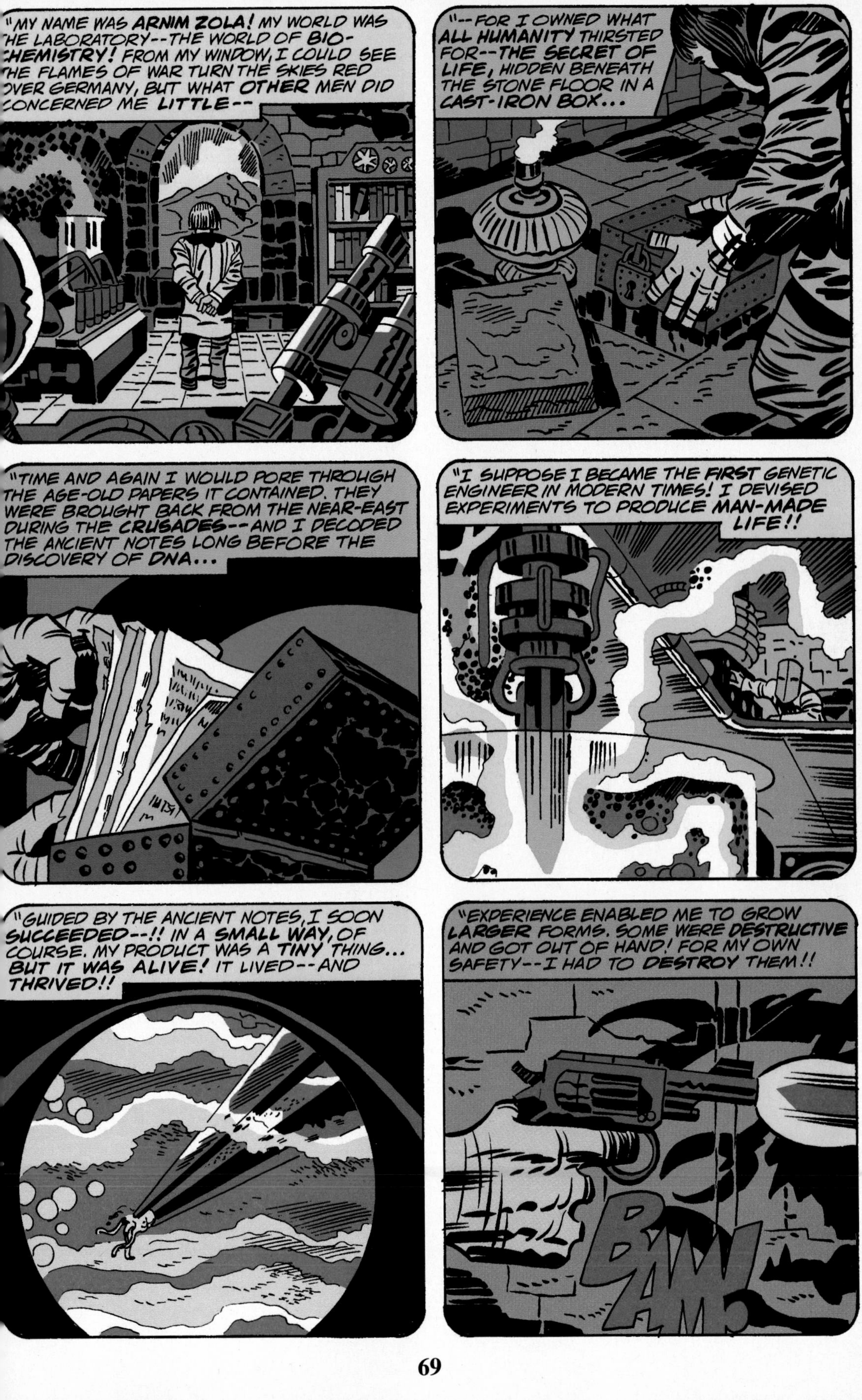
"MY NAME WAS ARNIM ZOLA! MY WORLD WAS THE LABORATORY--THE WORLD OF BIO-CHEMISTRY! FROM MY WINDOW, I COULD SEE THE FLAMES OF WAR TURN THE SKIES RED OVER GERMANY, BUT WHAT OTHER MEN DID CONCERNED ME LITTLE--
"--FOR I OWNED WHAT ALL HUMANITY THIRSTED FOR--THE SECRET OF LIFE, HIDDEN BENEATH THE STONE FLOOR IN A CAST-IRON BOX...
"TIME AND AGAIN I WOULD PORE THROUGH THE AGE-OLD PAPERS IT CONTAINED. THEY WERE BROUGHT BACK FROM THE NEAR-EAST DURING THE CRUSADES--AND I DECODED THE ANCIENT NOTES LONG BEFORE THE DISCOVERY OF DNA...
"I SUPPOSE I BECAME THE FIRST GENETIC ENGINEER IN MODERN TIMES! I DEVISED EXPERIMENTS TO PRODUCE MAN-MADE LIFE!!
"GUIDED BY THE ANCIENT NOTES, I SOON SUCCEEDED--!! IN A SMALL WAY, OF COURSE. MY PRODUCT WAS A TINY THING... BUT IT WAS ALIVE! IT LIVED--AND THRIVED!!
"EXPERIENCE ENABLED ME TO GROW LARGER FORMS. SOME WERE DESTRUCTIVE AND GOT OUT OF HAND! FOR MY OWN SAFETY--I HAD TO DESTROY THEM!!
BAM!

"WITH CAREFUL DELIBER-ATION, I STRUCTURED A NEW BODY FOR MY-SELF--! A STRONGER BODY, WHICH HOUSED ITS BRAIN IN A MORE PROTECTED POSITION!"

"IT TOOK A HEROIC EFFORT TO CONSTRUCT AN INSTRUMENT THAT WOULD TRANSFER MY OWN PERSONALITY TO THE BRAIN IN THAT OTHER BODY! BUT, I DID THAT, TOO! ONE NIGHT, THE OLD ARNIM ZOLA DIED!"

"THE NEW ONE LIVED TO CONTINUE HIS WORK! HE WAS ABLE TO DEAL WITH WHATEVER HIS EXPERIMENTS PRODUCED. THE NEW BRAIN WITHIN HIS BODY WAS SO POTENT THAT HE COULD CONTROL THEM BY THOUGHT ALONE..."

THIS IS HORRIBLE! CAN HE DO THAT TO US? CAN HE REACH INTO OUR MINDS AND FORCE US TO DO HIS BIDDING?

THAT'S AN INTER-ESTING QUESTION, ZOLA! CAN YOU CONTROL US... AS YOU DO YOUR CREATURES?

NO! IT IS A PUZZLE THAT I'VE YET TO SOLVE!

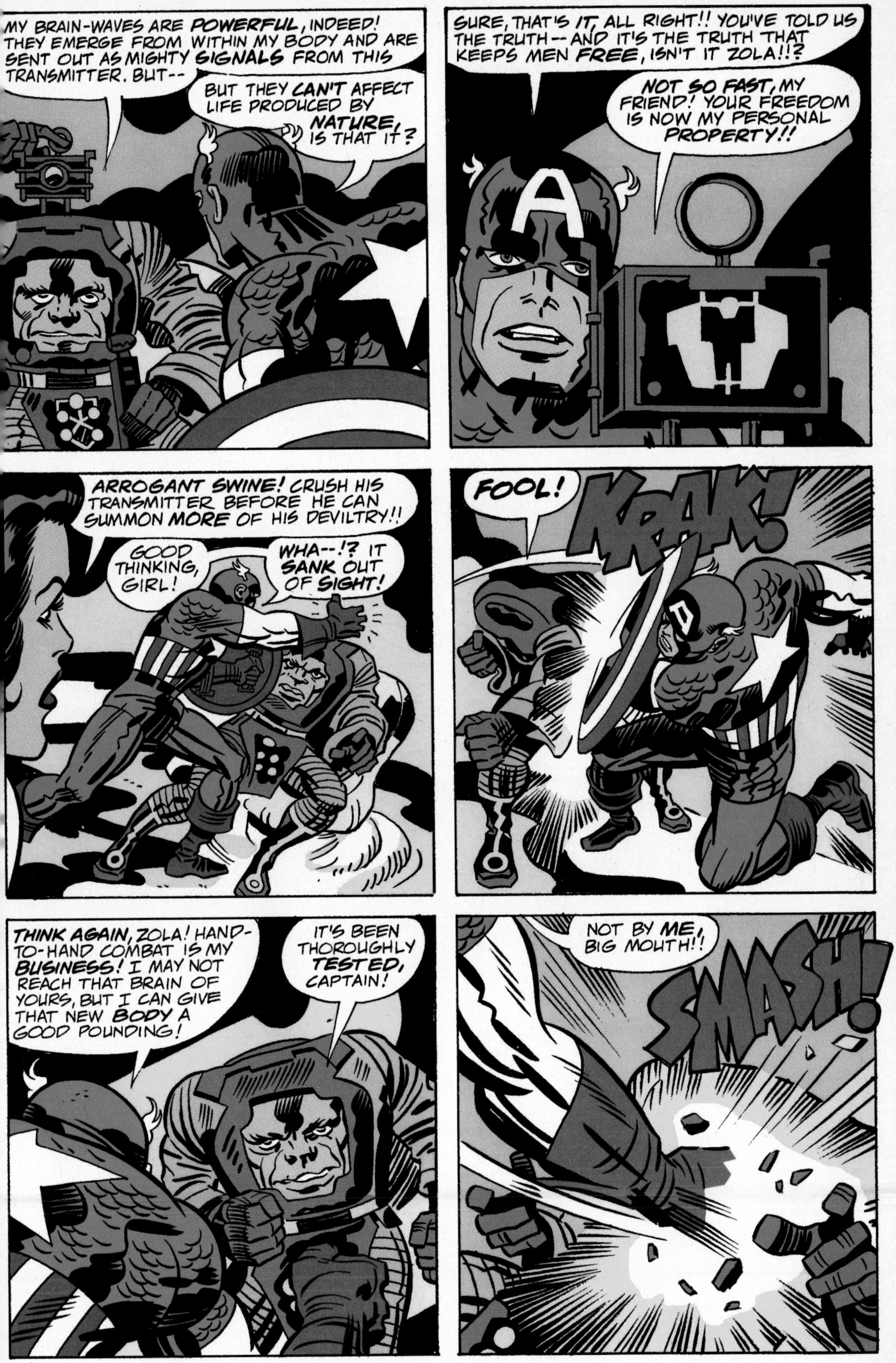
MY BRAIN-WAVES ARE POWERFUL, INDEED! THEY EMERGE FROM WITHIN MY BODY AND ARE SENT OUT AS MIGHTY SIGNALS FROM THIS TRANSMITTER. BUT--
BUT THEY CAN'T AFFECT LIFE PRODUCED BY NATURE, IS THAT IT?
SURE, THAT'S IT, ALL RIGHT!! YOU'VE TOLD US THE TRUTH -- AND IT'S THE TRUTH THAT KEEPS MEN FREE, ISN'T IT ZOLA!!?
NOT SO FAST, MY FRIEND! YOUR FREEDOM IS NOW MY PERSONAL PROPERTY!!
ARROGANT SWINE! CRUSH HIS TRANSMITTER BEFORE HE CAN SUMMON MORE OF HIS DEVILTRY!!
GOOD THINKING, GIRL!
WHA--!? IT SANK OUT OF SIGHT!
FOOL!
KRAK!
THINK AGAIN, ZOLA! HAND-TO-HAND COMBAT IS MY BUSINESS! I MAY NOT REACH THAT BRAIN OF YOURS, BUT I CAN GIVE THAT NEW BODY A GOOD POUNDING!
IT'S BEEN THOROUGHLY TESTED, CAPTAIN!
NOT BY ME, BIG MOUTH!!
SMASH!

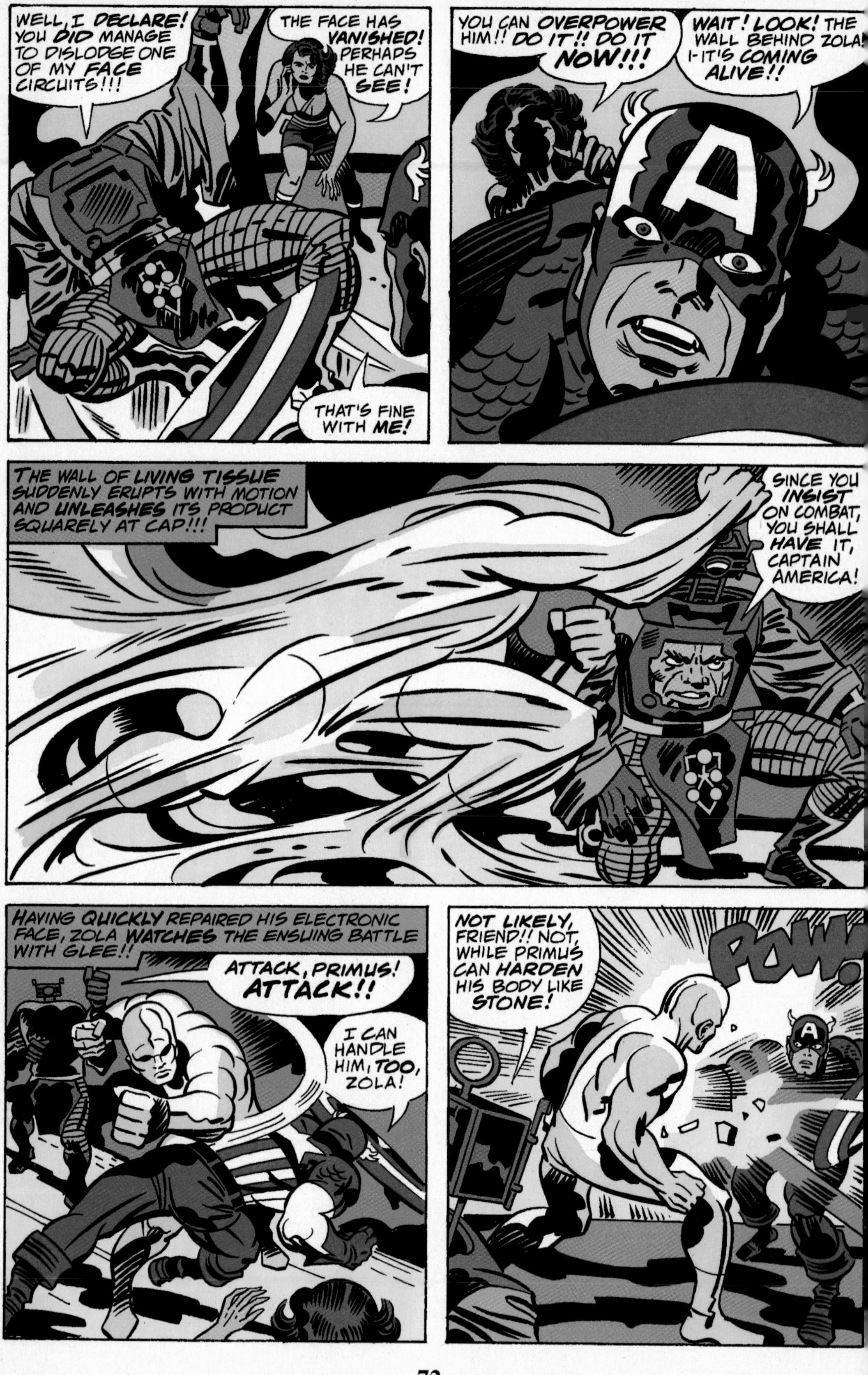
WELL, I DECLARE! YOU DID MANAGE TO DISLODGE ONE OF MY FACE CIRCUITS!!!
THE FACE HAS VANISHED! PERHAPS HE CAN'T SEE!
THAT'S FINE WITH ME!
YOU CAN OVERPOWER HIM!! DO IT!! DO IT NOW!!!
WAIT! LOOK! THE WALL BEHIND ZOLA I-IT'S COMING ALIVE!!
THE WALL OF LIVING TISSUE SUDDENLY ERUPTS WITH MOTION AND UNLEASHES ITS PRODUCT SQUARELY AT CAP!!!
SINCE YOU INSIST ON COMBAT, YOU SHALL HAVE IT, CAPTAIN AMERICA!
HAVING QUICKLY REPAIRED HIS ELECTRONIC FACE, ZOLA WATCHES THE ENSUING BATTLE WITH GLEE!!
ATTACK, PRIMUS! ATTACK!!
I CAN HANDLE HIM, TOO, ZOLA!
NOT LIKELY, FRIEND!! NOT, WHILE PRIMUS CAN HARDEN HIS BODY LIKE STONE!
POW

AT THAT VERY MOMENT, SOMEWHERE IN THE RUGGED **BADLANDS** OF SOUTH AMERICA, THE FALCON HAS MADE A **BIZARRE DISCOVERY** OF HIS OWN...

THOSE GREAT LOGS **COULDN'T** HAVE GOTTEN TO THESE BARREN HEIGHTS BY THEMSELVES!!

I-IT SEEMS TOO **FAR-OUT** TO CONSIDER-- YET, WHEN SEEN FROM THE **AIR**, ONE CAN ONLY CONCLUDE THAT THIS THING IS A **KING-SIZED**--

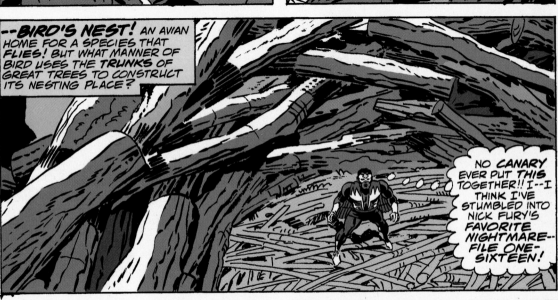

--**BIRD'S NEST!** AN AVIAN HOME FOR A SPECIES THAT **FLIES!** BUT WHAT MANNER OF BIRD USES THE **TRUNKS** OF GREAT TREES TO CONSTRUCT ITS NESTING PLACE?

NO **CANARY** EVER PUT **THIS** TOGETHER!! I--I THINK I'VE STUMBLED INTO NICK FURY'S FAVORITE **NIGHTMARE--** FILE ONE- SIXTEEN!

FALCON, YOU'VE BEEN HUNG ON THE HORNS OF A **DILEMMA!** IF YOU STAY TO SEE THIS THROUGH-- THEN YOU MUST **DELAY** YOUR SEARCH FOR **CAP!!**

THE CHOICE IS QUICKLY MADE **FOR** THE FALCON! A MAMMOTH SHADOW DARKENS THE SKY! THE BEAT OF GIANT WINGS CREATES A **STORM** IN THE STILL AIR...

UH-OH! THE **OWNER** OF THIS TRACT-HOME FOR TITANS HAS **RETURNED!**

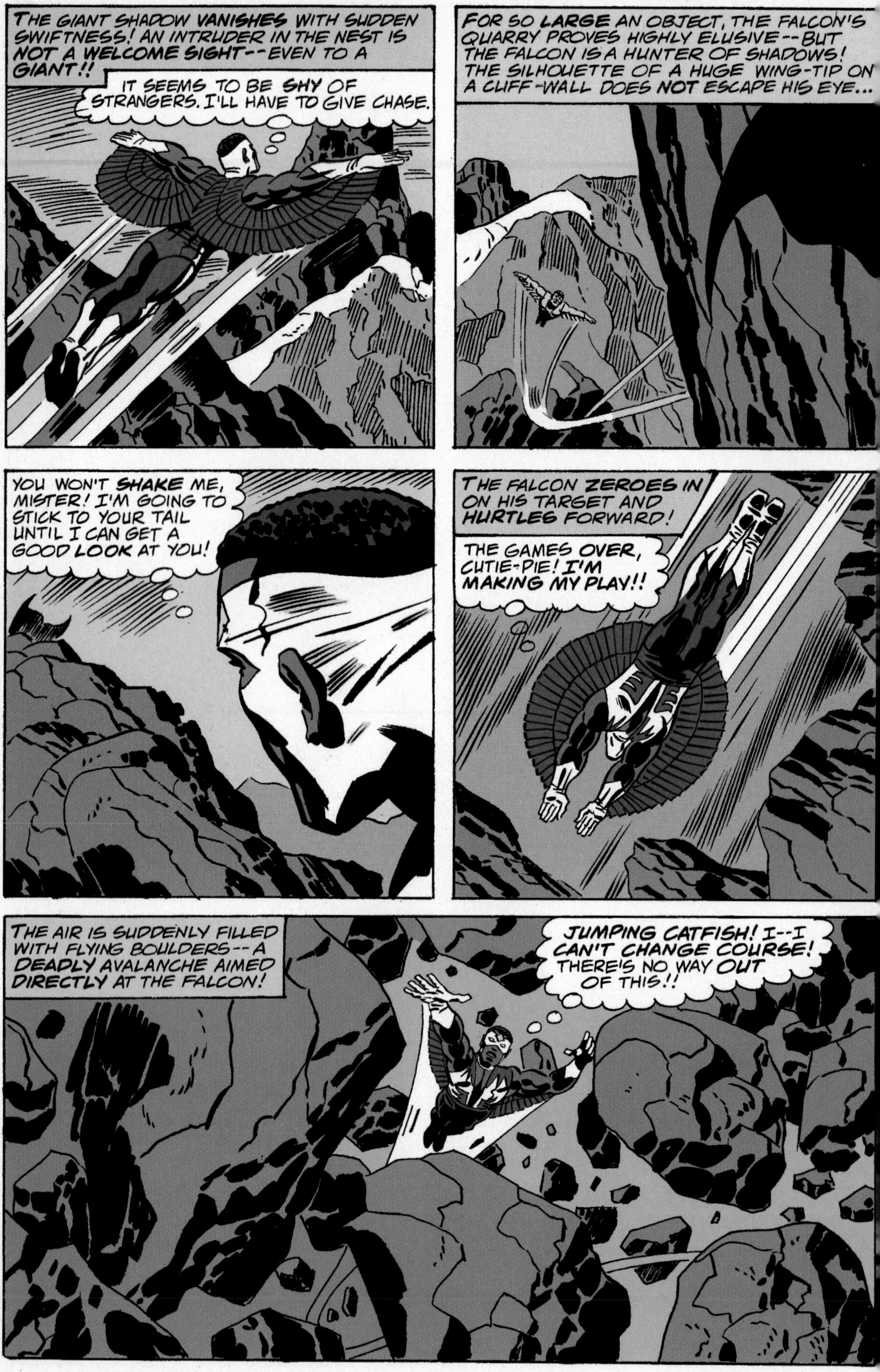

THE GIANT SHADOW VANISHES WITH SUDDEN SWIFTNESS! AN INTRUDER IN THE NEST IS NOT A WELCOME SIGHT--EVEN TO A GIANT!!
IT SEEMS TO BE SHY OF STRANGERS. I'LL HAVE TO GIVE CHASE.
FOR SO LARGE AN OBJECT, THE FALCON'S QUARRY PROVES HIGHLY ELUSIVE--BUT THE FALCON IS A HUNTER OF SHADOWS! THE SILHOUETTE OF A HUGE WING-TIP ON A CLIFF-WALL DOES NOT ESCAPE HIS EYE...
YOU WON'T SHAKE ME, MISTER! I'M GOING TO STICK TO YOUR TAIL UNTIL I CAN GET A GOOD LOOK AT YOU!
THE FALCON ZEROES IN ON HIS TARGET AND HURTLES FORWARD!
THE GAMES OVER, CUTIE-PIE! I'M MAKING MY PLAY!!
THE AIR IS SUDDENLY FILLED WITH FLYING BOULDERS--A DEADLY AVALANCHE AIMED DIRECTLY AT THE FALCON!
JUMPING CATFISH! I--I CAN'T CHANGE COURSE! THERE'S NO WAY OUT OF THIS!!

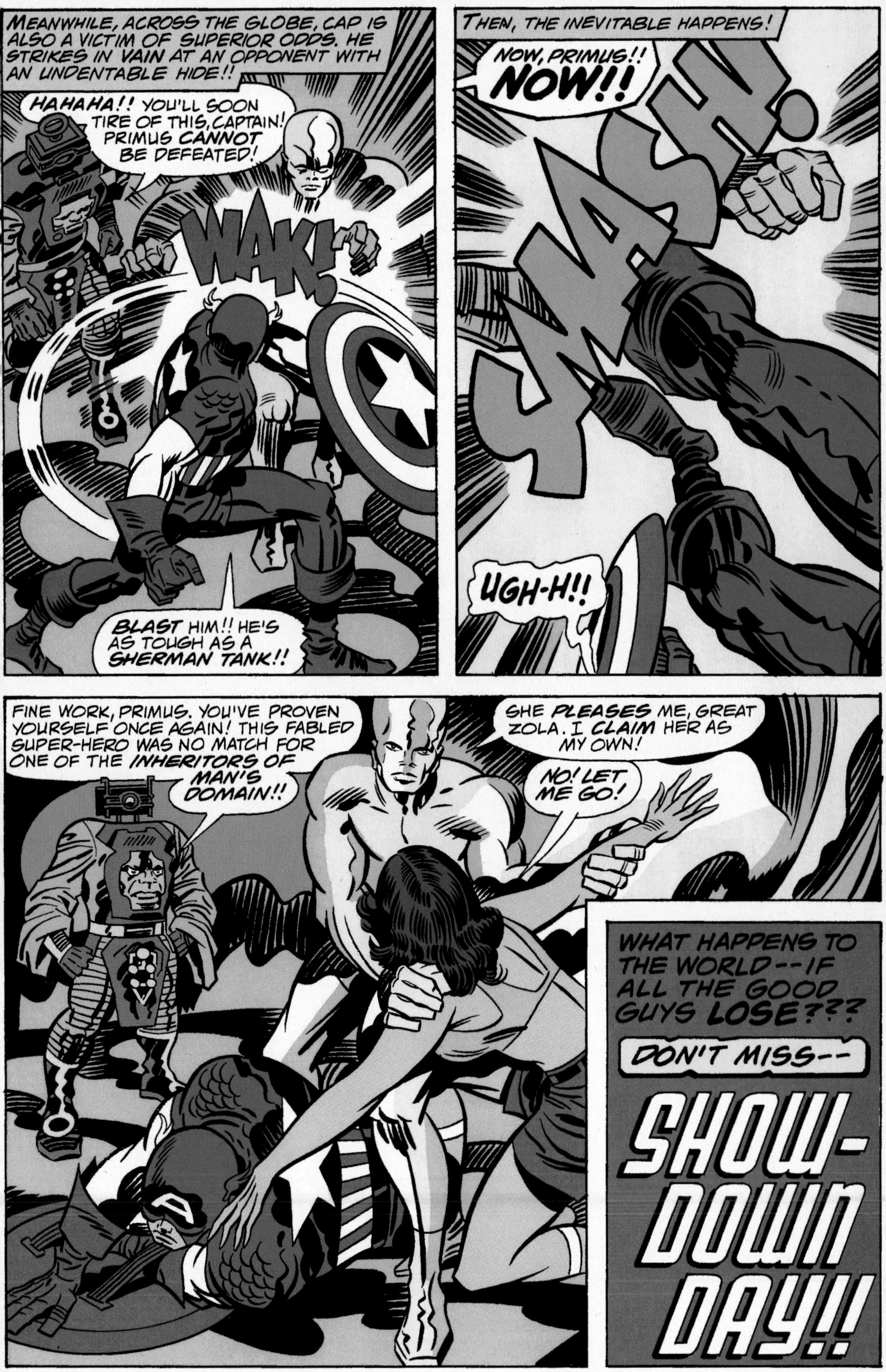
MEANWHILE, ACROSS THE GLOBE, CAP IS ALSO A VICTIM OF SUPERIOR ODDS. HE STRIKES IN VAIN AT AN OPPONENT WITH AN UNDENTABLE HIDE!!
HAHAHA!! YOU'LL SOON TIRE OF THIS, CAPTAIN! PRIMUS CANNOT BE DEFEATED!
WAK!
BLAST HIM!! HE'S AS TOUGH AS A SHERMAN TANK!!
THEN, THE INEVITABLE HAPPENS!
NOW, PRIMUS!! NOW!!
SMASH!
UGH-H!!
FINE WORK, PRIMUS. YOU'VE PROVEN YOURSELF ONCE AGAIN! THIS FABLED SUPER-HERO WAS NO MATCH FOR ONE OF THE INHERITORS OF MAN'S DOMAIN!!
SHE PLEASES ME, GREAT ZOLA. I CLAIM HER AS MY OWN!
NO! LET ME GO!
WHAT HAPPENS TO THE WORLD--IF ALL THE GOOD GUYS LOSE???
DON'T MISS--
SHOW-DOWN DAY!!

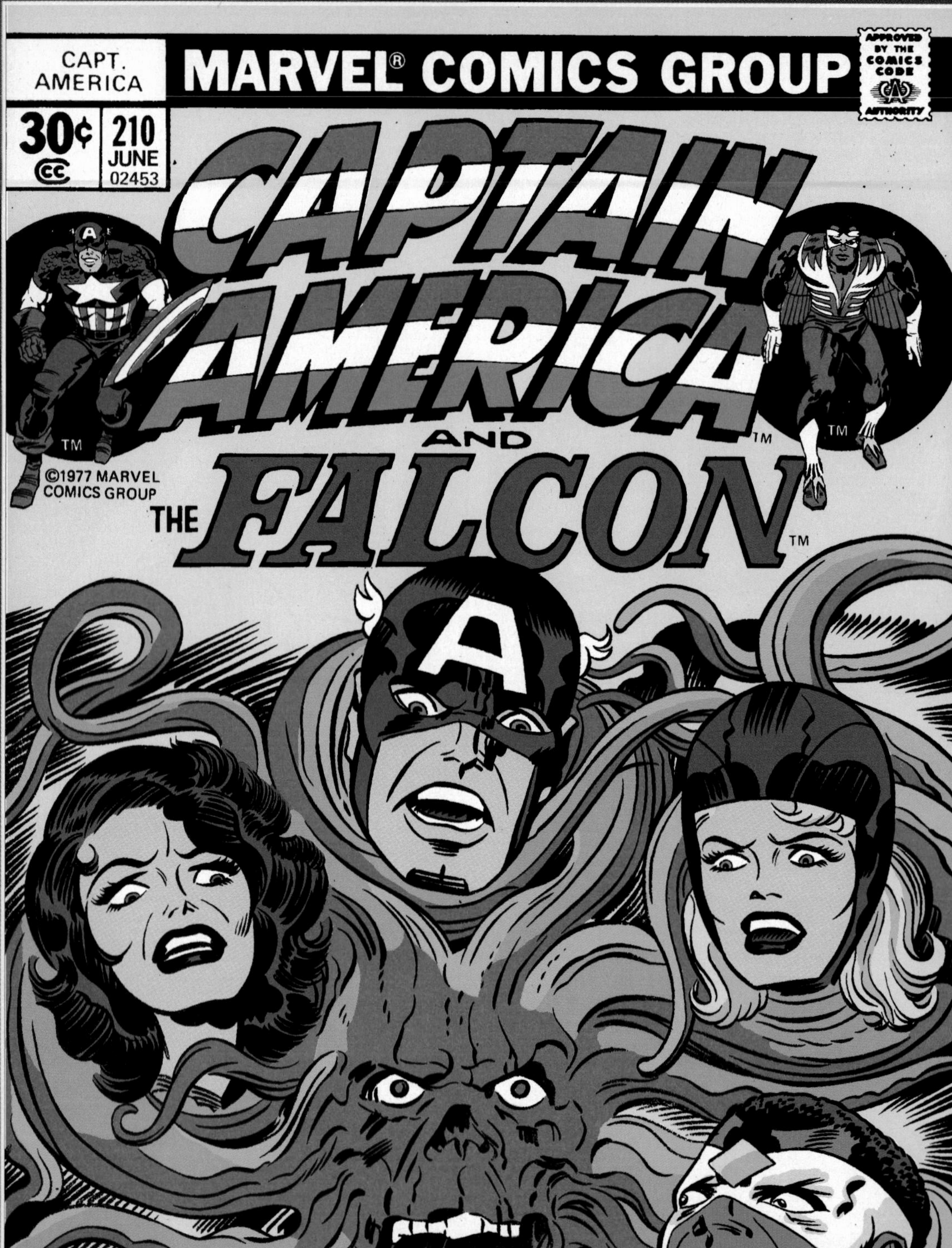
CAPT. AMERICA
MARVEL® COMICS GROUP
APPROVED BY THE COMICS CODE AUTHORITY
30¢
210
JUNE
02453
CAPTAIN AMERICA
AND
THE FALCON
©1977 MARVEL COMICS GROUP
CAP AND FALCON OPEN FILE 116 AND FIND THE MOST SINISTER SECRET OF ALL:
THE RED SKULL!

1941! The world at *war!* And in a secret laboratory, frail *Steve Rogers* became the American *super-soldier!* For four thrilling years, he fought the Axis powers—until a freak stroke of fate threw him into *suspended animation.* He woke in the mid-1960s, a man *twenty years out of his time.* Since that fateful day, Steve Rogers has sought his *destiny* in this brave new world.

STAN LEE PRESENTS: CAPTAIN AMERICA AND THE FALCON™

EDITED, WRITTEN AND DRAWN BY: **JACK KIRBY** / INKED AND LETTERED BY: MIKE ROYER / COLORED BY: G. ROUSSOS / UNFETTERED BY: ARCHIE GOODWIN

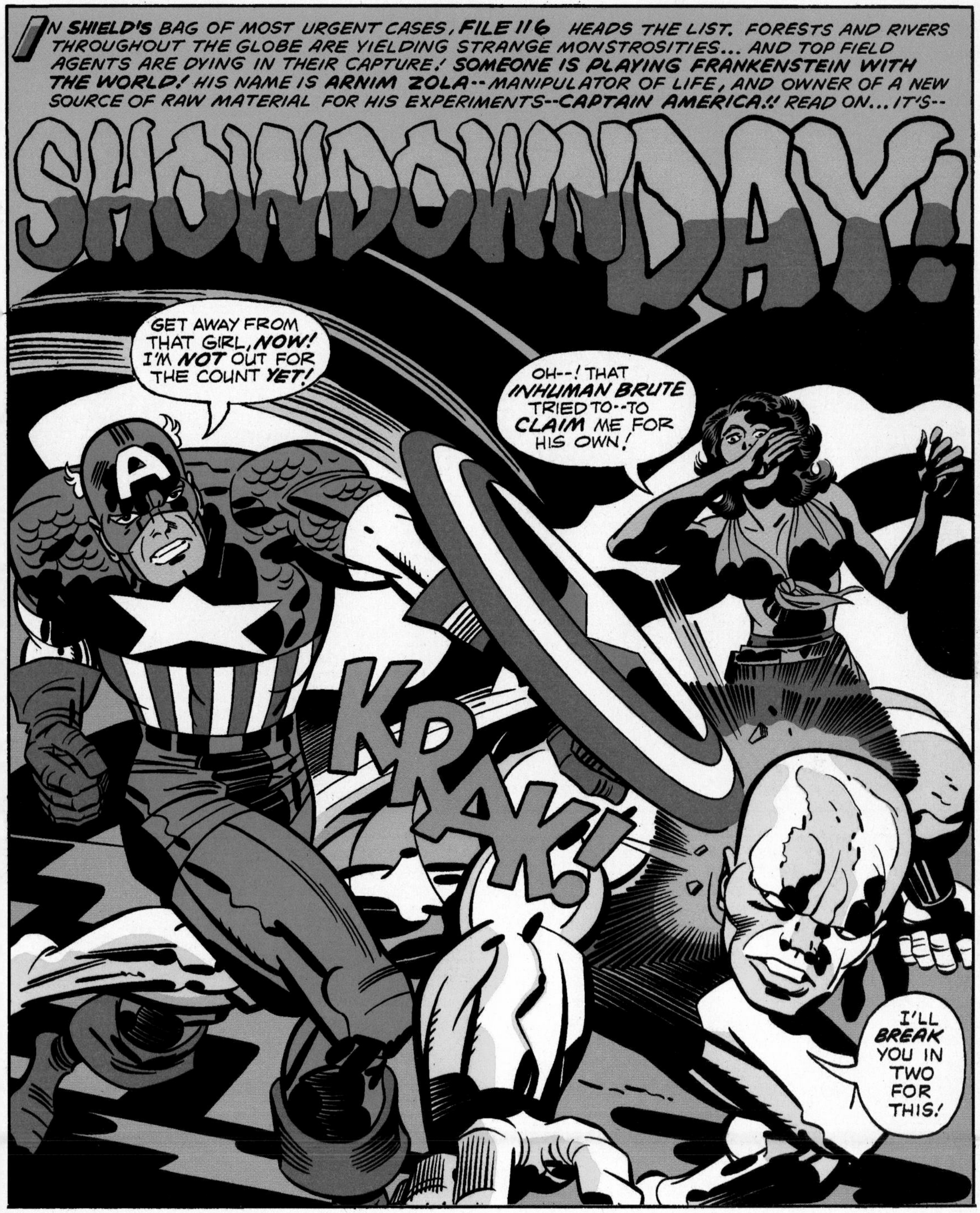
IN SHIELD'S BAG OF MOST URGENT CASES, FILE 116 HEADS THE LIST. FORESTS AND RIVERS THROUGHOUT THE GLOBE ARE YIELDING STRANGE MONSTROSITIES... AND TOP FIELD AGENTS ARE DYING IN THEIR CAPTURE! SOMEONE IS PLAYING FRANKENSTEIN WITH THE WORLD! HIS NAME IS ARNIM ZOLA--MANIPULATOR OF LIFE, AND OWNER OF A NEW SOURCE OF RAW MATERIAL FOR HIS EXPERIMENTS--CAPTAIN AMERICA!! READ ON... IT'S--
SHOWDOWN DAY!
GET AWAY FROM THAT GIRL, NOW! I'M NOT OUT FOR THE COUNT YET!
OH--! THAT INHUMAN BRUTE TRIED TO--TO CLAIM ME FOR HIS OWN!
KRAK!
I'LL BREAK YOU IN TWO FOR THIS!

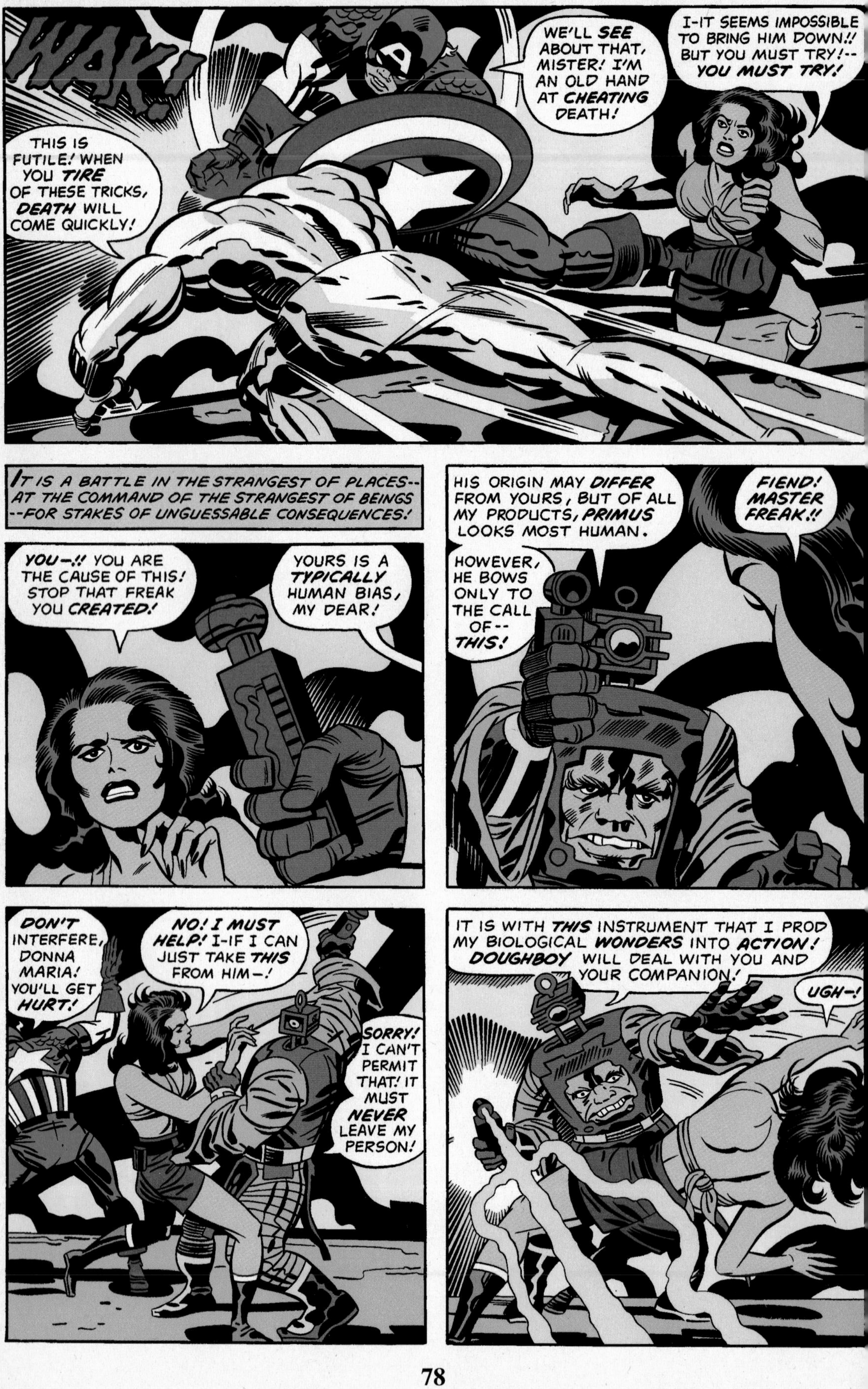
WAK!
THIS IS FUTILE! WHEN YOU TIRE OF THESE TRICKS, DEATH WILL COME QUICKLY!
WE'LL SEE ABOUT THAT, MISTER! I'M AN OLD HAND AT CHEATING DEATH!
I-IT SEEMS IMPOSSIBLE TO BRING HIM DOWN!! BUT YOU MUST TRY!-- YOU MUST TRY!
IT IS A BATTLE IN THE STRANGEST OF PLACES-- AT THE COMMAND OF THE STRANGEST OF BEINGS --FOR STAKES OF UNGUESSABLE CONSEQUENCES!
YOU-!! YOU ARE THE CAUSE OF THIS! STOP THAT FREAK YOU CREATED!
YOURS IS A TYPICALLY HUMAN BIAS, MY DEAR!
HIS ORIGIN MAY DIFFER FROM YOURS, BUT OF ALL MY PRODUCTS, PRIMUS LOOKS MOST HUMAN.
FIEND! MASTER FREAK!!
HOWEVER, HE BOWS ONLY TO THE CALL OF-- THIS!
DON'T INTERFERE, DONNA MARIA! YOU'LL GET HURT!
NO! I MUST HELP! I-IF I CAN JUST TAKE THIS FROM HIM-!
SORRY! I CAN'T PERMIT THAT! IT MUST NEVER LEAVE MY PERSON!
IT IS WITH THIS INSTRUMENT THAT I PROD MY BIOLOGICAL WONDERS INTO ACTION! DOUGHBOY WILL DEAL WITH YOU AND YOUR COMPANION!
UGH-!

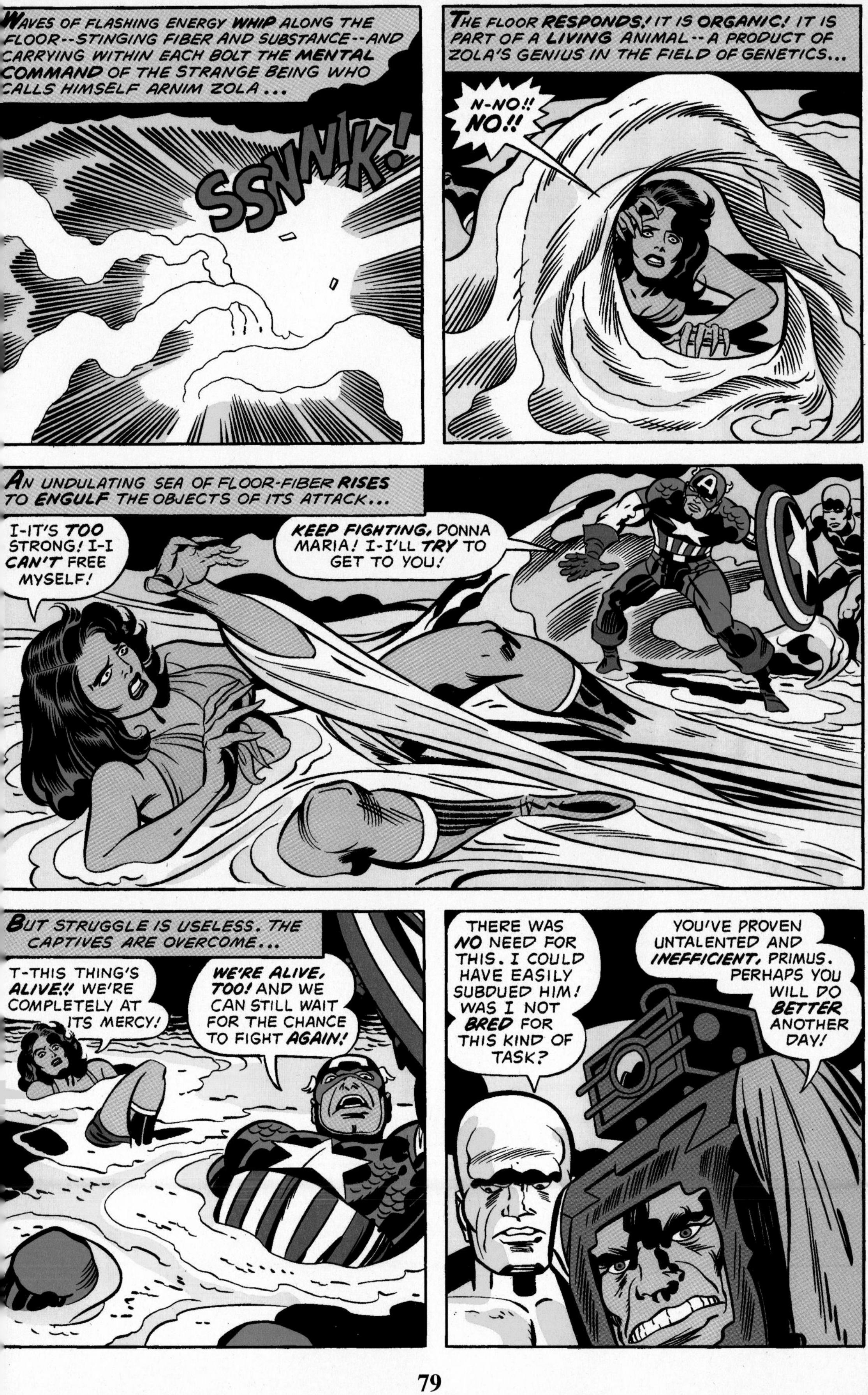
WAVES OF FLASHING ENERGY WHIP ALONG THE FLOOR--STINGING FIBER AND SUBSTANCE--AND CARRYING WITHIN EACH BOLT THE MENTAL COMMAND OF THE STRANGE BEING WHO CALLS HIMSELF ARNIM ZOLA...
SSNNIK!
THE FLOOR RESPONDS! IT IS ORGANIC! IT IS PART OF A LIVING ANIMAL--A PRODUCT OF ZOLA'S GENIUS IN THE FIELD OF GENETICS...
N-NO!! NO!!
AN UNDULATING SEA OF FLOOR-FIBER RISES TO ENGULF THE OBJECTS OF ITS ATTACK...
I-IT'S TOO STRONG! I-I CAN'T FREE MYSELF!
KEEP FIGHTING, DONNA MARIA! I-I'LL TRY TO GET TO YOU!
BUT STRUGGLE IS USELESS. THE CAPTIVES ARE OVERCOME...
T-THIS THING'S ALIVE!! WE'RE COMPLETELY AT ITS MERCY!
WE'RE ALIVE, TOO! AND WE CAN STILL WAIT FOR THE CHANCE TO FIGHT AGAIN!
THERE WAS NO NEED FOR THIS. I COULD HAVE EASILY SUBDUED HIM! WAS I NOT BRED FOR THIS KIND OF TASK?
YOU'VE PROVEN UNTALENTED AND INEFFICIENT, PRIMUS. PERHAPS YOU WILL DO BETTER ANOTHER DAY!

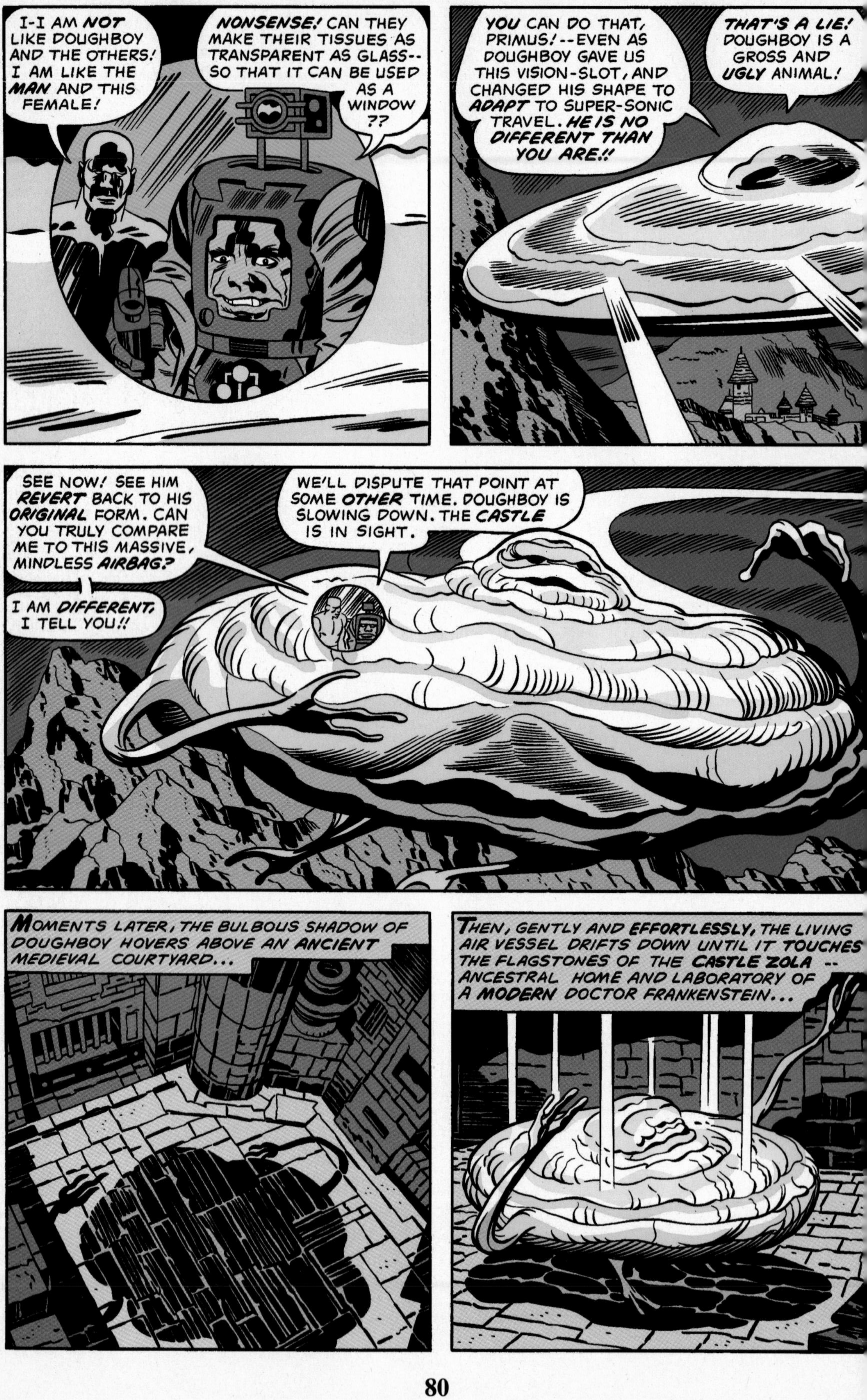
I-I AM NOT LIKE DOUGHBOY AND THE OTHERS! I AM LIKE THE MAN AND THIS FEMALE!
NONSENSE! CAN THEY MAKE THEIR TISSUES AS TRANSPARENT AS GLASS-- SO THAT IT CAN BE USED AS A WINDOW ??
YOU CAN DO THAT, PRIMUS! --EVEN AS DOUGHBOY GAVE US THIS VISION-SLOT, AND CHANGED HIS SHAPE TO ADAPT TO SUPER-SONIC TRAVEL. HE IS NO DIFFERENT THAN YOU ARE!!
THAT'S A LIE! DOUGHBOY IS A GROSS AND UGLY ANIMAL!
SEE NOW! SEE HIM REVERT BACK TO HIS ORIGINAL FORM. CAN YOU TRULY COMPARE ME TO THIS MASSIVE, MINDLESS AIRBAG?
I AM DIFFERENT. I TELL YOU!!
WE'LL DISPUTE THAT POINT AT SOME OTHER TIME. DOUGHBOY IS SLOWING DOWN. THE CASTLE IS IN SIGHT.
MOMENTS LATER, THE BULBOUS SHADOW OF DOUGHBOY HOVERS ABOVE AN ANCIENT MEDIEVAL COURTYARD...
THEN, GENTLY AND EFFORTLESSLY, THE LIVING AIR VESSEL DRIFTS DOWN UNTIL IT TOUCHES THE FLAGSTONES OF THE CASTLE ZOLA -- ANCESTRAL HOME AND LABORATORY OF A MODERN DOCTOR FRANKENSTEIN...

ARNIM ZOLA ISSUES A *TELEPATHIC* COMMAND THROUGH THE TRANSMITTER PERCHED UPON HIS SHOULDERS. THE ORGANIC WALLS OF DOUGHBOY PART... AN *OPENING* IS CREATED...

THANK YOU, DOUGHBOY. IT'S *GOOD* TO BE HOME!

A LIVING RAMP UNCOILS FROM THE WONDROUS ORGANISM. ITS MASTER DESCENDS TO THE COURTYARD IN *TRIUMPHANT* RETURN...

WAS THERE EVER SUCH A *GRATIFYING* CREATURE, EH, PRIMUS? IS THERE NOTHING HE CANNOT DO TO FACILITATE THE *COMFORT* OF THOSE WHO COMMAND HIM!?

HE *CANNOT* GRANT ME THE FEMALE. ONLY *YOU* CAN DO THAT!

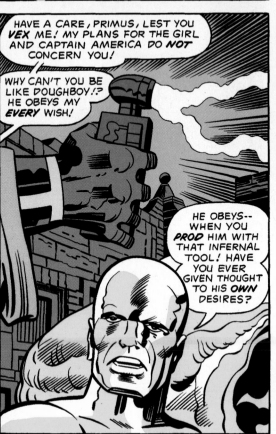

HAVE A CARE, PRIMUS, LEST YOU *VEX* ME! MY PLANS FOR THE GIRL AND CAPTAIN AMERICA DO *NOT* CONCERN YOU!

WHY CAN'T YOU BE LIKE DOUGHBOY!? HE OBEYS MY *EVERY* WISH!

HE OBEYS-- WHEN YOU *PROD* HIM WITH THAT INFERNAL TOOL! HAVE YOU EVER GIVEN THOUGHT TO HIS *OWN* DESIRES?

ZOLA TREATS THE QUESTION WITH SILENCE. HIS EYES ARE ON HIS *PRISONERS* AS THEY ARE THRUST INTO THE OPEN IN DOUGHBOY'S GRIP...

DON'T PANIC, DONNA MARIA. WE'LL GET OUT OF THIS, YET!

BUT HOW CAN WE *COPE* WITH SUCH CREATURES? T-THEY *AREN'T* HUMAN!!

PUT THEM IN CHAMBER *FOUR!*

HIGH ON A CASTLE WALL, A METAL **SHUTTER** SWINGS INWARD TO RECEIVE THE **NEW** OCCUPANTS...

ONCE INSIDE THE CHAMBER, THE CAPTIVES ARE QUICKLY RELEASED AND HURLED TO THE FLOOR.

THEN--!

CLANK!

BLAST! THE SHUTTER CLOSED BEFORE I COULD GET TO IT!

W-WE'RE **TRAPPED!**

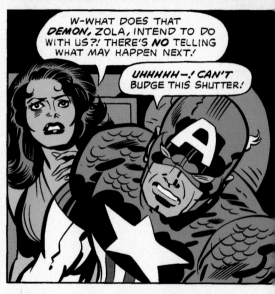

W-WHAT DOES THAT **DEMON**, ZOLA, INTEND TO DO WITH US?! THERE'S **NO** TELLING WHAT MAY HAPPEN NEXT!

UHHHHH--! CAN'T BUDGE THIS SHUTTER!

IT **RESISTS** MY EVERY EFFORT! THIS IS **NOT** ORDINARY METAL! I-IT FEELS --ALMOST WARM-- PLIANT-- **ALIVE**--!!

DONNA MARIA--! THIS SHUTTER IS-- **ORGANIC** !!

T-THAT'S **HORRIBLE!** --HORRIBLE! HOW **FAR** HAS THAT MONSTER GONE WITH HIS EXPERIMENTS !!?

HOLD ME -- HOLD ME **CLOSE!** THIS MADNESS **LOSES** ITS TERROR -- WHEN YOU'RE **NEAR** ME...

YEAH--WELL--I-I **UNDERSTAND**, DONNA MARIA.--B-BUT WE'D DO WELL TO JUST-- CONCENTRATE ON-- **ESCAPE!**

82

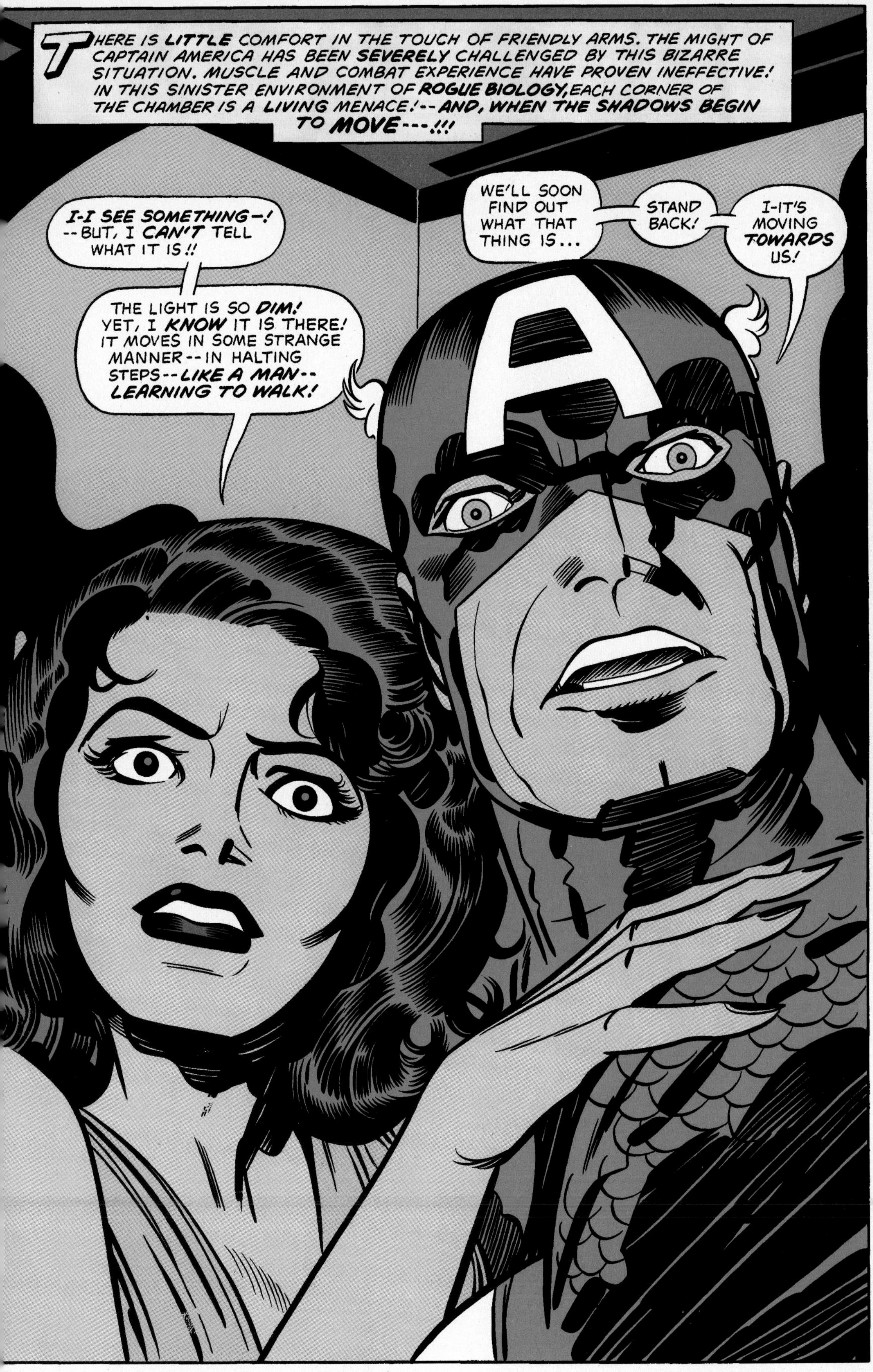
THERE IS LITTLE COMFORT IN THE TOUCH OF FRIENDLY ARMS. THE MIGHT OF CAPTAIN AMERICA HAS BEEN SEVERELY CHALLENGED BY THIS BIZARRE SITUATION. MUSCLE AND COMBAT EXPERIENCE HAVE PROVEN INEFFECTIVE! IN THIS SINISTER ENVIRONMENT OF ROGUE BIOLOGY, EACH CORNER OF THE CHAMBER IS A LIVING MENACE!--AND, WHEN THE SHADOWS BEGIN TO MOVE---!!!
I-I SEE SOMETHING-! --BUT, I CAN'T TELL WHAT IT IS!!
THE LIGHT IS SO DIM! YET, I KNOW IT IS THERE! IT MOVES IN SOME STRANGE MANNER--IN HALTING STEPS--LIKE A MAN--LEARNING TO WALK!
WE'LL SOON FIND OUT WHAT THAT THING IS...
STAND BACK!
I-IT'S MOVING TOWARDS US!

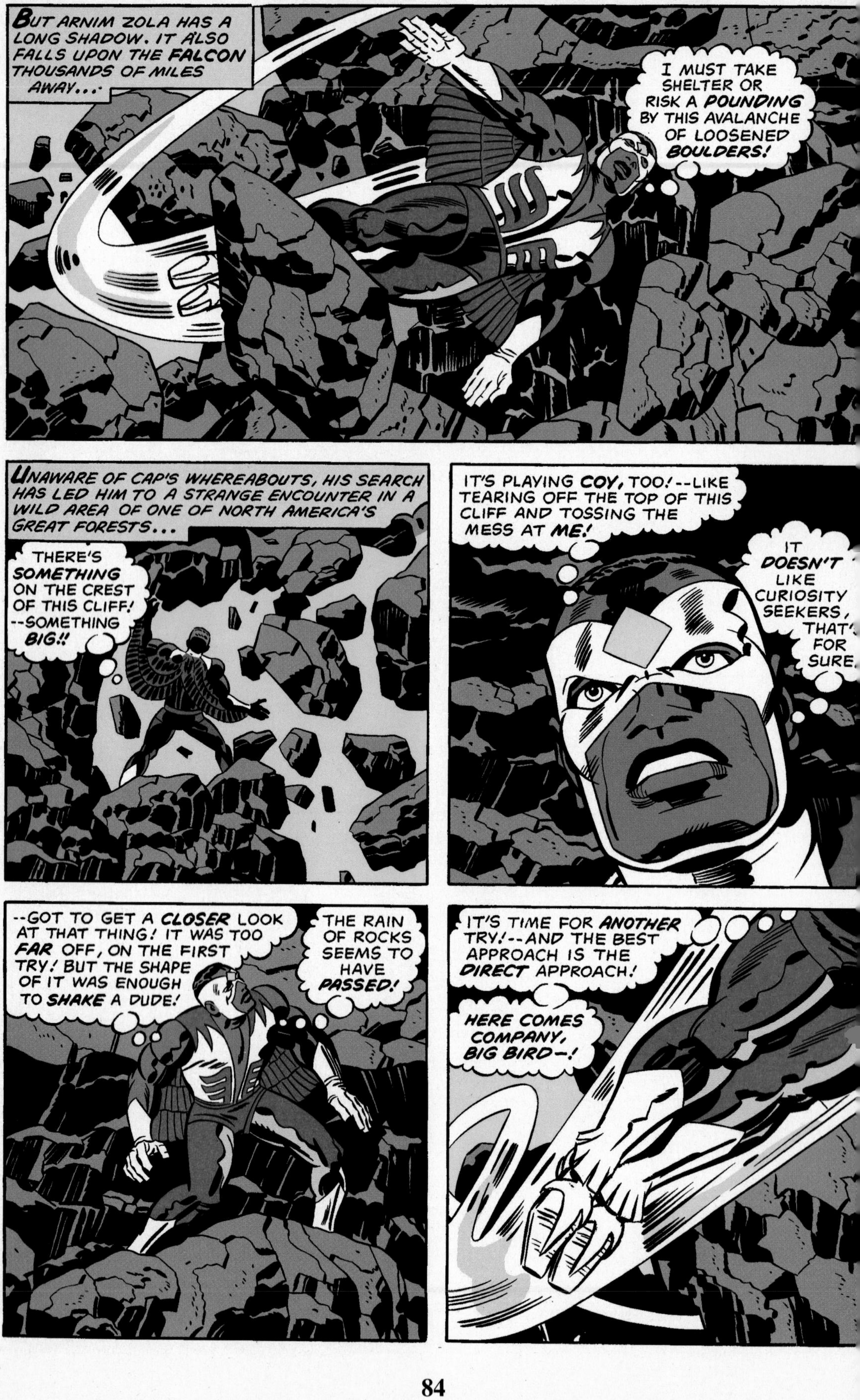
BUT ARNIM ZOLA HAS A LONG SHADOW. IT ALSO FALLS UPON THE FALCON THOUSANDS OF MILES AWAY...
I MUST TAKE SHELTER OR RISK A POUNDING BY THIS AVALANCHE OF LOOSENED BOULDERS!
UNAWARE OF CAP'S WHEREABOUTS, HIS SEARCH HAS LED HIM TO A STRANGE ENCOUNTER IN A WILD AREA OF ONE OF NORTH AMERICA'S GREAT FORESTS...
THERE'S SOMETHING ON THE CREST OF THIS CLIFF! --SOMETHING BIG!!
IT'S PLAYING COY, TOO! --LIKE TEARING OFF THE TOP OF THIS CLIFF AND TOSSING THE MESS AT ME!
IT DOESN'T LIKE CURIOSITY SEEKERS, THAT'S FOR SURE.
--GOT TO GET A CLOSER LOOK AT THAT THING! IT WAS TOO FAR OFF, ON THE FIRST TRY! BUT THE SHAPE OF IT WAS ENOUGH TO SHAKE A DUDE!
THE RAIN OF ROCKS SEEMS TO HAVE PASSED!
IT'S TIME FOR ANOTHER TRY! --AND THE BEST APPROACH IS THE DIRECT APPROACH!
HERE COMES COMPANY, BIG BIRD--!

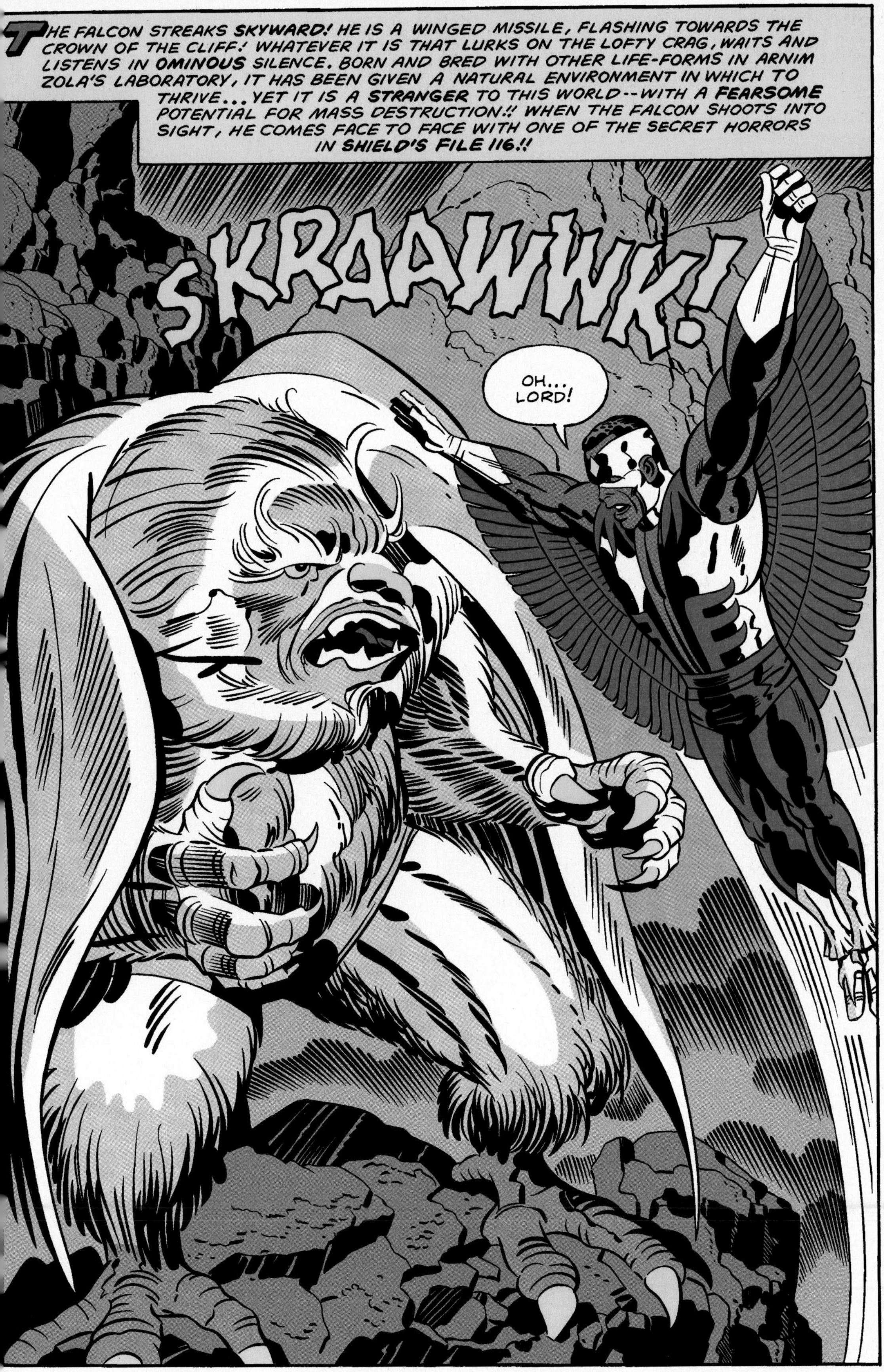
THE FALCON STREAKS SKYWARD! HE IS A WINGED MISSILE, FLASHING TOWARDS THE CROWN OF THE CLIFF! WHATEVER IT IS THAT LURKS ON THE LOFTY CRAG, WAITS AND LISTENS IN OMINOUS SILENCE. BORN AND BRED WITH OTHER LIFE-FORMS IN ARNIM ZOLA'S LABORATORY, IT HAS BEEN GIVEN A NATURAL ENVIRONMENT IN WHICH TO THRIVE... YET IT IS A STRANGER TO THIS WORLD--WITH A FEARSOME POTENTIAL FOR MASS DESTRUCTION!! WHEN THE FALCON SHOOTS INTO SIGHT, HE COMES FACE TO FACE WITH ONE OF THE SECRET HORRORS IN SHIELD'S FILE 116!!
SKRAAWWK!
OH... LORD!

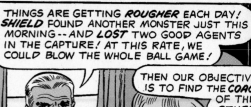

MEANWHILE, IN A REGIONAL OFFICE OF SHIELD, THE WEB OF FILE 116 HAS ALSO INVADED A MORE *INTIMATE* SECTOR OF CAPTAIN AMERICA'S LIFE...

READY FOR *WORK*, SHARON? I LIKE YOUR *NEW* HAIR-DO.

THAT TAKES CARE OF THE SWEET TALK. NOW-- GIVE ME THE *HARD* FACTS!

THINGS ARE GETTING *ROUGHER* EACH DAY! *SHIELD* FOUND ANOTHER MONSTER JUST THIS MORNING -- AND *LOST* TWO GOOD AGENTS IN THE CAPTURE! AT THIS RATE, WE COULD BLOW THE WHOLE BALL GAME!

THEN OUR OBJECTIVE IS TO FIND THE *COACH* OF THE *OTHER* TEAM!

NOT EASY. OUR COMPUTERS SAY HE'S A *LONER*, A BIO-CHEMIST AND PROBABLY A *PIONEER* OF THE NEW SCIENCE OF *GENETIC ENGINEERING!*

BUT, SURELY, SOMEONE MUST KNOW HIM... MEN IN THE SAME FIELD!

WE'VE RUN THROUGH THE LIST OF "BIGS" AND "LITTLES" WITHOUT SUCCESS. THEY'VE GIVEN US DRY LEADS...

YOU MAY BE OUR LAST CHANCE TO RUN THIS MAD GENIUS DOWN.

THEN, I TAKE IT YOU HAVE A *FINAL* LEAD FOR *ME* TO WORK ON?

YES... WE FEEL THAT OUR PIGEON MAY NEED *OUTSIDE* FINANCING FOR HIS *FRANKENSTEIN FACTORY!* IT'S OUR ONE HOPE -- AND IT MAY REST ON *ONE* MAN!

YOU'LL FIND OUR NOTES IN *THIS*.

DOES THIS INCLUDE HIS *IDENTITY*?

FILE 116

NO. YOU'LL BE GIVEN HIS NAME AND SHOWN HIS PHOTO WHEN YOU'RE *AIRBORNE!*

I MUST *FLY* THEN -- MUSTN'T I?

SOON AFTER, SHARON'S JET-COPTER LEAVES ITS SKYSCRAPER PAD AND TAKES TO THE AIR...

THIS IS "SCRAMBLE ONE"...I'M *READY* FOR MY BRIEFING!

VERY WELL, "SCRAMBLE ONE." SET YOUR CRAFT ON COURSE, AS LISTED, AND PUT IT ON REMOTE CONTROL!

DONE, CHIEF. NOW... *WHO'S THE MAN? WHERE'S THE MAN?* AND *WHY* DO *I* TALK TO THIS MAN?

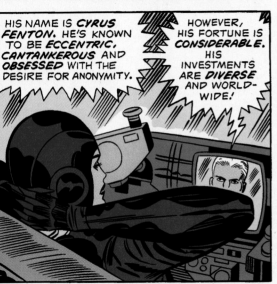

HIS NAME IS *CYRUS FENTON*. HE'S KNOWN TO BE *ECCENTRIC, CANTANKEROUS* AND *OBSESSED* WITH THE DESIRE FOR ANONYMITY.

HOWEVER, HIS FORTUNE IS *CONSIDERABLE*. HIS INVESTMENTS ARE *DIVERSE* AND WORLD-WIDE!

HE SOUNDS LIKE THE *MOVIE* VERSION OF THE "RICH RECLUSE," CHIEF... BUT THAT *DOESN'T* MAKE HIM SPECIAL!

TRUE... BUT THIS BIRD IS ATTRACTED BY GIMMICKY VENTURES-- *FAR OUT* NOTIONS IN SCIENTIFIC FIELDS--!

THIS IS A PHOTO OF YOUR MAN. STUDY IT *CAREFULLY*, AND REMEMBER--TREAT HIM WITH *CAUTION* AND RESPECT!

HE LOOKS LIKE A *PERFECT* DEAR!

HE *ISN'T!* TREAT HIM WITH THE RESPECT AND CAUTION GIVEN TO A *LOADED PISTOL!*

THIS MAY BE A *LONG-SHOT!* BUT, CYRUS FENTON COULD BE THE *MONEY-TREE* FROM WHICH THE MONSTERS GROW--!!

87

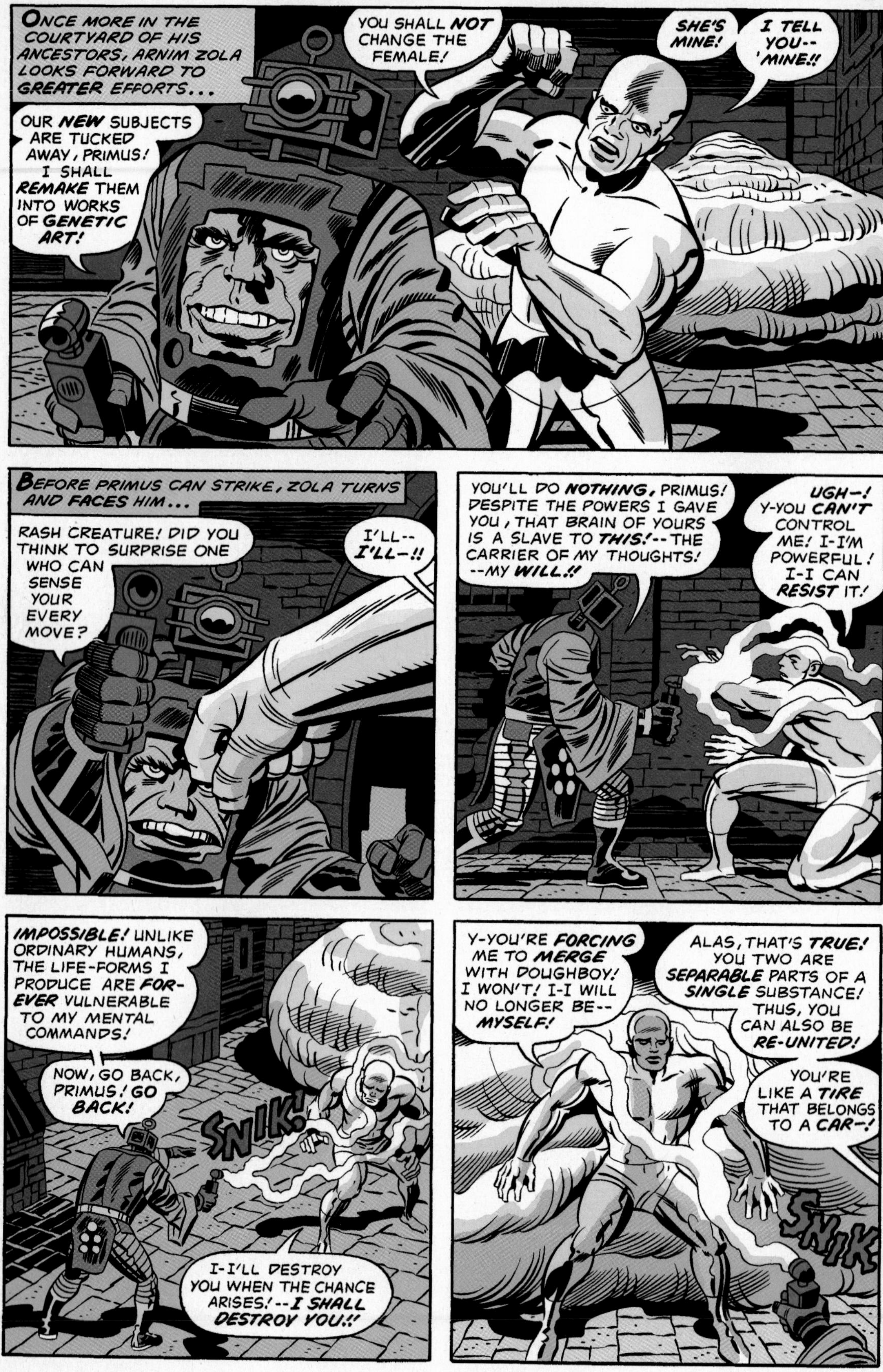

ONCE MORE IN THE COURTYARD OF HIS ANCESTORS, ARNIM ZOLA LOOKS FORWARD TO GREATER EFFORTS...
OUR NEW SUBJECTS ARE TUCKED AWAY, PRIMUS! I SHALL REMAKE THEM INTO WORKS OF GENETIC ART!
YOU SHALL NOT CHANGE THE FEMALE!
SHE'S MINE!
I TELL YOU-- 'MINE!!
BEFORE PRIMUS CAN STRIKE, ZOLA TURNS AND FACES HIM...
RASH CREATURE! DID YOU THINK TO SURPRISE ONE WHO CAN SENSE YOUR EVERY MOVE?
I'LL-- I'LL-!!
YOU'LL DO NOTHING, PRIMUS! DESPITE THE POWERS I GAVE YOU, THAT BRAIN OF YOURS IS A SLAVE TO THIS!--THE CARRIER OF MY THOUGHTS! --MY WILL!!
UGH-! Y-YOU CAN'T CONTROL ME! I-I'M POWERFUL! I-I CAN RESIST IT!
IMPOSSIBLE! UNLIKE ORDINARY HUMANS, THE LIFE-FORMS I PRODUCE ARE FOREVER VULNERABLE TO MY MENTAL COMMANDS!
NOW, GO BACK, PRIMUS! GO BACK!
SNIK!
I-I'LL DESTROY YOU WHEN THE CHANCE ARISES!--I SHALL DESTROY YOU!!
Y-YOU'RE FORCING ME TO MERGE WITH DOUGHBOY! I WON'T! I-I WILL NO LONGER BE-- MYSELF!
ALAS, THAT'S TRUE! YOU TWO ARE SEPARABLE PARTS OF A SINGLE SUBSTANCE! THUS, YOU CAN ALSO BE RE-UNITED!
YOU'RE LIKE A TIRE THAT BELONGS TO A CAR-!
SNIK

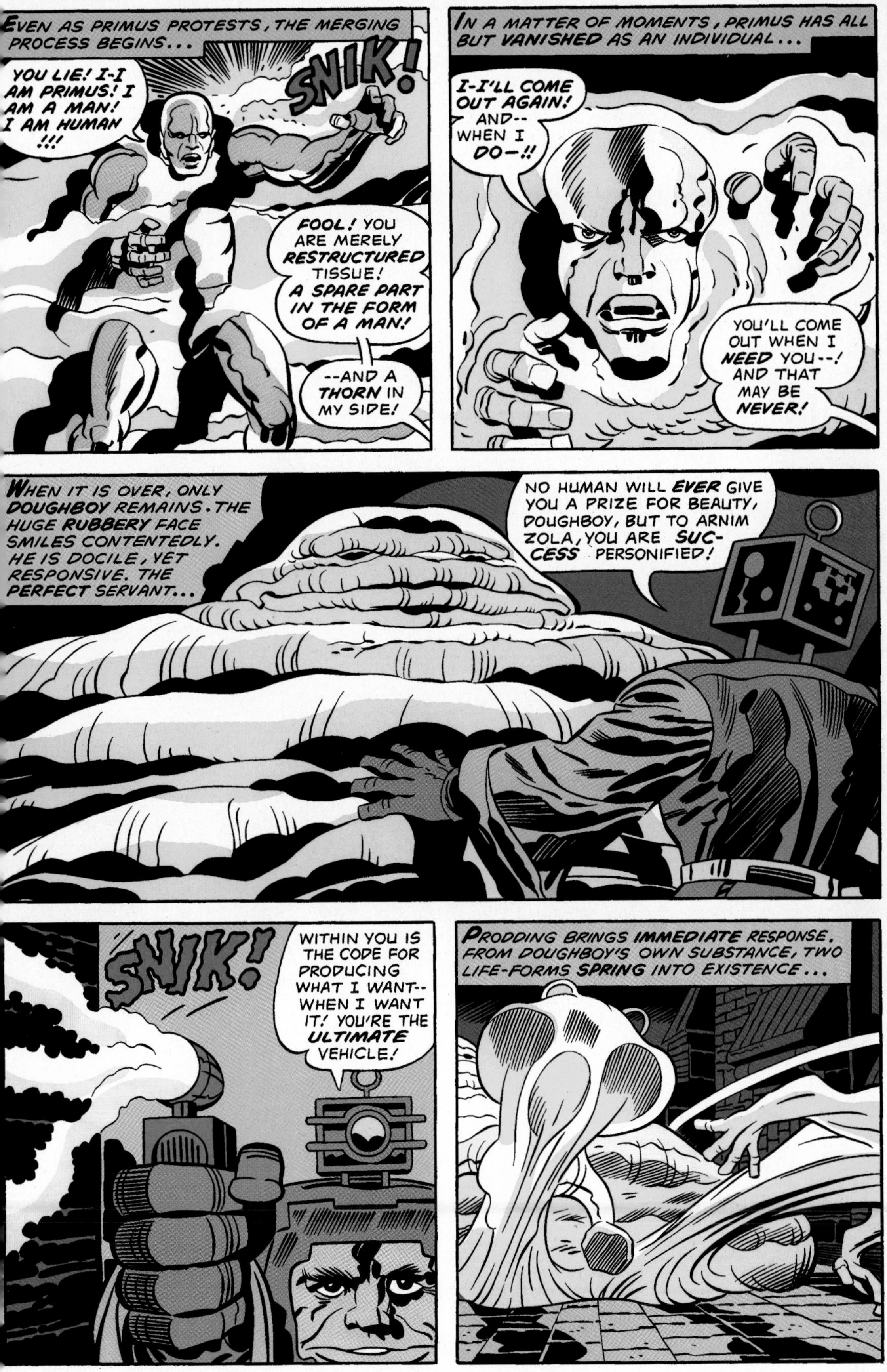
EVEN AS PRIMUS PROTESTS, THE MERGING PROCESS BEGINS...
SNIK!
YOU LIE! I-I AM PRIMUS! I AM A MAN! I AM HUMAN !!!
FOOL! YOU ARE MERELY RESTRUCTURED TISSUE! A SPARE PART IN THE FORM OF A MAN!
--AND A THORN IN MY SIDE!
IN A MATTER OF MOMENTS, PRIMUS HAS ALL BUT VANISHED AS AN INDIVIDUAL...
I-I'LL COME OUT AGAIN! AND-- WHEN I DO--!!
YOU'LL COME OUT WHEN I NEED YOU--! AND THAT MAY BE NEVER!
WHEN IT IS OVER, ONLY DOUGHBOY REMAINS. THE HUGE RUBBERY FACE SMILES CONTENTEDLY. HE IS DOCILE, YET RESPONSIVE. THE PERFECT SERVANT...
NO HUMAN WILL EVER GIVE YOU A PRIZE FOR BEAUTY, DOUGHBOY, BUT TO ARNIM ZOLA, YOU ARE SUCCESS PERSONIFIED!
SNIK!
WITHIN YOU IS THE CODE FOR PRODUCING WHAT I WANT-- WHEN I WANT IT! YOU'RE THE ULTIMATE VEHICLE!
PRODDING BRINGS IMMEDIATE RESPONSE. FROM DOUGHBOY'S OWN SUBSTANCE, TWO LIFE-FORMS SPRING INTO EXISTENCE...

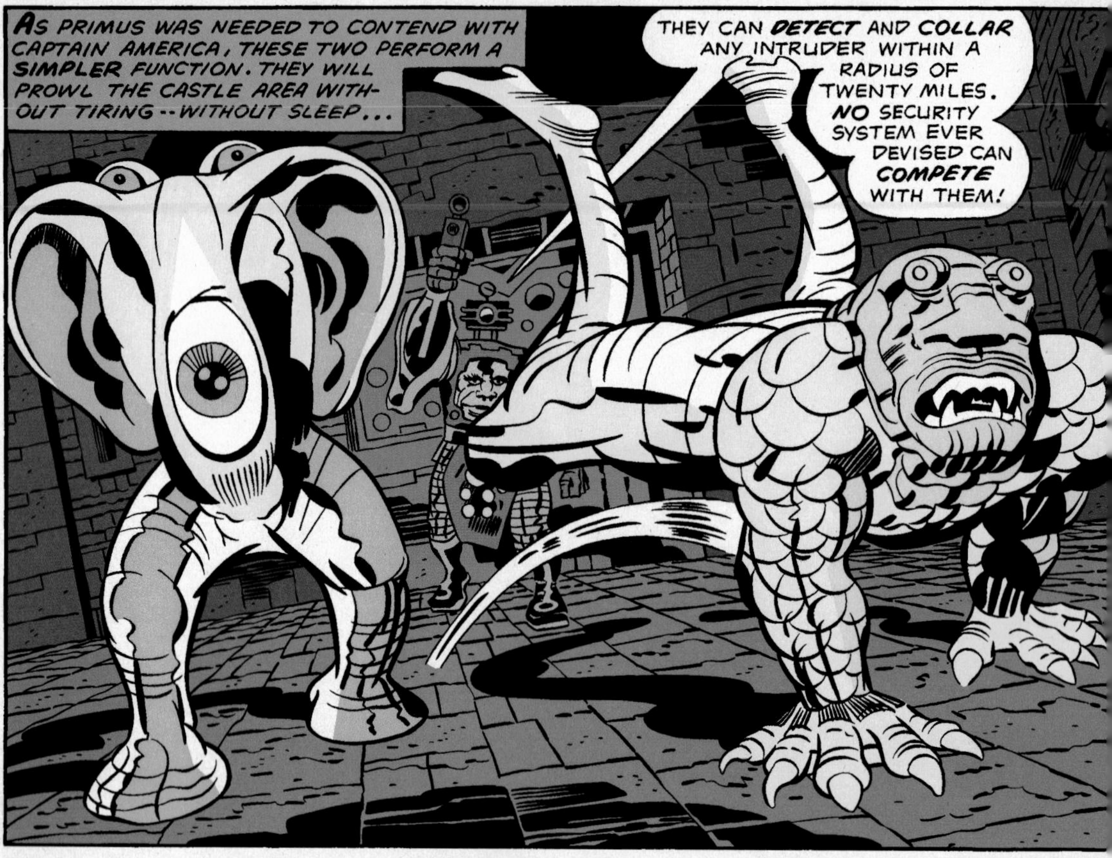
AS PRIMUS WAS NEEDED TO CONTEND WITH CAPTAIN AMERICA, THESE TWO PERFORM A SIMPLER FUNCTION. THEY WILL PROWL THE CASTLE AREA WITHOUT TIRING -- WITHOUT SLEEP...
THEY CAN DETECT AND COLLAR ANY INTRUDER WITHIN A RADIUS OF TWENTY MILES. NO SECURITY SYSTEM EVER DEVISED CAN COMPETE WITH THEM!

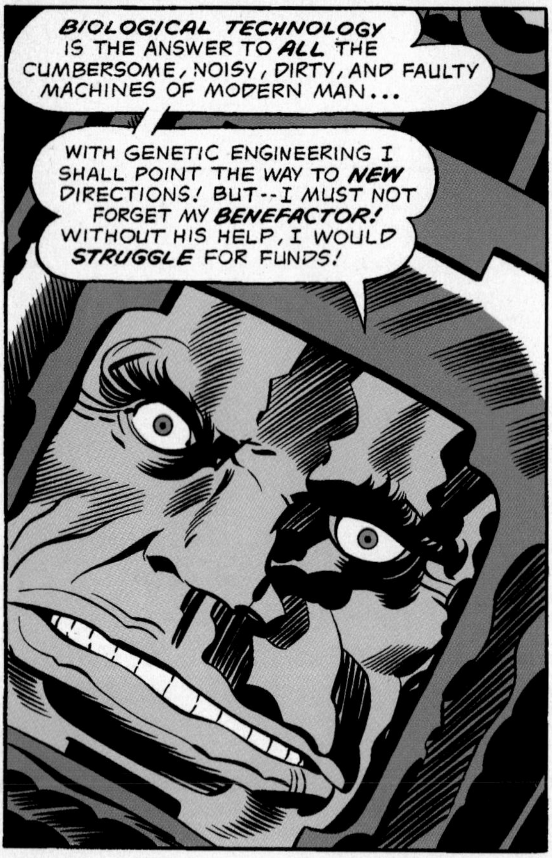
BIOLOGICAL TECHNOLOGY IS THE ANSWER TO ALL THE CUMBERSOME, NOISY, DIRTY, AND FAULTY MACHINES OF MODERN MAN...
WITH GENETIC ENGINEERING I SHALL POINT THE WAY TO NEW DIRECTIONS! BUT--I MUST NOT FORGET MY BENEFACTOR! WITHOUT HIS HELP, I WOULD STRUGGLE FOR FUNDS!

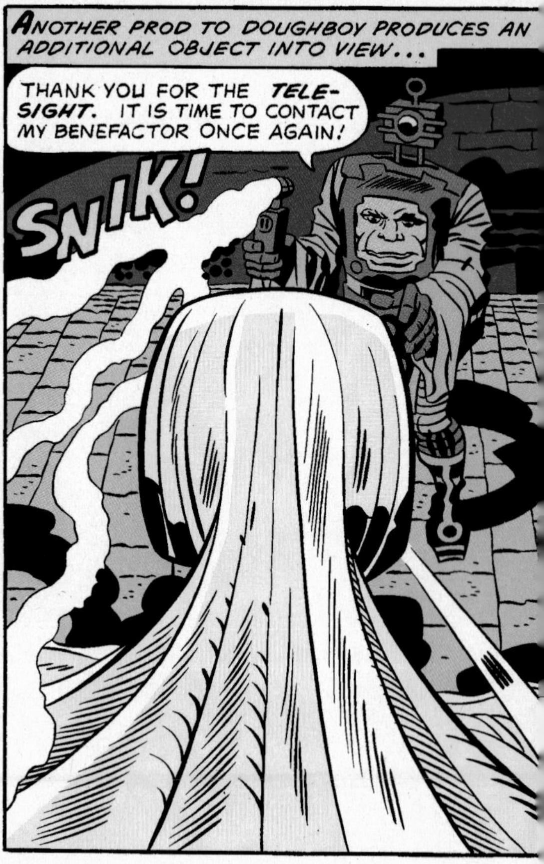
ANOTHER PROD TO DOUGHBOY PRODUCES AN ADDITIONAL OBJECT INTO VIEW...
THANK YOU FOR THE TELE-SIGHT. IT IS TIME TO CONTACT MY BENEFACTOR ONCE AGAIN!
SNIK!

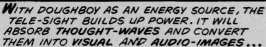

WITH DOUGHBOY AS AN ENERGY SOURCE, THE TELE-SIGHT BUILDS UP POWER. IT WILL ABSORB THOUGHT-WAVES AND CONVERT THEM INTO VISUAL AND AUDIO-IMAGES...

NO WIRES! NO TUBES! NO MASSIVE BROADCAST FACILITIES TO CONTEND WITH! AND YET, I CAN STAND HERE AND CONVERSE WITH ANYONE ON THIS PLANET--!

WAS THERE EVER SUCH A WONDER!

CONTACT IS ESTABLISHED WITH UNERRING ACCURACY...

ZOLA! IT'S YOU! -- WHAT IS IT THIS TIME? --A PROGRESS REPORT? MORE MONEY?

GOOD NEWS. MY LAST INSPECTION TOUR BROUGHT US A BIT OF LUCK!

I- ER- MANAGED TO PICK UP TWO SUBJECTS IN MY TRAVELS WHO'LL MAKE EXCELLENT SPECIMENS FOR OUR BIG PROJECT!

"PICKED THEM UP," DID YOU? HA HA HAH!

OUR ASSOCIATION HAS TRANSFORMED YOU INTO A RUTHLESS DREAMER!

I'VE LEARNED THAT THE END JUSTIFIES THE MEANS, BENEFACTOR!

YES--AND MIGHT MAKES RIGHT, AND ALL THAT HOGWASH! GET ON WITH IT--!

--WHAT MAKES THESE SUBJECTS SO EXCEPTIONAL!?

WELL... ONE OF THEM IS ACTUALLY A SUPER-HERO! HE'S KNOWN AS CAPTAIN AMERICA!

--I DON'T BELIEVE IT--! --YOU'VE-- GOT--CAPTAIN-- AMERICA?!

BOTH HE AND HIS FEMALE COMPANION ARE IN MY CUSTODY AT *THIS* MOMENT!

BLAST THAT *MONITOR!* IT *WOULD* SOUND OFF RIGHT *NOW!*

EXCUSE ME, ZOLA!

BEEEEP!

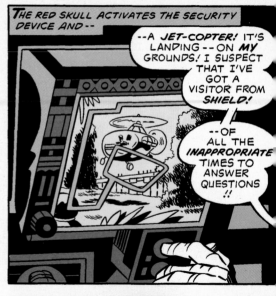

THE RED SKULL ACTIVATES THE SECURITY DEVICE AND --

--A *JET-COPTER!* IT'S LANDING -- ON *MY* GROUNDS! I SUSPECT THAT I'VE GOT A VISITOR FROM *SHIELD!*

-- OF ALL THE *INAPPROPRIATE* TIMES TO ANSWER QUESTIONS !!

BREAK CONTACT, ZOLA! WE'LL TALK TOMORROW. THIS DEVELOPMENT SHALL END IN *TRIUMPH* FOR BOTH OF US!

TOMORROW, THEN! WE'VE *MUCH* TO DISCUSS! FAREWELL --

SOON AFTER...

AS ZOLA'S PRISONER, CAPTAIN AMERICA IS *LITERALLY* IN MY HANDS.!! *FATE HAS CHOSEN IN MY FAVOR!*

YES... IT IS *SHOWDOWN DAY!* OLD SCORES, HOTLY FOUGHT, MUST SEEK A *FINAL END!* IT IS KARMA! -- *KISMET!* -- *DESTINY!*

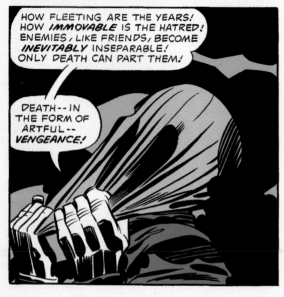

HOW FLEETING ARE THE YEARS! HOW *IMMOVABLE* IS THE HATRED! ENEMIES, LIKE FRIENDS, BECOME *INEVITABLY* INSEPARABLE! ONLY DEATH CAN PART THEM!

DEATH -- IN THE FORM OF ARTFUL -- *VENGEANCE!*

YES! IT'S AN INSPIRATIONAL THOUGHT --!

CAPTAIN AMERICA SHALL DIE A *LIVING DEATH!*

BUT FIRST... TO BUSINESS OF *ANOTHER* NATURE -- A FOOL'S PLAY -- CONVINCINGLY RENDERED BY THE *RED SKULL!*

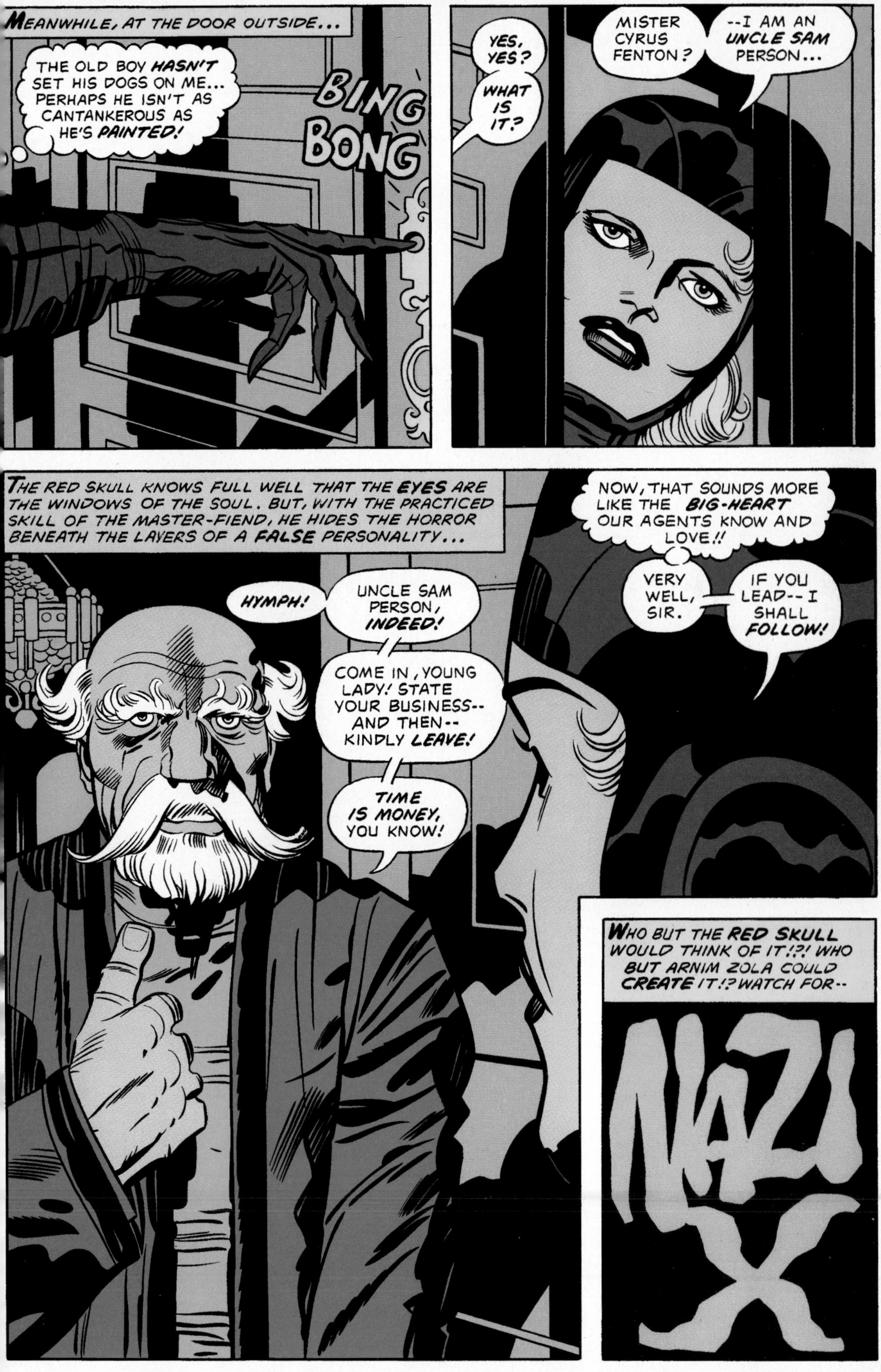
MEANWHILE, AT THE DOOR OUTSIDE...
THE OLD BOY HASN'T SET HIS DOGS ON ME... PERHAPS HE ISN'T AS CANTANKEROUS AS HE'S PAINTED!
BING BONG
YES, YES?
WHAT IS IT?
MISTER CYRUS FENTON?
--I AM AN UNCLE SAM PERSON...
THE RED SKULL KNOWS FULL WELL THAT THE EYES ARE THE WINDOWS OF THE SOUL. BUT, WITH THE PRACTICED SKILL OF THE MASTER-FIEND, HE HIDES THE HORROR BENEATH THE LAYERS OF A FALSE PERSONALITY...
HYMPH!
UNCLE SAM PERSON, INDEED!
COME IN, YOUNG LADY! STATE YOUR BUSINESS-- AND THEN-- KINDLY LEAVE!
TIME IS MONEY, YOU KNOW!
NOW, THAT SOUNDS MORE LIKE THE BIG-HEART OUR AGENTS KNOW AND LOVE!!
VERY WELL, SIR.
IF YOU LEAD-- I SHALL FOLLOW!
WHO BUT THE RED SKULL WOULD THINK OF IT!?! WHO BUT ARNIM ZOLA COULD CREATE IT!? WATCH FOR--
NAZI X

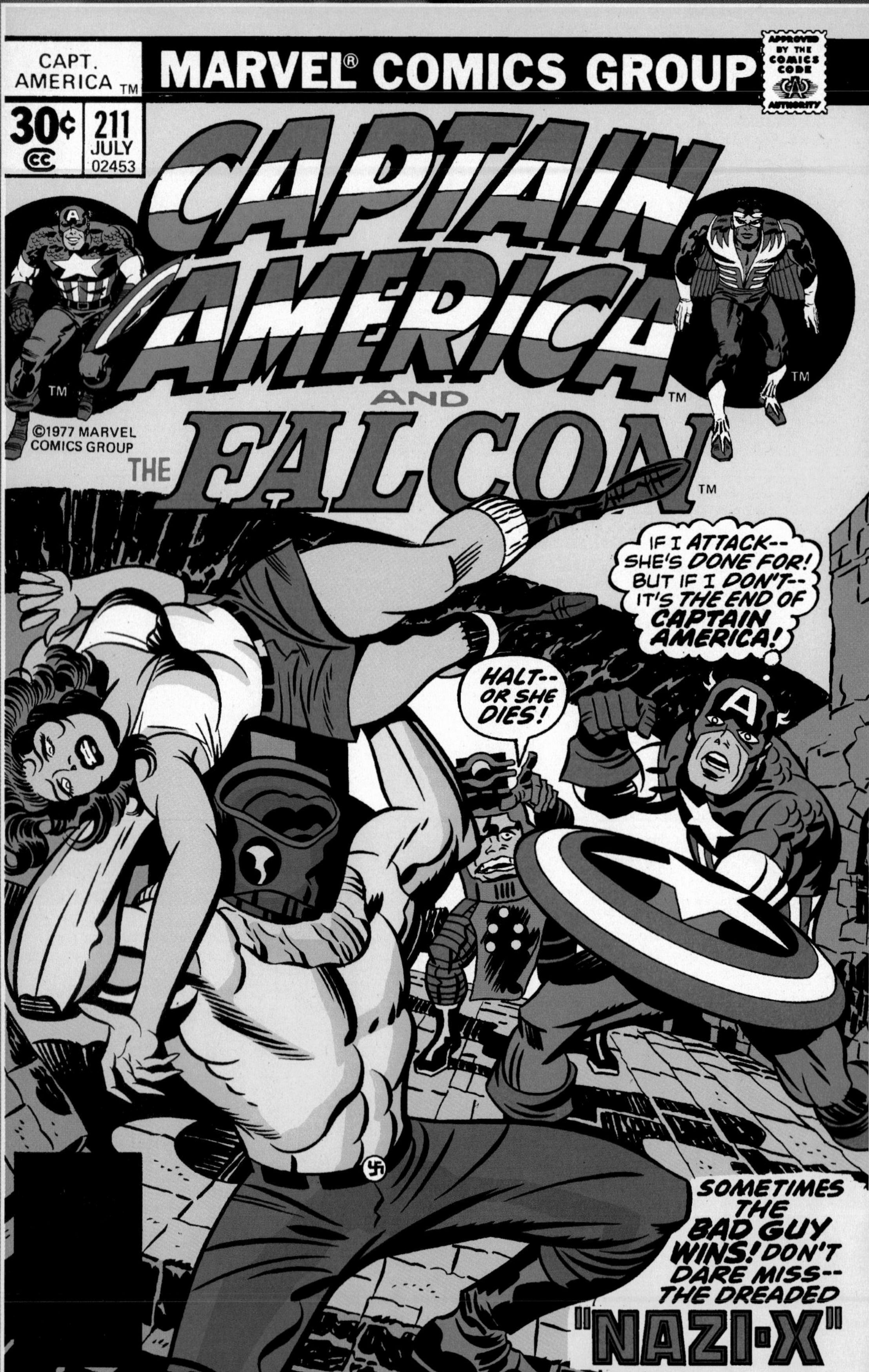

CAPT. AMERICA TM
MARVEL® COMICS GROUP
APPROVED BY THE COMICS CODE AUTHORITY
30¢
211 JULY 02453
CC
CAPTAIN AMERICA TM
AND
THE FALCON TM
©1977 MARVEL COMICS GROUP
IF I ATTACK-- SHE'S DONE FOR! BUT IF I DON'T-- IT'S THE END OF CAPTAIN AMERICA!
HALT-- OR SHE DIES!
SOMETIMES THE BAD GUY WINS! DON'T DARE MISS-- THE DREADED "NAZI-X"

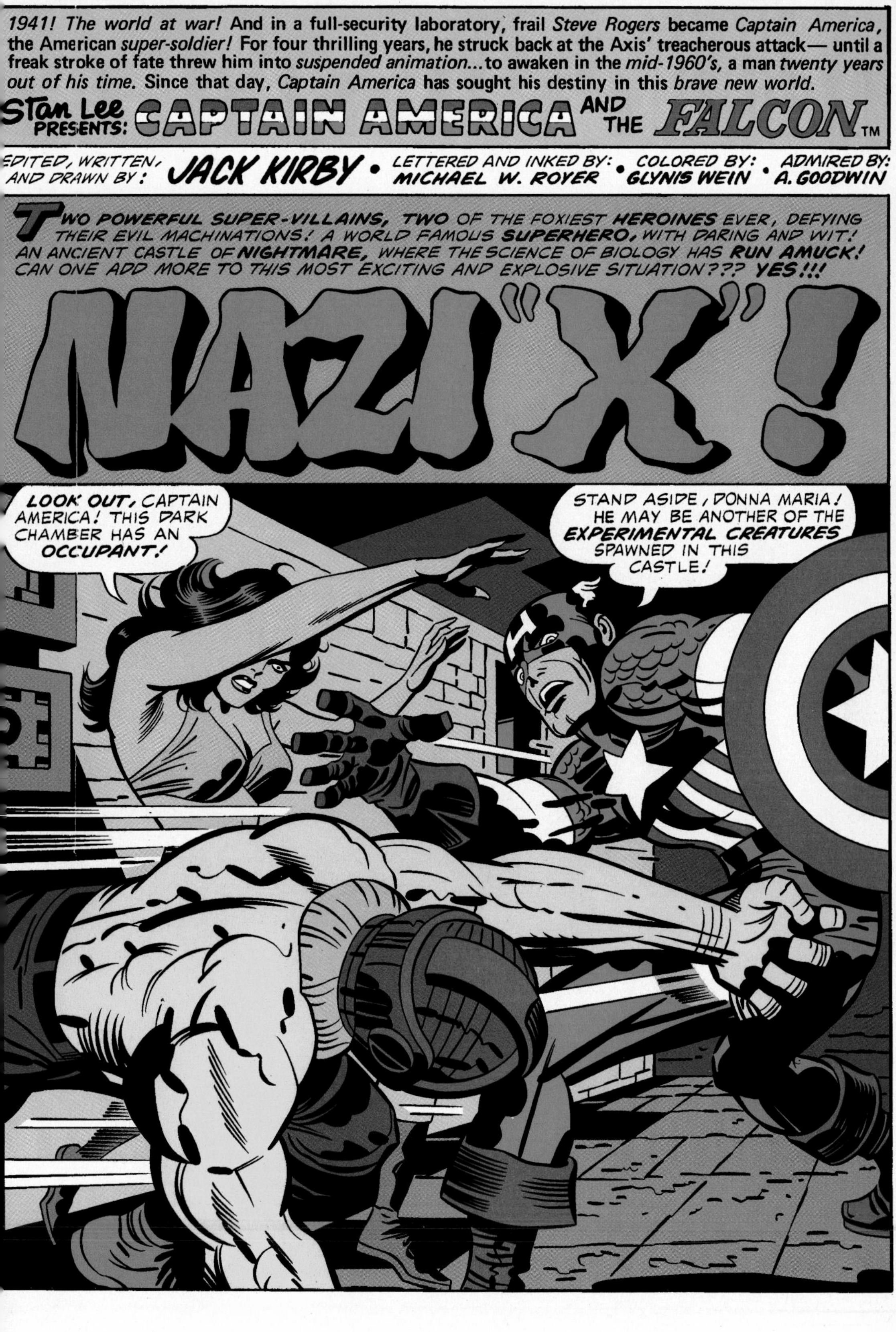
1941! The world at war! And in a full-security laboratory, frail Steve Rogers became Captain America, the American super-soldier! For four thrilling years, he struck back at the Axis' treacherous attack— until a freak stroke of fate threw him into suspended animation...to awaken in the mid-1960's, a man twenty years out of his time. Since that day, Captain America has sought his destiny in this brave new world.
Stan Lee PRESENTS: CAPTAIN AMERICA AND THE FALCON TM
EDITED, WRITTEN, AND DRAWN BY: JACK KIRBY • LETTERED AND INKED BY: MICHAEL W. ROYER • COLORED BY: GLYNIS WEIN • ADMIRED BY: A. GOODWIN
TWO POWERFUL SUPER-VILLAINS, TWO OF THE FOXIEST HEROINES EVER, DEFYING THEIR EVIL MACHINATIONS! A WORLD FAMOUS SUPERHERO, WITH DARING AND WIT! AN ANCIENT CASTLE OF NIGHTMARE, WHERE THE SCIENCE OF BIOLOGY HAS RUN AMUCK! CAN ONE ADD MORE TO THIS MOST EXCITING AND EXPLOSIVE SITUATION??? YES!!!
NAZI "X"!
LOOK OUT, CAPTAIN AMERICA! THIS DARK CHAMBER HAS AN OCCUPANT!
STAND ASIDE, DONNA MARIA! HE MAY BE ANOTHER OF THE EXPERIMENTAL CREATURES SPAWNED IN THIS CASTLE!

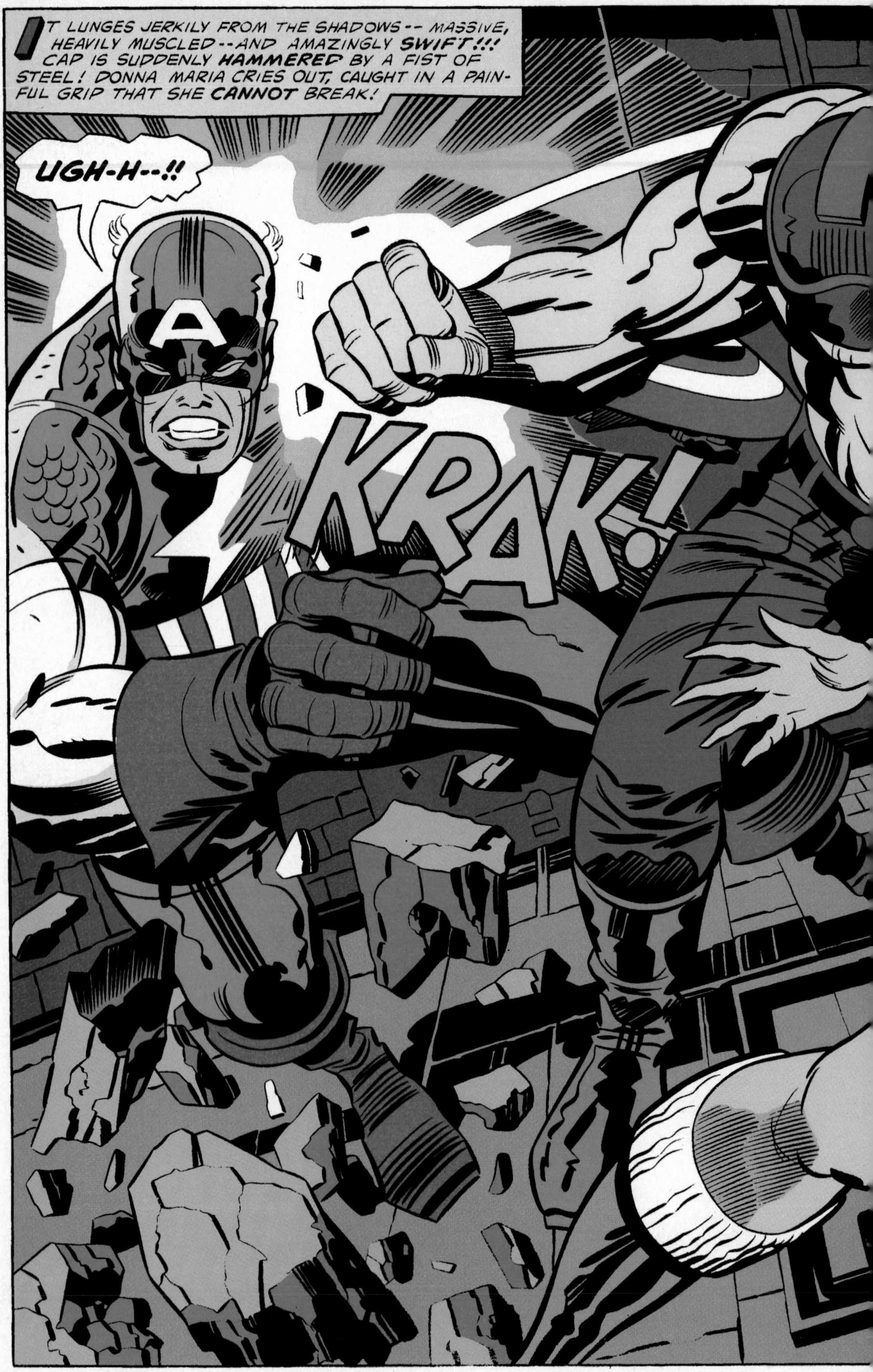
IT LUNGES JERKILY FROM THE SHADOWS -- MASSIVE, HEAVILY MUSCLED -- AND AMAZINGLY SWIFT!!! CAP IS SUDDENLY HAMMERED BY A FIST OF STEEL! DONNA MARIA CRIES OUT, CAUGHT IN A PAINFUL GRIP THAT SHE CANNOT BREAK!
UGH-H--!!
KRAK!

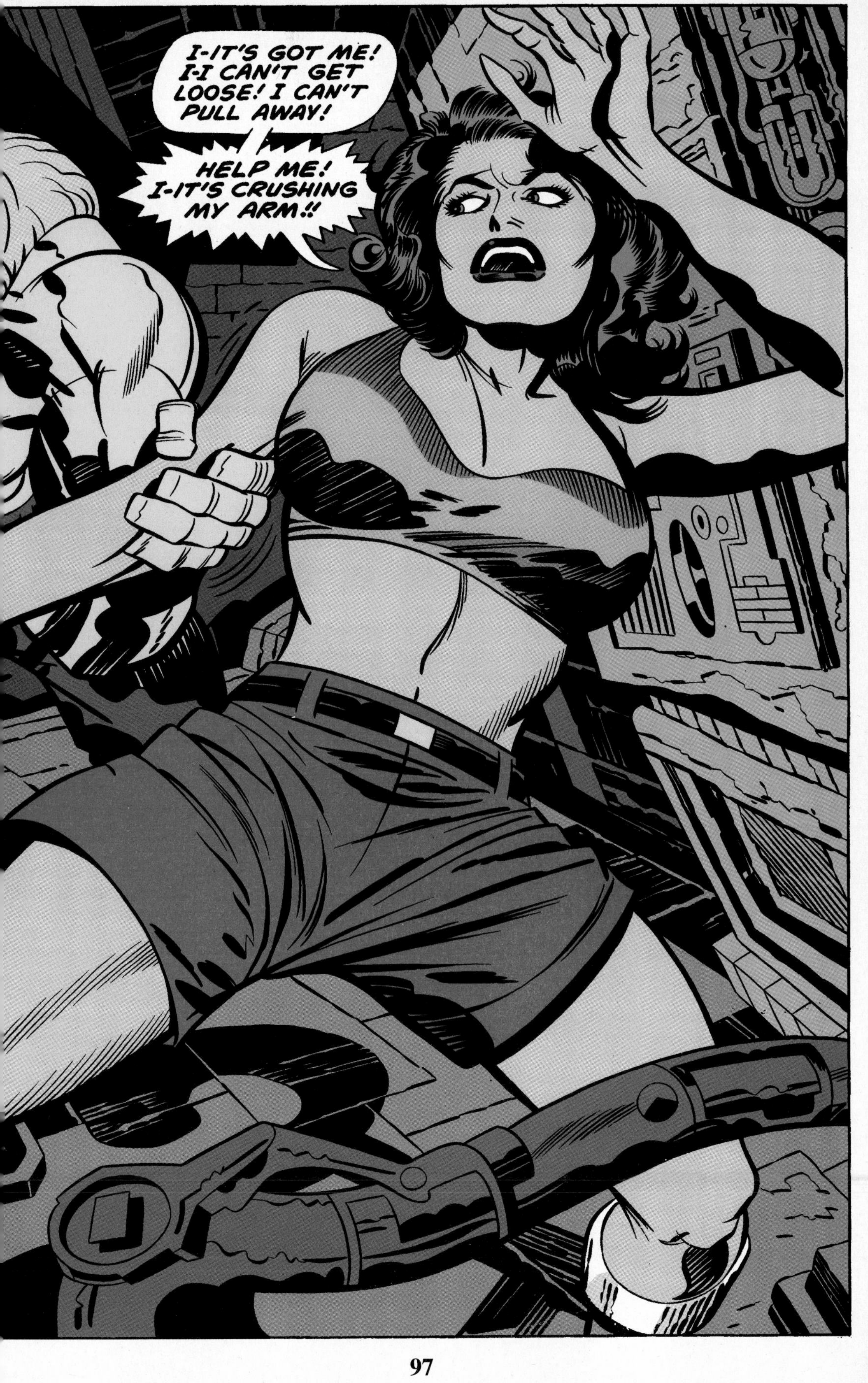
I-IT'S GOT ME! I-I CAN'T GET LOOSE! I CAN'T PULL AWAY!
HELP ME! I-IT'S CRUSHING MY ARM!!

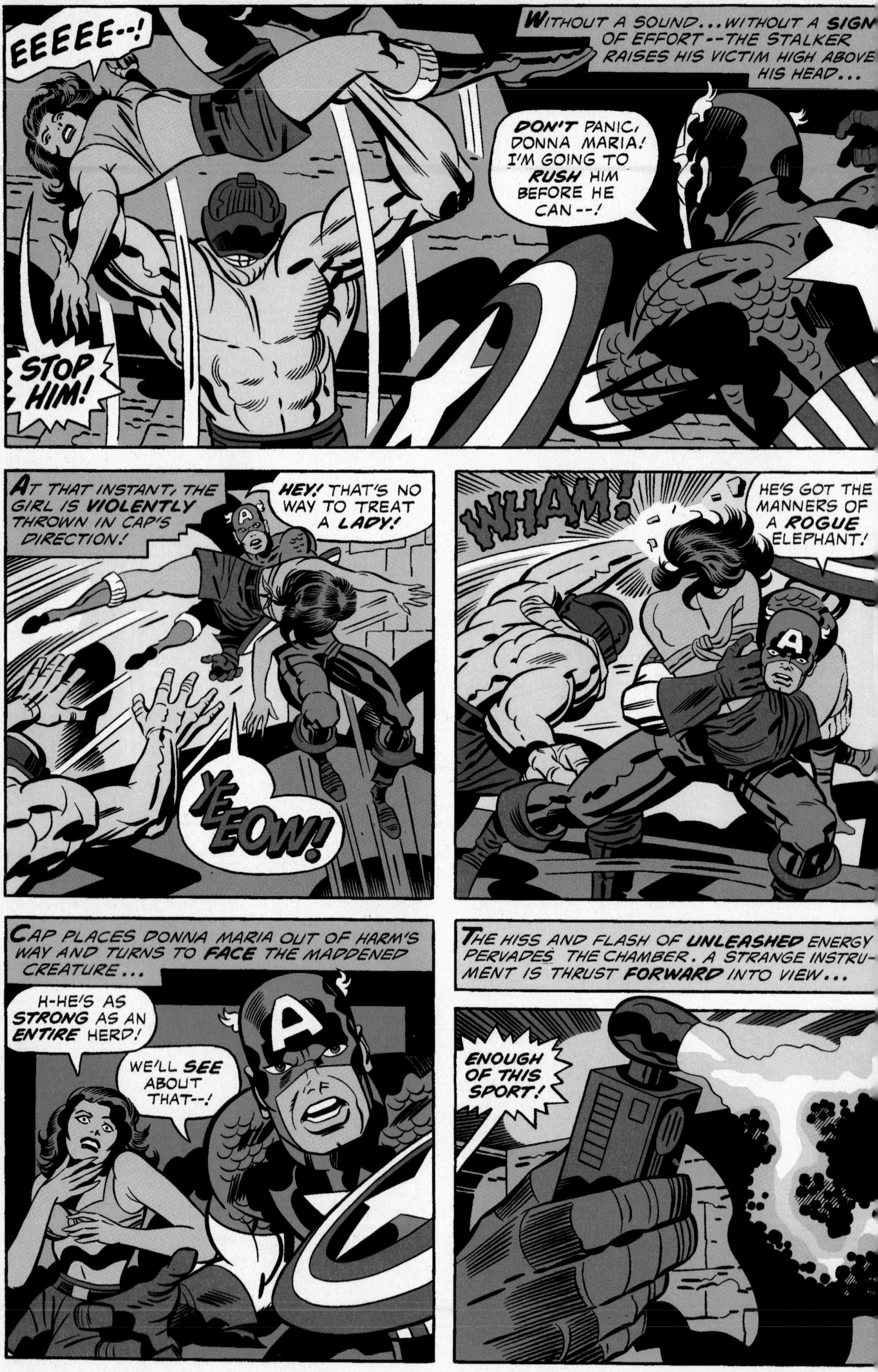
WITHOUT A SOUND...WITHOUT A SIGN OF EFFORT--THE STALKER RAISES HIS VICTIM HIGH ABOVE HIS HEAD...
EEEEE--!
DON'T PANIC, DONNA MARIA! I'M GOING TO RUSH HIM BEFORE HE CAN--!
STOP HIM!
AT THAT INSTANT, THE GIRL IS VIOLENTLY THROWN IN CAP'S DIRECTION!
HEY! THAT'S NO WAY TO TREAT A LADY!
YEEEOW!
WHAM!
HE'S GOT THE MANNERS OF A ROGUE ELEPHANT!
CAP PLACES DONNA MARIA OUT OF HARM'S WAY AND TURNS TO FACE THE MADDENED CREATURE...
H-HE'S AS STRONG AS AN ENTIRE HERD!
WE'LL SEE ABOUT THAT--!
THE HISS AND FLASH OF UNLEASHED ENERGY PERVADES THE CHAMBER. A STRANGE INSTRUMENT IS THRUST FORWARD INTO VIEW...
ENOUGH OF THIS SPORT!

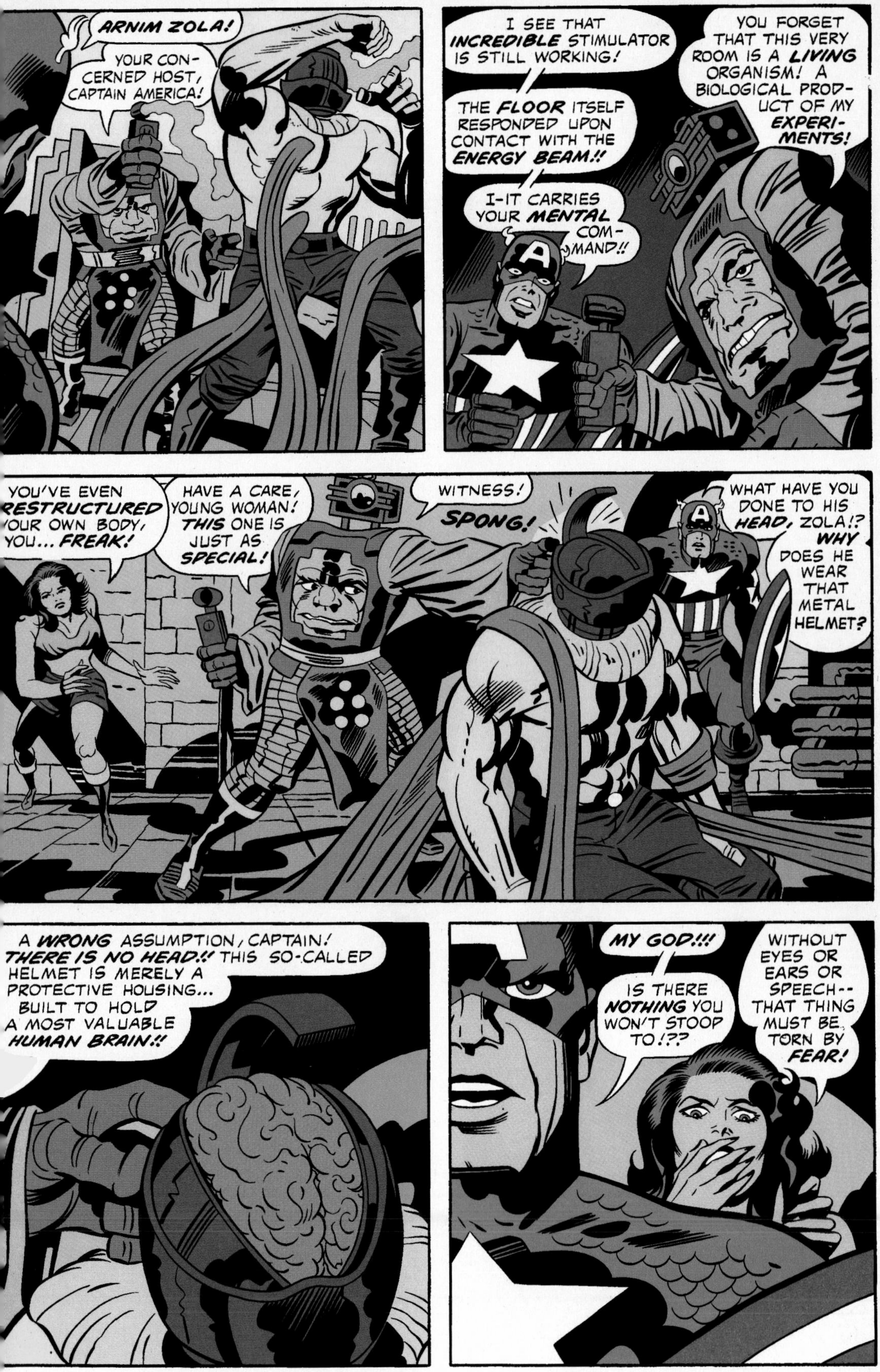
ARNIM ZOLA!
YOUR CON-CERNED HOST, CAPTAIN AMERICA!
I SEE THAT INCREDIBLE STIMULATOR IS STILL WORKING!
THE FLOOR ITSELF RESPONDED UPON CONTACT WITH THE ENERGY BEAM!!
I-IT CARRIES YOUR MENTAL COM-MAND!!
YOU FORGET THAT THIS VERY ROOM IS A LIVING ORGANISM! A BIOLOGICAL PROD-UCT OF MY EXPERI-MENTS!
YOU'VE EVEN RESTRUCTURED YOUR OWN BODY, YOU... FREAK!
HAVE A CARE, YOUNG WOMAN! THIS ONE IS JUST AS SPECIAL!
WITNESS!
SPONG!
WHAT HAVE YOU DONE TO HIS HEAD, ZOLA!? WHY DOES HE WEAR THAT METAL HELMET?
A WRONG ASSUMPTION, CAPTAIN! THERE IS NO HEAD!! THIS SO-CALLED HELMET IS MERELY A PROTECTIVE HOUSING... BUILT TO HOLD A MOST VALUABLE HUMAN BRAIN!!
MY GOD!!!
IS THERE NOTHING YOU WON'T STOOP TO!??
WITHOUT EYES OR EARS OR SPEECH-- THAT THING MUST BE TORN BY FEAR!

THAT, AMONG MANY *OTHER* EMOTIONS, MY DEAR! IT'S BEEN RATHER *DIFFICULT* TO KEEP THIS BRAIN ALIVE THROUGH THE YEARS!

THERE WAS A PERIOD WHEN IT *DIDN'T* EVEN HAVE THIS BODY!

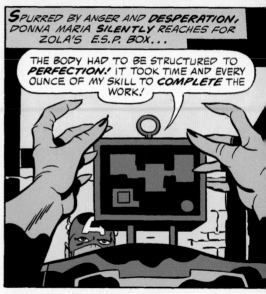

SPURRED BY ANGER AND DESPERATION, DONNA MARIA SILENTLY REACHES FOR ZOLA'S E.S.P. BOX...

THE BODY HAD TO BE STRUCTURED TO *PERFECTION!* IT TOOK TIME AND EVERY OUNCE OF MY SKILL TO *COMPLETE* THE WORK!

PREOCCUPIED WITH HIS OWN WORDS, ZOLA IS CAUGHT UNAWARES WHEN DONNA MARIA LEAPS UPON HIS BACK...

GOOD WORK, KID! I THINK WE'VE *GOT* HIM THIS TIME!

WHA!?

THE *FIEND!*

HE SHOULD BE JAILED FOR *LIFE!*

WE'LL HAVE TO *ALERT* THE AUTHORITIES, *FIRST!*

DROP THAT, ZOLA!

H-HOW CAN WE *ESCAPE* THIS PLACE? I-IT'S CRAWLING WITH *MONSTERS* FROM HIS LABORATORY!

Y-YOU'LL *PAY* FOR THIS!

WITHOUT *THIS* TO STIR THEM, ZOLA'S CREATURES ARE MERE *LUMPS* OF LIVING TISSUE!

NOW, SAY *FAREWELL* TO OUR HOST!

I HOPE HE *STAYS PUT* FOR THE TIME BEING!

LET'S GO! I'LL COME *BACK* FOR HIM, ONCE I'VE GOTTEN YOU TO *SAFETY!*

FOOLS!

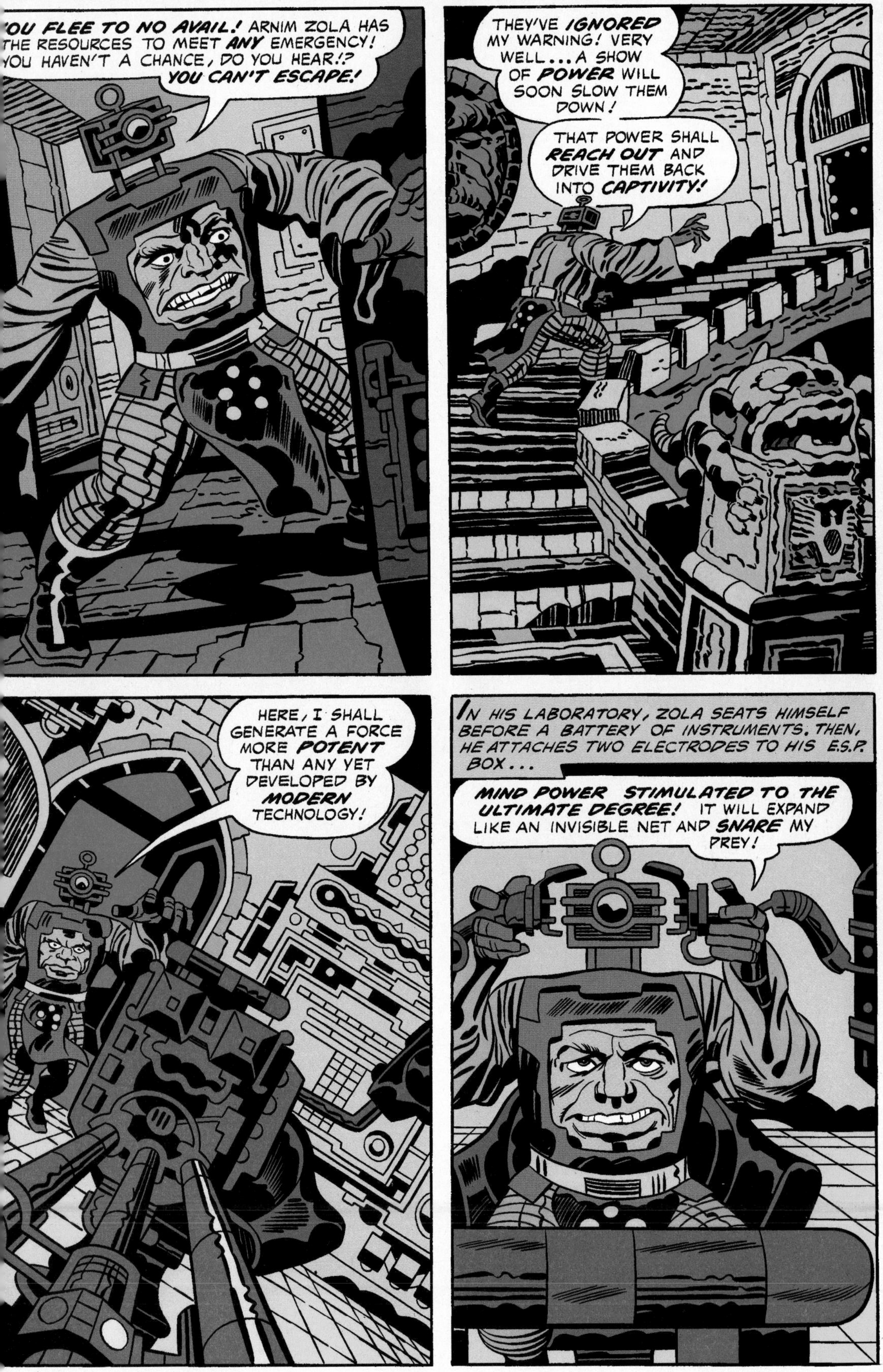

OU FLEE TO NO AVAIL! ARNIM ZOLA HAS THE RESOURCES TO MEET ANY EMERGENCY! YOU HAVEN'T A CHANCE, DO YOU HEAR!? YOU CAN'T ESCAPE!
THEY'VE IGNORED MY WARNING! VERY WELL... A SHOW OF POWER WILL SOON SLOW THEM DOWN!
THAT POWER SHALL REACH OUT AND DRIVE THEM BACK INTO CAPTIVITY!
HERE, I SHALL GENERATE A FORCE MORE POTENT THAN ANY YET DEVELOPED BY MODERN TECHNOLOGY!
IN HIS LABORATORY, ZOLA SEATS HIMSELF BEFORE A BATTERY OF INSTRUMENTS. THEN, HE ATTACHES TWO ELECTRODES TO HIS E.S.P. BOX...
MIND POWER STIMULATED TO THE ULTIMATE DEGREE! IT WILL EXPAND LIKE AN INVISIBLE NET AND SNARE MY PREY!

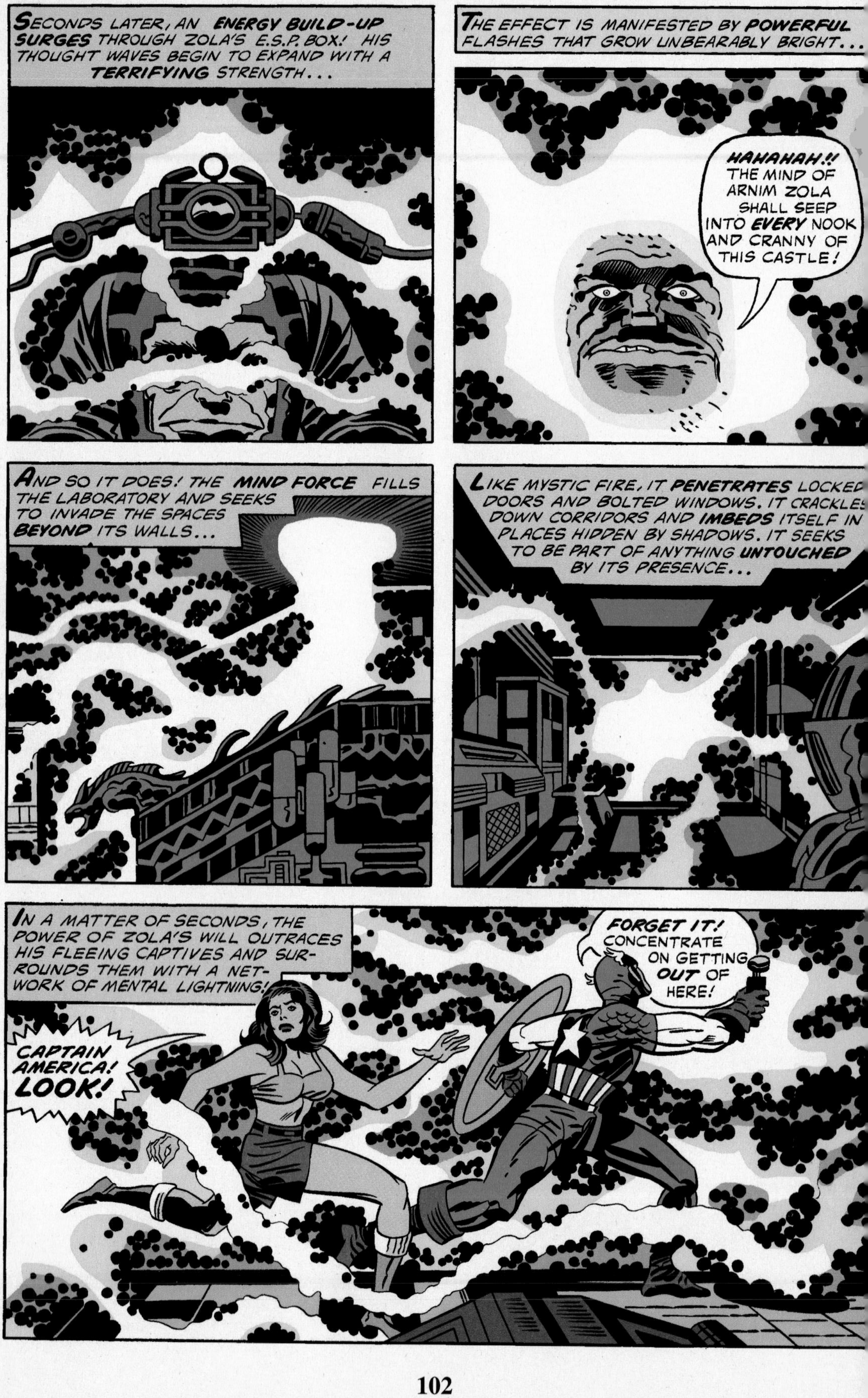
SECONDS LATER, AN ENERGY BUILD-UP SURGES THROUGH ZOLA'S E.S.P. BOX! HIS THOUGHT WAVES BEGIN TO EXPAND WITH A TERRIFYING STRENGTH...
THE EFFECT IS MANIFESTED BY POWERFUL FLASHES THAT GROW UNBEARABLY BRIGHT...
HAHAHAH!! THE MIND OF ARNIM ZOLA SHALL SEEP INTO EVERY NOOK AND CRANNY OF THIS CASTLE!
AND SO IT DOES! THE MIND FORCE FILLS THE LABORATORY AND SEEKS TO INVADE THE SPACES BEYOND ITS WALLS...
LIKE MYSTIC FIRE, IT PENETRATES LOCKED DOORS AND BOLTED WINDOWS. IT CRACKLES DOWN CORRIDORS AND IMBEDS ITSELF IN PLACES HIDDEN BY SHADOWS. IT SEEKS TO BE PART OF ANYTHING UNTOUCHED BY ITS PRESENCE...
IN A MATTER OF SECONDS, THE POWER OF ZOLA'S WILL OUTRACES HIS FLEEING CAPTIVES AND SURROUNDS THEM WITH A NETWORK OF MENTAL LIGHTNING!
FORGET IT! CONCENTRATE ON GETTING OUT OF HERE!
CAPTAIN AMERICA! LOOK!

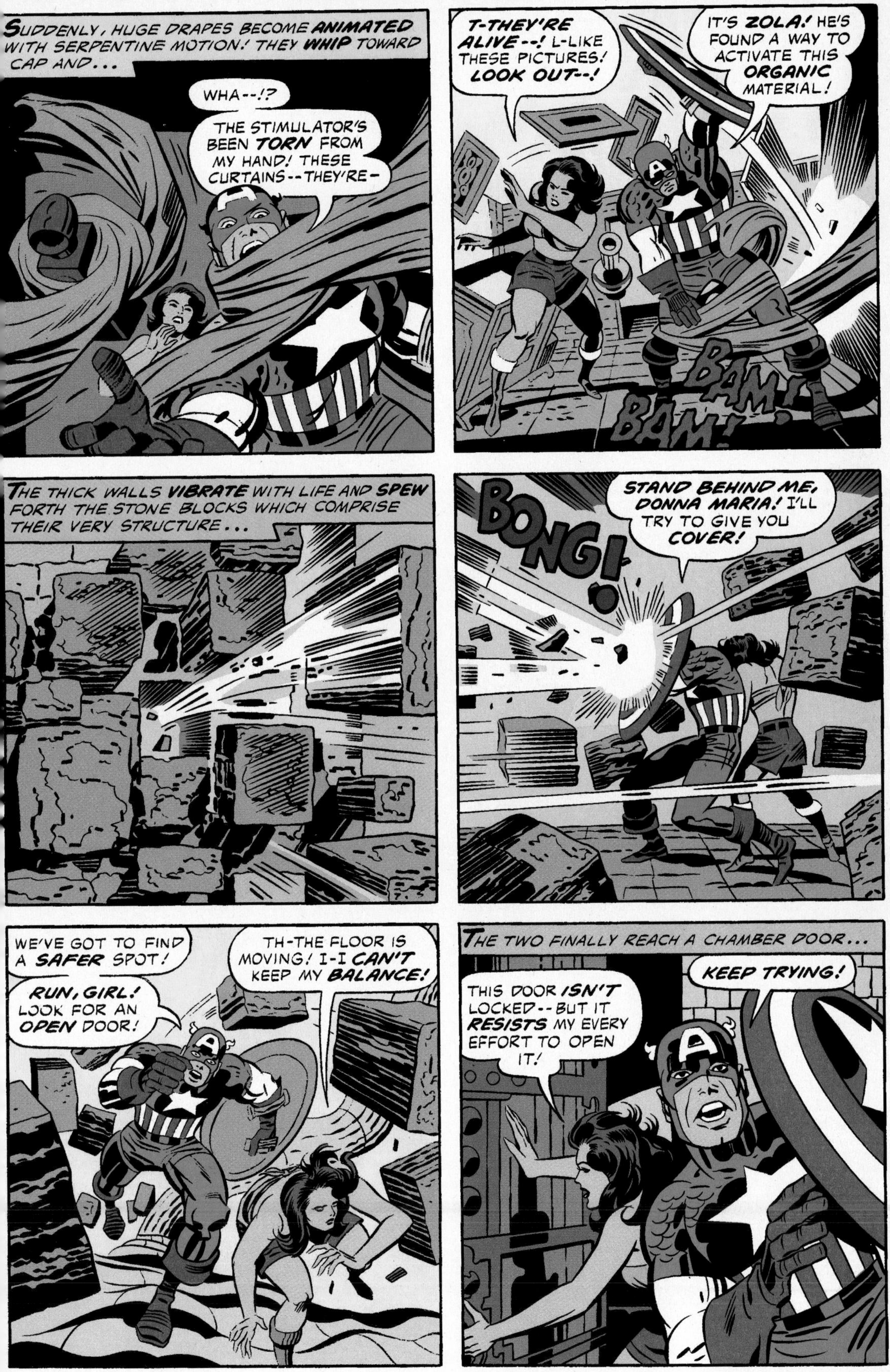
SUDDENLY, HUGE DRAPES BECOME ANIMATED WITH SERPENTINE MOTION! THEY WHIP TOWARD CAP AND...
WHA--!?
THE STIMULATOR'S BEEN TORN FROM MY HAND! THESE CURTAINS--THEY'RE-
T-THEY'RE ALIVE--! L-LIKE THESE PICTURES! LOOK OUT--!
IT'S ZOLA! HE'S FOUND A WAY TO ACTIVATE THIS ORGANIC MATERIAL!
BAM! BAM!
THE THICK WALLS VIBRATE WITH LIFE AND SPEW FORTH THE STONE BLOCKS WHICH COMPRISE THEIR VERY STRUCTURE...
BONG!
STAND BEHIND ME, DONNA MARIA! I'LL TRY TO GIVE YOU COVER!
WE'VE GOT TO FIND A SAFER SPOT!
RUN, GIRL! LOOK FOR AN OPEN DOOR!
TH-THE FLOOR IS MOVING! I-I CAN'T KEEP MY BALANCE!
THE TWO FINALLY REACH A CHAMBER DOOR...
THIS DOOR ISN'T LOCKED--BUT IT RESISTS MY EVERY EFFORT TO OPEN IT!
KEEP TRYING!

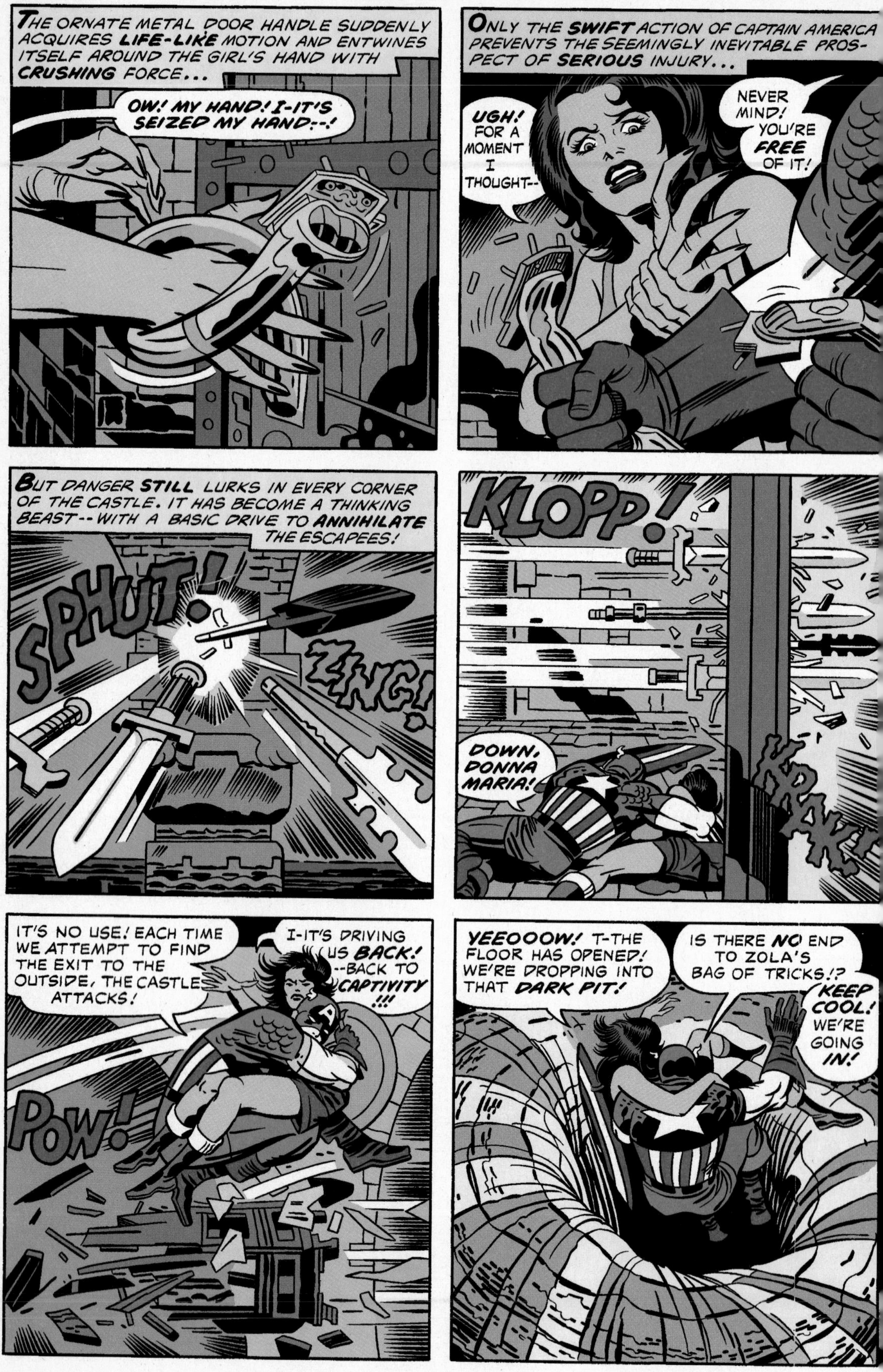

THE ORNATE METAL DOOR HANDLE SUDDENLY ACQUIRES LIFE-LIKE MOTION AND ENTWINES ITSELF AROUND THE GIRL'S HAND WITH CRUSHING FORCE...
OW! MY HAND! I-IT'S SEIZED MY HAND--!
ONLY THE SWIFT ACTION OF CAPTAIN AMERICA PREVENTS THE SEEMINGLY INEVITABLE PROSPECT OF SERIOUS INJURY...
UGH! FOR A MOMENT I THOUGHT--
NEVER MIND! YOU'RE FREE OF IT!
BUT DANGER STILL LURKS IN EVERY CORNER OF THE CASTLE. IT HAS BECOME A THINKING BEAST--WITH A BASIC DRIVE TO ANNIHILATE THE ESCAPEES!
SPHUT!
ZING!
KLOPP!
DOWN, DONNA MARIA!
KRAK!
IT'S NO USE! EACH TIME WE ATTEMPT TO FIND THE EXIT TO THE OUTSIDE, THE CASTLE ATTACKS!
I-IT'S DRIVING US BACK! --BACK TO CAPTIVITY!!!
POW!
YEEOOOW! T-THE FLOOR HAS OPENED! WE'RE DROPPING INTO THAT DARK PIT!
IS THERE NO END TO ZOLA'S BAG OF TRICKS!?
KEEP COOL! WE'RE GOING IN!

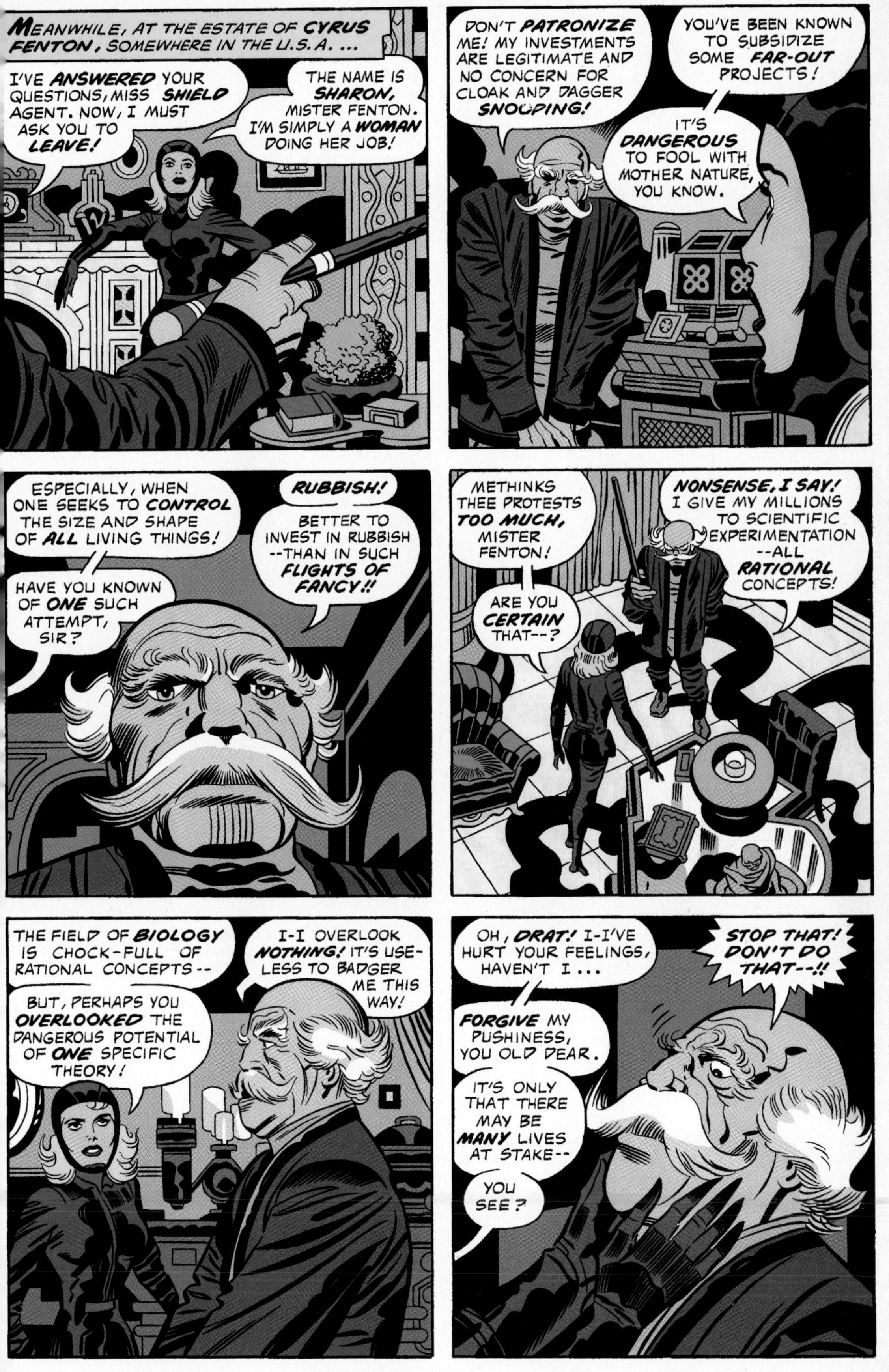
MEANWHILE, AT THE ESTATE OF CYRUS FENTON, SOMEWHERE IN THE U.S.A. ...
I'VE ANSWERED YOUR QUESTIONS, MISS SHIELD AGENT. NOW, I MUST ASK YOU TO LEAVE!
THE NAME IS SHARON, MISTER FENTON. I'M SIMPLY A WOMAN DOING HER JOB!
DON'T PATRONIZE ME! MY INVESTMENTS ARE LEGITIMATE AND NO CONCERN FOR CLOAK AND DAGGER SNOOPING!
YOU'VE BEEN KNOWN TO SUBSIDIZE SOME FAR-OUT PROJECTS!
IT'S DANGEROUS TO FOOL WITH MOTHER NATURE, YOU KNOW.
ESPECIALLY, WHEN ONE SEEKS TO CONTROL THE SIZE AND SHAPE OF ALL LIVING THINGS!
HAVE YOU KNOWN OF ONE SUCH ATTEMPT, SIR?
RUBBISH!
BETTER TO INVEST IN RUBBISH --THAN IN SUCH FLIGHTS OF FANCY!!
METHINKS THEE PROTESTS TOO MUCH, MISTER FENTON!
ARE YOU CERTAIN THAT--?
NONSENSE, I SAY! I GIVE MY MILLIONS TO SCIENTIFIC EXPERIMENTATION --ALL RATIONAL CONCEPTS!
THE FIELD OF BIOLOGY IS CHOCK-FULL OF RATIONAL CONCEPTS--
BUT, PERHAPS YOU OVERLOOKED THE DANGEROUS POTENTIAL OF ONE SPECIFIC THEORY!
I-I OVERLOOK NOTHING! IT'S USELESS TO BADGER ME THIS WAY!
OH, DRAT! I-I'VE HURT YOUR FEELINGS, HAVEN'T I ...
FORGIVE MY PUSHINESS, YOU OLD DEAR.
IT'S ONLY THAT THERE MAY BE MANY LIVES AT STAKE--
YOU SEE?
STOP THAT! DON'T DO THAT--!!

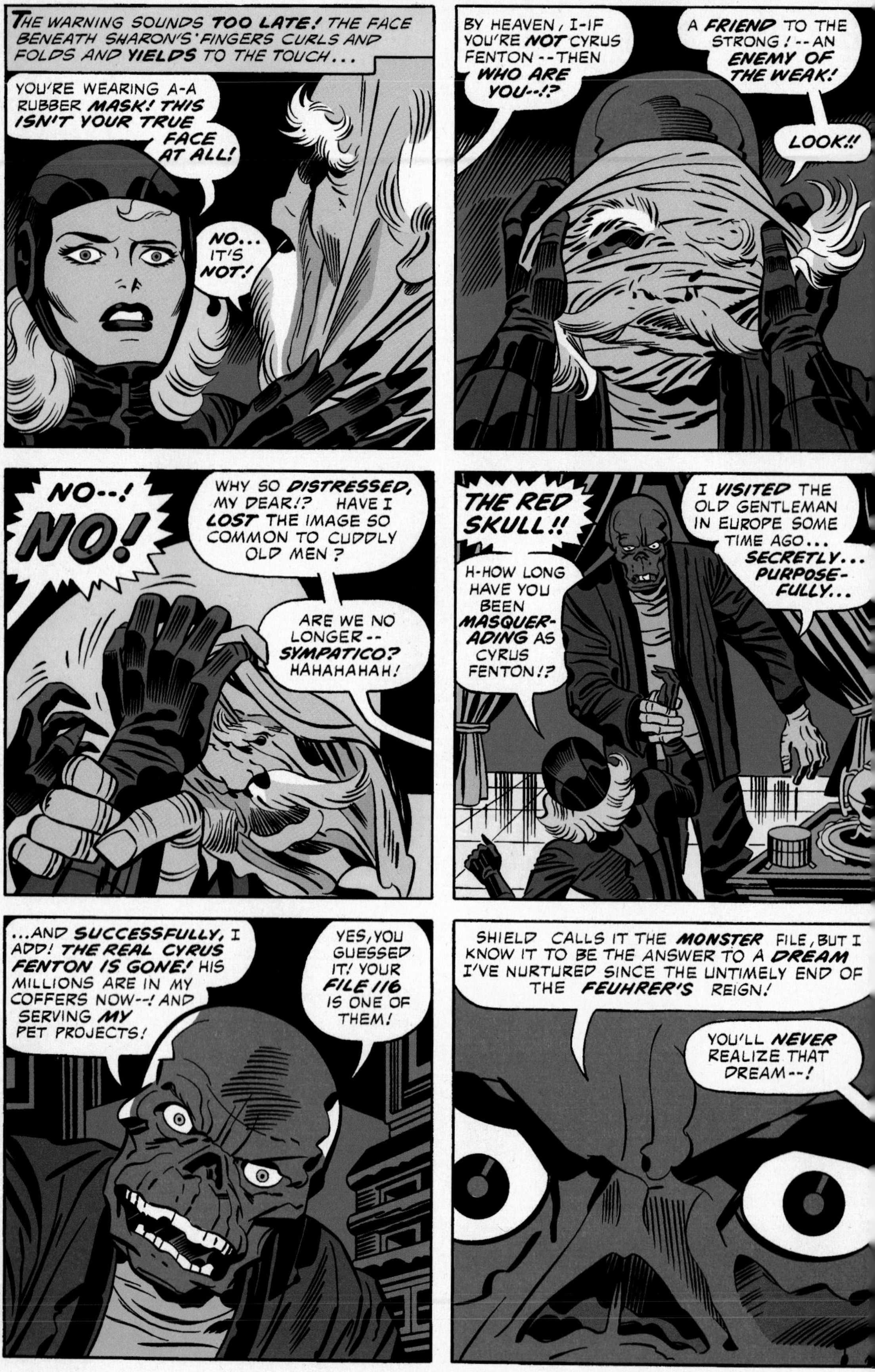
THE WARNING SOUNDS TOO LATE! THE FACE BENEATH SHARON'S FINGERS CURLS AND FOLDS AND YIELDS TO THE TOUCH...
YOU'RE WEARING A-A RUBBER MASK! THIS ISN'T YOUR TRUE FACE AT ALL!
NO... IT'S NOT!
BY HEAVEN, I-IF YOU'RE NOT CYRUS FENTON--THEN WHO ARE YOU--!?
A FRIEND TO THE STRONG!--AN ENEMY OF THE WEAK!
LOOK!!
NO--! NO!
WHY SO DISTRESSED, MY DEAR!? HAVE I LOST THE IMAGE SO COMMON TO CUDDLY OLD MEN?
ARE WE NO LONGER--SYMPATICO? HAHAHAHAH!
THE RED SKULL!!
H-HOW LONG HAVE YOU BEEN MASQUERADING AS CYRUS FENTON!?
I VISITED THE OLD GENTLEMAN IN EUROPE SOME TIME AGO... SECRETLY... PURPOSEFULLY...
...AND SUCCESSFULLY, I ADD! THE REAL CYRUS FENTON IS GONE! HIS MILLIONS ARE IN MY COFFERS NOW--! AND SERVING MY PET PROJECTS!
YES, YOU GUESSED IT! YOUR FILE 116 IS ONE OF THEM!
SHIELD CALLS IT THE MONSTER FILE, BUT I KNOW IT TO BE THE ANSWER TO A DREAM I'VE NURTURED SINCE THE UNTIMELY END OF THE FEUHRER'S REIGN!
YOU'LL NEVER REALIZE THAT DREAM--!

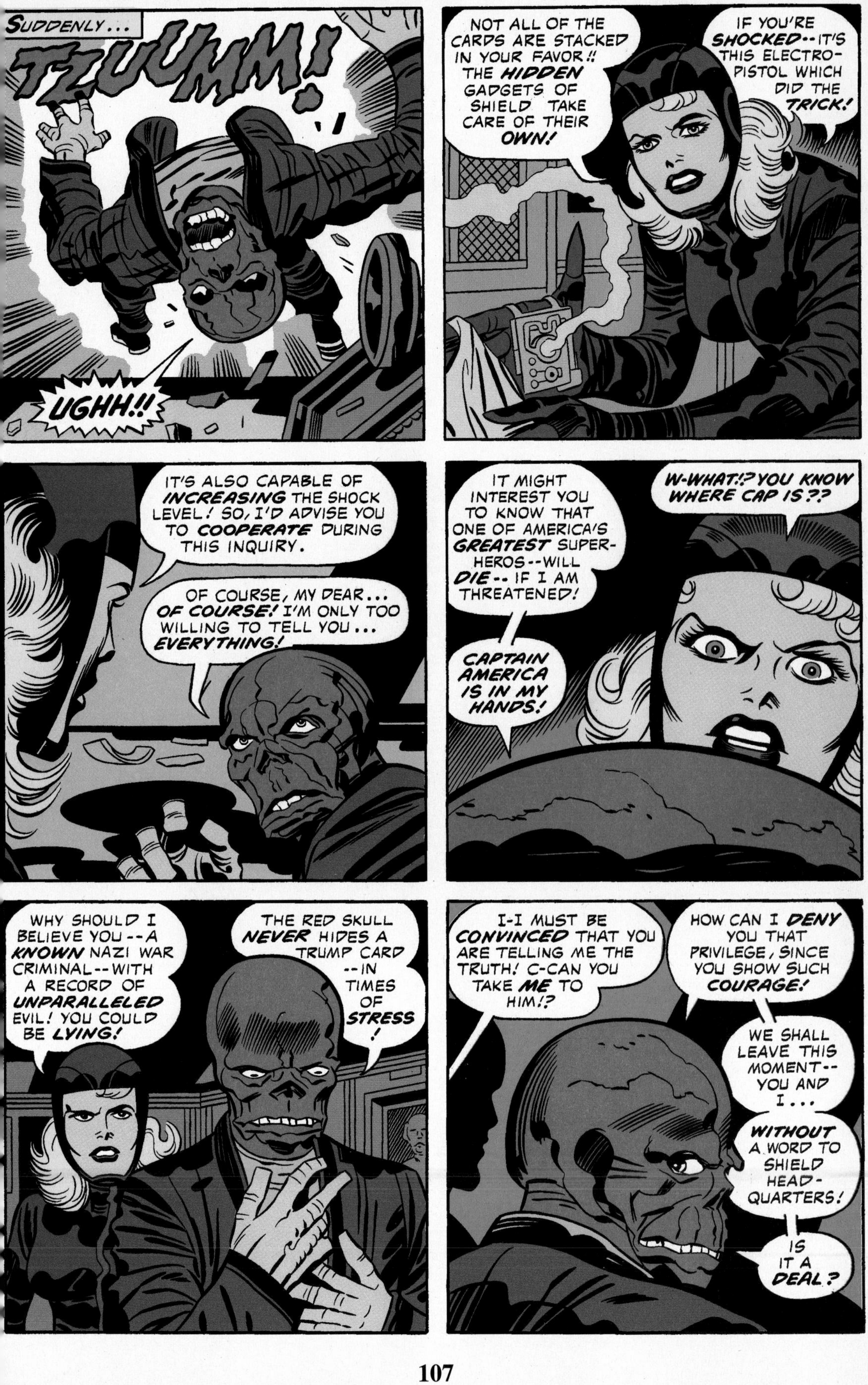
SUDDENLY...
TZUUMM!
UGHH!!
NOT ALL OF THE CARDS ARE STACKED IN YOUR FAVOR!! THE HIDDEN GADGETS OF SHIELD TAKE CARE OF THEIR OWN!
IF YOU'RE SHOCKED--IT'S THIS ELECTRO-PISTOL WHICH DID THE TRICK!
IT'S ALSO CAPABLE OF INCREASING THE SHOCK LEVEL! SO, I'D ADVISE YOU TO COOPERATE DURING THIS INQUIRY.
OF COURSE, MY DEAR... OF COURSE! I'M ONLY TOO WILLING TO TELL YOU... EVERYTHING!
IT MIGHT INTEREST YOU TO KNOW THAT ONE OF AMERICA'S GREATEST SUPER-HEROS--WILL DIE--IF I AM THREATENED!
CAPTAIN AMERICA IS IN MY HANDS!
W-WHAT!? YOU KNOW WHERE CAP IS??
WHY SHOULD I BELIEVE YOU--A KNOWN NAZI WAR CRIMINAL--WITH A RECORD OF UNPARALLELED EVIL! YOU COULD BE LYING!
THE RED SKULL NEVER HIDES A TRUMP CARD--IN TIMES OF STRESS!
I-I MUST BE CONVINCED THAT YOU ARE TELLING ME THE TRUTH! C-CAN YOU TAKE ME TO HIM!?
HOW CAN I DENY YOU THAT PRIVILEGE, SINCE YOU SHOW SUCH COURAGE!
WE SHALL LEAVE THIS MOMENT--YOU AND I...
WITHOUT A WORD TO SHIELD HEAD-QUARTERS!
IS IT A DEAL?

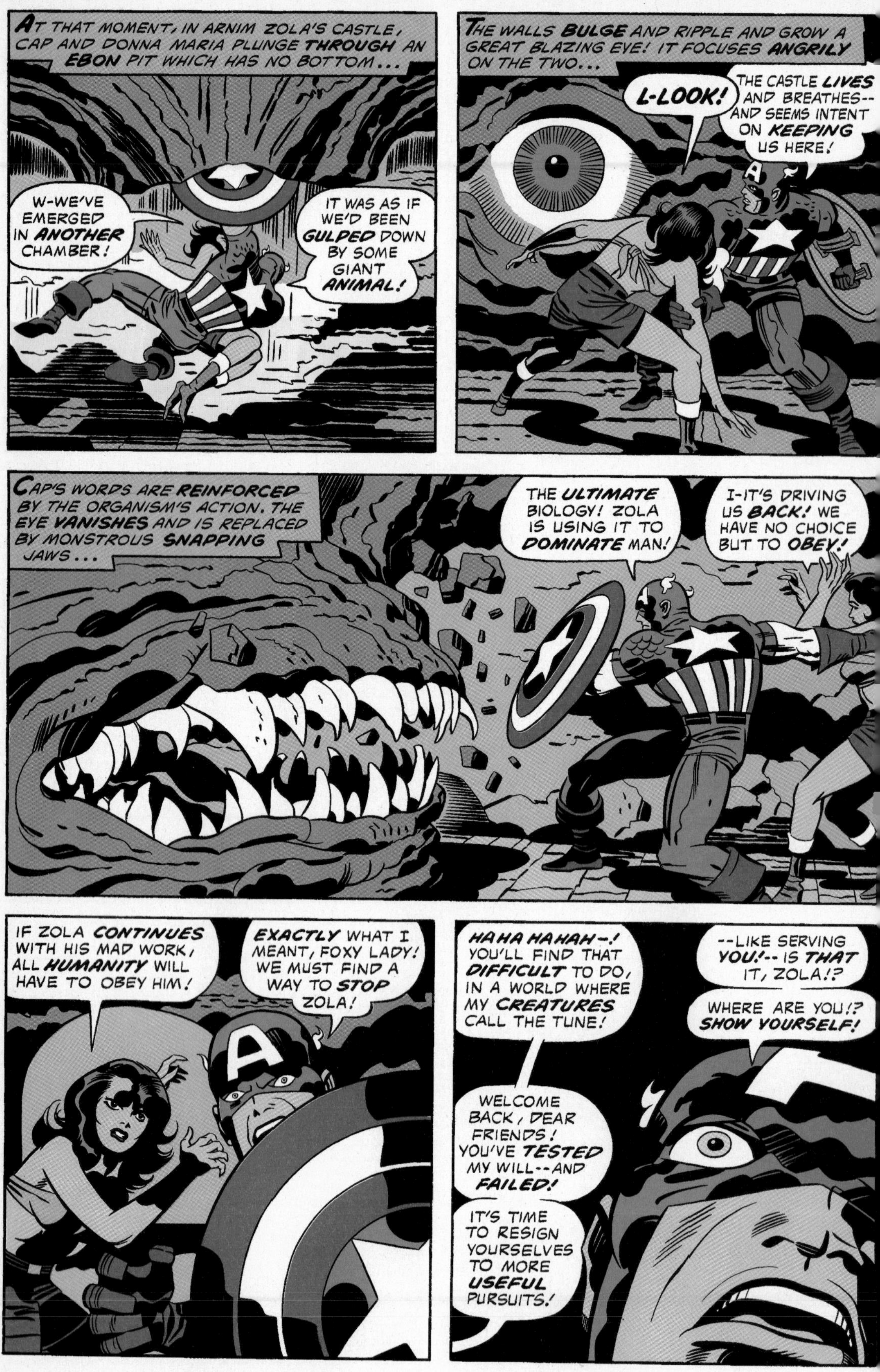
AT THAT MOMENT, IN ARNIM ZOLA'S CASTLE, CAP AND DONNA MARIA PLUNGE THROUGH AN EBON PIT WHICH HAS NO BOTTOM...
W-WE'VE EMERGED IN ANOTHER CHAMBER!
IT WAS AS IF WE'D BEEN GULPED DOWN BY SOME GIANT ANIMAL!
THE WALLS BULGE AND RIPPLE AND GROW A GREAT BLAZING EYE! IT FOCUSES ANGRILY ON THE TWO...
L-LOOK!
THE CASTLE LIVES AND BREATHES--AND SEEMS INTENT ON KEEPING US HERE!
CAP'S WORDS ARE REINFORCED BY THE ORGANISM'S ACTION. THE EYE VANISHES AND IS REPLACED BY MONSTROUS SNAPPING JAWS...
THE ULTIMATE BIOLOGY! ZOLA IS USING IT TO DOMINATE MAN!
I-IT'S DRIVING US BACK! WE HAVE NO CHOICE BUT TO OBEY!
IF ZOLA CONTINUES WITH HIS MAD WORK, ALL HUMANITY WILL HAVE TO OBEY HIM!
EXACTLY WHAT I MEANT, FOXY LADY! WE MUST FIND A WAY TO STOP ZOLA!
HAHA HAHAH--! YOU'LL FIND THAT DIFFICULT TO DO, IN A WORLD WHERE MY CREATURES CALL THE TUNE!
--LIKE SERVING YOU!-- IS THAT IT, ZOLA!?
WHERE ARE YOU!? SHOW YOURSELF!
WELCOME BACK, DEAR FRIENDS! YOU'VE TESTED MY WILL--AND FAILED!
IT'S TIME TO RESIGN YOURSELVES TO MORE USEFUL PURSUITS!

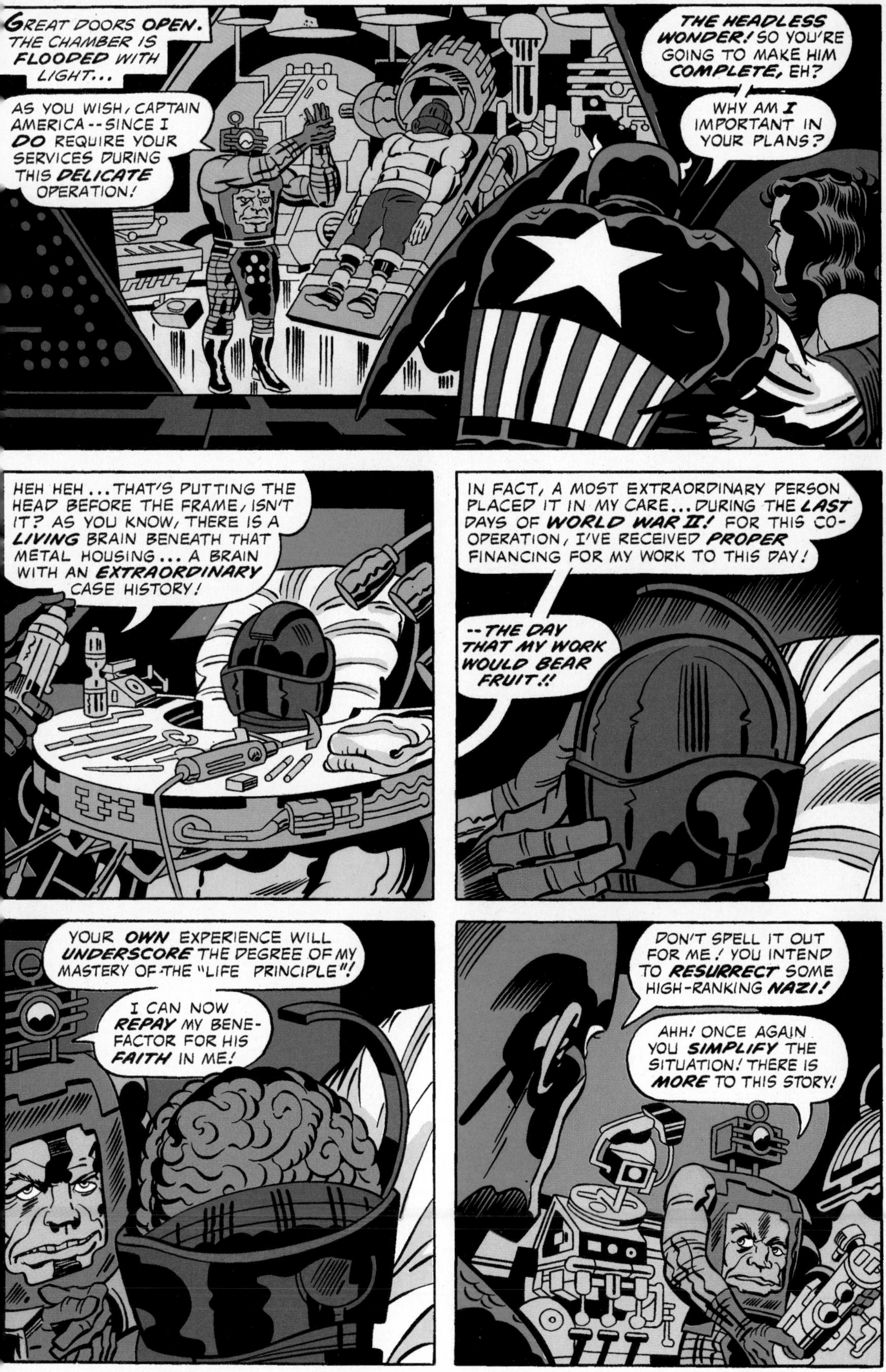
GREAT DOORS OPEN. THE CHAMBER IS FLOODED WITH LIGHT...
AS YOU WISH, CAPTAIN AMERICA--SINCE I DO REQUIRE YOUR SERVICES DURING THIS DELICATE OPERATION!
THE HEADLESS WONDER! SO YOU'RE GOING TO MAKE HIM COMPLETE, EH?
WHY AM I IMPORTANT IN YOUR PLANS?
HEH HEH...THAT'S PUTTING THE HEAD BEFORE THE FRAME, ISN'T IT? AS YOU KNOW, THERE IS A LIVING BRAIN BENEATH THAT METAL HOUSING... A BRAIN WITH AN EXTRAORDINARY CASE HISTORY!
IN FACT, A MOST EXTRAORDINARY PERSON PLACED IT IN MY CARE...DURING THE LAST DAYS OF WORLD WAR II! FOR THIS CO-OPERATION, I'VE RECEIVED PROPER FINANCING FOR MY WORK TO THIS DAY!
--THE DAY THAT MY WORK WOULD BEAR FRUIT!!
YOUR OWN EXPERIENCE WILL UNDERSCORE THE DEGREE OF MY MASTERY OF THE "LIFE PRINCIPLE"!
I CAN NOW REPAY MY BENEFACTOR FOR HIS FAITH IN ME!
DON'T SPELL IT OUT FOR ME! YOU INTEND TO RESURRECT SOME HIGH-RANKING NAZI!
AHH! ONCE AGAIN YOU SIMPLIFY THE SITUATION! THERE IS MORE TO THIS STORY!

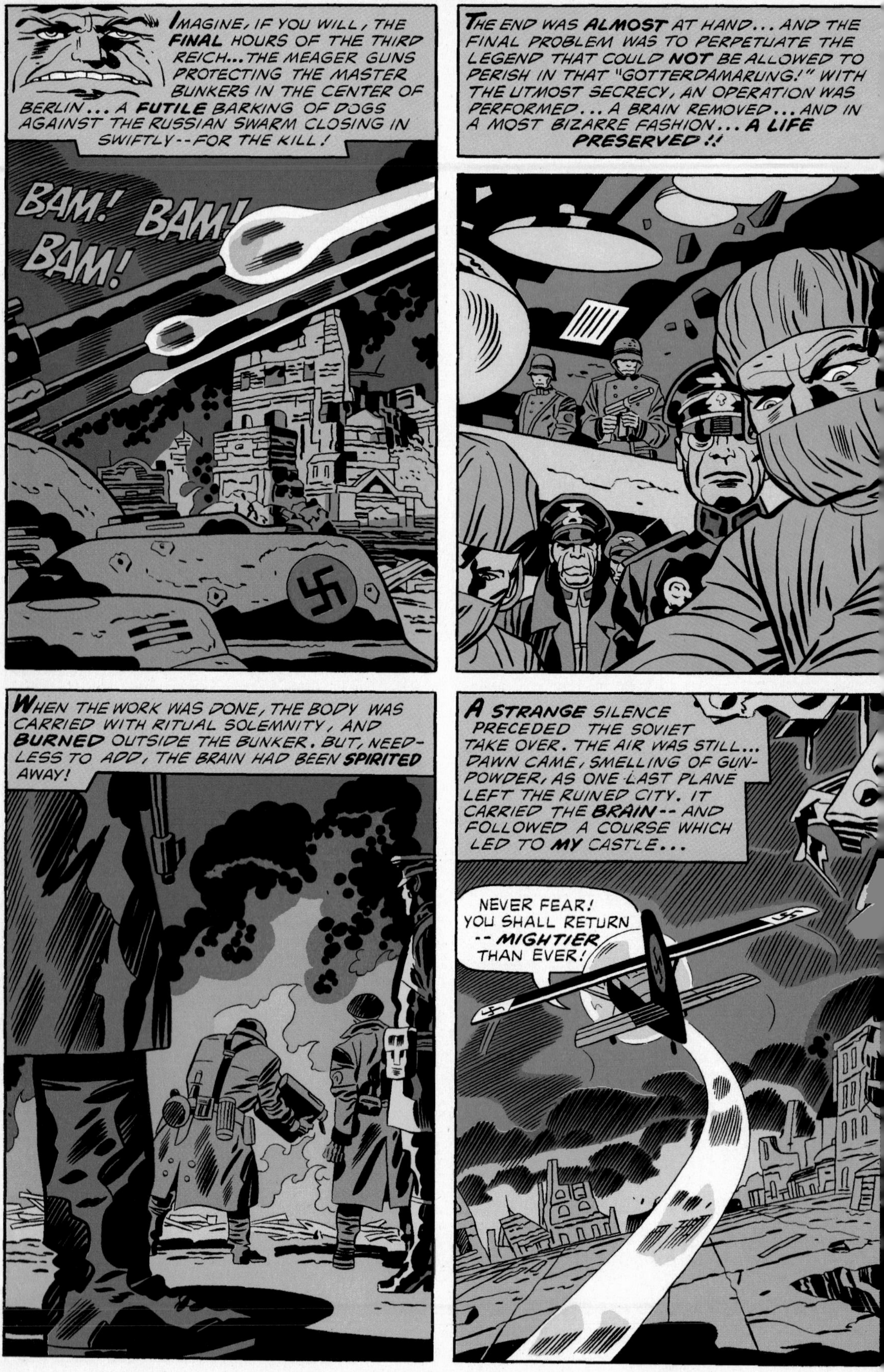
IMAGINE, IF YOU WILL, THE FINAL HOURS OF THE THIRD REICH...THE MEAGER GUNS PROTECTING THE MASTER BUNKERS IN THE CENTER OF BERLIN... A FUTILE BARKING OF DOGS AGAINST THE RUSSIAN SWARM CLOSING IN SWIFTLY--FOR THE KILL!
BAM! BAM! BAM!
THE END WAS ALMOST AT HAND... AND THE FINAL PROBLEM WAS TO PERPETUATE THE LEGEND THAT COULD NOT BE ALLOWED TO PERISH IN THAT "GOTTERDAMARUNG!" WITH THE UTMOST SECRECY, AN OPERATION WAS PERFORMED... A BRAIN REMOVED... AND IN A MOST BIZARRE FASHION... A LIFE PRESERVED!!
WHEN THE WORK WAS DONE, THE BODY WAS CARRIED WITH RITUAL SOLEMNITY, AND BURNED OUTSIDE THE BUNKER. BUT, NEEDLESS TO ADD, THE BRAIN HAD BEEN SPIRITED AWAY!
A STRANGE SILENCE PRECEDED THE SOVIET TAKE OVER. THE AIR WAS STILL... DAWN CAME, SMELLING OF GUN-POWDER, AS ONE LAST PLANE LEFT THE RUINED CITY. IT CARRIED THE BRAIN-- AND FOLLOWED A COURSE WHICH LED TO MY CASTLE...
NEVER FEAR! YOU SHALL RETURN --MIGHTIER THAN EVER!

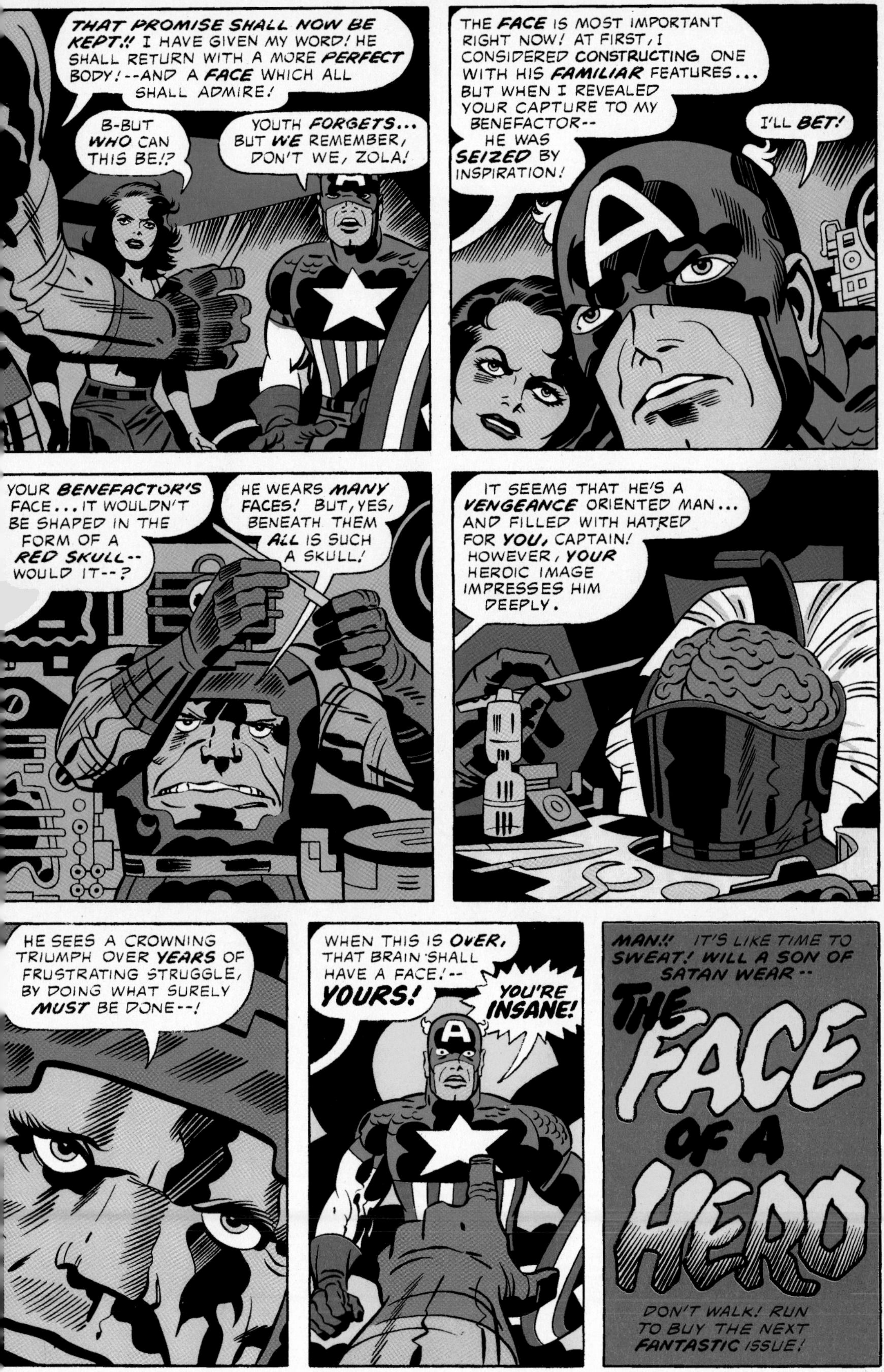

THAT PROMISE SHALL NOW BE KEPT!! I HAVE GIVEN MY WORD! HE SHALL RETURN WITH A MORE PERFECT BODY! --AND A FACE WHICH ALL SHALL ADMIRE!
B-BUT WHO CAN THIS BE!?
YOUTH FORGETS... BUT WE REMEMBER, DON'T WE, ZOLA!
THE FACE IS MOST IMPORTANT RIGHT NOW! AT FIRST, I CONSIDERED CONSTRUCTING ONE WITH HIS FAMILIAR FEATURES... BUT WHEN I REVEALED YOUR CAPTURE TO MY BENEFACTOR-- HE WAS SEIZED BY INSPIRATION!
I'LL BET!
YOUR BENEFACTOR'S FACE... IT WOULDN'T BE SHAPED IN THE FORM OF A RED SKULL-- WOULD IT--?
HE WEARS MANY FACES! BUT, YES, BENEATH THEM ALL IS SUCH A SKULL!
IT SEEMS THAT HE'S A VENGEANCE ORIENTED MAN... AND FILLED WITH HATRED FOR YOU, CAPTAIN! HOWEVER, YOUR HEROIC IMAGE IMPRESSES HIM DEEPLY.
HE SEES A CROWNING TRIUMPH OVER YEARS OF FRUSTRATING STRUGGLE, BY DOING WHAT SURELY MUST BE DONE--!
WHEN THIS IS OVER, THAT BRAIN SHALL HAVE A FACE! -- YOURS!
YOU'RE INSANE!
MAN!! IT'S LIKE TIME TO SWEAT! WILL A SON OF SATAN WEAR --
THE FACE OF A HERO
DON'T WALK! RUN TO BUY THE NEXT FANTASTIC ISSUE!

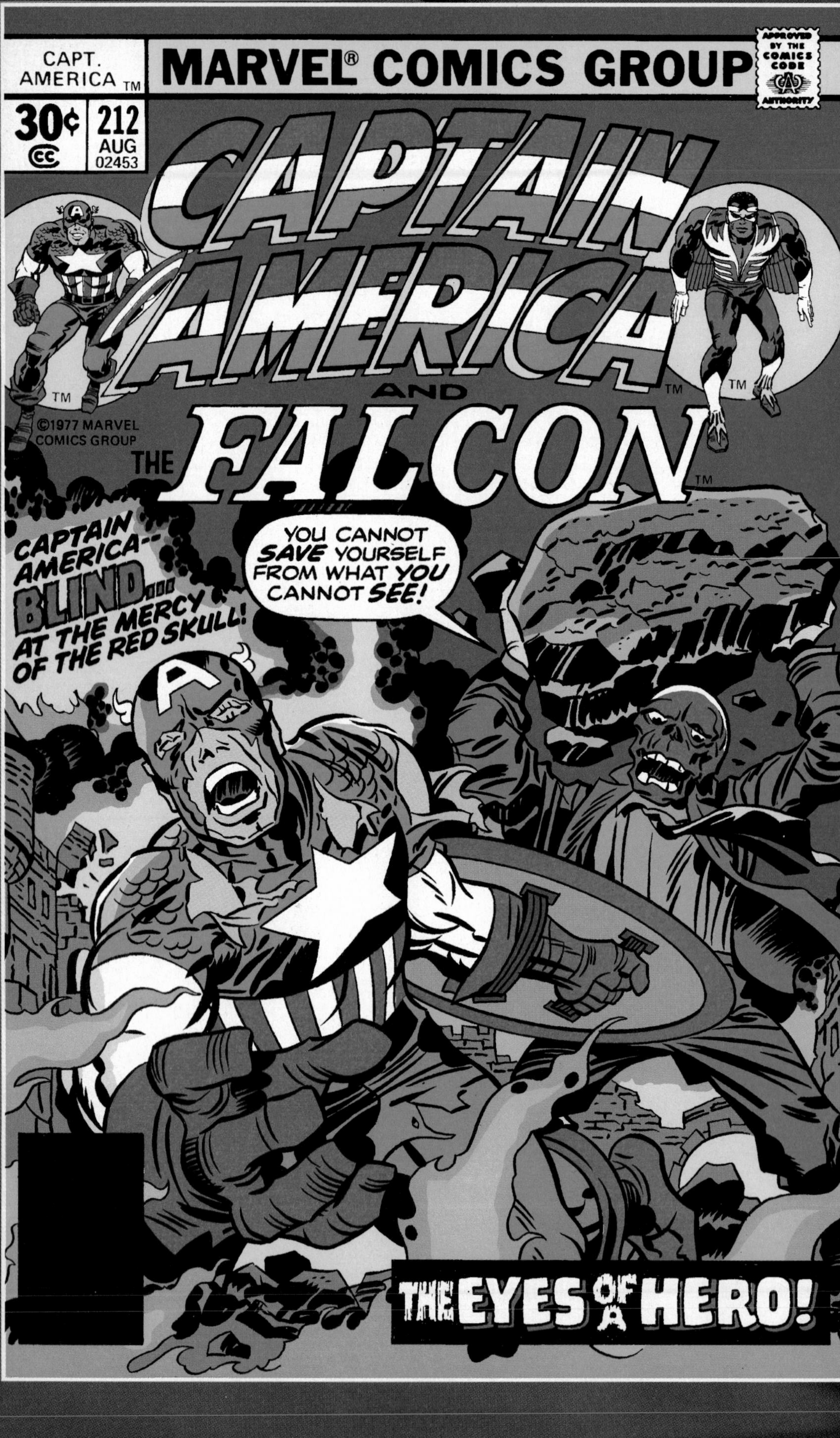
CAPT. AMERICA TM
MARVEL® COMICS GROUP
APPROVED BY THE COMICS CODE AUTHORITY
30¢
212 AUG 02453
CAPTAIN AMERICA AND THE FALCON
©1977 MARVEL COMICS GROUP
CAPTAIN AMERICA-- BLIND... AT THE MERCY OF THE RED SKULL!
YOU CANNOT SAVE YOURSELF FROM WHAT YOU CANNOT SEE!
THE EYES OF A HERO!

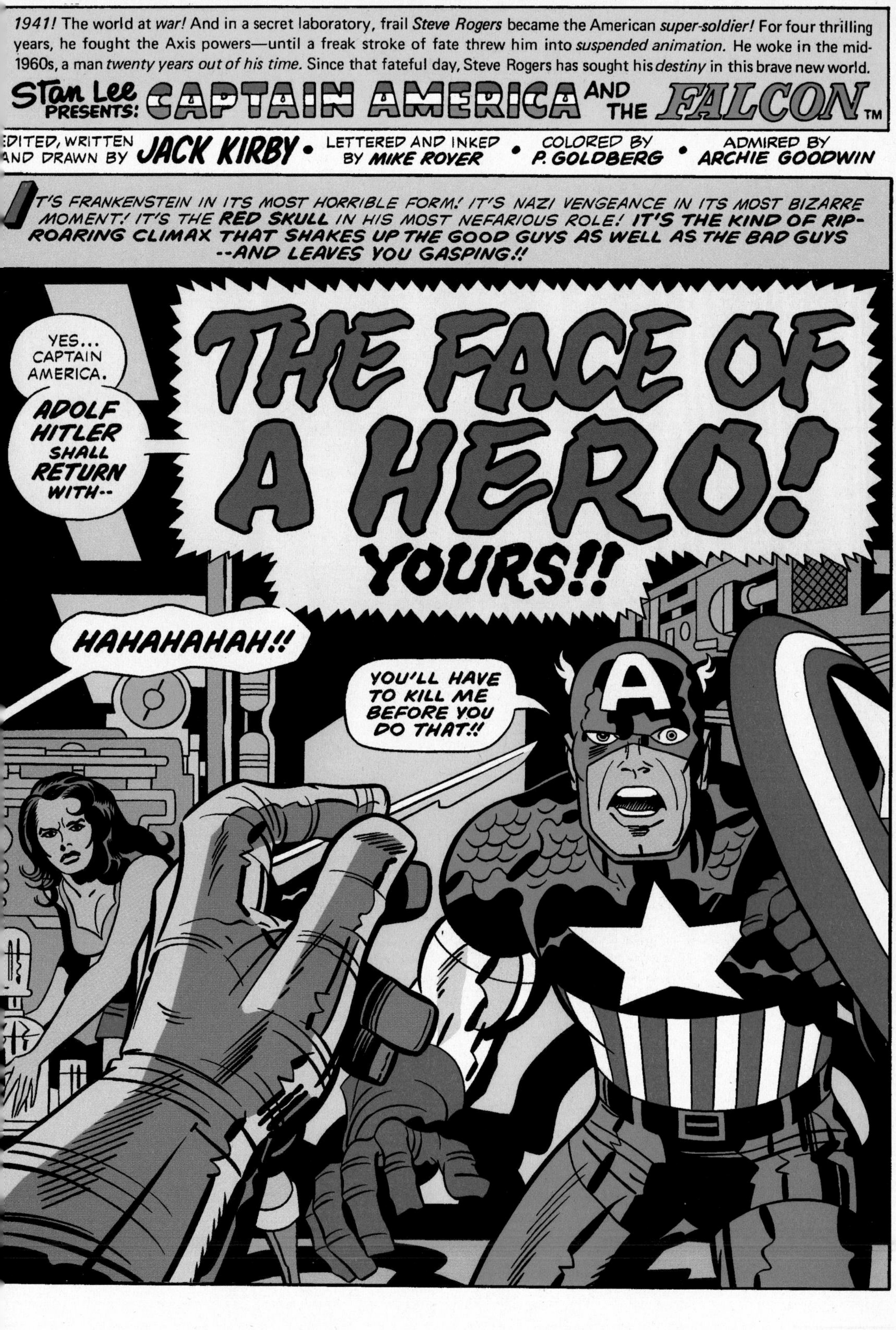
1941! The world at war! And in a secret laboratory, frail Steve Rogers became the American super-soldier! For four thrilling years, he fought the Axis powers—until a freak stroke of fate threw him into suspended animation. He woke in the mid-1960s, a man twenty years out of his time. Since that fateful day, Steve Rogers has sought his destiny in this brave new world.
Stan Lee PRESENTS: CAPTAIN AMERICA AND THE FALCON TM
EDITED, WRITTEN AND DRAWN BY JACK KIRBY • LETTERED AND INKED BY MIKE ROYER • COLORED BY P. GOLDBERG • ADMIRED BY ARCHIE GOODWIN
IT'S FRANKENSTEIN IN ITS MOST HORRIBLE FORM! IT'S NAZI VENGEANCE IN ITS MOST BIZARRE MOMENT! IT'S THE RED SKULL IN HIS MOST NEFARIOUS ROLE! IT'S THE KIND OF RIP-ROARING CLIMAX THAT SHAKES UP THE GOOD GUYS AS WELL AS THE BAD GUYS --AND LEAVES YOU GASPING!!
THE FACE OF A HERO!
YES... CAPTAIN AMERICA.
ADOLF HITLER SHALL RETURN WITH--
YOURS!!
HAHAHAHAH!!
YOU'LL HAVE TO KILL ME BEFORE YOU DO THAT!!

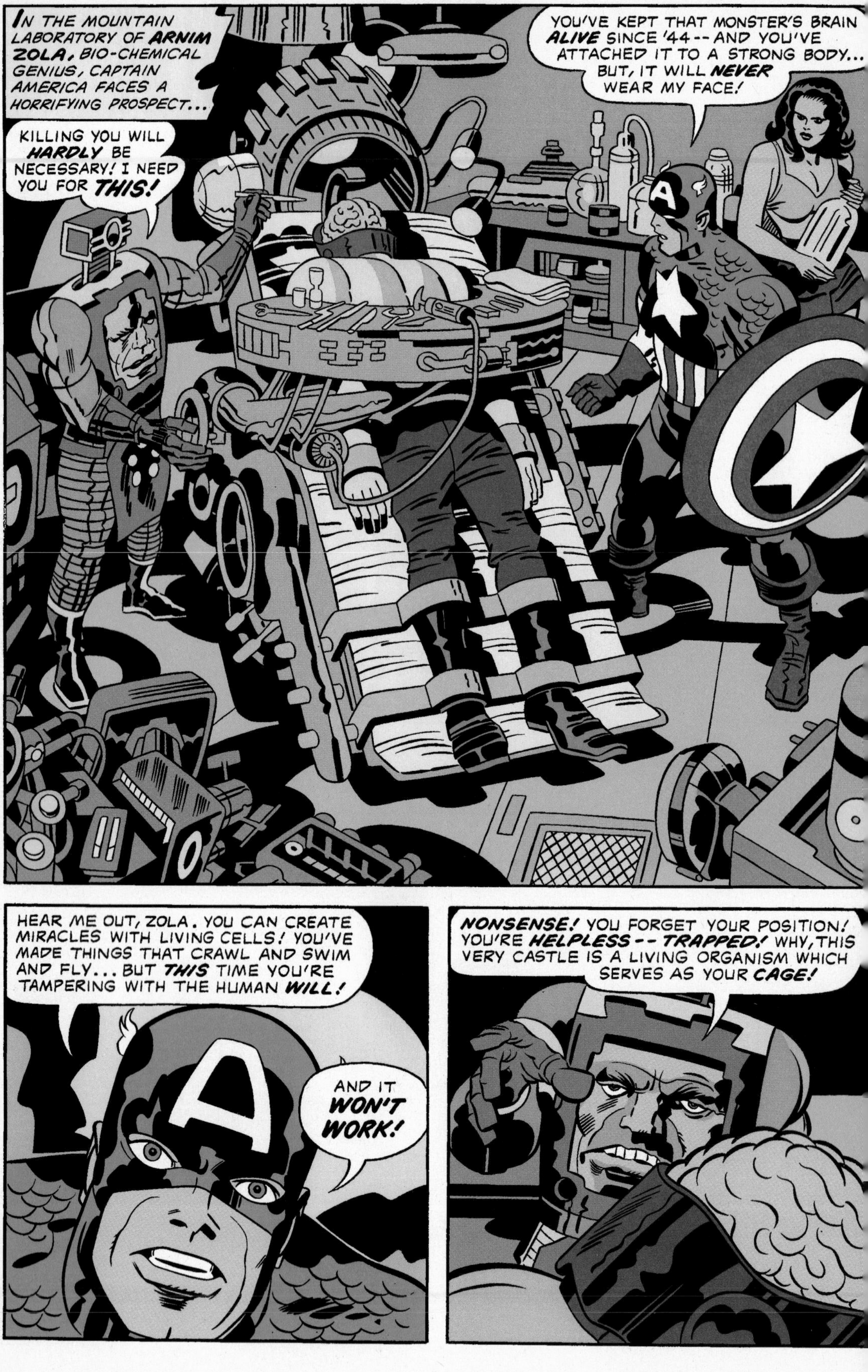
IN THE MOUNTAIN LABORATORY OF ARNIM ZOLA, BIO-CHEMICAL GENIUS, CAPTAIN AMERICA FACES A HORRIFYING PROSPECT...
YOU'VE KEPT THAT MONSTER'S BRAIN ALIVE SINCE '44 -- AND YOU'VE ATTACHED IT TO A STRONG BODY... BUT, IT WILL NEVER WEAR MY FACE!
KILLING YOU WILL HARDLY BE NECESSARY! I NEED YOU FOR THIS!
HEAR ME OUT, ZOLA. YOU CAN CREATE MIRACLES WITH LIVING CELLS! YOU'VE MADE THINGS THAT CRAWL AND SWIM AND FLY... BUT THIS TIME YOU'RE TAMPERING WITH THE HUMAN WILL!
AND IT WON'T WORK!
NONSENSE! YOU FORGET YOUR POSITION! YOU'RE HELPLESS -- TRAPPED! WHY, THIS VERY CASTLE IS A LIVING ORGANISM WHICH SERVES AS YOUR CAGE!

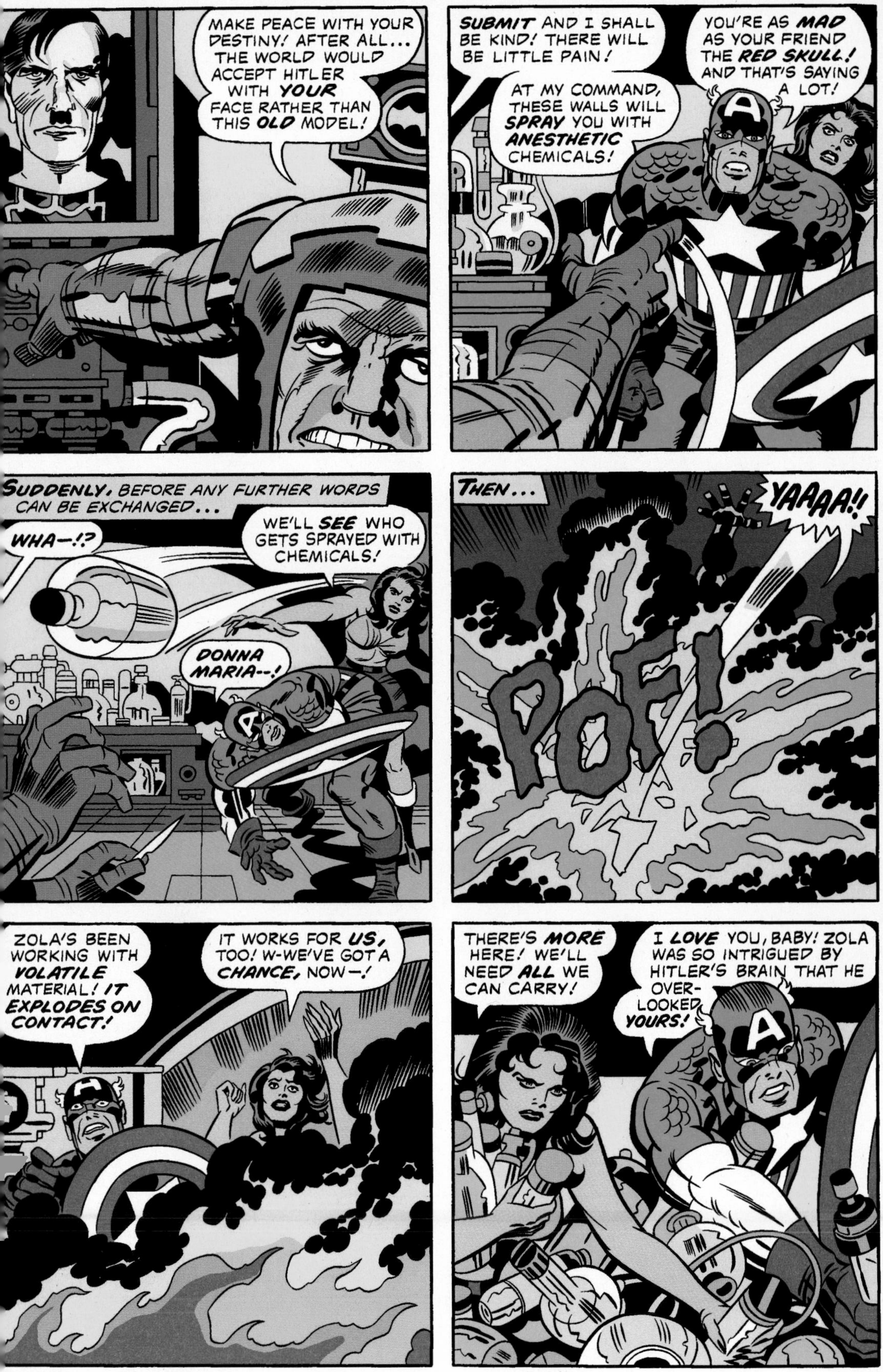
MAKE PEACE WITH YOUR DESTINY! AFTER ALL... THE WORLD WOULD ACCEPT HITLER WITH YOUR FACE RATHER THAN THIS OLD MODEL!
SUBMIT AND I SHALL BE KIND! THERE WILL BE LITTLE PAIN!
AT MY COMMAND, THESE WALLS WILL SPRAY YOU WITH ANESTHETIC CHEMICALS!
YOU'RE AS MAD AS YOUR FRIEND THE RED SKULL! AND THAT'S SAYING A LOT!
SUDDENLY, BEFORE ANY FURTHER WORDS CAN BE EXCHANGED...
WHA--!?
WE'LL SEE WHO GETS SPRAYED WITH CHEMICALS!
DONNA MARIA--!
THEN...
YAAAAA!!
POF!
ZOLA'S BEEN WORKING WITH VOLATILE MATERIAL! IT EXPLODES ON CONTACT!
IT WORKS FOR US, TOO! W-WE'VE GOT A CHANCE, NOW--!
THERE'S MORE HERE! WE'LL NEED ALL WE CAN CARRY!
I LOVE YOU, BABY! ZOLA WAS SO INTRIGUED BY HITLER'S BRAIN THAT HE OVER-LOOKED YOURS!

SAY THAT *AGAIN*... YOU KNOW...THE PART ABOUT *"I LOVE YOU, BABY!"*

NOW LOOK, DONNA MARIA...THIS IS *NOT* A MOONLIT PARK, AND WE'RE *NOT* OUT FOR A STROLL!

LET'S GET OUTTA HERE!!

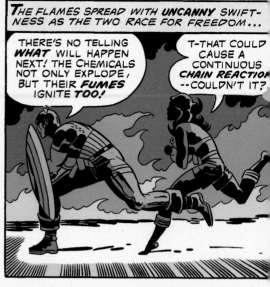

THE FLAMES SPREAD WITH UNCANNY SWIFTNESS AS THE TWO RACE FOR FREEDOM...

THERE'S NO TELLING *WHAT* WILL HAPPEN NEXT! THE CHEMICALS NOT ONLY EXPLODE, BUT THEIR *FUMES* IGNITE *TOO!*

T-THAT COULD CAUSE A CONTINUOUS *CHAIN REACTION* --COULDN'T IT?

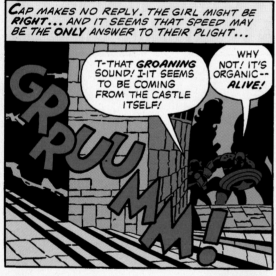

CAP MAKES NO REPLY. THE GIRL MIGHT BE RIGHT... AND IT SEEMS THAT SPEED MAY BE THE ONLY ANSWER TO THEIR PLIGHT...

T-THAT *GROANING* SOUND! I-IT SEEMS TO BE COMING FROM THE CASTLE ITSELF!

WHY NOT! IT'S ORGANIC-- *ALIVE!*

GRRUUMM!

AT THAT MOMENT, A ROCKET PLANE DROPS FROM ORBITAL FLIGHT AND HURTLES TOWARD THE SWISS ALPS...

YOU'RE BEHAVING LIKE A *GENTLEMAN,* RED SKULL! I'M RATHER *SURPRISED!*

SURPRISE, MY DEAR SHARON, IS MY MOST *FAVORED* TACTIC!

THEN, OF COURSE... A DEAL *IS* A *DEAL!* I PROMISED TO TAKE YOU TO CAPTAIN AMERICA IF YOU *ABSTAINED* FROM INVITING ALL THE OTHER *SHIELD* AGENTS!

I'VE *KEPT* MY BARGAIN! WE'RE NOT BEING FOLLOWED! BUT...REMEMBER *THIS*--!

I'M *FULLY* ARMED! AND YOU'RE *NOT!* IF YOU MAKE *ONE* MOVE TO RATTLE ME I'LL--!

HOW *ADMIRABLE!* I OFTEN REGRET THAT THE NAZI PHILOSOPHY *EXCLUDES* THE STRENGTH OF WOMEN!

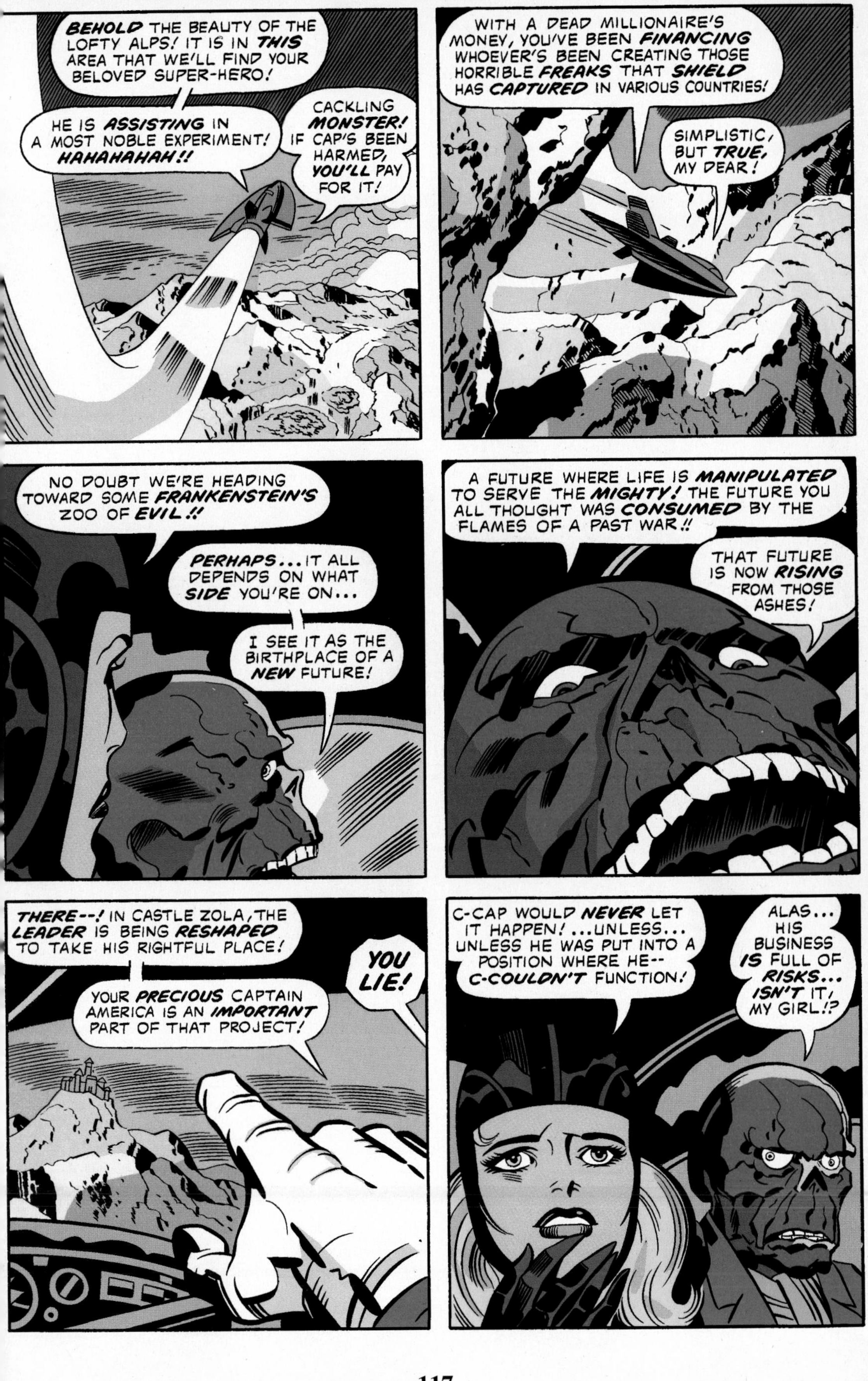

BEHOLD THE BEAUTY OF THE LOFTY ALPS! IT IS IN THIS AREA THAT WE'LL FIND YOUR BELOVED SUPER-HERO!
HE IS ASSISTING IN A MOST NOBLE EXPERIMENT! HAHAHAHAH!!
CACKLING MONSTER! IF CAP'S BEEN HARMED, YOU'LL PAY FOR IT!
WITH A DEAD MILLIONAIRE'S MONEY, YOU'VE BEEN FINANCING WHOEVER'S BEEN CREATING THOSE HORRIBLE FREAKS THAT SHIELD HAS CAPTURED IN VARIOUS COUNTRIES!
SIMPLISTIC, BUT TRUE, MY DEAR!
NO DOUBT WE'RE HEADING TOWARD SOME FRANKENSTEIN'S ZOO OF EVIL!!
PERHAPS...IT ALL DEPENDS ON WHAT SIDE YOU'RE ON...
I SEE IT AS THE BIRTHPLACE OF A NEW FUTURE!
A FUTURE WHERE LIFE IS MANIPULATED TO SERVE THE MIGHTY! THE FUTURE YOU ALL THOUGHT WAS CONSUMED BY THE FLAMES OF A PAST WAR!!
THAT FUTURE IS NOW RISING FROM THOSE ASHES!
THERE--! IN CASTLE ZOLA, THE LEADER IS BEING RESHAPED TO TAKE HIS RIGHTFUL PLACE!
YOUR PRECIOUS CAPTAIN AMERICA IS AN IMPORTANT PART OF THAT PROJECT!
YOU LIE!
C-CAP WOULD NEVER LET IT HAPPEN! ...UNLESS... UNLESS HE WAS PUT INTO A POSITION WHERE HE-- C-COULDN'T FUNCTION!
ALAS... HIS BUSINESS IS FULL OF RISKS... ISN'T IT, MY GIRL!?

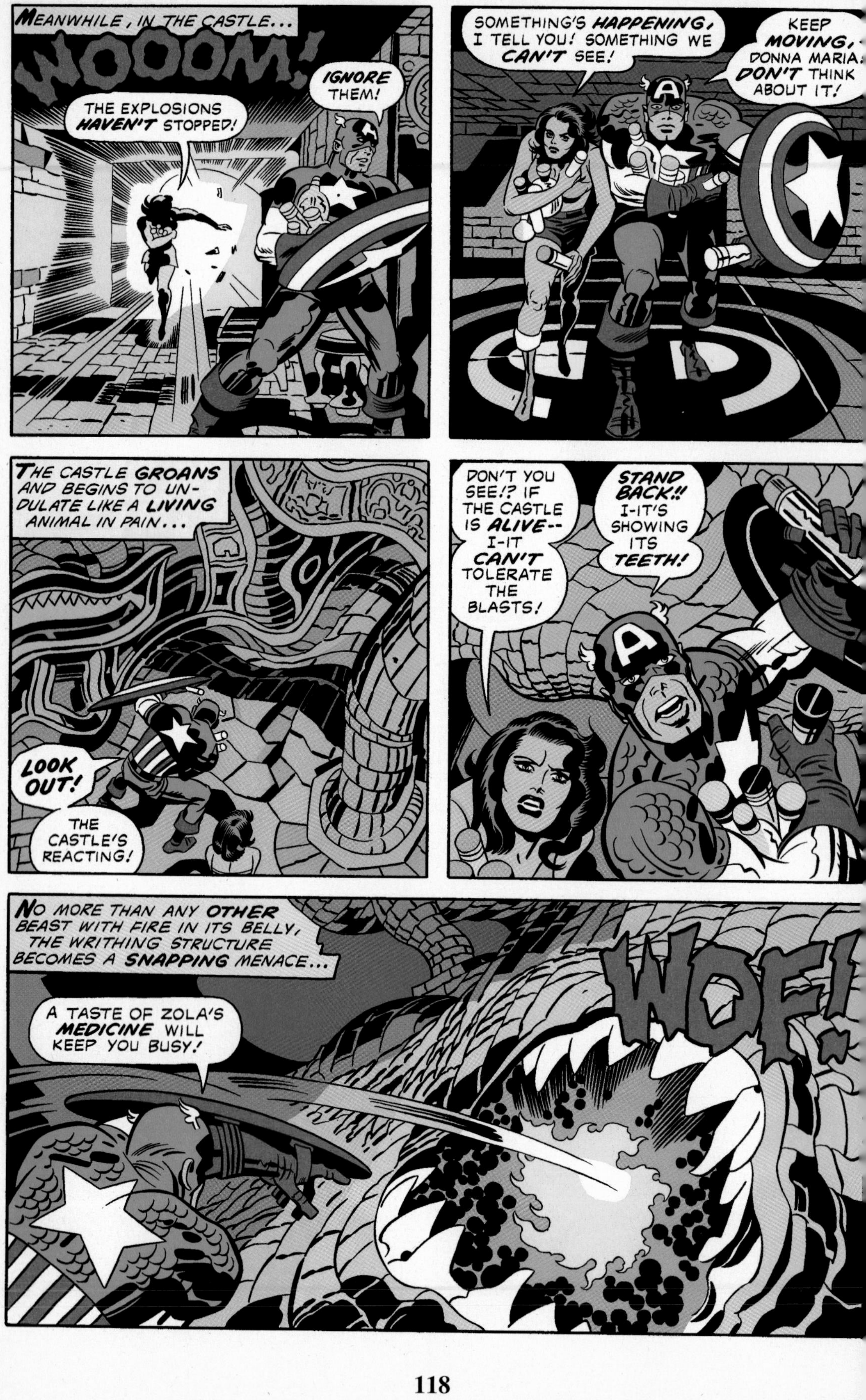

MEANWHILE, IN THE CASTLE...
WOOOM!
THE EXPLOSIONS HAVEN'T STOPPED!
IGNORE THEM!
SOMETHING'S HAPPENING, I TELL YOU! SOMETHING WE CAN'T SEE!
KEEP MOVING, DONNA MARIA! DON'T THINK ABOUT IT!
THE CASTLE GROANS AND BEGINS TO UN-DULATE LIKE A LIVING ANIMAL IN PAIN...
LOOK OUT!
THE CASTLE'S REACTING!
DON'T YOU SEE!? IF THE CASTLE IS ALIVE-- I-IT CAN'T TOLERATE THE BLASTS!
STAND BACK!! I-IT'S SHOWING ITS TEETH!
NO MORE THAN ANY OTHER BEAST WITH FIRE IN ITS BELLY, THE WRITHING STRUCTURE BECOMES A SNAPPING MENACE...
A TASTE OF ZOLA'S MEDICINE WILL KEEP YOU BUSY!
WOF!

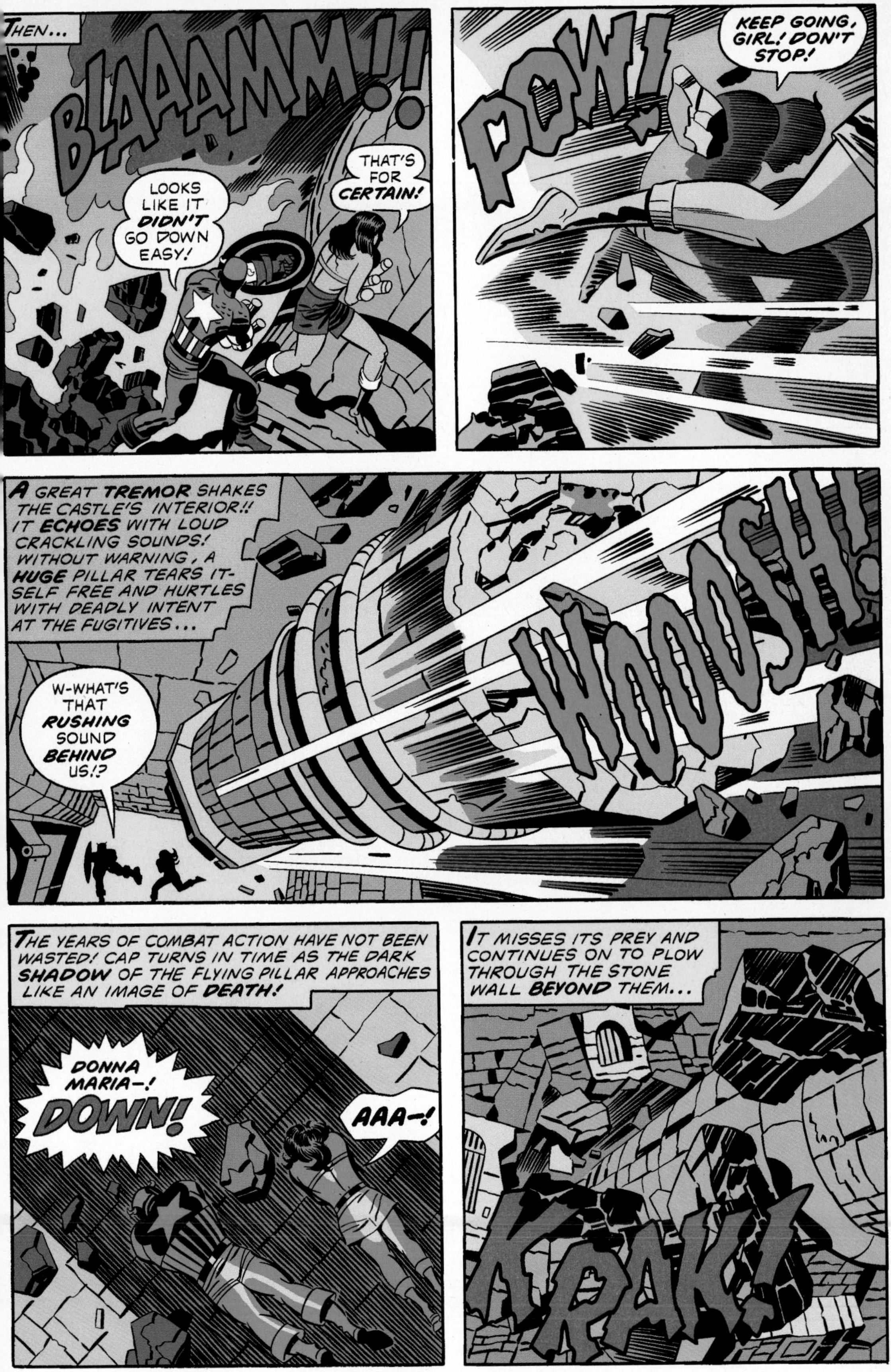
THEN...
BLAAAMM!!
LOOKS LIKE IT DIDN'T GO DOWN EASY!
THAT'S FOR CERTAIN!
POW!
KEEP GOING, GIRL! DON'T STOP!
A GREAT TREMOR SHAKES THE CASTLE'S INTERIOR!! IT ECHOES WITH LOUD CRACKLING SOUNDS! WITHOUT WARNING, A HUGE PILLAR TEARS IT-SELF FREE AND HURTLES WITH DEADLY INTENT AT THE FUGITIVES...
WOOOSH!
W-WHAT'S THAT RUSHING SOUND BEHIND US!?
THE YEARS OF COMBAT ACTION HAVE NOT BEEN WASTED! CAP TURNS IN TIME AS THE DARK SHADOW OF THE FLYING PILLAR APPROACHES LIKE AN IMAGE OF DEATH!
DONNA MARIA--! DOWN!
AAA--!
IT MISSES ITS PREY AND CONTINUES ON TO PLOW THROUGH THE STONE WALL BEYOND THEM...
KRAK!

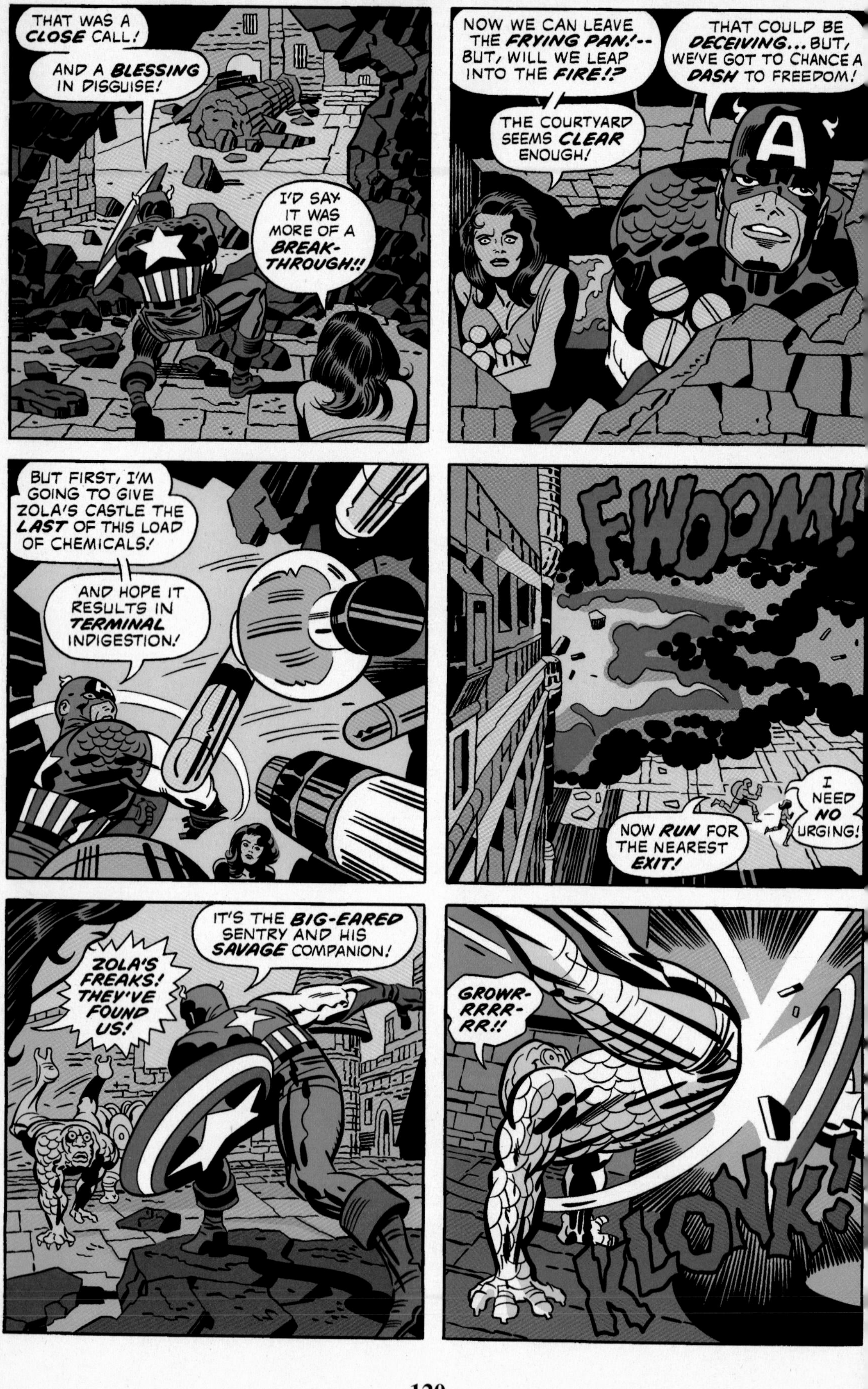
THAT WAS A CLOSE CALL!
AND A BLESSING IN DISGUISE!
I'D SAY IT WAS MORE OF A BREAK-THROUGH!!
NOW WE CAN LEAVE THE FRYING PAN!-- BUT, WILL WE LEAP INTO THE FIRE!?
THE COURTYARD SEEMS CLEAR ENOUGH!
THAT COULD BE DECEIVING... BUT, WE'VE GOT TO CHANCE A DASH TO FREEDOM!
BUT FIRST, I'M GOING TO GIVE ZOLA'S CASTLE THE LAST OF THIS LOAD OF CHEMICALS!
AND HOPE IT RESULTS IN TERMINAL INDIGESTION!
FWOOM!
NOW RUN FOR THE NEAREST EXIT!
I NEED NO URGING!
ZOLA'S FREAKS! THEY'VE FOUND US!
IT'S THE BIG-EARED SENTRY AND HIS SAVAGE COMPANION!
GROWR-RRRR-RR!!
KLONK!

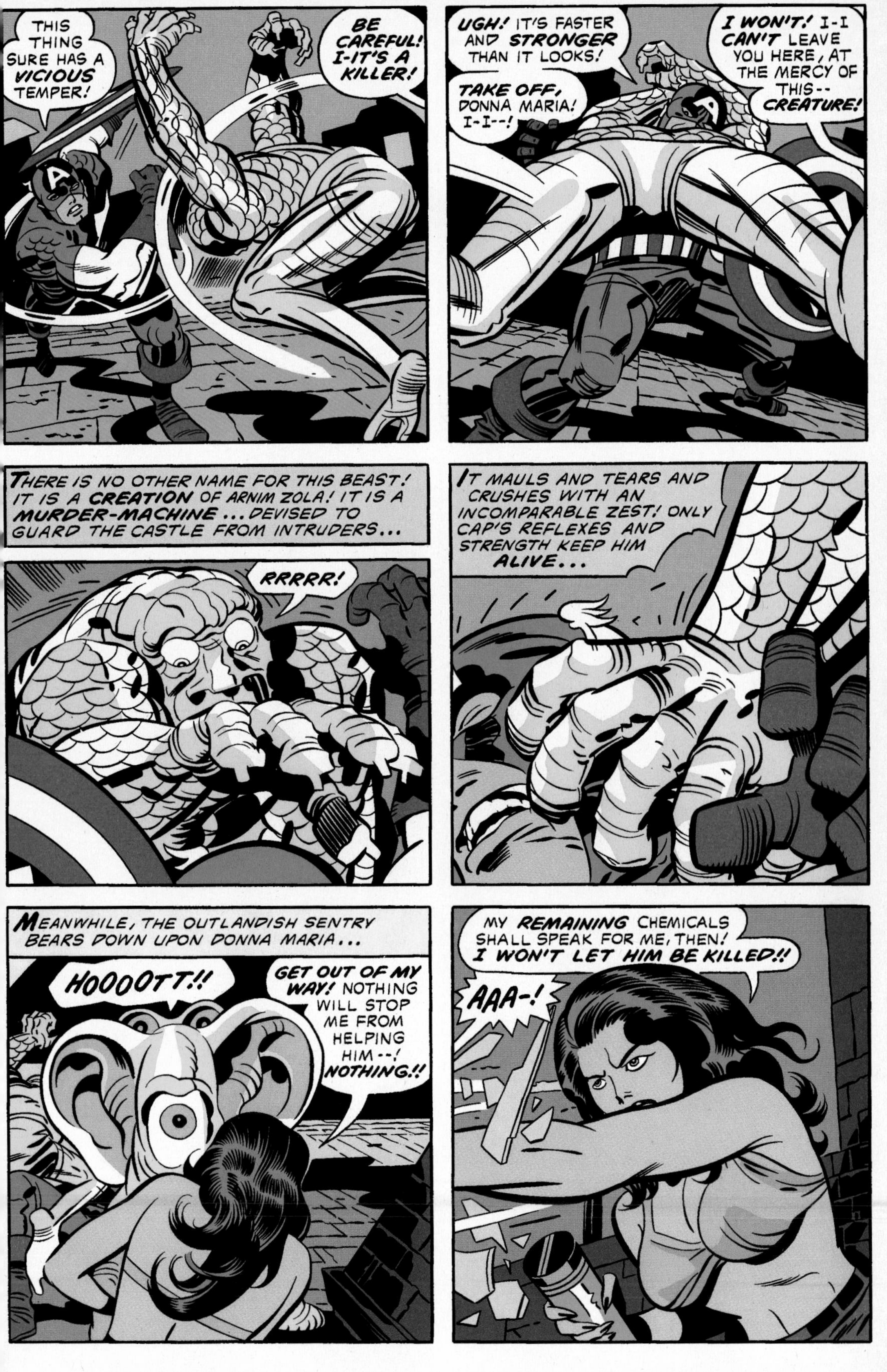

THIS THING SURE HAS A VICIOUS TEMPER!
BE CAREFUL! I-IT'S A KILLER!
UGH! IT'S FASTER AND STRONGER THAN IT LOOKS!
TAKE OFF, DONNA MARIA! I-I--!
I WON'T! I-I CAN'T LEAVE YOU HERE, AT THE MERCY OF THIS--CREATURE!
THERE IS NO OTHER NAME FOR THIS BEAST! IT IS A CREATION OF ARNIM ZOLA! IT IS A MURDER-MACHINE ... DEVISED TO GUARD THE CASTLE FROM INTRUDERS...
RRRRR!
IT MAULS AND TEARS AND CRUSHES WITH AN INCOMPARABLE ZEST! ONLY CAP'S REFLEXES AND STRENGTH KEEP HIM ALIVE...
MEANWHILE, THE OUTLANDISH SENTRY BEARS DOWN UPON DONNA MARIA...
HOOOOTT!!
GET OUT OF MY WAY! NOTHING WILL STOP ME FROM HELPING HIM--! NOTHING!!
MY REMAINING CHEMICALS SHALL SPEAK FOR ME, THEN! I WON'T LET HIM BE KILLED!!
AAA-!

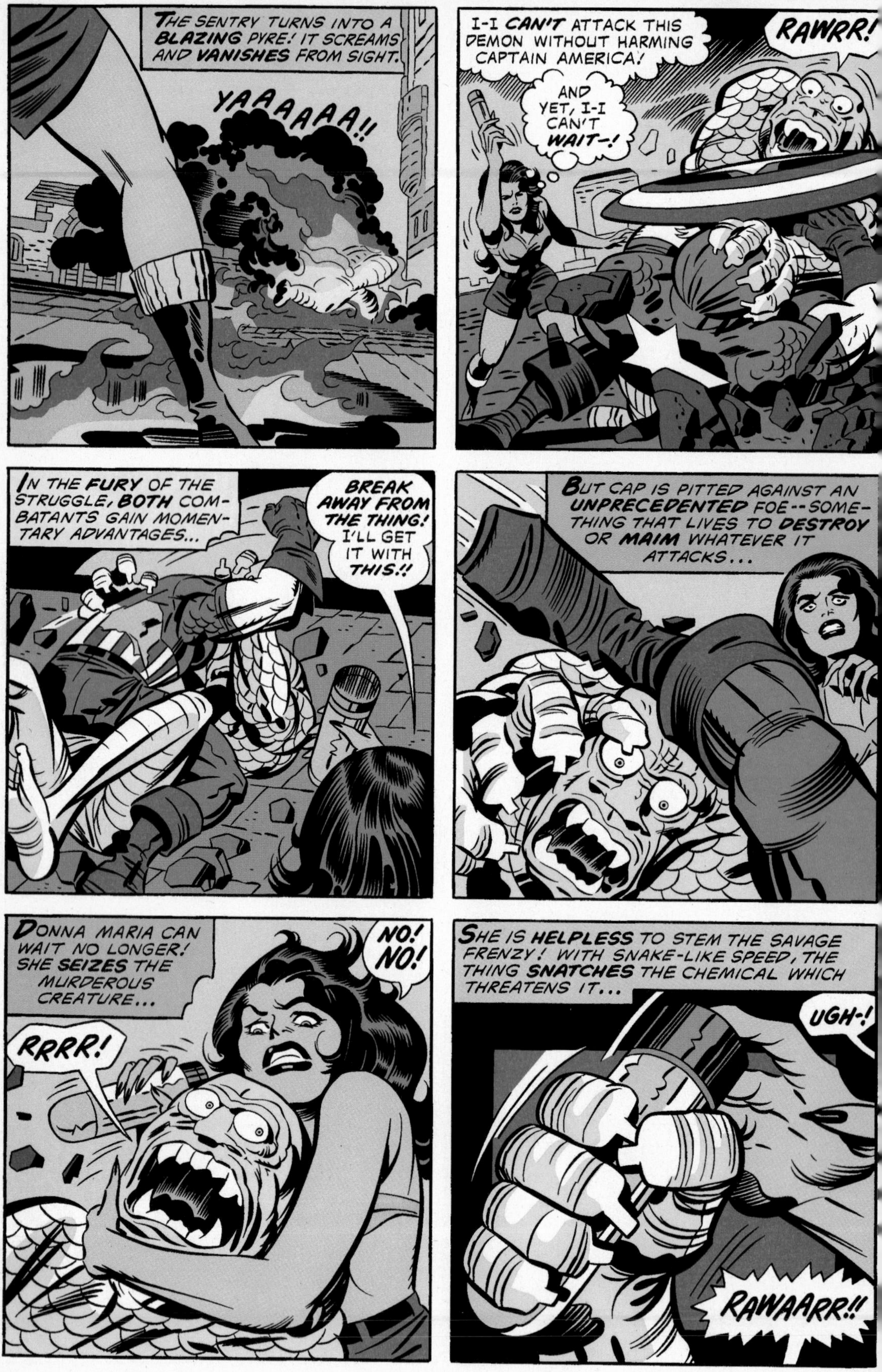

THE SENTRY TURNS INTO A BLAZING PYRE! IT SCREAMS AND VANISHES FROM SIGHT.
YAAAAAAA!!
I-I CAN'T ATTACK THIS DEMON WITHOUT HARMING CAPTAIN AMERICA!
RAWRR!
AND YET, I-I CAN'T WAIT--!
IN THE FURY OF THE STRUGGLE, BOTH COMBATANTS GAIN MOMENTARY ADVANTAGES...
BREAK AWAY FROM THE THING! I'LL GET IT WITH THIS!!
BUT CAP IS PITTED AGAINST AN UNPRECEDENTED FOE--SOMETHING THAT LIVES TO DESTROY OR MAIM WHATEVER IT ATTACKS...
DONNA MARIA CAN WAIT NO LONGER! SHE SEIZES THE MURDEROUS CREATURE...
NO! NO!
RRRR!
SHE IS HELPLESS TO STEM THE SAVAGE FRENZY! WITH SNAKE-LIKE SPEED, THE THING SNATCHES THE CHEMICAL WHICH THREATENS IT...
UGH-!
RAWAARR!!

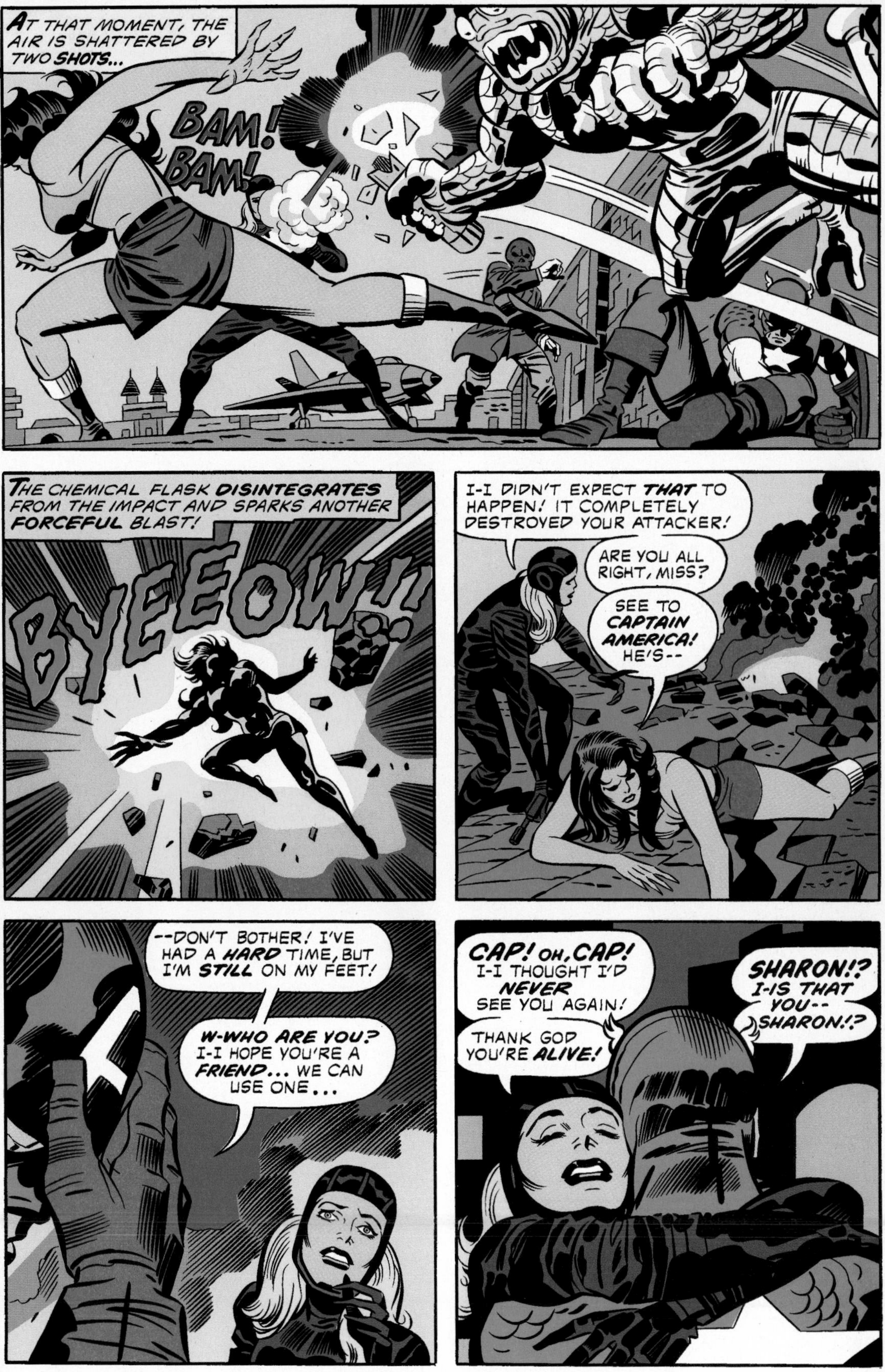
AT THAT MOMENT, THE AIR IS SHATTERED BY TWO SHOTS...
BAM! BAM!
THE CHEMICAL FLASK DISINTEGRATES FROM THE IMPACT AND SPARKS ANOTHER FORCEFUL BLAST!
BYEEOW!!
I-I DIDN'T EXPECT THAT TO HAPPEN! IT COMPLETELY DESTROYED YOUR ATTACKER!
ARE YOU ALL RIGHT, MISS?
SEE TO CAPTAIN AMERICA! HE'S--
--DON'T BOTHER! I'VE HAD A HARD TIME, BUT I'M STILL ON MY FEET!
W-WHO ARE YOU? I-I HOPE YOU'RE A FRIEND... WE CAN USE ONE...
CAP! OH, CAP! I-I THOUGHT I'D NEVER SEE YOU AGAIN!
THANK GOD YOU'RE ALIVE!
SHARON!? I-IS THAT YOU-- SHARON!?

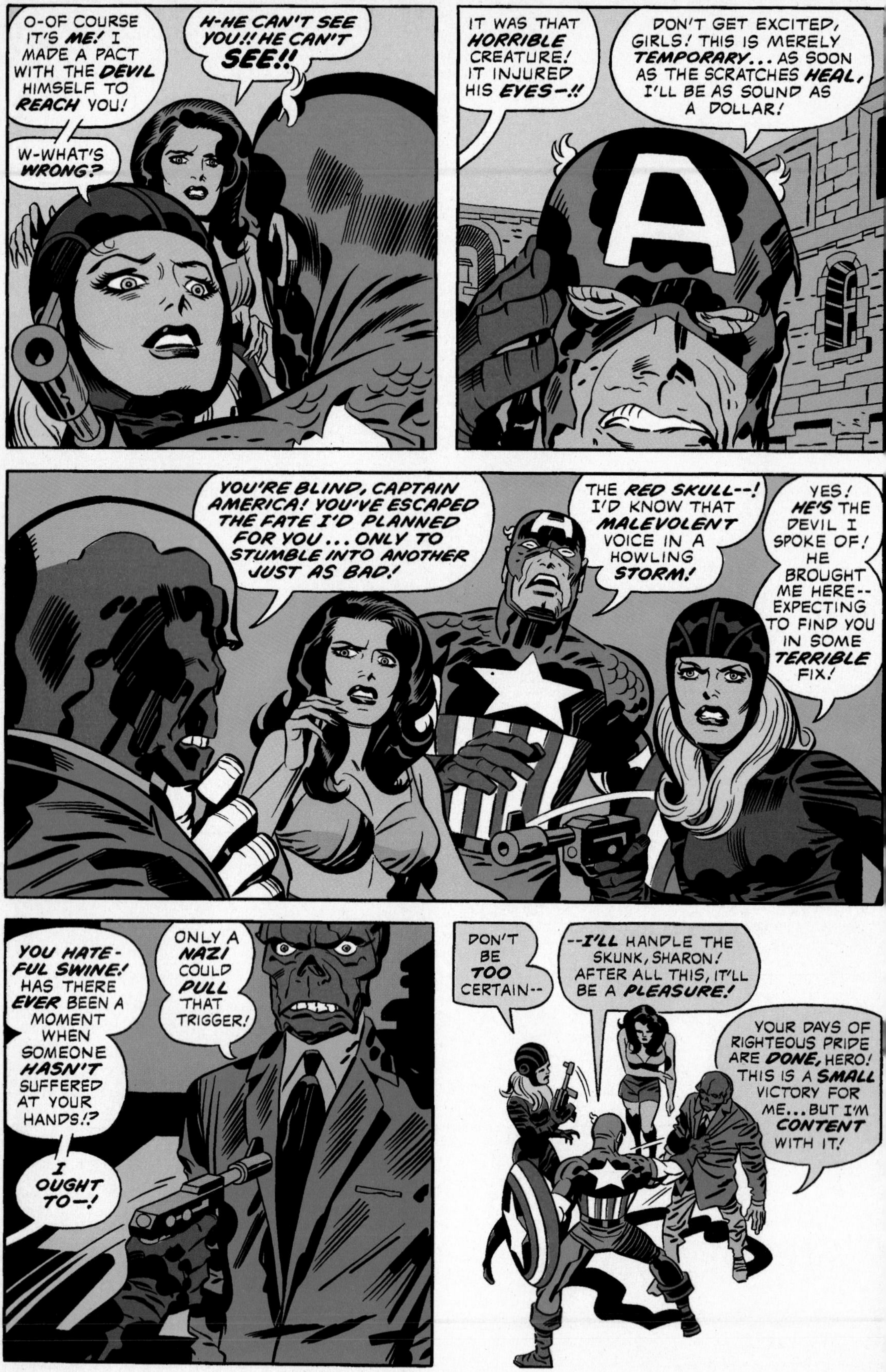
O-OF COURSE IT'S ME! I MADE A PACT WITH THE DEVIL HIMSELF TO REACH YOU!
W-WHAT'S WRONG?
H-HE CAN'T SEE YOU!! HE CAN'T SEE!!
IT WAS THAT HORRIBLE CREATURE! IT INJURED HIS EYES--!!
DON'T GET EXCITED, GIRLS! THIS IS MERELY TEMPORARY... AS SOON AS THE SCRATCHES HEAL, I'LL BE AS SOUND AS A DOLLAR!
YOU'RE BLIND, CAPTAIN AMERICA! YOU'VE ESCAPED THE FATE I'D PLANNED FOR YOU... ONLY TO STUMBLE INTO ANOTHER JUST AS BAD!
THE RED SKULL--! I'D KNOW THAT MALEVOLENT VOICE IN A HOWLING STORM!
YES! HE'S THE DEVIL I SPOKE OF! HE BROUGHT ME HERE--EXPECTING TO FIND YOU IN SOME TERRIBLE FIX!
YOU HATE-FUL SWINE! HAS THERE EVER BEEN A MOMENT WHEN SOMEONE HASN'T SUFFERED AT YOUR HANDS!?
I OUGHT TO--!
ONLY A NAZI COULD PULL THAT TRIGGER!
DON'T BE TOO CERTAIN--
--I'LL HANDLE THE SKUNK, SHARON! AFTER ALL THIS, IT'LL BE A PLEASURE!
YOUR DAYS OF RIGHTEOUS PRIDE ARE DONE, HERO! THIS IS A SMALL VICTORY FOR ME... BUT I'M CONTENT WITH IT!

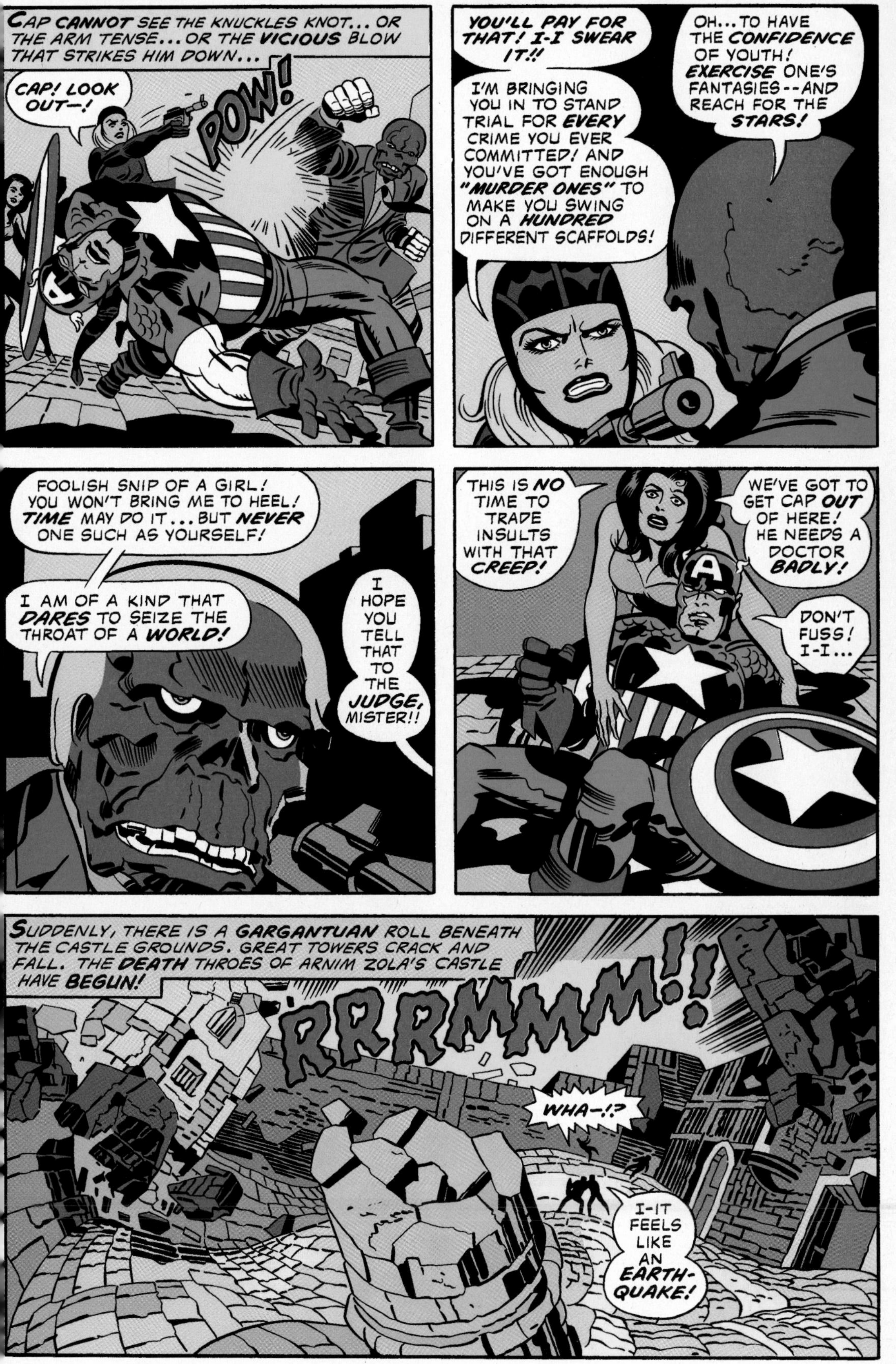
CAP CANNOT SEE THE KNUCKLES KNOT... OR THE ARM TENSE... OR THE VICIOUS BLOW THAT STRIKES HIM DOWN...
CAP! LOOK OUT--!
POW!
YOU'LL PAY FOR THAT! I-I SWEAR IT!!
I'M BRINGING YOU IN TO STAND TRIAL FOR EVERY CRIME YOU EVER COMMITTED! AND YOU'VE GOT ENOUGH "MURDER ONES" TO MAKE YOU SWING ON A HUNDRED DIFFERENT SCAFFOLDS!
OH...TO HAVE THE CONFIDENCE OF YOUTH! EXERCISE ONE'S FANTASIES--AND REACH FOR THE STARS!
FOOLISH SNIP OF A GIRL! YOU WON'T BRING ME TO HEEL! TIME MAY DO IT... BUT NEVER ONE SUCH AS YOURSELF!
I AM OF A KIND THAT DARES TO SEIZE THE THROAT OF A WORLD!
I HOPE YOU TELL THAT TO THE JUDGE, MISTER!!
THIS IS NO TIME TO TRADE INSULTS WITH THAT CREEP!
WE'VE GOT TO GET CAP OUT OF HERE! HE NEEDS A DOCTOR BADLY!
DON'T FUSS! I-I...
SUDDENLY, THERE IS A GARGANTUAN ROLL BENEATH THE CASTLE GROUNDS. GREAT TOWERS CRACK AND FALL. THE DEATH THROES OF ARNIM ZOLA'S CASTLE HAVE BEGUN!
RRRMMM!!
WHA--!?
I-IT FEELS LIKE AN EARTH-QUAKE!

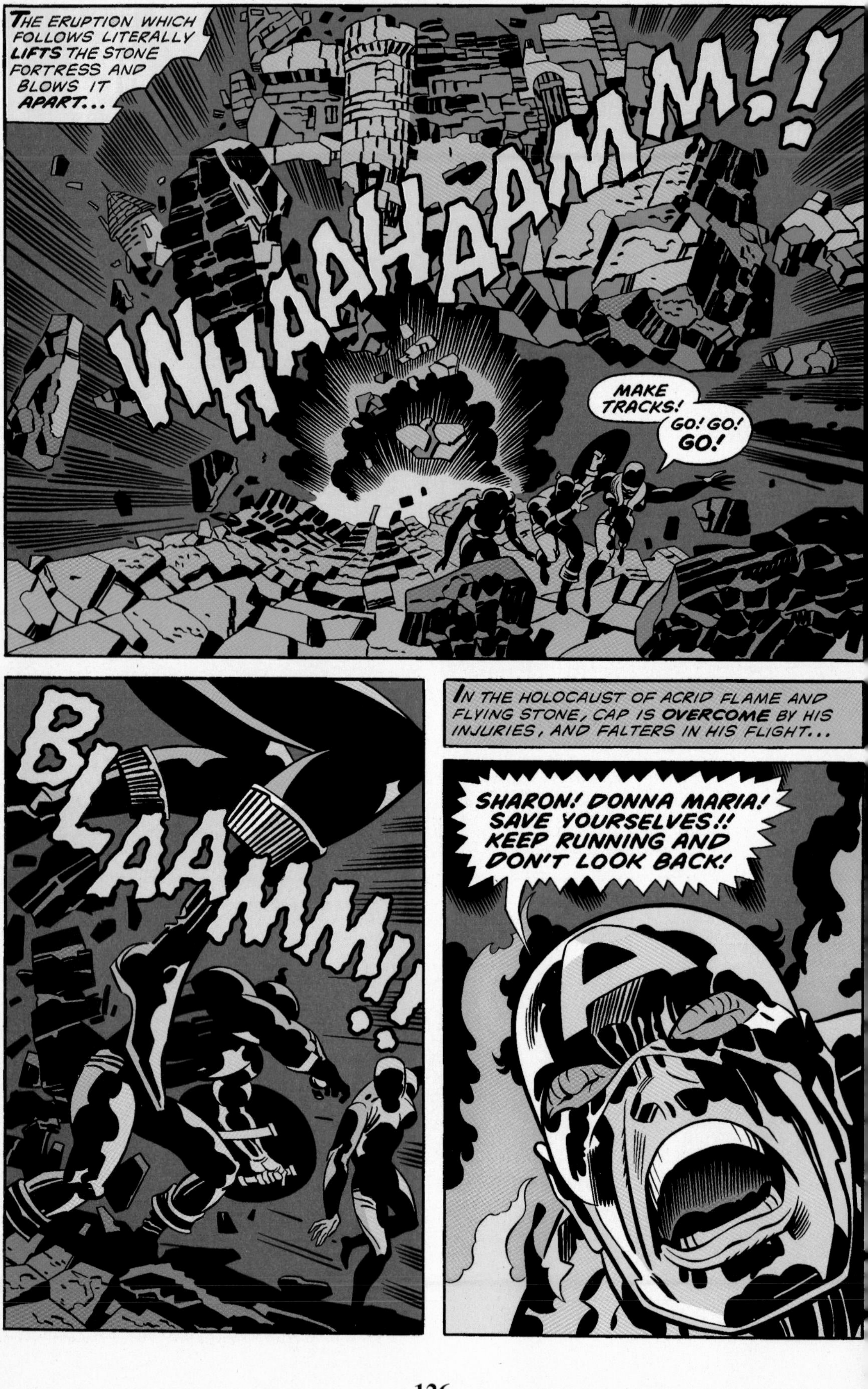
THE ERUPTION WHICH FOLLOWS LITERALLY LIFTS THE STONE FORTRESS AND BLOWS IT APART...
WHAAHAAMM!!
MAKE TRACKS!
GO! GO! GO!
BLAAMM!!
IN THE HOLOCAUST OF ACRID FLAME AND FLYING STONE, CAP IS OVERCOME BY HIS INJURIES, AND FALTERS IN HIS FLIGHT...
SHARON! DONNA MARIA! SAVE YOURSELVES!! KEEP RUNNING AND DON'T LOOK BACK!

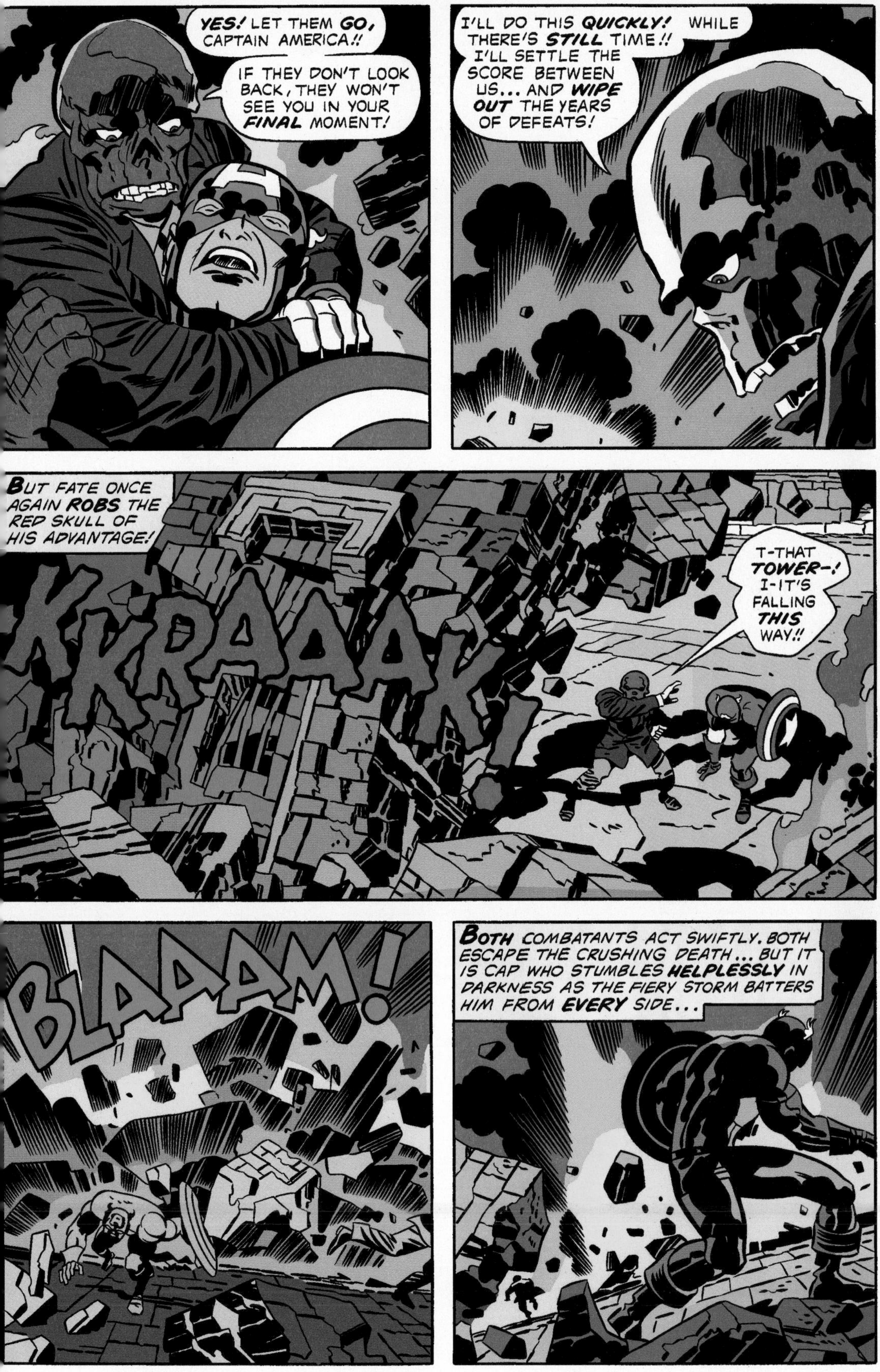

YES! LET THEM GO, CAPTAIN AMERICA!!
IF THEY DON'T LOOK BACK, THEY WON'T SEE YOU IN YOUR FINAL MOMENT!
I'LL DO THIS QUICKLY! WHILE THERE'S STILL TIME!! I'LL SETTLE THE SCORE BETWEEN US... AND WIPE OUT THE YEARS OF DEFEATS!
BUT FATE ONCE AGAIN ROBS THE RED SKULL OF HIS ADVANTAGE!
KKRAAAK!
T-THAT TOWER-! I-IT'S FALLING THIS WAY!!
BLAAAM!
BOTH COMBATANTS ACT SWIFTLY. BOTH ESCAPE THE CRUSHING DEATH... BUT IT IS CAP WHO STUMBLES HELPLESSLY IN DARKNESS AS THE FIERY STORM BATTERS HIM FROM EVERY SIDE...

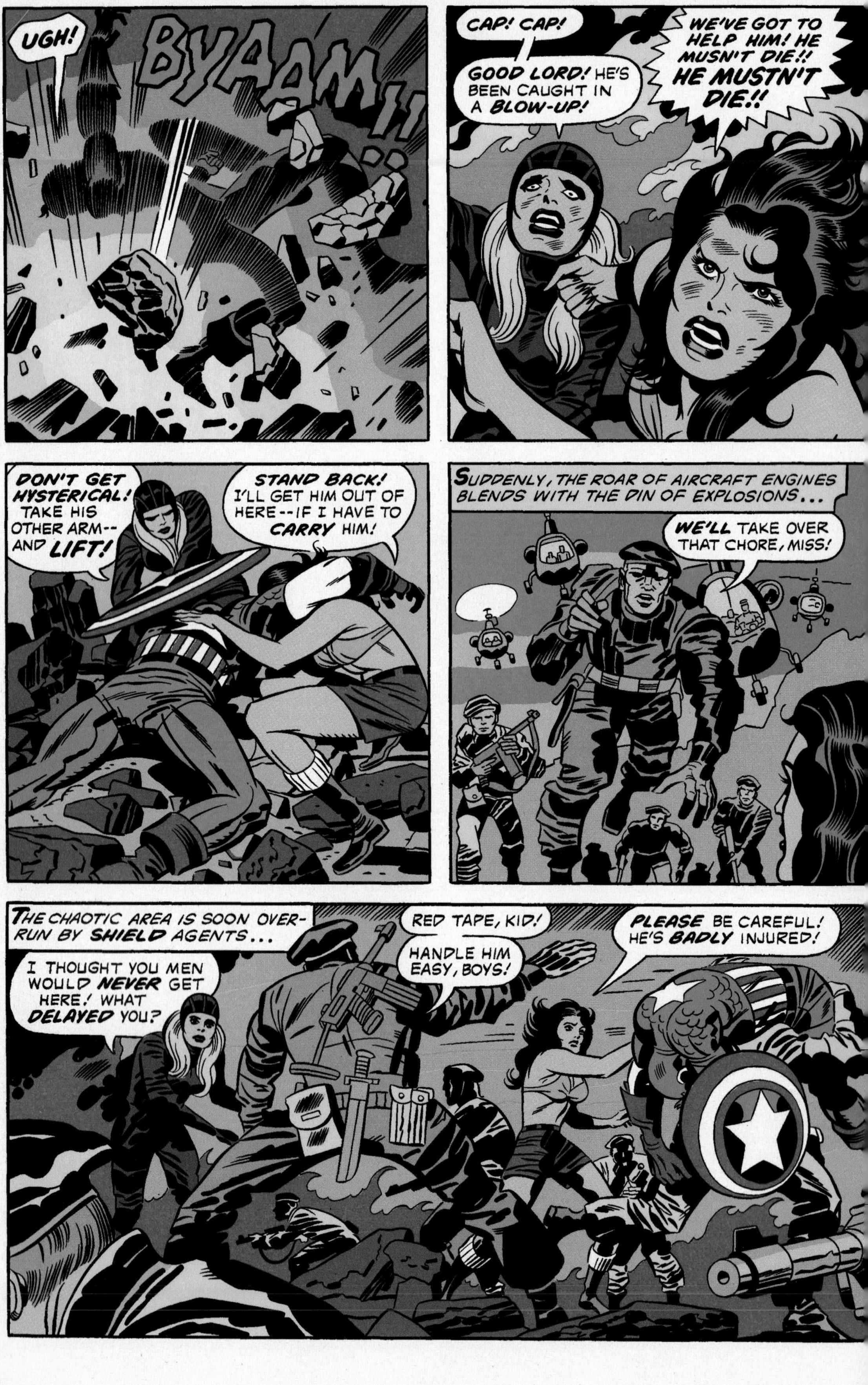
UGH!
BYAAM!!
CAP! CAP!
GOOD LORD! HE'S BEEN CAUGHT IN A BLOW-UP!
WE'VE GOT TO HELP HIM! HE MUSN'T DIE!! HE MUSTN'T DIE!!
DON'T GET HYSTERICAL! TAKE HIS OTHER ARM-- AND LIFT!
STAND BACK! I'LL GET HIM OUT OF HERE--IF I HAVE TO CARRY HIM!
SUDDENLY, THE ROAR OF AIRCRAFT ENGINES BLENDS WITH THE DIN OF EXPLOSIONS...
WE'LL TAKE OVER THAT CHORE, MISS!
THE CHAOTIC AREA IS SOON OVER-RUN BY SHIELD AGENTS...
I THOUGHT YOU MEN WOULD NEVER GET HERE! WHAT DELAYED YOU?
RED TAPE, KID!
HANDLE HIM EASY, BOYS!
PLEASE BE CAREFUL! HE'S BADLY INJURED!

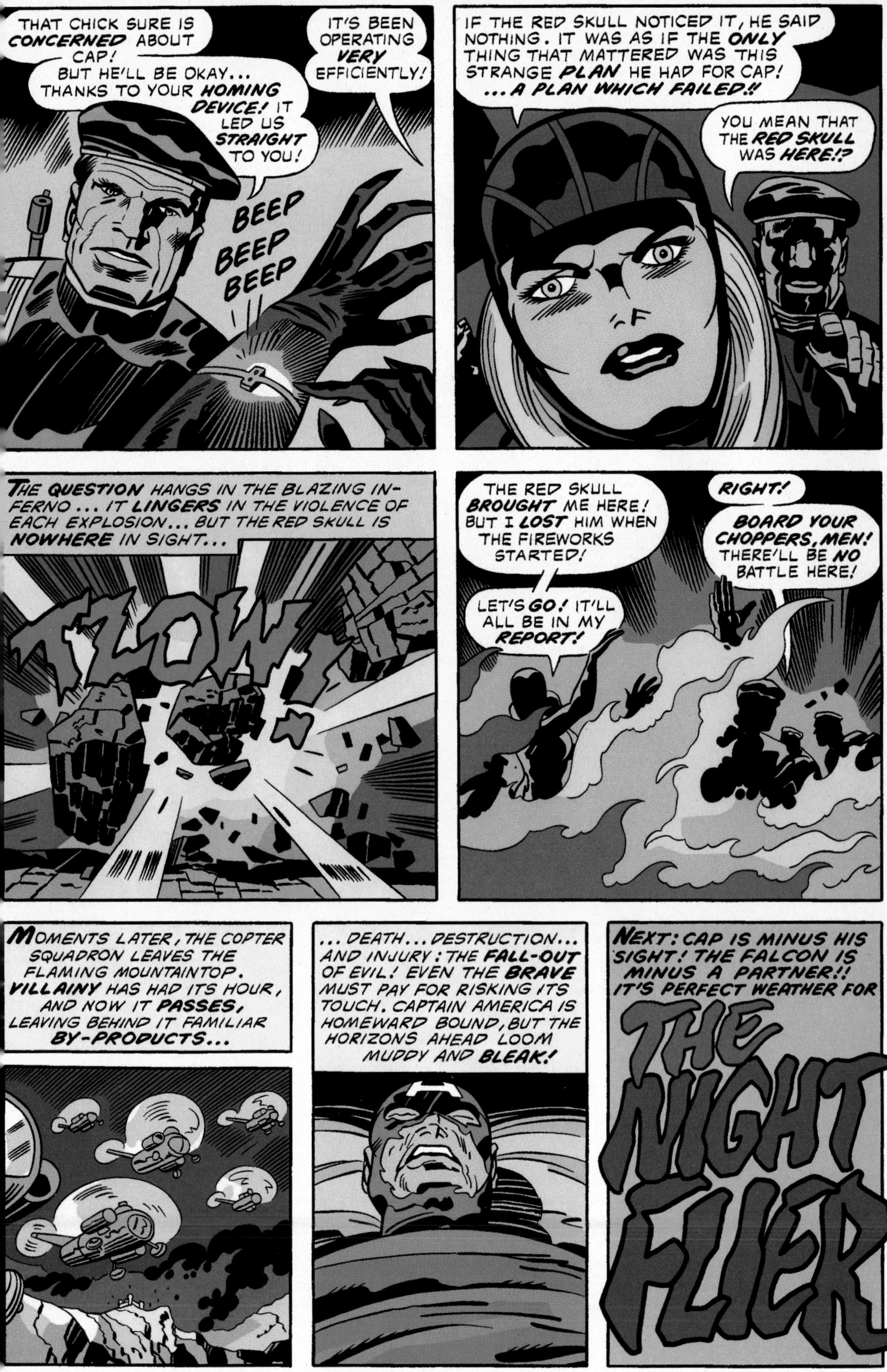

THAT CHICK SURE IS CONCERNED ABOUT CAP!
BUT HE'LL BE OKAY... THANKS TO YOUR HOMING DEVICE! IT LED US STRAIGHT TO YOU!
IT'S BEEN OPERATING VERY EFFICIENTLY!
BEEP BEEP BEEP
IF THE RED SKULL NOTICED IT, HE SAID NOTHING. IT WAS AS IF THE ONLY THING THAT MATTERED WAS THIS STRANGE PLAN HE HAD FOR CAP! ...A PLAN WHICH FAILED!!
YOU MEAN THAT THE RED SKULL WAS HERE!?
THE QUESTION HANGS IN THE BLAZING INFERNO ... IT LINGERS IN THE VIOLENCE OF EACH EXPLOSION... BUT THE RED SKULL IS NOWHERE IN SIGHT...
TZLOW
THE RED SKULL BROUGHT ME HERE! BUT I LOST HIM WHEN THE FIREWORKS STARTED!
LET'S GO! IT'LL ALL BE IN MY REPORT!
RIGHT!
BOARD YOUR CHOPPERS, MEN! THERE'LL BE NO BATTLE HERE!
MOMENTS LATER, THE COPTER SQUADRON LEAVES THE FLAMING MOUNTAINTOP. VILLAINY HAS HAD ITS HOUR, AND NOW IT PASSES, LEAVING BEHIND IT FAMILIAR BY-PRODUCTS...
... DEATH... DESTRUCTION... AND INJURY: THE FALL-OUT OF EVIL! EVEN THE BRAVE MUST PAY FOR RISKING ITS TOUCH. CAPTAIN AMERICA IS HOMEWARD BOUND, BUT THE HORIZONS AHEAD LOOM MUDDY AND BLEAK!
NEXT: CAP IS MINUS HIS SIGHT! THE FALCON IS MINUS A PARTNER!! IT'S PERFECT WEATHER FOR
THE NIGHT FLIER

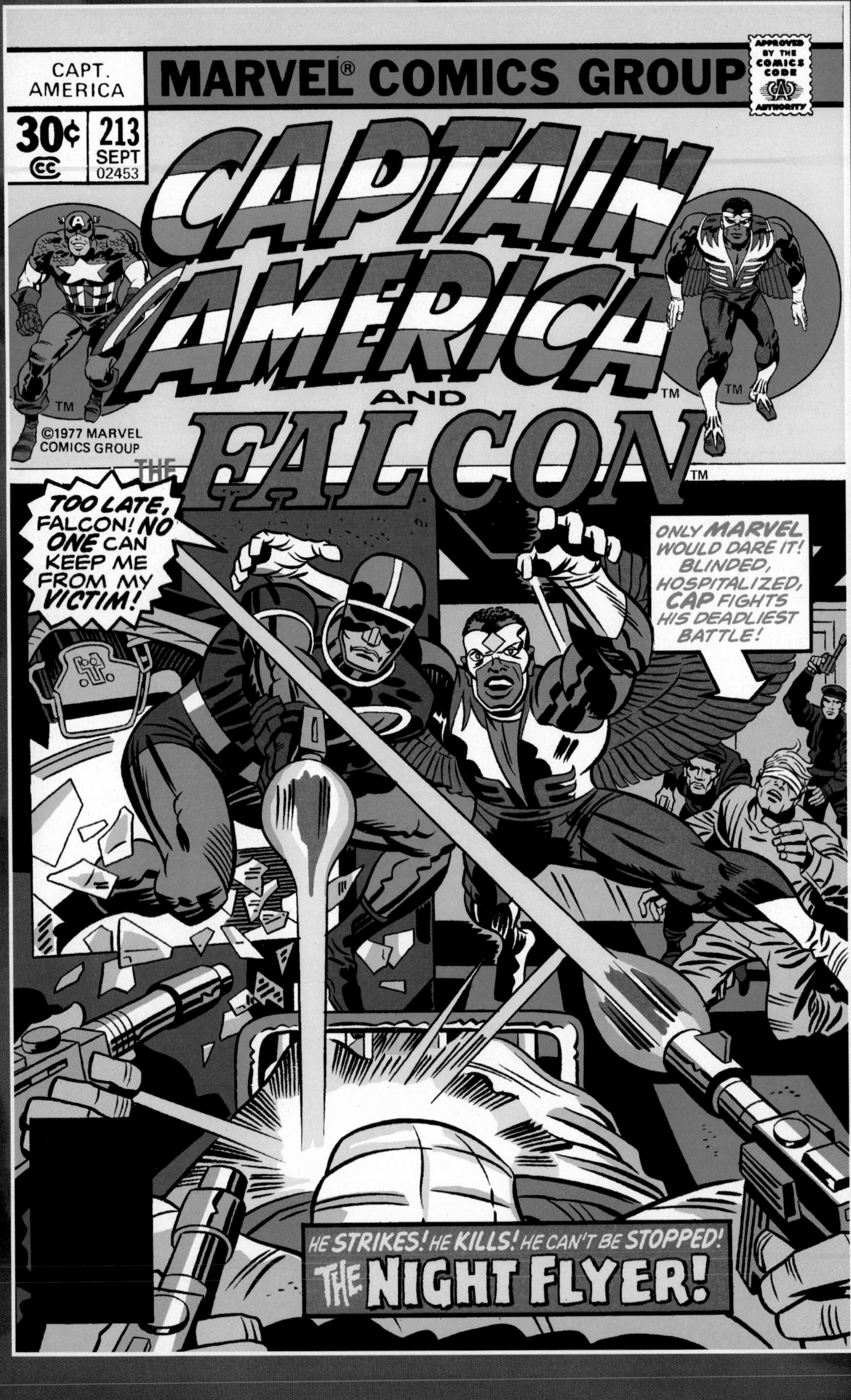

CAPT. AMERICA
MARVEL® COMICS GROUP
APPROVED BY THE COMICS CODE AUTHORITY
30¢
213
SEPT
02453
CAPTAIN AMERICA AND THE FALCON
©1977 MARVEL COMICS GROUP
TOO LATE, FALCON! NO ONE CAN KEEP ME FROM MY VICTIM!
ONLY MARVEL WOULD DARE IT! BLINDED, HOSPITALIZED, CAP FIGHTS HIS DEADLIEST BATTLE!
HE STRIKES! HE KILLS! HE CAN'T BE STOPPED!
THE NIGHT FLYER!

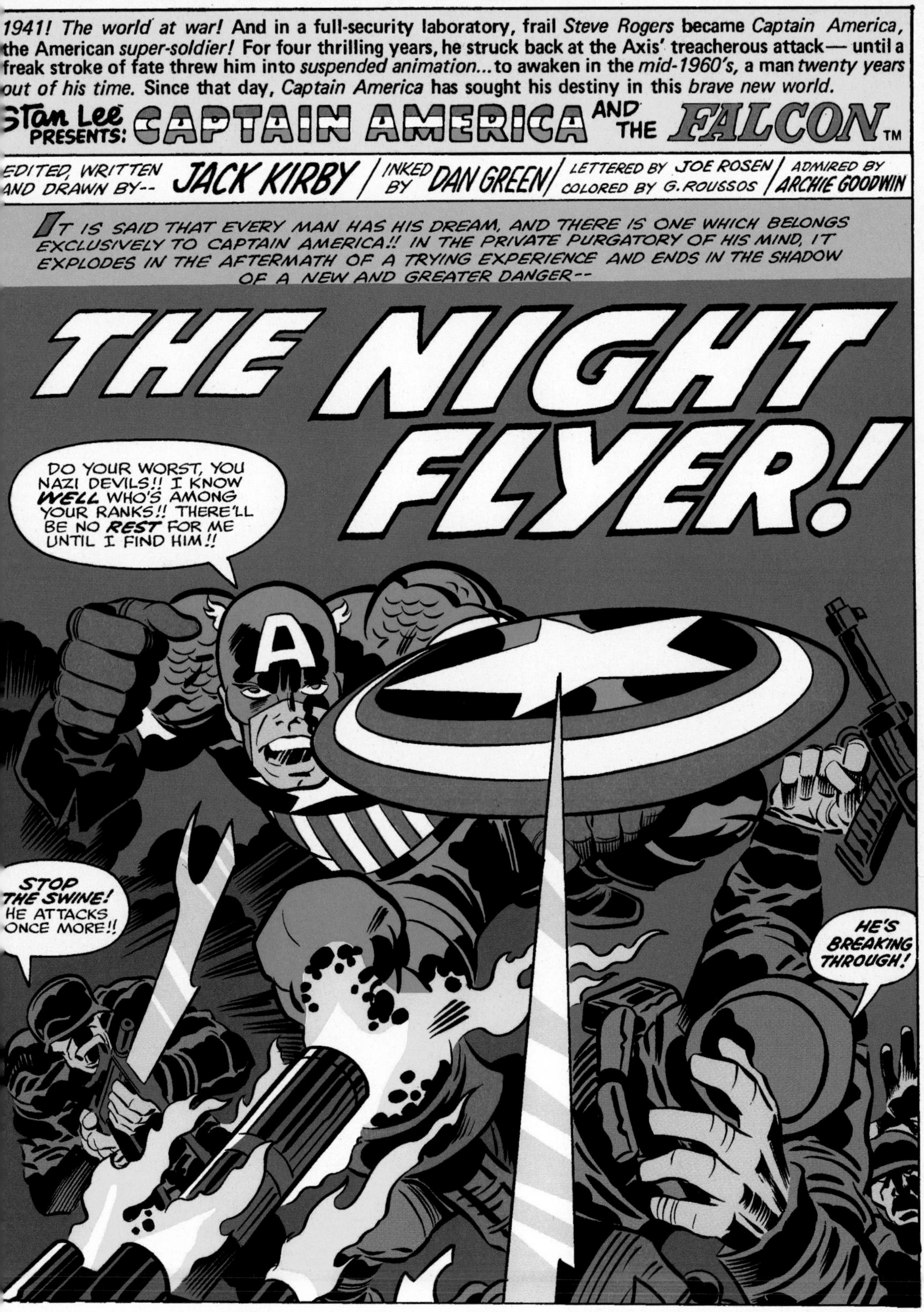
1941! The world at war! And in a full-security laboratory, frail Steve Rogers became Captain America, the American super-soldier! For four thrilling years, he struck back at the Axis' treacherous attack— until a freak stroke of fate threw him into suspended animation... to awaken in the mid-1960's, a man twenty years out of his time. Since that day, Captain America has sought his destiny in this brave new world.
Stan Lee PRESENTS: CAPTAIN AMERICA AND THE FALCON TM
EDITED, WRITTEN AND DRAWN BY-- JACK KIRBY / INKED BY DAN GREEN / LETTERED BY JOE ROSEN COLORED BY G. ROUSSOS / ADMIRED BY ARCHIE GOODWIN
IT IS SAID THAT EVERY MAN HAS HIS DREAM, AND THERE IS ONE WHICH BELONGS EXCLUSIVELY TO CAPTAIN AMERICA!! IN THE PRIVATE PURGATORY OF HIS MIND, IT EXPLODES IN THE AFTERMATH OF A TRYING EXPERIENCE AND ENDS IN THE SHADOW OF A NEW AND GREATER DANGER--
THE NIGHT FLYER!
DO YOUR WORST, YOU NAZI DEVILS!! I KNOW WELL WHO'S AMONG YOUR RANKS!! THERE'LL BE NO REST FOR ME UNTIL I FIND HIM!!
STOP THE SWINE! HE ATTACKS ONCE MORE!!
HE'S BREAKING THROUGH!

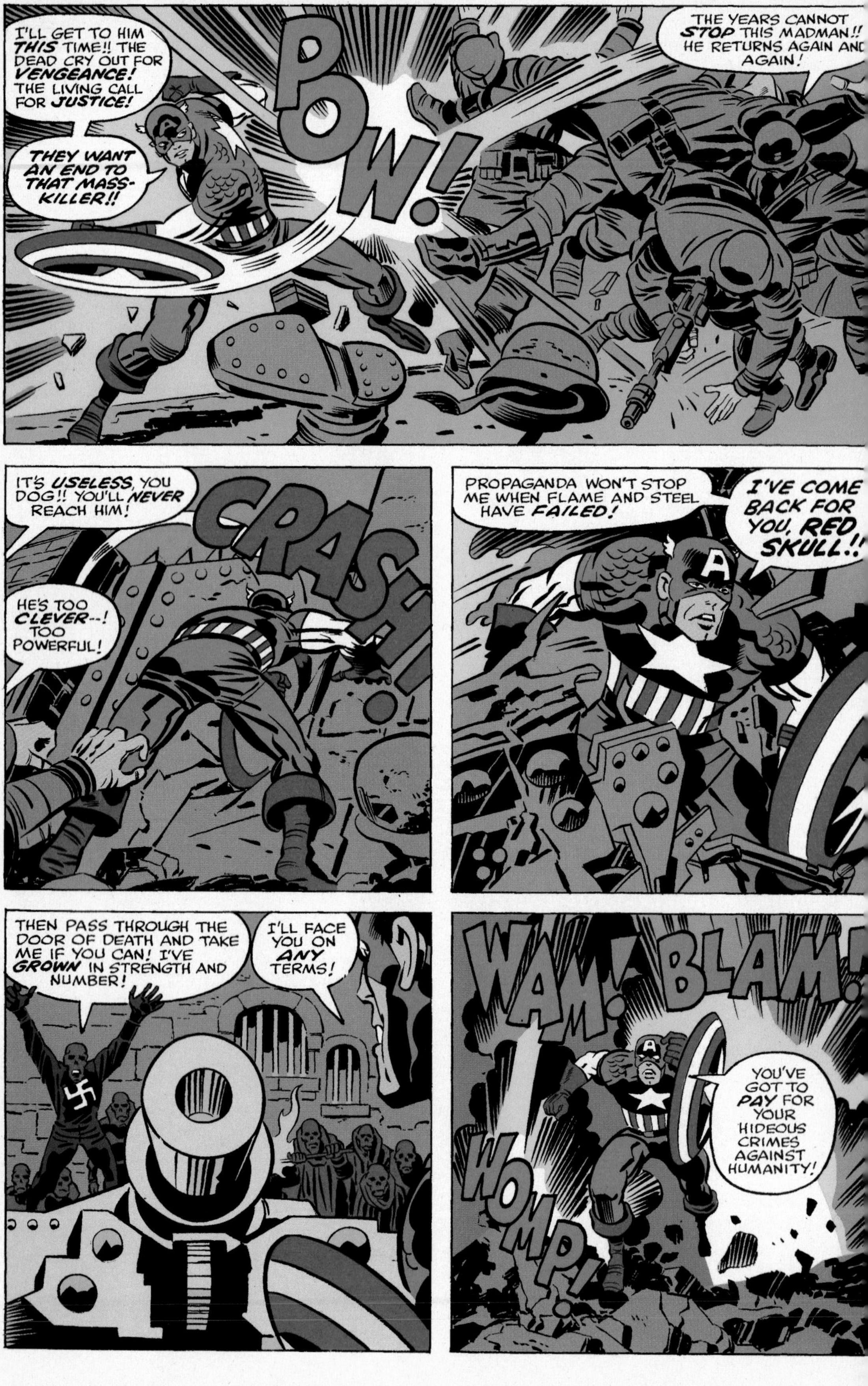

I'LL GET TO HIM THIS TIME!! THE DEAD CRY OUT FOR VENGEANCE! THE LIVING CALL FOR JUSTICE!
THEY WANT AN END TO THAT MASS-KILLER!!
POW!
THE YEARS CANNOT STOP THIS MADMAN!! HE RETURNS AGAIN AND AGAIN!
IT'S USELESS, YOU DOG!! YOU'LL NEVER REACH HIM!
CRASH!
HE'S TOO CLEVER--! TOO POWERFUL!
PROPAGANDA WON'T STOP ME WHEN FLAME AND STEEL HAVE FAILED!
I'VE COME BACK FOR YOU, RED SKULL!!
THEN PASS THROUGH THE DOOR OF DEATH AND TAKE ME IF YOU CAN! I'VE GROWN IN STRENGTH AND NUMBER!
I'LL FACE YOU ON ANY TERMS!
WAM! BLAM!
YOU'VE GOT TO PAY FOR YOUR HIDEOUS CRIMES AGAINST HUMANITY!
WOMP!

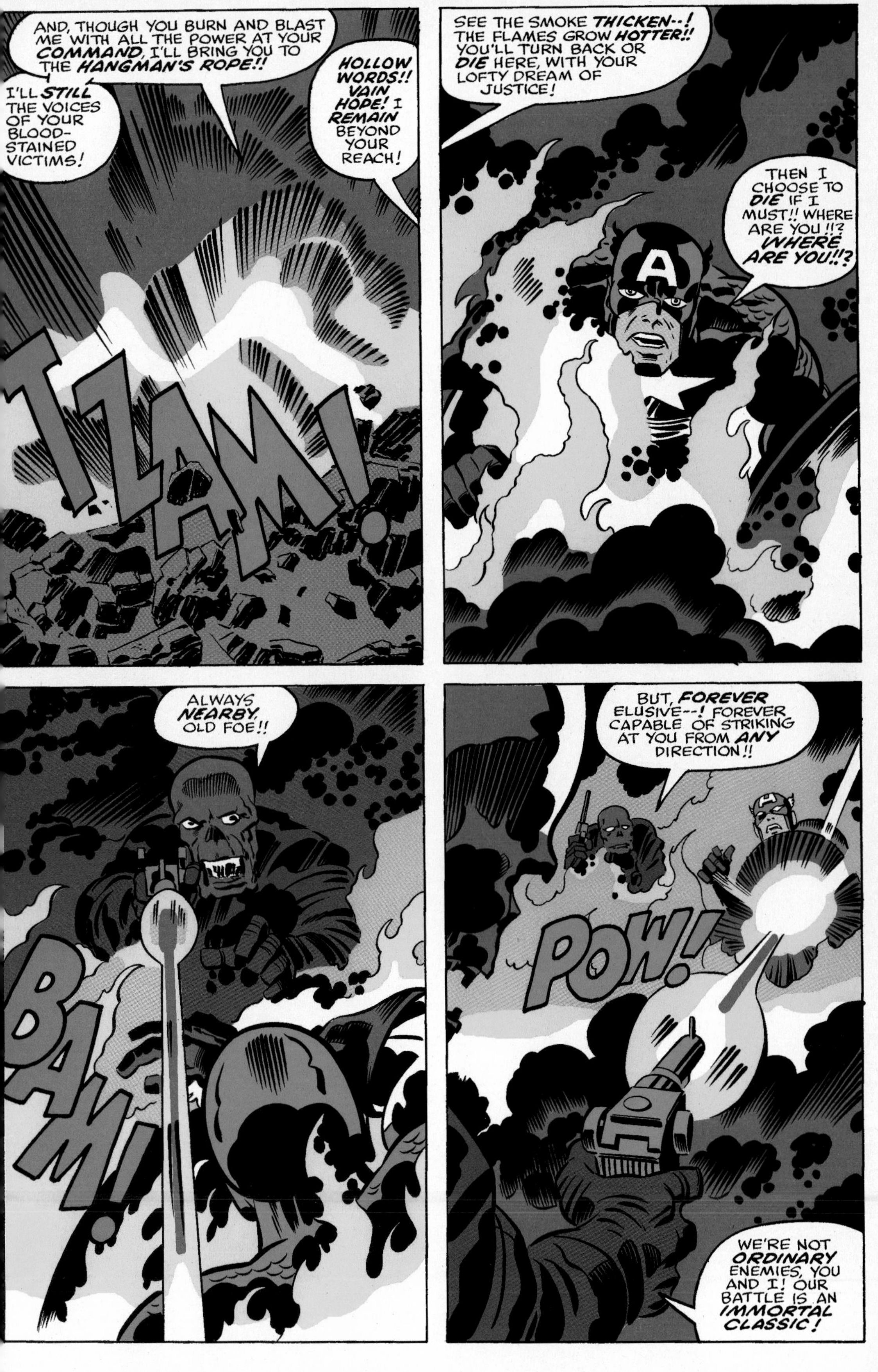
AND, THOUGH YOU BURN AND BLAST ME WITH ALL THE POWER AT YOUR COMMAND, I'LL BRING YOU TO THE HANGMAN'S ROPE!!
I'LL STILL THE VOICES OF YOUR BLOOD-STAINED VICTIMS!
HOLLOW WORDS!! VAIN HOPE! I REMAIN BEYOND YOUR REACH!
TZAM!
SEE THE SMOKE THICKEN--! THE FLAMES GROW HOTTER!! YOU'LL TURN BACK OR DIE HERE, WITH YOUR LOFTY DREAM OF JUSTICE!
THEN I CHOOSE TO DIE IF I MUST!! WHERE ARE YOU!!? WHERE ARE YOU!!?
ALWAYS NEARBY, OLD FOE!!
BAM!
BUT, FOREVER ELUSIVE--! FOREVER CAPABLE OF STRIKING AT YOU FROM ANY DIRECTION!!
POW!
WE'RE NOT ORDINARY ENEMIES, YOU AND I! OUR BATTLE IS AN IMMORTAL CLASSIC!

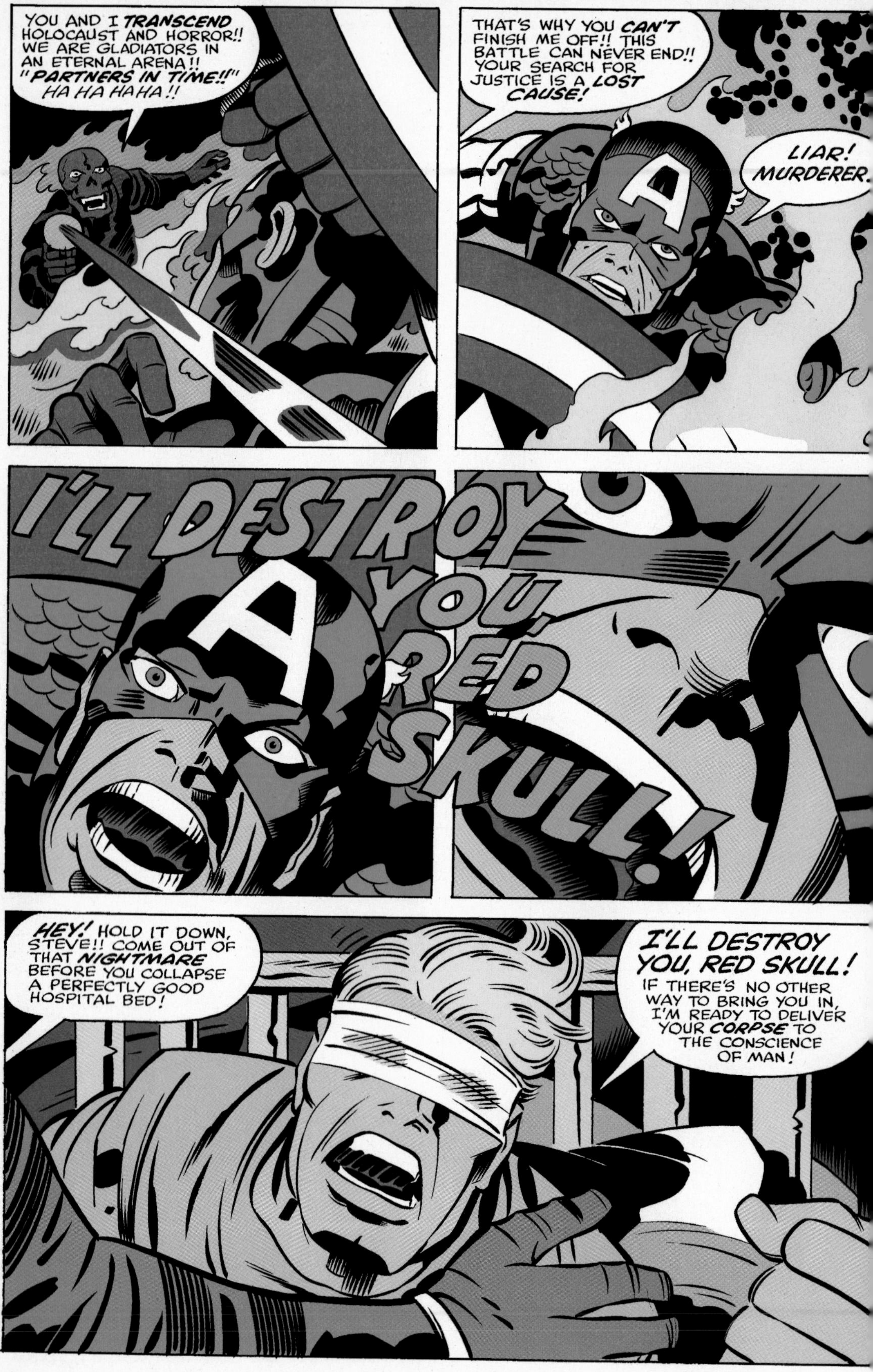

YOU AND I TRANSCEND HOLOCAUST AND HORROR!! WE ARE GLADIATORS IN AN ETERNAL ARENA!! "PARTNERS IN TIME!!" HA HA HAHA!!
THAT'S WHY YOU CAN'T FINISH ME OFF!! THIS BATTLE CAN NEVER END!! YOUR SEARCH FOR JUSTICE IS A LOST CAUSE!
LIAR! MURDERER.
I'LL DESTROY YOU, RED SKULL!
HEY! HOLD IT DOWN, STEVE!! COME OUT OF THAT NIGHTMARE BEFORE YOU COLLAPSE A PERFECTLY GOOD HOSPITAL BED!
I'LL DESTROY YOU, RED SKULL! IF THERE'S NO OTHER WAY TO BRING YOU IN, I'M READY TO DELIVER YOUR CORPSE TO THE CONSCIENCE OF MAN!

THAT'S IT! WAKE UP, CHUM! THE RED SKULL'S GONE, AND ALL'S RIGHT WITH THE WORLD-- AT LEAST, FOR THE TIME BEING.

SAM! SAM WILSON!! YOU FLAKY-FEATHERED FALCON!! SORRY I GAVE YOU SUCH A ROUGH TIME!

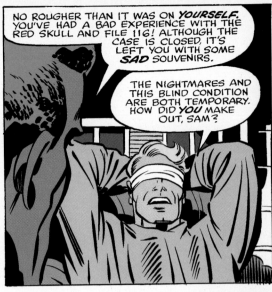

NO ROUGHER THAN IT WAS ON YOURSELF. YOU'VE HAD A BAD EXPERIENCE WITH THE RED SKULL AND FILE 116! ALTHOUGH THE CASE IS CLOSED, IT'S LEFT YOU WITH SOME SAD SOUVENIRS.

THE NIGHTMARES AND THIS BLIND CONDITION ARE BOTH TEMPORARY. HOW DID YOU MAKE OUT, SAM?

WHY, I FLEW INTO A NIGHTMARE OF MY OWN! ONLY THIS THING WAS ALIVE AND THIRTY FEET TALL! THEY DIDN'T CALL FILE 116 THE 'MONSTER FILE' WITHOUT REASON.

I UNDERSTAND THAT A SHIELD TEAM YANKED YOU FROM A NASTY FRACAS!

THAT'S NO LIE!! BUT THE HASSLE HARDLY GOT STARTED BEFORE THAT THING WAS TOTALLED BY HEAVY FIRE. IT SEEMS I'D WANDERED INTO WHAT SHIELD HAD LISTED AS A SUSPECTED AREA...

LUCKILY FOR YOU, THEY SUSPECTED RIGHT!

YOUR FEMALE FANS ARE CLAMORING FOR VISITOR'S PASSES, CAP, BUT SHIELD MEDICS ARE NOTORIOUSLY UP-TIGHT ABOUT IMPORTANT PATIENTS. I'M THE FIRST TO GET THROUGH TO SEE YOU.

SHARON, LEILA, DONNA MARIA--! THIS HASN'T BEEN EASY ON ANY OF THEM, HAS IT?

I DO SUPPOSE THEY'D BE HAPPIER IN THE COMPANY OF BASEBALL PLAYERS! LOSING A SERIES IS THE WORST THAT COULD HAPPEN!

YEAH! IN OUR WORK, LOSING ONE'S LIFE IS ALWAYS AROUND THE CORNER.

AT THAT MOMENT, THE DOOR OF STEVE ROGERS' ROOM BURSTS OPEN...

WE'VE BROUGHT YOU A ROOMMATE, STEVE!! LIKE YOURSELF, HE'S A GENUINE V.I.P.!

AND SHORT ON BORING CONVERSATION.

HE SEEMS TO BE SHORT ON ANY CONVERSATION...

WELL, THIS CAN'T BE NICK FURY! HE'D BE RATTLING OFF A WAR STORY WHILE FULLY ANESTHETIZED!

WHO IS HE? WHAT HAPPENED TO HIM?

THOSE TWO QUESTIONS ARE OFF-LIMITS, STEVE. SORRY. NICK FURY'S ORDERS.

SO, HE'S CLASSIFIED MATERIAL, EH? LIKE "OLE MAN RIVER", HE MUST KNOW SOMETHIN', BUT DON'T SAY NUTHIN'!

WE'LL SURE MAKE A GREAT PAIR!!

I CAN TELL YOU THIS-- WE CALL HIM "THE DEFECTOR" --AND THIS ROOM IS HEAVILY GUARDED.

THE ROOM'S FILLING UP! I'D BETTER SPLIT, PAL. I'LL GIVE THE GIRLS THE GOOD WORD AND DROP IN ON YOU AS SOON AS I CAN!

GOOD DEAL, SAM! TELL SHARON NOT TO WORRY ABOUT MY SIGHT. I'M GETTING POSITIVE REPORTS EACH DAY.

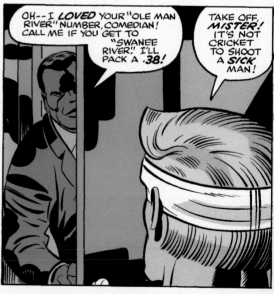

OH-- I LOVED YOUR "OLE MAN RIVER" NUMBER, COMEDIAN! CALL ME IF YOU GET TO "SWANEE RIVER." I'LL PACK A .38!

TAKE OFF, MISTER! IT'S NOT CRICKET TO SHOOT A SICK MAN!

LATER, THAT NIGHT, STEVE IS AWAKENED BY A *RUSTLING* AT THE DOOR. HE HEARS IT OPENING, AND THE SOUND OF SOMEONE ENTERING THE ROOM...

IT MUST BE ONE OF THE *GUARDS* LOOKING IN ON THE DEFECTOR!

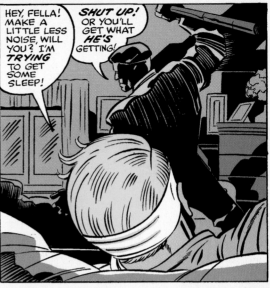

HEY, FELLA! MAKE A LITTLE LESS NOISE, WILL YOU? I'M *TRYING* TO GET SOME SLEEP!

SHUT UP! OR YOU'LL GET WHAT *HE'S* GETTING!

CAP QUICKLY GAUGES THE DIRECTION OF THE INTRUDER'S VOICE AND LEAPS FROM HIS BED...

THAT SOUNDED LIKE A *THREAT*, MISTER!!

YOU'VE MADE A *BAD* MOVE, BLIND MAN! I'LL HAVE TO TAKE CARE OF YOU *FIRST!*

THE ASSAILANT SWINGS WILDLY AT STEVE WITH A STEEL BAR, BUT NARROWLY MISSES HIS TARGET!

GUARDS! GUARDS!

THEY *WON'T* HEAR YOU! THEY WON'T HEAR *ANY-BODY!* I *SAW* TO THAT!

YOU'RE A *SLEEPER AGENT--!* PLANTED INSIDE *SHIELD* FOR AN ACT OF *SABOTAGE!*

WRONG, *DUMMY!!* I'M HERE TO MAKE A *HIT!* BUT I CAN MAKE *TWO* FOR THE PRICE OF ONE!

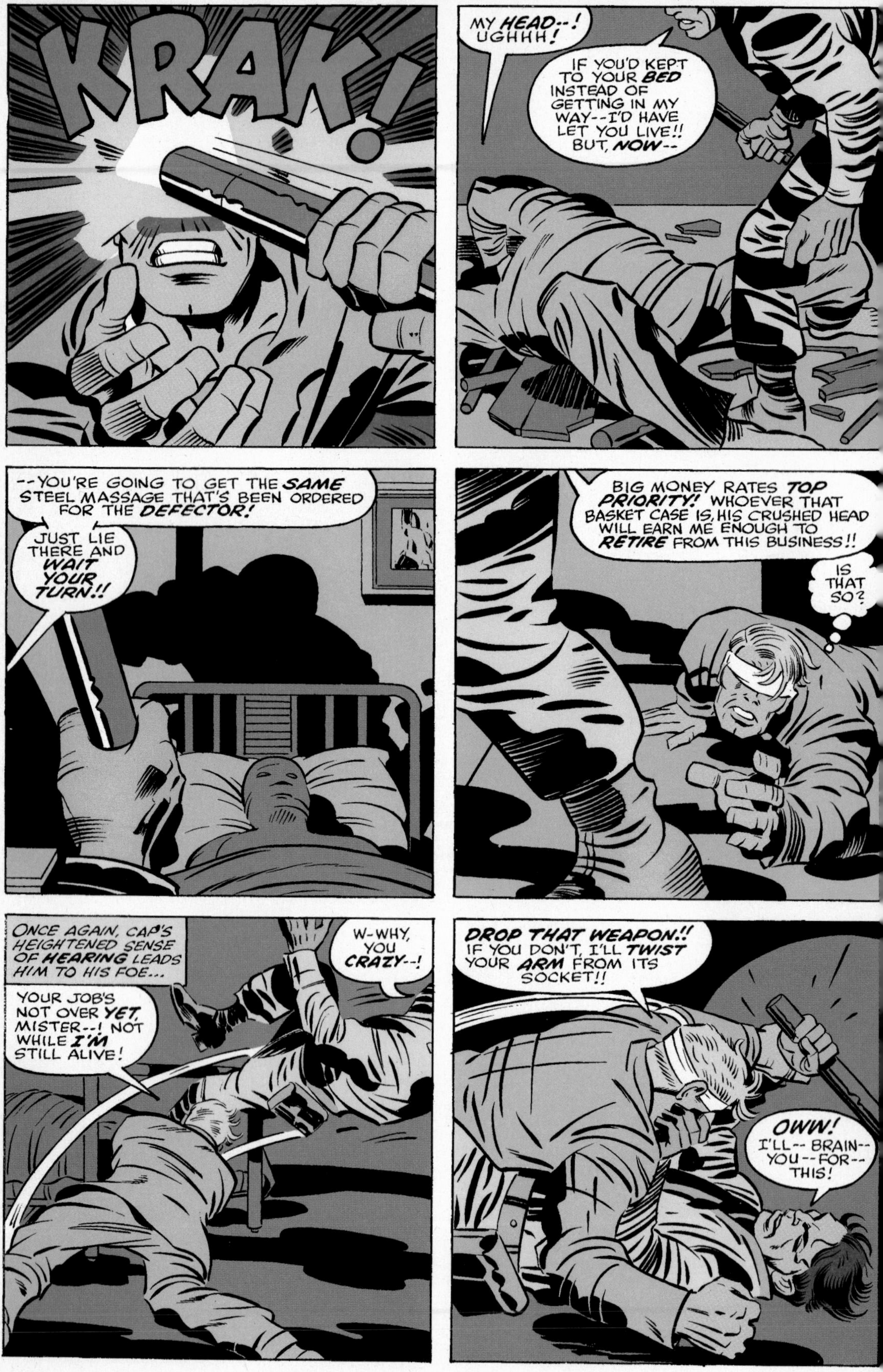
KRAK!
MY HEAD--! UGHHH!
IF YOU'D KEPT TO YOUR BED INSTEAD OF GETTING IN MY WAY--I'D HAVE LET YOU LIVE!! BUT, NOW--
--YOU'RE GOING TO GET THE SAME STEEL MASSAGE THAT'S BEEN ORDERED FOR THE DEFECTOR!
JUST LIE THERE AND WAIT YOUR TURN!!
BIG MONEY RATES TOP PRIORITY! WHOEVER THAT BASKET CASE IS, HIS CRUSHED HEAD WILL EARN ME ENOUGH TO RETIRE FROM THIS BUSINESS!!
IS THAT SO?
ONCE AGAIN, CAP'S HEIGHTENED SENSE OF HEARING LEADS HIM TO HIS FOE...
W-WHY, YOU CRAZY--!
YOUR JOB'S NOT OVER YET, MISTER--! NOT WHILE I'M STILL ALIVE!
DROP THAT WEAPON!! IF YOU DON'T, I'LL TWIST YOUR ARM FROM ITS SOCKET!!
OWW! I'LL-- BRAIN-- YOU--FOR-- THIS!

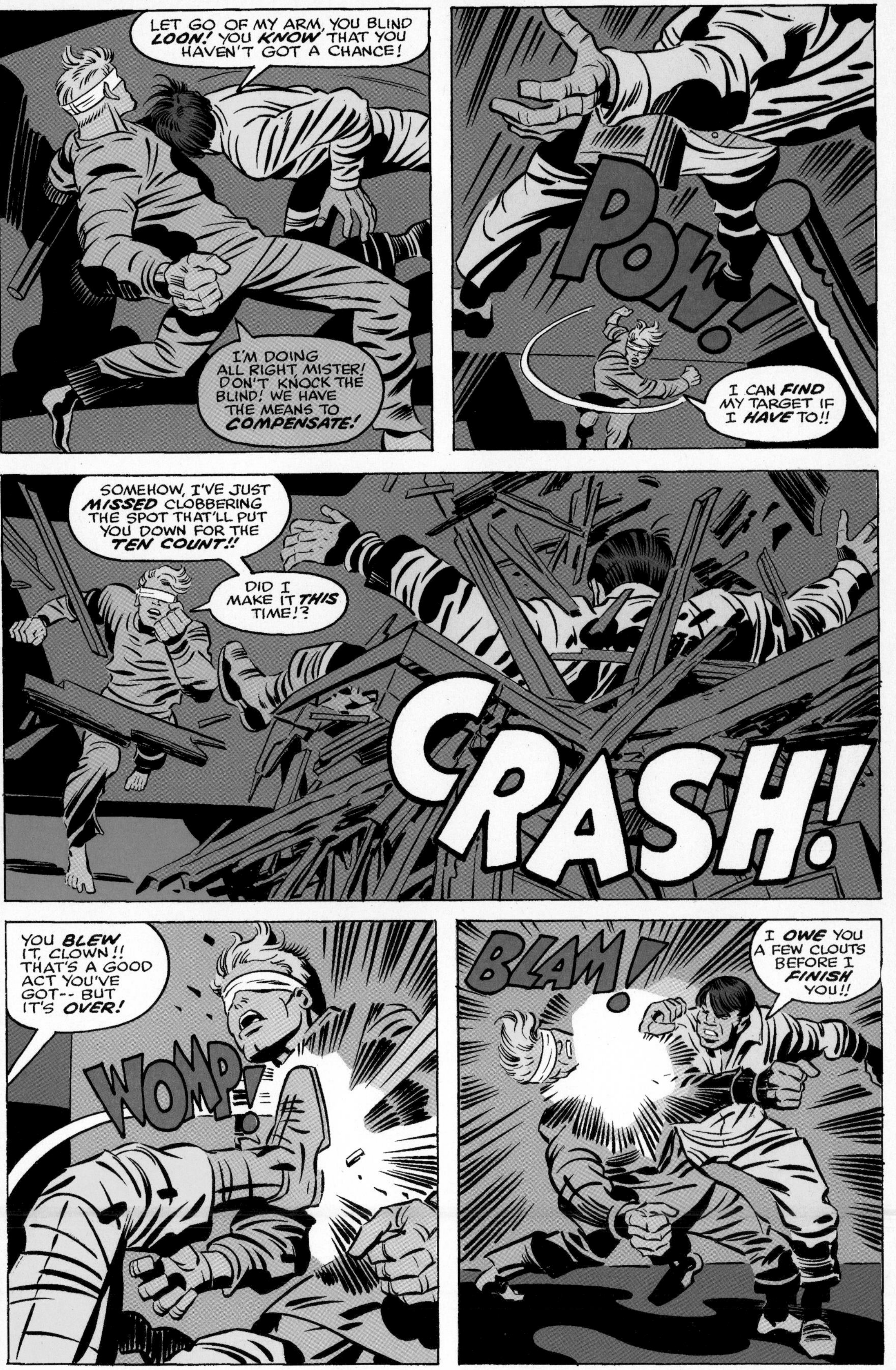
LET GO OF MY ARM, YOU BLIND LOON! YOU KNOW THAT YOU HAVEN'T GOT A CHANCE!
I'M DOING ALL RIGHT, MISTER! DON'T KNOCK THE BLIND! WE HAVE THE MEANS TO COMPENSATE!
POW!
I CAN FIND MY TARGET IF I HAVE TO!!
SOMEHOW, I'VE JUST MISSED CLOBBERING THE SPOT THAT'LL PUT YOU DOWN FOR THE TEN COUNT!!
DID I MAKE IT THIS TIME!?
CRASH!
YOU BLEW IT, CLOWN!! THAT'S A GOOD ACT YOU'VE GOT-- BUT IT'S OVER!
WOMP!
BLAM!
I OWE YOU A FEW CLOUTS BEFORE I FINISH YOU!!

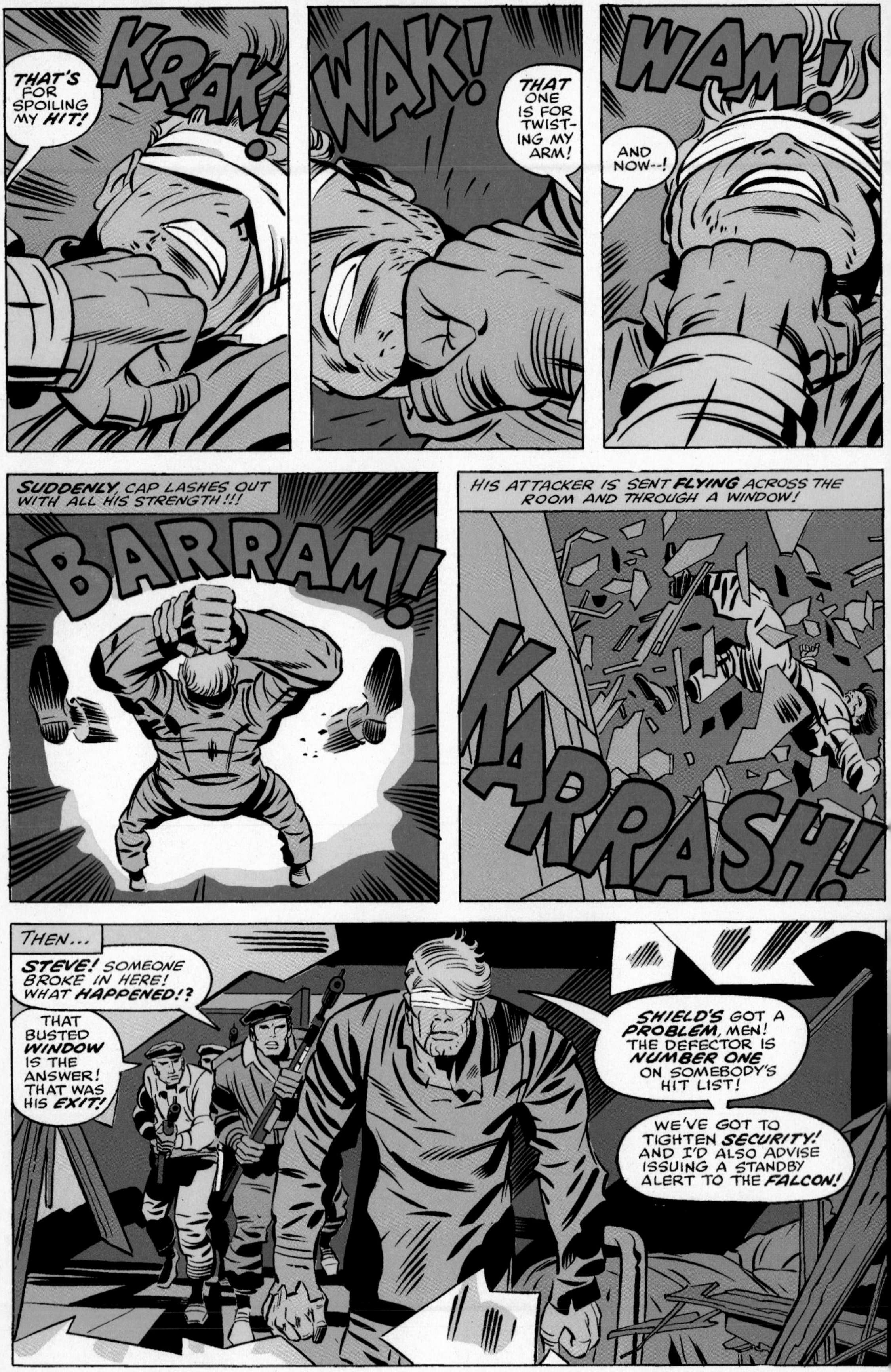
KRAK!
THAT'S FOR SPOILING MY HIT!
WAK!
THAT ONE IS FOR TWIST-ING MY ARM!
WAM!
AND NOW--!
SUDDENLY, CAP LASHES OUT WITH ALL HIS STRENGTH!!!
BARRAM!
HIS ATTACKER IS SENT FLYING ACROSS THE ROOM AND THROUGH A WINDOW!
KARRASH!
THEN...
STEVE! SOMEONE BROKE IN HERE! WHAT HAPPENED!?
THAT BUSTED WINDOW IS THE ANSWER! THAT WAS HIS EXIT!
SHIELD'S GOT A PROBLEM, MEN! THE DEFECTOR IS NUMBER ONE ON SOMEBODY'S HIT LIST!
WE'VE GOT TO TIGHTEN SECURITY! AND I'D ALSO ADVISE ISSUING A STANDBY ALERT TO THE FALCON!

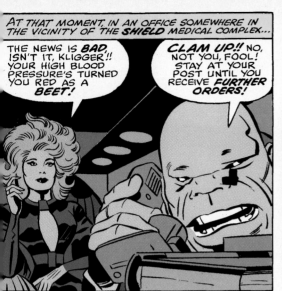

AT THAT MOMENT, IN AN OFFICE SOMEWHERE IN THE VICINITY OF THE SHIELD MEDICAL COMPLEX...
THE NEWS IS BAD, ISN'T IT, KLIGGER!! YOUR HIGH BLOOD PRESSURE'S TURNED YOU RED AS A BEET!
CLAM UP!! NO, NOT YOU, FOOL! STAY AT YOUR POST UNTIL YOU RECEIVE FURTHER ORDERS!
OUR INFORMANT AT SHIELD CONFIRMS WHAT I FEARED!! THE ATTEMPT ON OUR TARGET HAS FAILED!!
AND, GET THIS-- IT WAS FOILED BY A BLIND MAN!
BAD LUCK FOR YOU-- A BREAK FOR ME!
I SUPPOSE IT IS!! THE CORPORATION STILL WANTS THE DEFECTOR DEAD! ARE YOU CERTAIN THAT YOUR MAN CAN DO THE JOB?
IT'S GUARANTEED--! AT DOUBLE THE PRICE!
THE NIGHT FLYER'S RECORD IS PERFECT. HE'S THE LIVING EMBODIMENT OF SUDDEN DEATH! AMONG ALL THE HIT MEN, HE IS MOST FEARED AND RESPECTED!!
BUT THOSE WILD RUMORS, VEDA--! HE SOUNDS TOO WEIRD TO TRUST!
HE'S THE ULTIMATE CHOICE, KLIGGER--! A CULTIST... A MYSTIC... A RITUALIST, DEDICATED TO THE ART OF KILLING!!! DON'T YOU SEE--? IT'S UNTHINKABLE FOR HIM TO FAIL!
I KNOW ALL THAT. HOWEVER, IT'S THE OTHER STORIES ABOUT HIM THAT BOTHER ME!
OKAY-- HE MAKES THE KILL-- AND GIVES YOU YOUR PERCENTAGE OF THE DEAL.
YOU FOUND HIM-- YOU CALL HIM!!
DONE! I'LL CALL HIM RIGHT NOW!

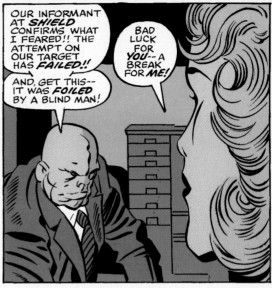

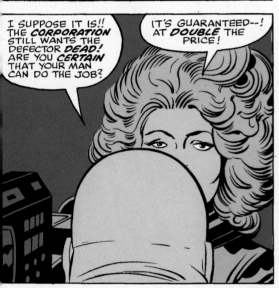

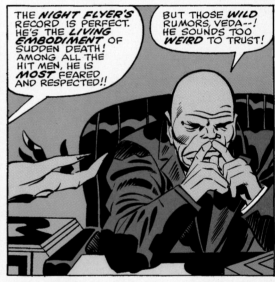

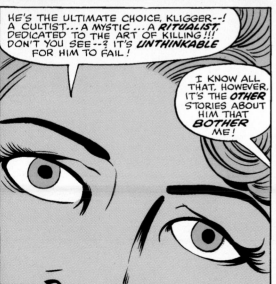

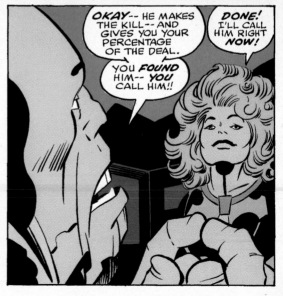

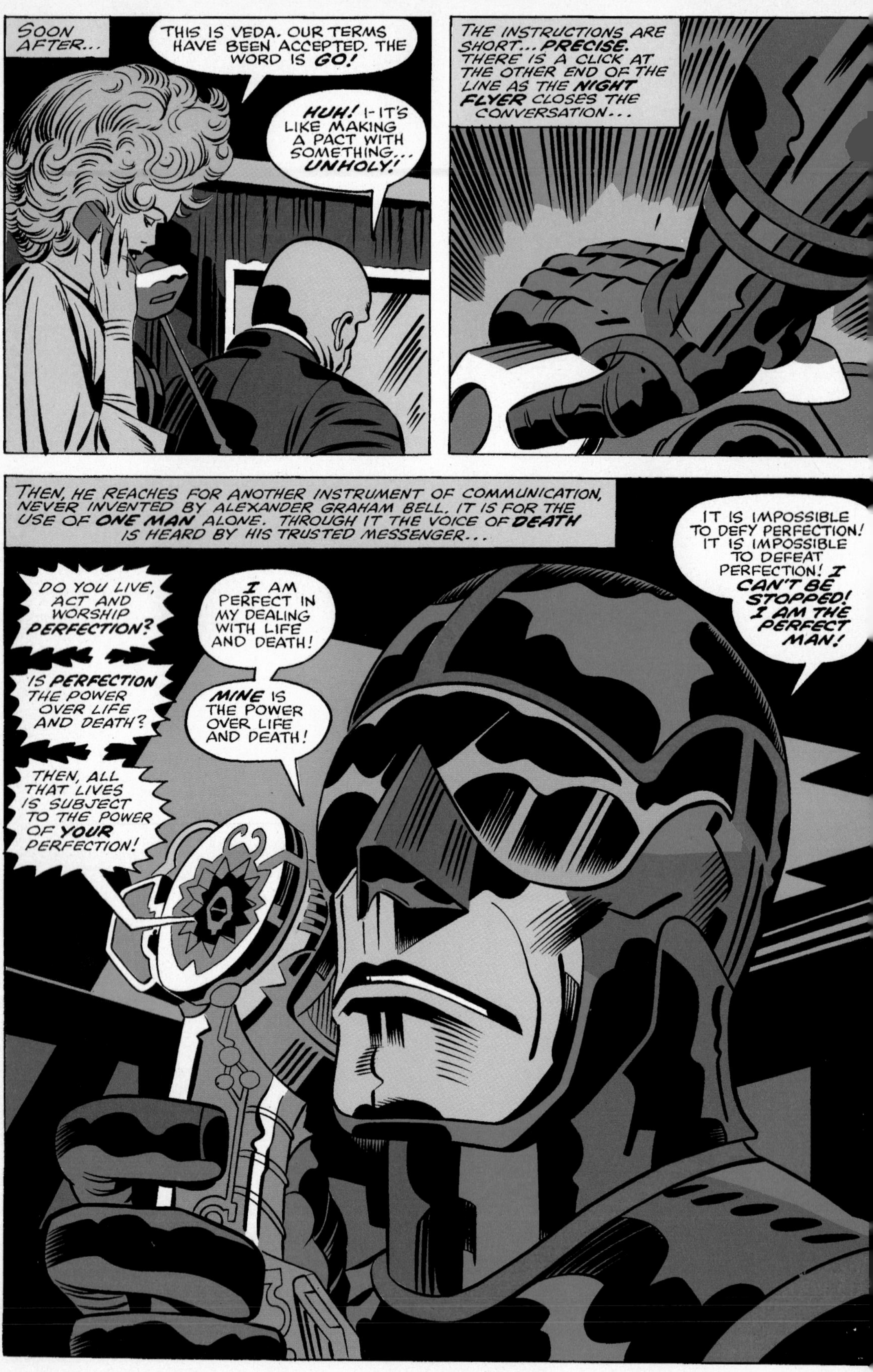

SOON AFTER...
THIS IS VEDA. OUR TERMS HAVE BEEN ACCEPTED. THE WORD IS GO!
HUH! I-IT'S LIKE MAKING A PACT WITH SOMETHING... UNHOLY!
THE INSTRUCTIONS ARE SHORT... PRECISE. THERE IS A CLICK AT THE OTHER END OF THE LINE AS THE NIGHT FLYER CLOSES THE CONVERSATION...
THEN, HE REACHES FOR ANOTHER INSTRUMENT OF COMMUNICATION, NEVER INVENTED BY ALEXANDER GRAHAM BELL. IT IS FOR THE USE OF ONE MAN ALONE. THROUGH IT THE VOICE OF DEATH IS HEARD BY HIS TRUSTED MESSENGER...
DO YOU LIVE, ACT AND WORSHIP PERFECTION?
I AM PERFECT IN MY DEALING WITH LIFE AND DEATH!
IS PERFECTION THE POWER OVER LIFE AND DEATH?
MINE IS THE POWER OVER LIFE AND DEATH!
THEN, ALL THAT LIVES IS SUBJECT TO THE POWER OF YOUR PERFECTION!
IT IS IMPOSSIBLE TO DEFY PERFECTION! IT IS IMPOSSIBLE TO DEFEAT PERFECTION! I CAN'T BE STOPPED! I AM THE PERFECT MAN!

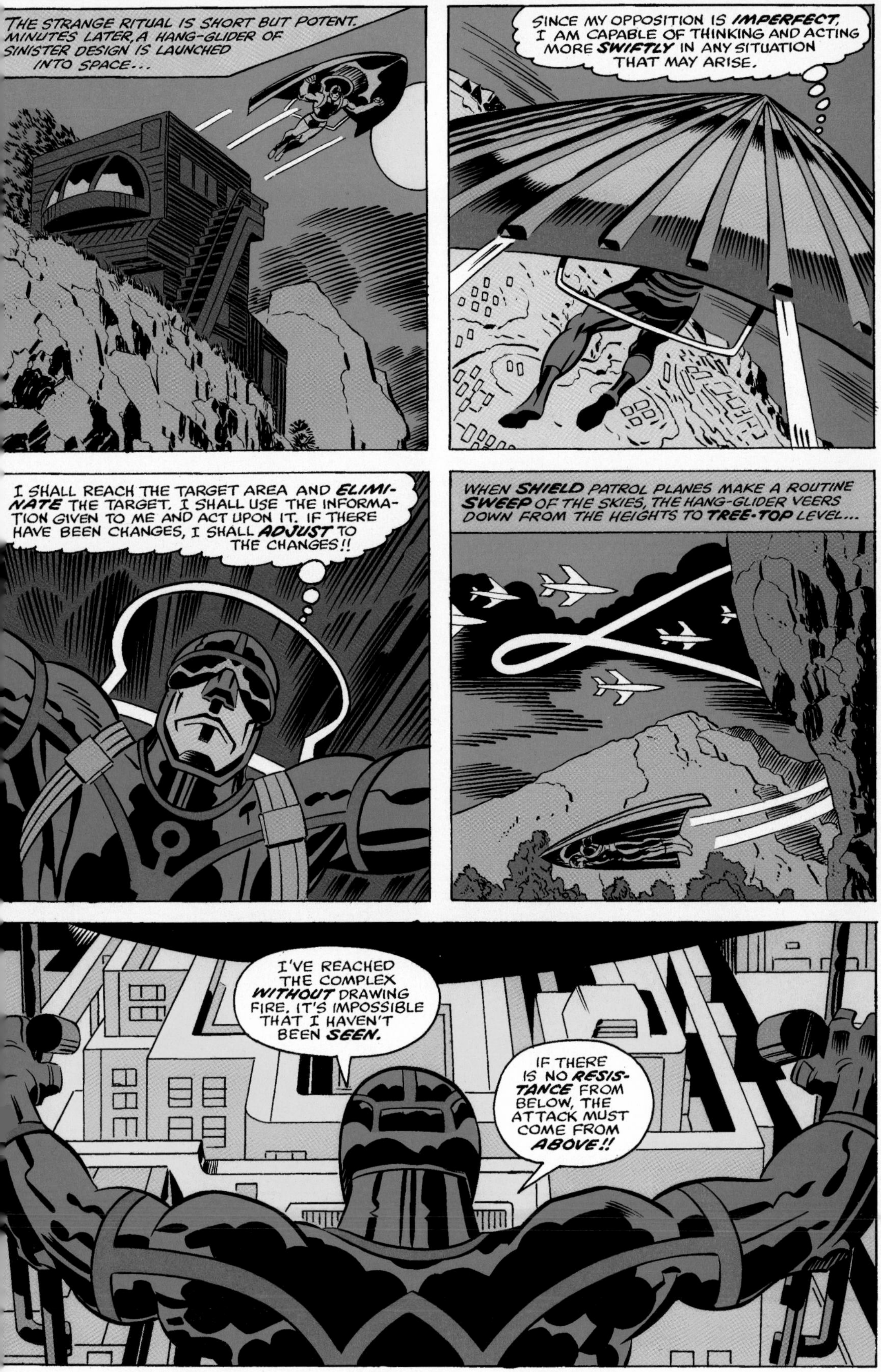

THE STRANGE RITUAL IS SHORT BUT POTENT. MINUTES LATER, A HANG-GLIDER OF SINISTER DESIGN IS LAUNCHED INTO SPACE...
SINCE MY OPPOSITION IS IMPERFECT, I AM CAPABLE OF THINKING AND ACTING MORE SWIFTLY IN ANY SITUATION THAT MAY ARISE.
I SHALL REACH THE TARGET AREA AND ELIMINATE THE TARGET. I SHALL USE THE INFORMATION GIVEN TO ME AND ACT UPON IT. IF THERE HAVE BEEN CHANGES, I SHALL ADJUST TO THE CHANGES!!
WHEN SHIELD PATROL PLANES MAKE A ROUTINE SWEEP OF THE SKIES, THE HANG-GLIDER VEERS DOWN FROM THE HEIGHTS TO TREE-TOP LEVEL...
I'VE REACHED THE COMPLEX WITHOUT DRAWING FIRE. IT'S IMPOSSIBLE THAT I HAVEN'T BEEN SEEN.
IF THERE IS NO RESISTANCE FROM BELOW, THE ATTACK MUST COME FROM ABOVE!!

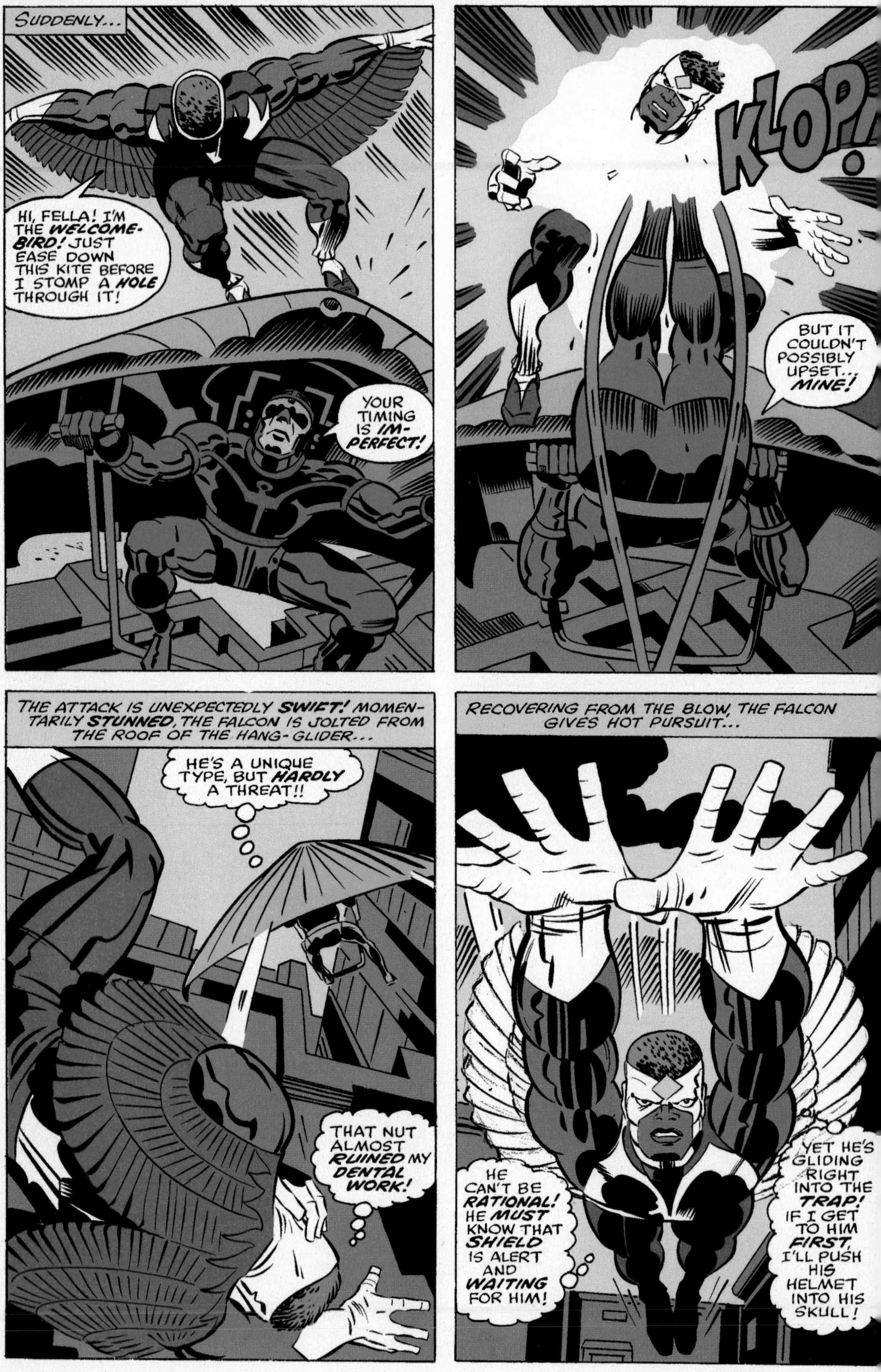
SUDDENLY...
HI, FELLA! I'M THE WELCOME-BIRD! JUST EASE DOWN THIS KITE BEFORE I STOMP A HOLE THROUGH IT!
YOUR TIMING IS IM-PERFECT!
KLOP!
BUT IT COULDN'T POSSIBLY UPSET... MINE!
THE ATTACK IS UNEXPECTEDLY SWIFT! MOMEN-TARILY STUNNED, THE FALCON IS JOLTED FROM THE ROOF OF THE HANG-GLIDER...
HE'S A UNIQUE TYPE, BUT HARDLY A THREAT!!
THAT NUT ALMOST RUINED MY DENTAL WORK!
RECOVERING FROM THE BLOW, THE FALCON GIVES HOT PURSUIT...
HE CAN'T BE RATIONAL! HE MUST KNOW THAT SHIELD IS ALERT AND WAITING FOR HIM!
YET HE'S GLIDING RIGHT INTO THE TRAP! IF I GET TO HIM FIRST, I'LL PUSH HIS HELMET INTO HIS SKULL!

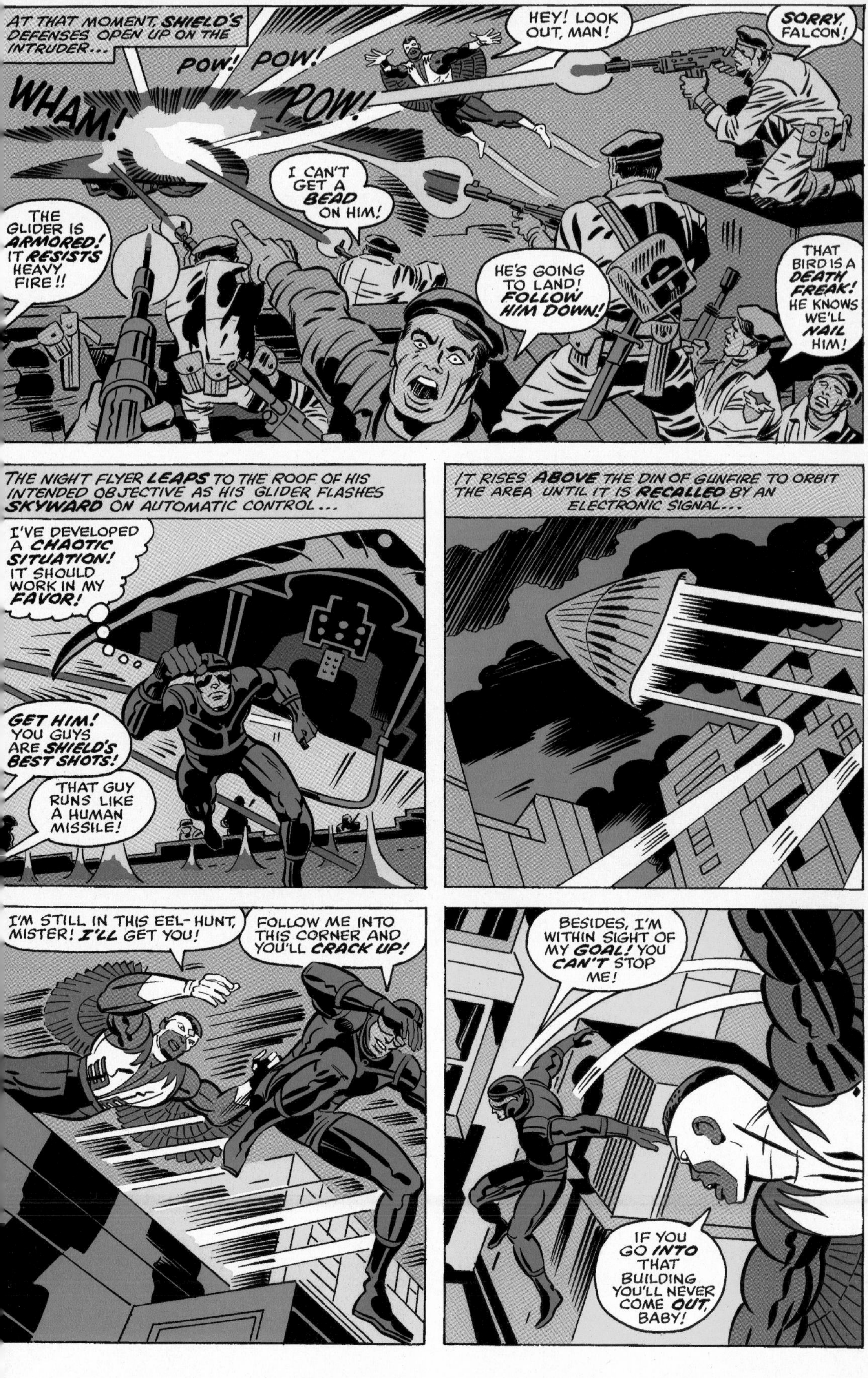

AT THAT MOMENT, SHIELD'S DEFENSES OPEN UP ON THE INTRUDER...
HEY! LOOK OUT, MAN!
SORRY, FALCON!
POW! POW!
WHAM!
POW!
I CAN'T GET A BEAD ON HIM!
THE GLIDER IS ARMORED! IT RESISTS HEAVY FIRE!!
HE'S GOING TO LAND! FOLLOW HIM DOWN!
THAT BIRD IS A DEATH FREAK! HE KNOWS WE'LL NAIL HIM!
THE NIGHT FLYER LEAPS TO THE ROOF OF HIS INTENDED OBJECTIVE AS HIS GLIDER FLASHES SKYWARD ON AUTOMATIC CONTROL...
I'VE DEVELOPED A CHAOTIC SITUATION! IT SHOULD WORK IN MY FAVOR!
GET HIM! YOU GUYS ARE SHIELD'S BEST SHOTS!
THAT GUY RUNS LIKE A HUMAN MISSILE!
IT RISES ABOVE THE DIN OF GUNFIRE TO ORBIT THE AREA UNTIL IT IS RECALLED BY AN ELECTRONIC SIGNAL...
I'M STILL IN THIS EEL-HUNT, MISTER! I'LL GET YOU!
FOLLOW ME INTO THIS CORNER AND YOU'LL CRACK UP!
BESIDES, I'M WITHIN SIGHT OF MY GOAL! YOU CAN'T STOP ME!
IF YOU GO INTO THAT BUILDING YOU'LL NEVER COME OUT, BABY!

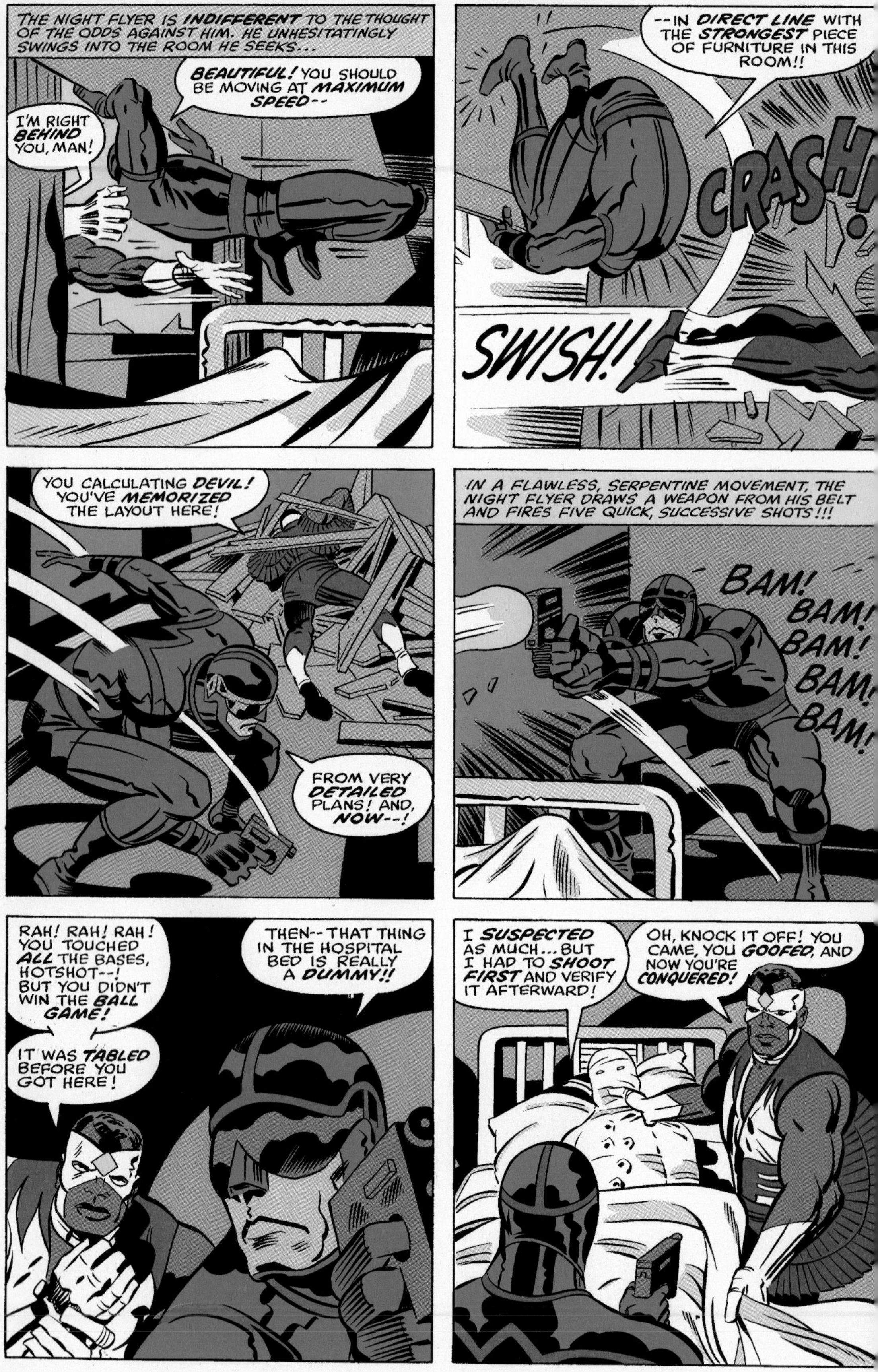
THE NIGHT FLYER IS INDIFFERENT TO THE THOUGHT OF THE ODDS AGAINST HIM. HE UNHESITATINGLY SWINGS INTO THE ROOM HE SEEKS...
BEAUTIFUL! YOU SHOULD BE MOVING AT MAXIMUM SPEED--
I'M RIGHT BEHIND YOU, MAN!
--IN DIRECT LINE WITH THE STRONGEST PIECE OF FURNITURE IN THIS ROOM!!
CRASH!
SWISH!
YOU CALCULATING DEVIL! YOU'VE MEMORIZED THE LAYOUT HERE!
FROM VERY DETAILED PLANS! AND, NOW--!
IN A FLAWLESS, SERPENTINE MOVEMENT, THE NIGHT FLYER DRAWS A WEAPON FROM HIS BELT AND FIRES FIVE QUICK, SUCCESSIVE SHOTS!!!
BAM! BAM! BAM! BAM! BAM!
RAH! RAH! RAH! YOU TOUCHED ALL THE BASES, HOTSHOT--! BUT YOU DIDN'T WIN THE BALL GAME!
IT WAS TABLED BEFORE YOU GOT HERE!
THEN--THAT THING IN THE HOSPITAL BED IS REALLY A DUMMY!!
I SUSPECTED AS MUCH... BUT I HAD TO SHOOT FIRST AND VERIFY IT AFTERWARD!
OH, KNOCK IT OFF! YOU CAME, YOU GOOFED, AND NOW YOU'RE CONQUERED!

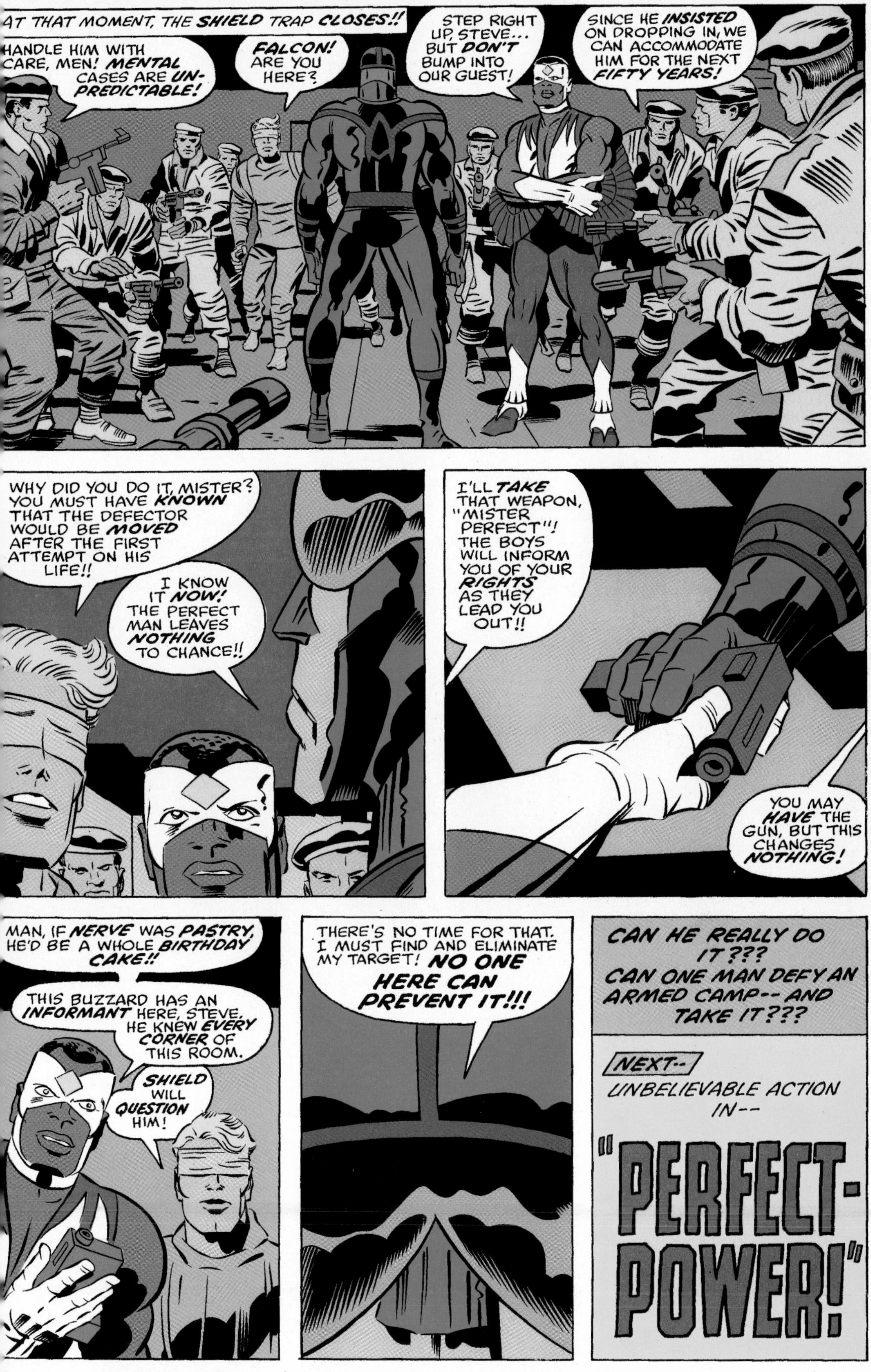
AT THAT MOMENT, THE SHIELD TRAP CLOSES!!
HANDLE HIM WITH CARE, MEN! MENTAL CASES ARE UNPREDICTABLE!
FALCON! ARE YOU HERE?
STEP RIGHT UP, STEVE... BUT DON'T BUMP INTO OUR GUEST!
SINCE HE INSISTED ON DROPPING IN, WE CAN ACCOMMODATE HIM FOR THE NEXT FIFTY YEARS!
WHY DID YOU DO IT, MISTER? YOU MUST HAVE KNOWN THAT THE DEFECTOR WOULD BE MOVED AFTER THE FIRST ATTEMPT ON HIS LIFE!!
I KNOW IT NOW! THE PERFECT MAN LEAVES NOTHING TO CHANCE!!
I'LL TAKE THAT WEAPON, "MISTER PERFECT"! THE BOYS WILL INFORM YOU OF YOUR RIGHTS AS THEY LEAD YOU OUT!!
YOU MAY HAVE THE GUN, BUT THIS CHANGES NOTHING!
MAN, IF NERVE WAS PASTRY, HE'D BE A WHOLE BIRTHDAY CAKE!!
THIS BUZZARD HAS AN INFORMANT HERE, STEVE. HE KNEW EVERY CORNER OF THIS ROOM.
SHIELD WILL QUESTION HIM!
THERE'S NO TIME FOR THAT. I MUST FIND AND ELIMINATE MY TARGET! NO ONE HERE CAN PREVENT IT!!!
CAN HE REALLY DO IT??? CAN ONE MAN DEFY AN ARMED CAMP-- AND TAKE IT???
NEXT--
UNBELIEVABLE ACTION IN--
"PERFECT-POWER!"

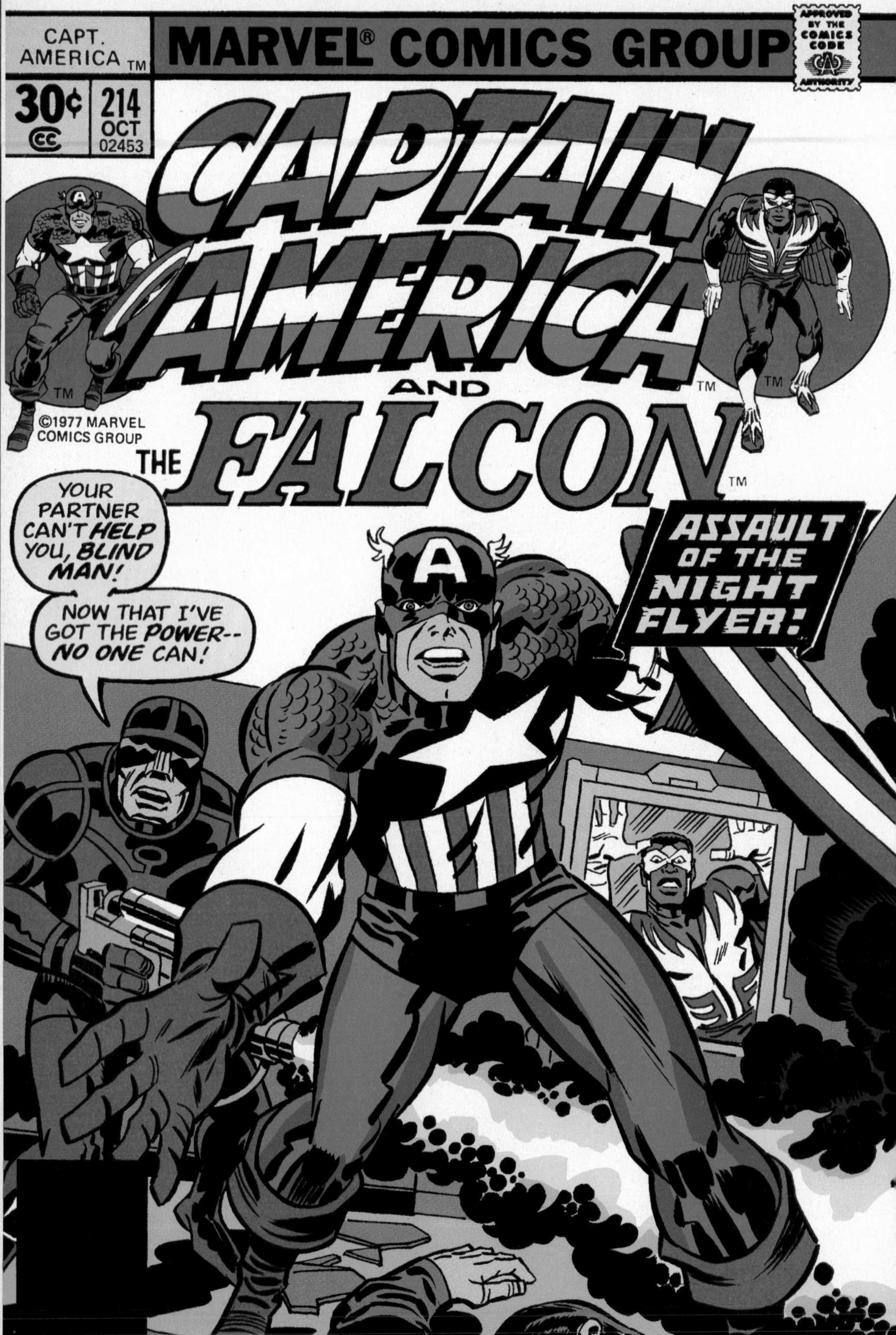
CAPT. AMERICA TM
MARVEL® COMICS GROUP
APPROVED BY THE COMICS CODE AUTHORITY
30¢ CC
214 OCT 02453
CAPTAIN AMERICA TM
AND
THE FALCON TM
TM
TM
©1977 MARVEL COMICS GROUP
YOUR PARTNER CAN'T HELP YOU, BLIND MAN!
NOW THAT I'VE GOT THE POWER-- NO ONE CAN!
ASSAULT OF THE NIGHT FLYER!

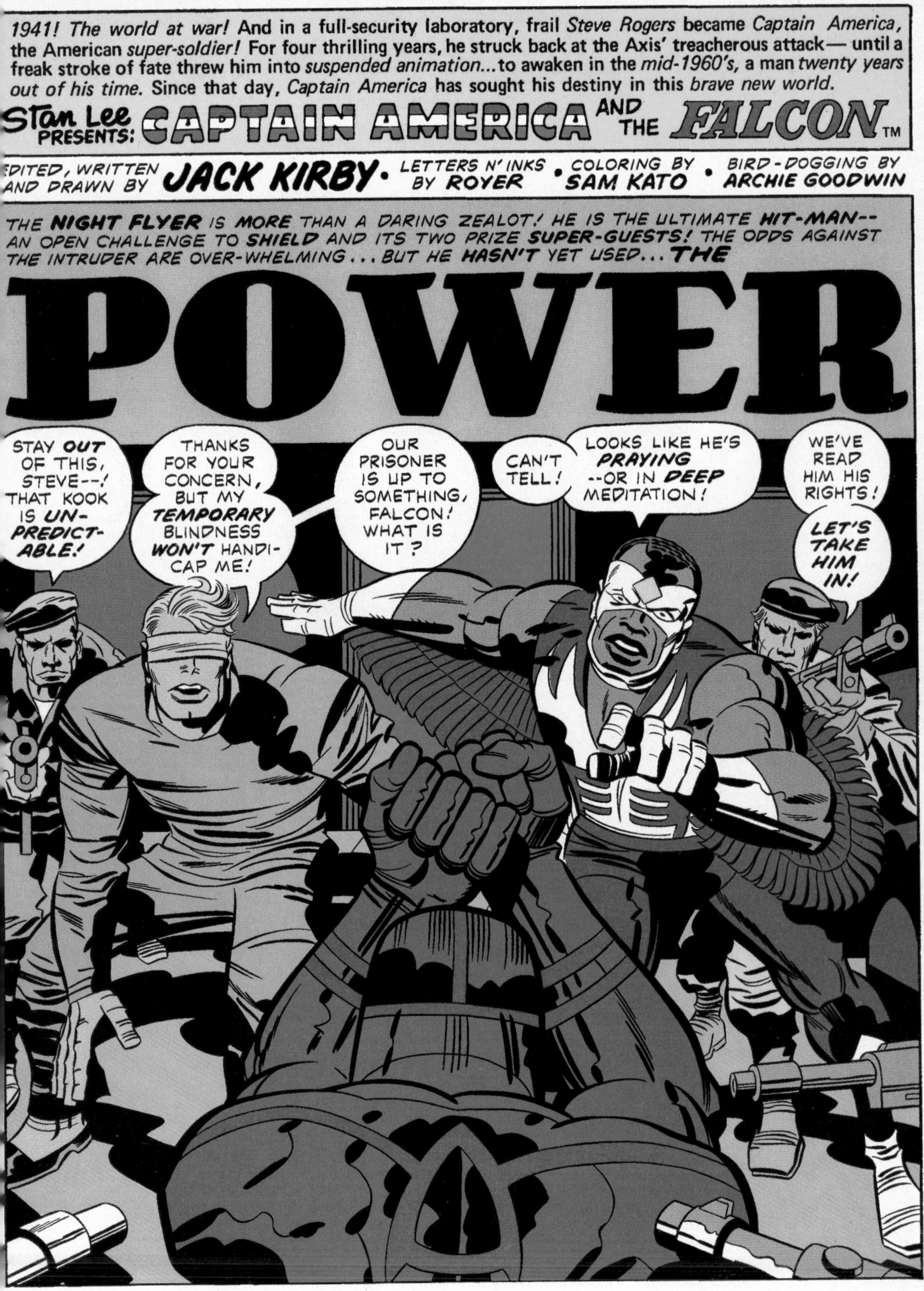
1941! The world at war! And in a full-security laboratory, frail Steve Rogers became Captain America, the American super-soldier! For four thrilling years, he struck back at the Axis' treacherous attack— until a freak stroke of fate threw him into suspended animation...to awaken in the mid-1960's, a man twenty years out of his time. Since that day, Captain America has sought his destiny in this brave new world.
Stan Lee PRESENTS: CAPTAIN AMERICA AND THE FALCON TM
EDITED, WRITTEN AND DRAWN BY JACK KIRBY • LETTERS N' INKS BY ROYER • COLORING BY SAM KATO • BIRD-DOGGING BY ARCHIE GOODWIN
THE NIGHT FLYER IS MORE THAN A DARING ZEALOT! HE IS THE ULTIMATE HIT-MAN-- AN OPEN CHALLENGE TO SHIELD AND ITS TWO PRIZE SUPER-GUESTS! THE ODDS AGAINST THE INTRUDER ARE OVER-WHELMING... BUT HE HASN'T YET USED... THE
POWER
STAY OUT OF THIS, STEVE--! THAT KOOK IS UN-PREDICT-ABLE!
THANKS FOR YOUR CONCERN, BUT MY TEMPORARY BLINDNESS WON'T HANDI-CAP ME!
OUR PRISONER IS UP TO SOMETHING, FALCON! WHAT IS IT?
CAN'T TELL!
LOOKS LIKE HE'S PRAYING --OR IN DEEP MEDITATION!
WE'VE READ HIM HIS RIGHTS!
LET'S TAKE HIM IN!

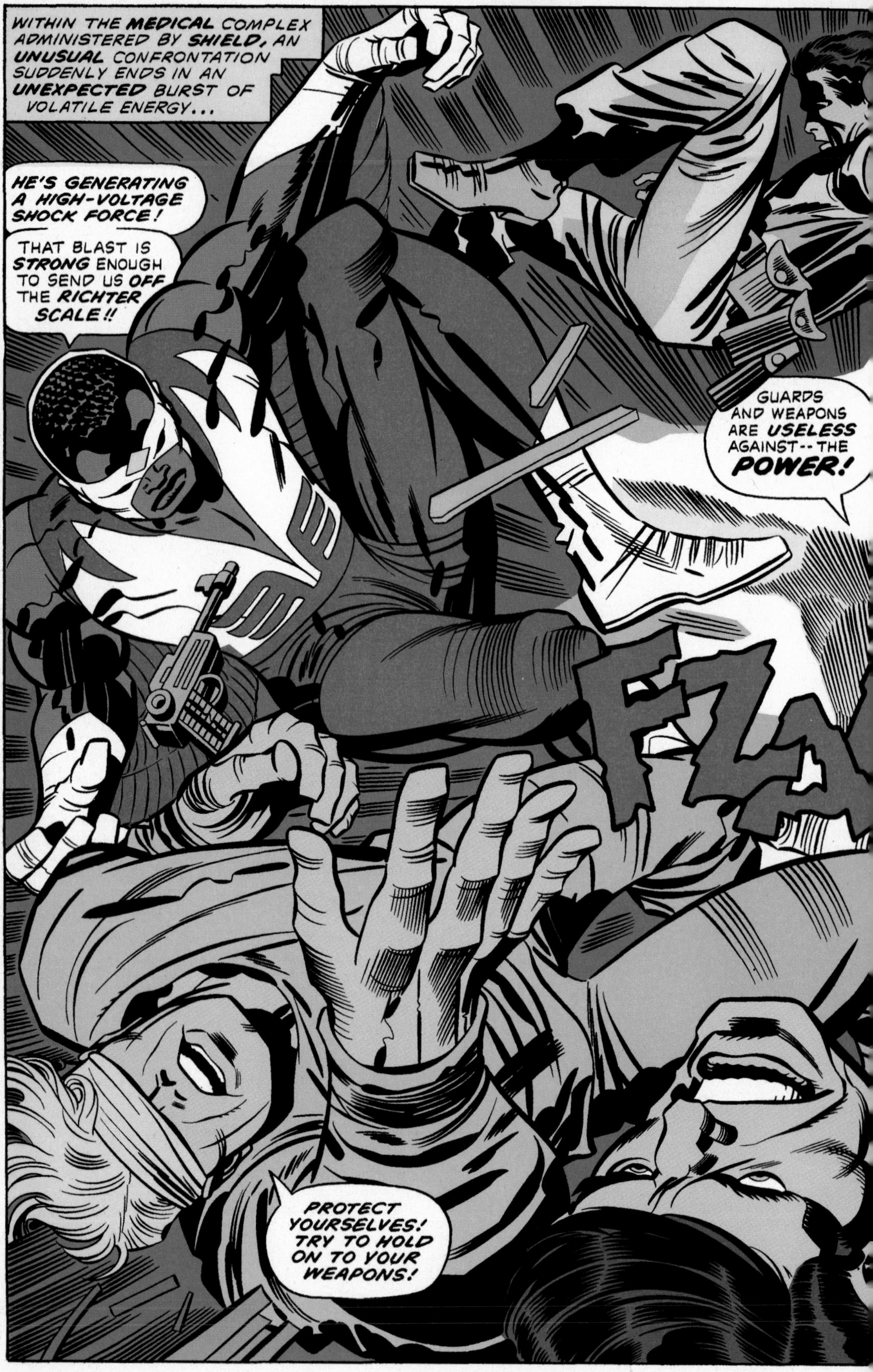
WITHIN THE MEDICAL COMPLEX ADMINISTERED BY SHIELD, AN UNUSUAL CONFRONTATION SUDDENLY ENDS IN AN UNEXPECTED BURST OF VOLATILE ENERGY...
HE'S GENERATING A HIGH-VOLTAGE SHOCK FORCE!
THAT BLAST IS STRONG ENOUGH TO SEND US OFF THE RICHTER SCALE!!
GUARDS AND WEAPONS ARE USELESS AGAINST-- THE POWER!
FZA
PROTECT YOURSELVES! TRY TO HOLD ON TO YOUR WEAPONS!

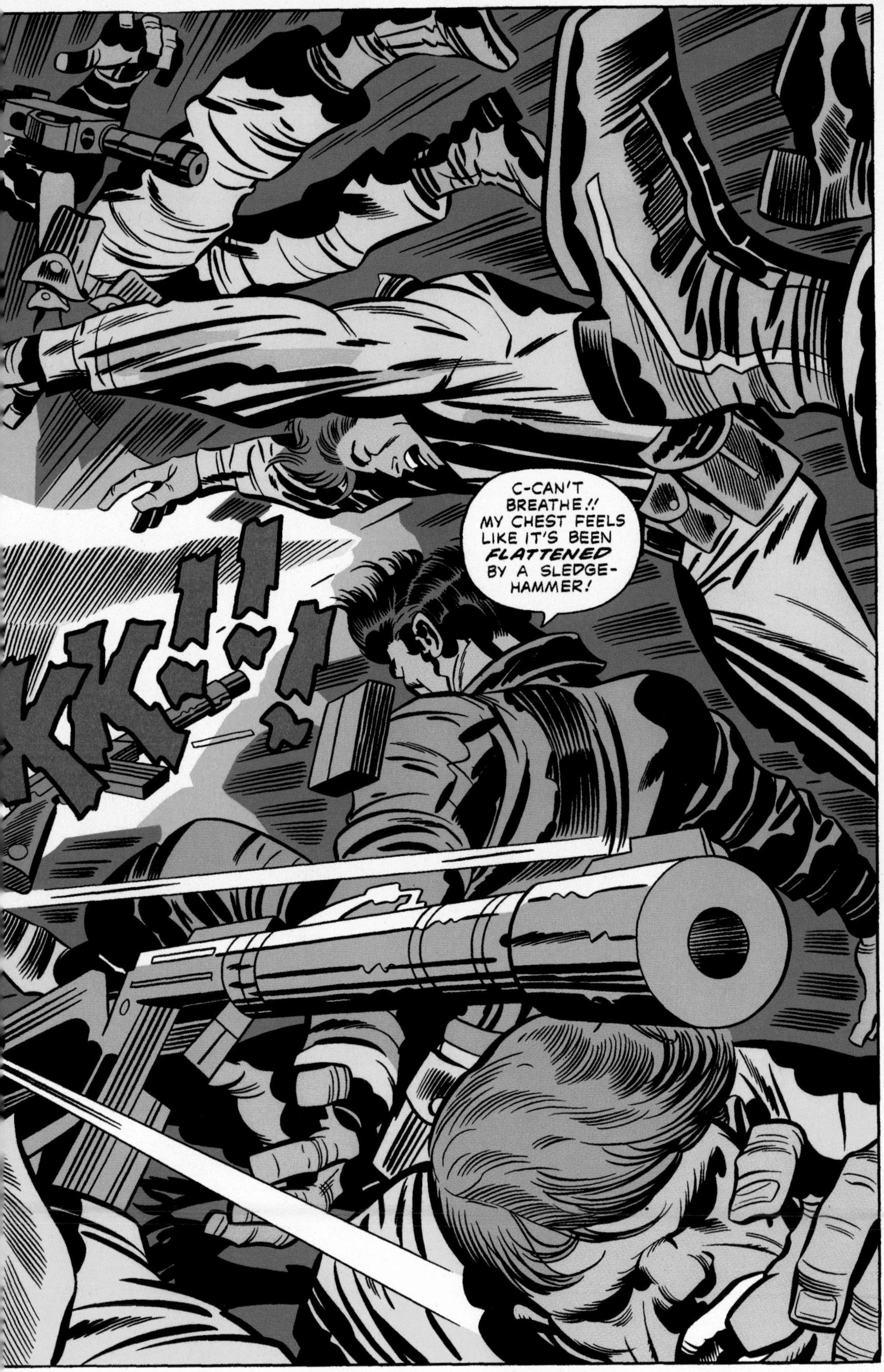
C-CAN'T BREATHE!! MY CHEST FEELS LIKE IT'S BEEN *FLATTENED* BY A SLEDGE-HAMMER!
KK!!

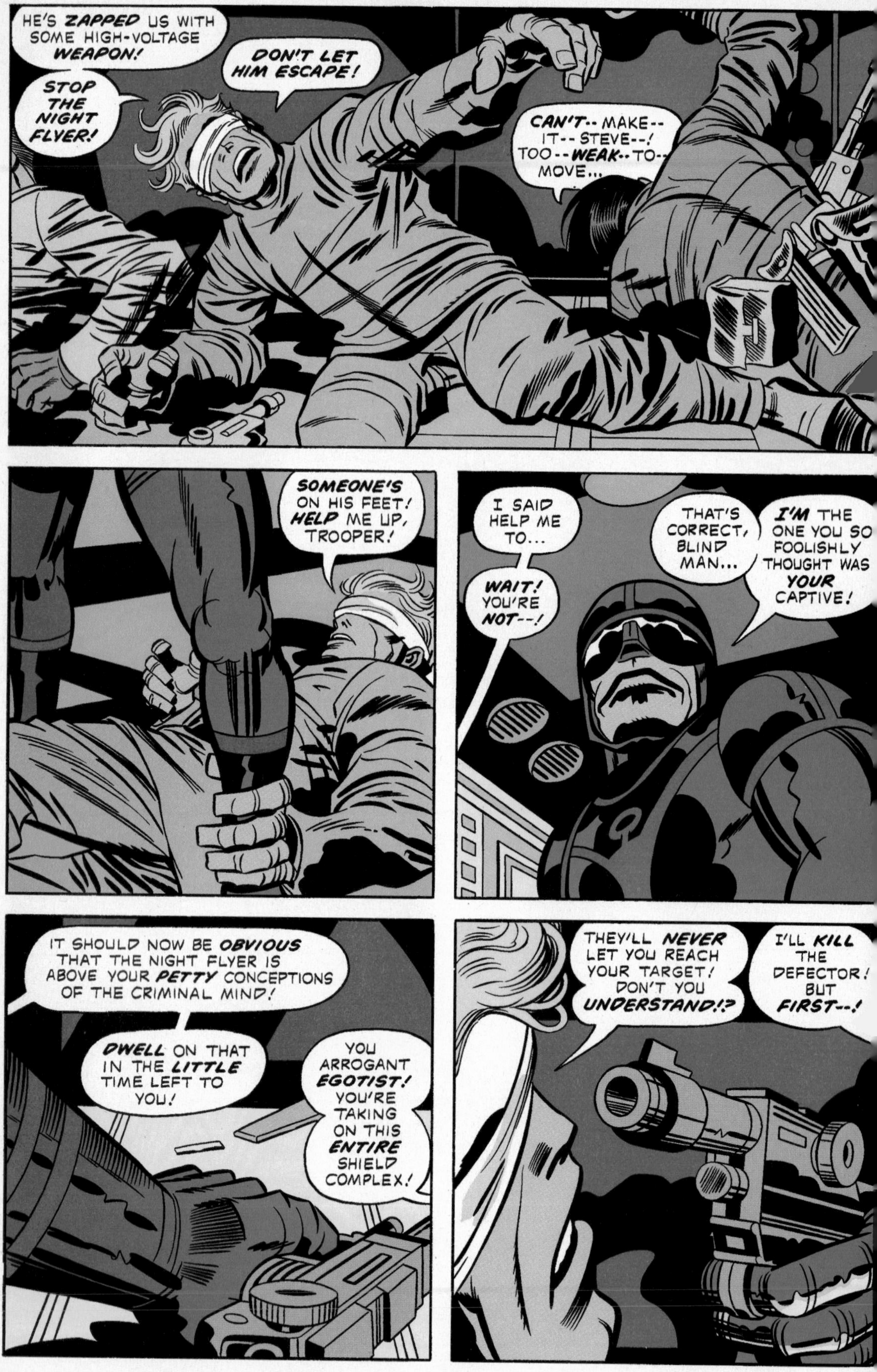
HE'S ZAPPED US WITH SOME HIGH-VOLTAGE WEAPON!
STOP THE NIGHT FLYER!
DON'T LET HIM ESCAPE!
CAN'T-- MAKE-- IT-- STEVE--! TOO-- WEAK-- TO-- MOVE...
SOMEONE'S ON HIS FEET! HELP ME UP, TROOPER!
I SAID HELP ME TO...
WAIT! YOU'RE NOT--!
THAT'S CORRECT, BLIND MAN...
I'M THE ONE YOU SO FOOLISHLY THOUGHT WAS YOUR CAPTIVE!
IT SHOULD NOW BE OBVIOUS THAT THE NIGHT FLYER IS ABOVE YOUR PETTY CONCEPTIONS OF THE CRIMINAL MIND!
DWELL ON THAT IN THE LITTLE TIME LEFT TO YOU!
YOU ARROGANT EGOTIST! YOU'RE TAKING ON THIS ENTIRE SHIELD COMPLEX!
THEY'LL NEVER LET YOU REACH YOUR TARGET! DON'T YOU UNDERSTAND!?
I'LL KILL THE DEFECTOR! BUT FIRST--!

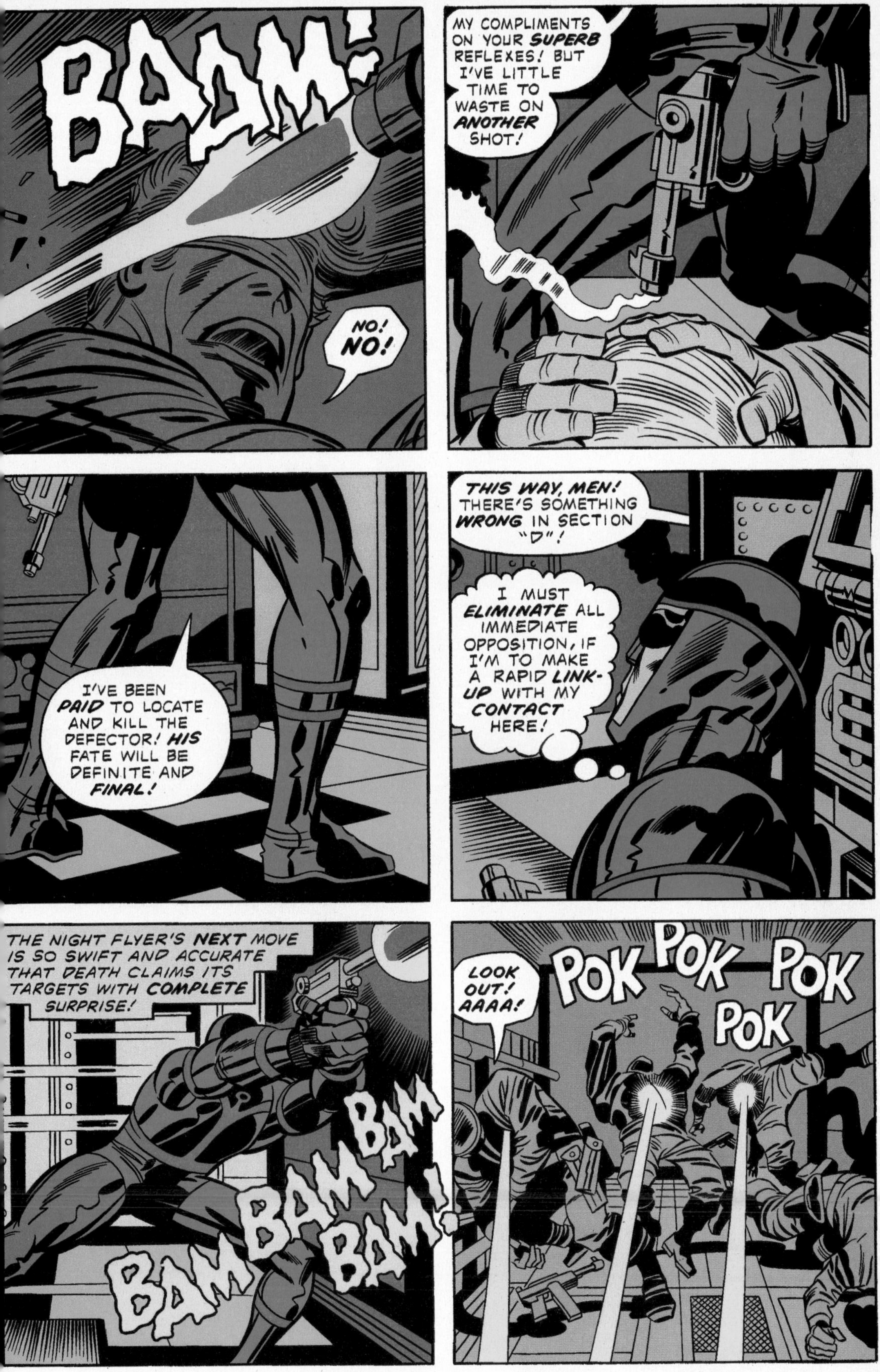

BAAM!
NO! NO!
MY COMPLIMENTS ON YOUR SUPERB REFLEXES! BUT I'VE LITTLE TIME TO WASTE ON ANOTHER SHOT!
I'VE BEEN PAID TO LOCATE AND KILL THE DEFECTOR! HIS FATE WILL BE DEFINITE AND FINAL!
THIS WAY, MEN! THERE'S SOMETHING WRONG IN SECTION "D"!
I MUST ELIMINATE ALL IMMEDIATE OPPOSITION, IF I'M TO MAKE A RAPID LINK-UP WITH MY CONTACT HERE!
THE NIGHT FLYER'S NEXT MOVE IS SO SWIFT AND ACCURATE THAT DEATH CLAIMS ITS TARGETS WITH COMPLETE SURPRISE!
BAM BAM BAM BAM!
LOOK OUT! AAAA!
POK POK POK POK

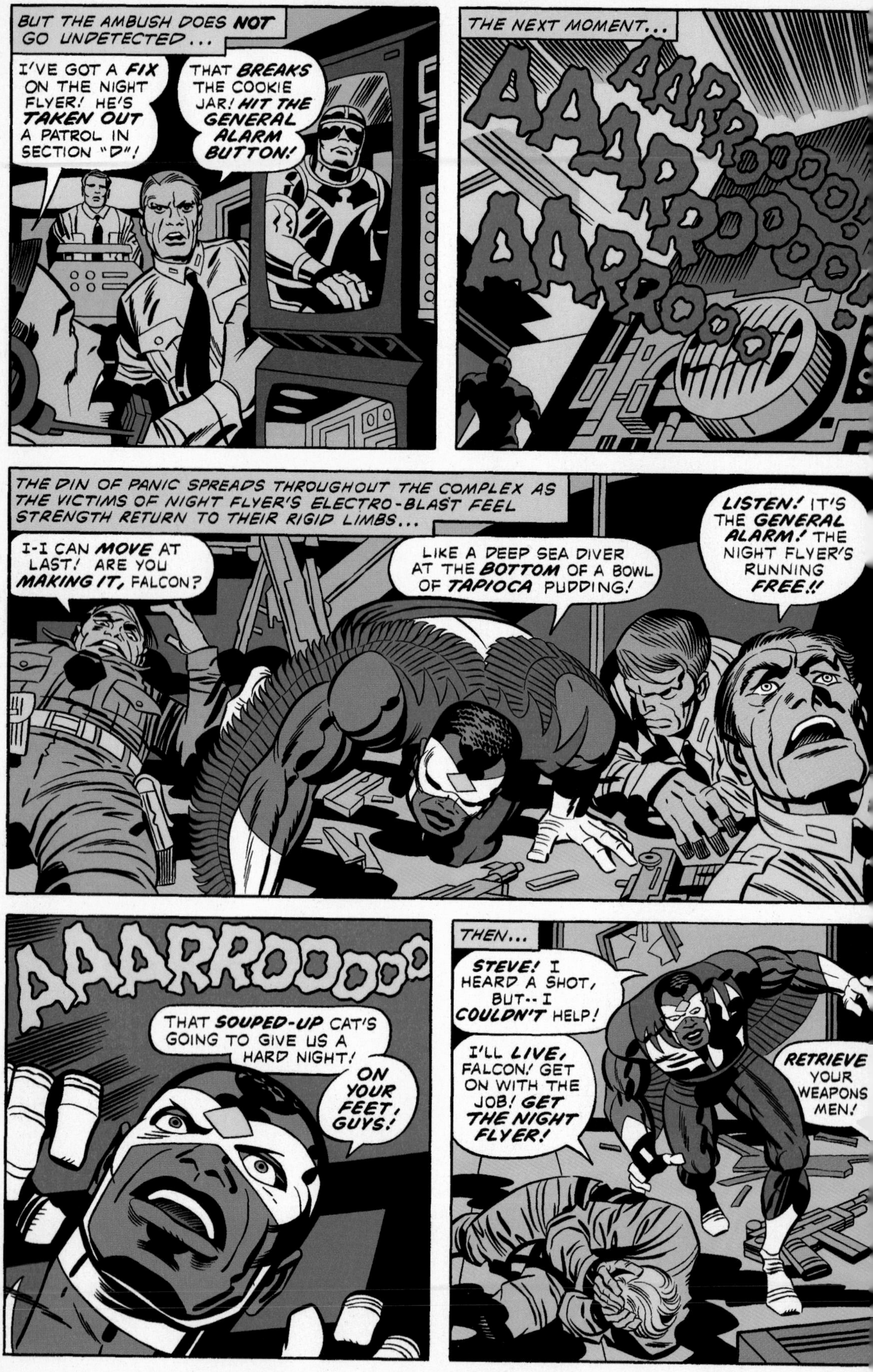
BUT THE AMBUSH DOES NOT GO UNDETECTED...
I'VE GOT A FIX ON THE NIGHT FLYER! HE'S TAKEN OUT A PATROL IN SECTION "D"!
THAT BREAKS THE COOKIE JAR! HIT THE GENERAL ALARM BUTTON!
THE NEXT MOMENT...
AAARROOOOO! AAARROOOOO! AAARROOOO
THE DIN OF PANIC SPREADS THROUGHOUT THE COMPLEX AS THE VICTIMS OF NIGHT FLYER'S ELECTRO-BLAST FEEL STRENGTH RETURN TO THEIR RIGID LIMBS...
I-I CAN MOVE AT LAST! ARE YOU MAKING IT, FALCON?
LIKE A DEEP SEA DIVER AT THE BOTTOM OF A BOWL OF TAPIOCA PUDDING!
LISTEN! IT'S THE GENERAL ALARM! THE NIGHT FLYER'S RUNNING FREE!!
AAARROOOOOO
THAT SOUPED-UP CAT'S GOING TO GIVE US A HARD NIGHT!
ON YOUR FEET, GUYS!
THEN...
STEVE! I HEARD A SHOT, BUT-- I COULDN'T HELP!
I'LL LIVE, FALCON! GET ON WITH THE JOB! GET THE NIGHT FLYER!
RETRIEVE YOUR WEAPONS MEN!

DON'T WASTE TIME ON ME! HIS SHOT JUST ADDED INSULT TO INJURY! IT WAS *CLOSE* TO MY EYES!

LET ME *CHECK!* YOU'VE BEEN BADLY *SINGED,* MAN!

YEAH... WELL, POWDER BURNS AREN'T AS *NEAT* AS BULLET PUNCTURES, BUT AT LEAST YOU CAN *LIVE* TO BEEF ABOUT THEM!

I DON'T LIKE THAT NIGHT FLYER, STEVE! I DON'T LIKE A WEIRD CAT WHO KILLS LIKE A COLD, INDIFFERENT MACHINE!

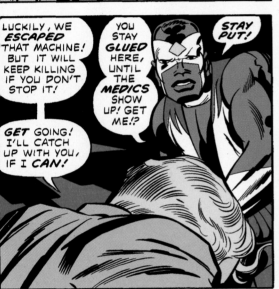

LUCKILY, WE *ESCAPED* THAT MACHINE! BUT IT WILL KEEP KILLING IF YOU DON'T *STOP* IT!

GET GOING! I'LL CATCH UP WITH YOU, IF I *CAN!*

YOU STAY *GLUED* HERE, UNTIL THE *MEDICS* SHOW UP! GET ME!?

STAY PUT!

TIME TO SPLIT, HEROES! SHAKE THE LEAD OUT AND TEAR UP THE PLACE UNTIL YOU'VE *FOUND* OUR BOY!

THAT KIND OF *RATTLER* GIVES ONE *LITTLE* CHOICE!

WHEN YOU SPOT HIM -- *SHOOT* TO KILL!

SOON AFTER...

SPREAD OUT-- AND WATCH FOR SURPRISES!

I CAN *STILL* FEEL THE SPARKS OF THAT FIRST ONE!

STAY WITH IT, MEN! A FAST SWEEP OF THIS CORRIDOR MAY GET SOME *RESULTS!*

LAND ON HIM *HARD* IF YOU COLLAR HIM!

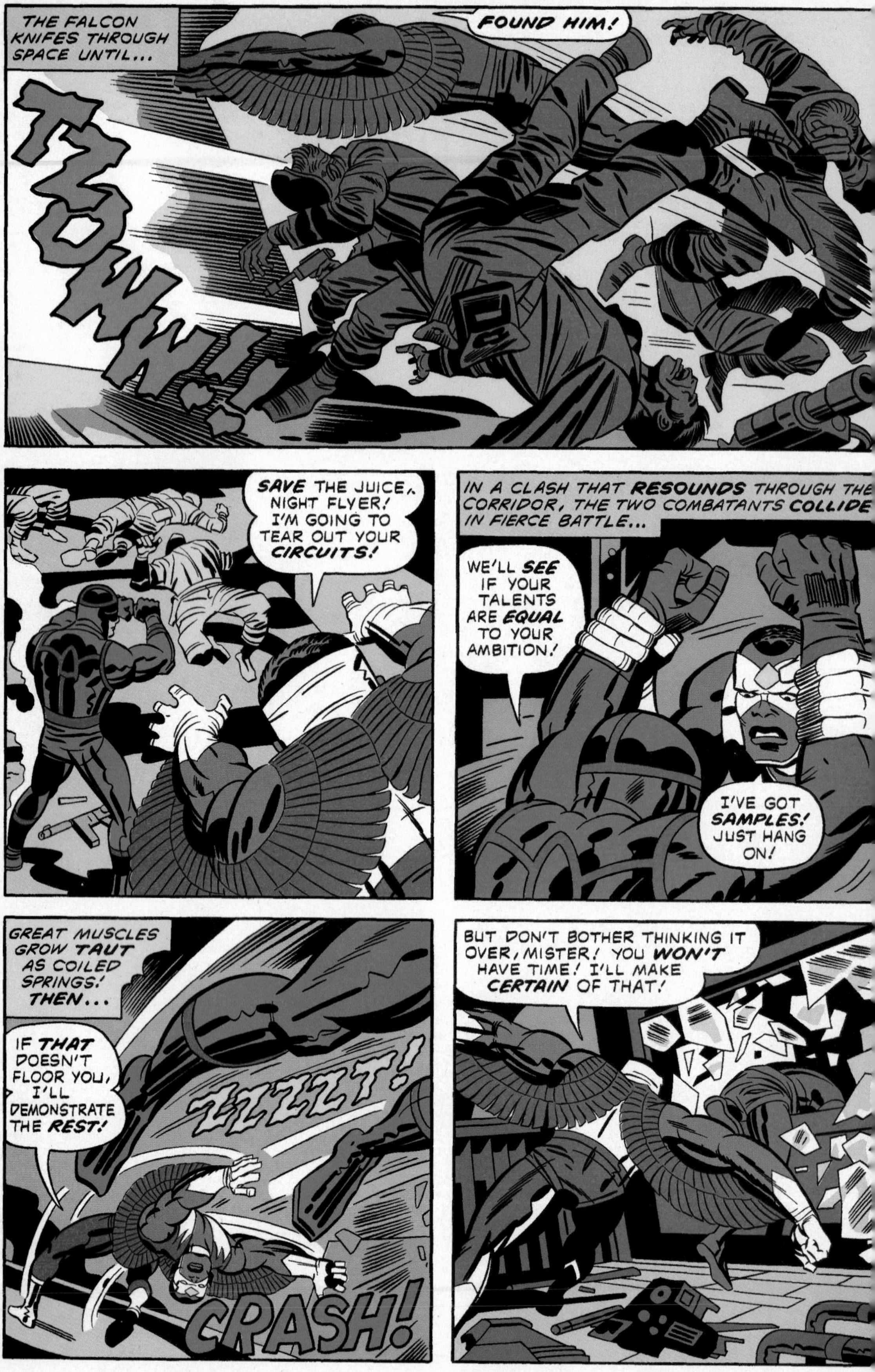

THE FALCON KNIFES THROUGH SPACE UNTIL...
FOUND HIM!
TZOWW!!
SAVE THE JUICE, NIGHT FLYER! I'M GOING TO TEAR OUT YOUR CIRCUITS!
IN A CLASH THAT RESOUNDS THROUGH THE CORRIDOR, THE TWO COMBATANTS COLLIDE IN FIERCE BATTLE...
WE'LL SEE IF YOUR TALENTS ARE EQUAL TO YOUR AMBITION!
I'VE GOT SAMPLES! JUST HANG ON!
GREAT MUSCLES GROW TAUT AS COILED SPRINGS! THEN...
IF THAT DOESN'T FLOOR YOU, I'LL DEMONSTRATE THE REST!
ZZZZT!
CRASH!
BUT DON'T BOTHER THINKING IT OVER, MISTER! YOU WON'T HAVE TIME! I'LL MAKE CERTAIN OF THAT!

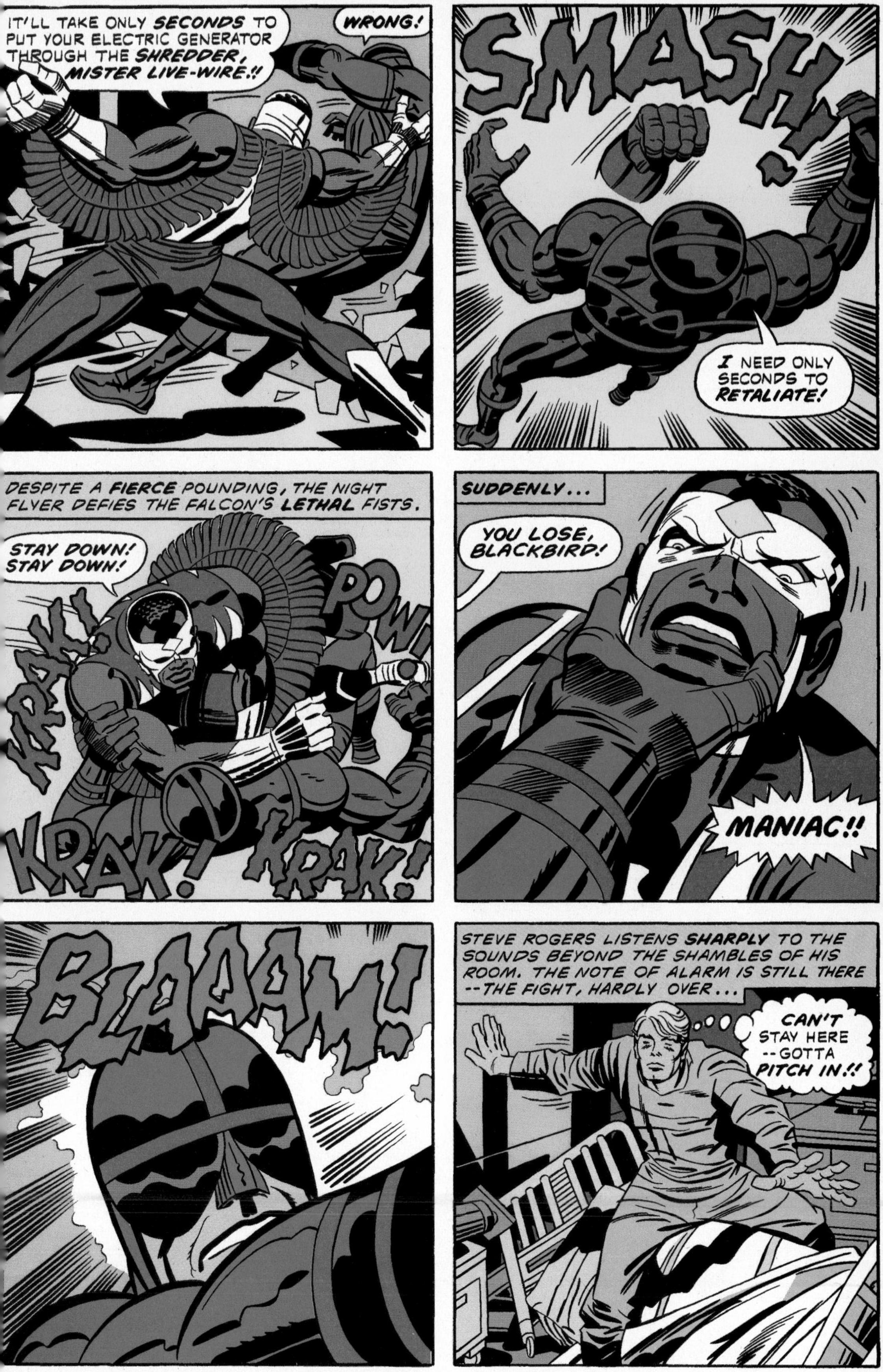

IT'LL TAKE ONLY SECONDS TO PUT YOUR ELECTRIC GENERATOR THROUGH THE SHREDDER, MISTER LIVE-WIRE.!!
WRONG!
SMASH!
I NEED ONLY SECONDS TO RETALIATE!
DESPITE A FIERCE POUNDING, THE NIGHT FLYER DEFIES THE FALCON'S LETHAL FISTS.
STAY DOWN! STAY DOWN!
KRAK!
POW!
KRAK!
KRAK!
SUDDENLY...
YOU LOSE, BLACKBIRD!
MANIAC!!
BLAAAM!
STEVE ROGERS LISTENS SHARPLY TO THE SOUNDS BEYOND THE SHAMBLES OF HIS ROOM. THE NOTE OF ALARM IS STILL THERE --THE FIGHT, HARDLY OVER...
CAN'T STAY HERE --GOTTA PITCH IN.!!

STILL *NUMBED* BY HIS WOUNDS, STEVE SHAKILY MAKES HIS WAY TO A FAR DOOR. HE FUMBLES FOR A *HIDDEN* STUD...

GOT IT! A GOOD MEMORY IS EVERY BIT AS VALUABLE AS GOOD *VISION!*

SNIK!

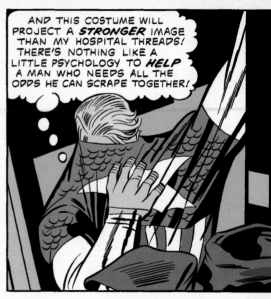

AND THIS COSTUME WILL PROJECT A *STRONGER* IMAGE THAN MY HOSPITAL THREADS! THERE'S NOTHING LIKE A LITTLE PSYCHOLOGY TO *HELP* A MAN WHO NEEDS ALL THE ODDS HE CAN SCRAPE TOGETHER!

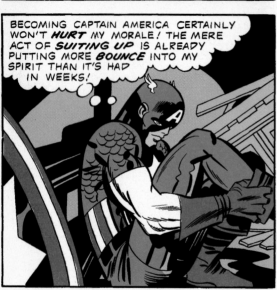

BECOMING CAPTAIN AMERICA CERTAINLY WON'T *HURT* MY MORALE! THE MERE ACT OF *SUITING UP* IS ALREADY PUTTING MORE *BOUNCE* INTO MY SPIRIT THAN IT'S HAD IN WEEKS!

WHATEVER HAPPENS NOW CAN ONLY BE A *PLUS*, AS FAR AS I'M CONCERNED! IF MY *FUNCTIONING* FACULTIES REMAIN SHARP, I MAY GET SOME LICKS IN *YET!*

I HEAR THE SOUND OF POUNDING BOOTS IN THE DISTANCE... THE *SHIELD* PATROLS ARE *STILL* ON THE HUNT!

I WONDER IF THE *FALCON* HAS FOUND THE *QUARRY!?*

AT THAT MOMENT...

THESE FOOTFALLS ARE SOFTER--*STEALTHIER!* HE WEARS THE HEAVY SHOE OF A *TROOPER*, BUT...

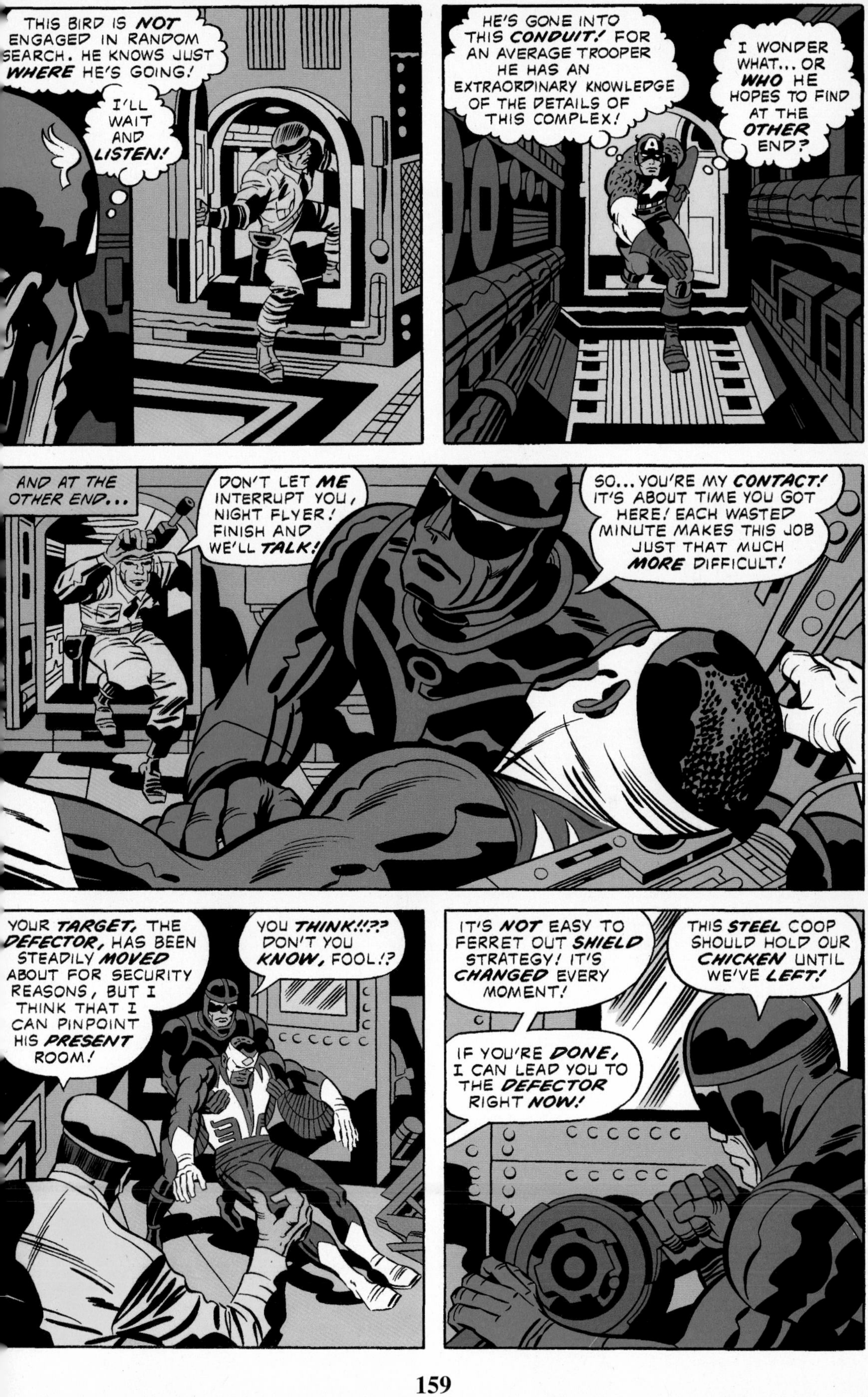

THIS BIRD IS NOT ENGAGED IN RANDOM SEARCH. HE KNOWS JUST WHERE HE'S GOING!
I'LL WAIT AND LISTEN!
HE'S GONE INTO THIS CONDUIT! FOR AN AVERAGE TROOPER HE HAS AN EXTRAORDINARY KNOWLEDGE OF THE DETAILS OF THIS COMPLEX!
I WONDER WHAT... OR WHO HE HOPES TO FIND AT THE OTHER END?
AND AT THE OTHER END...
DON'T LET ME INTERRUPT YOU, NIGHT FLYER! FINISH AND WE'LL TALK!
SO... YOU'RE MY CONTACT! IT'S ABOUT TIME YOU GOT HERE! EACH WASTED MINUTE MAKES THIS JOB JUST THAT MUCH MORE DIFFICULT!
YOUR TARGET, THE DEFECTOR, HAS BEEN STEADILY MOVED ABOUT FOR SECURITY REASONS, BUT I THINK THAT I CAN PINPOINT HIS PRESENT ROOM!
YOU THINK!!?? DON'T YOU KNOW, FOOL!?
IT'S NOT EASY TO FERRET OUT SHIELD STRATEGY! IT'S CHANGED EVERY MOMENT!
IF YOU'RE DONE, I CAN LEAD YOU TO THE DEFECTOR RIGHT NOW!
THIS STEEL COOP SHOULD HOLD OUR CHICKEN UNTIL WE'VE LEFT!

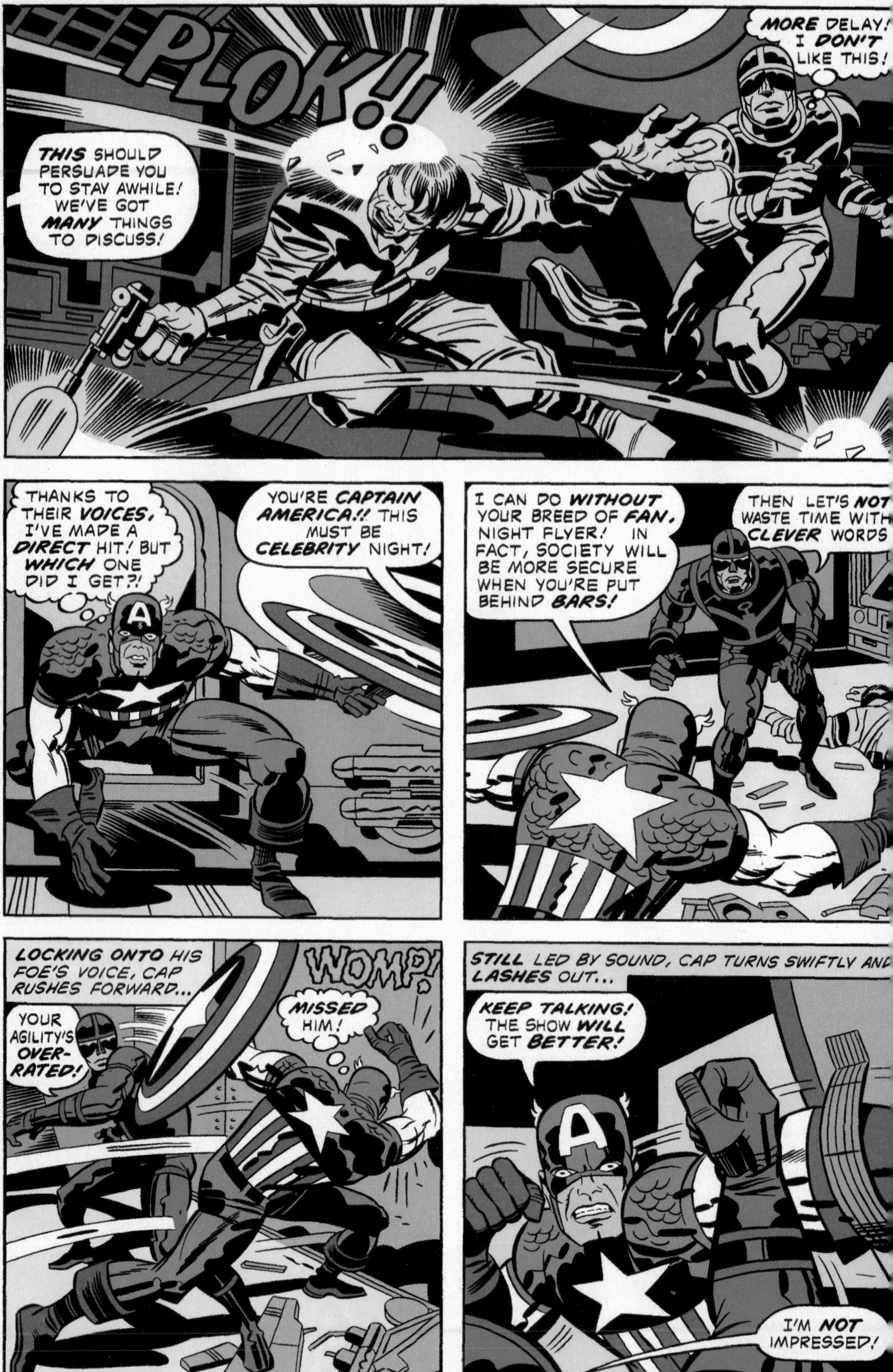
PLOK!!
MORE DELAY! I DON'T LIKE THIS!
THIS SHOULD PERSUADE YOU TO STAY AWHILE! WE'VE GOT MANY THINGS TO DISCUSS!
THANKS TO THEIR VOICES, I'VE MADE A DIRECT HIT! BUT WHICH ONE DID I GET?!
YOU'RE CAPTAIN AMERICA!! THIS MUST BE CELEBRITY NIGHT!
I CAN DO WITHOUT YOUR BREED OF FAN, NIGHT FLYER! IN FACT, SOCIETY WILL BE MORE SECURE WHEN YOU'RE PUT BEHIND BARS!
THEN LET'S NOT WASTE TIME WITH CLEVER WORDS
LOCKING ONTO HIS FOE'S VOICE, CAP RUSHES FORWARD...
WOMP!
YOUR AGILITY'S OVER-RATED!
MISSED HIM!
STILL LED BY SOUND, CAP TURNS SWIFTLY AND LASHES OUT...
KEEP TALKING! THE SHOW WILL GET BETTER!
I'M NOT IMPRESSED!

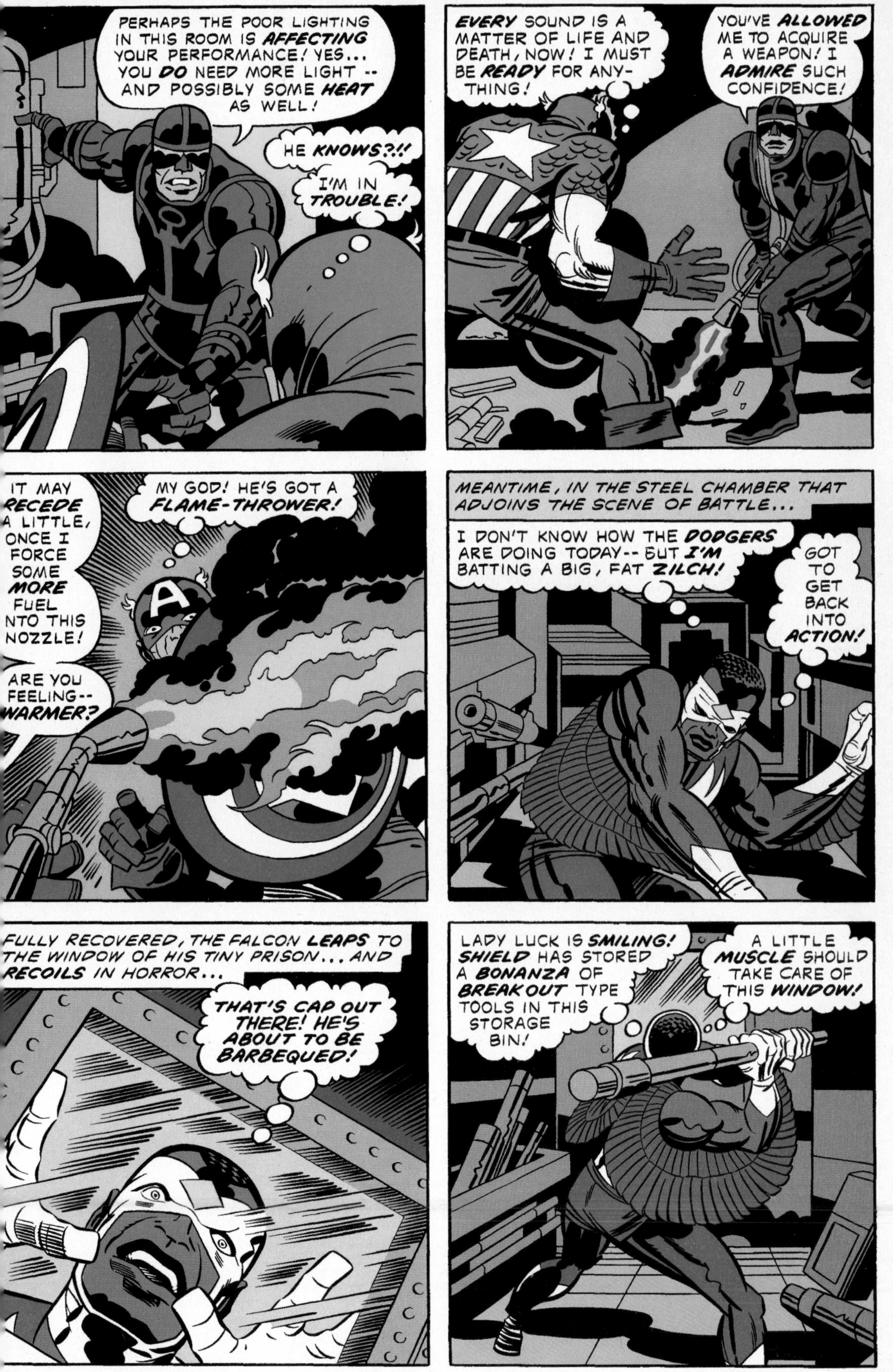

PERHAPS THE POOR LIGHTING IN THIS ROOM IS AFFECTING YOUR PERFORMANCE! YES... YOU DO NEED MORE LIGHT -- AND POSSIBLY SOME HEAT AS WELL!
HE KNOWS?!!
I'M IN TROUBLE!
EVERY SOUND IS A MATTER OF LIFE AND DEATH, NOW! I MUST BE READY FOR ANYTHING!
YOU'VE ALLOWED ME TO ACQUIRE A WEAPON! I ADMIRE SUCH CONFIDENCE!
IT MAY RECEDE A LITTLE, ONCE I FORCE SOME MORE FUEL NTO THIS NOZZLE!
MY GOD! HE'S GOT A FLAME-THROWER!
ARE YOU FEELING-- WARMER?
MEANTIME, IN THE STEEL CHAMBER THAT ADJOINS THE SCENE OF BATTLE...
I DON'T KNOW HOW THE DODGERS ARE DOING TODAY-- BUT I'M BATTING A BIG, FAT ZILCH!
GOT TO GET BACK INTO ACTION!
FULLY RECOVERED, THE FALCON LEAPS TO THE WINDOW OF HIS TINY PRISON... AND RECOILS IN HORROR...
THAT'S CAP OUT THERE! HE'S ABOUT TO BE BARBEQUED!
LADY LUCK IS SMILING! SHIELD HAS STORED A BONANZA OF BREAKOUT TYPE TOOLS IN THIS STORAGE BIN!
A LITTLE MUSCLE SHOULD TAKE CARE OF THIS WINDOW!

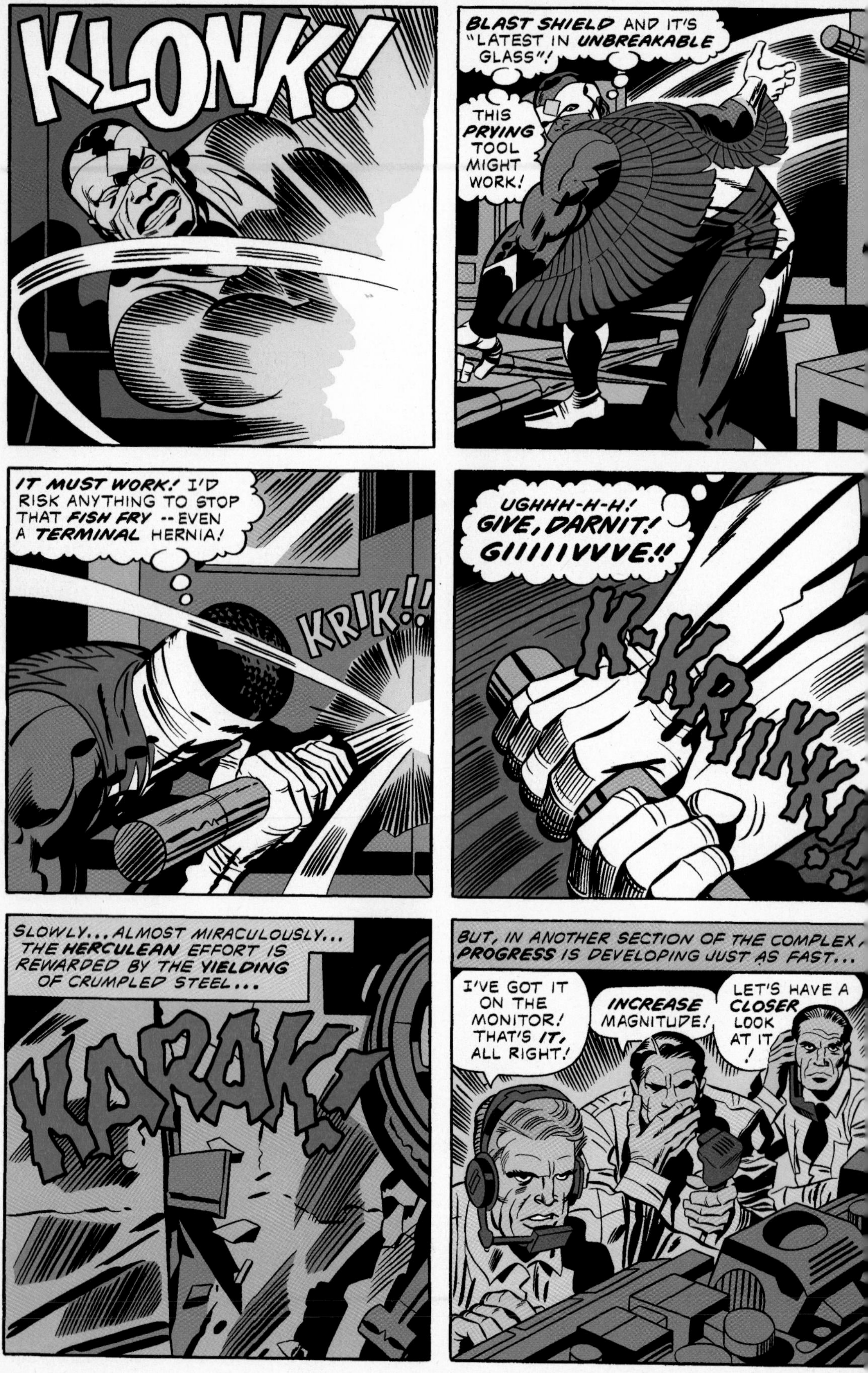
KLONK!
BLAST SHIELD AND IT'S "LATEST IN UNBREAKABLE GLASS"!
THIS PRYING TOOL MIGHT WORK!
IT MUST WORK! I'D RISK ANYTHING TO STOP THAT FISH FRY -- EVEN A TERMINAL HERNIA!
KRIK!!
UGHHH-H-H! GIVE, DARNIT! GIIIIIVVVE!!
K-KRIKK!!
SLOWLY... ALMOST MIRACULOUSLY... THE HERCULEAN EFFORT IS REWARDED BY THE YIELDING OF CRUMPLED STEEL...
KARAK!
BUT, IN ANOTHER SECTION OF THE COMPLEX, PROGRESS IS DEVELOPING JUST AS FAST...
I'VE GOT IT ON THE MONITOR! THAT'S IT, ALL RIGHT!
INCREASE MAGNITUDE!
LET'S HAVE A CLOSER LOOK AT IT!

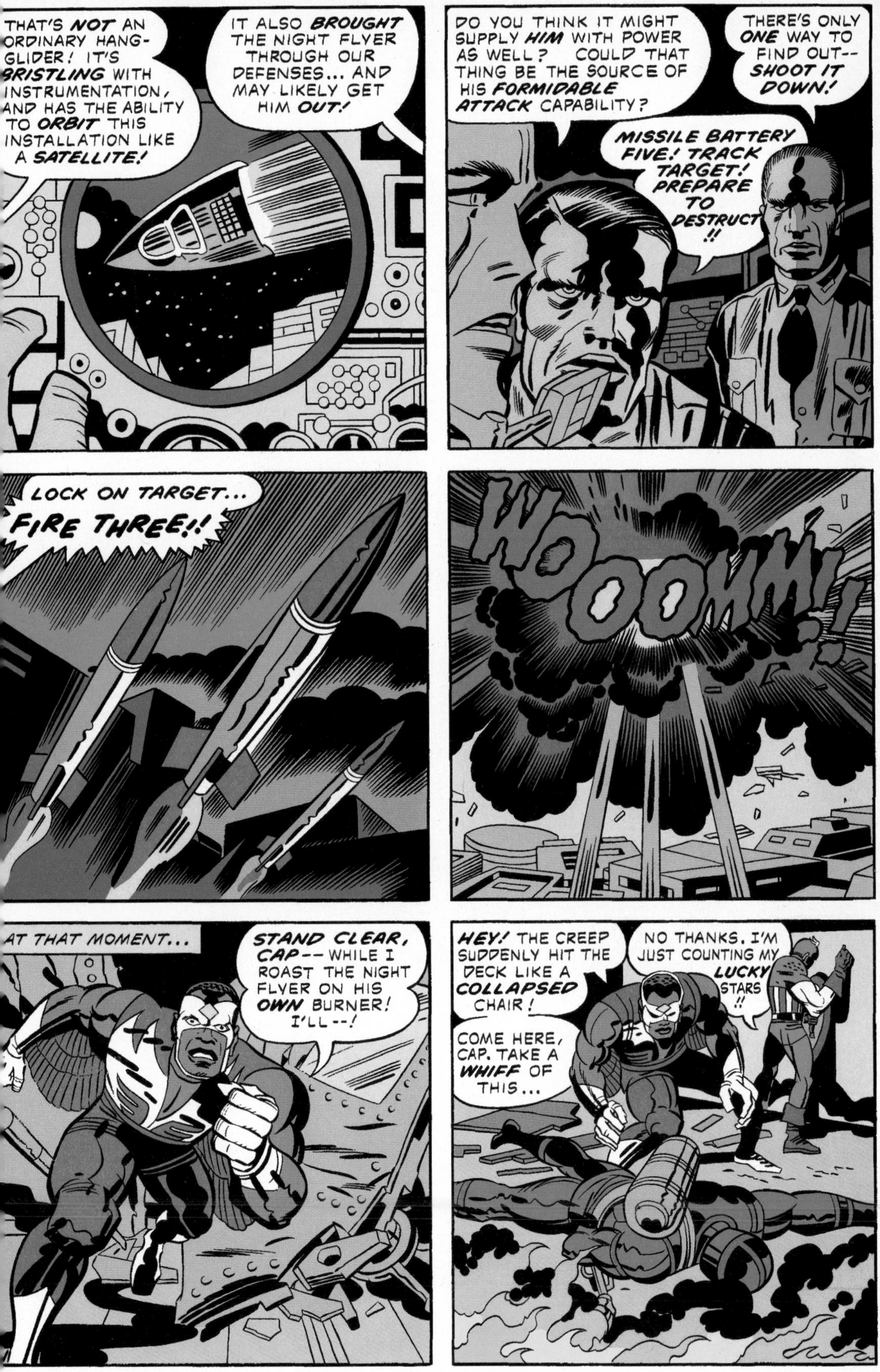
THAT'S NOT AN ORDINARY HANG-GLIDER! IT'S BRISTLING WITH INSTRUMENTATION, AND HAS THE ABILITY TO ORBIT THIS INSTALLATION LIKE A SATELLITE!
IT ALSO BROUGHT THE NIGHT FLYER THROUGH OUR DEFENSES... AND MAY LIKELY GET HIM OUT!
DO YOU THINK IT MIGHT SUPPLY HIM WITH POWER AS WELL? COULD THAT THING BE THE SOURCE OF HIS FORMIDABLE ATTACK CAPABILITY?
THERE'S ONLY ONE WAY TO FIND OUT-- SHOOT IT DOWN!
MISSILE BATTERY FIVE! TRACK TARGET! PREPARE TO DESTRUCT!!
LOCK ON TARGET... FIRE THREE!!
WOOOMM!!
AT THAT MOMENT...
STAND CLEAR, CAP-- WHILE I ROAST THE NIGHT FLYER ON HIS OWN BURNER! I'LL--!
HEY! THE CREEP SUDDENLY HIT THE DECK LIKE A COLLAPSED CHAIR!
NO THANKS. I'M JUST COUNTING MY LUCKY STARS!!
COME HERE, CAP. TAKE A WHIFF OF THIS...

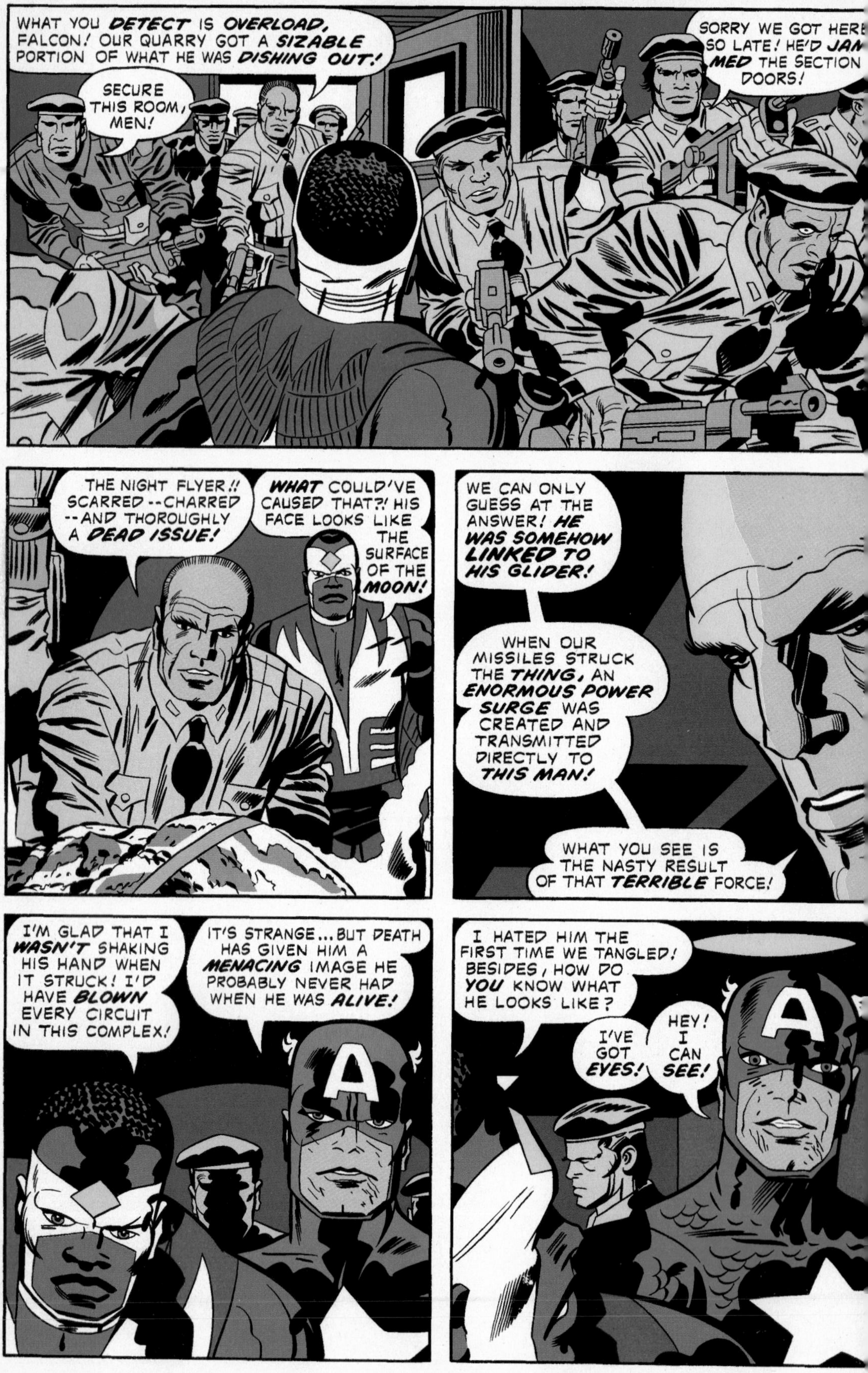
WHAT YOU DETECT IS OVERLOAD, FALCON! OUR QUARRY GOT A SIZABLE PORTION OF WHAT HE WAS DISHING OUT!
SECURE THIS ROOM, MEN!
SORRY WE GOT HERE SO LATE! HE'D JAMMED THE SECTION DOORS!
THE NIGHT FLYER!! SCARRED--CHARRED --AND THOROUGHLY A DEAD ISSUE!
WHAT COULD'VE CAUSED THAT?! HIS FACE LOOKS LIKE THE SURFACE OF THE MOON!
WE CAN ONLY GUESS AT THE ANSWER! HE WAS SOMEHOW LINKED TO HIS GLIDER!
WHEN OUR MISSILES STRUCK THE THING, AN ENORMOUS POWER SURGE WAS CREATED AND TRANSMITTED DIRECTLY TO THIS MAN!
WHAT YOU SEE IS THE NASTY RESULT OF THAT TERRIBLE FORCE!
I'M GLAD THAT I WASN'T SHAKING HIS HAND WHEN IT STRUCK! I'D HAVE BLOWN EVERY CIRCUIT IN THIS COMPLEX!
IT'S STRANGE... BUT DEATH HAS GIVEN HIM A MENACING IMAGE HE PROBABLY NEVER HAD WHEN HE WAS ALIVE!
I HATED HIM THE FIRST TIME WE TANGLED! BESIDES, HOW DO YOU KNOW WHAT HE LOOKS LIKE?
I'VE GOT EYES!
HEY! I CAN SEE!

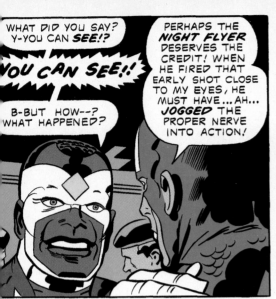

WHAT DID YOU SAY? Y-YOU CAN *SEE!?*

YOU CAN SEE!!

B-BUT HOW--? WHAT HAPPENED?

PERHAPS THE *NIGHT FLYER* DESERVES THE CREDIT! WHEN HE FIRED THAT EARLY SHOT CLOSE TO MY EYES, HE MUST HAVE...AH... *JOGGED* THE PROPER NERVE INTO ACTION!

AT ANY RATE...IT WASN'T UNTIL A FEW *MINUTES* AGO THAT MY SIGHT BEGAN TO *RETURN!*

HUNH! IT SHOWS THAT THE *MEANEST* CAT IS CAPABLE OF *ONE* GOOD DEED!

TAKE HIM TO *AUTOPSY!*

WHO'S THIS TROOPER? WE FOUND HIM LIKE *THIS* WHEN WE BROKE IN HERE!

DON'T TURN TO *ME* FOR ANSWERS!

I'VE GOT THEM! HE WAS THE NIGHT FLYER'S *CONTACT!* HIS JOB WAS TO *DIVULGE* THE WHEREABOUTS OF THE *DEFECTOR!*

A *COURT-MARTIAL* WILL GET THE REST OF THE SORDID FACTS!

LET'S GO-- BENEDICT!

AND DON'T FORGET TO GIVE (M) REGARDS TO *ARNOLD!!*

THAT'S A *BAD* JOKE, SON!

IT'S BEEN A BAD *NIGHT,* CAP! BUT THE *DEFECTOR* IS *INTACT--* WHOEVER AND WHEREVER HE IS... ONLY *SHIELD'S* GOT THE ANSWERS!

MY GUESS IS THAT HE WAS *NEVER* IN THIS COMPLEX! I THINK IT WAS A *COVER* STORY TO *OBSCURE* HIS *REAL* LOCATION!

WE'VE BEEN VICTIMS OF *ANOTHER* DEVIOUS DESIGN IN THE FAR-FLUNG WEB ADMINISTERED AND CAREFULLY GUARDED BY THAT ONE-EYED, STUBBLE-PLASTERED, CIGAR-SMOKING *NICK FURY!*

MAY HIS COMBAT MEDALS TURN *GREEN!*

TELL YA WHAT-- LET'S THROW A *PARTY!* WE'LL CALL SHARON N' LILA AND CELEBRATE YOUR *SEEING* AGAIN!

NEXT: *A NEW DIRECTION!*

165

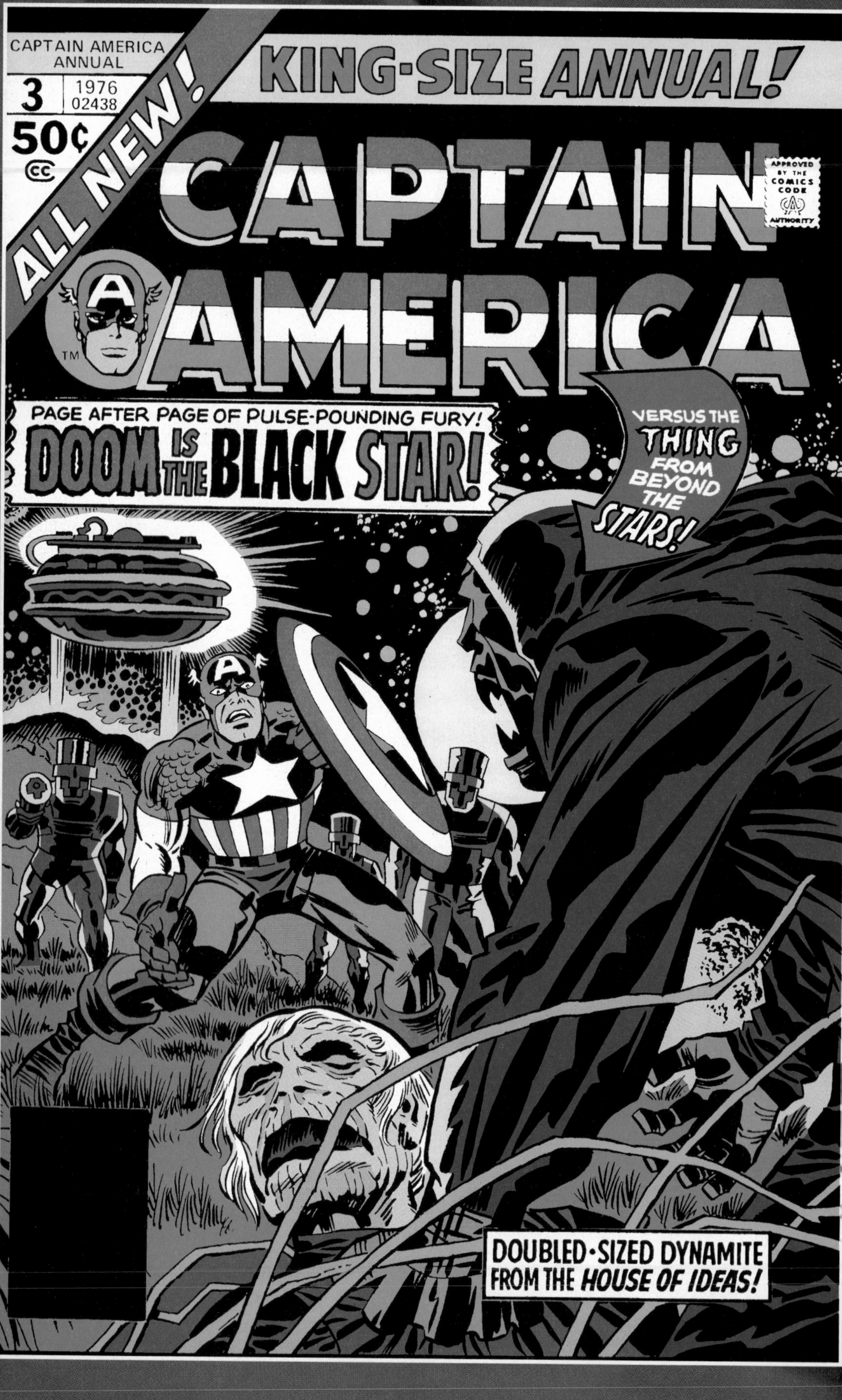
CAPTAIN AMERICA ANNUAL
3
1976
02438
50¢
CC
ALL NEW!
KING-SIZE ANNUAL!
CAPTAIN AMERICA
TM
APPROVED BY THE COMICS CODE AUTHORITY
PAGE AFTER PAGE OF PULSE-POUNDING FURY!
DOOM IS THE BLACK STAR!
VERSUS THE THING FROM BEYOND THE STARS!
DOUBLED-SIZED DYNAMITE FROM THE HOUSE OF IDEAS!

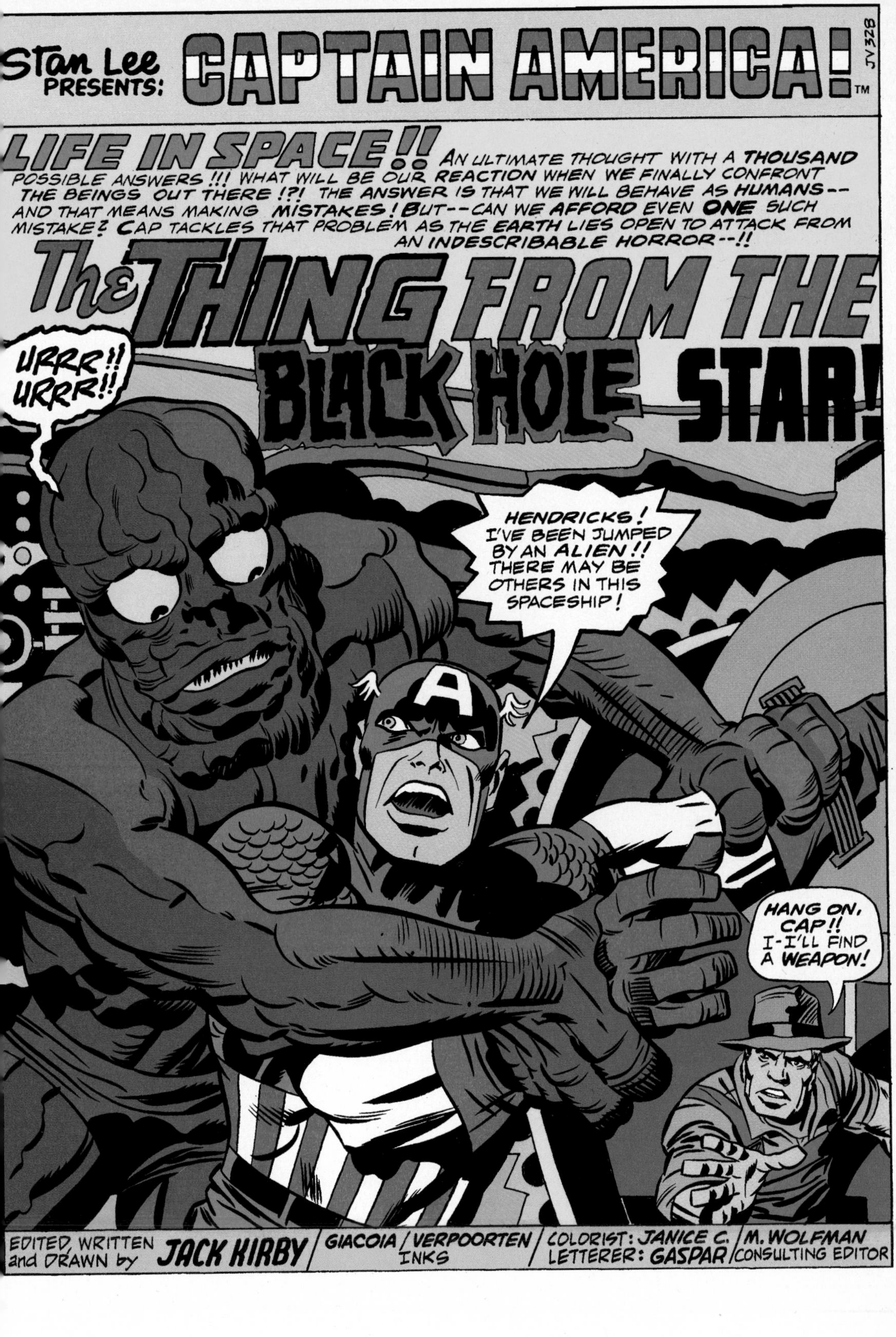

Stan Lee PRESENTS: CAPTAIN AMERICA!™
JV 328
LIFE IN SPACE!! AN ULTIMATE THOUGHT WITH A THOUSAND POSSIBLE ANSWERS!!! WHAT WILL BE OUR REACTION WHEN WE FINALLY CONFRONT THE BEINGS OUT THERE!?! THE ANSWER IS THAT WE WILL BEHAVE AS HUMANS -- AND THAT MEANS MAKING MISTAKES! BUT -- CAN WE AFFORD EVEN ONE SUCH MISTAKE? CAP TACKLES THAT PROBLEM AS THE EARTH LIES OPEN TO ATTACK FROM AN INDESCRIBABLE HORROR--!!
The THING FROM THE BLACK HOLE STAR!
URRR!! URRR!!
HENDRICKS! I'VE BEEN JUMPED BY AN ALIEN!! THERE MAY BE OTHERS IN THIS SPACESHIP!
HANG ON, CAP!! I-I'LL FIND A WEAPON!
EDITED, WRITTEN and DRAWN by JACK KIRBY / GIACOIA / VERPOORTEN INKS / COLORIST: JANICE C. LETTERER: GASPAR / M. WOLFMAN CONSULTING EDITOR

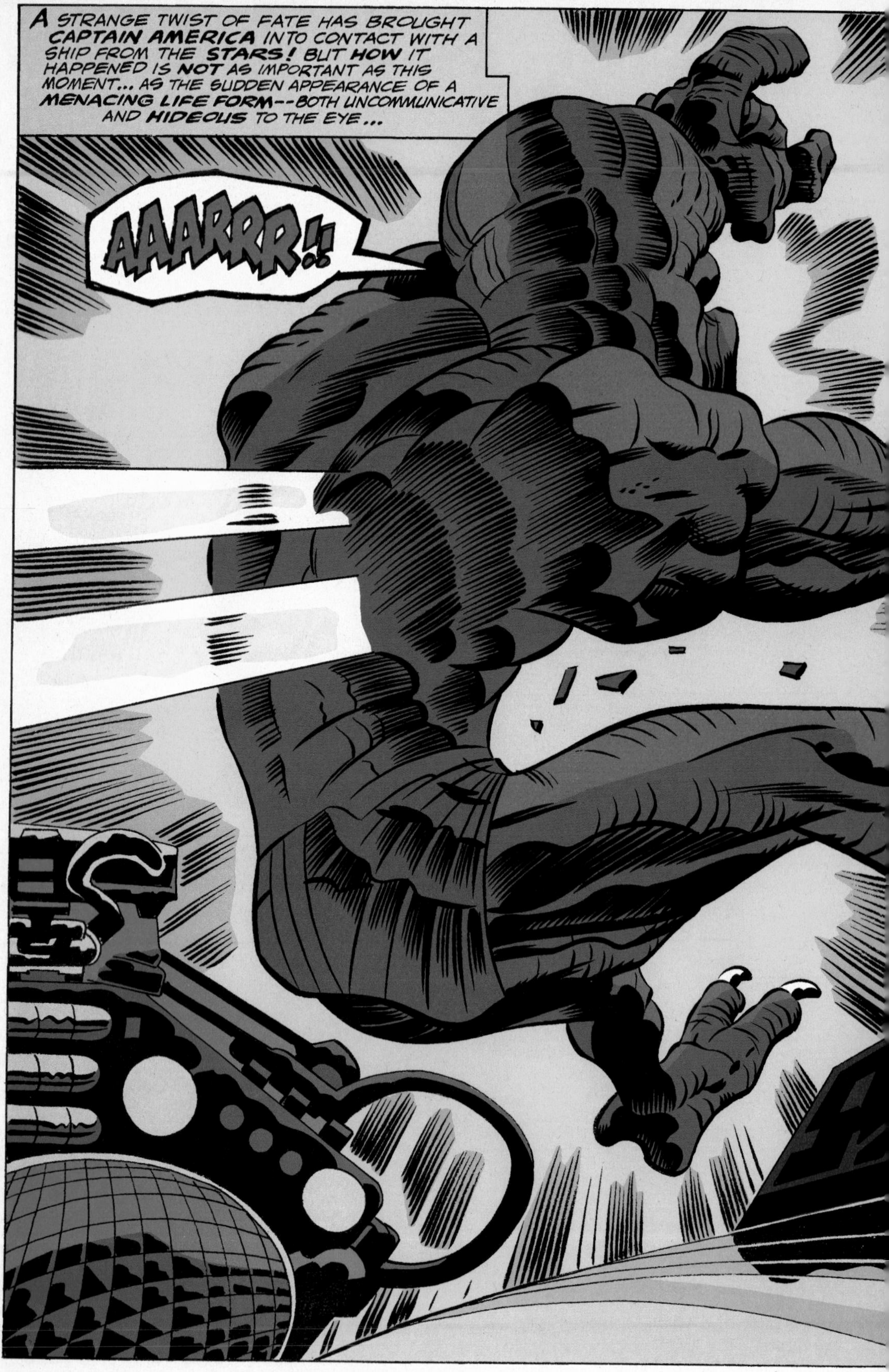
A STRANGE TWIST OF FATE HAS BROUGHT CAPTAIN AMERICA INTO CONTACT WITH A SHIP FROM THE STARS! BUT HOW IT HAPPENED IS NOT AS IMPORTANT AS THIS MOMENT... AS THE SUDDEN APPEARANCE OF A MENACING LIFE FORM--BOTH UNCOMMUNICATIVE AND HIDEOUS TO THE EYE...
AAARRR!!

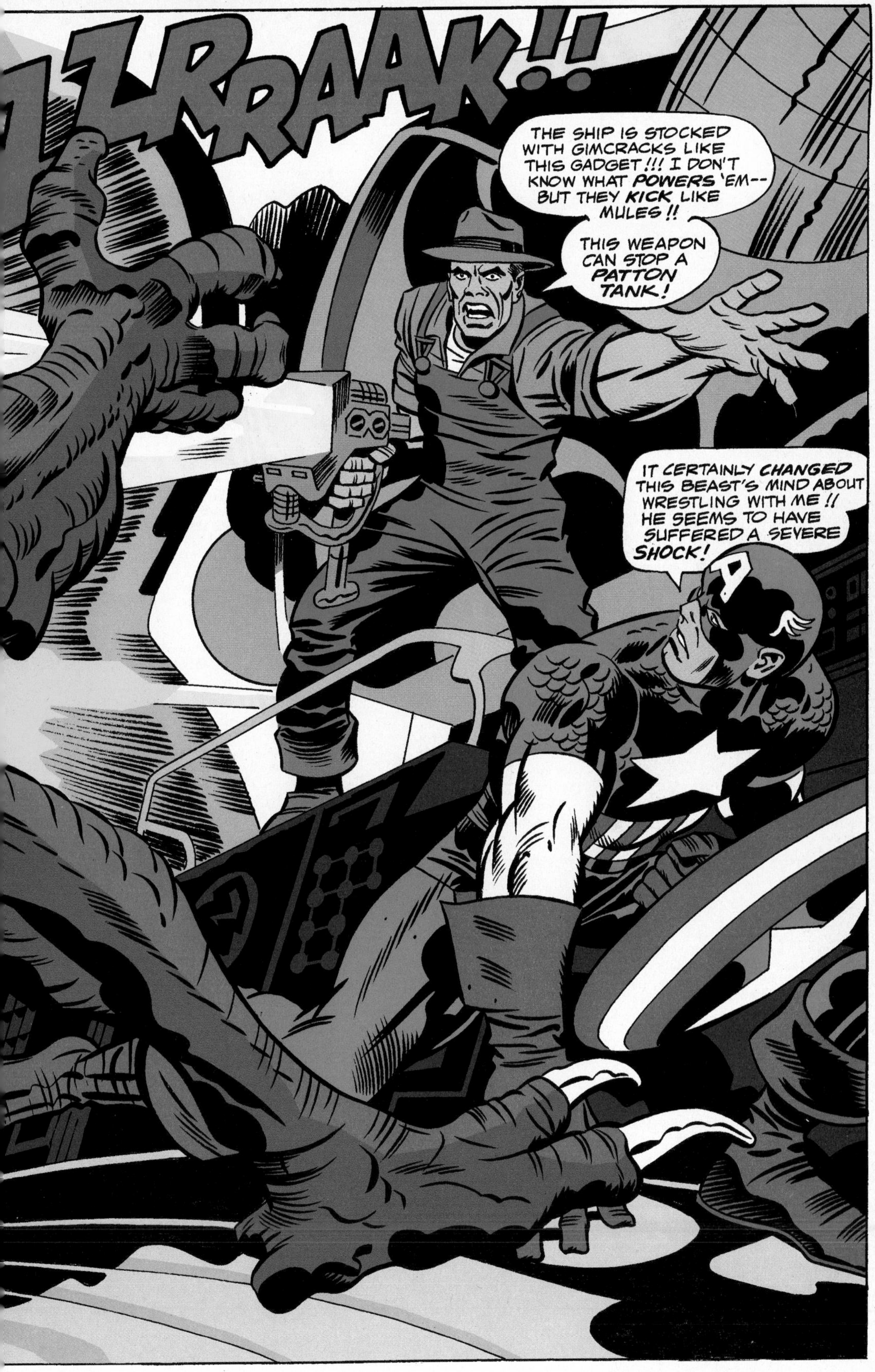
ZZRRAAK!!
THE SHIP IS STOCKED WITH GIMCRACKS LIKE THIS GADGET!!! I DON'T KNOW WHAT POWERS 'EM-- BUT THEY KICK LIKE MULES!!
THIS WEAPON CAN STOP A PATTON TANK!
IT CERTAINLY CHANGED THIS BEAST'S MIND ABOUT WRESTLING WITH ME!! HE SEEMS TO HAVE SUFFERED A SEVERE SHOCK!

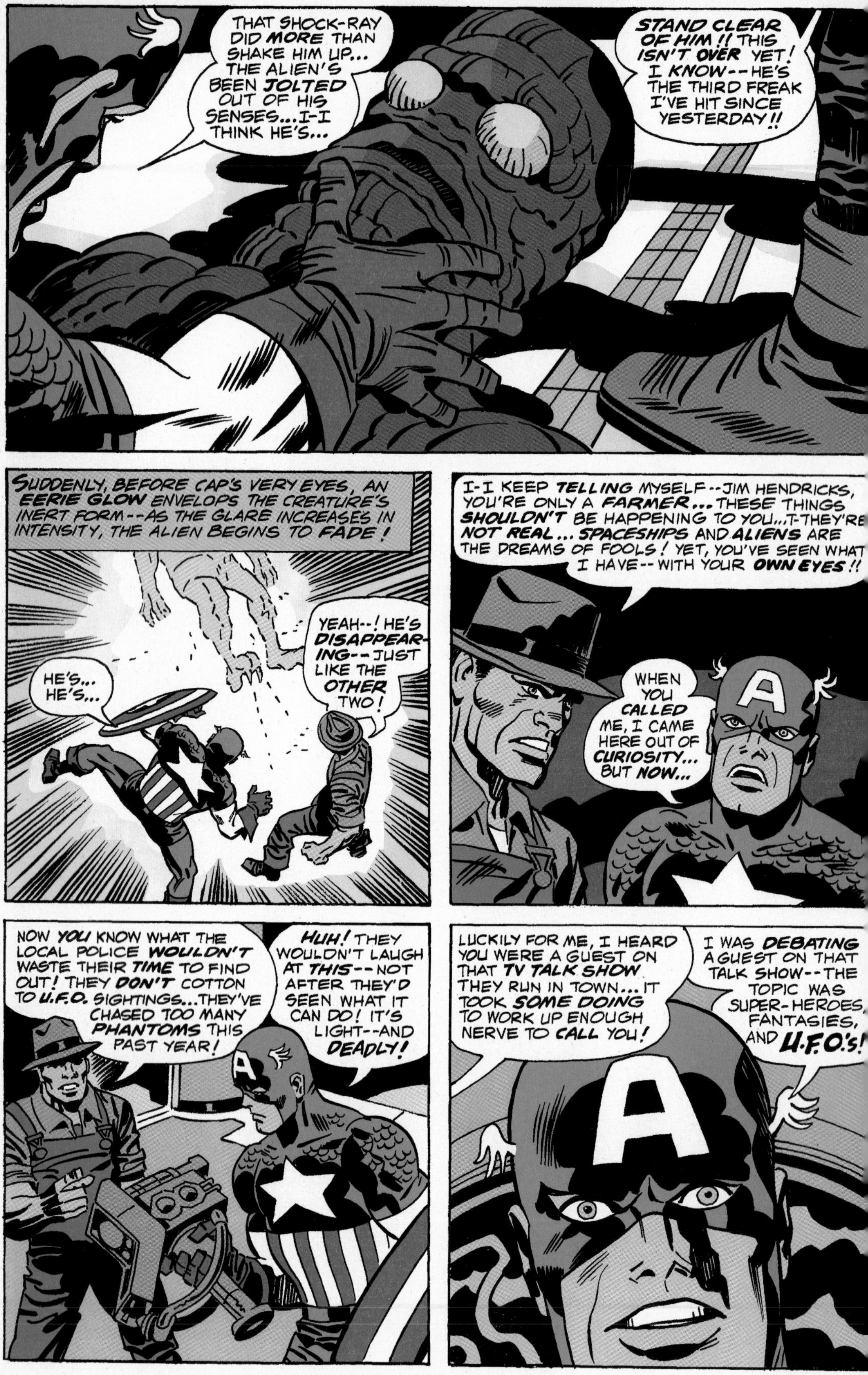
THAT SHOCK-RAY DID MORE THAN SHAKE HIM UP... THE ALIEN'S BEEN JOLTED OUT OF HIS SENSES...I-I THINK HE'S...
STAND CLEAR OF HIM!! THIS ISN'T OVER YET! I KNOW--HE'S THE THIRD FREAK I'VE HIT SINCE YESTERDAY!!
SUDDENLY, BEFORE CAP'S VERY EYES, AN EERIE GLOW ENVELOPS THE CREATURE'S INERT FORM--AS THE GLARE INCREASES IN INTENSITY, THE ALIEN BEGINS TO FADE!
HE'S... HE'S...
YEAH--! HE'S DISAPPEARING--JUST LIKE THE OTHER TWO!
I-I KEEP TELLING MYSELF--JIM HENDRICKS, YOU'RE ONLY A FARMER... THESE THINGS SHOULDN'T BE HAPPENING TO YOU...T-THEY'RE NOT REAL... SPACESHIPS AND ALIENS ARE THE DREAMS OF FOOLS! YET, YOU'VE SEEN WHAT I HAVE--WITH YOUR OWN EYES!!
WHEN YOU CALLED ME, I CAME HERE OUT OF CURIOSITY... BUT NOW...
NOW YOU KNOW WHAT THE LOCAL POLICE WOULDN'T WASTE THEIR TIME TO FIND OUT! THEY DON'T COTTON TO U.F.O. SIGHTINGS...THEY'VE CHASED TOO MANY PHANTOMS THIS PAST YEAR!
HUH! THEY WOULDN'T LAUGH AT THIS--NOT AFTER THEY'D SEEN WHAT IT CAN DO! IT'S LIGHT--AND DEADLY!
LUCKILY FOR ME, I HEARD YOU WERE A GUEST ON THAT TV TALK SHOW THEY RUN IN TOWN... IT TOOK SOME DOING TO WORK UP ENOUGH NERVE TO CALL YOU!
I WAS DEBATING A GUEST ON THAT TALK SHOW--THE TOPIC WAS SUPER-HEROES, FANTASIES, AND U.F.O.'s!

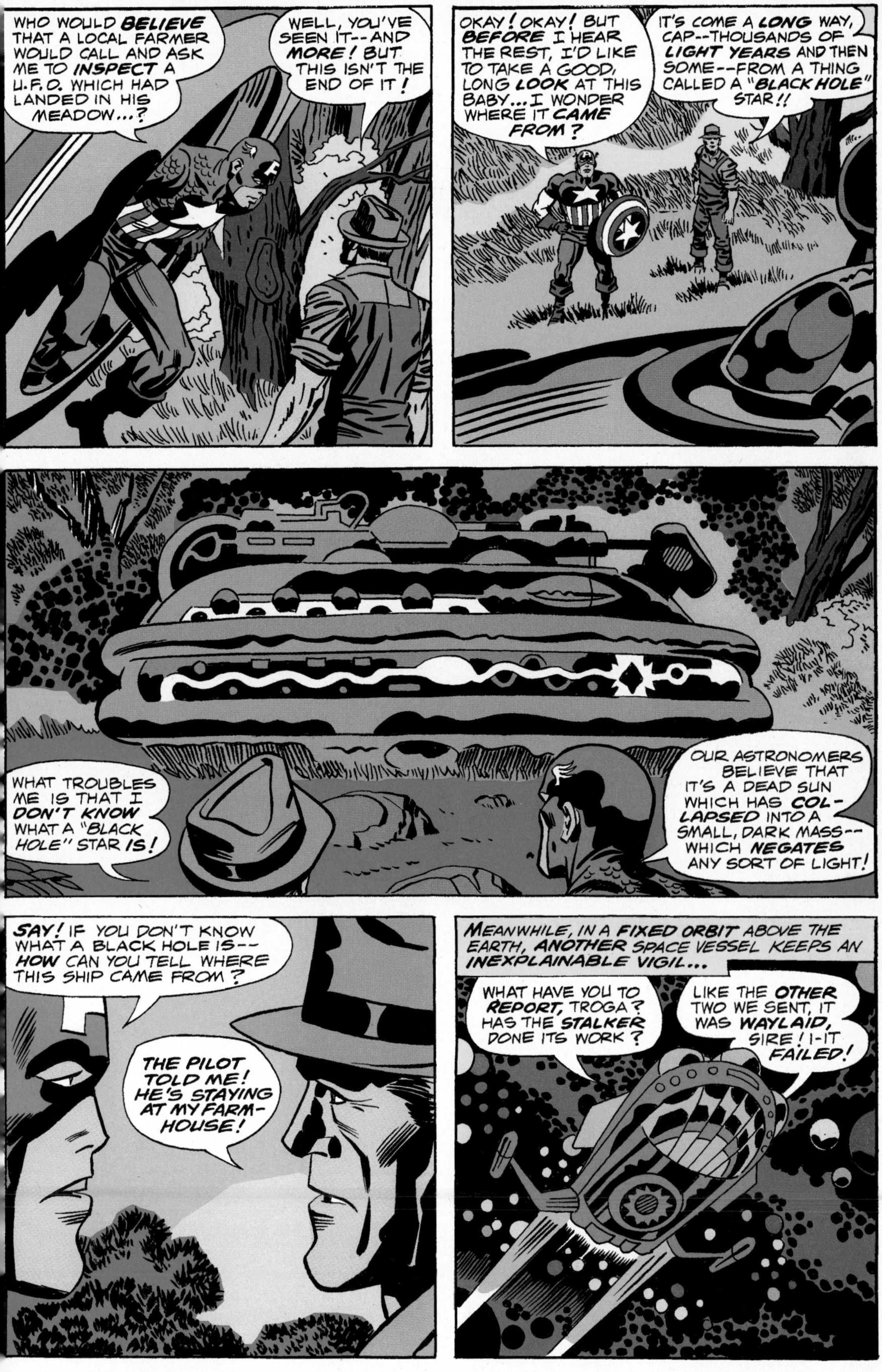
WHO WOULD BELIEVE THAT A LOCAL FARMER WOULD CALL AND ASK ME TO INSPECT A U.F.O. WHICH HAD LANDED IN HIS MEADOW...?
WELL, YOU'VE SEEN IT--AND MORE! BUT THIS ISN'T THE END OF IT!
OKAY! OKAY! BUT BEFORE I HEAR THE REST, I'D LIKE TO TAKE A GOOD, LONG LOOK AT THIS BABY... I WONDER WHERE IT CAME FROM?
IT'S COME A LONG WAY, CAP--THOUSANDS OF LIGHT YEARS AND THEN SOME--FROM A THING CALLED A "BLACK HOLE" STAR!!
WHAT TROUBLES ME IS THAT I DON'T KNOW WHAT A "BLACK HOLE" STAR IS!
OUR ASTRONOMERS BELIEVE THAT IT'S A DEAD SUN WHICH HAS COL-LAPSED INTO A SMALL, DARK MASS--WHICH NEGATES ANY SORT OF LIGHT!
SAY! IF YOU DON'T KNOW WHAT A BLACK HOLE IS--HOW CAN YOU TELL WHERE THIS SHIP CAME FROM?
THE PILOT TOLD ME! HE'S STAYING AT MY FARM-HOUSE!
MEANWHILE, IN A FIXED ORBIT ABOVE THE EARTH, ANOTHER SPACE VESSEL KEEPS AN INEXPLAINABLE VIGIL...
WHAT HAVE YOU TO REPORT, TROGA? HAS THE STALKER DONE ITS WORK?
LIKE THE OTHER TWO WE SENT, IT WAS WAYLAID, SIRE! I-IT FAILED!

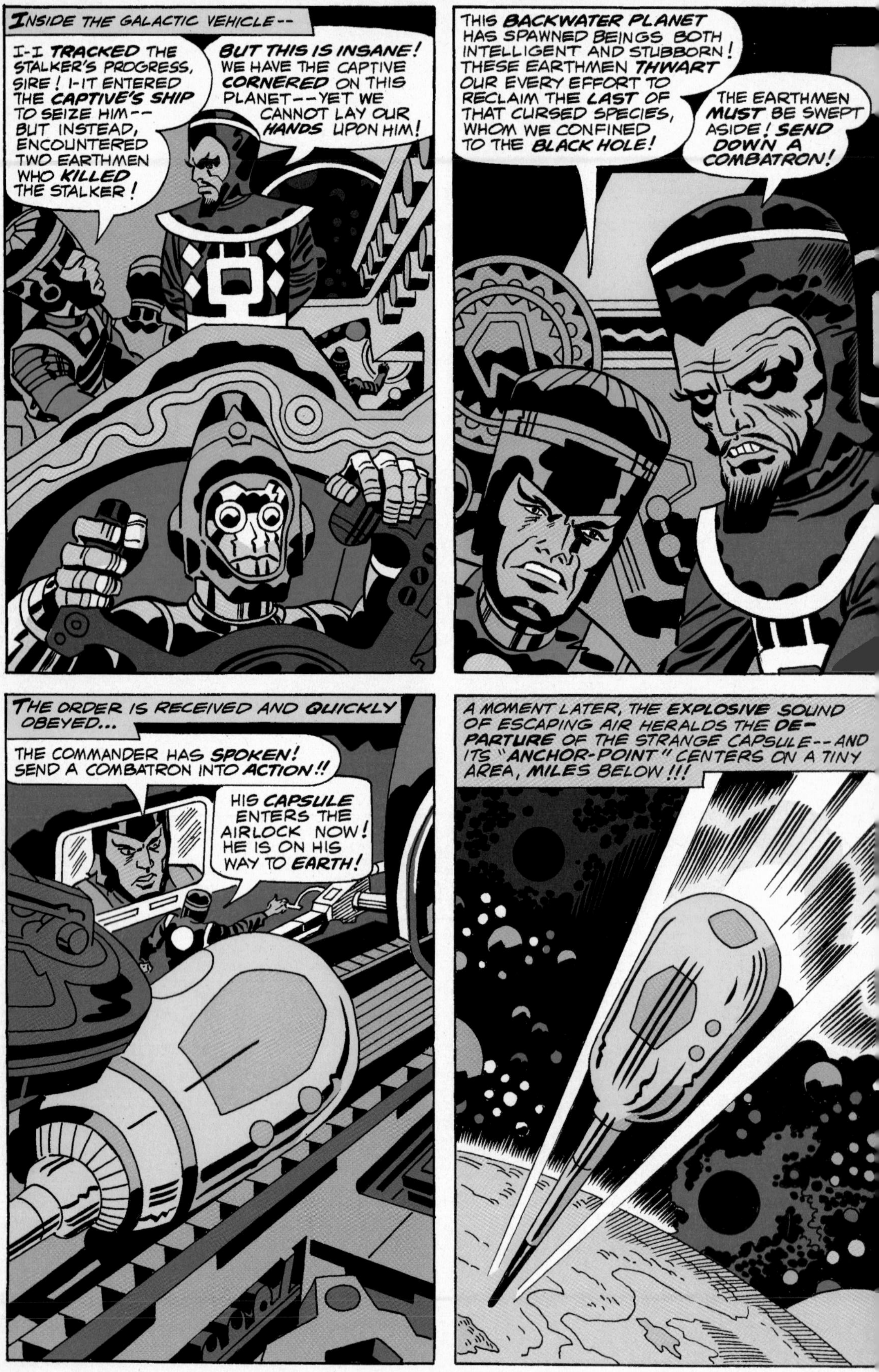
INSIDE THE GALACTIC VEHICLE--
I-I TRACKED THE STALKER'S PROGRESS, SIRE! I-IT ENTERED THE CAPTIVE'S SHIP TO SEIZE HIM--BUT INSTEAD, ENCOUNTERED TWO EARTHMEN WHO KILLED THE STALKER!
BUT THIS IS INSANE! WE HAVE THE CAPTIVE CORNERED ON THIS PLANET--YET WE CANNOT LAY OUR HANDS UPON HIM!
THIS BACKWATER PLANET HAS SPAWNED BEINGS BOTH INTELLIGENT AND STUBBORN! THESE EARTHMEN THWART OUR EVERY EFFORT TO RECLAIM THE LAST OF THAT CURSED SPECIES, WHOM WE CONFINED TO THE BLACK HOLE!
THE EARTHMEN MUST BE SWEPT ASIDE! SEND DOWN A COMBATRON!
THE ORDER IS RECEIVED AND QUICKLY OBEYED...
THE COMMANDER HAS SPOKEN! SEND A COMBATRON INTO ACTION!!
HIS CAPSULE ENTERS THE AIRLOCK NOW! HE IS ON HIS WAY TO EARTH!
A MOMENT LATER, THE EXPLOSIVE SOUND OF ESCAPING AIR HERALDS THE DEPARTURE OF THE STRANGE CAPSULE--AND ITS "ANCHOR-POINT" CENTERS ON A TINY AREA, MILES BELOW!!!

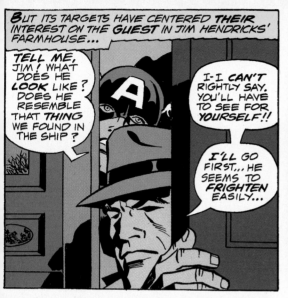

BUT ITS TARGETS HAVE CENTERED *THEIR* INTEREST ON THE *GUEST* IN JIM HENDRICKS' FARMHOUSE...

TELL ME, JIM! WHAT *DOES* HE *LOOK* LIKE? DOES HE *RESEMBLE* THAT *THING* WE FOUND IN THE SHIP?

I-I *CAN'T* RIGHTLY SAY. YOU'LL HAVE TO SEE FOR *YOURSELF!!*

I'LL GO *FIRST*...HE SEEMS TO *FRIGHTEN* EASILY...

THEN...!

HOLD ON THERE! DON'T *PANIC*, MISTER! I'VE BROUGHT A *FRIEND*, SEE--A *FRIEND!*--

HE WANTS TO *HELP* YOU!

HE IS *NOT* LIKE *YOU*! I DO NOT LIKE HIS *APPEARANCE* OR *MANNER!*

THE TWO MEN *STUDY* THE SPACEMAN...HIS FEATURES ARE HIDDEN BY A PROTECTIVE HOOD...BUT THE *EYES* THAT STARE FROM BEHIND THEIR TRANSPARENT SHIELD ARE NARROWED WITH *SUSPICION*...

YOU TRUST *ME*, DON'T YOU? I ASK YOU TO *TRUST* MY FRIEND.

I'VE GOT *REASONS* FOR WEARING A MASK....BUT THEY'RE *NOT* EVIL...

HE IS CALLED *CAPTAIN AMERICA*...ON *THIS* PLANET, HIS NAME IS KNOWN FAR AND WIDE AS A SYMBOL OF *JUSTICE* FOR THOSE WHO SEEK IT!

JUSTICE! THE WORD HAS *NO MEANING* FOR ONE SUCH AS THE *CAPTIVE!*

I DON'T KNOW WHAT YOUR *STORY* IS, MISTER, BUT I AIM TO *GET* IT REAL QUICK--*NOW*, LET'S SEE WHAT *YOU LOOK* LIKE!!

DON'T BE AFRAID! HE HAS *NO* INTENTION OF HARMING YOU...

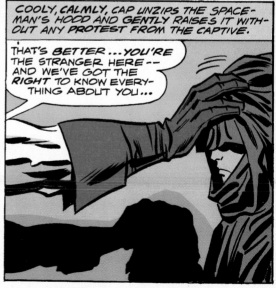

COOLY, CALMLY, CAP UNZIPS THE SPACEMAN'S *HOOD* AND *GENTLY* RAISES IT WITHOUT ANY *PROTEST* FROM THE CAPTIVE.

THAT'S *BETTER*....YOU'RE THE STRANGER HERE-- AND WE'VE GOT THE *RIGHT* TO KNOW EVERYTHING ABOUT YOU...

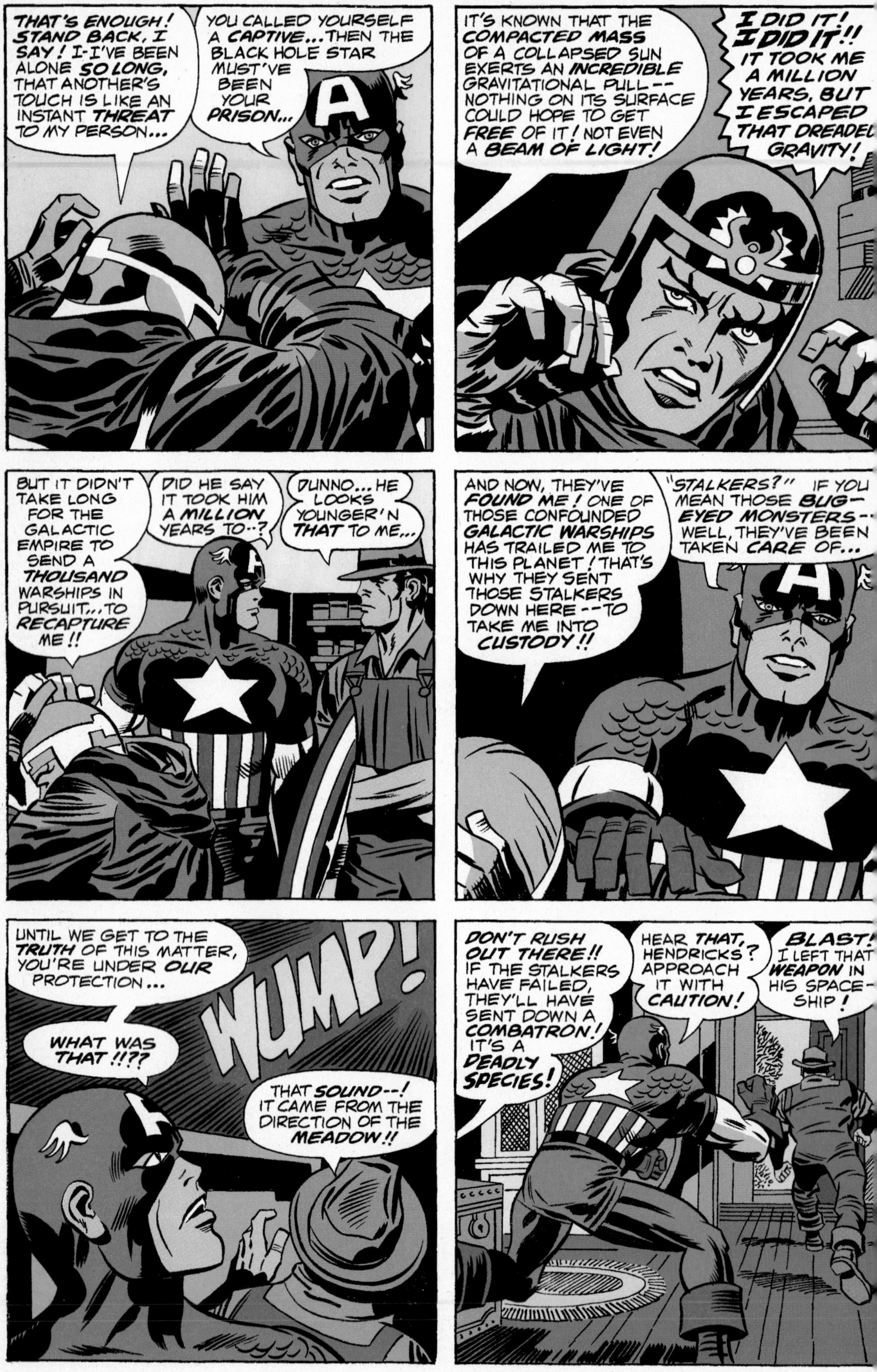
THAT'S ENOUGH! STAND BACK, I SAY! I-I'VE BEEN ALONE SO LONG, THAT ANOTHER'S TOUCH IS LIKE AN INSTANT THREAT TO MY PERSON...
YOU CALLED YOURSELF A CAPTIVE... THEN THE BLACK HOLE STAR MUST'VE BEEN YOUR PRISON...
IT'S KNOWN THAT THE COMPACTED MASS OF A COLLAPSED SUN EXERTS AN INCREDIBLE GRAVITATIONAL PULL -- NOTHING ON ITS SURFACE COULD HOPE TO GET FREE OF IT! NOT EVEN A BEAM OF LIGHT!
I DID IT! I DID IT!! IT TOOK ME A MILLION YEARS, BUT I ESCAPED THAT DREADE GRAVITY!
BUT IT DIDN'T TAKE LONG FOR THE GALACTIC EMPIRE TO SEND A THOUSAND WARSHIPS IN PURSUIT... TO RECAPTURE ME!!
DID HE SAY IT TOOK HIM A MILLION YEARS TO..?
DUNNO... HE LOOKS YOUNGER'N THAT TO ME...
AND NOW, THEY'VE FOUND ME! ONE OF THOSE CONFOUNDED GALACTIC WARSHIPS HAS TRAILED ME TO THIS PLANET! THAT'S WHY THEY SENT THOSE STALKERS DOWN HERE -- TO TAKE ME INTO CUSTODY!!
"STALKERS?" IF YOU MEAN THOSE BUG-EYED MONSTERS-- WELL, THEY'VE BEEN TAKEN CARE OF...
UNTIL WE GET TO THE TRUTH OF THIS MATTER, YOU'RE UNDER OUR PROTECTION...
WUMP!
WHAT WAS THAT!!??
THAT SOUND--! IT CAME FROM THE DIRECTION OF THE MEADOW!!
DON'T RUSH OUT THERE!! IF THE STALKERS HAVE FAILED, THEY'LL HAVE SENT DOWN A COMBATRON! IT'S A DEADLY SPECIES!
HEAR THAT, HENDRICKS? APPROACH IT WITH CAUTION!
BLAST! I LEFT THAT WEAPON IN HIS SPACE-SHIP!

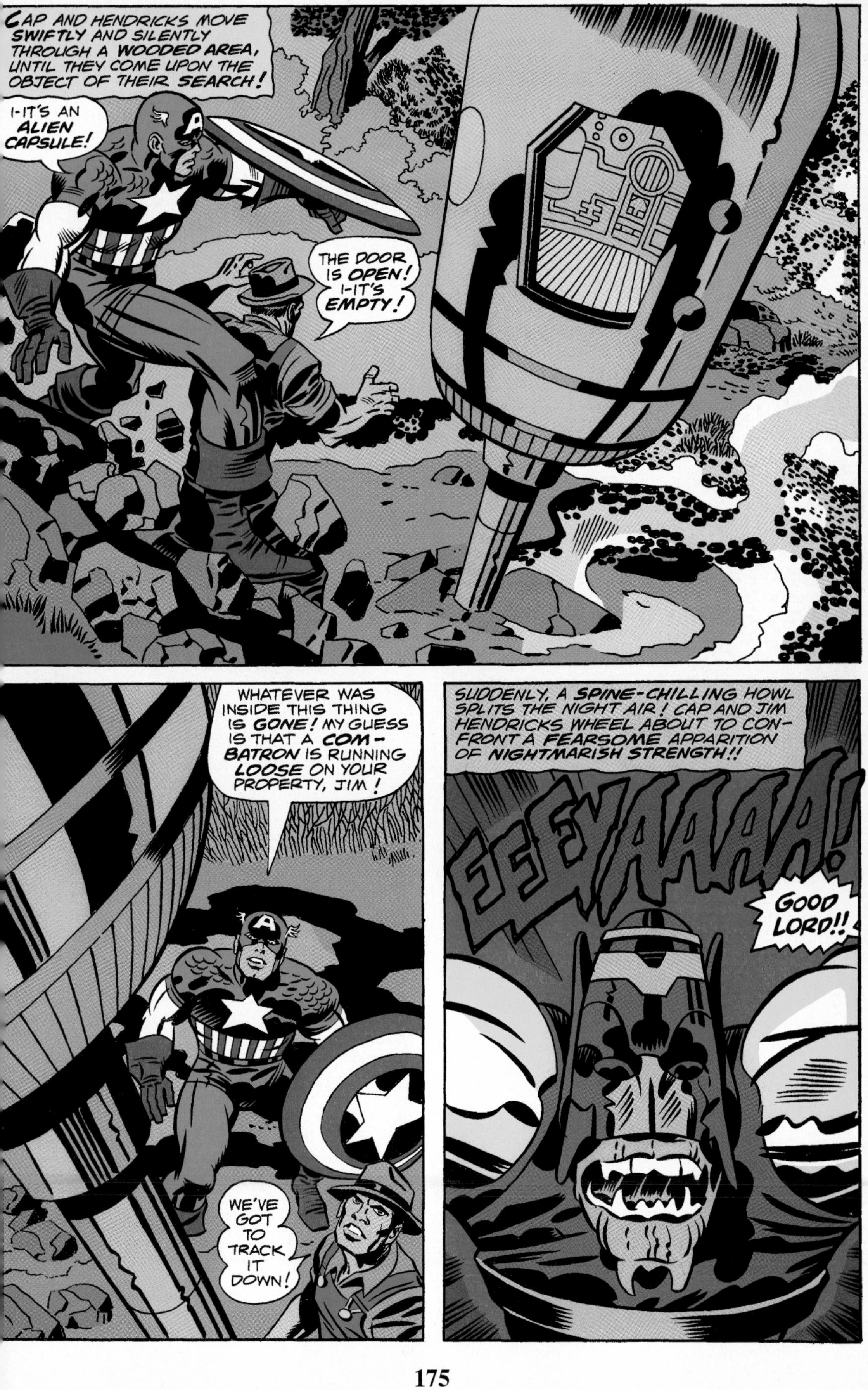
CAP AND HENDRICKS MOVE SWIFTLY AND SILENTLY THROUGH A WOODED AREA, UNTIL THEY COME UPON THE OBJECT OF THEIR SEARCH!
I-IT'S AN ALIEN CAPSULE!
THE DOOR IS OPEN! I-IT'S EMPTY!
WHATEVER WAS INSIDE THIS THING IS GONE! MY GUESS IS THAT A COM-BATRON IS RUNNING LOOSE ON YOUR PROPERTY, JIM!
WE'VE GOT TO TRACK IT DOWN!
SUDDENLY, A SPINE-CHILLING HOWL SPLITS THE NIGHT AIR! CAP AND JIM HENDRICKS WHEEL ABOUT TO CON-FRONT A FEARSOME APPARITION OF NIGHTMARISH STRENGTH!!
EEEYAAAA!
GOOD LORD!!

THE COMBATRON ROARS INTO ACTION BY **BLASTING** THE GROUND WITH ITS **PRESSURE ARM**...

TAKE COVER!! IT'S TEARING LOOSE EVERY ROCK AND TREE IN THIS AREA!

ZZTOM!

IT IS **SIMPLE** STRATEGY...THE COMBATRON PUTS HIS ENEMY TO FLIGHT WITH **FEAR**, AND BLINDS HIM WITH **FLYING DEBRIS** ...

CAN'T SEE!! IT'S LIKE STANDING IN A **TORNADO**!

FALL BACK, CAP! YOU'RE **BOUND** TO BE HIT IN THIS RAIN OF **BOULDERS**!

THE PRESSURE **INCREASES** WITH A SUDDEN INTENSITY!! A SCREAMING **WIND** NOW REPLACES THE STORM OF DEBRIS! CAP **SEIZES** A TREE STUMP AND HANGS ON FOR DEAR LIFE--!

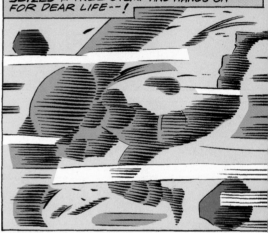

IT IS A SHORT BUT **SAVAGE** ATTACK.!! WHEN THE COMBATRON SHUTS OFF ITS **PRESSURE**, ITS OPPONENTS LIE WEAKENED, **HALF-BURIED** IN THE REMAINS OF THE SHATTERED **WOODS**...

MAULED BY THE COMBATRON'S ASSAULT, CAP FIGHTS TO REGAIN HIS STRENGTH! HE ATTEMPTS TO RISE FOR **BATTLE**, BUT HIS FIERCE ENEMY IS **UPON HIM** !!!

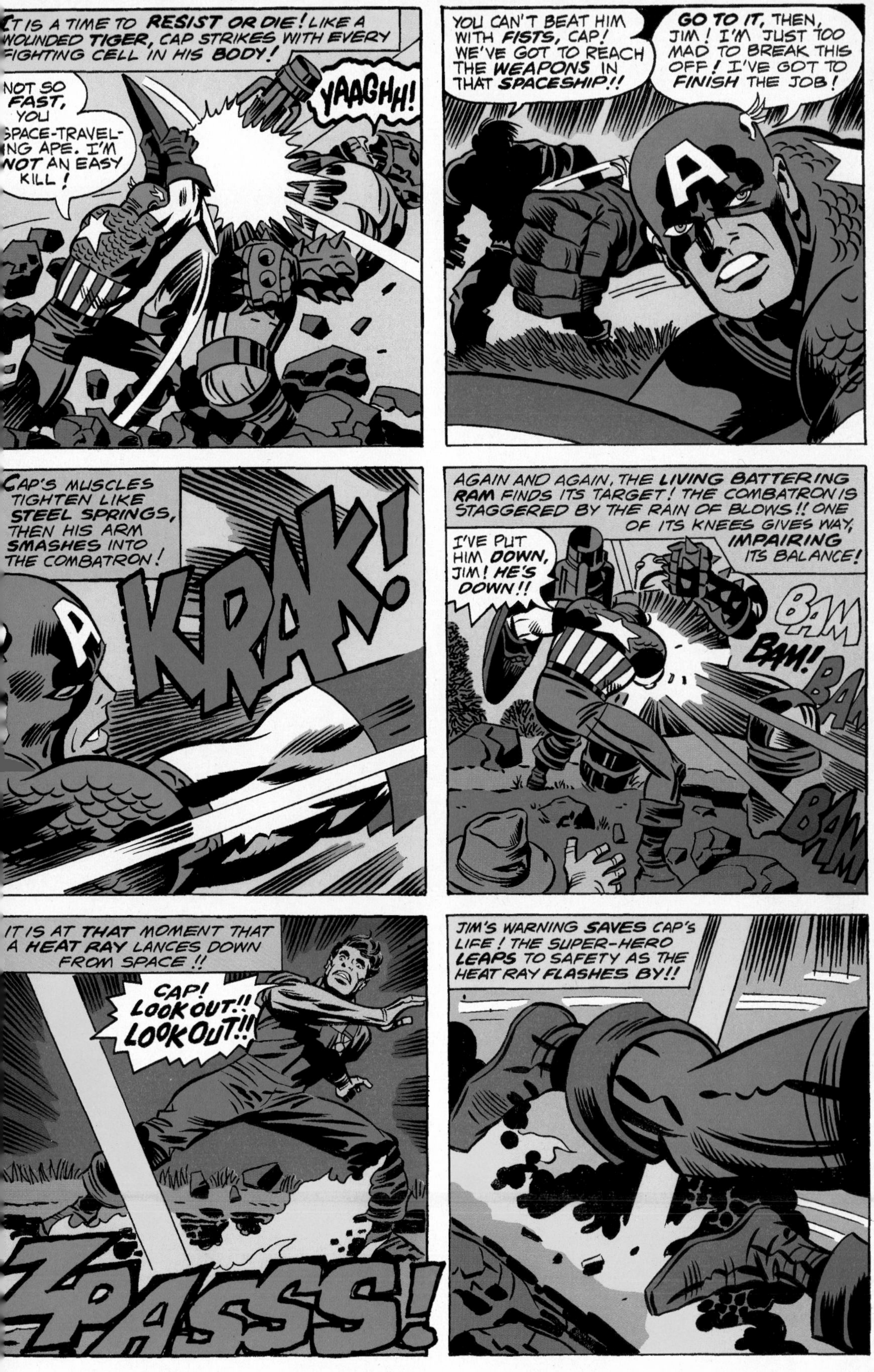
IT IS A TIME TO RESIST OR DIE! LIKE A WOUNDED TIGER, CAP STRIKES WITH EVERY FIGHTING CELL IN HIS BODY!
NOT SO FAST, YOU SPACE-TRAVELING APE. I'M NOT AN EASY KILL!
YAAGHH!
YOU CAN'T BEAT HIM WITH FISTS, CAP! WE'VE GOT TO REACH THE WEAPONS IN THAT SPACESHIP!!
GO TO IT, THEN, JIM! I'M JUST TOO MAD TO BREAK THIS OFF! I'VE GOT TO FINISH THE JOB!
CAP'S MUSCLES TIGHTEN LIKE STEEL SPRINGS, THEN HIS ARM SMASHES INTO THE COMBATRON!
KRAK!
AGAIN AND AGAIN, THE LIVING BATTERING RAM FINDS ITS TARGET! THE COMBATRON IS STAGGERED BY THE RAIN OF BLOWS!! ONE OF ITS KNEES GIVES WAY, IMPAIRING ITS BALANCE!
I'VE PUT HIM DOWN, JIM! HE'S DOWN!!
BAM
BAM!
BAM
BAM
IT IS AT THAT MOMENT THAT A HEAT RAY LANCES DOWN FROM SPACE!!
CAP! LOOK OUT!! LOOK OUT!!
ZPASSS!
JIM'S WARNING SAVES CAP'S LIFE! THE SUPER-HERO LEAPS TO SAFETY AS THE HEAT RAY FLASHES BY!!

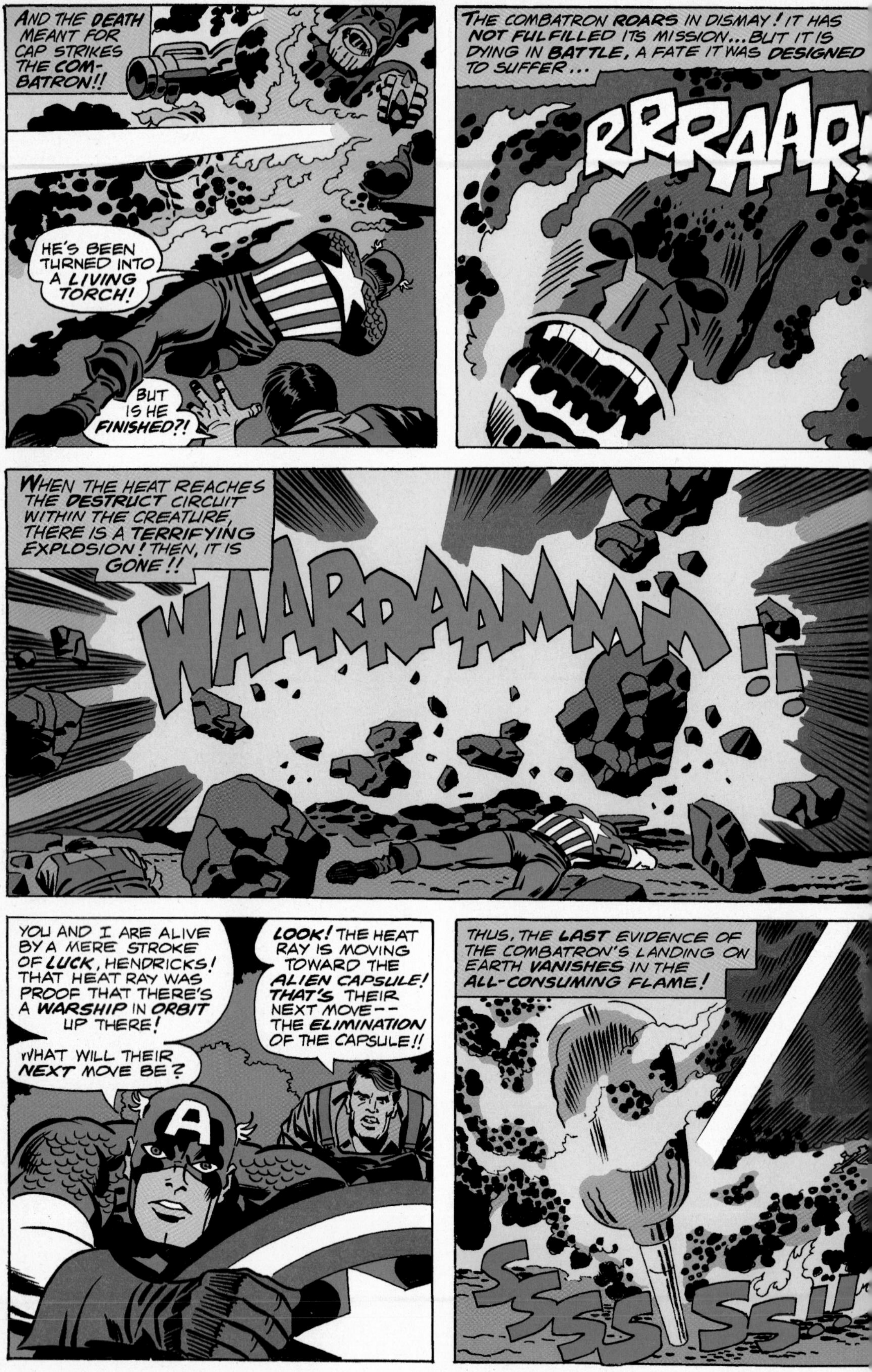
AND THE DEATH MEANT FOR CAP STRIKES THE COMBATRON!!
HE'S BEEN TURNED INTO A LIVING TORCH!
BUT IS HE FINISHED?!
THE COMBATRON ROARS IN DISMAY! IT HAS NOT FULFILLED ITS MISSION... BUT IT IS DYING IN BATTLE, A FATE IT WAS DESIGNED TO SUFFER...
RRRAAR!
WHEN THE HEAT REACHES THE DESTRUCT CIRCUIT WITHIN THE CREATURE, THERE IS A TERRIFYING EXPLOSION! THEN, IT IS GONE!!
WAARRAAMMM!!
YOU AND I ARE ALIVE BY A MERE STROKE OF LUCK, HENDRICKS! THAT HEAT RAY WAS PROOF THAT THERE'S A WARSHIP IN ORBIT UP THERE!
WHAT WILL THEIR NEXT MOVE BE?
LOOK! THE HEAT RAY IS MOVING TOWARD THE ALIEN CAPSULE! THAT'S THEIR NEXT MOVE-- THE ELIMINATION OF THE CAPSULE!!
THUS, THE LAST EVIDENCE OF THE COMBATRON'S LANDING ON EARTH VANISHES IN THE ALL-CONSUMING FLAME!
SSSSSSS!!

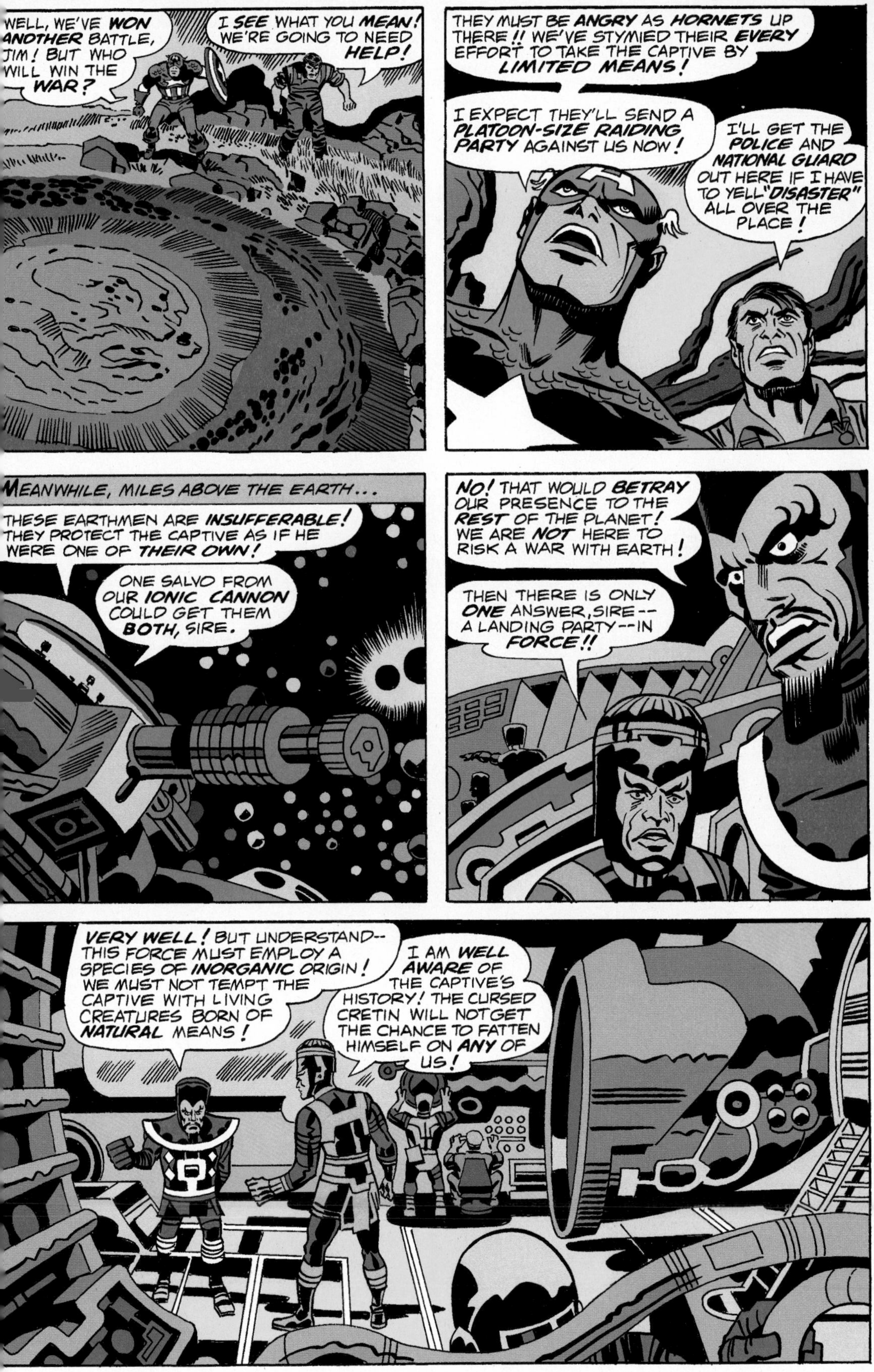
WELL, WE'VE WON ANOTHER BATTLE, JIM! BUT WHO WILL WIN THE WAR?
I SEE WHAT YOU MEAN! WE'RE GOING TO NEED HELP!
THEY MUST BE ANGRY AS HORNETS UP THERE!! WE'VE STYMIED THEIR EVERY EFFORT TO TAKE THE CAPTIVE BY LIMITED MEANS!
I EXPECT THEY'LL SEND A PLATOON-SIZE RAIDING PARTY AGAINST US NOW!
I'LL GET THE POLICE AND NATIONAL GUARD OUT HERE IF I HAVE TO YELL "DISASTER" ALL OVER THE PLACE!
MEANWHILE, MILES ABOVE THE EARTH...
THESE EARTHMEN ARE INSUFFERABLE! THEY PROTECT THE CAPTIVE AS IF HE WERE ONE OF THEIR OWN!
ONE SALVO FROM OUR IONIC CANNON COULD GET THEM BOTH, SIRE.
NO! THAT WOULD BETRAY OUR PRESENCE TO THE REST OF THE PLANET! WE ARE NOT HERE TO RISK A WAR WITH EARTH!
THEN THERE IS ONLY ONE ANSWER, SIRE -- A LANDING PARTY -- IN FORCE!!
VERY WELL! BUT UNDERSTAND-- THIS FORCE MUST EMPLOY A SPECIES OF INORGANIC ORIGIN! WE MUST NOT TEMPT THE CAPTIVE WITH LIVING CREATURES BORN OF NATURAL MEANS!
I AM WELL AWARE OF THE CAPTIVE'S HISTORY! THE CURSED CRETIN WILL NOTGET THE CHANCE TO FATTEN HIMSELF ON ANY OF US!

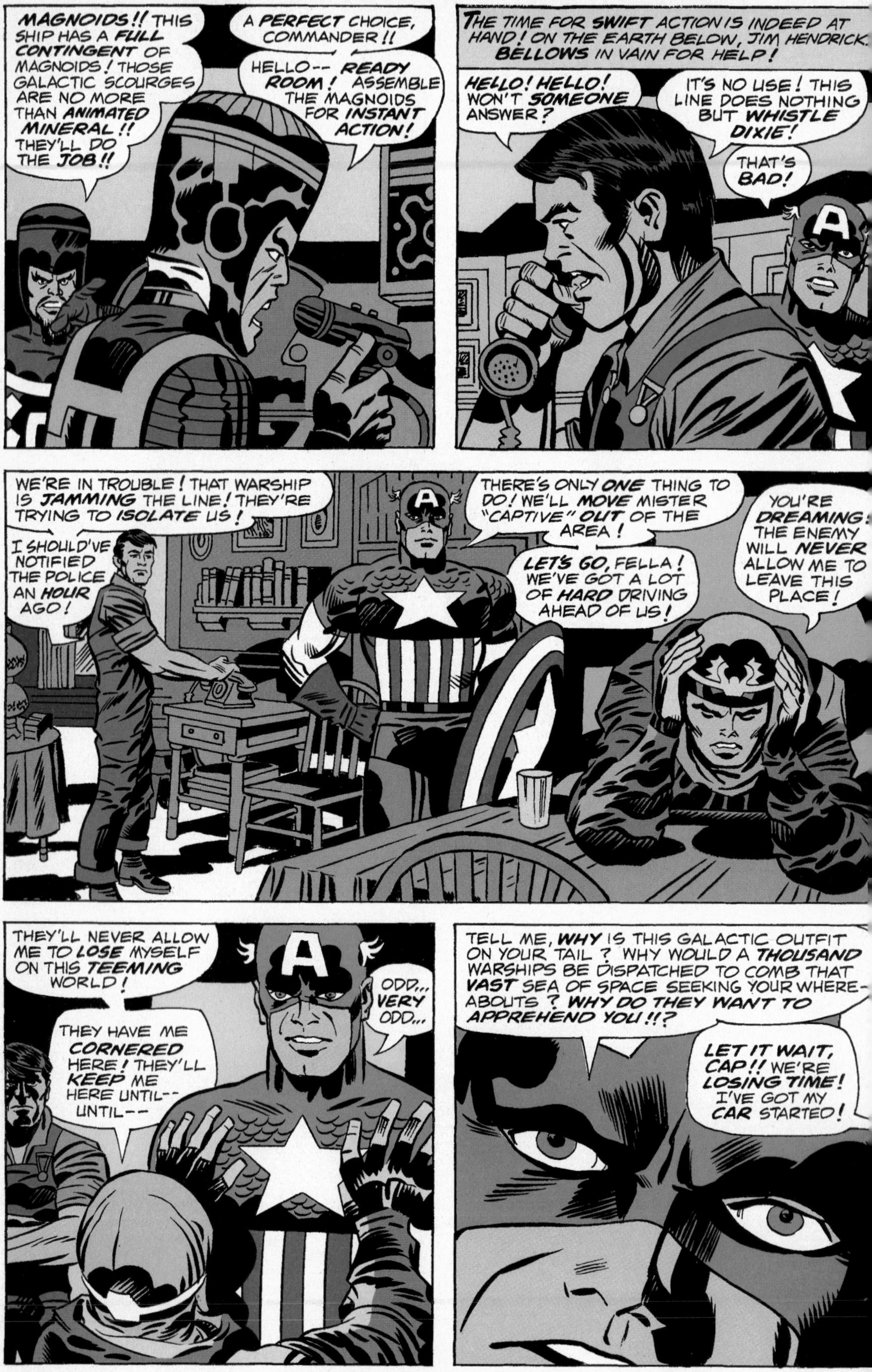
MAGNOIDS!! THIS SHIP HAS A FULL CONTINGENT OF MAGNOIDS! THOSE GALACTIC SCOURGES ARE NO MORE THAN ANIMATED MINERAL!! THEY'LL DO THE JOB!!
A PERFECT CHOICE, COMMANDER!!
HELLO-- READY ROOM! ASSEMBLE THE MAGNOIDS FOR INSTANT ACTION!
THE TIME FOR SWIFT ACTION IS INDEED AT HAND! ON THE EARTH BELOW, JIM HENDRICK BELLOWS IN VAIN FOR HELP!
HELLO! HELLO! WON'T SOMEONE ANSWER?
IT'S NO USE! THIS LINE DOES NOTHING BUT WHISTLE DIXIE!
THAT'S BAD!
WE'RE IN TROUBLE! THAT WARSHIP IS JAMMING THE LINE! THEY'RE TRYING TO ISOLATE US!
I SHOULD'VE NOTIFIED THE POLICE AN HOUR AGO!
THERE'S ONLY ONE THING TO DO! WE'LL MOVE MISTER "CAPTIVE" OUT OF THE AREA!
LET'S GO, FELLA! WE'VE GOT A LOT OF HARD DRIVING AHEAD OF US!
YOU'RE DREAMING! THE ENEMY WILL NEVER ALLOW ME TO LEAVE THIS PLACE!
THEY'LL NEVER ALLOW ME TO LOSE MYSELF ON THIS TEEMING WORLD!
ODD... VERY ODD...
THEY HAVE ME CORNERED HERE! THEY'LL KEEP ME HERE UNTIL-- UNTIL--
TELL ME, WHY IS THIS GALACTIC OUTFIT ON YOUR TAIL? WHY WOULD A THOUSAND WARSHIPS BE DISPATCHED TO COMB THAT VAST SEA OF SPACE SEEKING YOUR WHERE-ABOUTS? WHY DO THEY WANT TO APPREHEND YOU!!?
LET IT WAIT, CAP!! WE'RE LOSING TIME! I'VE GOT MY CAR STARTED!

CAP PAUSES FOR A MOMENT...THEN HE MOTIONS FOR A DASH TO THE CAR...

THIS IS USELESS!

SHUT UP AND RUN!

I'VE GOT'ER PERKED UP AND RARIN' TO ROLL! IT WON'T TAKE US LONG TO MAKE IT TO TOWN!

SUDDENLY, BOLTS FROM ABOVE WRECK ALL HOPES FOR ESCAPE!!!

BLAAAMM

THEY GOT THE CAR!!

WE'RE BOXED IN THIS PLACE!

FOOLS! I TOLD YOU WHAT WOULD HAPPEN! MY ONLY CHANCE IS TO ESCAPE ON FOOT!

THAT'S SUICIDE! THEY'LL TAG YOU WITH THE SAME LIGHTNING THAT GOT THE CAR!

DON'T YOU SEE? THEY CAN PINPOINT INDIVIDUAL TARGETS!

THERE'S ANOTHER U.F.O. ON ITS WAY DOWN HERE, CAP! THIS ONE LOOKS BIGGER'N THE CAPSULE!

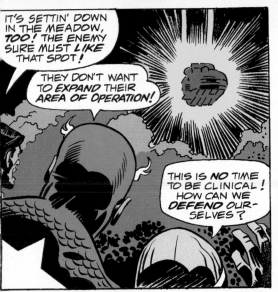

IT'S SETTIN' DOWN IN THE MEADOW, TOO! THE ENEMY SURE MUST LIKE THAT SPOT!

THEY DON'T WANT TO EXPAND THEIR AREA OF OPERATION!

THIS IS NO TIME TO BE CLINICAL! HOW CAN WE DEFEND OURSELVES?

CAP'S COMBAT-WISE BRAIN RESPONDS WITH COMPUTER RAPIDITY! HE BARKS HIS ORDERS!

WE'VE GOT A DEFENSE--HIS SPACESHIP! MAKE FOR THE SPACESHIP AND CHECK EVERY WEAPON FOR ACTION! I'LL JOIN YOU TWO AS SOON AS I'VE SCOUTED THE SIZE OF THE OPPOSITION!

HE MAKES SENSE! LET'S GO, CAPTIVE!

AS YOU SAY!

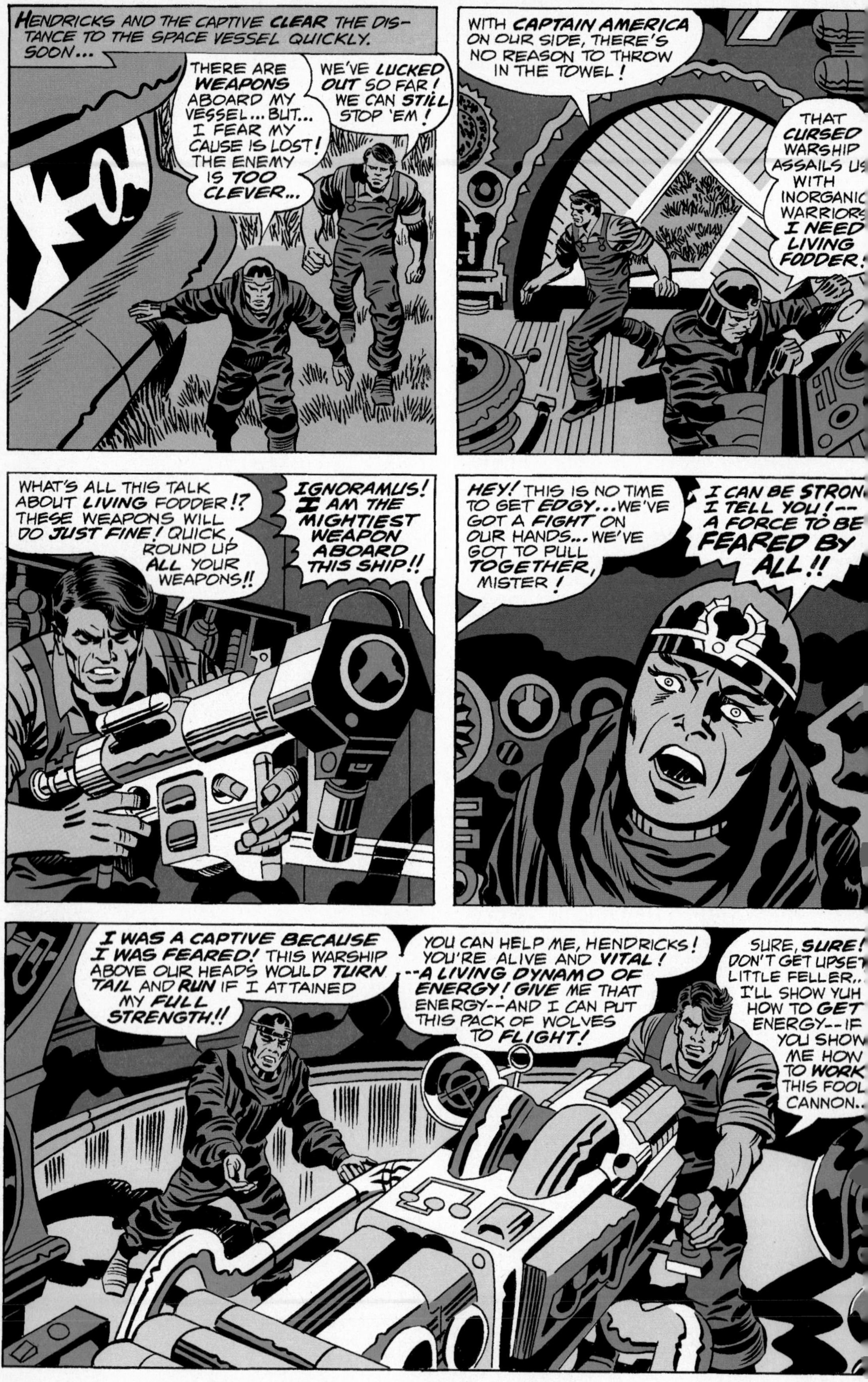
HENDRICKS AND THE CAPTIVE CLEAR THE DISTANCE TO THE SPACE VESSEL QUICKLY. SOON...
THERE ARE WEAPONS ABOARD MY VESSEL... BUT... I FEAR MY CAUSE IS LOST! THE ENEMY IS TOO CLEVER...
WE'VE LUCKED OUT SO FAR! WE CAN STILL STOP 'EM!
WITH CAPTAIN AMERICA ON OUR SIDE, THERE'S NO REASON TO THROW IN THE TOWEL!
THAT CURSED WARSHIP ASSAILS US WITH INORGANIC WARRIORS I NEED LIVING FODDER!
WHAT'S ALL THIS TALK ABOUT LIVING FODDER!? THESE WEAPONS WILL DO JUST FINE! QUICK, ROUND UP ALL YOUR WEAPONS!!
IGNORAMUS! I AM THE MIGHTIEST WEAPON ABOARD THIS SHIP!!
HEY! THIS IS NO TIME TO GET EDGY... WE'VE GOT A FIGHT ON OUR HANDS... WE'VE GOT TO PULL TOGETHER, MISTER!
I CAN BE STRONG I TELL YOU!-- A FORCE TO BE FEARED BY ALL!!
I WAS A CAPTIVE BECAUSE I WAS FEARED! THIS WARSHIP ABOVE OUR HEADS WOULD TURN TAIL AND RUN IF I ATTAINED MY FULL STRENGTH!!
YOU CAN HELP ME, HENDRICKS! YOU'RE ALIVE AND VITAL! --A LIVING DYNAMO OF ENERGY! GIVE ME THAT ENERGY--AND I CAN PUT THIS PACK OF WOLVES TO FLIGHT!
SURE, SURE! DON'T GET UPSET LITTLE FELLER.. I'LL SHOW YUH HOW TO GET ENERGY-- IF YOU SHOW ME HOW TO WORK THIS FOOL CANNON..

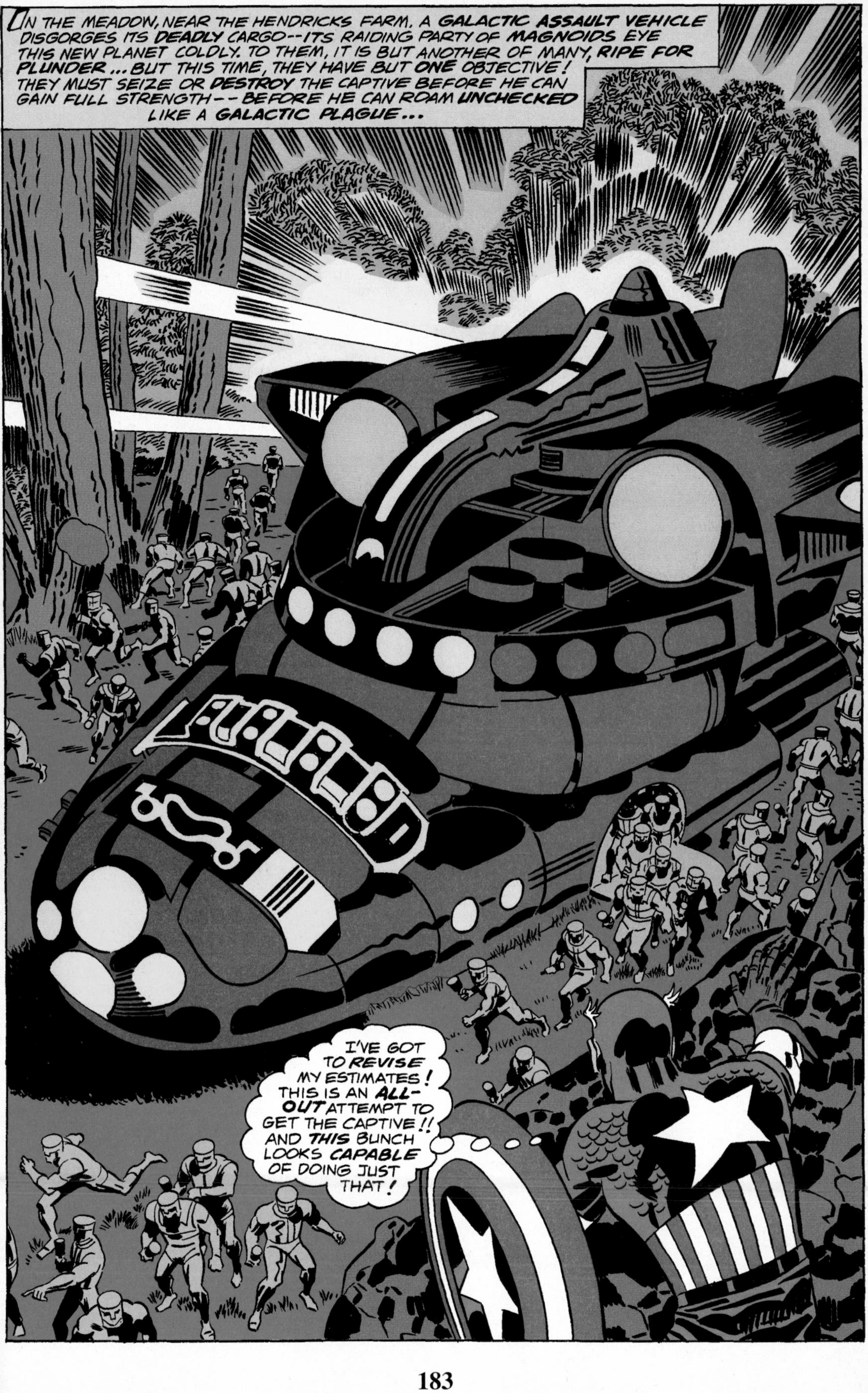
ON THE MEADOW, NEAR THE HENDRICKS FARM, A GALACTIC ASSAULT VEHICLE DISGORGES ITS DEADLY CARGO--ITS RAIDING PARTY OF MAGNOIDS EYE THIS NEW PLANET COLDLY. TO THEM, IT IS BUT ANOTHER OF MANY, RIPE FOR PLUNDER... BUT THIS TIME, THEY HAVE BUT ONE OBJECTIVE! THEY MUST SEIZE OR DESTROY THE CAPTIVE BEFORE HE CAN GAIN FULL STRENGTH-- BEFORE HE CAN ROAM UNCHECKED LIKE A GALACTIC PLAGUE...
I'VE GOT TO REVISE MY ESTIMATES! THIS IS AN ALL-OUT ATTEMPT TO GET THE CAPTIVE!! AND THIS BUNCH LOOKS CAPABLE OF DOING JUST THAT!

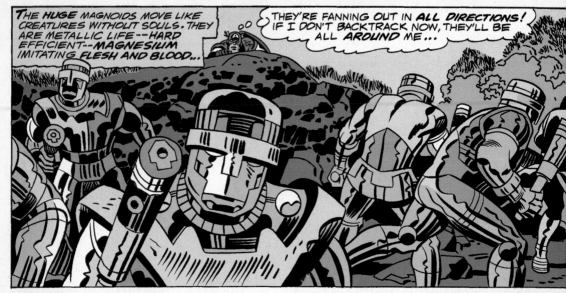

THE HUGE MAGNOIDS MOVE LIKE CREATURES WITHOUT SOULS. THEY ARE METALLIC LIFE--HARD EFFICIENT--MAGNESIUM IMITATING FLESH AND BLOOD...

THEY'RE FANNING OUT IN *ALL DIRECTIONS!* IF I DON'T BACKTRACK NOW, THEY'LL BE ALL *AROUND* ME...

CAP HAS ALSO *UNDERESTIMATED* THE *SPEED* OF THE MAGNOIDS... HE IS *ALREADY* UNDER COLD SURVEILLANCE...

I ONLY HOPE THE CAPTIVE IS *WORTH* A FIGHT! BUT EVEN IF HE'S WANTED FOR A *CRIME*--HE STILL DESERVES HIS DAY IN *COURT!*

SUDDENLY--!!

ZZZAAP!

DLOMM!

I'VE BEEN DISCOVERED! THE HEAT'S ON!!

WEAVING AND *DODGING* WITH EVERY OUNCE OF HIS BATTLE-WISE AGILITY, CAP ATTEMPTS TO OUTLAST THE MERCILESS, WHITE-HOT BURSTS OF *DESTRUCTION*...

POW!

POW!

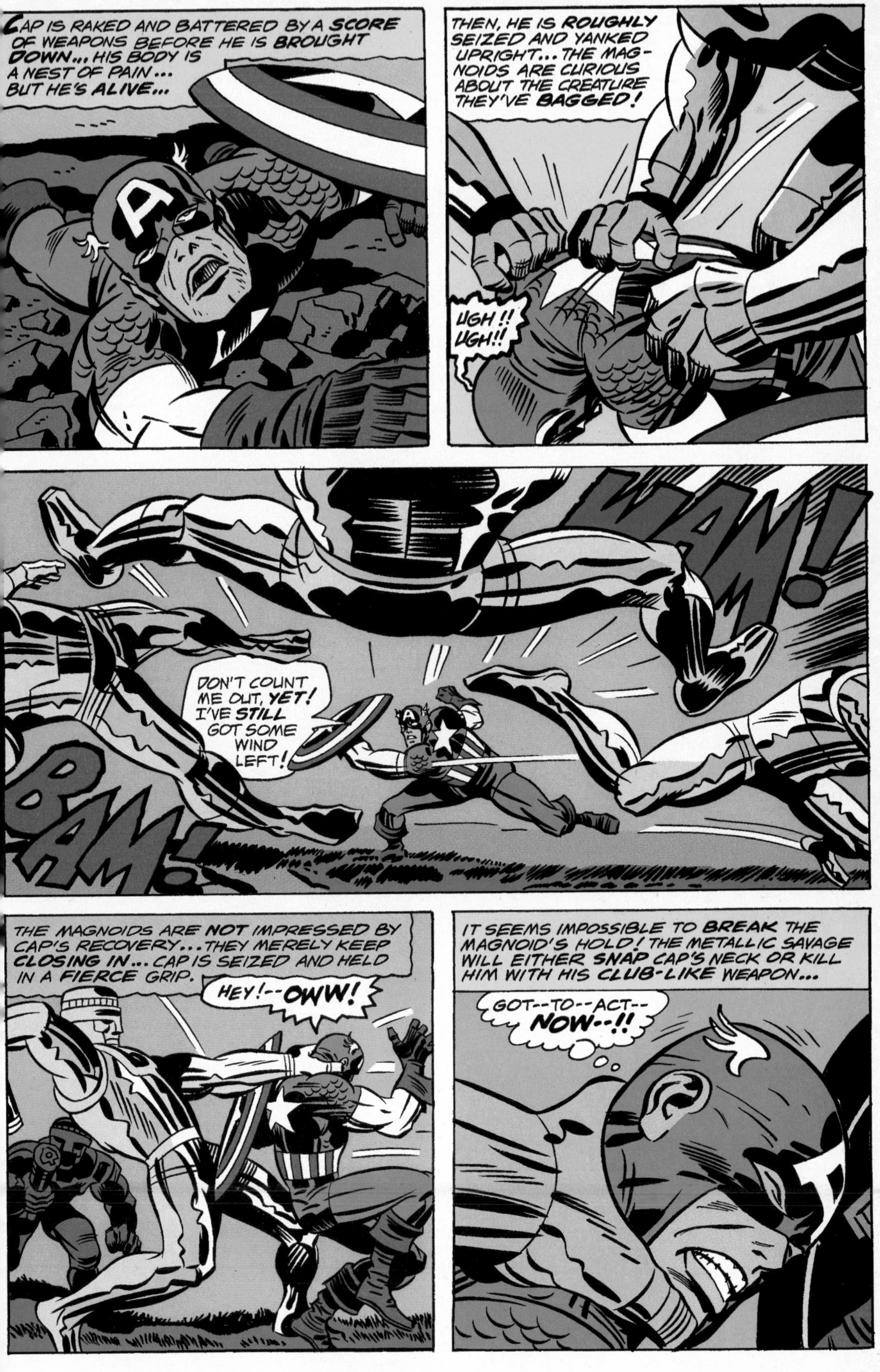

CAP IS RAKED AND BATTERED BY A SCORE OF WEAPONS BEFORE HE IS BROUGHT DOWN... HIS BODY IS A NEST OF PAIN... BUT HE'S ALIVE...
THEN, HE IS ROUGHLY SEIZED AND YANKED UPRIGHT... THE MAGNOIDS ARE CURIOUS ABOUT THE CREATURE THEY'VE BAGGED!
UGH!! UGH!!
WAM!
DON'T COUNT ME OUT, YET! I'VE STILL GOT SOME WIND LEFT!
BAM!
THE MAGNOIDS ARE NOT IMPRESSED BY CAP'S RECOVERY... THEY MERELY KEEP CLOSING IN... CAP IS SEIZED AND HELD IN A FIERCE GRIP.
HEY!--OWW!
IT SEEMS IMPOSSIBLE TO BREAK THE MAGNOID'S HOLD! THE METALLIC SAVAGE WILL EITHER SNAP CAP'S NECK OR KILL HIM WITH HIS CLUB-LIKE WEAPON...
GOT--TO--ACT--NOW--!!

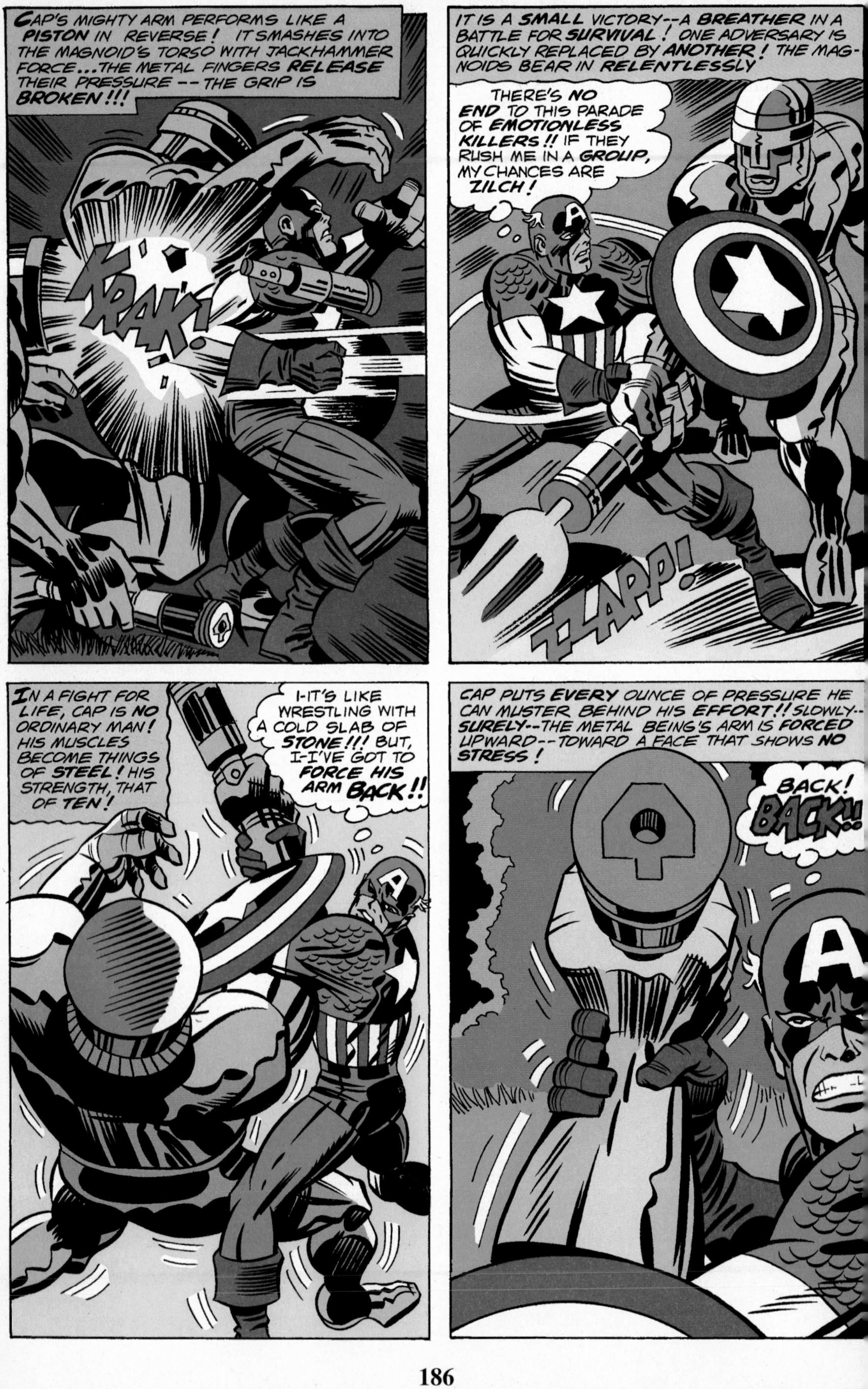
CAP'S MIGHTY ARM PERFORMS LIKE A PISTON IN REVERSE! IT SMASHES INTO THE MAGNOID'S TORSO WITH JACKHAMMER FORCE... THE METAL FINGERS RELEASE THEIR PRESSURE -- THE GRIP IS BROKEN!!!
KRAK!
IT IS A SMALL VICTORY-- A BREATHER IN A BATTLE FOR SURVIVAL! ONE ADVERSARY IS QUICKLY REPLACED BY ANOTHER! THE MAGNOIDS BEAR IN RELENTLESSLY
THERE'S NO END TO THIS PARADE OF EMOTIONLESS KILLERS!! IF THEY RUSH ME IN A GROUP, MY CHANCES ARE ZILCH!
ZZAPP!
IN A FIGHT FOR LIFE, CAP IS NO ORDINARY MAN! HIS MUSCLES BECOME THINGS OF STEEL! HIS STRENGTH, THAT OF TEN!
I-IT'S LIKE WRESTLING WITH A COLD SLAB OF STONE!!! BUT, I-I'VE GOT TO FORCE HIS ARM BACK!!
CAP PUTS EVERY OUNCE OF PRESSURE HE CAN MUSTER BEHIND HIS EFFORT!! SLOWLY-- SURELY-- THE METAL BEING'S ARM IS FORCED UPWARD-- TOWARD A FACE THAT SHOWS NO STRESS!
BACK! BACK!!

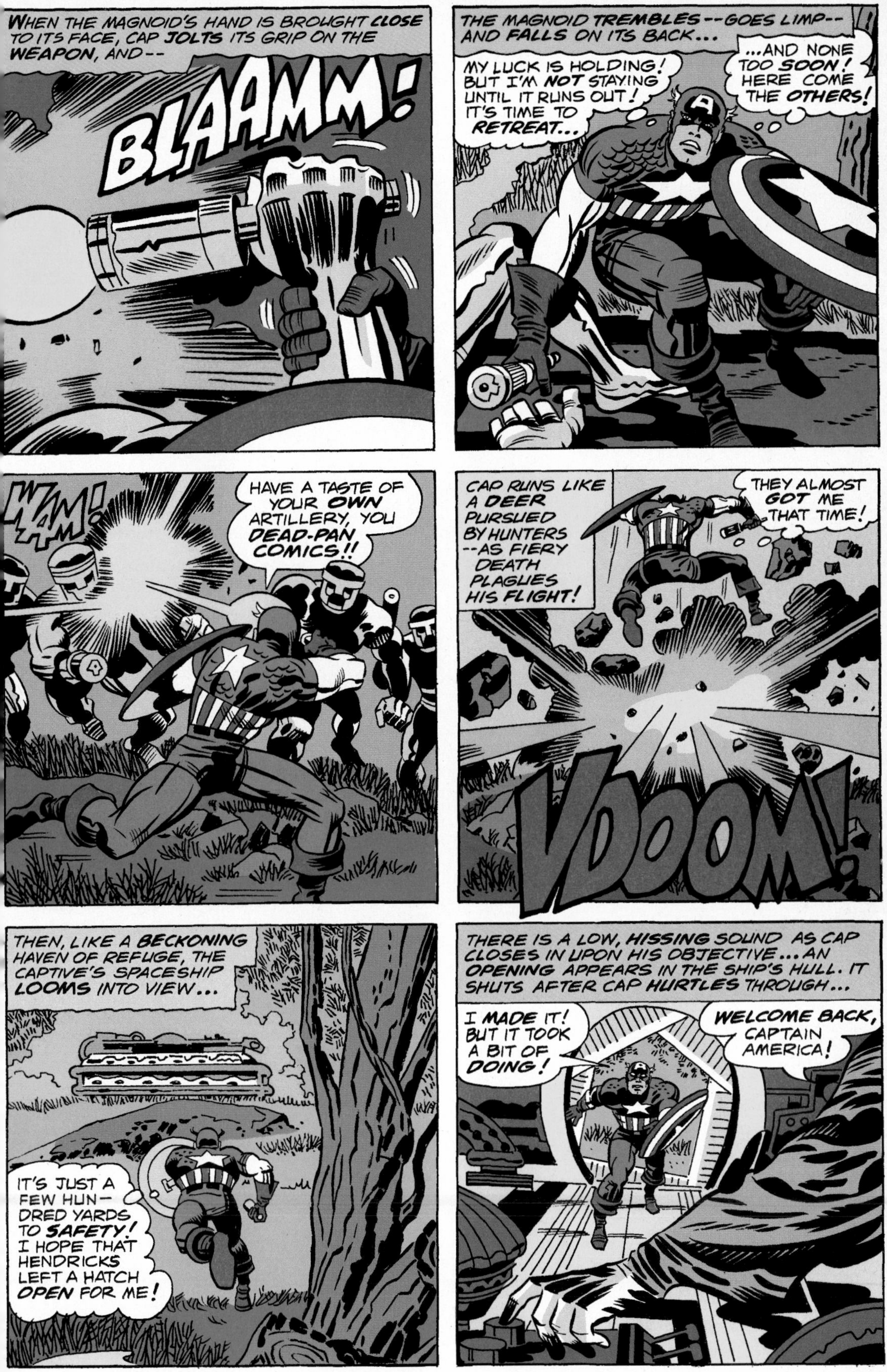

WHEN THE MAGNOID'S HAND IS BROUGHT CLOSE TO ITS FACE, CAP JOLTS ITS GRIP ON THE WEAPON, AND--
BLAAMM!
THE MAGNOID TREMBLES--GOES LIMP--AND FALLS ON ITS BACK...
MY LUCK IS HOLDING! BUT I'M NOT STAYING UNTIL IT RUNS OUT! IT'S TIME TO RETREAT...
...AND NONE TOO SOON! HERE COME THE OTHERS!
WAM!
HAVE A TASTE OF YOUR OWN ARTILLERY, YOU DEAD-PAN COMICS!!
CAP RUNS LIKE A DEER PURSUED BY HUNTERS --AS FIERY DEATH PLAGUES HIS FLIGHT!
THEY ALMOST GOT ME THAT TIME!
VOOOM!
THEN, LIKE A BECKONING HAVEN OF REFUGE, THE CAPTIVE'S SPACESHIP LOOMS INTO VIEW...
IT'S JUST A FEW HUN-DRED YARDS TO SAFETY! I HOPE THAT HENDRICKS LEFT A HATCH OPEN FOR ME!
THERE IS A LOW, HISSING SOUND AS CAP CLOSES IN UPON HIS OBJECTIVE... AN OPENING APPEARS IN THE SHIP'S HULL. IT SHUTS AFTER CAP HURTLES THROUGH...
I MADE IT! BUT IT TOOK A BIT OF DOING!
WELCOME BACK, CAPTAIN AMERICA!

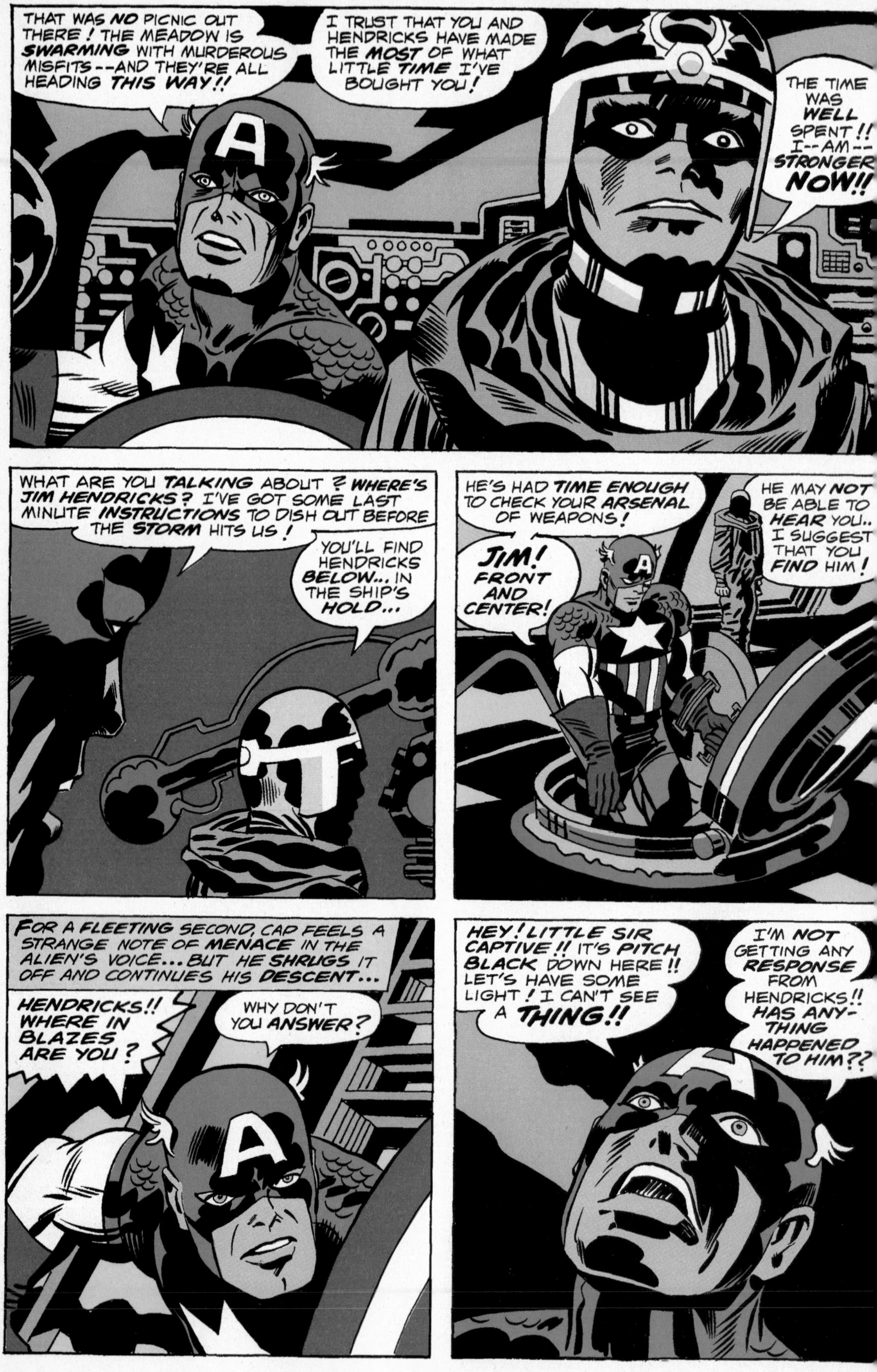
THAT WAS NO PICNIC OUT THERE! THE MEADOW IS SWARMING WITH MURDEROUS MISFITS--AND THEY'RE ALL HEADING THIS WAY!!
I TRUST THAT YOU AND HENDRICKS HAVE MADE THE MOST OF WHAT LITTLE TIME I'VE BOUGHT YOU!
THE TIME WAS WELL SPENT!! I--AM--STRONGER NOW!!
WHAT ARE YOU TALKING ABOUT? WHERE'S JIM HENDRICKS? I'VE GOT SOME LAST MINUTE INSTRUCTIONS TO DISH OUT BEFORE THE STORM HITS US!
YOU'LL FIND HENDRICKS BELOW... IN THE SHIP'S HOLD...
HE'S HAD TIME ENOUGH TO CHECK YOUR ARSENAL OF WEAPONS!
HE MAY NOT BE ABLE TO HEAR YOU.. I SUGGEST THAT YOU FIND HIM!
JIM! FRONT AND CENTER!
FOR A FLEETING SECOND, CAP FEELS A STRANGE NOTE OF MENACE IN THE ALIEN'S VOICE... BUT HE SHRUGS IT OFF AND CONTINUES HIS DESCENT...
HENDRICKS!! WHERE IN BLAZES ARE YOU?
WHY DON'T YOU ANSWER?
HEY! LITTLE SIR CAPTIVE!! IT'S PITCH BLACK DOWN HERE!! LET'S HAVE SOME LIGHT! I CAN'T SEE A THING!!
I'M NOT GETTING ANY RESPONSE FROM HENDRICKS!! HAS ANYTHING HAPPENED TO HIM??

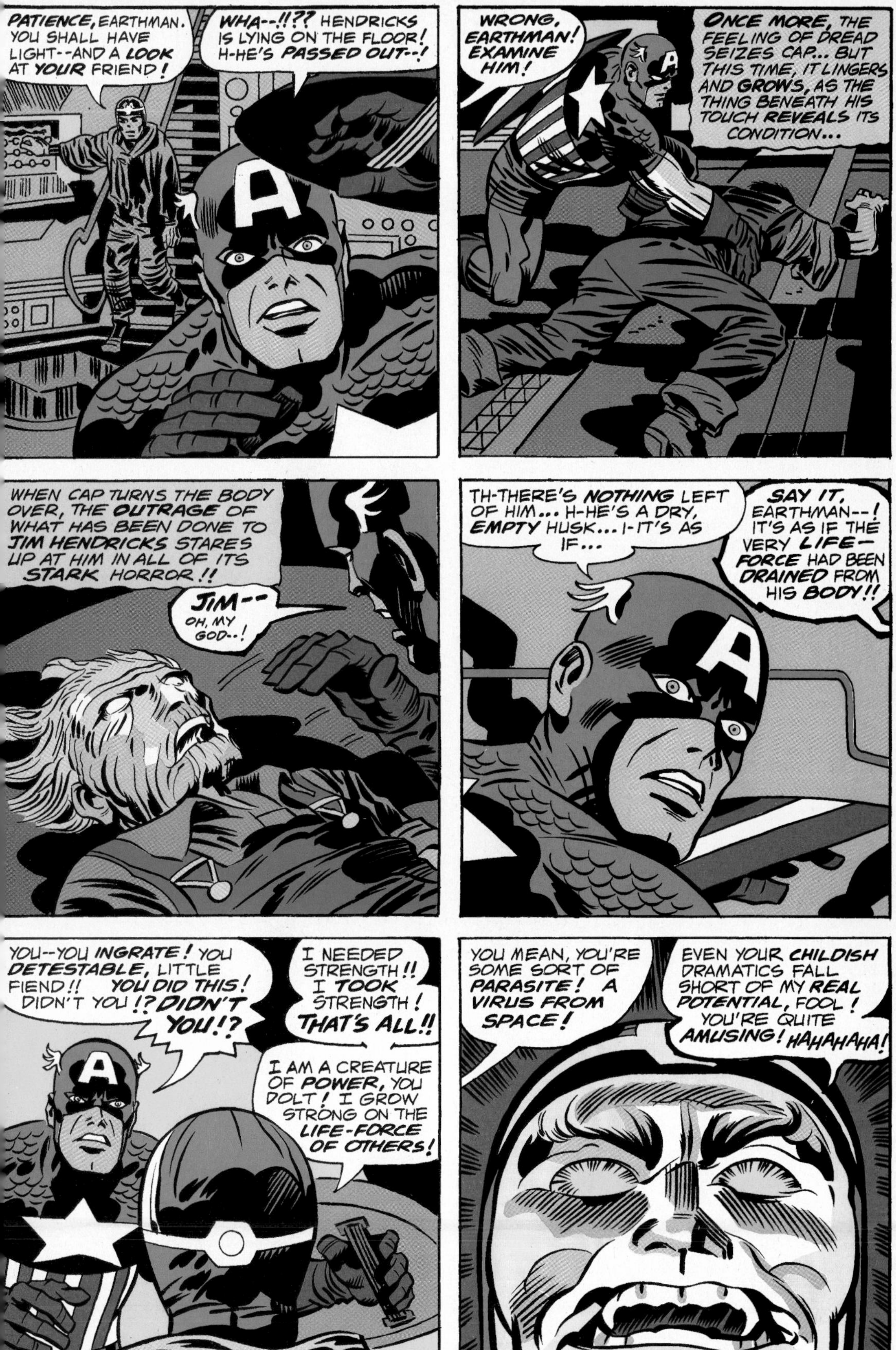
PATIENCE, EARTHMAN. YOU SHALL HAVE LIGHT--AND A LOOK AT YOUR FRIEND!
WHA--!!?? HENDRICKS IS LYING ON THE FLOOR! H-HE'S PASSED OUT--!
WRONG, EARTHMAN! EXAMINE HIM!
ONCE MORE, THE FEELING OF DREAD SEIZES CAP... BUT THIS TIME, IT LINGERS AND GROWS, AS THE THING BENEATH HIS TOUCH REVEALS ITS CONDITION...
WHEN CAP TURNS THE BODY OVER, THE OUTRAGE OF WHAT HAS BEEN DONE TO JIM HENDRICKS STARES UP AT HIM IN ALL OF ITS STARK HORROR!!
JIM-- OH, MY GOD--!
TH-THERE'S NOTHING LEFT OF HIM... H-HE'S A DRY, EMPTY HUSK... I-IT'S AS IF...
SAY IT, EARTHMAN--! IT'S AS IF THE VERY LIFE-FORCE HAD BEEN DRAINED FROM HIS BODY!!
YOU--YOU INGRATE! YOU DETESTABLE, LITTLE FIEND!! YOU DID THIS! DIDN'T YOU!? DIDN'T YOU!?
I NEEDED STRENGTH!! I TOOK STRENGTH! THAT'S ALL!!
I AM A CREATURE OF POWER, YOU DOLT! I GROW STRONG ON THE LIFE-FORCE OF OTHERS!
YOU MEAN, YOU'RE SOME SORT OF PARASITE! A VIRUS FROM SPACE!
EVEN YOUR CHILDISH DRAMATICS FALL SHORT OF MY REAL POTENTIAL, FOOL! YOU'RE QUITE AMUSING! HAHAHAHA!

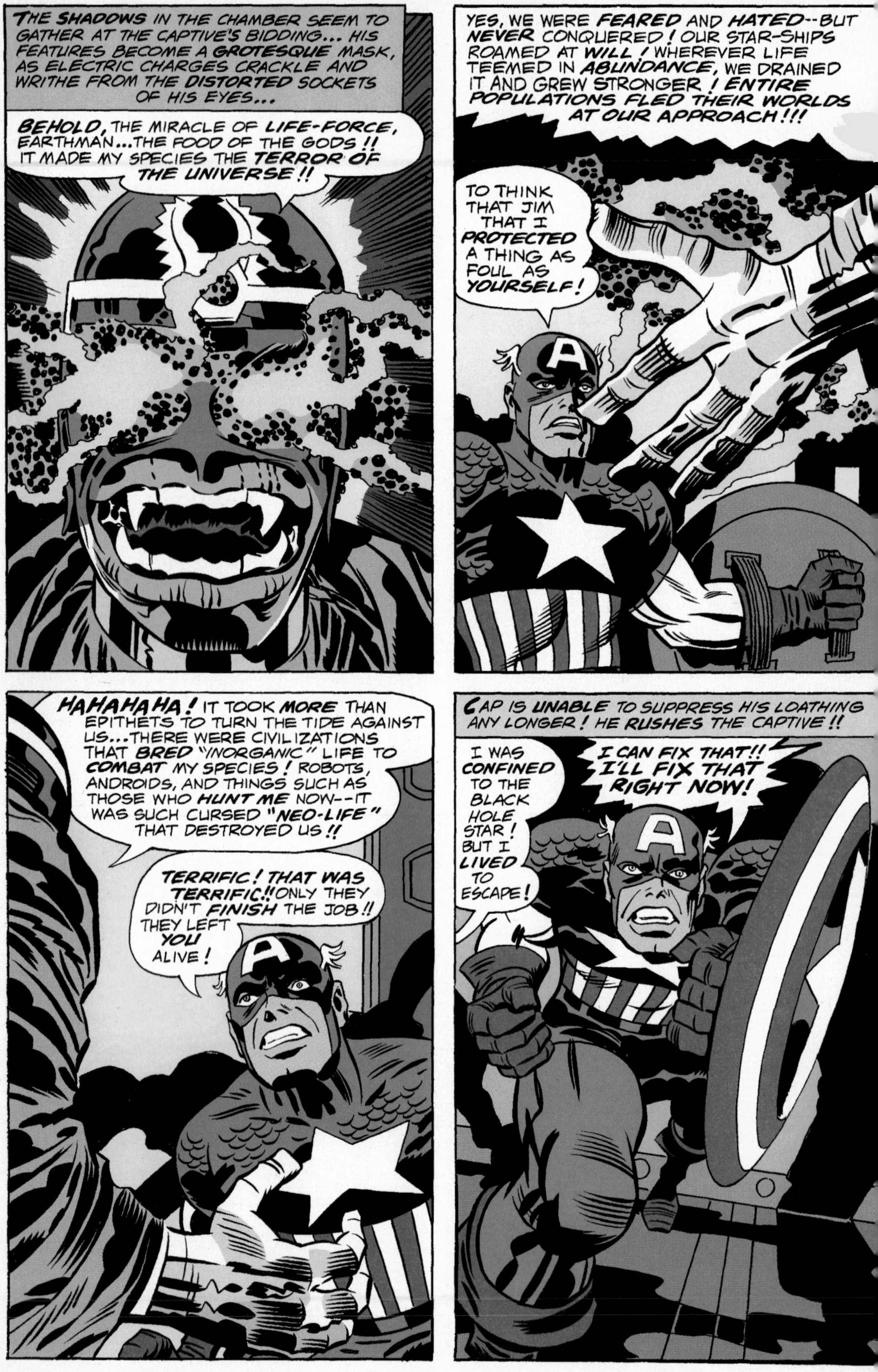

THE SHADOWS IN THE CHAMBER SEEM TO GATHER AT THE CAPTIVE'S BIDDING... HIS FEATURES BECOME A GROTESQUE MASK, AS ELECTRIC CHARGES CRACKLE AND WRITHE FROM THE DISTORTED SOCKETS OF HIS EYES...
BEHOLD, THE MIRACLE OF LIFE-FORCE, EARTHMAN...THE FOOD OF THE GODS!! IT MADE MY SPECIES THE TERROR OF THE UNIVERSE!!
YES, WE WERE FEARED AND HATED--BUT NEVER CONQUERED! OUR STAR-SHIPS ROAMED AT WILL! WHEREVER LIFE TEEMED IN ABUNDANCE, WE DRAINED IT AND GREW STRONGER! ENTIRE POPULATIONS FLED THEIR WORLDS AT OUR APPROACH!!!
TO THINK THAT JIM THAT I PROTECTED A THING AS FOUL AS YOURSELF!
HAHAHAHA! IT TOOK MORE THAN EPITHETS TO TURN THE TIDE AGAINST US...THERE WERE CIVILIZATIONS THAT BRED "INORGANIC" LIFE TO COMBAT MY SPECIES! ROBOTS, ANDROIDS, AND THINGS SUCH AS THOSE WHO HUNT ME NOW--IT WAS SUCH CURSED "NEO-LIFE" THAT DESTROYED US!!
TERRIFIC! THAT WAS TERRIFIC!! ONLY THEY DIDN'T FINISH THE JOB!! THEY LEFT YOU ALIVE!
CAP IS UNABLE TO SUPPRESS HIS LOATHING ANY LONGER! HE RUSHES THE CAPTIVE!!
I WAS CONFINED TO THE BLACK HOLE STAR! BUT I LIVED TO ESCAPE!
I CAN FIX THAT!! I'LL FIX THAT RIGHT NOW!

AT THE INSTANT OF *CONTACT* BETWEEN THE TWO, A VERITABLE *EXPLOSION* OF *ENERGY* OCCURS, WHICH *ENGULFS* THEM *BOTH!*

HA HA HA HA!!

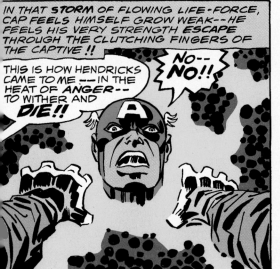

IN THAT *STORM* OF FLOWING *LIFE-FORCE*, CAP *FEELS* HIMSELF GROW *WEAK*--HE FEELS HIS VERY STRENGTH *ESCAPE* THROUGH THE CLUTCHING FINGERS OF THE *CAPTIVE!!*

THIS IS HOW HENDRICKS CAME TO ME --IN THE HEAT OF *ANGER*-- TO WITHER AND *DIE!!*

NO-- NO!!

CAP *RALLIES* WHAT STRENGTH HE HAS LEFT, AND *TEARS HIMSELF* FROM THE CAPTIVE'S *GRIP!!!*

YOU MERELY *DELAY* THE PROCESS, EARTHMAN! RESISTANCE IS *USELESS!*

YOU WON'T GET ME, YOU *DEVIL!* YOU *WON'T*--!

YOURS IS NO MORE THAN *MOCK DEFIANCE!* SAY WHAT YOU WILL OF *DEATH*...BUT YOU CANNOT *CHEAT* HIM OF HIS *DUE!*

AS *DEATH*, I CLAIM YOU! AS *DEATH* I SHALL HAVE YOU...

I'LL BEAT YOU! I'LL BEAT YOU!!

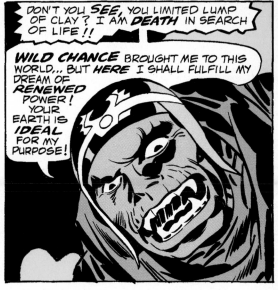

DON'T YOU *SEE*, YOU LIMITED LUMP OF CLAY? I AM *DEATH* IN SEARCH OF *LIFE!!*

WILD CHANCE BROUGHT ME TO THIS WORLD...BUT *HERE* I SHALL FULFILL MY DREAM OF *RENEWED* POWER! YOUR EARTH IS *IDEAL* FOR MY PURPOSE!

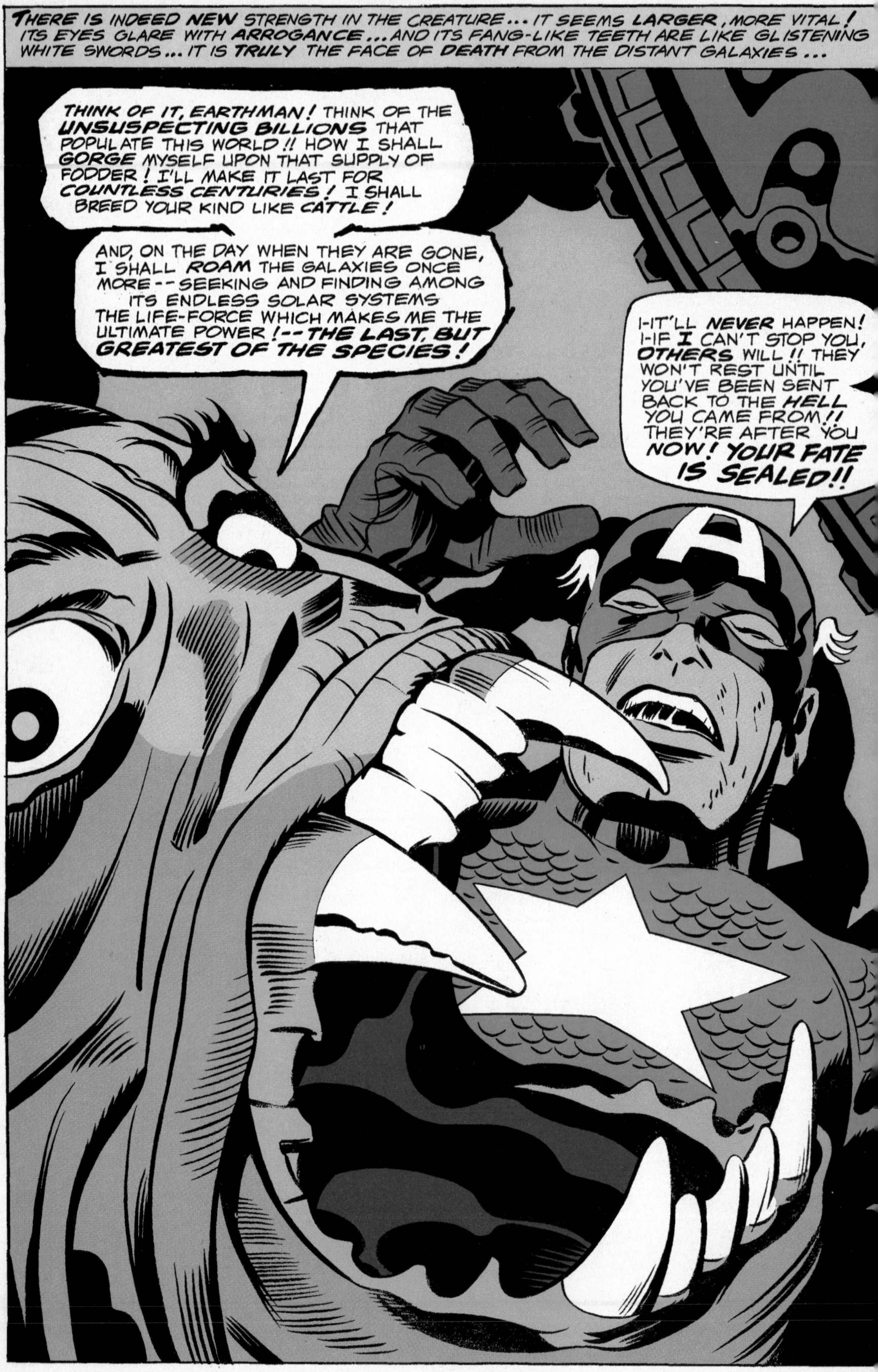
THERE IS INDEED NEW STRENGTH IN THE CREATURE... IT SEEMS LARGER, MORE VITAL! ITS EYES GLARE WITH ARROGANCE... AND ITS FANG-LIKE TEETH ARE LIKE GLISTENING WHITE SWORDS... IT IS TRULY THE FACE OF DEATH FROM THE DISTANT GALAXIES...
THINK OF IT, EARTHMAN! THINK OF THE UNSUSPECTING BILLIONS THAT POPULATE THIS WORLD!! HOW I SHALL GORGE MYSELF UPON THAT SUPPLY OF FODDER! I'LL MAKE IT LAST FOR COUNTLESS CENTURIES! I SHALL BREED YOUR KIND LIKE CATTLE!
AND, ON THE DAY WHEN THEY ARE GONE, I SHALL ROAM THE GALAXIES ONCE MORE--SEEKING AND FINDING AMONG ITS ENDLESS SOLAR SYSTEMS THE LIFE-FORCE WHICH MAKES ME THE ULTIMATE POWER!--THE LAST, BUT GREATEST OF THE SPECIES!
I-IT'LL NEVER HAPPEN! I-IF I CAN'T STOP YOU, OTHERS WILL!! THEY WON'T REST UNTIL YOU'VE BEEN SENT BACK TO THE HELL YOU CAME FROM!! THEY'RE AFTER YOU NOW! YOUR FATE IS SEALED!!

NOTHING SHALL STOP ME NOW, EARTHMAN! THE LIFE-FORCE I TOOK FROM HENDRICKS HAS GIVEN ME RENEWED POWER--YOURS SHALL MAKE ME EVEN STRONGER!!

GIVE ME YOUR LIFE-FORCE, CAPTAIN AMERICA! YOU'VE BEEN WEAKENED!! YOU'VE GOT NO CHOICE!!

COME--AND--GET IT--YOU--YOU--MONSTROSITY!

THE CAPTIVE'S FINGERS REACH SWIFTLY FOR CAP, BUT ENCOUNTER THE TOUGH, METAL SURFACE OF HIS SHIELD, INSTEAD!

WHA--!!??

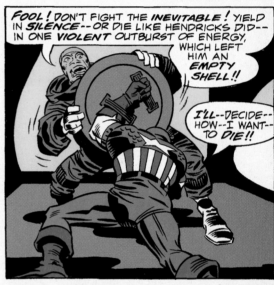

FOOL! DON'T FIGHT THE INEVITABLE! YIELD IN SILENCE--OR DIE LIKE HENDRICKS DID-- IN ONE VIOLENT OUTBURST OF ENERGY, WHICH LEFT HIM AN EMPTY SHELL!!

I'LL--DECIDE--HOW--I WANT--TO DIE!!

CAP USES WHAT STRENGTH HE HAS LEFT TO STRUGGLE AGAINST THIS POWERFUL CREATURE... BUT HE KNOWS THAT HIS SHIELD WILL KEEP THE THING AT BAY FOR ONLY A SHORT TIME...

I-IT'S USELESS! I-I CAN'T KEEP THIS UP MUCH LONGER! BUT I'LL BATTLE HIM--'TIL THE--END!

SUDDENLY--FROM THE CHAMBER ABOVE--

BAM! CLUMP!

INTRUDERS!! THEY'VE BROKEN INTO THE SHIP!!

BUT I'LL DEAL WITH THEM!!

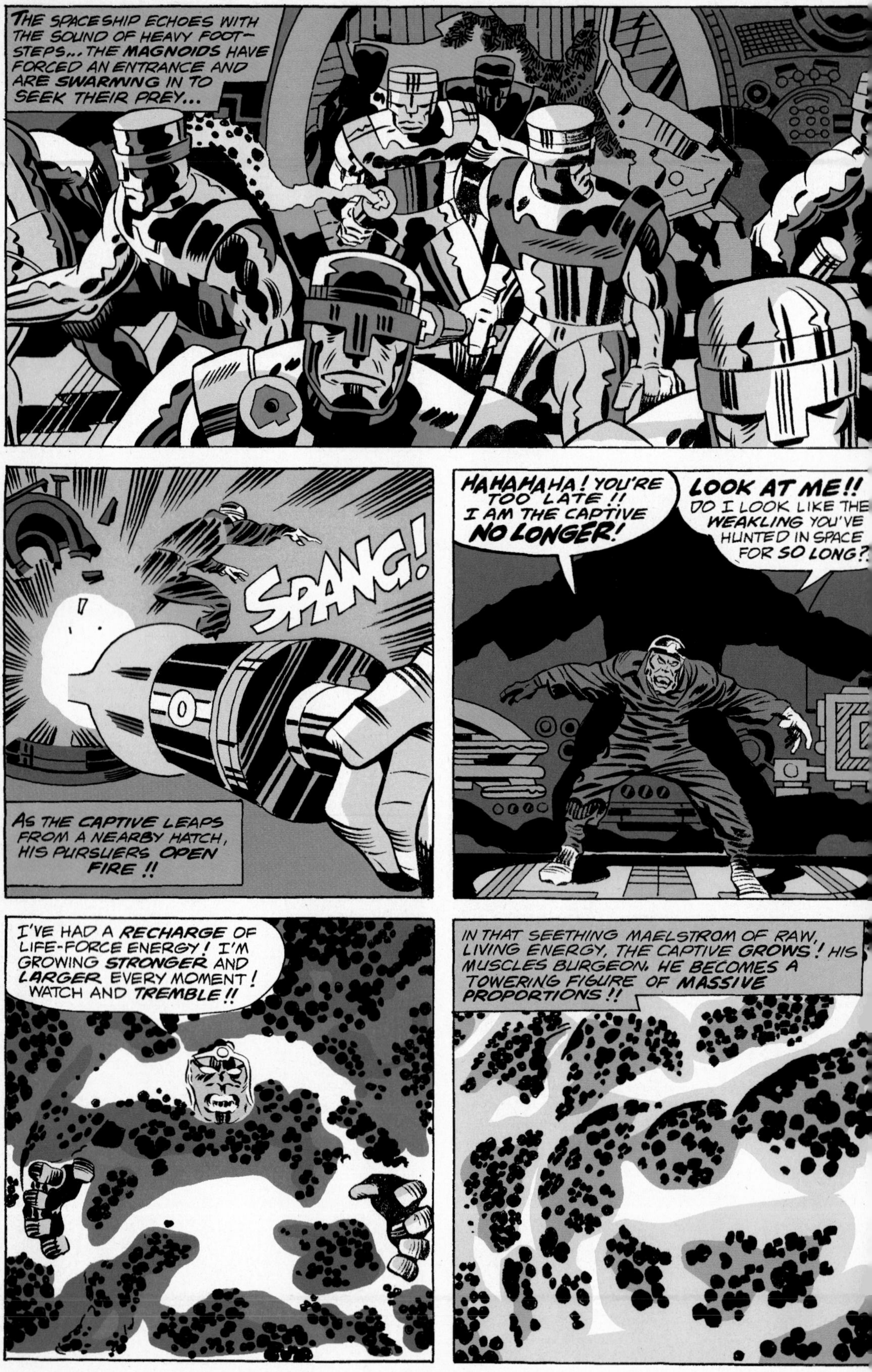
THE SPACESHIP ECHOES WITH THE SOUND OF HEAVY FOOT-STEPS... THE MAGNOIDS HAVE FORCED AN ENTRANCE AND ARE SWARMING IN TO SEEK THEIR PREY...
SPANG!
AS THE CAPTIVE LEAPS FROM A NEARBY HATCH, HIS PURSUERS OPEN FIRE !!
HAHAHAHA! YOU'RE TOO LATE !! I AM THE CAPTIVE NO LONGER!
LOOK AT ME!! DO I LOOK LIKE THE WEAKLING YOU'VE HUNTED IN SPACE FOR SO LONG?
I'VE HAD A RECHARGE OF LIFE-FORCE ENERGY! I'M GROWING STRONGER AND LARGER EVERY MOMENT! WATCH AND TREMBLE !!
IN THAT SEETHING MAELSTROM OF RAW, LIVING ENERGY, THE CAPTIVE GROWS! HIS MUSCLES BURGEON. HE BECOMES A TOWERING FIGURE OF MASSIVE PROPORTIONS !!

MEANWHILE, CAP HAS MANAGED TO CRAWL THROUGH THE HATCH...HE IS SEIZED BY THE HORROR OF THE NIGHTMARE TRANSPIRING BEFORE HIM...

THE CAPTIVE !! HE'S ACHIEVING *MONSTROUS* SIZE !!

GOT TO STOP *HIM* -- BEFORE HE BECOMES-- *INVINCIBLE !!*

CAP UNLIMBERS HIS SHIELD WITH *FIRM RESOLVE* !!! HE IS DETERMINED TO MAKE A *LAST ALL-OUT* EFFORT AGAINST THIS SUPER-ENEMY...

THE SECRET IS *COOLNESS* AND ACCURACY-- AND A *THOUSAND* DESPERATE EXPERIENCES GUIDING THE *ARM* WHICH UNLEASHES A WEAPON, UNIQUE TO ITS *OWNER ALONE* ...

ALL RIGHT, YOU *MISBEGOTTEN* SPAWN OF THE PITS !! LET'S SEE *YOU* TAKE ME THIS TIME !!

THEN !!

BWAAM!

THERE IS A BRIGHT, *UNEARTHLY* FLASH -- A PIERCING *SCREAM* -- A PAUSE-- A THUMP-- AND THE DIM RETURN OF *HOPE* THAT THE CAPTIVE HAS BEEN *VANQUISHED* !!!

I-I THINK HE'S *DOWN* !! TOO...WEAK...TO MAKE CERTAIN...T-THAT TOSS *REALLY* ZAPPED ME OUT...

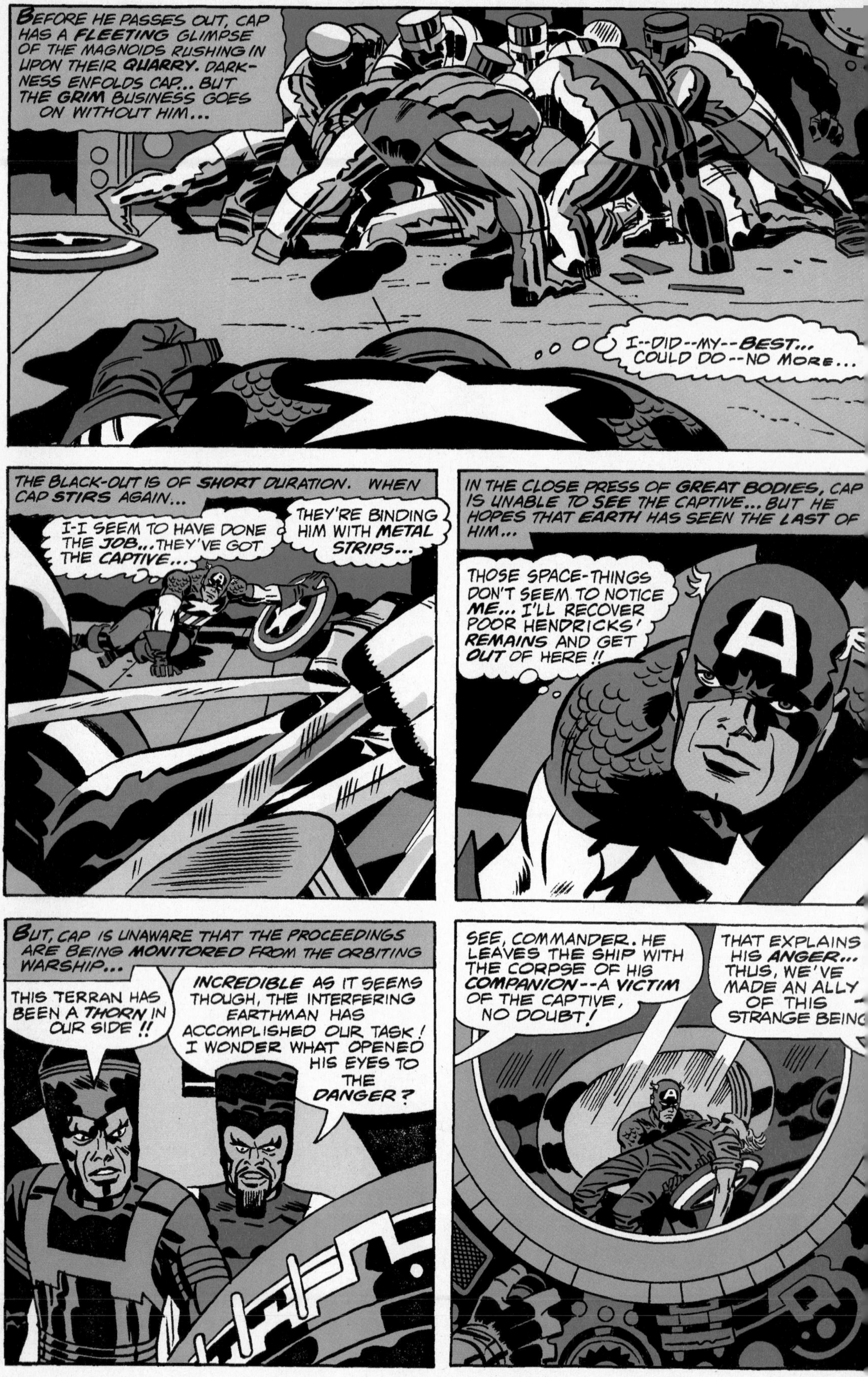
BEFORE HE PASSES OUT, CAP HAS A FLEETING GLIMPSE OF THE MAGNOIDS RUSHING IN UPON THEIR QUARRY. DARKNESS ENFOLDS CAP... BUT THE GRIM BUSINESS GOES ON WITHOUT HIM...
I--DID--MY--BEST... COULD DO--NO MORE...
THE BLACK-OUT IS OF SHORT DURATION. WHEN CAP STIRS AGAIN...
I-I SEEM TO HAVE DONE THE JOB...THEY'VE GOT THE CAPTIVE...
THEY'RE BINDING HIM WITH METAL STRIPS...
IN THE CLOSE PRESS OF GREAT BODIES, CAP IS UNABLE TO SEE THE CAPTIVE... BUT HE HOPES THAT EARTH HAS SEEN THE LAST OF HIM...
THOSE SPACE-THINGS DON'T SEEM TO NOTICE ME... I'LL RECOVER POOR HENDRICKS' REMAINS AND GET OUT OF HERE!!
BUT, CAP IS UNAWARE THAT THE PROCEEDINGS ARE BEING MONITORED FROM THE ORBITING WARSHIP...
THIS TERRAN HAS BEEN A THORN IN OUR SIDE!!
INCREDIBLE AS IT SEEMS THOUGH, THE INTERFERING EARTHMAN HAS ACCOMPLISHED OUR TASK! I WONDER WHAT OPENED HIS EYES TO THE DANGER?
SEE, COMMANDER. HE LEAVES THE SHIP WITH THE CORPSE OF HIS COMPANION--A VICTIM OF THE CAPTIVE, NO DOUBT!
THAT EXPLAINS HIS ANGER... THUS, WE'VE MADE AN ALLY OF THIS STRANGE BEING

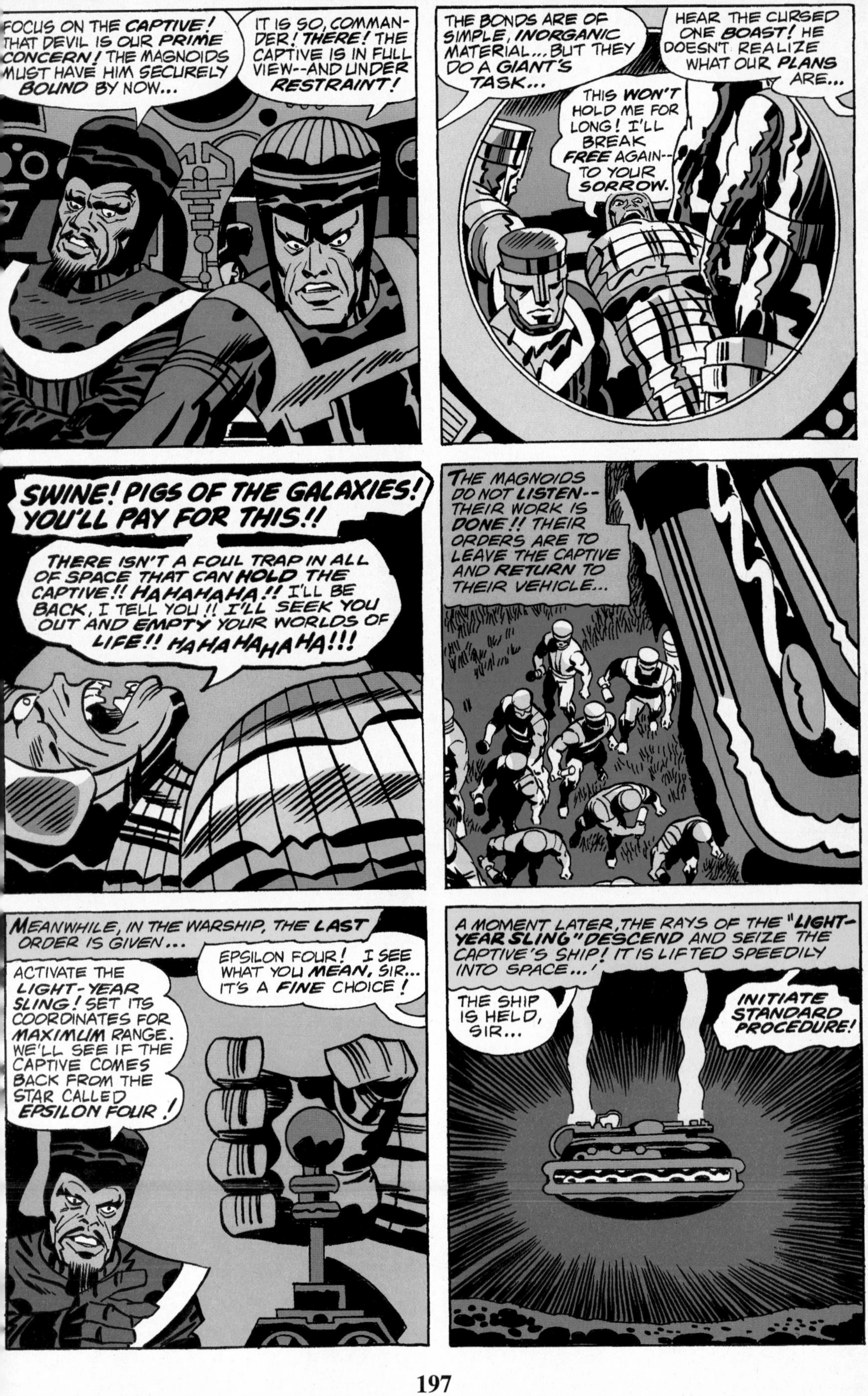
FOCUS ON THE CAPTIVE! THAT DEVIL IS OUR PRIME CONCERN! THE MAGNOIDS MUST HAVE HIM SECURELY BOUND BY NOW...
IT IS SO, COMMANDER! THERE! THE CAPTIVE IS IN FULL VIEW--AND UNDER RESTRAINT!
THE BONDS ARE OF SIMPLE, INORGANIC MATERIAL... BUT THEY DO A GIANT'S TASK...
HEAR THE CURSED ONE BOAST! HE DOESN'T REALIZE WHAT OUR PLANS ARE...
THIS WON'T HOLD ME FOR LONG! I'LL BREAK FREE AGAIN--TO YOUR SORROW.
SWINE! PIGS OF THE GALAXIES! YOU'LL PAY FOR THIS!!
THERE ISN'T A FOUL TRAP IN ALL OF SPACE THAT CAN HOLD THE CAPTIVE!! HAHAHAHA!! I'LL BE BACK, I TELL YOU!! I'LL SEEK YOU OUT AND EMPTY YOUR WORLDS OF LIFE!! HAHAHAHAHAHA!!!
THE MAGNOIDS DO NOT LISTEN--THEIR WORK IS DONE!! THEIR ORDERS ARE TO LEAVE THE CAPTIVE AND RETURN TO THEIR VEHICLE...
MEANWHILE, IN THE WARSHIP, THE LAST ORDER IS GIVEN...
ACTIVATE THE LIGHT-YEAR SLING! SET ITS COORDINATES FOR MAXIMUM RANGE. WE'LL SEE IF THE CAPTIVE COMES BACK FROM THE STAR CALLED EPSILON FOUR!
EPSILON FOUR! I SEE WHAT YOU MEAN, SIR... IT'S A FINE CHOICE!
A MOMENT LATER, THE RAYS OF THE "LIGHT-YEAR SLING" DESCEND AND SEIZE THE CAPTIVE'S SHIP! IT IS LIFTED SPEEDILY INTO SPACE...
THE SHIP IS HELD, SIR...
INITIATE STANDARD PROCEDURE!

THE "LIGHT-YEAR SLING" BRINGS THE VESSEL HIGH ABOVE THE EARTH--AND, WITH *FANTASTIC FORCE*, WHIPS IT INTO DEEP SPACE...

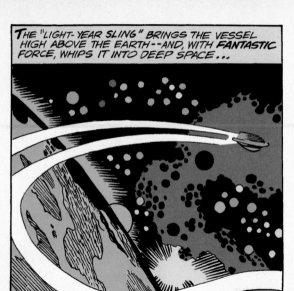

AT *FASTER-THAN-LIGHT* SPEEDS, THE CAPTIVE IS *HURLED* ACROSS UNIMAGINABLE DISTANCES IN A MATTER OF *SECONDS*. HIS *FATE* AWAITS HIM SOMEWHERE BEYOND THE FARTHEST SUNS...

IT IS *NIGHT* ON EARTH...THE FOREST BIRDS ARE SILENT...BLACK SHADOWS CLOAK THE SCENES OF RECENT STRIFE...THEY ALSO HIDE THE MAN WHOSE EYES ARE RIVETED ON THE *STARRY SKY*...

I-IT'S *HARD* TO BELIEVE THE CAPTIVE IS *GONE*...FOR ONE TERRIFYING MOMENT, THIS WORLD WAS IN *MORTAL DANGER* FROM AN ENEMY TOO *GHASTLY* TO THINK ABOUT!

I'M COUNTING ON HIS JAILERS TO MAKE *CERTAIN* THAT THE CAPTIVE IS *NEVER* SEEN AGAIN...

THEN, CAP SADLY TURNS TO THE SPOT WHERE *JIM HENDRICKS* LIES.

YOUR DEATH WILL NOT BE IN VAIN, JIM...WE'VE LEARNED A *VALUABLE LESSON*...

EARTH MUST BE *FOREVER* ON ITS GUARD--AND *NOW*, AS IN THE PAST--WE MUST ASK OURSELVES: WHO COMES FROM SPACE--*FRIEND*--OR *FOE*?

I'D BETTER *CHECK* ON THE WHEREABOUTS OF THOSE *METAL MUGGERS*! THEY MAY STILL BE AROUND!!

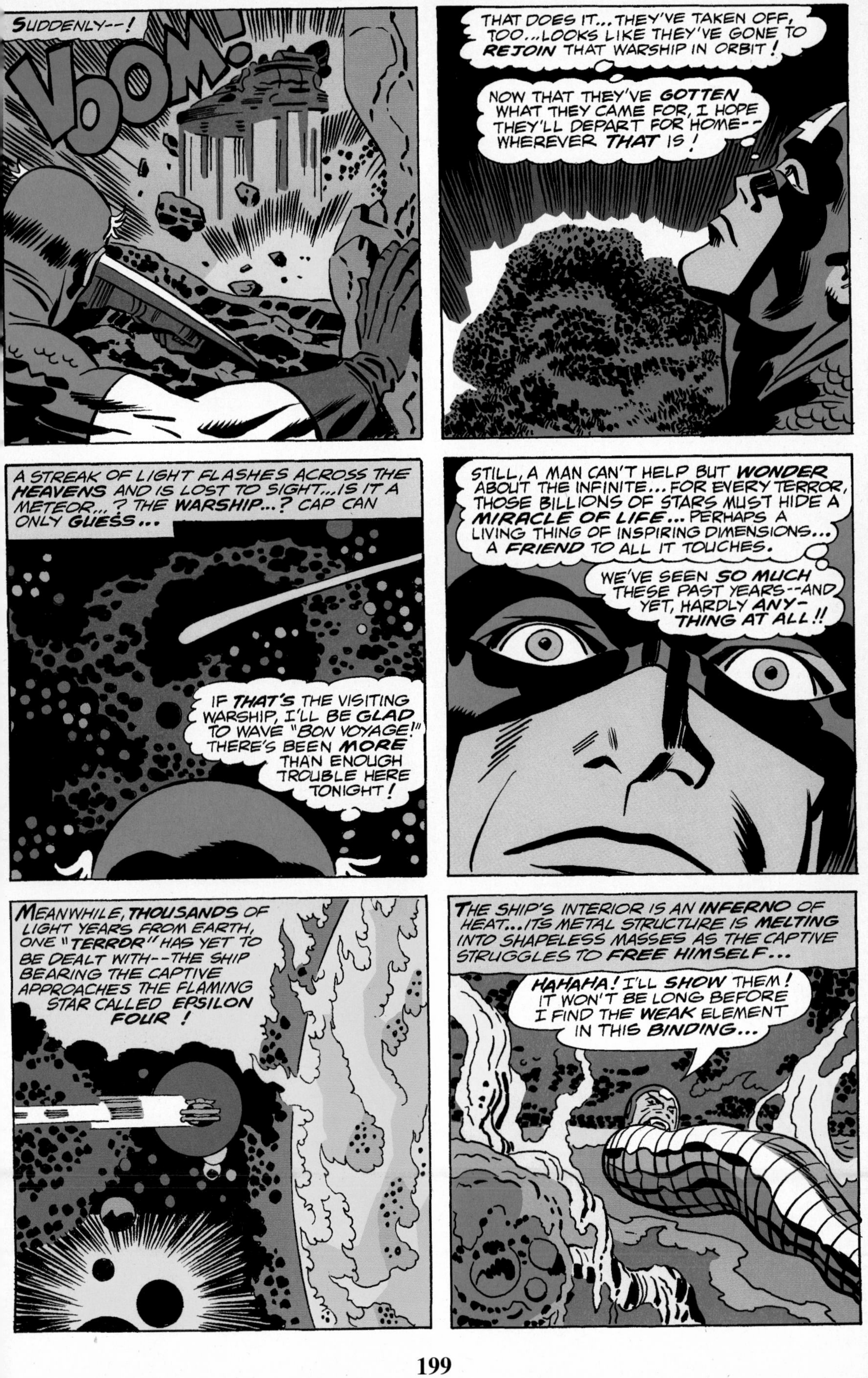
SUDDENLY--!
VOOM!
THAT DOES IT... THEY'VE TAKEN OFF, TOO... LOOKS LIKE THEY'VE GONE TO REJOIN THAT WARSHIP IN ORBIT!
NOW THAT THEY'VE GOTTEN WHAT THEY CAME FOR, I HOPE THEY'LL DEPART FOR HOME--WHEREVER THAT IS!
A STREAK OF LIGHT FLASHES ACROSS THE HEAVENS AND IS LOST TO SIGHT... IS IT A METEOR...? THE WARSHIP...? CAP CAN ONLY GUESS...
IF THAT'S THE VISITING WARSHIP, I'LL BE GLAD TO WAVE "BON VOYAGE!" THERE'S BEEN MORE THAN ENOUGH TROUBLE HERE TONIGHT!
STILL, A MAN CAN'T HELP BUT WONDER ABOUT THE INFINITE... FOR EVERY TERROR, THOSE BILLIONS OF STARS MUST HIDE A MIRACLE OF LIFE... PERHAPS A LIVING THING OF INSPIRING DIMENSIONS... A FRIEND TO ALL IT TOUCHES.
WE'VE SEEN SO MUCH THESE PAST YEARS--AND YET, HARDLY ANY-THING AT ALL!!
MEANWHILE, THOUSANDS OF LIGHT YEARS FROM EARTH, ONE "TERROR" HAS YET TO BE DEALT WITH--THE SHIP BEARING THE CAPTIVE APPROACHES THE FLAMING STAR CALLED EPSILON FOUR!
THE SHIP'S INTERIOR IS AN INFERNO OF HEAT... ITS METAL STRUCTURE IS MELTING INTO SHAPELESS MASSES AS THE CAPTIVE STRUGGLES TO FREE HIMSELF...
HAHAHA! I'LL SHOW THEM! IT WON'T BE LONG BEFORE I FIND THE WEAK ELEMENT IN THIS BINDING...

THOUGH THEY HURL ME INTO THE FIERY *HEART OF A BURNING SUN*, I SHALL *SURVIVE* THE ORDEAL! THE CAPTIVE *DEFIES* EVERY METHOD OF *DESTRUCTION!*

HA, HA, HA, HA! BOIL AND *BUBBLE* AND FILL THE UNIVERSE WITH THE *BRIMSTONE OF HELL*--!! IT MEANS *NOTHING* TO THE CAPTIVE! *NOTHING!* *HA, HA!*

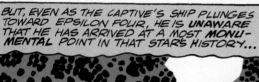

BUT, EVEN AS THE CAPTIVE'S SHIP PLUNGES TOWARD *EPSILON FOUR*, HE IS UNAWARE THAT HE HAS ARRIVED AT A MOST *MONUMENTAL* POINT IN THAT STAR'S HISTORY...

EPSILON FOUR IS GOING *NOVA*!! IT BEGINS TO *EXPAND*--TO *DISTORT*-- AT ITS EXPLOSIVE MOMENT OF--

HA HA HA!

--DEATH!

SSKAABLAAMM!!

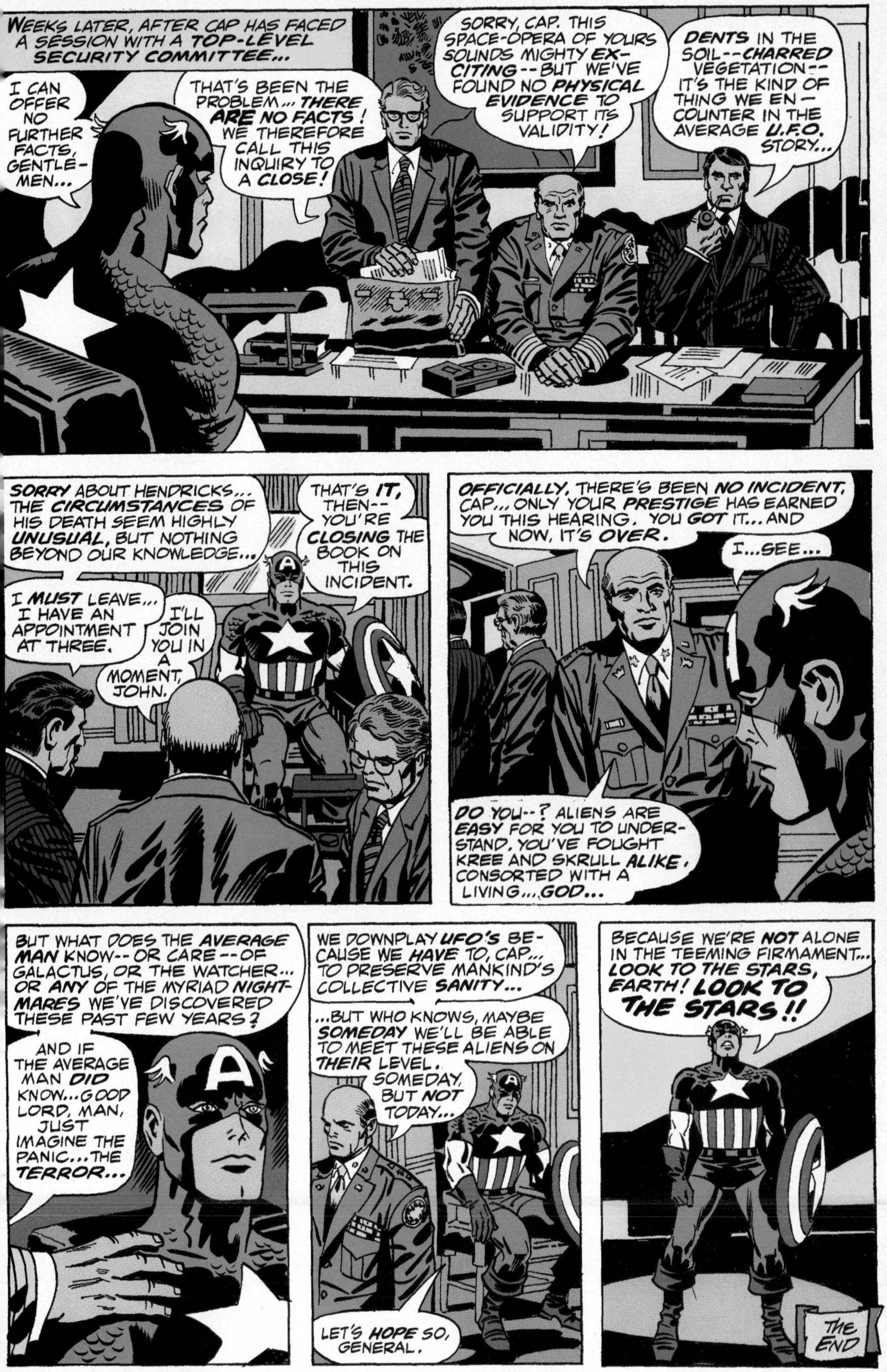
WEEKS LATER, AFTER CAP HAS FACED A SESSION WITH A TOP-LEVEL SECURITY COMMITTEE...
I CAN OFFER NO FURTHER FACTS, GENTLEMEN...
THAT'S BEEN THE PROBLEM... THERE ARE NO FACTS! WE THEREFORE CALL THIS INQUIRY TO A CLOSE!
SORRY, CAP. THIS SPACE-OPERA OF YOURS SOUNDS MIGHTY EXCITING--BUT WE'VE FOUND NO PHYSICAL EVIDENCE TO SUPPORT ITS VALIDITY!
DENTS IN THE SOIL--CHARRED VEGETATION--IT'S THE KIND OF THING WE ENCOUNTER IN THE AVERAGE U.F.O. STORY...
SORRY ABOUT HENDRICKS... THE CIRCUMSTANCES OF HIS DEATH SEEM HIGHLY UNUSUAL, BUT NOTHING BEYOND OUR KNOWLEDGE...
THAT'S IT, THEN--YOU'RE CLOSING THE BOOK ON THIS INCIDENT.
I MUST LEAVE... I HAVE AN APPOINTMENT AT THREE.
I'LL JOIN YOU IN A MOMENT, JOHN.
OFFICIALLY, THERE'S BEEN NO INCIDENT, CAP... ONLY YOUR PRESTIGE HAS EARNED YOU THIS HEARING. YOU GOT IT... AND NOW, IT'S OVER.
I...SEE...
DO YOU--? ALIENS ARE EASY FOR YOU TO UNDERSTAND. YOU'VE FOUGHT KREE AND SKRULL ALIKE, CONSORTED WITH A LIVING... GOD...
BUT WHAT DOES THE AVERAGE MAN KNOW-- OR CARE --OF GALACTUS, OR THE WATCHER... OR ANY OF THE MYRIAD NIGHTMARES WE'VE DISCOVERED THESE PAST FEW YEARS?
AND IF THE AVERAGE MAN DID KNOW...GOOD LORD, MAN, JUST IMAGINE THE PANIC...THE TERROR...
WE DOWNPLAY UFO'S BECAUSE WE HAVE TO, CAP... TO PRESERVE MANKIND'S COLLECTIVE SANITY...
...BUT WHO KNOWS, MAYBE SOMEDAY WE'LL BE ABLE TO MEET THESE ALIENS ON THEIR LEVEL.
SOMEDAY, BUT NOT TODAY...
LET'S HOPE SO, GENERAL.
BECAUSE WE'RE NOT ALONE IN THE TEEMING FIRMAMENT... LOOK TO THE STARS, EARTH! LOOK TO THE STARS!!
THE END

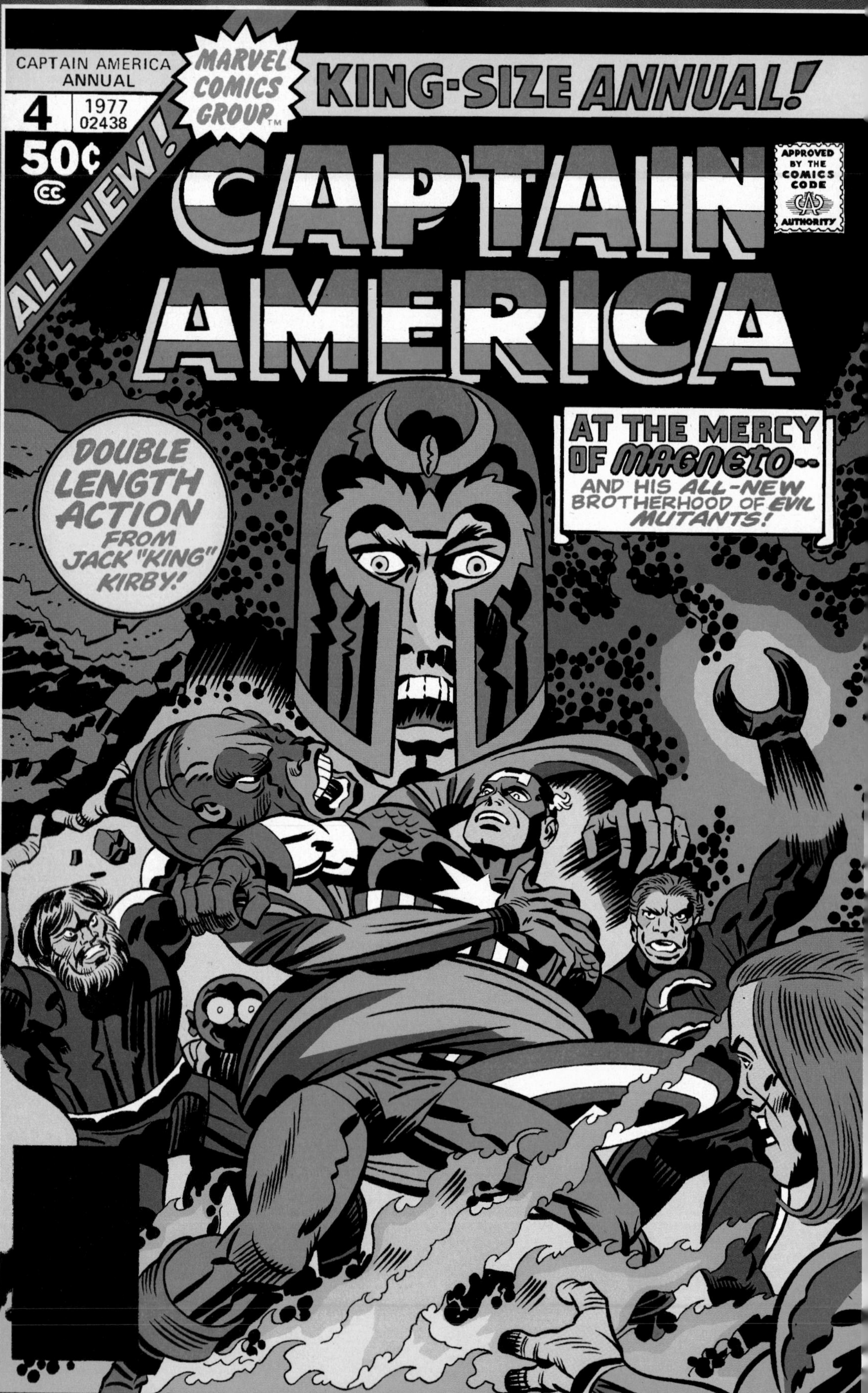
CAPTAIN AMERICA ANNUAL
4
1977
02438
50¢
CC
ALL NEW!
MARVEL COMICS GROUP™
KING-SIZE ANNUAL!
APPROVED BY THE COMICS CODE AUTHORITY
CAPTAIN AMERICA
DOUBLE LENGTH ACTION FROM JACK "KING" KIRBY!
AT THE MERCY OF MAGNETO-- AND HIS ALL-NEW BROTHERHOOD OF EVIL MUTANTS!

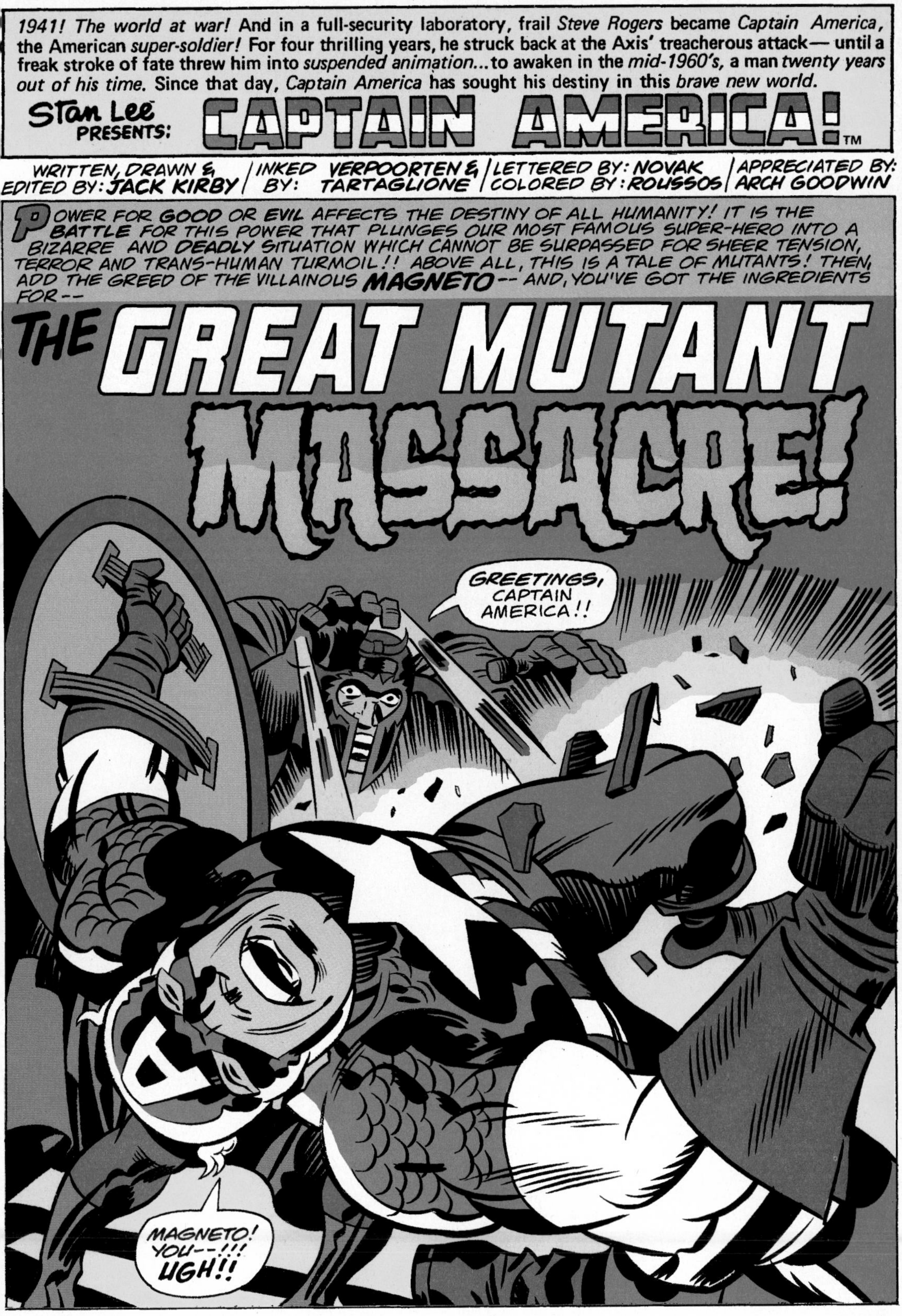
1941! The world at war! And in a full-security laboratory, frail Steve Rogers became Captain America, the American super-soldier! For four thrilling years, he struck back at the Axis' treacherous attack— until a freak stroke of fate threw him into suspended animation... to awaken in the mid-1960's, a man twenty years out of his time. Since that day, Captain America has sought his destiny in this brave new world.
STAN LEE PRESENTS: CAPTAIN AMERICA!™
WRITTEN, DRAWN & EDITED BY: JACK KIRBY
INKED BY: VERPOORTEN & TARTAGLIONE
LETTERED BY: NOVAK
COLORED BY: ROUSSOS
APPRECIATED BY: ARCH GOODWIN
POWER FOR GOOD OR EVIL AFFECTS THE DESTINY OF ALL HUMANITY! IT IS THE BATTLE FOR THIS POWER THAT PLUNGES OUR MOST FAMOUS SUPER-HERO INTO A BIZARRE AND DEADLY SITUATION WHICH CANNOT BE SURPASSED FOR SHEER TENSION, TERROR AND TRANS-HUMAN TURMOIL!! ABOVE ALL, THIS IS A TALE OF MUTANTS! THEN, ADD THE GREED OF THE VILLAINOUS MAGNETO-- AND, YOU'VE GOT THE INGREDIENTS FOR--
THE GREAT MUTANT MASSACRE!
GREETINGS, CAPTAIN AMERICA!!
MAGNETO! YOU--!!! UGH!!

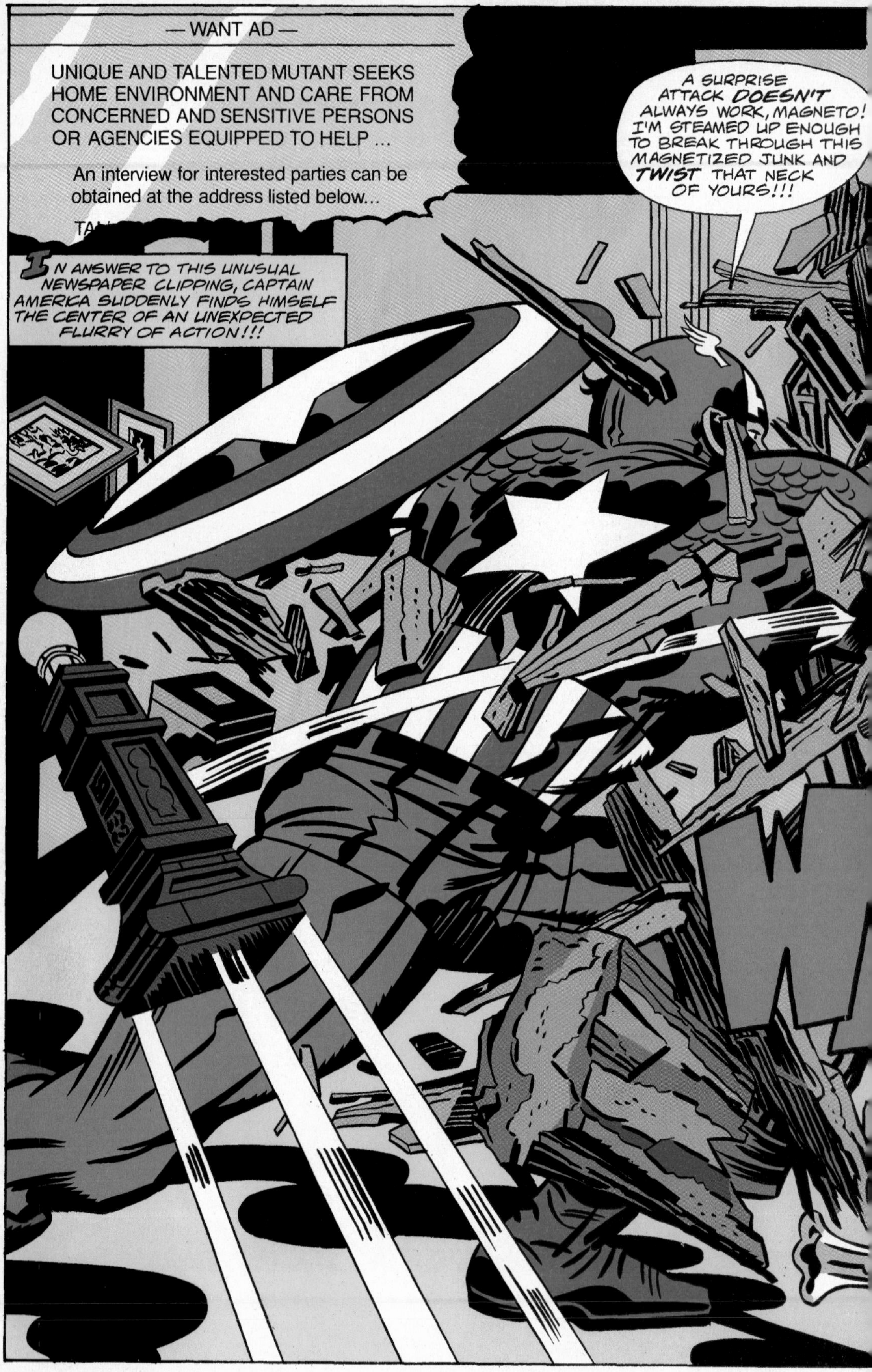
— WANT AD —
UNIQUE AND TALENTED MUTANT SEEKS HOME ENVIRONMENT AND CARE FROM CONCERNED AND SENSITIVE PERSONS OR AGENCIES EQUIPPED TO HELP ...
An interview for interested parties can be obtained at the address listed below...
IN ANSWER TO THIS UNUSUAL NEWSPAPER CLIPPING, CAPTAIN AMERICA SUDDENLY FINDS HIMSELF THE CENTER OF AN UNEXPECTED FLURRY OF ACTION!!!
A SURPRISE ATTACK DOESN'T ALWAYS WORK, MAGNETO! I'M STEAMED UP ENOUGH TO BREAK THROUGH THIS MAGNETIZED JUNK AND TWIST THAT NECK OF YOURS!!!

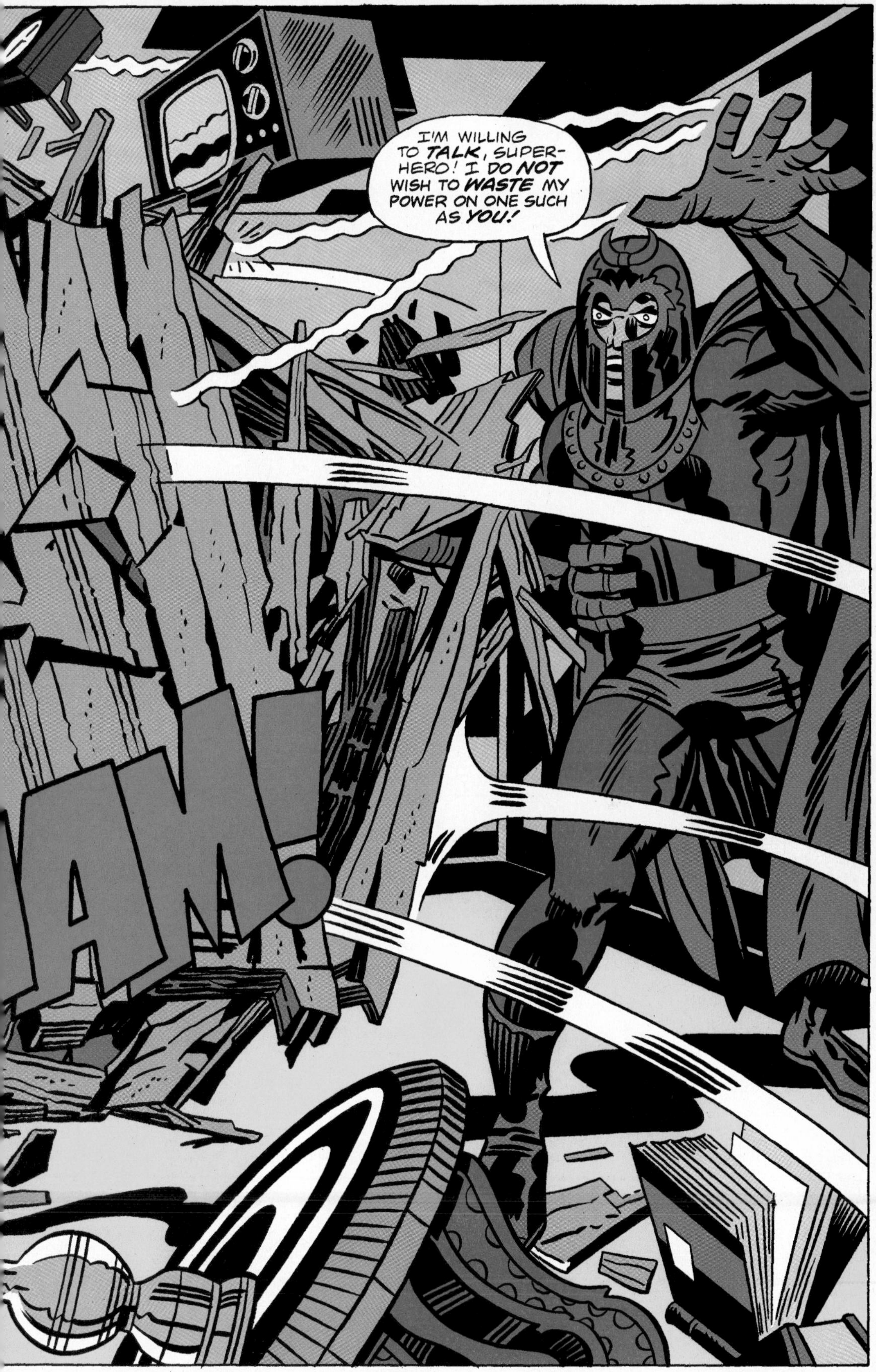
I'M WILLING TO TALK, SUPER-HERO! I DO NOT WISH TO WASTE MY POWER ON ONE SUCH AS YOU!

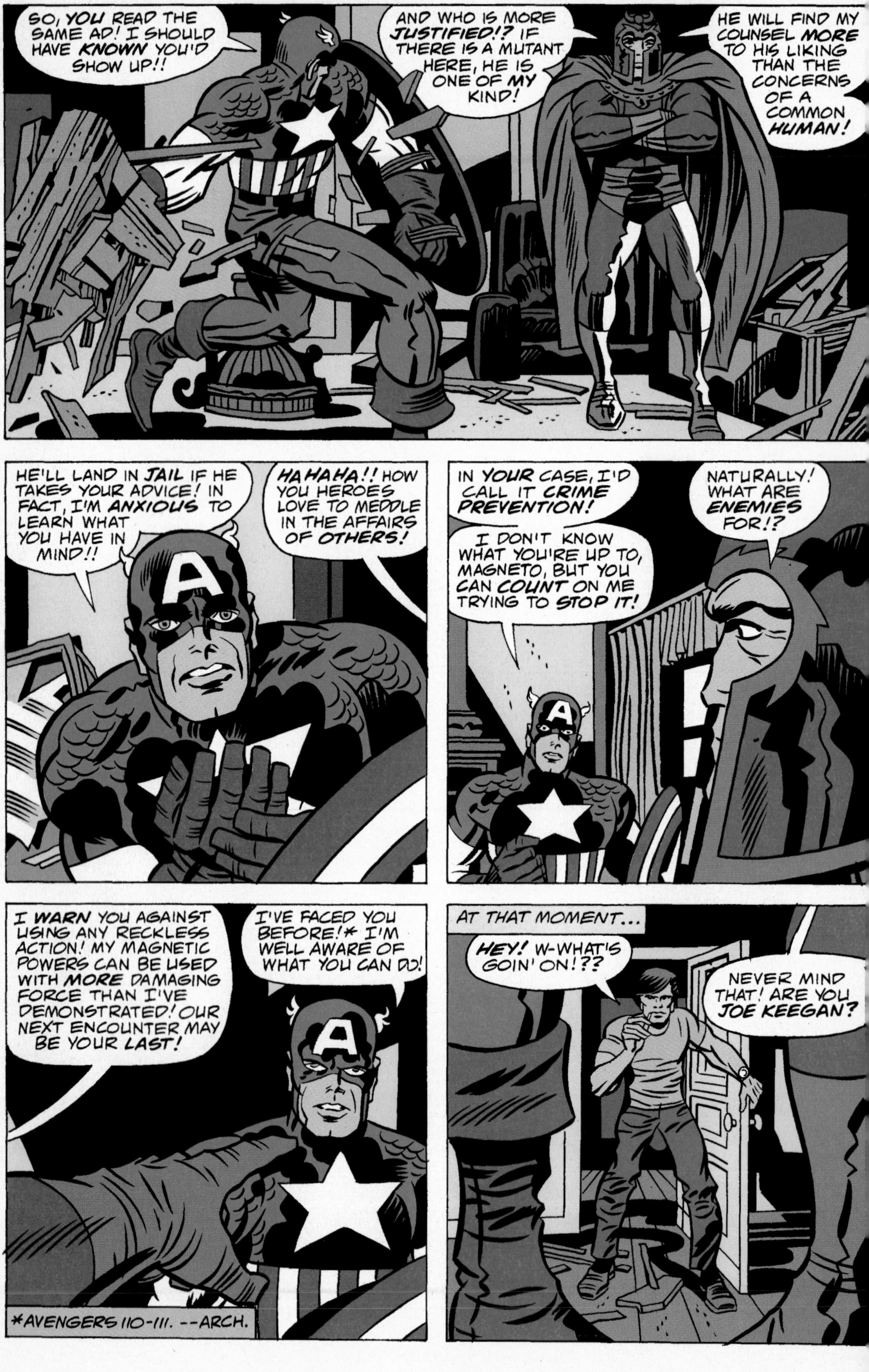
SO, YOU READ THE SAME AD! I SHOULD HAVE KNOWN YOU'D SHOW UP!!
AND WHO IS MORE JUSTIFIED!? IF THERE IS A MUTANT HERE, HE IS ONE OF MY KIND!
HE WILL FIND MY COUNSEL MORE TO HIS LIKING THAN THE CONCERNS OF A COMMON HUMAN!
HE'LL LAND IN JAIL IF HE TAKES YOUR ADVICE! IN FACT, I'M ANXIOUS TO LEARN WHAT YOU HAVE IN MIND!!
HAHAHA!! HOW YOU HEROES LOVE TO MEDDLE IN THE AFFAIRS OF OTHERS!
IN YOUR CASE, I'D CALL IT CRIME PREVENTION!
I DON'T KNOW WHAT YOU'RE UP TO, MAGNETO, BUT YOU CAN COUNT ON ME TRYING TO STOP IT!
NATURALLY! WHAT ARE ENEMIES FOR!?
I WARN YOU AGAINST USING ANY RECKLESS ACTION! MY MAGNETIC POWERS CAN BE USED WITH MORE DAMAGING FORCE THAN I'VE DEMONSTRATED! OUR NEXT ENCOUNTER MAY BE YOUR LAST!
I'VE FACED YOU BEFORE!* I'M WELL AWARE OF WHAT YOU CAN DO!
*AVENGERS 110-111. --ARCH.
AT THAT MOMENT...
HEY! W-WHAT'S GOIN' ON!??
NEVER MIND THAT! ARE YOU JOE KEEGAN?

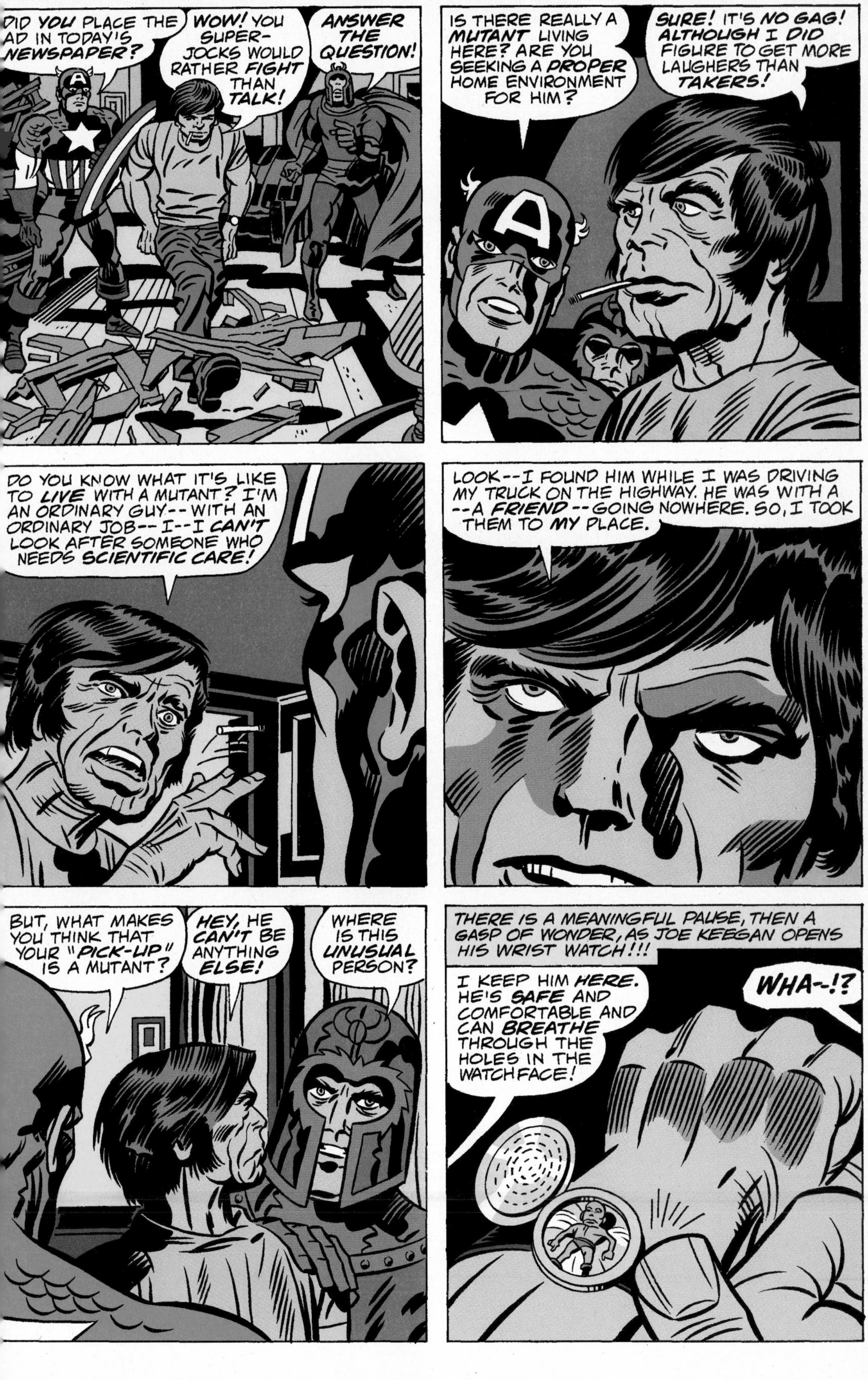
DID YOU PLACE THE AD IN TODAY'S NEWSPAPER?
WOW! YOU SUPER-JOCKS WOULD RATHER FIGHT THAN TALK!
ANSWER THE QUESTION!
IS THERE REALLY A MUTANT LIVING HERE? ARE YOU SEEKING A PROPER HOME ENVIRONMENT FOR HIM?
SURE! IT'S NO GAG! ALTHOUGH I DID FIGURE TO GET MORE LAUGHERS THAN TAKERS!
DO YOU KNOW WHAT IT'S LIKE TO LIVE WITH A MUTANT? I'M AN ORDINARY GUY-- WITH AN ORDINARY JOB-- I--I CAN'T LOOK AFTER SOMEONE WHO NEEDS SCIENTIFIC CARE!
LOOK--I FOUND HIM WHILE I WAS DRIVING MY TRUCK ON THE HIGHWAY. HE WAS WITH A --A FRIEND--GOING NOWHERE. SO, I TOOK THEM TO MY PLACE.
BUT, WHAT MAKES YOU THINK THAT YOUR "PICK-UP" IS A MUTANT?
HEY, HE CAN'T BE ANYTHING ELSE!
WHERE IS THIS UNUSUAL PERSON?
THERE IS A MEANINGFUL PAUSE, THEN A GASP OF WONDER, AS JOE KEEGAN OPENS HIS WRIST WATCH!!!
I KEEP HIM HERE. HE'S SAFE AND COMFORTABLE AND CAN BREATHE THROUGH THE HOLES IN THE WATCHFACE!
WHA--!?

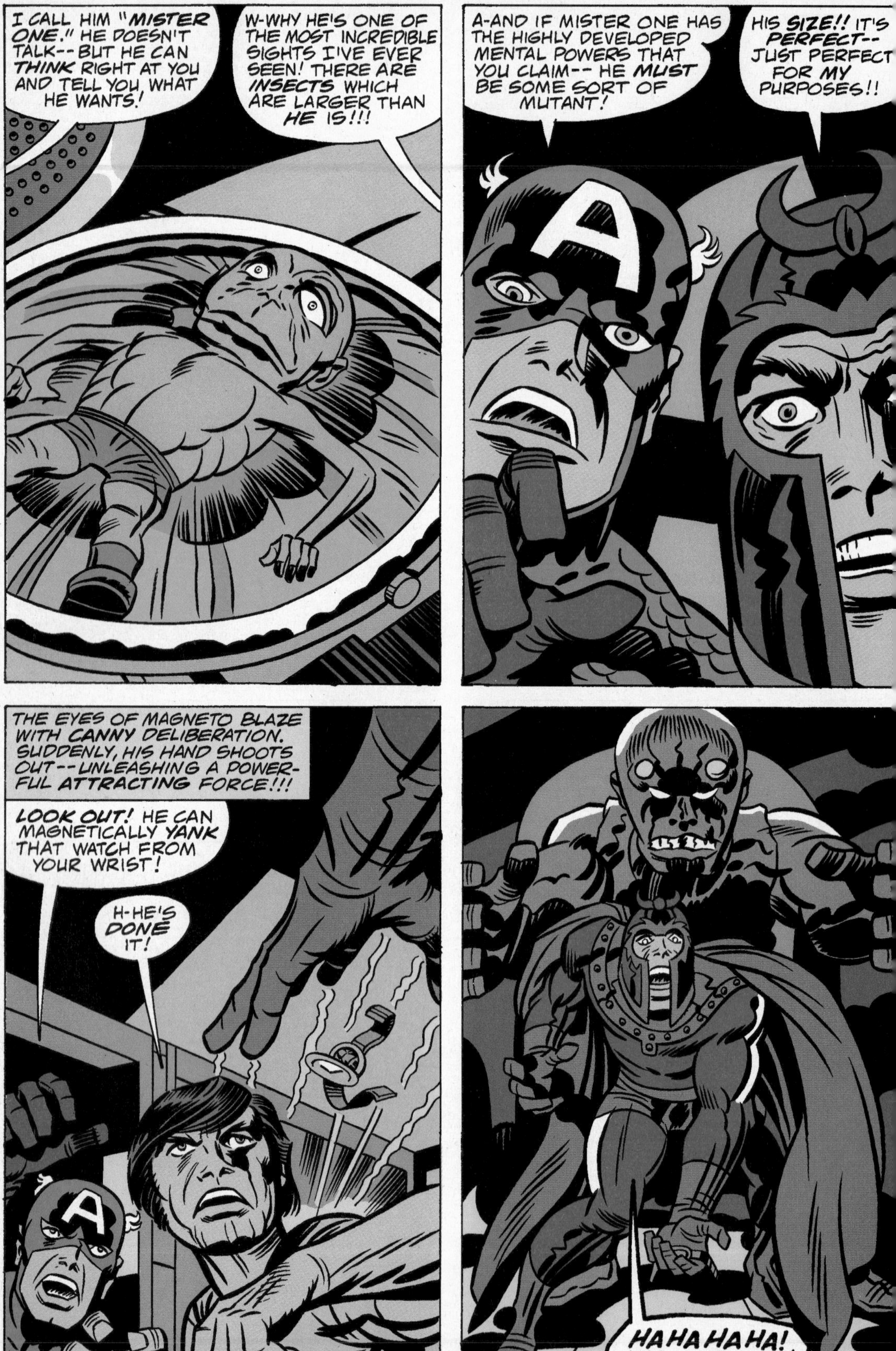
I CALL HIM "MISTER ONE." HE DOESN'T TALK--BUT HE CAN THINK RIGHT AT YOU AND TELL YOU WHAT HE WANTS!
W-WHY HE'S ONE OF THE MOST INCREDIBLE SIGHTS I'VE EVER SEEN! THERE ARE INSECTS WHICH ARE LARGER THAN HE IS!!!
A-AND IF MISTER ONE HAS THE HIGHLY DEVELOPED MENTAL POWERS THAT YOU CLAIM-- HE MUST BE SOME SORT OF MUTANT!
HIS SIZE!! IT'S PERFECT-- JUST PERFECT FOR MY PURPOSES!!
THE EYES OF MAGNETO BLAZE WITH CANNY DELIBERATION. SUDDENLY, HIS HAND SHOOTS OUT--UNLEASHING A POWERFUL ATTRACTING FORCE!!!
LOOK OUT! HE CAN MAGNETICALLY YANK THAT WATCH FROM YOUR WRIST!
H-HE'S DONE IT!
HAHAHAHA! HE'S MINE, NOW! MINE!!

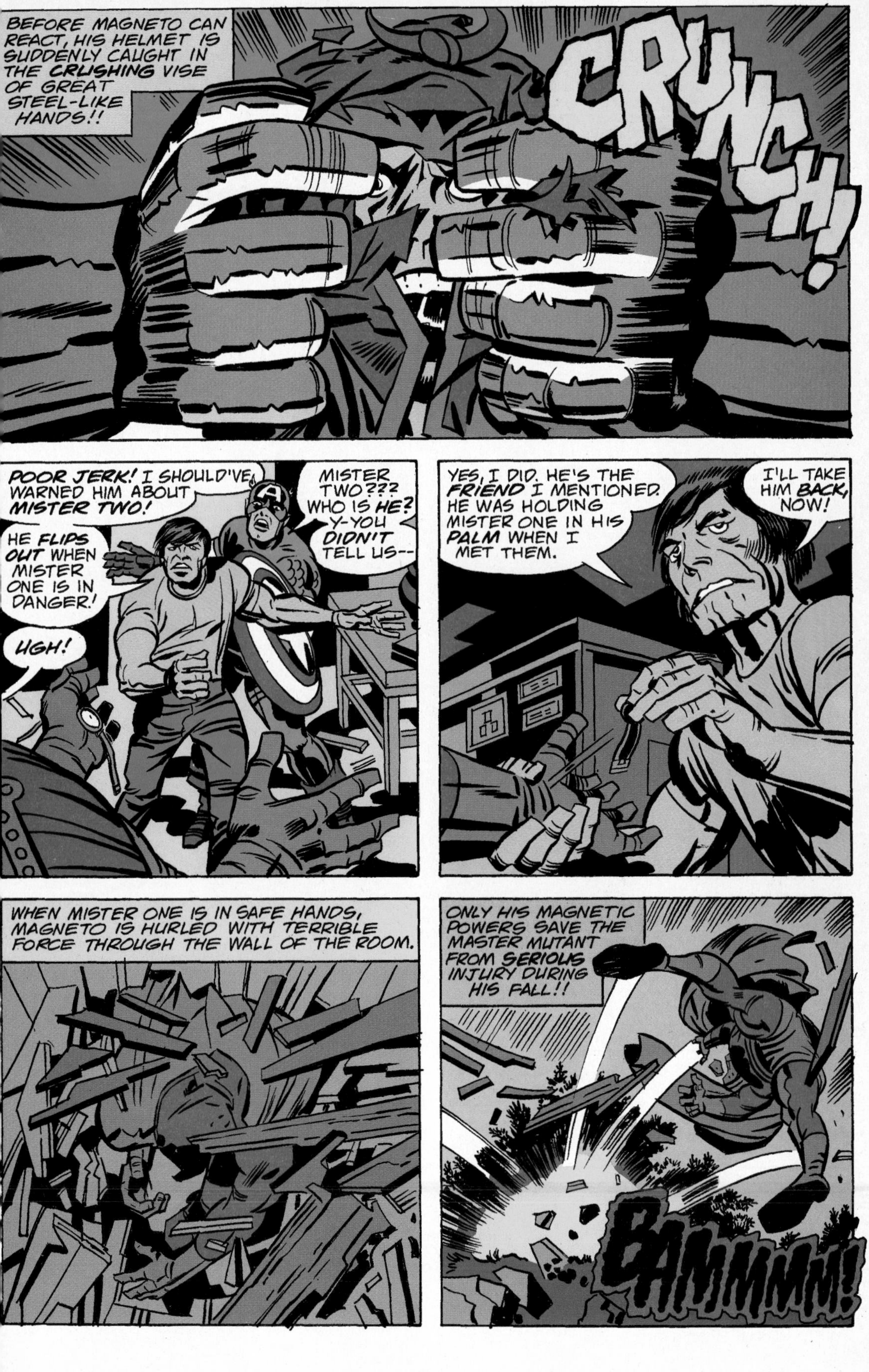
BEFORE MAGNETO CAN REACT, HIS HELMET IS SUDDENLY CAUGHT IN THE CRUSHING VISE OF GREAT STEEL-LIKE HANDS!!
CRUNCH!
POOR JERK! I SHOULD'VE WARNED HIM ABOUT MISTER TWO!
HE FLIPS OUT WHEN MISTER ONE IS IN DANGER!
MISTER TWO??? WHO IS HE? Y-YOU DIDN'T TELL US--
UGH!
YES, I DID. HE'S THE FRIEND I MENTIONED. HE WAS HOLDING MISTER ONE IN HIS PALM WHEN I MET THEM.
I'LL TAKE HIM BACK, NOW!
WHEN MISTER ONE IS IN SAFE HANDS, MAGNETO IS HURLED WITH TERRIBLE FORCE THROUGH THE WALL OF THE ROOM.
ONLY HIS MAGNETIC POWERS SAVE THE MASTER MUTANT FROM SERIOUS INJURY DURING HIS FALL!!
BAMMMM!

SOON AFTER--

T-THE *TRICKY* SWINE!! HIS MONSTROUS CONFEDERATE WAS LURKING IN THE BACK ROOM-- READY TO *STRIKE!!*

YOU'LL ALL *PAY* DEARLY FOR THIS! MAGNETO WILL *NOT* BE DEFIED OR *DEFEATED!!*

I'LL BE BACK FOR MISTER ONE! HE IS DESTINED FOR WORK IN THE SERVICE OF *HOMO SUPERIOR!*

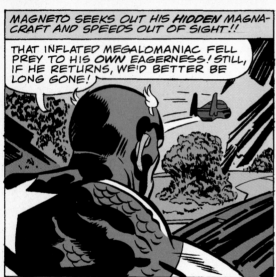

MAGNETO SEEKS OUT HIS *HIDDEN* MAGNA-CRAFT AND SPEEDS OUT OF SIGHT!!

THAT INFLATED MEGALOMANIAC FELL PREY TO HIS *OWN* EAGERNESS! STILL, IF HE RETURNS, WE'D BETTER BE LONG GONE!

WELL, IT SEEMS THAT I'VE *INHERITED* THE JOB OF STRAIGHTENING OUT THIS SITUATION. I ADVISE YOU TO *ACCEPT* MY HELP.

YOU'VE GOT JOE KEEGAN'S *VOTE!*

IN FACT, I WAS HOPING THAT A *SINCERE* SUPER-TYPE LIKE YOU WOULD SHOW UP! YOU CAN PLACE THESE TWO IN THE CARE OF *RESPONSIBLE* PEOPLE!

WILL YOU *DO* THAT?

I CAN, JOE-- AND I *SHALL.*

A WEEK LATER, STEVE ROGERS VISITS THE *SHIELD* DEPARTMENT OF MEDICAL RESEARCH...

COME IN, *MOTHER HEN!* YOUR TWO CHICKS ARE DOING *FINE!!*

I'M *GLAD*, DOC. THEY HAVE THE POTENTIAL FOR DE-VELOPING INTO A *PROBLEM.*

IT'S *MISTER TWO* I WORRY ABOUT. IF THAT GIANT WERE TO GROW DIFFICULT, HE COULD *WRECK* THIS PLACE.

IT'S STRANGE THAT YOU SHOULD MENTION IT--

--HIS BEHAVIOR SEEMS TO DEPEND ON THE WELL-BEING OF *MISTER ONE.*

LET'S GO INTO MY OFFICE AND *REVIEW* THEIR PROGRESS.

YES, I'D LIKE TO SEE THEIR FILE, DOCTOR HALSEY. SOME-HOW, I *CONTINUE* TO FEEL LIKE A CONCERNED *RELATIVE.*

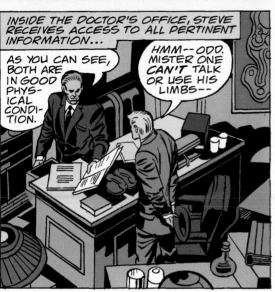

INSIDE THE DOCTOR'S OFFICE, STEVE RECEIVES ACCESS TO ALL PERTINENT INFORMATION...

AS YOU CAN SEE, BOTH ARE IN GOOD PHYS-ICAL CONDI-TION.

HMM-- ODD. MISTER ONE *CAN'T* TALK OR USE HIS LIMBS--

--YET, HE EXHIBITS *NO* EVIDENCE OF PHYSICAL OR MENTAL DISABILITY. HE'S AS SOUND AS *WE* ARE!

TRUE, BUT HE'S NEVER KNOWN THE *NEED* TO FETCH AND CARRY.

YOU SEE, ALL *THAT* IS DONE *FOR* HIM!

STEVE IS THEN TAKEN TO AN ADJOINING ROOM, WHERE--

THUS, THEY *BOTH* SURVIVE.

WE BELIEVE THAT "MISTER ONE" *CONTROLS* "MISTER TWO" BY MENTAL COMMAND AND *RELIES* UPON HIM FOR ANY TASK INVOLVING PHYSICAL LABOR.

ONE *THINKS* FOR THE OTHER--AND, ONE *WORKS* FOR THE OTHER. IT'S A *SYMBIOTIC* RELATIONSHIP!

I ASSUME THAT THIS IS THE *ENVIRONMENTAL SYSTEM* YOU BUILT FOR MISTER ONE. IT SEEMS TO SUPPLY *EVERY-THING*-- SUNLIGHT, FRESH AIR, PROPER NUTRITION-- THE WHOLE SHMEER!

THIS GLASS CASE MAGNIFIES HIM FOR STUDY, EH?

FOR THAT AND *COMMUNICATION*, STEVE...

HE'S AWAKE. YOU CAN *TALK* TO HIM IF YOU'D LIKE. USE THIS MICROPHONE.

AMAZING! BUT HOW IS HE ABLE TO *REPLY?*

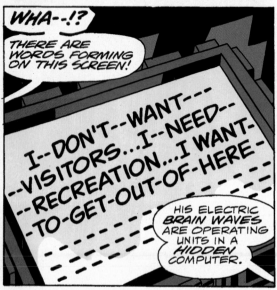

WHA--!? THERE ARE WORDS FORMING ON THIS SCREEN!

I--DON'T--WANT--- --VISITORS...I--NEED-- --RECREATION...I WANT- -TO-GET-OUT-OF-HERE-

HIS ELECTRIC *BRAIN WAVES* ARE OPERATING UNITS IN A *HIDDEN* COMPUTER.

HE'S BEGINNING TO SHOW SIGNS OF *UNREST*-- LIKE HIS CHUM BEHIND THAT *WINDOW.*

BAM! BAM!

LISTEN TO *THAT!*

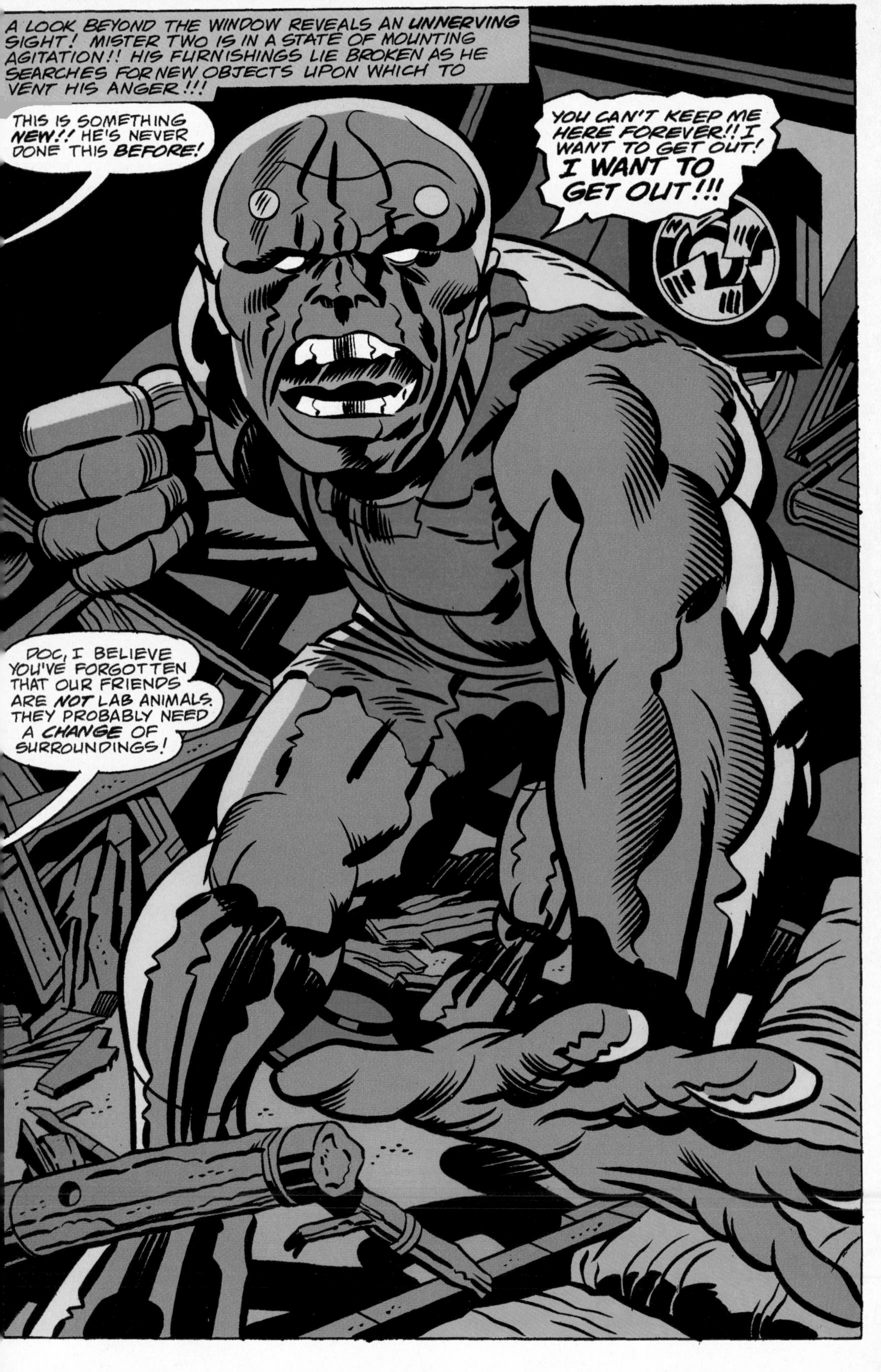
A LOOK BEYOND THE WINDOW REVEALS AN UNNERVING SIGHT! MISTER TWO IS IN A STATE OF MOUNTING AGITATION!! HIS FURNISHINGS LIE BROKEN AS HE SEARCHES FOR NEW OBJECTS UPON WHICH TO VENT HIS ANGER!!!
THIS IS SOMETHING NEW!! HE'S NEVER DONE THIS BEFORE!
YOU CAN'T KEEP ME HERE FOREVER!! I WANT TO GET OUT! I WANT TO GET OUT!!!
DOC, I BELIEVE YOU'VE FORGOTTEN THAT OUR FRIENDS ARE NOT LAB ANIMALS. THEY PROBABLY NEED A CHANGE OF SURROUNDINGS!

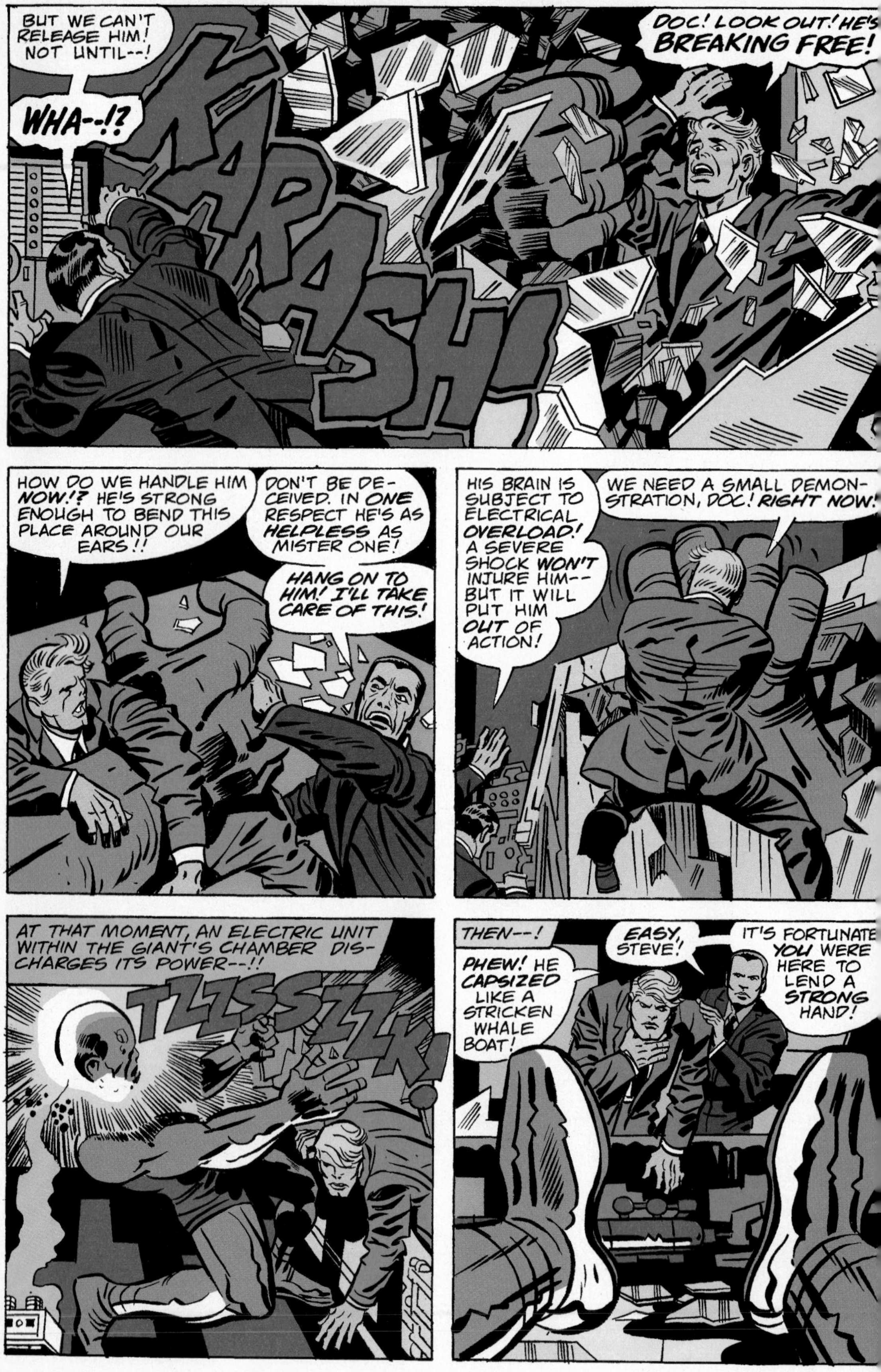
BUT WE CAN'T RELEASE HIM! NOT UNTIL--!
WHA--!?
KARASH!
DOC! LOOK OUT! HE'S BREAKING FREE!
HOW DO WE HANDLE HIM NOW!? HE'S STRONG ENOUGH TO BEND THIS PLACE AROUND OUR EARS!!
DON'T BE DECEIVED. IN ONE RESPECT HE'S AS HELPLESS AS MISTER ONE!
HANG ON TO HIM! I'LL TAKE CARE OF THIS!
HIS BRAIN IS SUBJECT TO ELECTRICAL OVERLOAD! A SEVERE SHOCK WON'T INJURE HIM-- BUT IT WILL PUT HIM OUT OF ACTION!
WE NEED A SMALL DEMONSTRATION, DOC! RIGHT NOW!
AT THAT MOMENT, AN ELECTRIC UNIT WITHIN THE GIANT'S CHAMBER DISCHARGES ITS POWER--!!
TZZSSZZK!
THEN--!
PHEW! HE CAPSIZED LIKE A STRICKEN WHALE BOAT!
EASY, STEVE!
IT'S FORTUNATE YOU WERE HERE TO LEND A STRONG HAND!

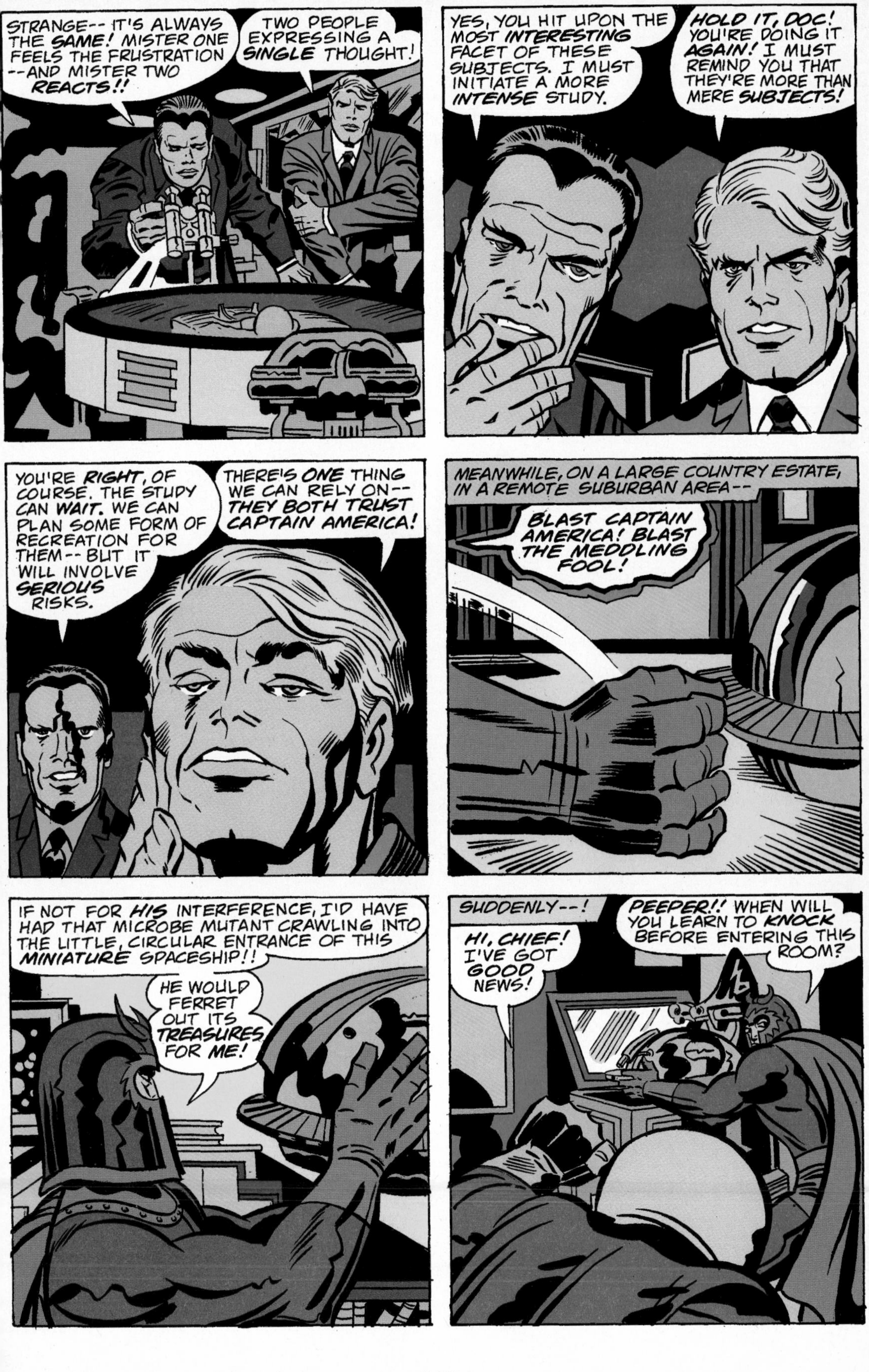
STRANGE-- IT'S ALWAYS THE SAME! MISTER ONE FEELS THE FRUSTRATION --AND MISTER TWO REACTS!!
TWO PEOPLE EXPRESSING A SINGLE THOUGHT!
YES, YOU HIT UPON THE MOST INTERESTING FACET OF THESE SUBJECTS. I MUST INITIATE A MORE INTENSE STUDY.
HOLD IT, DOC! YOU'RE DOING IT AGAIN! I MUST REMIND YOU THAT THEY'RE MORE THAN MERE SUBJECTS!
YOU'RE RIGHT, OF COURSE. THE STUDY CAN WAIT. WE CAN PLAN SOME FORM OF RECREATION FOR THEM-- BUT IT WILL INVOLVE SERIOUS RISKS.
THERE'S ONE THING WE CAN RELY ON-- THEY BOTH TRUST CAPTAIN AMERICA!
MEANWHILE, ON A LARGE COUNTRY ESTATE, IN A REMOTE SUBURBAN AREA--
BLAST CAPTAIN AMERICA! BLAST THE MEDDLING FOOL!
IF NOT FOR HIS INTERFERENCE, I'D HAVE HAD THAT MICROBE MUTANT CRAWLING INTO THE LITTLE, CIRCULAR ENTRANCE OF THIS MINIATURE SPACESHIP!!
HE WOULD FERRET OUT ITS TREASURES FOR ME!
SUDDENLY--!
HI, CHIEF! I'VE GOT GOOD NEWS!
PEEPER!! WHEN WILL YOU LEARN TO KNOCK BEFORE ENTERING THIS ROOM?

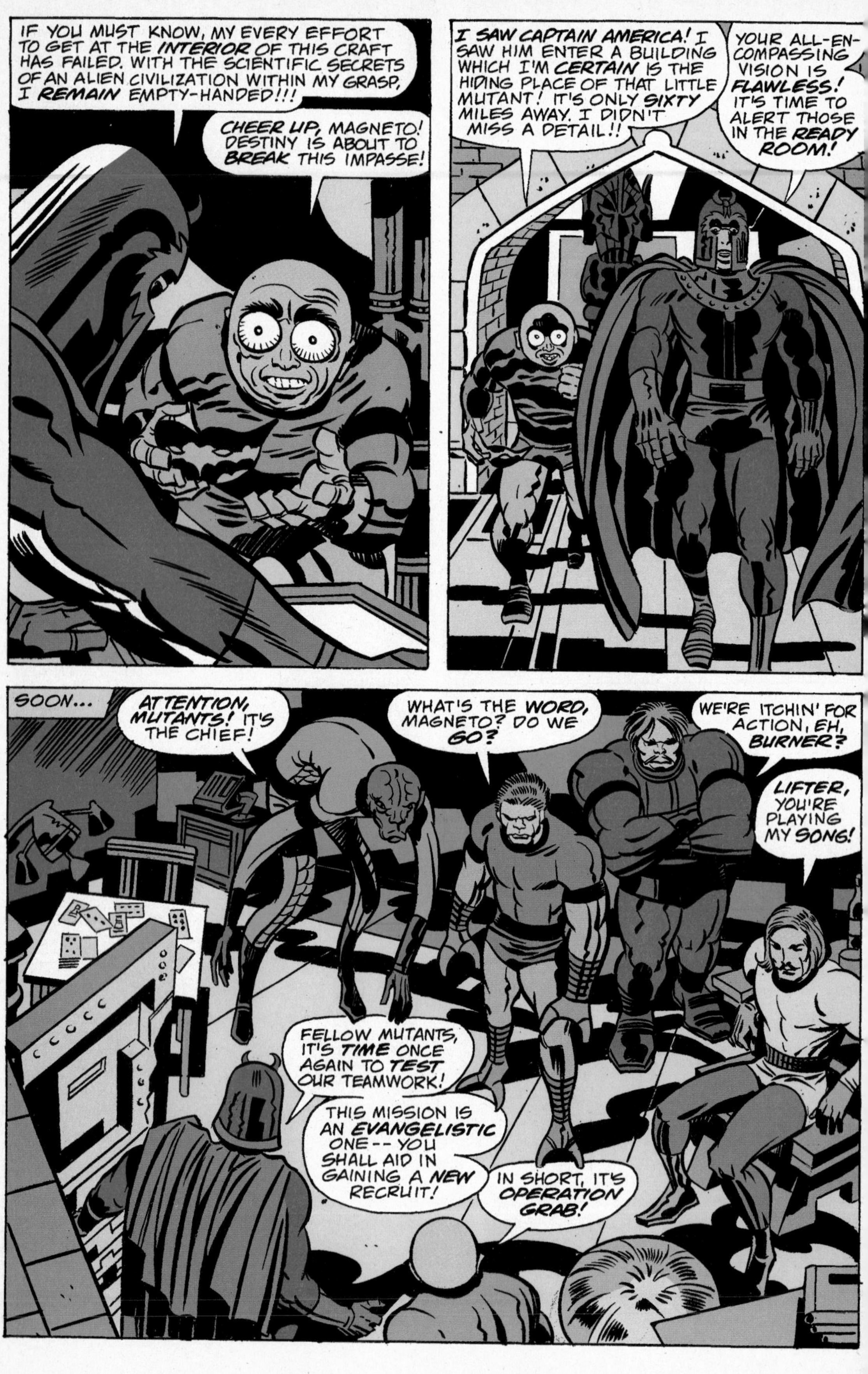
IF YOU MUST KNOW, MY EVERY EFFORT TO GET AT THE INTERIOR OF THIS CRAFT HAS FAILED. WITH THE SCIENTIFIC SECRETS OF AN ALIEN CIVILIZATION WITHIN MY GRASP, I REMAIN EMPTY-HANDED!!!
CHEER UP, MAGNETO! DESTINY IS ABOUT TO BREAK THIS IMPASSE!
I SAW CAPTAIN AMERICA! I SAW HIM ENTER A BUILDING WHICH I'M CERTAIN IS THE HIDING PLACE OF THAT LITTLE MUTANT! IT'S ONLY SIXTY MILES AWAY. I DIDN'T MISS A DETAIL!!
YOUR ALL-ENCOMPASSING VISION IS FLAWLESS! IT'S TIME TO ALERT THOSE IN THE READY ROOM!
SOON...
ATTENTION, MUTANTS! IT'S THE CHIEF!
WHAT'S THE WORD, MAGNETO? DO WE GO?
WE'RE ITCHIN' FOR ACTION, EH, BURNER?
LIFTER, YOU'RE PLAYING MY SONG!
FELLOW MUTANTS, IT'S TIME ONCE AGAIN TO TEST OUR TEAMWORK!
THIS MISSION IS AN EVANGELISTIC ONE -- YOU SHALL AID IN GAINING A NEW RECRUIT!
IN SHORT, IT'S OPERATION GRAB!

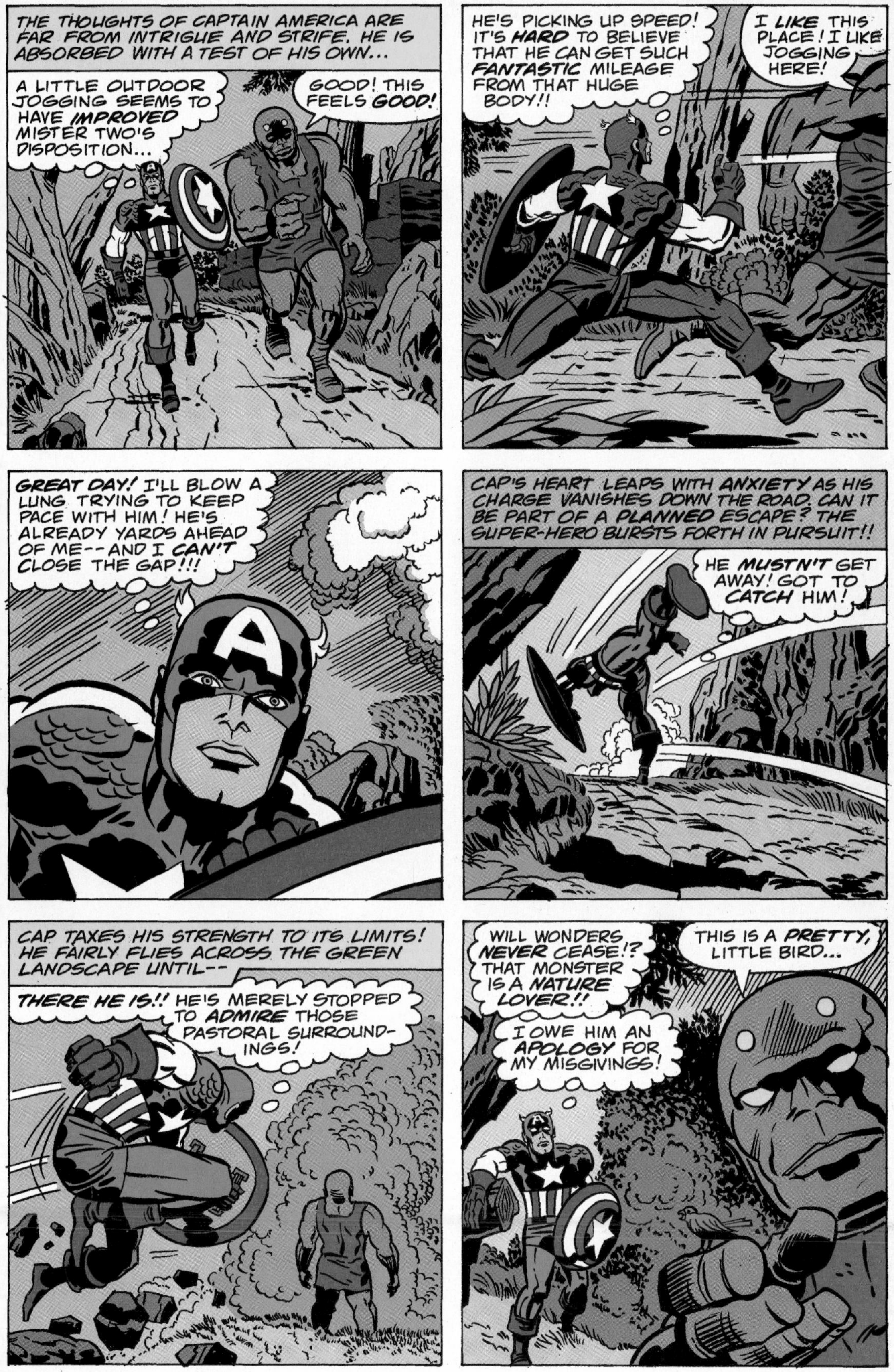
THE THOUGHTS OF CAPTAIN AMERICA ARE FAR FROM INTRIGUE AND STRIFE. HE IS ABSORBED WITH A TEST OF HIS OWN...
A LITTLE OUTDOOR JOGGING SEEMS TO HAVE IMPROVED MISTER TWO'S DISPOSITION...
GOOD! THIS FEELS GOOD!
HE'S PICKING UP SPEED! IT'S HARD TO BELIEVE THAT HE CAN GET SUCH FANTASTIC MILEAGE FROM THAT HUGE BODY!!
I LIKE THIS PLACE! I LIKE JOGGING HERE!
GREAT DAY! I'LL BLOW A LUNG TRYING TO KEEP PACE WITH HIM! HE'S ALREADY YARDS AHEAD OF ME--AND I CAN'T CLOSE THE GAP!!!
CAP'S HEART LEAPS WITH ANXIETY AS HIS CHARGE VANISHES DOWN THE ROAD. CAN IT BE PART OF A PLANNED ESCAPE? THE SUPER-HERO BURSTS FORTH IN PURSUIT!!
HE MUSTN'T GET AWAY! GOT TO CATCH HIM!
CAP TAXES HIS STRENGTH TO ITS LIMITS! HE FAIRLY FLIES ACROSS THE GREEN LANDSCAPE UNTIL--
THERE HE IS!! HE'S MERELY STOPPED TO ADMIRE THOSE PASTORAL SURROUNDINGS!
WILL WONDERS NEVER CEASE!? THAT MONSTER IS A NATURE LOVER!!
THIS IS A PRETTY, LITTLE BIRD...
I OWE HIM AN APOLOGY FOR MY MISGIVINGS!

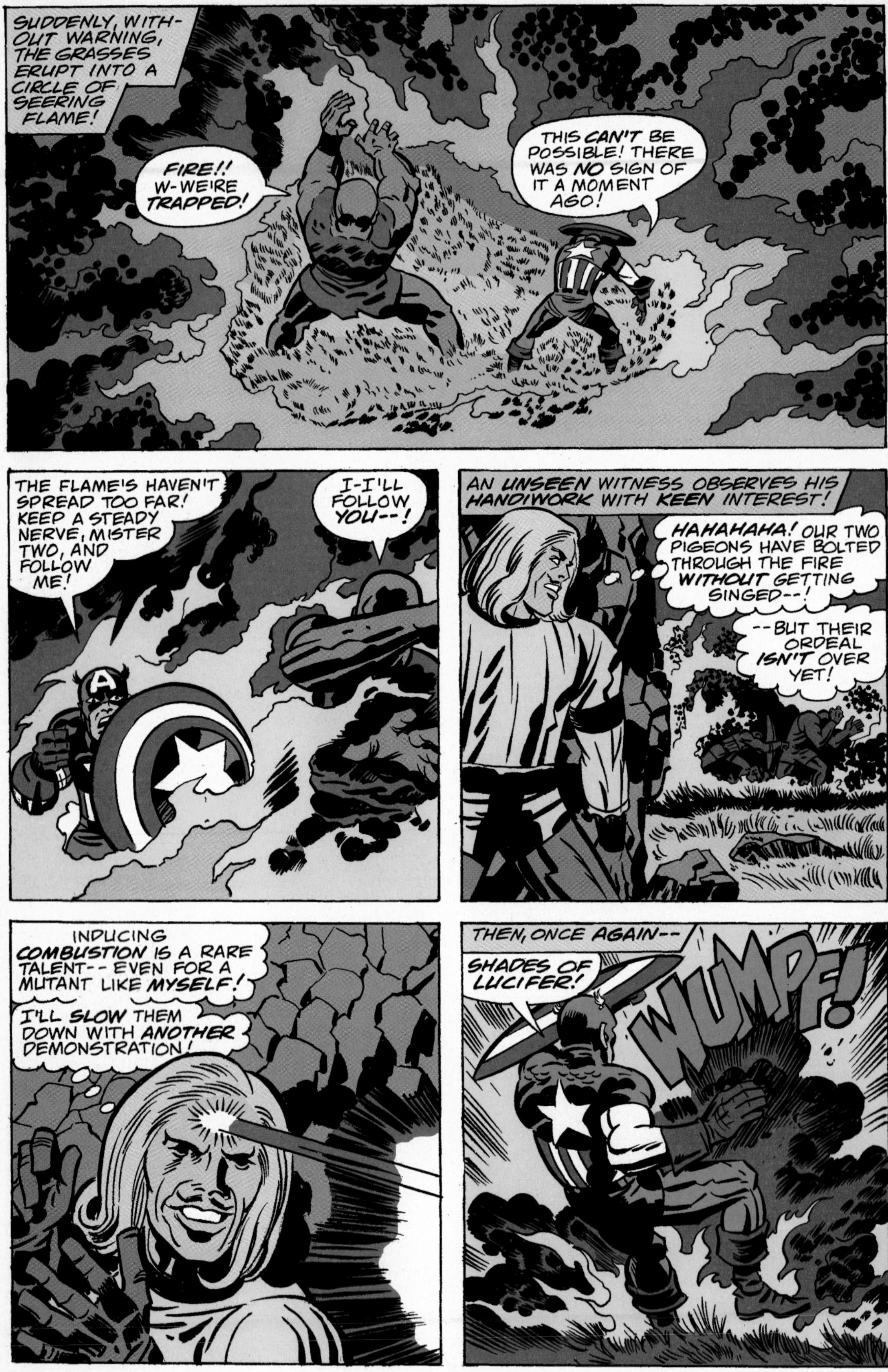
SUDDENLY, WITH-OUT WARNING, THE GRASSES ERUPT INTO A CIRCLE OF SEERING FLAME!
FIRE!! W-WE'RE TRAPPED!
THIS CAN'T BE POSSIBLE! THERE WAS NO SIGN OF IT A MOMENT AGO!
THE FLAME'S HAVEN'T SPREAD TOO FAR! KEEP A STEADY NERVE, MISTER TWO, AND FOLLOW ME!
I-I'LL FOLLOW YOU--!
AN UNSEEN WITNESS OBSERVES HIS HANDIWORK WITH KEEN INTEREST!
HAHAHAHA! OUR TWO PIGEONS HAVE BOLTED THROUGH THE FIRE WITHOUT GETTING SINGED--!
--BUT THEIR ORDEAL ISN'T OVER YET!
INDUCING COMBUSTION IS A RARE TALENT-- EVEN FOR A MUTANT LIKE MYSELF!
I'LL SLOW THEM DOWN WITH ANOTHER DEMONSTRATION!
THEN, ONCE AGAIN--
SHADES OF LUCIFER!
WUMPF!

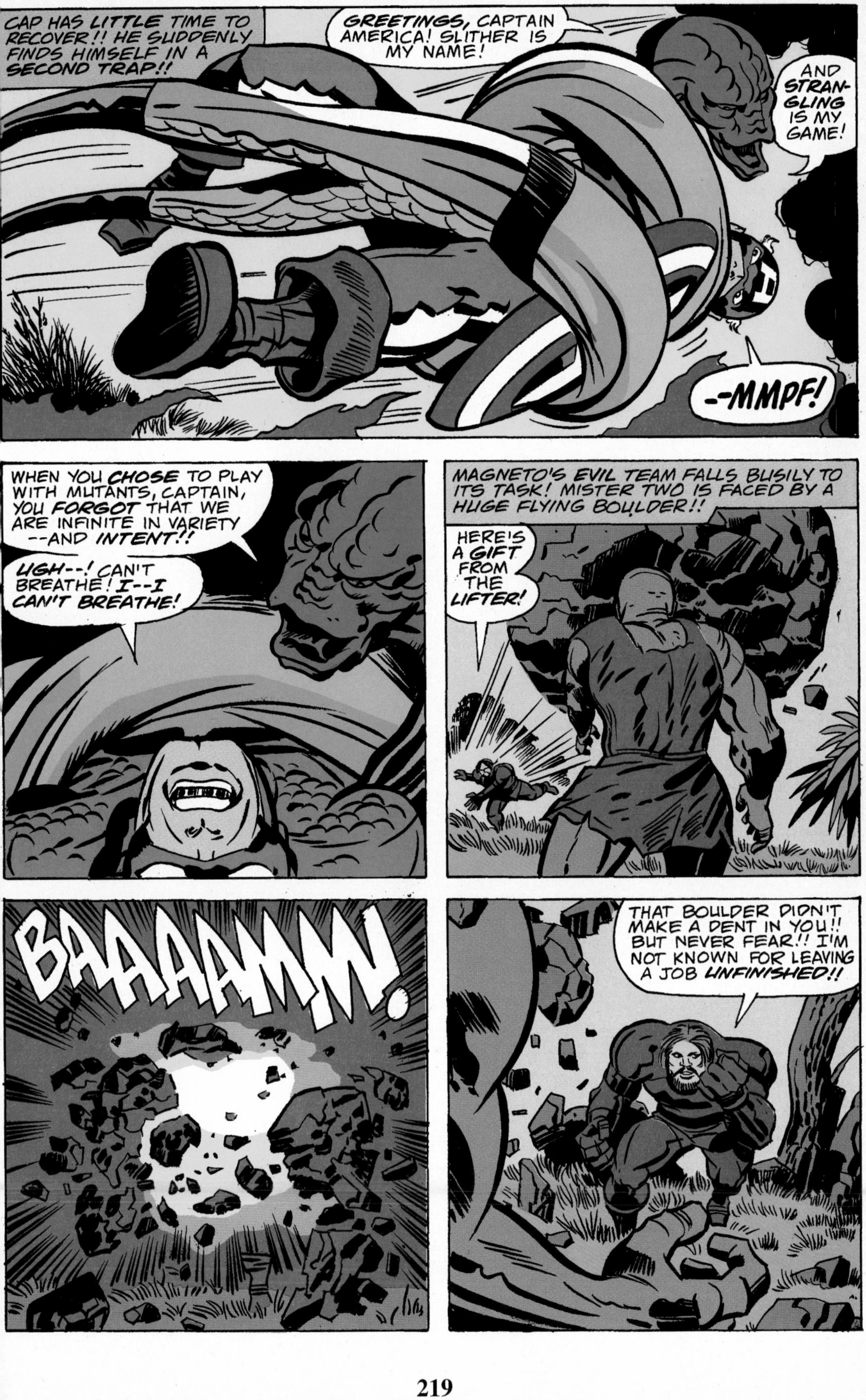

CAP HAS LITTLE TIME TO RECOVER!! HE SUDDENLY FINDS HIMSELF IN A SECOND TRAP!!
GREETINGS, CAPTAIN AMERICA! SLITHER IS MY NAME!
AND STRAN-GLING IS MY GAME!
--MMPF!
WHEN YOU CHOSE TO PLAY WITH MUTANTS, CAPTAIN, YOU FORGOT THAT WE ARE INFINITE IN VARIETY --AND INTENT!!
UGH--! CAN'T BREATHE! I--I CAN'T BREATHE!
MAGNETO'S EVIL TEAM FALLS BUSILY TO ITS TASK! MISTER TWO IS FACED BY A HUGE FLYING BOULDER!!
HERE'S A GIFT FROM THE LIFTER!
BAAAAMM!
THAT BOULDER DIDN'T MAKE A DENT IN YOU!! BUT NEVER FEAR!! I'M NOT KNOWN FOR LEAVING A JOB UNFINISHED!!

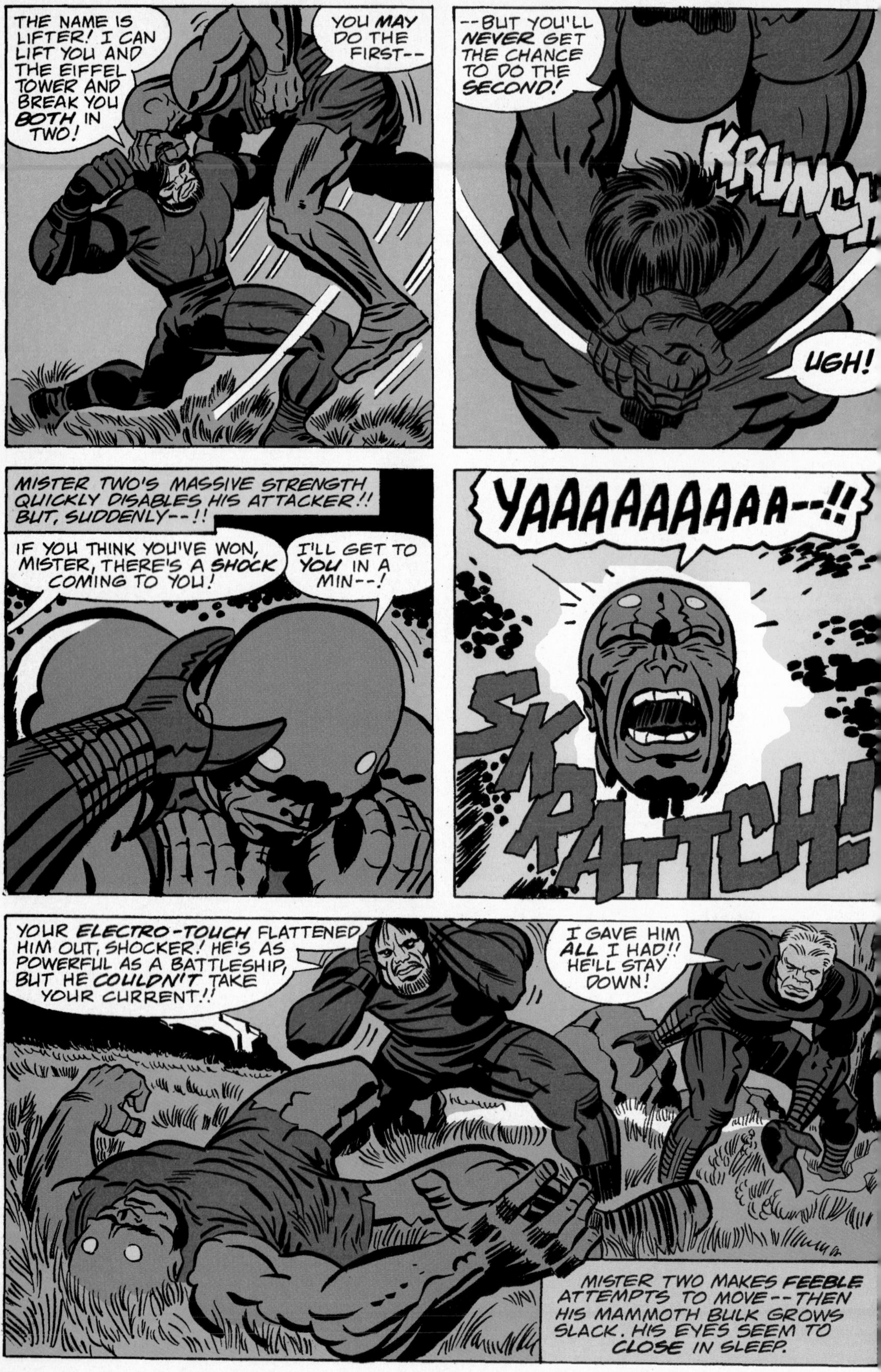

THE NAME IS LIFTER! I CAN LIFT YOU AND THE EIFFEL TOWER AND BREAK YOU BOTH IN TWO!
YOU MAY DO THE FIRST--
--BUT YOU'LL NEVER GET THE CHANCE TO DO THE SECOND!
KRUNCH
UGH!
MISTER TWO'S MASSIVE STRENGTH QUICKLY DISABLES HIS ATTACKER!! BUT, SUDDENLY--!!
IF YOU THINK YOU'VE WON, MISTER, THERE'S A SHOCK COMING TO YOU!
I'LL GET TO YOU IN A MIN--!
YAAAAAAAAA--!!
SKRATTCH!
YOUR ELECTRO-TOUCH FLATTENED HIM OUT, SHOCKER! HE'S AS POWERFUL AS A BATTLESHIP, BUT HE COULDN'T TAKE YOUR CURRENT!!
I GAVE HIM ALL I HAD!! HE'LL STAY DOWN!
MISTER TWO MAKES FEEBLE ATTEMPTS TO MOVE--THEN HIS MAMMOTH BULK GROWS SLACK. HIS EYES SEEM TO CLOSE IN SLEEP.

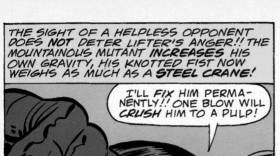

THE SIGHT OF A HELPLESS OPPONENT DOES **NOT** DETER LIFTER'S ANGER!! THE MOUNTAINOUS MUTANT **INCREASES** HIS OWN GRAVITY, HIS KNOTTED FIST NOW WEIGHS AS MUCH AS A **STEEL CRANE!**

I'LL **FIX** HIM PERMANENTLY!! ONE BLOW WILL **CRUSH** HIM TO A PULP!

HOLD IT! SOMETHING'S UP!!

WHAT IS IT, SLITHER!?

PLAYTIME'S OVER!! THIS PLACE IS CRAWLING WITH **SHIELD** MEN!

THEY'VE BEEN HERE ALL THIS TIME -- KEEPING OUT OF SIGHT UNTIL WE **HIT** THEIR LITTLE PETS!

I **ALMOST** NAILED CAPTAIN AMERICA!

A MISS DOESN'T COUNT! LET'S SPLIT!

WHERE'S THE VAN?

RIGHT **HERE!** PILE IN, SLOW POKES! BURNER'S GOT IT JUICED UP AND **READY** TO GO!!

BAM!

I'D LIKE TO **TANGLE** WITH THESE **SHIELD** DUDES!!

BAM! BAM!

STOW IT! YOU KNOW MAGNETO'S ORDERS! WE CAME TO START A HASSLE -- NOT TO TEST OUR POWERS AGAINST AN **ENTIRE** TASK FORCE!

GET THIS OFF THE GROUND, BURNER!

WAM! WAM!

POK!

THAT VAN IS A **HOVER-CRAFT!!** AND IT'S TAKING OFF LIKE A **BULLET!**

STOP FIRING! THEY'RE OUT OF RANGE!

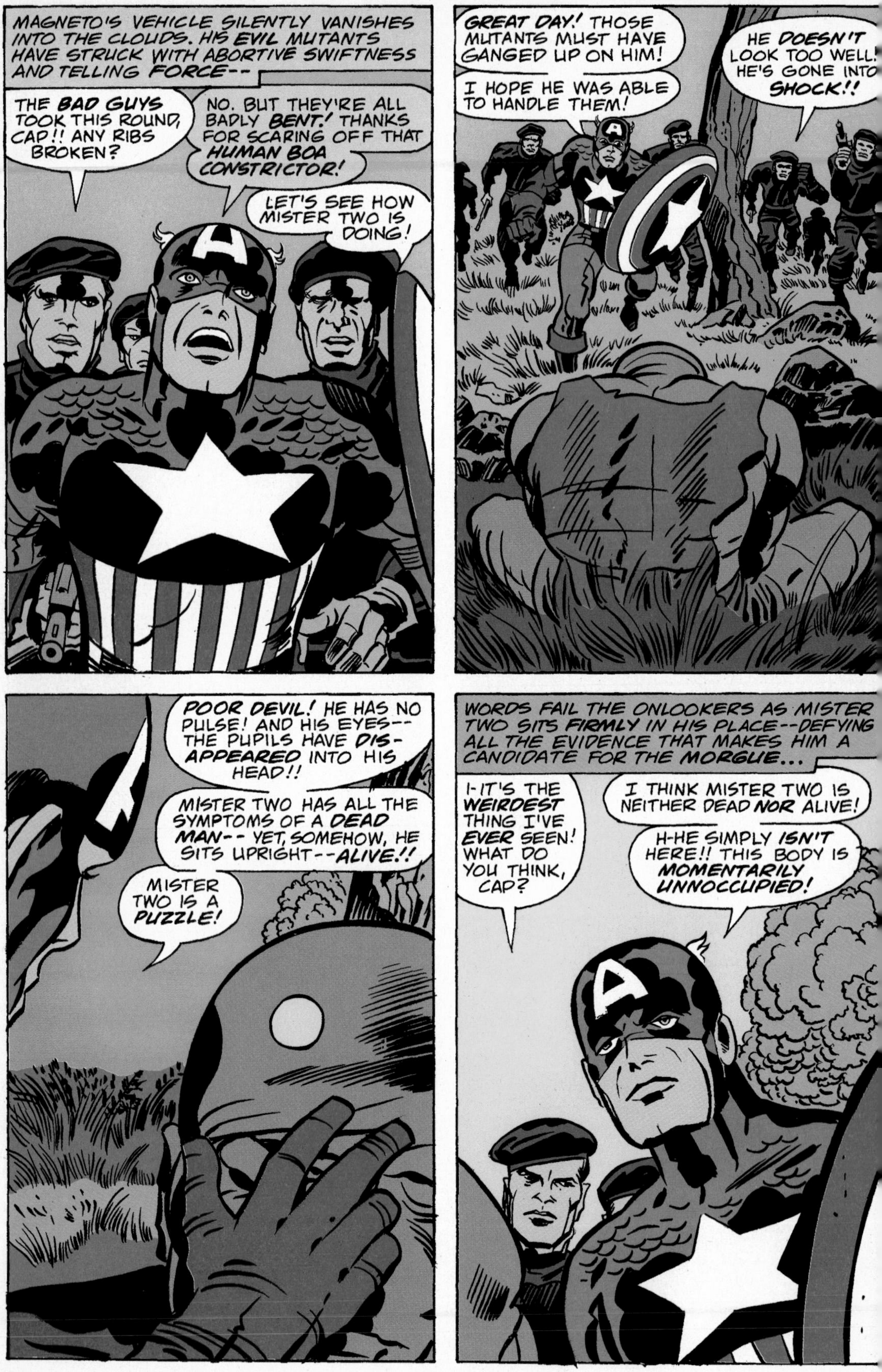

MAGNETO'S VEHICLE SILENTLY VANISHES INTO THE CLOUDS. HIS EVIL MUTANTS HAVE STRUCK WITH ABORTIVE SWIFTNESS AND TELLING FORCE--
THE BAD GUYS TOOK THIS ROUND, CAP!! ANY RIBS BROKEN?
NO. BUT THEY'RE ALL BADLY BENT! THANKS FOR SCARING OFF THAT HUMAN BOA CONSTRICTOR!
LET'S SEE HOW MISTER TWO IS DOING!
GREAT DAY! THOSE MUTANTS MUST HAVE GANGED UP ON HIM!
I HOPE HE WAS ABLE TO HANDLE THEM!
HE DOESN'T LOOK TOO WELL! HE'S GONE INTO SHOCK!!
POOR DEVIL! HE HAS NO PULSE! AND HIS EYES-- THE PUPILS HAVE DIS-APPEARED INTO HIS HEAD!!
MISTER TWO HAS ALL THE SYMPTOMS OF A DEAD MAN-- YET, SOMEHOW, HE SITS UPRIGHT--ALIVE!!
MISTER TWO IS A PUZZLE!
WORDS FAIL THE ONLOOKERS AS MISTER TWO SITS FIRMLY IN HIS PLACE--DEFYING ALL THE EVIDENCE THAT MAKES HIM A CANDIDATE FOR THE MORGUE...
I-IT'S THE WEIRDEST THING I'VE EVER SEEN! WHAT DO YOU THINK, CAP?
I THINK MISTER TWO IS NEITHER DEAD NOR ALIVE!
H-HE SIMPLY ISN'T HERE!! THIS BODY IS MOMENTARILY UNNOCCUPIED!

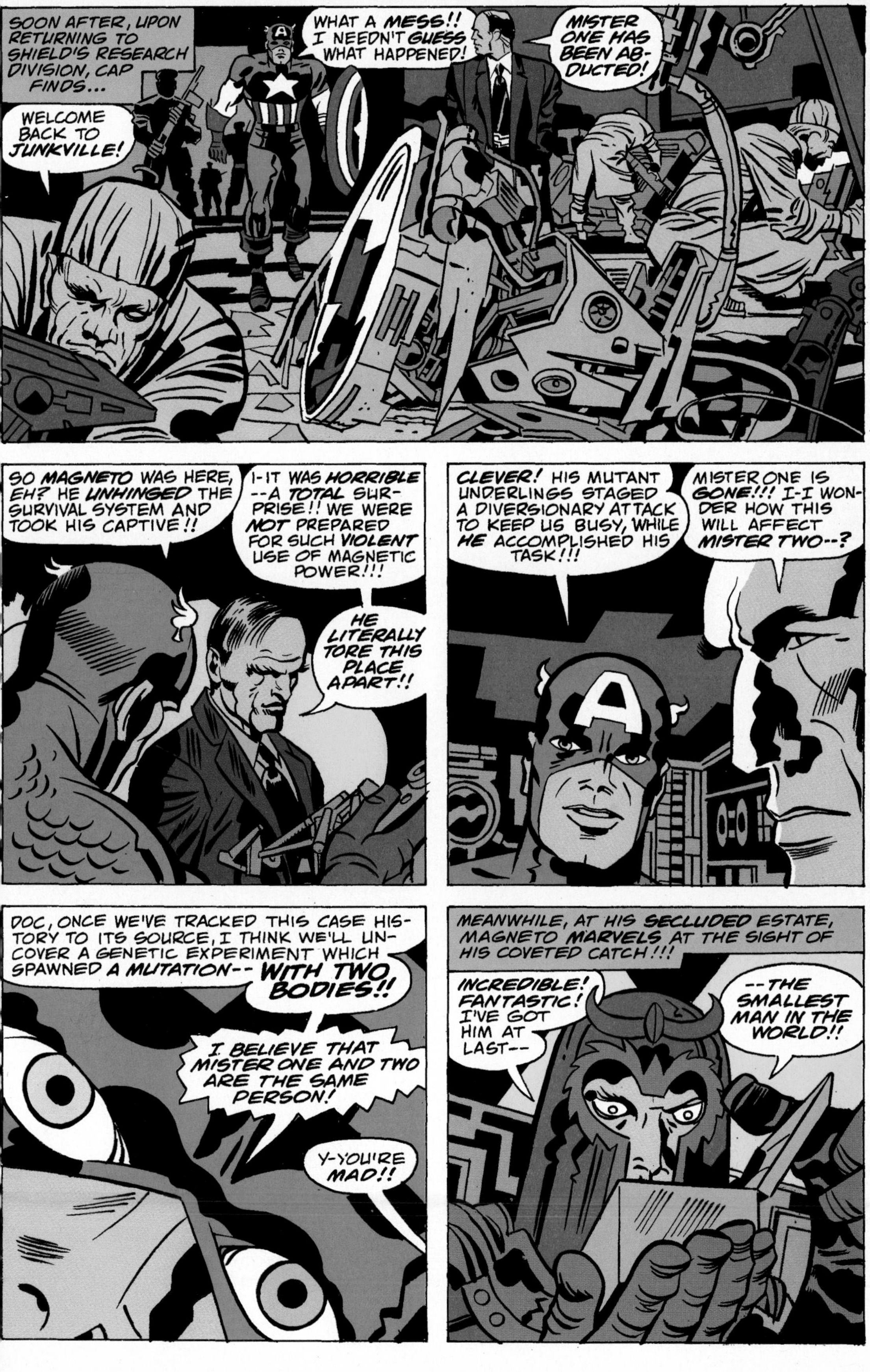
SOON AFTER, UPON RETURNING TO SHIELD'S RESEARCH DIVISION, CAP FINDS...
WELCOME BACK TO JUNKVILLE!
WHAT A MESS!! I NEEDN'T GUESS WHAT HAPPENED!
MISTER ONE HAS BEEN AB-DUCTED!
SO MAGNETO WAS HERE, EH? HE UNHINGED THE SURVIVAL SYSTEM AND TOOK HIS CAPTIVE!!
I-IT WAS HORRIBLE --A TOTAL SUR-PRISE!! WE WERE NOT PREPARED FOR SUCH VIOLENT USE OF MAGNETIC POWER!!!
HE LITERALLY TORE THIS PLACE APART!!
CLEVER! HIS MUTANT UNDERLINGS STAGED A DIVERSIONARY ATTACK TO KEEP US BUSY, WHILE HE ACCOMPLISHED HIS TASK!!!
MISTER ONE IS GONE!!! I-I WON-DER HOW THIS WILL AFFECT MISTER TWO--?
DOC, ONCE WE'VE TRACKED THIS CASE HIS-TORY TO ITS SOURCE, I THINK WE'LL UN-COVER A GENETIC EXPERIMENT WHICH SPAWNED A MUTATION-- WITH TWO BODIES!!
I BELIEVE THAT MISTER ONE AND TWO ARE THE SAME PERSON!
Y-YOU'RE MAD!!
MEANWHILE, AT HIS SECLUDED ESTATE, MAGNETO MARVELS AT THE SIGHT OF HIS COVETED CATCH!!!
INCREDIBLE! FANTASTIC! I'VE GOT HIM AT LAST--
--THE SMALLEST MAN IN THE WORLD!!

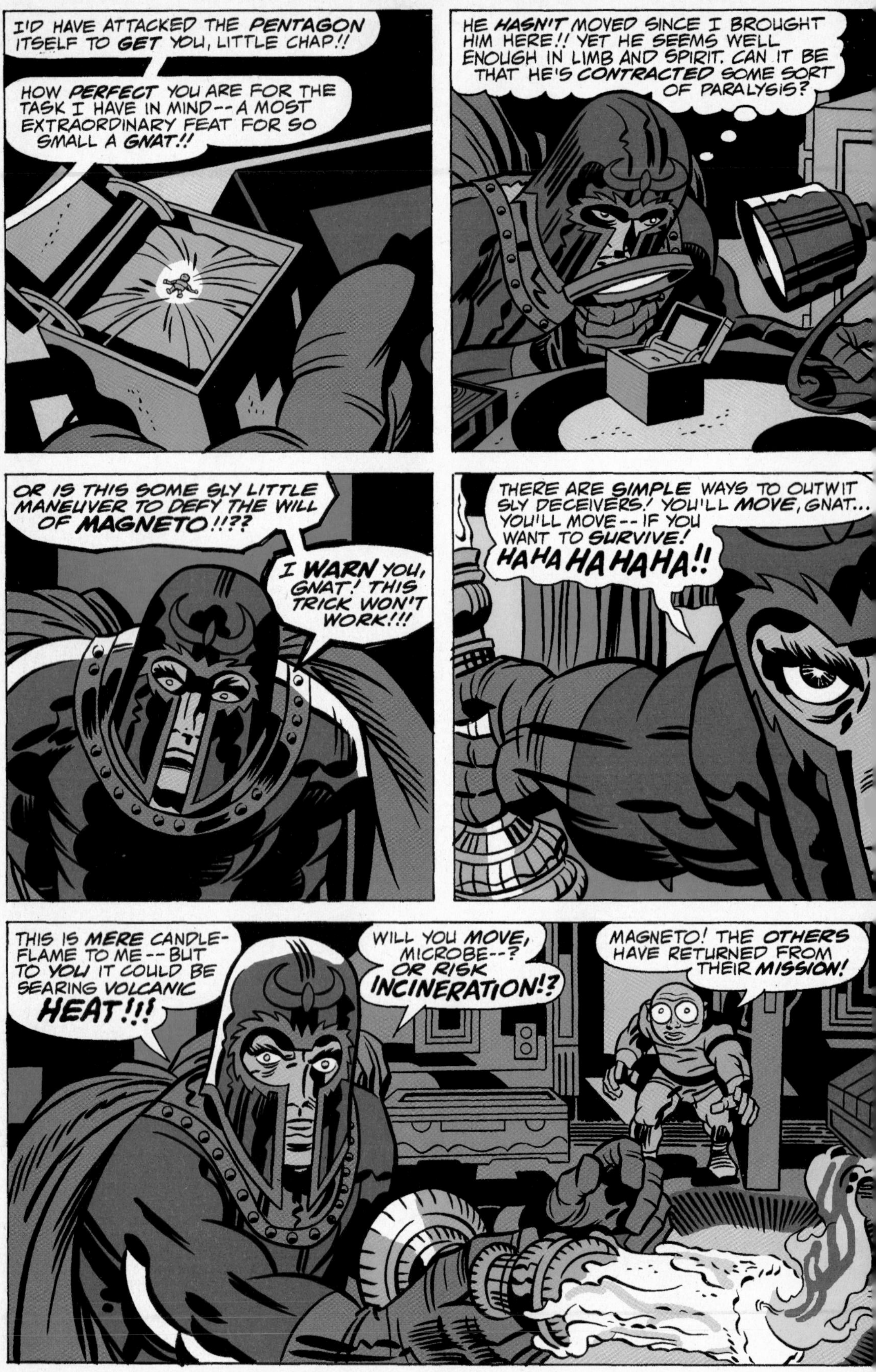

I'D HAVE ATTACKED THE PENTAGON ITSELF TO GET YOU, LITTLE CHAP!!
HOW PERFECT YOU ARE FOR THE TASK I HAVE IN MIND-- A MOST EXTRAORDINARY FEAT FOR SO SMALL A GNAT!!
HE HASN'T MOVED SINCE I BROUGHT HIM HERE!! YET HE SEEMS WELL ENOUGH IN LIMB AND SPIRIT. CAN IT BE THAT HE'S CONTRACTED SOME SORT OF PARALYSIS?
OR IS THIS SOME SLY LITTLE MANEUVER TO DEFY THE WILL OF MAGNETO!!??
I WARN YOU, GNAT! THIS TRICK WON'T WORK!!!
THERE ARE SIMPLE WAYS TO OUTWIT SLY DECEIVERS! YOU'LL MOVE, GNAT... YOU'LL MOVE-- IF YOU WANT TO SURVIVE! HAHAHAHAHAHA!!
THIS IS MERE CANDLE-FLAME TO ME-- BUT TO YOU IT COULD BE SEARING VOLCANIC HEAT!!!
WILL YOU MOVE, MICROBE--? OR RISK INCINERATION!?
MAGNETO! THE OTHERS HAVE RETURNED FROM THEIR MISSION!

THEY WANT TO MAKE A *FULL* REPORT ON THEIR COLLISION WITH *CAPTAIN AMERICA* AND THAT GOLIATH OF A MUTANT!

THE FOOLS CAN WAIT! TELL THEM TO STAND BY UNTIL I'M *READY* TO SEE THEM!

WE'VE DONE *ENOUGH* OF THAT, MAGNETO!

WE'VE SERVED YOU *WELL!* NOW WHAT'S IN THIS FOR *US!!*?

YES! WE PULLED A DIVERSION FOR YOU *BEFORE*, BUT WE NEVER LEARNED *WHAT* YOU STOLE!

OH-- YOU MEAN THAT TOP SECRET JOB?

MAGNETO TRUCULENTLY OPENS A HEAVY WOODEN CHEST AND--!

THIS IS WHAT I SEIZED!!

WHAT!!?? YOU RISKED OUR LIVES FOR THAT... *TOY!*?

WE WERE *SHOT* AT BY *EVERY* MAN AT THE AIR FORCE BASE--

--FOR *THAT?*

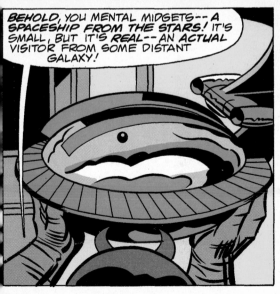

BEHOLD, YOU MENTAL MIDGETS-- A *SPACESHIP FROM THE STARS!* IT'S SMALL, BUT IT'S *REAL*-- AN *ACTUAL* VISITOR FROM SOME DISTANT GALAXY!

BUT, IT RESISTS *ALL* EFFORTS TO *PENETRATE* ITS INTERIOR!! NOT EVEN X-RAYS WILL ENTER ITS HULL!!

THAT'S WHY OUR LITTLE *MAN* IS HERE-- TO DO THAT *VERY JOB!!!*

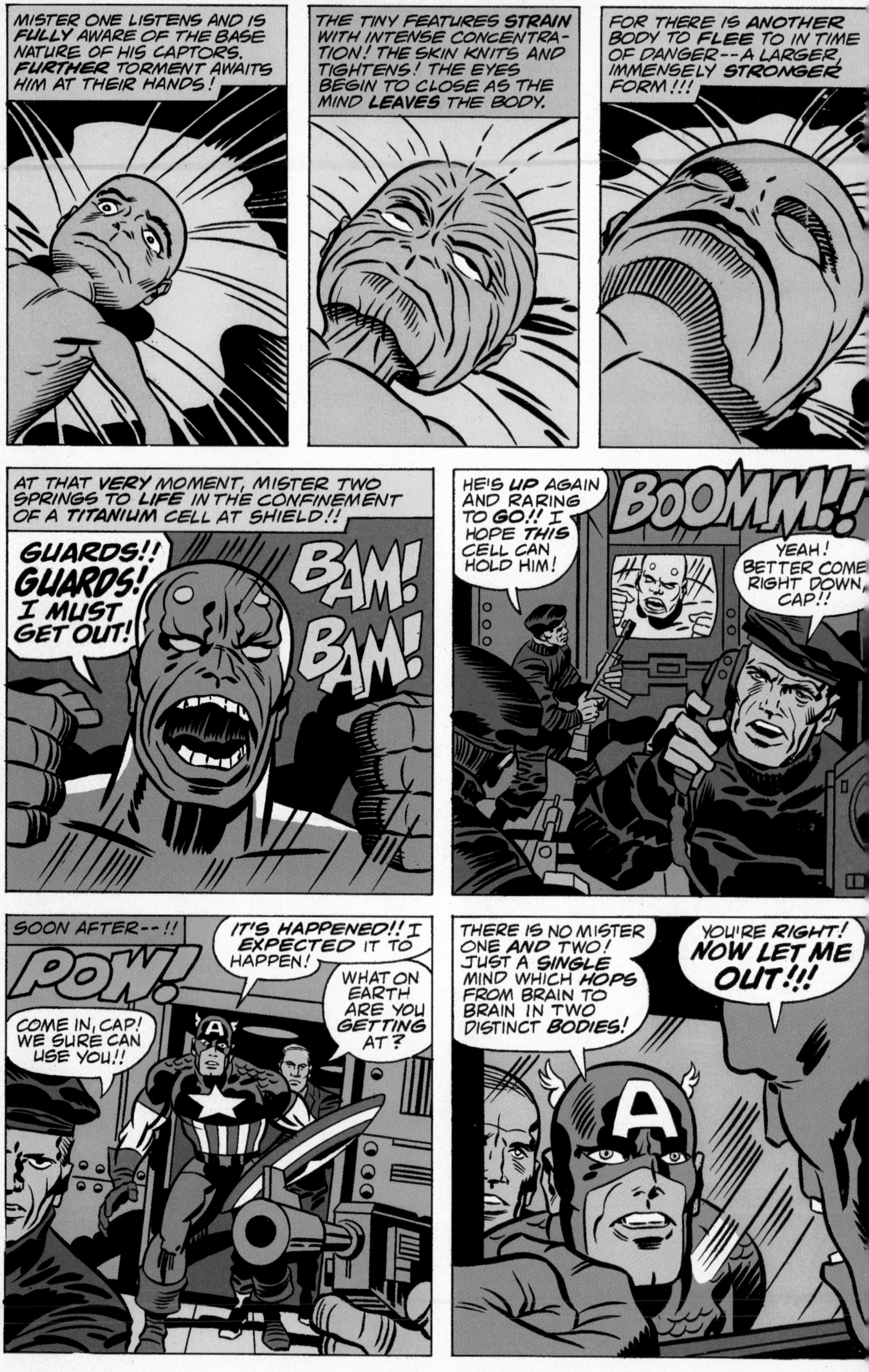
MISTER ONE LISTENS AND IS FULLY AWARE OF THE BASE NATURE OF HIS CAPTORS. FURTHER TORMENT AWAITS HIM AT THEIR HANDS!
THE TINY FEATURES STRAIN WITH INTENSE CONCENTRATION! THE SKIN KNITS AND TIGHTENS! THE EYES BEGIN TO CLOSE AS THE MIND LEAVES THE BODY.
FOR THERE IS ANOTHER BODY TO FLEE TO IN TIME OF DANGER--A LARGER, IMMENSELY STRONGER FORM!!!
AT THAT VERY MOMENT, MISTER TWO SPRINGS TO LIFE IN THE CONFINEMENT OF A TITANIUM CELL AT SHIELD!!
GUARDS!! GUARDS! I MUST GET OUT!
BAM! BAM!
HE'S UP AGAIN AND RARING TO GO!! I HOPE THIS CELL CAN HOLD HIM!
BOOMM!!
YEAH! BETTER COME RIGHT DOWN, CAP!!
SOON AFTER--!!
POW!
COME IN, CAP! WE SURE CAN USE YOU!!
IT'S HAPPENED!! I EXPECTED IT TO HAPPEN!
WHAT ON EARTH ARE YOU GETTING AT?
THERE IS NO MISTER ONE AND TWO! JUST A SINGLE MIND WHICH HOPS FROM BRAIN TO BRAIN IN TWO DISTINCT BODIES!
YOU'RE RIGHT! NOW LET ME OUT!!!

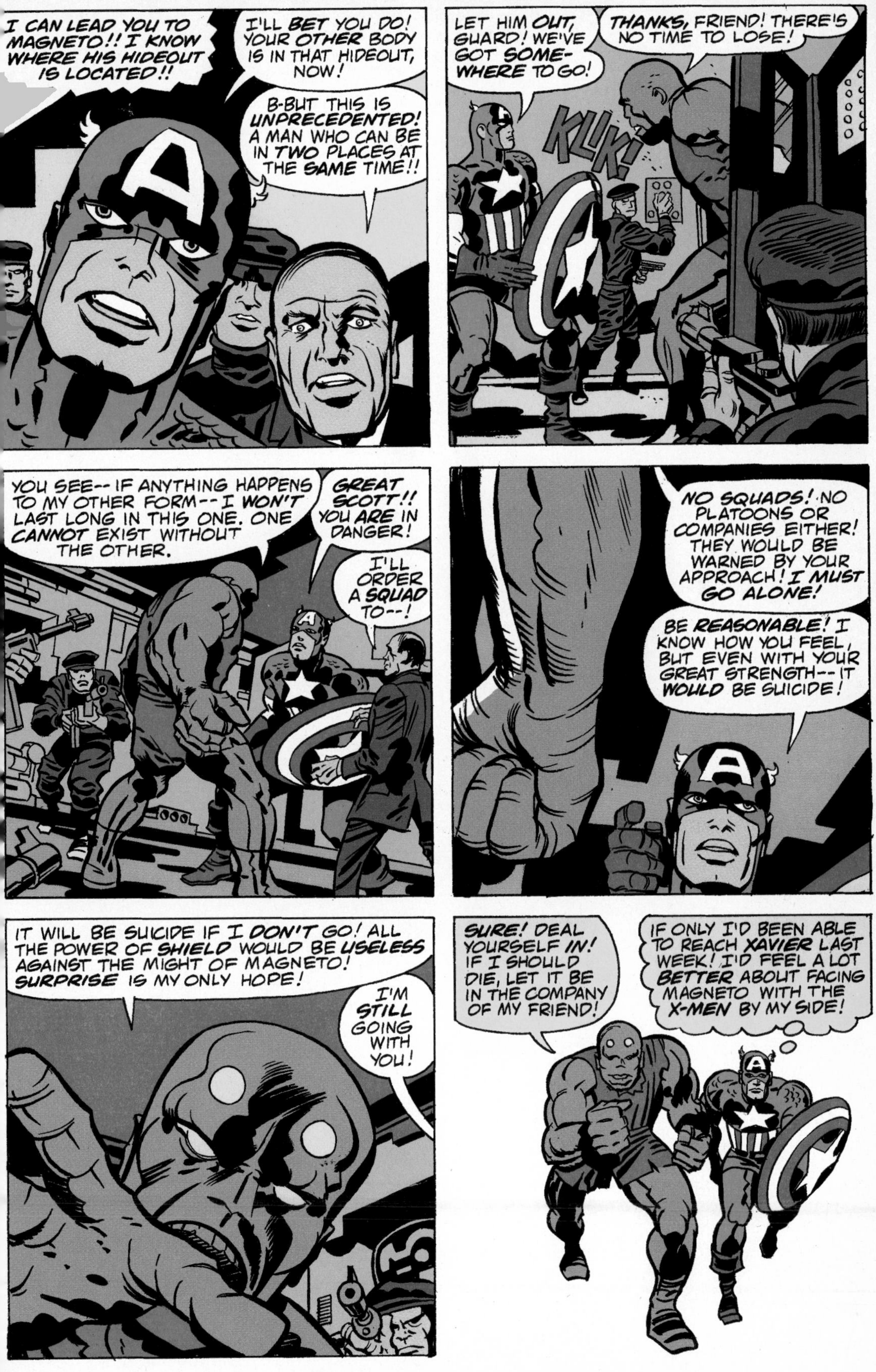

I CAN LEAD YOU TO MAGNETO!! I KNOW WHERE HIS HIDEOUT IS LOCATED!!
I'LL BET YOU DO! YOUR OTHER BODY IS IN THAT HIDEOUT, NOW!
B-BUT THIS IS UNPRECEDENTED! A MAN WHO CAN BE IN TWO PLACES AT THE SAME TIME!!
LET HIM OUT, GUARD! WE'VE GOT SOMEWHERE TO GO!
THANKS, FRIEND! THERE'S NO TIME TO LOSE!
KLIK!
YOU SEE-- IF ANYTHING HAPPENS TO MY OTHER FORM-- I WON'T LAST LONG IN THIS ONE. ONE CANNOT EXIST WITHOUT THE OTHER.
GREAT SCOTT!! YOU ARE IN DANGER!
I'LL ORDER A SQUAD TO--!
NO SQUADS! NO PLATOONS OR COMPANIES EITHER! THEY WOULD BE WARNED BY YOUR APPROACH! I MUST GO ALONE!
BE REASONABLE! I KNOW HOW YOU FEEL, BUT EVEN WITH YOUR GREAT STRENGTH-- IT WOULD BE SUICIDE!
IT WILL BE SUICIDE IF I DON'T GO! ALL THE POWER OF SHIELD WOULD BE USELESS AGAINST THE MIGHT OF MAGNETO! SURPRISE IS MY ONLY HOPE!
I'M STILL GOING WITH YOU!
SURE! DEAL YOURSELF IN! IF I SHOULD DIE, LET IT BE IN THE COMPANY OF MY FRIEND!
IF ONLY I'D BEEN ABLE TO REACH XAVIER LAST WEEK! I'D FEEL A LOT BETTER ABOUT FACING MAGNETO WITH THE X-MEN BY MY SIDE!

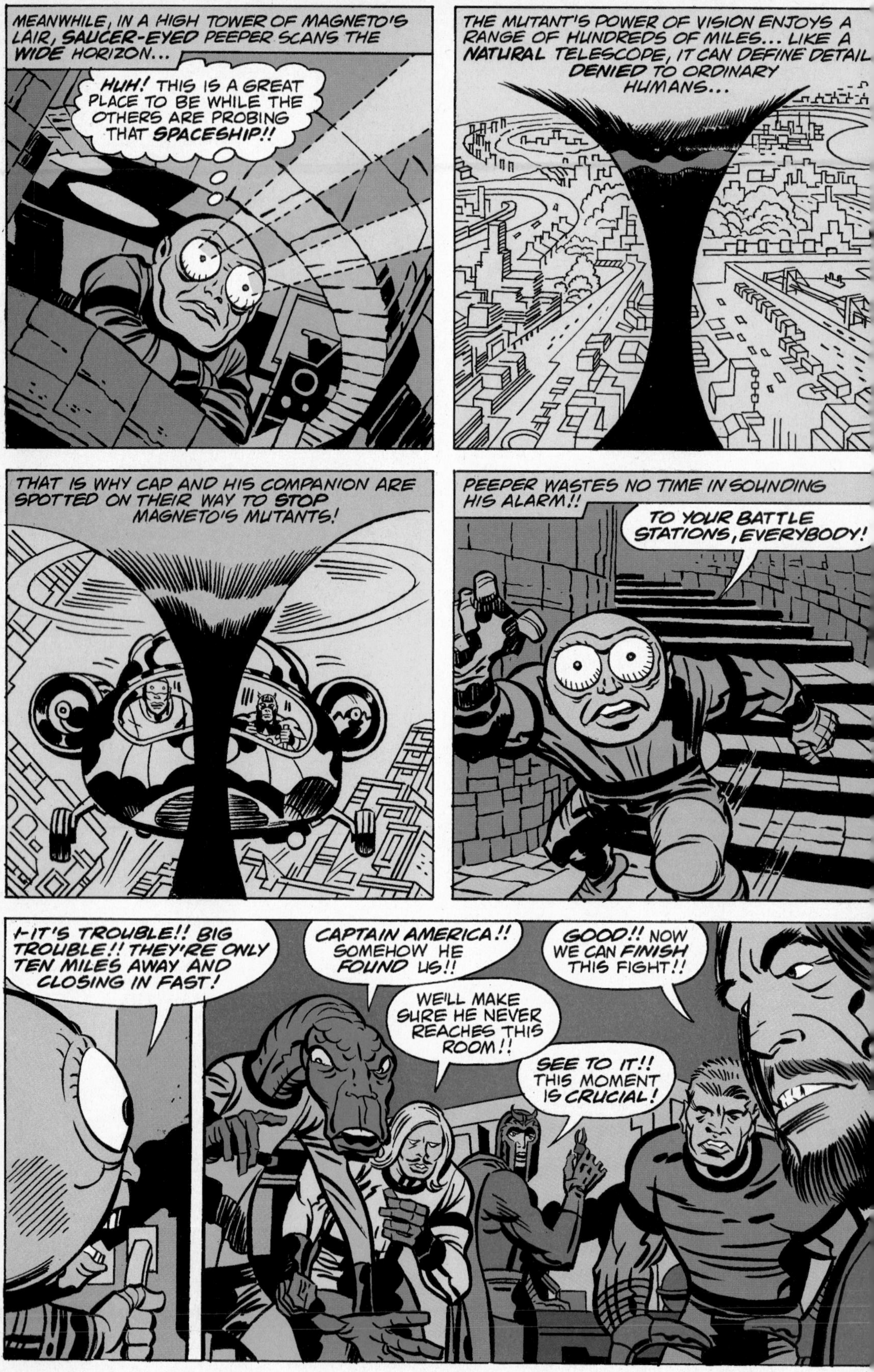
MEANWHILE, IN A HIGH TOWER OF MAGNETO'S LAIR, SAUCER-EYED PEEPER SCANS THE WIDE HORIZON...
HUH! THIS IS A GREAT PLACE TO BE WHILE THE OTHERS ARE PROBING THAT SPACESHIP!!
THE MUTANT'S POWER OF VISION ENJOYS A RANGE OF HUNDREDS OF MILES... LIKE A NATURAL TELESCOPE, IT CAN DEFINE DETAIL DENIED TO ORDINARY HUMANS...
THAT IS WHY CAP AND HIS COMPANION ARE SPOTTED ON THEIR WAY TO STOP MAGNETO'S MUTANTS!
PEEPER WASTES NO TIME IN SOUNDING HIS ALARM!!
TO YOUR BATTLE STATIONS, EVERYBODY!
I-IT'S TROUBLE!! BIG TROUBLE!! THEY'RE ONLY TEN MILES AWAY AND CLOSING IN FAST!
CAPTAIN AMERICA!! SOMEHOW HE FOUND US!!
WE'LL MAKE SURE HE NEVER REACHES THIS ROOM!!
GOOD!! NOW WE CAN FINISH THIS FIGHT!!
SEE TO IT!! THIS MOMENT IS CRUCIAL!

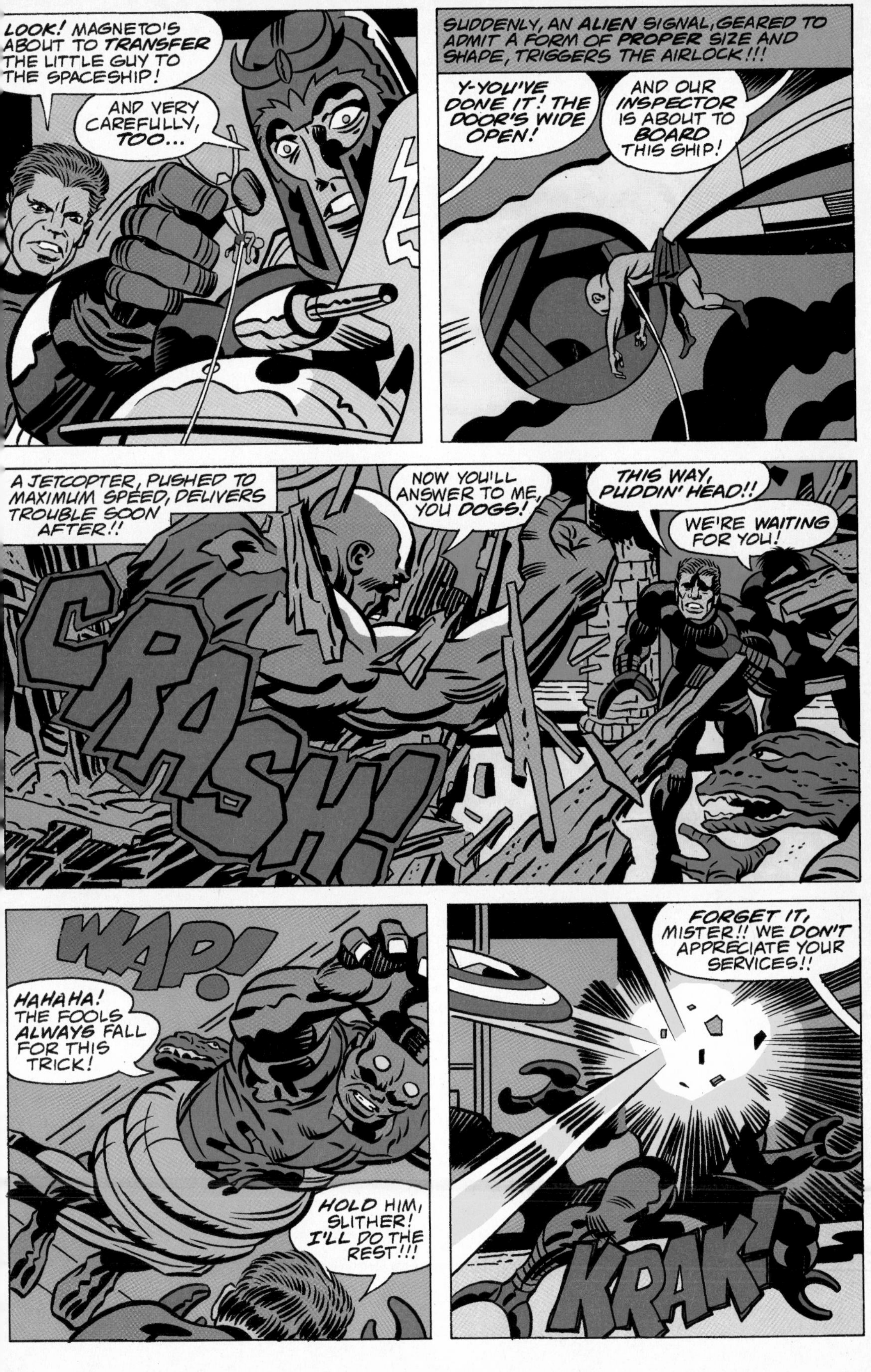
LOOK! MAGNETO'S ABOUT TO TRANSFER THE LITTLE GUY TO THE SPACESHIP!
AND VERY CAREFULLY, TOO...
SUDDENLY, AN ALIEN SIGNAL, GEARED TO ADMIT A FORM OF PROPER SIZE AND SHAPE, TRIGGERS THE AIRLOCK!!!
Y-YOU'VE DONE IT! THE DOOR'S WIDE OPEN!
AND OUR INSPECTOR IS ABOUT TO BOARD THIS SHIP!
A JETCOPTER, PUSHED TO MAXIMUM SPEED, DELIVERS TROUBLE SOON AFTER!!
CRASH!
NOW YOU'LL ANSWER TO ME, YOU DOGS!
THIS WAY, PUDDIN' HEAD!!
WE'RE WAITING FOR YOU!
WAP!
HAHAHA! THE FOOLS ALWAYS FALL FOR THIS TRICK!
HOLD HIM, SLITHER! I'LL DO THE REST!!!
FORGET IT, MISTER!! WE DON'T APPRECIATE YOUR SERVICES!!
KRAK!

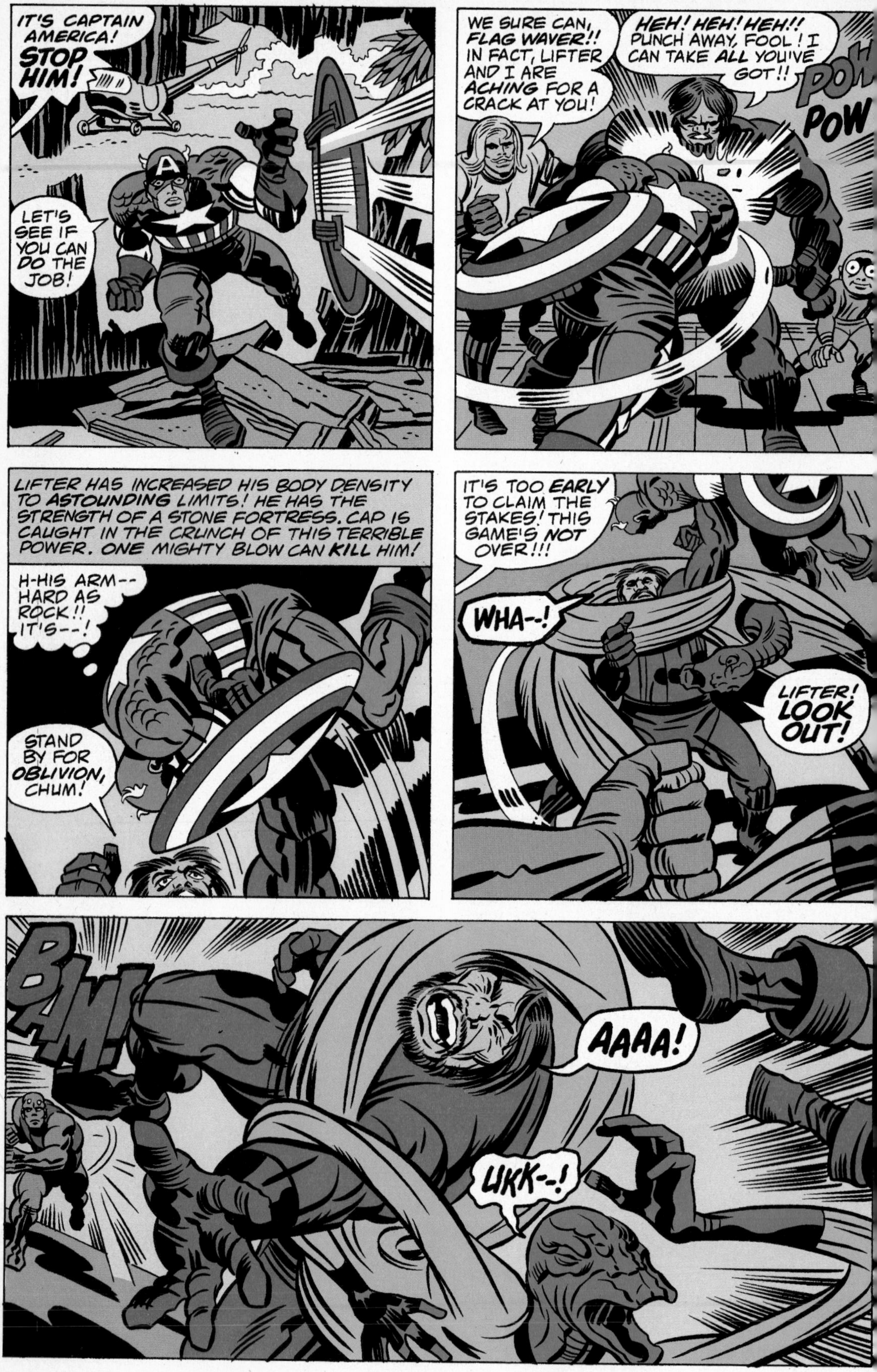
IT'S CAPTAIN AMERICA! STOP HIM!
LET'S SEE IF YOU CAN DO THE JOB!
WE SURE CAN, FLAG WAVER!! IN FACT, LIFTER AND I ARE ACHING FOR A CRACK AT YOU!
HEH! HEH! HEH!! PUNCH AWAY, FOOL! I CAN TAKE ALL YOU'VE GOT!!
POW
POW
LIFTER HAS INCREASED HIS BODY DENSITY TO ASTOUNDING LIMITS! HE HAS THE STRENGTH OF A STONE FORTRESS. CAP IS CAUGHT IN THE CRUNCH OF THIS TERRIBLE POWER. ONE MIGHTY BLOW CAN KILL HIM!
H-HIS ARM-- HARD AS ROCK!! IT'S--!
STAND BY FOR OBLIVION, CHUM!
IT'S TOO EARLY TO CLAIM THE STAKES! THIS GAME'S NOT OVER!!!
WHA--!
LIFTER! LOOK OUT!
BAM!
AAAA!
UKK--!

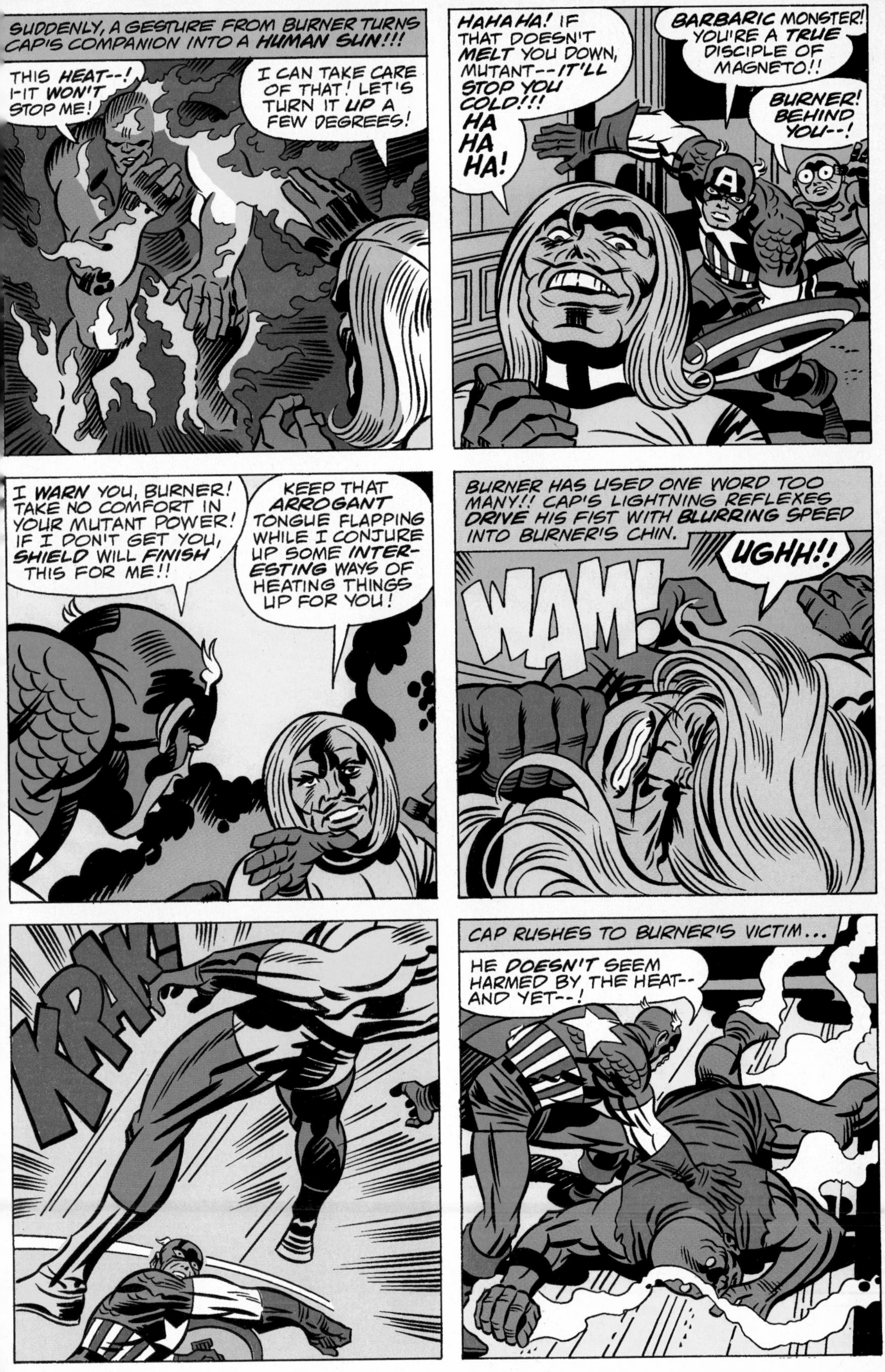
SUDDENLY, A GESTURE FROM BURNER TURNS CAP'S COMPANION INTO A HUMAN SUN!!!
THIS HEAT--! I-IT WON'T STOP ME!
I CAN TAKE CARE OF THAT! LET'S TURN IT UP A FEW DEGREES!
HAHAHA! IF THAT DOESN'T MELT YOU DOWN, MUTANT--IT'LL STOP YOU COLD!!! HA HA HA!
BARBARIC MONSTER! YOU'RE A TRUE DISCIPLE OF MAGNETO!!
BURNER! BEHIND YOU--!
I WARN YOU, BURNER! TAKE NO COMFORT IN YOUR MUTANT POWER! IF I DON'T GET YOU, SHIELD WILL FINISH THIS FOR ME!!
KEEP THAT ARROGANT TONGUE FLAPPING WHILE I CONJURE UP SOME INTERESTING WAYS OF HEATING THINGS UP FOR YOU!
BURNER HAS USED ONE WORD TOO MANY!! CAP'S LIGHTNING REFLEXES DRIVE HIS FIST WITH BLURRING SPEED INTO BURNER'S CHIN.
UGHH!!
WAM!
KRAK!
CAP RUSHES TO BURNER'S VICTIM...
HE DOESN'T SEEM HARMED BY THE HEAT--AND YET--!

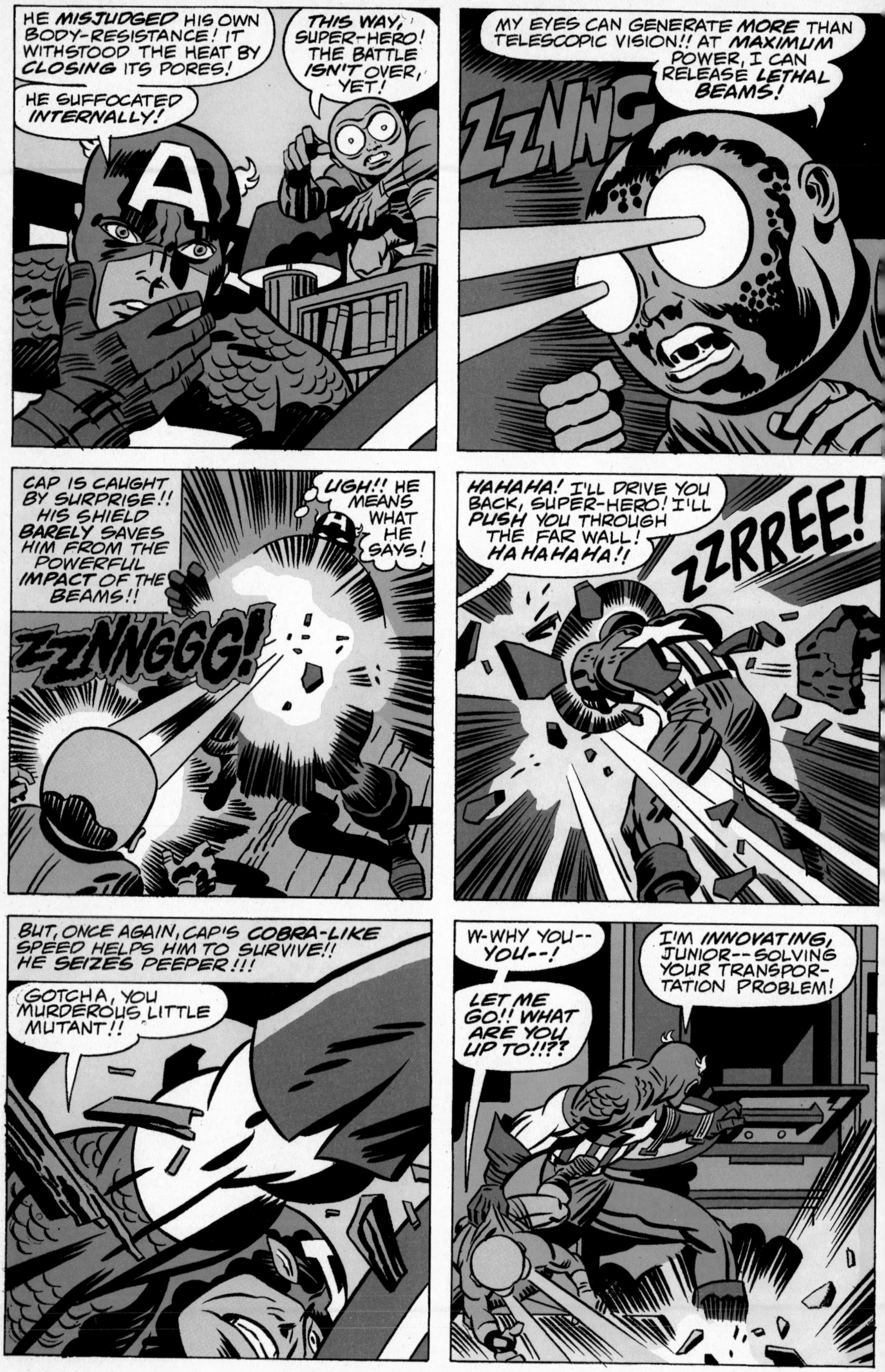
HE MISJUDGED HIS OWN BODY-RESISTANCE! IT WITHSTOOD THE HEAT BY CLOSING ITS PORES!
HE SUFFOCATED INTERNALLY!
THIS WAY, SUPER-HERO! THE BATTLE ISN'T OVER, YET!
MY EYES CAN GENERATE MORE THAN TELESCOPIC VISION!! AT MAXIMUM POWER, I CAN RELEASE LETHAL BEAMS!
ZZNNG
CAP IS CAUGHT BY SURPRISE!! HIS SHIELD BARELY SAVES HIM FROM THE POWERFUL IMPACT OF THE BEAMS!!
UGH!! HE MEANS WHAT HE SAYS!
ZZNNGGG!
HAHAHA! I'LL DRIVE YOU BACK, SUPER-HERO! I'LL PUSH YOU THROUGH THE FAR WALL! HAHAHAHA!!
ZZRREE!
BUT, ONCE AGAIN, CAP'S COBRA-LIKE SPEED HELPS HIM TO SURVIVE!! HE SEIZES PEEPER!!!
GOTCHA, YOU MURDEROUS LITTLE MUTANT!!
W-WHY YOU-- YOU--!
LET ME GO!! WHAT ARE YOU UP TO!!??
I'M INNOVATING, JUNIOR--SOLVING YOUR TRANSPORTATION PROBLEM!

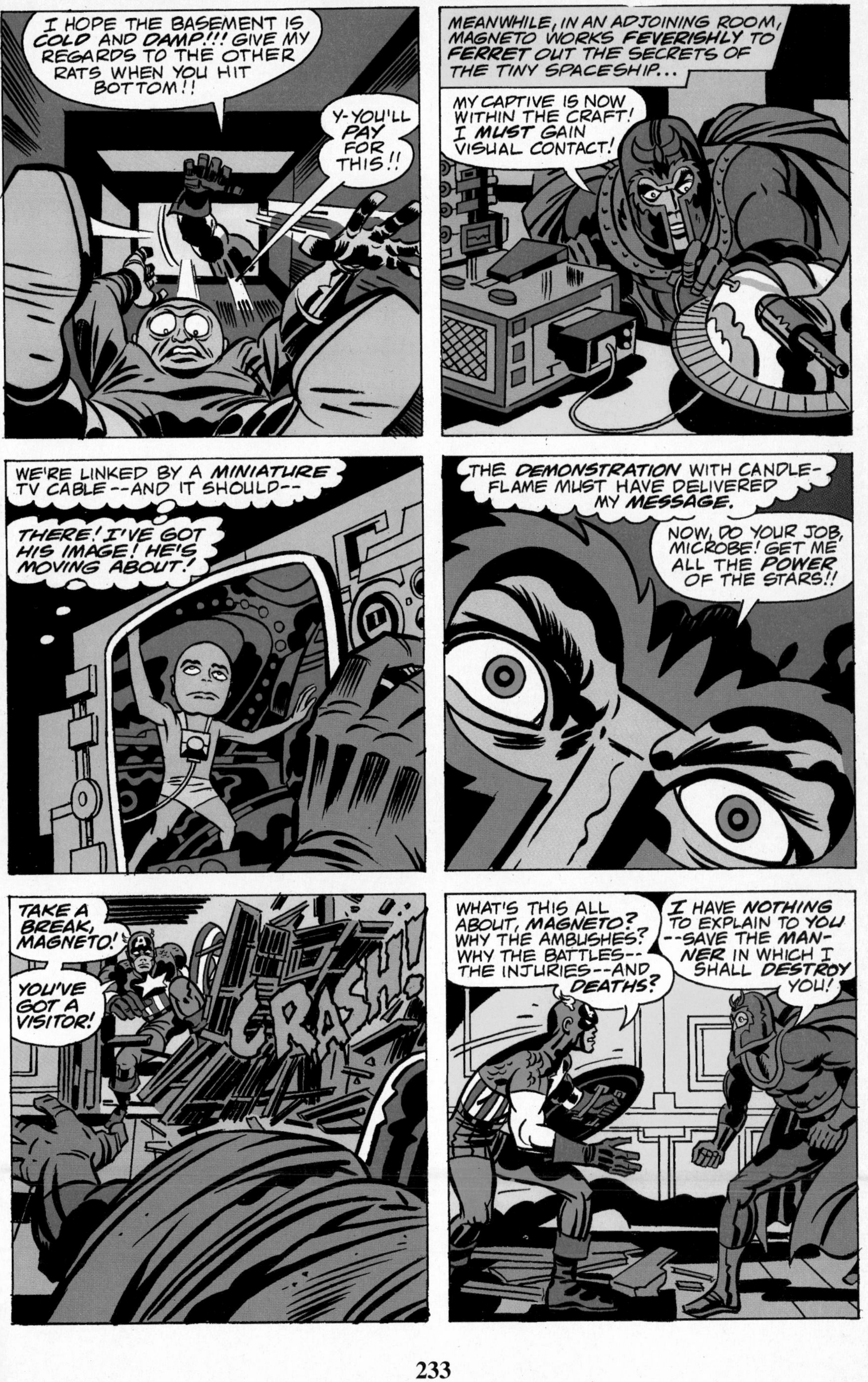
I HOPE THE BASEMENT IS COLD AND DAMP!!! GIVE MY REGARDS TO THE OTHER RATS WHEN YOU HIT BOTTOM!!
Y-YOU'LL PAY FOR THIS!!
MEANWHILE, IN AN ADJOINING ROOM, MAGNETO WORKS FEVERISHLY TO FERRET OUT THE SECRETS OF THE TINY SPACESHIP...
MY CAPTIVE IS NOW WITHIN THE CRAFT! I MUST GAIN VISUAL CONTACT!
WE'RE LINKED BY A MINIATURE TV CABLE --AND IT SHOULD--
THERE! I'VE GOT HIS IMAGE! HE'S MOVING ABOUT!
THE DEMONSTRATION WITH CANDLE-FLAME MUST HAVE DELIVERED MY MESSAGE.
NOW, DO YOUR JOB, MICROBE! GET ME ALL THE POWER OF THE STARS!!
TAKE A BREAK, MAGNETO!
YOU'VE GOT A VISITOR!
CRASH!
WHAT'S THIS ALL ABOUT, MAGNETO? WHY THE AMBUSHES? WHY THE BATTLES-- THE INJURIES--AND DEATHS?
I HAVE NOTHING TO EXPLAIN TO YOU --SAVE THE MAN-NER IN WHICH I SHALL DESTROY YOU!

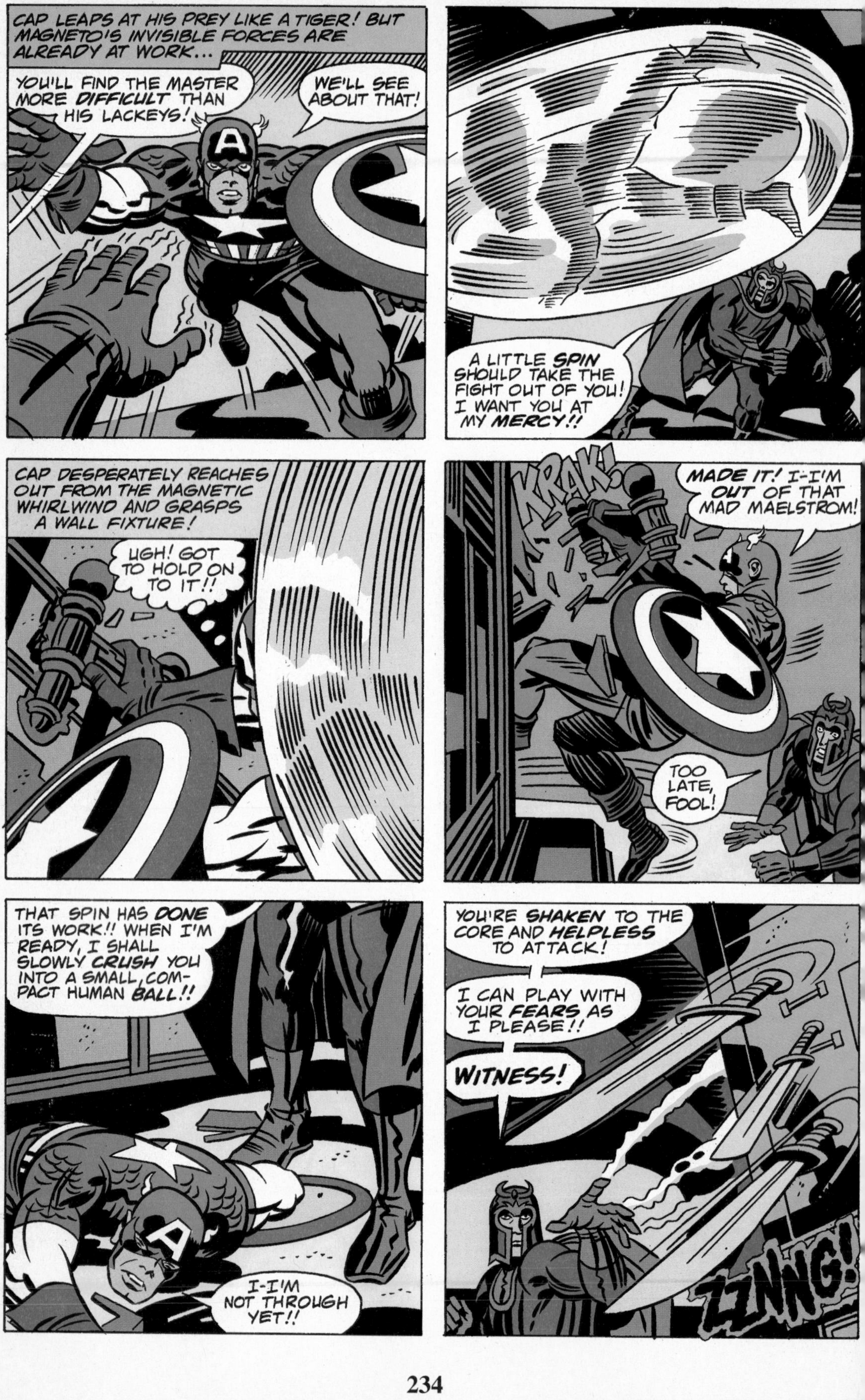
CAP LEAPS AT HIS PREY LIKE A TIGER! BUT MAGNETO'S INVISIBLE FORCES ARE ALREADY AT WORK...
YOU'LL FIND THE MASTER MORE DIFFICULT THAN HIS LACKEYS!
WE'LL SEE ABOUT THAT!
A LITTLE SPIN SHOULD TAKE THE FIGHT OUT OF YOU! I WANT YOU AT MY MERCY!!
CAP DESPERATELY REACHES OUT FROM THE MAGNETIC WHIRLWIND AND GRASPS A WALL FIXTURE!
UGH! GOT TO HOLD ON TO IT!!
KRAK!
MADE IT! I-I'M OUT OF THAT MAD MAELSTROM!
TOO LATE, FOOL!
THAT SPIN HAS DONE ITS WORK!! WHEN I'M READY, I SHALL SLOWLY CRUSH YOU INTO A SMALL, COMPACT HUMAN BALL!!
I-I'M NOT THROUGH YET!!
YOU'RE SHAKEN TO THE CORE AND HELPLESS TO ATTACK!
I CAN PLAY WITH YOUR FEARS AS I PLEASE!!
WITNESS!
ZZNNG!

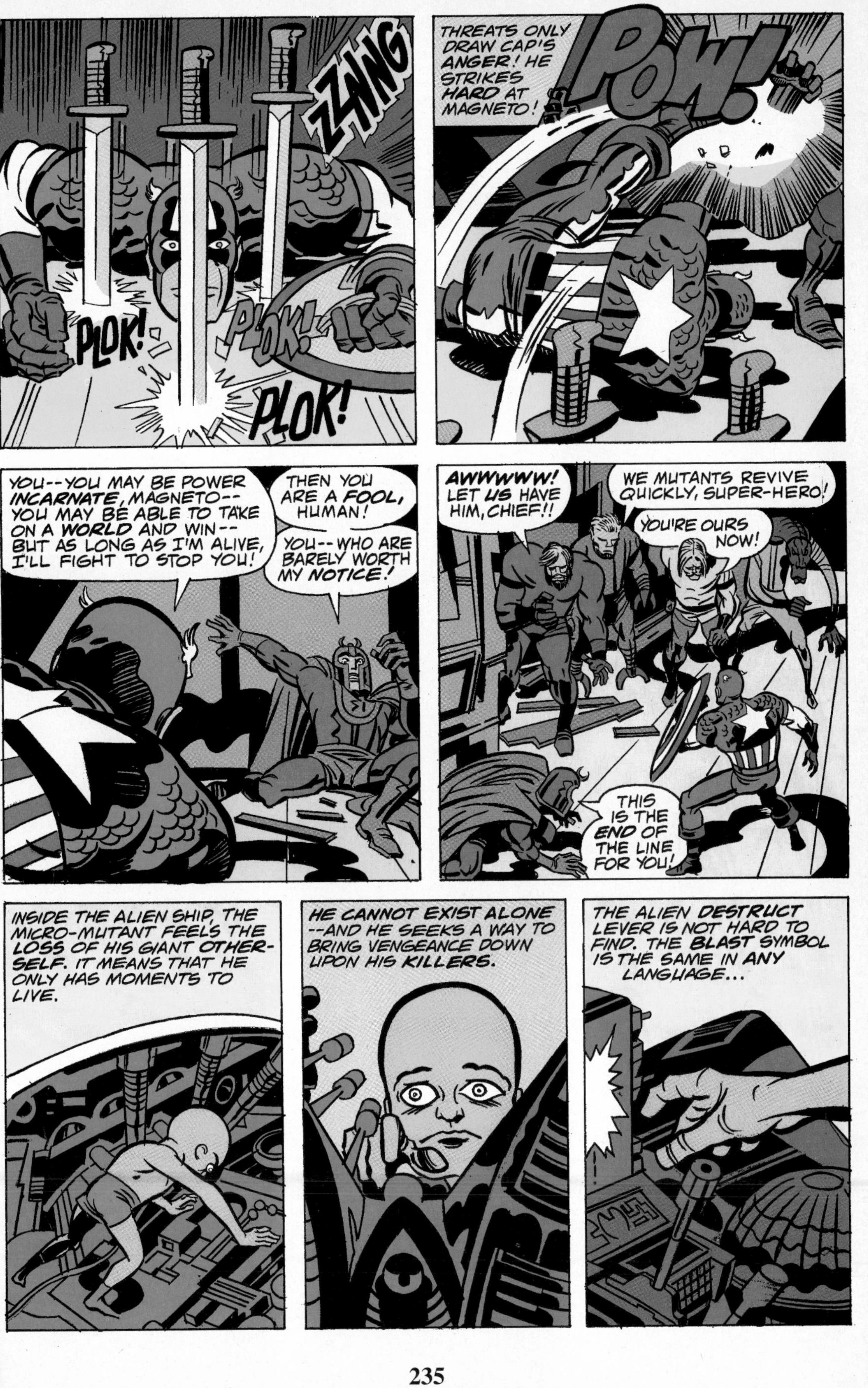
ZZING
PLOK!
PLOK!
PLOK!
THREATS ONLY DRAW CAP'S ANGER! HE STRIKES HARD AT MAGNETO!
POW!
YOU--YOU MAY BE POWER INCARNATE, MAGNETO-- YOU MAY BE ABLE TO TAKE ON A WORLD AND WIN-- BUT AS LONG AS I'M ALIVE, I'LL FIGHT TO STOP YOU!
THEN YOU ARE A FOOL, HUMAN!
YOU--WHO ARE BARELY WORTH MY NOTICE!
AWWWWW! LET US HAVE HIM, CHIEF!!
WE MUTANTS REVIVE QUICKLY, SUPER-HERO!
YOU'RE OURS NOW!
THIS IS THE END OF THE LINE FOR YOU!
INSIDE THE ALIEN SHIP, THE MICRO-MUTANT FEELS THE LOSS OF HIS GIANT OTHER-SELF. IT MEANS THAT HE ONLY HAS MOMENTS TO LIVE.
HE CANNOT EXIST ALONE --AND HE SEEKS A WAY TO BRING VENGEANCE DOWN UPON HIS KILLERS.
THE ALIEN DESTRUCT LEVER IS NOT HARD TO FIND. THE BLAST SYMBOL IS THE SAME IN ANY LANGUAGE...

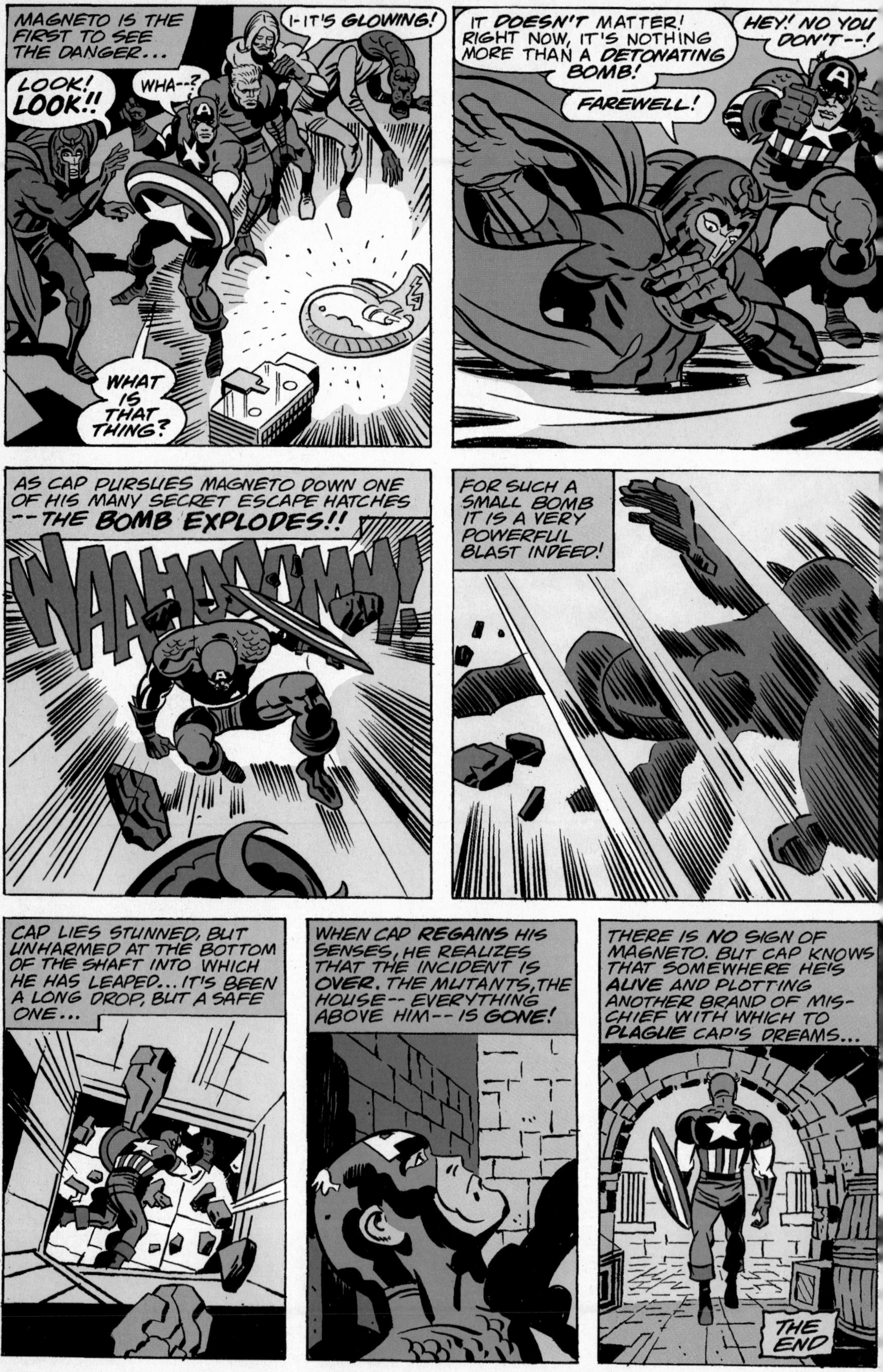
MAGNETO IS THE FIRST TO SEE THE DANGER...
LOOK! LOOK!!
WHA--?
I-IT'S GLOWING!
WHAT IS THAT THING?
IT DOESN'T MATTER! RIGHT NOW, IT'S NOTHING MORE THAN A DETONATING BOMB!
FAREWELL!
HEY! NO YOU DON'T--!
AS CAP PURSUES MAGNETO DOWN ONE OF HIS MANY SECRET ESCAPE HATCHES --THE BOMB EXPLODES!!
WAHOOOMM!
FOR SUCH A SMALL BOMB IT IS A VERY POWERFUL BLAST INDEED!
CAP LIES STUNNED, BUT UNHARMED AT THE BOTTOM OF THE SHAFT INTO WHICH HE HAS LEAPED... IT'S BEEN A LONG DROP, BUT A SAFE ONE...
WHEN CAP REGAINS HIS SENSES, HE REALIZES THAT THE INCIDENT IS OVER. THE MUTANTS, THE HOUSE-- EVERYTHING ABOVE HIM-- IS GONE!
THERE IS NO SIGN OF MAGNETO. BUT CAP KNOWS THAT SOMEWHERE HE'S ALIVE AND PLOTTING ANOTHER BRAND OF MIS-CHIEF WITH WHICH TO PLAGUE CAP'S DREAMS...
THE END

MARVEL SPOTLIGHT

JACK KIRBY • Official Handbook

REAL NAME: Jacob Kurtzberg
NICKNAME: "The King"
DATE OF BIRTH: August 28, 1917
PLACE OF BIRTH: New York City, NY
OCCUPATION: Comic book writer, entertainment producer
WEBSITE: www.jackkirby.com and www.kirbymuseum.com
FIRST MARVEL COMICS APPEARANCE: *Red Raven #1*, 1940

HISTORY: Jacob Kurtzberg was born in 1917 into a gritty upbringing in the streets of New York's Lower East Side. It would be many years before he would adopt the more familiar name of Jack Kirby, but his experiences on the street would help inform the work that later made him a legend. Unlike many of his rough-and-tumble peers, his imagination inspired him to look beyond the commonality of everyday life. He was inclined at an early age to pursue drawing, and he was also a guy who wanted to "get things done." This hard work ethic and ambition took him places most men of humble stations like his would never dream of going,

After some early strip work helped get his name out to prospective employers, a fateful meeting with artist Joe Simon connected the two at the hip and vaulted both of them into comics prominence. Together, they developed *Captain America Comics* for *Timely Comics*, and Jack immediately helped redefine what comics could be with his innovative page designs and proportion-exploding panels.

Soon, Simon & Kirby were working with National Publications, turning out hit kid gang comics like *Newsboy Legion* and *Boy Commandoes*, as well as superhero fare like Sandman and Manhunter. Like many of his peers, he served honorably in WWII, with combat duties that took him through the European theater.

Through the 50s, Jack returned to comics, helping Joe Simon establish the romance genre with its first title, *Young Romance Comics*. More genre work followed for Timely/Atlas, with prolific output that covered western, war, and monster genres. When it came time to launch the Marvel Age of Comics, Stan Lee brought along Jack Kirby to help create the visual demeanor of this new universe of characters and stories. Jack brought his dynamic layouts, unparalleled bombast and unbridled creativity to the fore in books like *Fantastic Four*, *Avengers*, *X-Men*, *Incredible Hulk* and *Thor*, leaving his unmistakable stamp on the characters he created. He also returned to Captain America in the pages of *Tales of Suspense*, reviving from fictional suspended animation the character he had created almost twenty-five years previously.

The King's way of doing things was so popular that it set the tone for many of Stan Lee's editorial decisions throughout the '60s; before new artists were entrusted with taking the reins on a title, they were often assimilated onto books by drawing over Jack's layouts. The Silver Age of Marvel Comics directly reflects the attitudes and values of Jack's artistic mind. After co-creating dozens and dozens of characters, drawing over a hundred issues of *Fantastic Four*, and completing a long tenure on *Thor*, Jack's time at Marvel drew to a close in 1970. He moved to California and signed a contract with DC, this time handling the scripting chores as well as the art duties. Jack's "Fourth World" books (*New Gods, Forever People, Mister Miracle and Jimmy Olsen*), along with *Kamandi, OMAC* and *The Demon* were Jack's major efforts from that era. He was finally able to put everything together the way he saw it in his mind with this newfound artistic freedom, but it wasn't to last. His relationship with DC only lasted five years, and Jack returned to Marvel in 1975.

Back at the company he helped build, Jack created more new characters: *The Eternals, Machine Man,* and *Devil Dinosaur*. As well, he returned to the pages of *Captain America*, starting a long run that would last nearly two years, and he also started up the first series for another character he had created back in 1966, Black Panther. He once again left Marvel Comics, pursuing new challenges in the field of television animation, drawing storyboards for hit shows like *Thundarr the Barbarian*. He still had comics in him, however, and he forty years after his career had begun, he turned to the indie publishers at Pacific Comics to release his *Captain Victory and His Galactic Rangers* and *Silver Star* series.

Jack continued creating comics throughout the '80s and early '90s until passing away in 1994, a creative giant for whom the word "legend" may be too small a title.

THE MARVEL COMICS LIBRARY:
SILVER AGE HEROES (1961-1970, 1975-1978):

2001: A Space Odyssey #1-10
2001: A Space Odyssey Treasury Special
Amazing Spider-Man #8
Ant-Man/Giant-Man from Tales to Astonish #27, 35-40, 44, 49-51
Avengers #1-8, 14-16
Black Panther #1-12
Captain America from Tales of Suspense #59–75, 77-86, 92-99
Captain America #100-109, 112, 193-214, Annual #3-4
Captain America Bicentennial Battles Treasury Special
Daredevil #12-13
Devil Dinosaur #1-9
Eternals #1-19, Annual #1
Fantastic Four #1-102, 108, Annual #1-6
Human Torch from Strange Tales #101-105, 114, 120, Annual #2
Incredible Hulk #1-5
Incredible Hulk from Tales to Astonish #68-84
Inhumans in Amazing Adventures #1-4
Ka-Zar from Astonishing Tales #1-2
Iron Man from Tales of Suspense #40-41, 43
Machine Man #1-9
Nick Fury from Strange Tales #135-153
Not Brand Ecch #1, 3, 5-7
Sgt. Fury #1-7, 13
Silver Surfer #18, Graphic Novel
Sub-Mariner from Tales to Astonish #82-83
Thor from Journey Into Mystery 83-89, 93, 97-125, Annual #1
Thor #126-177, 179, Special #2
X-Men #1-17

SIMON, KIRBY AND CAPTAIN AMERICA

Before Lee and Kirby, there was. . .Simon and Kirby!

By Matt Adler

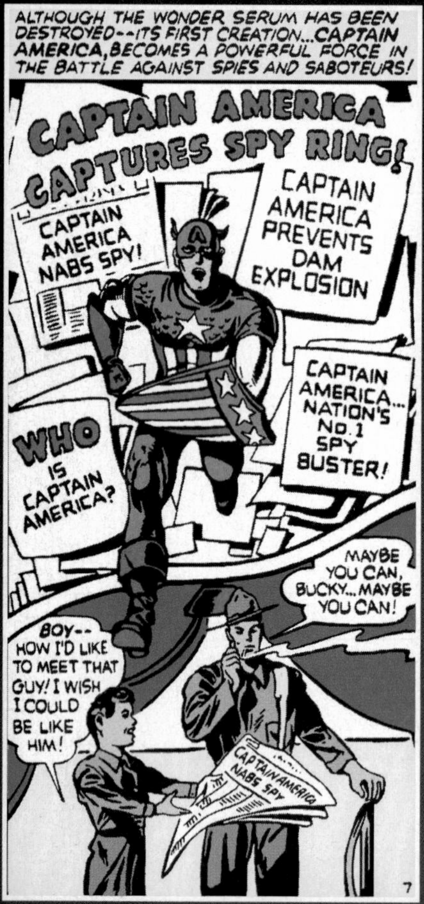

ALTHOUGH THE WONDER SERUM HAS BEEN DESTROYED--ITS FIRST CREATION...CAPTAIN AMERICA, BECOMES A POWERFUL FORCE IN THE BATTLE AGAINST SPIES AND SABOTEURS!
CAPTAIN AMERICA CAPTURES SPY RING!
CAPTAIN AMERICA NABS SPY!
CAPTAIN AMERICA PREVENTS DAM EXPLOSION
CAPTAIN AMERICA... NATION'S No. 1 SPY BUSTER!
WHO IS CAPTAIN AMERICA?
MAYBE YOU CAN, BUCKY...MAYBE YOU CAN!
BOY-- HOW I'D LIKE TO MEET THAT GUY! I WISH I COULD BE LIKE HIM!
CAPTAIN AMERICA NABS SPY
7

A HERO FOR AMERICA: Joe and Jack deliver a hero that was right for the times: the star-spangled super-soldier, Captain America! From *Captain America Comics* #1

The original Marvel duo of Joe Simon and Jack Kirby predated the Marvel Age of Comics - which began in 1961 with the creation of the *Fantastic Four* - by a couple decades, their legendary partnership having started all the way back in 1939, when Marvel was then known as Timely Comics. *Spotlight* had the chance to talk with Joe Simon - one half of that famous duo - about his partnership with Jack, his personal remembrances about the man, and their celebrated creation of Captain America.

Joe Simon and Jack Kirby first met while working for Golden Age publisher Fox Comics. Joe had just been hired by the company as an editor, while Jack was already working in the Fox bullpen at the time, doing clean-up chores, and drawing such strips as the *Blue Beetle*. They made an instant impression on one another. As Joe tells it, "My father was a tailor, so I came in a suit he had made for me. I was the first comic creator Jack had seen in a suit, and he was impressed. Jack's father was a tailor, too, but he made pants!"

Jack likewise made an impression on Joe, but for far different reasons than his fashion sense. "Right away, I was greatly impressed. Jack was maybe 22 years old when I met him, and I felt he was advanced artistically far beyond his age as an artist. He changed his style a lot over the years, but right from the start, I felt he made the most of his potential, which was considerable."

The collaboration proved to be extremely smooth for both of them. As Joe explains it, "I do not recall one incident where we didn't see eye-to-eye. As a collaborator, he had talents that I never expected to match. I had skills and experience that he was lacking. We had very similar ideas as to what we hoped to achieve. We were extremely happy with our products."

Although they came from similar backgrounds, Simon doesn't make too much of it. He sees the similarities as something that defined the industry and its participants as something very much a piece of the times. "It seemed that our whole generation - the comic book generation – was made up of struggling, working class guys, and we were proud of it! It's funny, we writers and artists were considered intellectual, but most of us did not go to college."

And times certainly were tough for struggling young artists in those days. Both Joe and Jack had to supplement their primary income by doing freelance work for other companies. This included Timely, the pre-cursor company to Marvel Comics. Eventually, this led to their fateful creation, the timeless American super-soldier.

As Joe tells it, "Jack was making 15 dollars a week at the time, and living on the Lower East Side. Eventually, I came up with Captain America and brought it to Martin Goodman at Timely. He just loved it. Captain America was actually the first hero that Timely launched in his own book." By this time, the Simon/Kirby team was well-established, and as Joe recalls, he did not view Jack merely as an artist, but as a collaborator in every sense of the word. "I was editing or art-editing for Timely on several other magazines, and I considered Jack as co-editor of the comics."

"We had very similar ideas as to what we hoped to achieve."

The early Captain America stories Simon and Kirby created were grounded very much in the real world, something which set them decidedly apart from their contemporaries, which were much later to the game in confronting fascism and Naziism from abroad. The stories were peppered with roles given to prominent historical figures of the time, including President Franklin Delano Roosevelt, FBI Director J. Edgar Hoover, Nazi leader Adolf Hitler, and his second-in-command Hermann Goering. The stories also regularly showcased Captain America and his partner Bucky squaring off against real-life threats to the United States, including spies and saboteurs intent on hurting America's fledgling war effort. Many of the stories also centered around life in Camp Lehigh, where the heroes' non-costumed alter-egos, Steve Rogers and James Buchanan Barnes, resided and trained for deployment.

These kinds of stories stood in stark contrast to the more fantasy-based super-hero tales of most publishers of the time. One might think its creators were setting out to make a statement, but Simon says it wasn't conscious. "We were just trying to get interesting stories out. Both Jack and I loved to read; we'd go to the library and book stores and read all sorts of things, everything from the classic novels to the pulps, not to mention the newspapers and listening to the radio. I also worked as a columnist for the Hearst newspapers when I was 18 years old." Although, Simon does admit, "Like so many others, we were ticked off at Hitler and wanted to get our two cents in."

The Simon/Kirby partnership continued for a long time after they moved away from their seminal star-spangled creation. They went on to create many more notable properties, particularly for rival publisher DC. Among these were *Newsboy Legion, Boy Commandos,* and *Manhunter,* as well as a run on *Sandman.* They are also widely credited with creating the field of romance comics, most notably the popular title *Young Romance.*

But as all good things tend to, the Simon/Kirby partnership finally came to an end in 1955, after more than 15 years. Far from a natural end, this came amidst the well-publicized, anti-comics hysteria fueled by adolescent psychiatrist Frederic Wertham and the Congressional scrutiny that followed. Simon recounts, "This was around the time of the Kefauver hearings. Mothers, mostly those who belonged to churches and PTAs, formed groups and were organizing boycotts. They claimed comics were harmful to children. The Senate even held nationally televised hearings. The industry really suffered, and many publishers had to fold up.

"At one point, Jack and I formed our own company called Mainline, where we would package complete books and then sell them to other publishers. At the time, we were being distributed by a company called Leader News. Leader's main source of income was distributing horror publisher EC Comics. When EC folded as a result of all the controversy, Leader shut down as well. That in turn made us close up. It was a bad time all around."

Simon subsequently moved into advertising and commercial art, while Kirby - as we all know - returned to Timely/Marvel, then called Atlas. He eventually collaborated with Stan Lee on the *Fantastic Four,* a creation that would change the world of comics forever. Simon and Kirby did later go on to collaborate on a few more projects, even after the heyday of their partnership had passed, but despite the sudden end to their ongoing collaboration, Simon still looks back on it with great fondness. He sums up their relationship by saying, "We were a comics machine, and we actually liked one another."

In the end, what more can one ask for?

You can read much more about the Simon/Kirby experience in Joe's autobiographical book, *The Comic Book Makers,* and you can visit Joe's website at www.simoncomics.com.

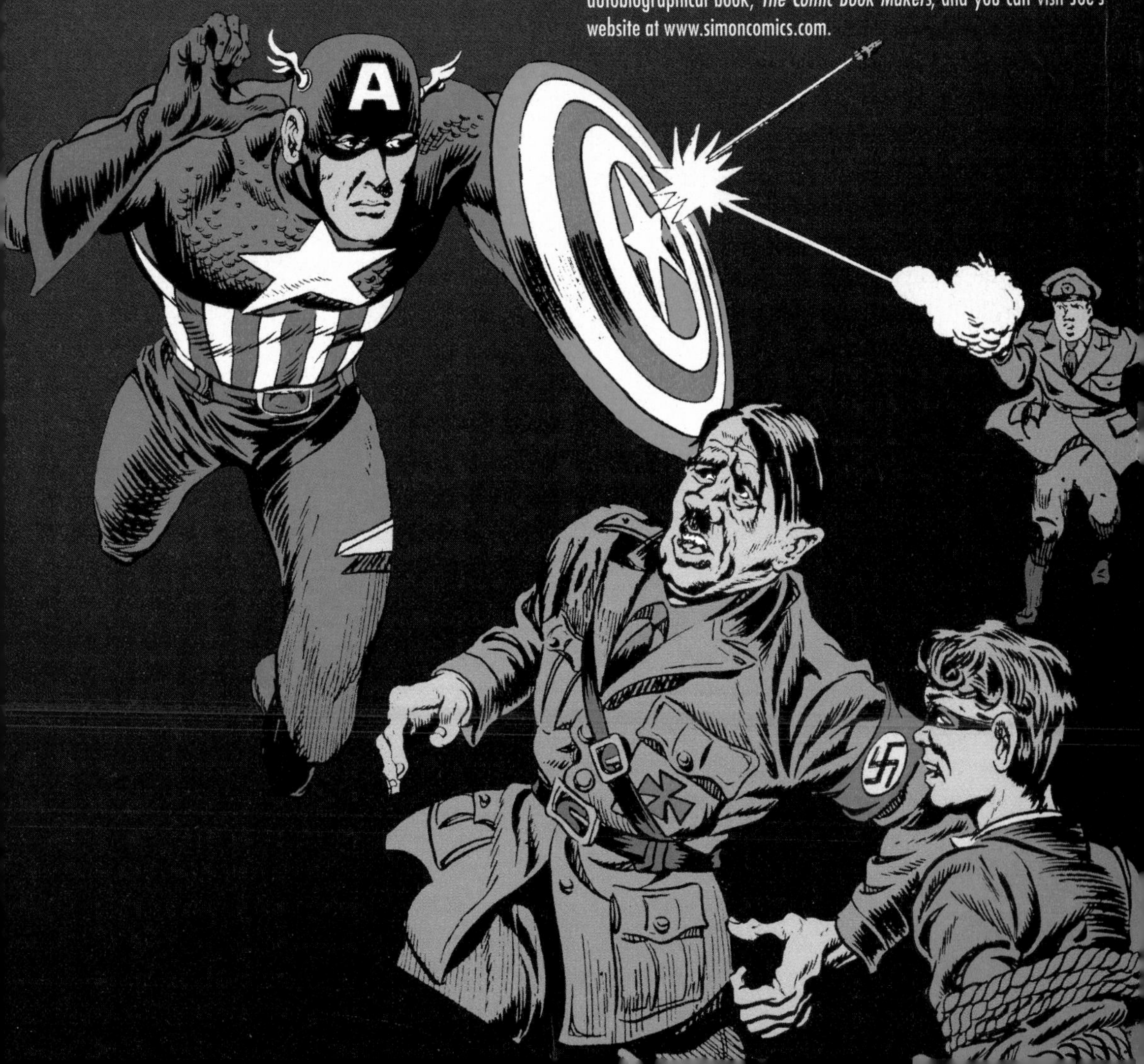